THE BLOODY WHITE BARON

The Bloody White Baron

JAMES PALMER

ff

faber and faber

First published in 2008
by Faber and Faber Limited
3 Queen Square London WC1N 3AU

Typeset by RefineCatch Ltd
Printed in England by Mackays of Chatham, plc

A CIP record for this book
is available from the British Library

ISBN 978-0-571-23023-5

2 4 6 8 10 9 7 5 3 1

For my mother and father

Contents

Acknowledgements

Thanks go first of all to Colin Thubron, who both encouraged me to propose the book in the first place and said ridiculously kind and reassuring things about my writing. My father, Martin Palmer, read and criticised the book at all stages, as well as supporting me through the inevitable financial travails of roaming across Asia; my mother, Sandra Palmer, provided an English home base filled with love and encouragement in those travels. Vicki Finlay helped greatly with the proposal and provided tips on dealing with the publishing process.

Neil Belton improved this book immensely through his careful and intelligent editing, as did Henry Volans. Trevor Horwood's thoughtful and detailed copy-editing was a pleasure to endure and András Bereznay tracked down even the most obscure Mongolian towns for the maps. Many thanks also go to my agents, Gillon Aitken and Jon Jackson.

Willard Sunderland suggested Russian materials, read and criticised the manuscript and caught several important errors; I owe a great debt to his scholarly generosity, and am greatly looking forward to reading his own book on Ungern. Jamie Bisher's *White Terror* was an invaluable source for information on Semenov and the Whites in Siberia, and his enthusiasm and kindness in providing further information an inspiration. My debt to the collections of materials and documents on Ungern compiled by S. L. Kuzmin is immense.

Tjalling Halbertsma, Machiavelli of the steppe, encouraged me to come to Mongolia; Guido Verboom provided a warm welcome when I was there. 'Jack' drove me around the country in a beaten-up taxi that really shouldn't have gone as far as it did. Urantsatsral Chimedsengee was an excellent translator, as was Anna. Shamefully, I have lost the name of my excellent half-Buriat translator and guide.

My friend Christiane Mackenzie died the year before I started working on the book, after a long and loving correspondence in which she never stopped pushing me to write; her last letter to me was titled 'Mongolia'. Arthur Hertzberg taught me that all good books stem from obsession. Olga Bryskine tried to introduce me to Russian many years ago; it wasn't her fault that I was more interested in her than the language. Che Yiping made living in a dust-filled provincial city in Hebei a positive joy; so, in *very* different ways, did George Dent and Ian Sherman.

I'd also like to thank James and Allison Holloway, Julia von dem Knesebeck, Evgenie Medvedev, Sergei Bojalensky, Christopher Kaplonski, Nicholas Goodrick-Clarke, Nick Middleton, Jasper Becker, Tom McGrenery, Professor Khisight, Thierry Michel, Gareth Hanrahan, Elizabeth and Scott Akehurst-Moore, my aunts Roxie, Ralou, Sheila and Yan Chi, my uncle Nigel, my aged grandsire Rudolf Fischer and his wife Dagmar, all of whom gave advice, commentary, or support, as well as many others who provided hospitality or directions in Russia, Mongolia and Estonia.

My girlfriend, Claudia He, put up with my wandering about Mongolia and Russia from the very start of our relationship three years ago, and kept a loving home in Beijing for me when I came back. She insisted, out of a Confucian sense of filial piety, that this book be dedicated to my parents alone; the next one is just for her.

Maps

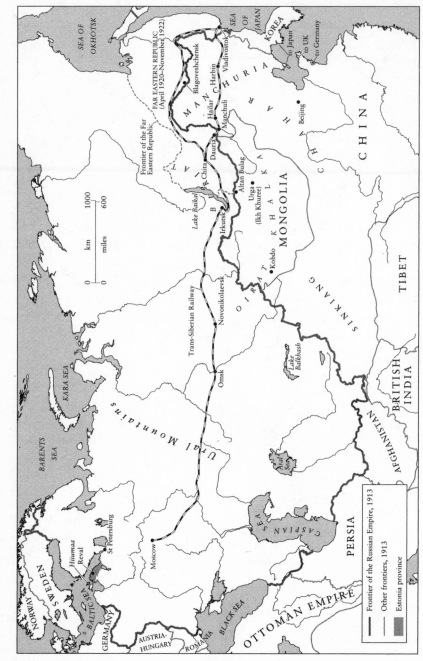

The Russian Empire and her neighbours, 1913

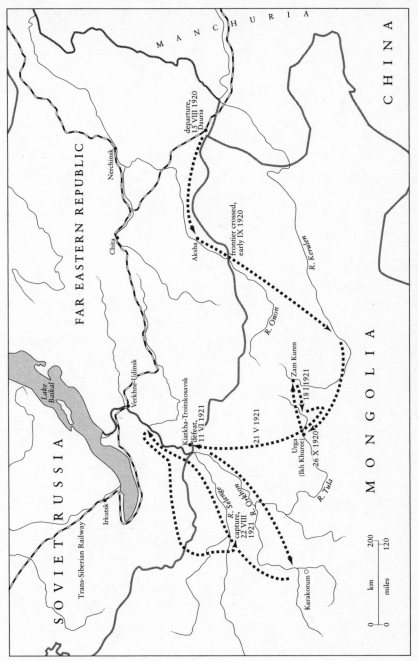

Ungern's movements in Mongolia

SOVIET RUSSIA

FAR EASTERN REPUBLIC

MANCHURIA

CHINA

MONGOLIA

Lake Baikal

Irkutsk

Trans-Siberian Railway

Verkhne-Udinsk

Chita

Nerchinsk

Kiakhta-Troitskosavsk
defeat,
11 VII 1921

Aksha

departure,
15 VIII 1920
Dauria

frontier crossed,
early IX 1920

R. Onon

R. Kerulen

Zam Kuren

18 III 1921

Urga
(Ikh Khuree)
26 X 1920

21 V 1921

R. Tula

capture,
22 VIII
1921

R. Selenge

R. Orkhon

Karakorum

km   200
       0
miles 120
       0

xiii

Introduction

My name is surrounded with such hate and fear
that no one can judge what is the truth and what is
false, what is history and what myth.

BARON UNGERN-STERNBERG, 1921

I imagine that he would like to be remembered riding through a horde
of terrified revolutionary soldiers, scything them down with his sabre
as bullets whizzed around him, passing through his cloak, but never so
much as scraping him; the warrior-king of Mongolia, receiving
reports, tribute and prisoners, like his hero Genghis Khan, in a hastily
pitched campaign tent. My chief image of him, though, is less heroic;
I picture him on the steps of a temple, hearing – and believing – that
he has only a hundred and thirty days left to live, his mutilated face
suddenly contorted by terror.

This book tells the story of Freiherr Roman Nikolai Maximilian
von Ungern-Sternberg, the last khan of Mongolia, who in one short
year rose from being a Russian nobleman to incarnate God of War
and returned Khan. In Mongolia he was lauded as a hero, feared as a
demon and, briefly, worshipped as a god.

I first stumbled upon his story in one of Peter Hopkirk's brilliant
accounts of central Asian espionage, *Setting the East Ablaze*. In late
1920 a White Russian baron and cavalry major-general, thin, intense and hideously scarred, had cut his way into Mongolia,
defeated the Chinese occupiers, taken over the country, ruled it
briefly and brutally, and raised a Mongolian army to lead back
against Russia.

It could have been just another bloody episode in the long horror
of the Russian Civil War, but what made it unusual was the sheer

oddness of Ungern-Sternberg. Most of the Russian leaders, whether the Bolshevik Reds or their opponents the Whites,[1] were a vicious bunch who were not averse to the slaughter of a few thousand citizens, the Reds in the name of the people, the Whites in the name of the tsar, but none of the others did it in the name of Buddha. According to his Russian companions, Ungern-Sternberg was a pious, if unorthodox, Buddhist, and he lived in a world of gods and prophecies that contrasted starkly with the one inhabited by most of his contemporaries. He had not seized Mongolia out of a grand strategic plan, but because, it was claimed, he believed himself to be the returned Genghis Khan, flail of the Bolshevik unbelievers and head of an empire that would stretch from China to the Urals.

It was an almost unbelievable story. One of his chief war aims was to free the Bogd Khan, the huge, blind Living Buddha who had been imprisoned by the Chinese, so that he could act as a rallying point for his crusade. Like all good conquerors, he was rumoured to have left hidden treasure behind him, plundered from monasteries and buried somewhere on the steppe. Ungern-Sternberg did not seem to belong to a century of tanks and telephones but to an earlier, cruder age. Like his Baltic forefathers, he was a lost crusader, a bloody-handed pillager driven by both an intense religious fanaticism and devotion to the joy of slaughter. His hatred was focused, though: Jews and Bolsheviks were killed by his troops on sight, presaging a later, greater evil.

His adventures were made all the stranger by their location. Mongolia can sometimes seem half-imaginary, a storybook country that has no business being real. Most countries project their own mental image, however muddle-headed or stereotypical: skyscrapers and hamburgers, berets and the Eiffel Tower, the willow pattern and the Great Wall, bowler hats and big red buses. Mongolia's popular images are emptiness and exile; Outer Mongolia is a metaphor for as far from anywhere as you can be. When the current president of Mongolia, Enkhbayar, came to England to study as a young man, he was detained by a sceptical immigration official who refused to believe that Mongolia was a real country – 'You're having me on, son' – until Enkhbayar produced an atlas to prove his homeland's reality.

There was a time, though, when the Mongols ruled the world, or at least a substantial chunk of it. Under Genghis Khan (1162–1227), arguably the most successful conqueror in history,[2] the Mongols were transformed from a group of infighting backward steppe tribes to become the masters of Asia, a ruthless, streamlined war machine whose speed, force and flexibility massively outclassed any other army of the era. By the time of Ungern's invasion, however, the Mongol Empire had long collapsed, swallowed up by Russia and China, once again a collection of scattered and feuding clans. They left behind them deep cultural memories of massacred peoples and burnt-out cities.

Tolstoy, writing gloomily of the brutalities of the tsarist system in the nineteenth century, feared the onset of 'Genghis Khan with the telegraph',[3] and perhaps a greater soldier could have made something of the combination of Mongol ferocity and modern strategy. Ungern was not that man. His agenda was set by the rantings of shamans and his chaotic dreams, not by railway timetables or quartermasters' reports. How, I thought, do you come to behave like this? How does a Baltic-Russian aristocrat end up a fanatical Buddhist?

And yet, there seemed to be more to his leadership than sheer despotic terror. He was undoubtedly popular among his Mongolian troops, who fought for him with a fury which appeared to some European observers to be close to devil-worship. Everything about the story seemed uncertain, even Ungern's appearance, tall in some sources, short in others, grey-eyed, green-eyed, blue-eyed – nobody was able to pin him down. In one account he came across as a detached fanatic, willing to muse on philosophy and history, in another as a sadist and butcher, hands steeped in blood. Stories about him were a morass of rumour, myth and supposition. His personal beliefs were murky; his Buddhism might have been inherited from an equally eccentric grandfather, or the result of a personal conversion during his early years in Mongolia, and he seemed happy to use the most respectable, if mystical and apocalyptic, language of Russian Orthodoxy at points, despite his family being Lutheran. The changes in his appearance suggest an atavistic religious progress. In one of the few surviving photographs he appears in Russian army uniform, neatly groomed, but with an intense, monastic appearance, like an Orthodox mountain hermit, but near the end of his campaign he rode bare-chested, 'like a Neanderthal', hung with bones and charms, his beard sprouting in all directions and his chest smeared with dirt. He had gone from monk to shaman in a few years.

＋—✥✦✥—＋

The ferocity of Ungern's crusade was surprising, given his Buddhist connections. Buddhism has always been one of the most accessible Asian religions to Westerners; appealingly philosophical, pleasantly pacifist and, compared with Hinduism or much of Chinese religion, supposedly free of 'superstitious' or 'primitive' beliefs in the form of gods or magic. Many writers ignorant of Asian history – particularly, for some reason, anti-religious science writers – also claimed that Buddhism lacked the history of atrocities and intolerance that marked Western religion, despite, for instance, the many Buddhist-inspired messianic revolts in China, or the deep complicity of Zen Buddhism in Japanese militarism during the Second World War. It especially appealed to the English because, like the Church of England, it seemed not to demand that you believe in anything. To be a Westerner and call oneself a Muslim, or even a Hindu, makes some definite statement about your beliefs and perhaps your actions; calling yourself a Buddhist in the West, however, does not define your identity in any fixed way. Western Buddhism resembles Unitarianism without the harsh dogma.

The emphasis on the philosophical aspects of Buddhism in the West also means that the reality of Buddhist religious practice worldwide tends to be eclipsed. For instance, Buddhists are often portrayed in the West as not believing in a God or gods, and most Western Buddhists don't. The vast majority of Buddhists worldwide, however, are enthusiastic believers in all manner of gods and spirits, often drawn from local traditions or taken from older religions such as Hinduism or Daoism.

At first I found it hard to understand why Mongolian Buddhism made a particularly strong and fearful impact on Westerners such as Ungern. In the Chinese variety with which I was familiar the most ferocious of the gods are the guardians found at every temple entrance. Their expressions of earnest intensity, combined with their elaborate martial stances, make them look like Morris dancers. Temple complexes as a whole feel gentle and benign: quiet gardens, the slow chanting of prayers, the gods and Buddhas set to the back of spacious halls, their hands raised in benediction.

Buddhism in China, introduced by missionaries from India in the first century AD and rapidly incorporated into the happy melange of Chinese folk religion, was part of the mainstream of the Mahayana tradition, the largest school of Buddhism. It focused upon salvation, mercy and release from the wheel of suffering; although there were Buddhist monks and nuns, it remained a populist religion at heart. The chief figures were the various bodhisattvas, beings who had turned back at the threshold of enlightenment in order to work towards redemption for the rest of the world.

However, Chinese Buddhism was – and is – very different from the Mongolian variety. Mongolian Buddhism was an offshoot of the Tibetan religion, also known as Lamaist or Tantric Buddhism. The country had converted as a result of a deal struck in the sixteenth century, effectively giving the Mongol khans temporal authority over Tibet in return for the Tibetans assuming spiritual authority over Mongolia. The relationship was not particularly easy; the Fourth Dalai Lama had been Mongolian, and had been murdered by the Tibetans for being so. Though based in the Mahayana tradition, Tibetan Buddhism focused on magic, secret teachings, spirits and demons, the acquisition of special powers, and the superior status of the monk or lama – all of which were to play an important role in Ungern's story.

Many foreigners were suspicious of Tibetan Buddhism. One seventeenth-century Jesuit text on China depicts in wonderful hand-drawn illustrations the various idols the missionaries encountered. The pictures of solemn monks standing next to smiling statues of Chinese Buddhist gods, resting one affectionate hand on their backs, look like holiday snaps in comparison with the Tibetan deities, which stand on their own, sharp and fierce. There is a distant respect about the pictures, mixed, perhaps, with a touch of fear. By far the most commonly worshipped deity in Buddhism is Kwan Yin, the Goddess of Compassion, similar in many ways to the Virgin Mary in Christianity. Merciful goddesses have their place in Tibetan Buddhism, but more prominent is the child-devouring figure of Palden Llamo, a ferocious figure close to the Hindu death-goddess Kali.

The Jesuit illustrations capture something that photographs never can; in the harsh light of the lens the Buddhist deities appear cheap and gaudy, painted in bright colours and hung with fake jewellery. The accoutrements don't help; in most cases an excess of weapons, skulls, corpses, rats, and spikes serves only to make them look a little ridiculous, like a group of middle-aged heavy-metal fans.

In the flesh – or the wood, rather – the Mongolian gods have an even fiercer presence. I first encountered them at the Seven Towers Temple in Hohhut, the capital of Inner Mongolia. Squashed between old houses, with narrow hallways and tiny courtyards, it was a disturbing place. Despite the high, bright afternoon outside, almost everything was shadowed; the only light was from very dim, shuttered lanterns. I could hear a ragged chanting everywhere I went, adding to the general eeriness. I was reminded of the Yonghe Gong, the Lama Temple in Peking, where in the 1930s Western visitors were warned to keep to well-lit corridors for fear of assault by rogue monks.[4]

I entered the shrine of a gruesome god, his sharp teeth grinning and his head festooned with skulls. I wasn't certain who he was, since the Tibetan pantheon inherited by the Mongolians is replete with such figures. In a small dark room, with incense burning and other gargoyles looming, it seemed capable of an awful, twitching animation; I felt it might lick its lips at any moment. A rural Mongolian couple were kneeling on the floor before it, chanting and kowtowing; they'd brought oranges to feed the god, and cash to bribe him. Even after the pilgrims had left, I didn't want to stand in front of the thing, let alone examine it closely; it was the first time I'd had any concrete sense of the word 'idol'.

Elsewhere in the temple, small-denomination notes were tucked into the armpits and behind the ears of most of the gods, and ageing fruit lay before them. I wondered whether the purpose was prayer or appeasement. The assembled gods trampled bodies, gripped weapons and had fixed, bloody smiles. The last time I'd visited a Chinese temple I'd spent my time wisecracking about the 'war umbrellas' the gods carried, much to the horror of my Chinese companion, who, despite being Muslim, was convinced I was drawing some awful curse down on myself. I was raised Anglican, which takes most of the fear out of religion, but I wasn't making any jokes in this place. I could see chipped paint and worm-eaten wood, the cracks and hollows of years of neglect. It didn't make me feel any more at ease; it just made the gods seem older and darker and angrier.

The temple's gift shop sold plastic versions of the monstrosities inside, grinning horror reduced to plastic kitsch. I bought some oranges and a few sticks of incense before returning inside with a bunch of schoolchildren, their laughter and joking soon silenced in the shadows before the gods. I stuck the incense in the sandbox before the biggest and grisliest of the lot and placed a five-yuan note alongside the oranges at its feet. Better safe than sorry, after all.

Such a temple, with its close, fearful atmosphere would surely have made a deep and lasting impression on Ungern. He had not come to it a blank slate – he was a cruel and ruthless man long before his arrival in Mongolia – but the images of Mongolian Buddhism, filtered through the perspective of the equally murky world of Russian and European mysticism and its fascination with the 'Orient', had shaped his thinking and his actions. This fascination was mingled, in Ungern's time, with deep fears of the 'inevitable' rise of the East, creating the myth of the 'Yellow Peril', the hordes of sinister Orientals who threatened the West.

Beyond the religious aspects, Ungern's actions had to be understood as part of the regional clashes in the first half of the twentieth century between Russia, Japan and China. Mongolia and Manchuria had been the fault line for conflict between the old and crumbling tsarist and Chinese empires, but also the focus of the new imperialism of the Soviets and Japanese. Mongolia, an impoverished, seemingly unimportant country of fewer than two million people, became a key part of these struggles, and Ungern's thinking and strategy made sense only in the context of these conflicts.

I was beginning to develop a sense of what lay behind the Baron's terrible deeds, but definite information was still hard to come by. Even in the 1930s the Russian-French writer Vladimir Pozner had found that Ungern

> kept on escaping me. He confused the catalogues of books in the libraries. He muddled up the addresses of people who had once known him. He afflicted some of them with loss of memory. He struck others dead: for example, 'Prince' Tumbair-Malinovski, who was felled by paralysis and shot himself in a Nice hospital. He allowed no one to identify him.[5]

Nobody died while I was tracking Ungern, but he remained elusive.

My own travels through Mongolia, Russia and China made many aspects of Ungern's campaign clearer to me, as did the work of Russian and Mongolian scholars. I began to see how a small, brutal war in Mongolia fitted into the larger patterns of history, and how Ungern's actions had had a far greater impact than I had ever previously realised. The story often seems medieval, but Ungern's campaign is not even a century removed from us. In Asia the events of the twentieth century are written in the landscape and on the bodies of the people.[6] In China I met ancient communists who could just remember when China was an empire, and Mongolia a mere vassal state. I met, too, young nationalists who were all too eager to retake, even settle, Mongolia – and Mongolians who were keen to fight them.

In telling the story of Ungern's short life and brutal death, then, and of the consequences of his actions, I have drawn from many different sources. Some are accounts by his contemporaries, some are later works or my own impressions of a country or its culture. Much of the documentation concerning Ungern is clustered in the last three years of his life, and at times, when describing his early career and beliefs, I have projected later statements backward in time. I also had to make some difficult choices about what to believe; Ungern became a legendary figure even when alive, and his myth grew even more after his death. His own beliefs and actions were deeply bizarre, but so were those of his contemporaries, and often it was difficult to tell whether a particular story was a fantasy of Ungern's or of the witness reporting it. As it happened, I began the book in a greater spirit of scepticism than when I finished it; too many of the oddest stories turned out to be confirmed by reliable witnesses, often more than one. Who would have thought, after all, that Ungern really did keep wolves in his house? Or marry a Chinese princess? Or pause on a reconnaissance mission, in the middle of a hostile city, to chastise an enemy soldier for being asleep on duty?

There is very little to like about Ungern himself. He was an appalling human being in almost every way; virtually his only admirable characteristic was his fierce physical bravery, and perhaps parts of his fascination with the East. There seemed to be very few aspects of ordinary life which could please him; his pleasures were violent and he lived in a world increasingly – and rightfully – hostile to the values he believed in.

Yet he remains fascinating. His voice – strident, sarcastic, vicious – dominates his story. Other voices are absent, or at least muted: those of Ungern's victims and his communist successors'. Peasants, widows, nomads, and monks, they have left almost no accounts of the events of the year in which Ungern's horde tortured and murdered so many of them, or of the terrible years that followed. In the writings of Western or Chinese travellers, the Mongolians, with the exception of a few nobles or high-ranking lamas, are often ignored; it seems hideously appropriate that virtually the only accounts we have from ordinary Mongolians are the interrogation records of the old communist regime, voices bent by torture and distorted for propaganda.

The Mongolians were the tools, and the victims, of a delusional psychopath driven by a fusion of religious, imperial and reactionary ideology. Ungern's atrocities were a foreshadowing of worse things to come for the world, and both his life and the suffering he caused have been eclipsed by the greater horrors that followed. I hope that in this book I have, at least in part, given some accounting of his victims together with their – and his – place in history.

ONE

A Son of Crusaders and Privateers

Ungern was born in Graz, Austria, in 1885 to an Estonian father of German blood and a German mother. Within a few years of his birth his parents had divorced, his mother had remarried and he had moved back to Reval, Estonia (now Tallinn), where he was to spend the rest of his childhood. His sense of family and place was uncertain from his very birth, something reflected in his name. 'Sternberg', 'star mountain', an archetypal Jewish name, has an epic ring on its own, but its coupling with 'Ungern', which translates as 'unwillingly, reluctantly', is an odd one. It even inspired an anti-Semitic joke, popular during the 1930s: 'What's your name?' 'Ungern-Sternberg.' 'If I were *Sternberg*, I'd be unhappy about it too.' Though there is no evidence that Ungern possessed any trace of Jewish ancestry, he separated out the names, entirely incorrectly, often referring to himself as Ungern von Sternberg. It was clearly an uncomfortable name for him; when he translated it into Mongolian it disappeared entirely, and he became simply 'Great Star Mountain'.

Ungern was christened Nikolai Roman Maximilian, a mixture of Russian and German names befitting his heritage. He added a patronymic, in common with most Germans in Russia, transforming his father's German Theodor into the Russian Fyodorovich. Even the date of his birth reflects the split between these two worlds, for he was born in two separate years: on 10 January, 1886 by the Western Gregorian calendar and on 29 December, 1885 by the Russian Julian one, which ran twelve days behind. Errors in conversion from biographers and bureaucrats alike have produced birthdates ranging from 23 January to 16 December! Similar cross-cultural confusion and misinterpretation would mark Ungern's whole life.

In truth, he had barely any Russian ancestry, his family were thoroughly German and warlike; in his own words, 'crusaders and privateers'.[1] There was a weak family connection to Russian royalty many generations previously, true, through the Romanov intermarriage with German nobility, but this was hardly unusual for an aristocratic central European family. Through them there was an even more tenuous claim to distant Mongolian ancestry. The family had a tradition of pride bordering on arrogance. One of their ancestors was supposed to have been an ambassador to the court of Ivan the Terrible, and to have had his hat nailed to his head after he refused to lift it to the tsar; it was said that they would have boarded the Ark only reluctantly, hence the origin of the name. (The real origin of 'Ungern' lay in the family's distant Hungarian roots; 'unwilling' was a linguistic coincidence.)

Young Roman could, in fact, claim descent from any number of royal bloodlines, including the Plantagenets and the Habsburgs, but it was the Russian imperial connection that he always liked to assert and it was as a Russian that he always, first and foremost, presented himself. An intense programme of Russification had taken place during the 1860s as part of a wider Russian effort to strengthen the ties of the border provinces to the central Empire,[2] and it had had a deep effect on the Ungern-Sternbergs. Even so, the Baron's sense of attachment to the Russian Empire was almost pathologically intense; in some ways he had what Isaiah Berlin described as 'borderlands syndrome', the insecurity that comes from being on the fringes of a great empire, and which seems to produce an unusually high frequency of the most blindly cruel servants or leaders of these empires. Such men, including the Austrian Hitler, the Corsican Napoleon or the Georgian Stalin, developed, according to Berlin, either 'exaggerated sentiment or contempt for the dominant majority, or else over-intense admiration or even worship of it . . . which leads both to unusual insights, and – born of overwrought sensibilities – a neurotic distortion of the facts'.[3]

His homeland, Estonia – then known to both the Germans and the Russians as Estland – had been carved into existence by the crusading order of the Knights of the Sword in the twelfth and thirteenth centuries. The Northern Crusades against the pagans of Lithuania and Livonia have received scant attention compared with the crusades for the Holy Land, but they were long-lasting and bloody affairs, undertaken more out of a desire for land than any genuine missionary impulse. It was the first clash in what was to become the long history of German–Eastern conflict.

Initially the native peoples, primitive and idol-worshipping, had little hope against the iron-wrapped charges of the German crusaders, and were slaughtered in droves when they tried to confront the crusading armies directly. Some of them were not even pagan, but had been converted to Orthodoxy by Russian missionaries; this made little difference to the Germans. The locals fought viciously enough themselves when they had the chance, often targeting the preachers who followed in the armies' wake; many a priest was martyred, burnt as an offering to Perun the Sun God or quartered in homage to the Lord of Horses. After some time the pagan forces settled into a long colonial border war between Estonia and Lithuania, forcing the knights into the forests and swamps where their horses were useless, concealing themselves among the peasantry, and making hit-and-run attacks where the knights were weakest.

The Ungern-Sternbergs were direct descendants of these proud crusaders. The Knights themselves had been eclipsed by Lutheranism and the new Russian kingdoms, and eventually disbanded by Napoleon, but many of the Baltic Germans, including Ungern's father and stepfather, were members of the successor charitable organisation, the Honourable Knights of the Teutonic Order, based in Austria. This gave the family a somewhat ambiguous position within the Russian Empire; one of the foremost triumphs of Russian history, after all, was Alexandr Nevskii's defeat of the Teutonic Knights on the frozen ice of Lake Peipus in 1242, halting their advance to the east. Later, as a story of heroic Russian victory over German invasion, it was given great play during the Second World War. Nevskii's triumph was made possible only by his striking a submissive deal with the Mongols, turning his princedom of Novgorod into a tributary state, something that did not often feature in Russian histories.

Though unpopular with the masses, the Germans were regarded within the imperial system as the de facto equivalent of the Russian nobility. The high rate of intermarriage between the Romanovs and German royalty contributed to their social status, and a German was just as likely to rise to high military or civil rank as a Russian. There were mutterings, particularly during the First World War, of how much influence the Germans had; certainly a goodly number of the Russian commanders on the Eastern Front had German family names.

The division between conqueror and conquered was still highly visible in Ungern's day. As in Russia, the noble estates were surrounded by a sea of peasantry, but here the class distinction was also ethnic, a clear divide between poor Slavic natives and Teutonic aristocracy. What middle class there was comprised mainly later German immigrants, sometimes Jews, although by the turn of the century there was an emerging Estonian middle class. The whole country had just under a million people, roughly 5 per cent of them German, and maybe a fifth of those Jewish. The justice system was traditionally based around social class, and consequently ethnicity; the word of a baron or a knight weighed considerably heavier in the scales of evidence than that of a peasant, hence that of a German heavier than that of a Slav. Although this system had been reformed before Ungern's birth, the attitudes it reflected still survived.

As elsewhere in the Russian Empire, the peasantry lived a virtually medieval lifestyle, scraping a living from farming and fishing. An outward layer of deep devotion to the Lutheran Church concealed a multitude of incongruous, semi-pagan superstitions. There were some shamanic elements in the folk tales, similar to those of neighbouring Finland. During the 1920s these were formed into Tassi, an outlandish neo-pagan religion something like modern Wicca, which fused supposedly ancient beliefs with a nationalist, right-wing agenda. Tassi never attracted more than a few thousand believers and was crushed as counter-revolutionary in Soviet times, but it is, nevertheless, a fine example of the way nationalism and esoteric beliefs sometimes crossed. Tiny, near-medieval, aristocratic, freezing in winter but burning hot in summer, on the fringes of a great empire, with a muddle of earlier beliefs lying under a late-imposed religion – Estonia was not unlike Mongolia.

Ethnic Germans such as the Ungern-Sternbergs did not regard themselves as belonging to their adopted country. In some ways they were still colonists, overseers of vast estates powered by native labour, nostalgic for the bright lights of the city. Like Ungern's parents, they frequently holidayed in, or even moved back to, Austria or Germany.

They were widely known for being proud, even by Russian aristocratic standards, and looked down on Jews, 'native' Estonians and

Russians, roughly in that order. Until late in the nineteenth century there were hardly any Jews in Estonia, since it lay outside the Pale established for Jewish settlement in Russia. The Baltic Germans in all three countries, on the other hand, were effectively one community, having far more to do with each other than with the locals, and the Germans in Estonia picked up on the prejudices of their Latvian and Livonian relatives.

The incestuous nature of the community was reflected in their large manor houses, which frequently changed ownership as various nobles drank or gambled away their family fortunes, but which almost always passed to other German families rather than to Estonians, or even the Russian nobility. The Baltic German community was closely associated with the *Volkisch* pan-German movements, and produced a remarkably high number of Nazi leaders and thinkers; the Nazi 'philosopher' and neo-pagan Alfred Rosenberg, hanged at Nuremberg for his anti-Semitic propaganda and his brutal administration of occupied eastern Europe, grew up in Reval only a few years behind Ungern. Like most nineteenth-century aristocrats, Germans were frequently in debt, living a long way beyond their means in order to sustain their fantasies of noble life. Yet, like the Russian aristocracy, their children spent a lot of time among the peasantry, and some of them found the peasant lifestyle more appealing than the cold and restricting world of their parents.

The Germans in Estonia were divided between their identity as Germans and their role as servants of the Russian Empire. It was a conflict full of contradictions. The wider German world was more modern, more liberal, more civilised than most of the Russian Empire, but many Baltic Germans maintained virtually medieval privileges and prejudices, and it was the Russians who had begun to abolish much of the legal basis on which German superiority over the indigenous population rested. Reval reflected these tensions. In this fortress city the crusader-built castle set on a hill in the centre – a visible symbol of German power – vied for architectural prominence with the Orthodox cathedral, a glitzy pseudo-Muscovite construction built in the 1880s and designed to overshadow the Lutheran cathedral nearby. (It was named, none-too-subtly, after Alexandr Nevskii, the great Russian hero of the medieval wars against the German invaders.)

The Ungern-Sternbergs had traditionally identified themselves with both the German aristocracy and the Russian imperialists. In the early nineteenth century more members of the family began to pursue military careers, inevitably entangling them in the sprawling frontiers of Russia's eastern empire. Russia's nineteenth-century drive to the east, a continuation of the great expansions of the previous two centuries, saw the gradual absorption, by diplomacy or by force, of the various petty khanates, tribes and kingdoms of central Asia, followed by Russian colonisation of the newly conquered areas. This mirrored the Mongol conquests of the thirteenth and fourteenth centuries, when they had swept out of Mongolia to become the masters of Eurasia. In two centuries Russia had more than doubled in size, and a whole new class of diplomats, warriors and spies evolved to deal with the conquered territories, and the often rebellious locals. They fought against an array of small Muslim states, remnants of the Mongol Empire: set-piece battles during which Russian artillery pounded medieval mountain fortresses into dust, and cavalry skirmishes and massacres during which the Cossacks would be loosed against one or other unfortunate tribe. Asked whether 'his family had distinguished itself on Russian service', Ungern replied proudly 'Seventy-two killed during wartime!'[4]

It was a fusion of the Wild West and the Roman Empire, and the transmission of family stories and mementos of far-off campaigns left a deep impression on Ungern. A member of a minority in his homeland, an uncertain Russian, the core of his familial identity was not national but military. He always prided himself upon the warlike nature of his ancestors, talking enthusiastically of such figures as 'the Axe' and 'the Brother of Satan'. He was obsessed with their role in the Crusades in particular, a period of history he often referred to in conversation. The Ungern-Sternbergs did have their fair share of military heroes, but the family's history was not entirely glorious; one of their most famous Estonian forebears, Otto von Ungern-Sternberg (1744–1811), was a wrecker, using false lights to lure ships on to the harsh rocks of the coast of the Estonian island Hiiumaa, then killing the surviving crew and plundering the cargo. In his spare time Otto was a poet and mystic, neither of which stopped the Russian authorities from shipping him off to Siberia when he was found guilty of piracy and banditry. In Ungern's own account this gruesome heritage was transformed into the more glamorous practice of privateering. He claimed, entirely falsely, that his paternal grandfather had served under an Indian prince as a privateer against the British. It's a wonderfully swashbuckling image, and sounds exactly like the fantasy of a young boy.

His fantasies extended beyond the military to the religious. He claimed that the same grandfather had converted to Buddhism as a result of his experiences in India. Since Buddhism was barely known in India at the time, this is rather like saying that someone converted to Islam as a result of a trip to Spain. If anything, the opposite was the case; Western scholars and occultists were influential in *reintroducing* Buddhism to India and some, such as the Theosophist Henry Olcott, are still honoured for doing so. Claims such as this remain common among occult groups and new religious movements, adding an appealing veneer of antiquity to their beliefs.[5] In Ungern's case it indicates an interest in Buddhism coupled with a general ignorance of its practical and historical realities that was typical of the man.

Ungern's fantasies about his family's history were, perhaps, the result of one of the most mundane of childhood tragedies: an early parental divorce. His father, Theodor Leonhard Rudolf von Ungern-Sternberg, was an amateur geologist; his mother, Sophie Charlotte von Wimpffen, from Hesse in Germany, was an aristocrat. It was not a happy marriage. They divorced when Roman was six, and he was raised by his mother and her second husband, another baron, Oskar von Hoyningen-Huene. The cause of the divorce was probably his father's gradual mental collapse, which eventually necessitated his committal to a sanatorium at Hupfal for five years. The records tiptoe around the exact nature of his illness, describing him as 'mentally unsound'.[6] The early deaths of the first two children of the marriage, both girls, can't have helped. He may have been suffering from some form of schizophrenia, though he apparently made a strong recovery in later life. We can only speculate as to whether his young son ever witnessed any of his psychotic episodes, and the effect it might have had on him. His mother, unsurprisingly given her own experiences of the marriage, seems to have prevented him having much contact with his father, even after the latter's release from the asylum.

Sophie Charlotte remarried in 1894 and the family moved to his stepfather's estate at Jerwakant (Järvakandi in Estonian), around forty miles from Reval, the Estonian capital. There they occupied a substantial manor house, set back in the woods and deep in snow in the winter like something from a fairy tale. Hoyningen-Huene owned the land and controlled the rents for miles around, like any good German lordling. Most of the staff on the estate were German, most of the workers and peasants Estonian. The impact of the divorce on Ungern can, perhaps, be best gauged through silence; despite acting in loco parentis for all but his first six years, Ungern's stepfather receives no mention in any of his later letters or recorded conversations. A hint of their relationship is given from Ungern's school records, which note 'a bad attitude towards his stepfather'.7

Like the majority of the Baltic Germans, the family were Protestant Lutherans, but Ungern was inevitably exposed to Eastern Orthodoxy, the state religion of Russia which the Russian authorities were making strong efforts to press upon the Germans. The Lutheran cathedral in Reval was festooned with the heraldry of the Baltic German noble families, including the Ungern-Sternberg coat of arms: quartered roses and fleurs-de-lis. It was also full of images of death, plague and doom; one wall was hung with a *danse macabre* and carved skulls could be found among the coats of arms.

Young Roman's world was as multilingual as it was multicultural. His parents probably spoke German at home, but he was surrounded by Russian speakers and soon became fluent in both. In addition, he spoke French, required of any Russian with aspirations to culture, and English, also common among the Russian aristocracy. He may have spoken Estonian, perhaps learnt from servants or nurses. If so, it may have helped him with his later language acquisition. Estonian is distantly related to the Mongolian languages, and shares several characteristics with them, chief of which are agglutination[8] and an alarming number of cases.

Ungern holidayed with his relatives on Hiiumaa (Dago to the Germans), an isolated, beautiful Baltic island which the Ungern-Sternberg clan had ruled for two hundred years. It could be a disturbing place for outsiders. Two generations later, under Soviet rule, it would be garrisoned by Kazakh soldiers who lived in fear of the dark woods, the bitter cold and the tall blond 'fascists' around them. It was here that his infamous wrecker of a great-great-grandfather, Otto, had plied his grisly trade. Legends about him were still common on the island, and Ungern stayed in his forebear's vast, echoing manor, Suuremõisa, where, it was said, Otto would daily line up his servants and give them ten strokes of the rod apiece, just in case they had done something to deserve it.

— ✠ —

Contemplating a monster as a child is always a difficult business. Children are innocent, likeable creatures, full of hope. Picture the little Roman von Ungern-Sternberg (floppy hair, skinned knees, clear blue eyes, schoolbag) and within him there are wound-up futures: burnt villages, skinned bodies, lynched Jews. Such images are not irreconcilable; as anybody with an unclouded memory of their own childhood knows, children are frequently uncaring, sadistic, vicious and prejudiced, and readily absorb the various bigotries of schoolmates and parents.

We have no strong evidence of Ungern's childhood character. What fragments we do have indicate a violent and impulsive child. One of his neighbours, for instance, had a pet owl, which Ungern, for no good reason, tried to strangle when he was twelve. He was educated at home in German until he was fifteen, and then sent to the Nicholas Gymnasium in Reval, the school of choice for the upper class. It had a slight majority of Russians, a lot of Germans, and a few Estonians and Jews.

The school was a military-orientated, Russian version of *Stalky & Co.*, designed to prepare its charges for the burdens of empire, but Ungern did not take well to being taught. By the time he went to school he was a strong-willed young man, tall and athletic, unwilling to bend to school rules or obey teachers he saw as inferiors. He was naturally intelligent, but his grades were atrocious. In class he was obstinate and violent; I imagine him not to have been a bully as such, but, as his later behaviour suggests, rather one of those pupils of whom even the bullies are afraid, the kind who violate the unwritten rules of childhood fights, whom nobody wants to sit near, and who cannot be trusted with compasses or scissors. According to friends of his parents interviewed in exile in Paris, 'Roman was a terror to his fellow-pupils and his masters. Several of the pupils' mothers forbade their sons to speak to him. Roman took his revenge. He got into the habit of throwing his school-books out of the window in the middle of lessons, running out after them, and never coming back. His masters didn't dare to complain.'9 They may not have complained directly, but they did take discreet action, and Ungern's mother was asked to withdraw him from the school.

Despite this humiliation, his family came through for him. His stepfather, Baron Hoyningen-Huene, wrote a letter to the heads of the Marine Academy at St Petersburg, asking for him to be admitted and including – presumably somewhat reluctantly – his previous grade record. He resignedly noted that, 'If you feel it necessary to exclude him, [. . .] I undertake to take him back under my care without delay.'10 Clearly the family expected trouble.

It was an even higher-class school, full of the children of the empire's nobility, but Ungern did not take well to its strict military routine. His disciplinary record shows constant skirmishes with authority. Among his offences were returning from the holidays with long hair, smoking in bed, smoking on duty, fighting with his classmates, talking back to his teachers, standing in church, and skipping gymnastics. Told that his answer in an exam on naval architecture was unclear, he replied, 'Oh, what a shame!'11 – typical of his sense of humour, which even as an adult remained limited to brutal sarcasm. Locked up in detention, he compounded the original offence by escaping and stealing his supper from the kitchens.

For the first year his grades were passable, but in the second they had sunk to new depths. The only thing he consistently excelled in was physical exercise, including some forms peculiar to the naval academy, such as manoeuvring around masts and topstays. Humiliatingly, he was held back a year in May 1904, forced to study alongside younger boys. He showed no academic improvement. Combined with his lack of discipline, it was too much for the school, and his parents were asked to withdraw him the following February. From the tone of his long-suffering stepfather's reply to the school's letter, Ungern received a formidable rollicking.

Ungern, however, found a way out. The Russo-Japanese war was in full swing and, quixotically, he decided to volunteer as an ordinary soldier. The nominal cause of hostilities had been a dispute about forestry concessions, but the war released decades of pent-up Japanese resentment against Russia, which had become especially strong after the Russians pressured Japan out of the valuable Liaotung peninsula in 1895. Despite its name, the war was fought almost entirely on the territory of the collapsing Chinese Empire. The Russians had long been keen to extend their influence into Manchuria and the Pacific, and with China's weakness in the nineteenth century their time seemed to have come. Unfortunately, Russia's opportunity coincided with the rise of a new regional hegemony. The Japanese were radically transform-ing their nation into a modern power – and that meant an imperialis-tic one, with the crumbling Chinese Empire as their target. Korea and Manchuria would make ideal first colonies, since both were ethnically and culturally separate from most of China, close to Japan, and had many natural harbours.

A series of small conflicts, starting with the reckless Russian seizure of Japan's island naval base of Tsushima in 1861, had built inevitably into war. The Russians bullied the Japanese out of Manchuria in 1895, after the first Sino-Japanese war had left the Japanese in control of Korea, formerly a Chinese tributary. The Japanese resented it, and they felt that the rest of the developed world, to which they badly wanted to belong, had backed the Russians out of racial empathy. A clique of Russian officers around General Alexsei Kuropatkin, mean-while, saw the Japanese advance as part of the rise of the Asian peoples, a 'Yellow Peril' against which Russia had to stand firm.

When the two sides mutually declared war in February 1904, the Russians were still in control of most of Manchuria, outnumbered the Japanese, and were confident of an easy victory against soldiers many of them referred to as 'yellow monkeys'. By the time Ungern arrived at the front, the Russian army had suffered a series of humiliating defeats. The Japanese had outmanoeuvred them at every turn, crack-ing them out of established defensive positions, mauling them with superior artillery and inflicting terrible casualties. At school, Ungern would have heard of a series of shocking losses: Yalu, Mukden, Liaoyang, the fall of Port Arthur. For a young man steeped in Russian military tradition, with a strong sense of national pride, each new loss must have been a terrible shock. Perhaps, as nineteen-year-old boys tend to, he fantasised that he could somehow reverse the situation by some act of bravery or leadership that would turn the tide and bring Russian victory.

There would be no chance for heroism by the time Ungern arrived at the front, however. The Japanese were at the limits of their supply lines and their manpower. The Russians couldn't afford to reinforce failure, since any extra men would have to be drawn from regions which, rural and urban alike, were already brimming with unrest and bitterness, caused both by a long history of inequality and by a new wave of intellectual agitators. Conscription, always unpopular, could prove explosive. Neither side could cope with another of the hideous, slaughterhouse battles which had characterised the war so far, and so they had settled down along an extended line of trenches in exhausted stalemate to wait for their navies to decide things. The Baltic fleet had been dispatched at almost exactly the same time as Ungern had left Estonia, but it was still steaming around the world to its final reversal at Tsushima which would seal Russia's defeat.

Ungern's time as an ordinary soldier passed without great incident. Like many Russian officers, Japanese skill and courage made a considerable impression on him. Good relations with the Japanese army would be crucially important to him in the future, and he spoke of them in admiring terms. He learnt military routine and discipline himself, and took to it better than he had at the Marine Academy. The teachers there had been mere petty autocrats, but this was *war*, and it had to be treated seriously. By the end of the conflict he was a corporal, and had been awarded a service medal. It was not a heroic distinction, but impressive enough; he had certainly proved his dedication to the motherland. And he had seen the Far East for the first time, the region where he would later serve an empire – and attempt to carve out his own.

TWO

The Ends of the World

Back in Russia, the system that Ungern had volunteered to defend was falling apart. Under pressures from urbanisation, secularisation and radicalism, the old imperial order was beginning to crack. For many reactionaries this was a sign of the forthcoming End of Days, and their writings and meetings began to be filled with talk of the Apocalypse. In the Byzantine era the Eastern Orthodox Church considered the Book of Revelation semi-canonical at best, and tried to restrict it from being too widely circulated, rightfully fearful of the consequences. It was a restriction that went unheeded by the Russian Orthodox hierarchy, where imagery drawn from Revelation was common in both art and diatribe. Scenes of the Apocalypse were blazoned on the porticoes of their churches, burning themselves into the conscience of the laity.

As the imperial forces in the East stumbled from disaster to disaster, the authorities back home proved equally incapable of coping with social unrest. On Sunday 22 January, 1905, in St Petersburg, a huge demonstration assembled to present workers' grievances and petition for democratic representation. The petition was written in deferential terms, drawing upon old images of the 'Father-Tsar', deeply concerned for his people, and the marchers sung hymns and carried icons as they headed towards the Winter Palace. Piety was met with violence, as the army opened fire, heedless of the women and children in the front lines. Cossack troops charged down the survivors, sparking panic in the crowd. In a few minutes around a thousand people were killed, and any belief in the essential benevolence of the tsarist system shattered.

'Bloody Sunday' sparked dissent throughout Russia. In the countryside, groups of peasants seized land and burnt down manor houses as terrified nobles fled in fear of their lives. In the cities, workers downed tools and formed unions, calling for an elected parliament and a legal system that would guarantee their civil rights. For Ungern this was appalling, a breakdown of the natural order. As he put it later, 'the classes cannot exist by themselves, but are connected'. His vision of society was like the medieval Great Chain of Being, in which everyone from noble to peasant had their place, and to disturb one element was to disrupt the whole hierarchy.

He had a fundamental sense of arrogant privilege. The Ungern-Sternberg family had 'never taken orders from the working classes', and it was not the place of 'dirty workers who've never had any servants of their own, but still think they can command' to manage society.[1] Worst of all were the revolts of the peasantry, whom he considered the bedrock of the entire feudal-monarchical system.

There was a racial element here, too; in Ungern's view the Slavic peasants were naturally inferior, incapable of making their own decisions. Without the guidance of 'superior' peoples, he later stated, they would only fall for the manipulations of the Jews. This was a belief shared by many of the Russian nobility, who sometimes saw themselves as a race apart from the peasantry – for instance some believed, or claimed to believe, that the peasants literally had 'black blood'. In some cases such prejudice had been partly softened during childhood by contact with Russian peasant nurses and servants, but the staff at Jerwakant were all German, so Ungern lacked even this basic knowledge of the Russian peasantry.

The gap between the Germans and the locals was provoking trouble in rural Estonia. The main cause of unrest here was not socialism, but national revival. The Estonians had, in theory, already been granted equal legal rights with the Germans. In practice, though, the country was still dominated by a tiny foreign elite. Russian attempts to reduce the power of the Germans had resulted only in Russian administrators replacing German. Since they, too, rarely spoke Estonian, had no family ties with the region and were mainly interested in reaping as much profit from their post as possible before a comfortable retirement in St Petersburg, they managed to make themselves even less popular than the Germans.

During the 1905 revolutions the Estonian peasantry ran riot. Seven hundred years of political and economic oppression exploded in a joyous outpouring of violence. The burnt-out manor houses in the countryside were complemented by smashed windows and broken furniture in the cities. In just over a week in December 1905, one-fifth of all German-owned property was destroyed.[2] The Ungern-Sternberg clan owned several properties and suffered great losses from the Estonians' vengeful rage. These included the manor house at Jerwakant where Ungern has been raised, of which the local peasantry left nothing but a blackened shell.

With the arrival of twenty thousand Russian soldiers, the power of the Germans was restored and the rebels were put down without quarter. Three hundred were shot, another three hundred sentenced to death, and thousands sent to Siberia. It cemented, in Ungern's mind, all the prejudices of his family and class. The peasants were feral animals, fit only to be tamed and corralled, 'rough, untutored, wild and constantly angry, hating everybody and everything without understanding why'.[3]

Imperial rule was the natural order of things, and to threaten it threatened the world itself; revolution was the harbinger of 'famine, destruction, the death of culture, of glory, of honour and of spirit, the death of states and the death of peoples'.[4] The monarchical system was very dear to Ungern; it was the centrepiece of the hierarchies that governed his world. The Russian monarchy, however, was the most sacred of all, blessed, like Russia, by God himself. The revolution, seemingly spontaneous, was really controlled by Jews and intellectuals; it was 'the horrible harvest of the seed sowed by revolutionaries'. He dismissed any suggestion that the revolts might have arisen out of genuine social grievance, believing that 'in their hearts, the people remained loyal to Tsar, Faith, and Fatherland',[5] but had been led astray by the intelligentsia. The threat to the monarchy threatened the very order of things and foreshadowed the end of all.

Others shared his views; the end of the revolution saw over seven hundred pogroms, spurred on by rightist anti-Semitic organisations such as the Union of the Russian People and the Legion of the Archangel Michael. The paramilitary groups associated with them, which carried out over three thousand murders, were known as the 'Black Hundreds'. The tottering tsarist regime, sensing its own unpopularity, attempted to rouse popular anti-Semitism to bolster support for the monarchy and against Jews and revolutionaries, increasingly connected in rightist propaganda. The 'Protocols of the Elders of Zion', a tract which claimed that Jews were organised in a sinister, world-dominating conspiracy, circulated widely among reactionaries. Right-wing propaganda took on an increasingly eliminationist tone, looking not merely to 'contain', but to permanently eradicate the 'Jewish menace'.

For the moment, Ungern had to learn to defend that order, now barely stabilised by the introduction of the 'October Manifesto', which reformed the Russian constitution and provided a limited degree of both democracy and civil rights. For Ungern even this was an abomination, the beginning of the end, and he agreed with Tsar Nikolas II, who had been badgered and threatened into signing, that it was a betrayal of the rightful principles of autocratic monarchy. As a young soldier, however, there was nothing he could do about it, especially with his career to consider. Returning to Russia in 1906, yet more strings were pulled and, after briefly considering the Engineering Corps, he was able to enrol in the extremely prestigious Paul I (Pavlovskoe) Military Academy instead, switching from navy to army. The academy churned out military cadets, particularly for the cavalry, the most glamorous of the services. Here he seems to have settled down, though he was never anything other than a mediocre student; perhaps his temperament was simply more suited to the contemplation of hand-to-hand slaughter than the distant calculations of naval battle, or perhaps the experience of war had sharpened his commitment to the army.

While studying logistics, military engineering, and small unit tactics, Ungern was also beginning to develop his interest in more esoteric matters. He seems to have read widely on Buddhism, occultism, and religion in general, as well as Western philosophy and literature – he particularly liked Dostoevskii and Dante. Nietzsche, popular among the Pavlovskoe cadets, was another influence. He began to develop some of the classic traits of an intelligent but narrow-minded autodidact: contempt for the intelligentsia, a fervent belief in his own findings and reasoning, and a dangerous credulity for unusual fringe beliefs.

An interest in both Eastern religion and the occult tends today to be associated with a broad range of 'alternative' thought, and in general with radical, or at least mildly left-wing, politics.[6] This was certainly not the case in Ungern's time. Although plenty of radicals and socialists could be found in occult circles, at least as many occultists were reactionaries or fervent nationalists. One reason was the innate elitism of occultism. George Orwell, considering advertisements for astrologers in a French fascist magazine, brilliantly noted how 'the very concept of occultism carries with it the idea that knowledge must be a secret thing, limited to a small circle of initiates. [. . .] Those who dread the prospect of universal suffrage, popular education, freedom of thought, emancipation of women, will start off with a predilection towards secret cults.'[7] The high intensity of Russian patriotism and Orthodox mysticism, especially the near-deification of the tsar, easily bled over into the stranger fringes of belief.

We don't know precisely how Ungern first discovered Buddhism and mysticism, but he would hardly have been short of opportunities. St Petersburg was rife with occultism. One Orthodox priest, Father Dmitrevskii, was shocked at how, 'In bookstore display windows, at the train stations, all these books about spiritualism, chiromancy, occultism, and mysticism in general leap out at you. Even the most innocent books are sold in covers decorated with some kind of mystical emblems and symbols which assault the eye.'[8] Orthodox priests of the time seem to have spent their lives in a perpetual state of outrage at just about everything, but his account of the overwhelming interest in the occult is confirmed by numerous contemporaries. In St Petersburg alone, during Ungern's time there, there were thirty-five officially registered occult groups. Then, as now, alternative medicine was a mainstay of such movements, including a school of 'Tibetan medicine', frequented by the rich and gullible. In 1913 a Tibetan Buddhist temple was even established, affiliated with the Theosophist movement and established by the extraordinary Buriat monk and secret agent Agvan Dorjiev. Some took the rise in esoteric religions as synonymous with the supposed decadence of the time, railing against black magic, satanism and witchcraft; others perceived it as a vital outpouring of that national obsession, the Russian soul.

Orientalist trappings were very common among esoteric groups. Magazine and book covers of the time frequently appropriated Asian symbols; the *wuxing* (yin/yang symbol), the swastika, the Buddha, the *vajra* thunderbolt, the lotus and so forth.[9] Perhaps some of them seemed familiar to the Baron from his genuine experiences of the East; the boom in interest in Asian religion had, after all, been sparked largely by the imperial interests of Britain and Russia. His relative-by-marriage Hermann Keyserling, later to become an important figure in European occultism, observed that even as a young man he was interested in 'Tibetan and Hindu philosophy' and spoke of 'geometrical symbols'.[10] Keyserling thought him 'one of the most metaphysically and occultly gifted men I have met', and believed he possessed clairvoyant abilities. That Ungern could read minds was a common belief among those who knew him. Perhaps this impression was due to his distinctive gimlet eyes: small, deep-set, and unevenly spaced. There was something inconsistent about their colour, and nobody could seem to agree whether they were blue or grey. They fixed upon his interlocutors with a disconcerting intensity, 'like those of an animal from a cave', according to Keyserling.

'Tibetan and Hindu philosophy' was undoubtedly a reference to one of Keyserling's own interests, the peculiar new cult of Theosophy. Hugely popular in Russia, it often portrayed itself as a form of 'esoteric Buddhism'. The Theosophical Society had been founded in 1875 by, among others, a Russian mystic, traveller and con-artist named Helena Blavatsky (1831–1891), a woman of considerable creative intelligence, great charm and no little greed. Having read widely, if shallowly, in the literature of the Eastern religions, she cobbled together Hinduism, Buddhism, bits of existing Western occultism, elements of the novels of the popular fantasist Edward Bulwer-Lytton and her curious interpretations of contemporary scientific and pseudo-scientific theories to create her own religion. Her motives were muddled; she genuinely wished to bring Asian insight to Europe, but also took much delight in the gullibility of her disciples, whom she once offhandedly referred too as 'flap-doodles', and the financial benefits they provided.

Theosophy was a kind of stripped-down and generalised version of Hinduism and Tibetan Buddhism. Its most critical beliefs were in reincarnation, the fundamental unity of world religions, the existence of karma and the cyclical nature of the universe. Today Theosophy survives largely through the diligent work and wills of sweet little old ladies, but its wider influence is obvious to anybody familiar with alternative Western religious beliefs, particularly during the so-called 'New Age' of the 1980s. Crankish though its beliefs were, Blavatsky's society drew to it many talented and likeable individuals, and was a major influence on many artists and poets. It was especially popular in

Russia, where it had tens, perhaps hundreds, of thousands of followers, mostly from the upper classes. Among the Russian and German
aristocracy, belief in clairvoyance, poltergeists, telepathy, spiritualism,
astrology and the like were as common as belief in homeopathy
among the English middle classes today. Come the revolution, interest
had reached such a level among the White diaspora that priests in the
Russian-Chinese city of Harbin complained of being overwhelmed by
Theosophists.

Blavatsky's books occasionally leap into vivid, poetic passages, but
exhibit for the most part a tedious, prolix quality, replete with a high
degree of pseudo-scholarship; a typical page of Blavatsky's prose contains references to a half-dozen 'eminent Hindu scholars', a couple of
German professors, some kind of elaborate table of elements and a
few dubious etymologies of Sanskrit or Chinese words. Whole passages
are copied outright from other works. A touch of irony may be found
where she writes of one of her invented verses of the 'Secret Doctrine'
that 'this is, perhaps, the most difficult of the stanzas to explain. Its
language is comprehensible only to him who is well versed in Eastern
allegory and purportedly obscure phraseology'.[11] That her books ever
became best sellers beggars belief.

Theosophy was normally presented in Russia as a form of Buddhism
– Theosophical circles frequently opened 'Buddhist temples' – and
Ungern certainly perceived it as such. His term for his own faith, 'esoteric Buddhism', echoed a phrase which recurs throughout Blavatsky's
writings, and was a standard description for Theosophy in Russia. The
influence of Theosophical language and ideas is evident whenever
Ungern discusses religion. Of particular importance to Theosophists
was a belief in the 'Hidden Masters of the World' – great spiritual
figures who influenced the world through their mystical powers, and
whose benevolent teachings and guidance could aid the West. They
communicated through Madame Blavatsky, apparently by dropping
envelopes in the corners of rooms while nobody was looking through a
sort of mystical postal service.

Tied into the notion of the positive conspiracy of the Hidden
Masters was its inverse; the negative, manipulating, corrupting influence of evil forces. The notion of a conspiratorial elite could be traced
back, in part, to a confused misinterpretation of the Jewish belief
in thirty-six 'righteous men', living and suffering saints for whom

God continued to spare the universe from destruction. Unsurprisingly, this rapidly became tied in with the conspiratorial anti-Semitism of Jewish well-poisoners, bankers and revolutionary masterminds. Western occultism had often exhibited a traditionally philosemitic streak, but now it was almost as though the Wisdom of the East had come to replace the Wisdom of the Jews, the Kabbalah swapped for Tibetan magic.

Although mainstream Theosophy was not obsessed by conspiratorial anti-Semitism, Blavatsky was never averse to taking occasional sideswipes at Judaism. She wrote of it as 'theologically a religion of hate and malice towards everyone and everything about it'. In contrast to Aryan religion, 'the Semite interpretations emanated from, and were pre-eminently those of a small tribe, thus marking [. . .] the idiosyncratic defects that characterise many of the Jews to this day – gross realism, selfishness, and sensuality'. Not to mention that 'while the Egyptian emblem was spiritual, that of the Jews was purely materialistic'.

Theosophical ideas of the rise and fall of races and peoples meshed well with another popular Russian mystic and philosopher, Konstantin Leontiev, known as the 'Russian Nietzsche'. Although he died when Ungern was five, his books, particularly *Russia and Europe*, were still popular. They were exaltations of Russian character and will, in contrast to the weakness and softness of the West. Cultures began in simplicity and purity, became more intricate and entangled, and finally, burdened by their own complexities, decayed and died. Western society, with its unnatural commitment to egalitarianism rather than natural, healthy difference, was doomed. Leontiev praised the East, particularly its nomadic peoples, and felt that Russia's destiny lay with expansion into Asia. For now, Russia could be preserved by keeping everything exactly as it was – 'frozen so it doesn't stink' – and by the vigorous power of the tsar's will. Monarchy-dictatorship was the way forward. Ungern absorbed his ideas, and would regurgitate some of them later, along with those of other mystical and reactionary thinkers.

Ungern read in German as well as Russian, and among some German thinkers, a mixture of fear and respect for Asia was playing an increasingly strong role. The 1890s had spawned in the West the spectre of the 'Yellow Peril', the rise to dominance of the Asian peoples. The evidence cited was Asian population growth, immigration to the West (America and Australia in particular), and increased Chinese settlement along the Russian border. These demographic and political fears were accompanied by a vague and ominous dread of the mysterious powers supposedly possessed by the initiates of Eastern religions. There is a striking German picture of the 1890s, depicting the dream that inspired Kaiser Wilhelm II to coin the term 'Yellow Peril', that shows the union of these ideas. It depicts the nations of Europe, personified as heroic but vulnerable female figures guarded by the Archangel Michael, gazing apprehensively towards a dark cloud of smoke in the East, in which rests an eerily calm Buddha, wreathed in flame.

Indeed, Germans in particular seemed obsessed with the idea – partially because it reflected their fear of their enormous, half-civilised, neighbour Russia. Some, such as Wilhelm himself, could take a more positive view of Russia's role. In a letter to Tsar Nikolas, his cousin, in April 1895 he wrote: 'It is clearly the great task of the future for Russia to cultivate the Asian continent and defend Europe from the inroads of the Great Yellow Race.'[12] It was a sentiment shared by many in Russia, but it was far more common for Germans to identify Russia *with* the Asiatics.

Combined with this was a sense of the slow sinking of the *Abendland*, the 'Evening Land' of the West. This would be put most powerfully by thinkers such as Oswald Spengler in *The Decline of the West* (1917) and the Prussian philosopher Moeller van den Bruck, a Russian-speaker obsessed with the coming rise of the East. Both called for Germany to join the 'young nations' of Asia – through the adoption of such supposedly Asiatic practices as collectivism, 'inner barbarism' and despotic leadership. The identification of Russia with Asia would eventually overwhelm any such sympathies, instead leading to a more-or-less straightforward association of Germany with the values of 'the West', against the 'Asiatic barbarism' of Russia. This was most obvious during the Nazi era, when virtually every piece of anti-Russian propaganda talked of the 'Asiatic millions' or 'Mongolian hordes' which threatened to overrun Europe, but identification of the Russians as Asian – and especially as *Mongolian* – continued well into the Cold War era.

It was not an identity that most Russians shared. The East was the other, the opposite of civilised, Westernised Russia, and the Mongols the epitome of the Asian bogeyman. Nikolas II was just as concerned about the threat of the 'yellow' peoples as his cousin, and it had shaped

Russia's actions during the war with the Japanese. Nevertheless, some Russians, particularly artists, were becoming increasingly interested in the Mongolian heritage of the country. Russian intellectual identity was continually torn between Asia and Europe, both wanting to be part of European, 'civilised' culture and feeling the call of 'wild Asian blood'. Most of the time the first view prevailed, and the whole history of Russian–Mongol relations was rewritten into a myth of heroic resistance, the extensive collaboration between Russian kingdoms and the Mongols forgotten. The Mongols became the enemy – but at the same time they represented something heroic and wild, a romantic part of the Russians' self-image and yearning.

As a result, in the nineteenth century there was an increasing trend in Russia towards 'pan-Mongolism', a search for the origins of Russian customs and folk beliefs in Asiatic legend. This rested mainly upon a nebulous and romanticised image of Mongolia in which Mongols, Tatars and Scythians were bundled together into a vision of untamed and savage natural life. Serious interest in the cultures and religions of the Far East was limited to a tiny minority of ethnologists, linguists and hobbyists. There were also those who needed practical knowledge, the soldiers and bureaucrats who protected and governed Russia's far-flung eastern provinces, although they often arrived with a pre-forged image of the peoples and territories they were about to encounter. Ungern was soon to be numbered among them.

⊷ ⚒ ⊶

Despite his extracurricular readings, Ungern managed, finally, to pass through an institution without being expelled from it. He graduated in the middle of his class, and found that the best option open to him was service in a Cossack regiment. Around this time he was photographed in his dress uniform, sword to his side and a pair of gloves in one hand, a rather diffident looking young officer. The sword was the Cossack sabre, or *shashka*, for which he had a particular liking. This three-foot, slightly curved weapon was said to originate from a Mongolian design. Ungern would use it not only in war, but to chastise underlings or threaten recalcitrant bureaucrats. Offered a chance to serve in western Siberia, he instead chose a regiment stationed near

Manchuria. He was drawn back to the region by his twin interests in religion and war. It would offer him a chance to explore Eastern beliefs, but it would also be close to the front lines if war broke out with China or Japan. The East was full of possibilities.

Ungern's new home was the 1st Argun Regiment of the Zabaikal (Transbaikal) Cossack Host. He had chosen the 1st Argun for practical reasons – the Cossacks offered his best chance for a posting, and he hoped for the patronage of a powerful cousin, General Rennenkampf, a famous cavalry leader and an enthusiastic Asian adventurer who was affiliated with the regiment. There was a romantic attraction, too. The Cossacks were a strange collection of peoples, the descendants of outlaws and exiles who, four hundred years beforehand, had fled civilised life in Poland, Lithuania and Russia to carve out their own living on the steppe. They had 'gone Mongol', turning from towns-people and peasants into bandits and freebooters, forming patriarchal, violent, free-spirited kingdoms of their own. The Russians had gradu-ally absorbed them into the empire, but had always allowed them to keep their own territories and drafted them for military service not by head-count, as with most Russians, but in whole regiments, albeit with Russian commanders.

The Cossacks were famous throughout Europe, and often despised. Known as vicious anti-Semites, they often instigated their own pogroms. The Transbaikal Host was less subject to this particular prejudice than some, since there were so few Jews in the region, but Cossack brutality seemed to many to be a throwback to the Mongols themselves. The military historian John Keegan sums the relationship up well:

> The Cossacks showed a cruelty which stirred in their Western European victims a reminder of the visitations of the steppe peoples, pitiless, pony-riding nomads whose horsetail standards cast the shadow of death wherever their hordes galloped, visit-ations that lay buried in the darkest recesses of the collective memory.[13]

The Cossacks were also seen as cowards, preferring the easy work of spearing peasants and massacring Jews to the dangers of battle. They were rarely willing to face any form of resistance head-on, and during the nineteenth-century wars between Russia, Britain and France would often retreat when confronted by trained European forces, even when they outnumbered the enemy two-to-one. They saw this as simply the intelligent thing to do, preferring to use their mobility to strike at the vulnerable flanks of enemy formations. One of their favourite tactics was the 'fish hook', the old Mongol tactic of drawing an enemy beyond his lines with a faked retreat, then enveloping him from both sides. At the same time, they could be capable of tremendous bravery, making suicidal cavalry charges against fortified positions. Their forte was guerrilla-style raiding and pillaging, an approach to war that would leave a deep impression on Ungern.

While Europeans reviled Cossack brutality, they also romanticised and celebrated their egalitarian, free-spirited lifestyle. Russians, in particular, saw in them an alternative to the stifling, controlled lives they led in the cities, and many Russian writers, especially Tolstoy and Gogol, wrote novels or stories portraying Cossacks as dashing, heroic bandits. Not themselves 'Russian', they remained a fundamental part of an idea of 'Russia', a half-civilised barrier between Westernised Russia and the East. In many ways they were the acceptable version of the Mongols, decently Slavic rather than Asian, and nominally Christian.

This was not entirely true of Ungern's new regiment. The Transbaikal was one of the smallest and newest Cossack hosts (*voisko*) – the very name reminiscent of the Mongol armies. It had been founded in 1858 and with only a quarter of a million members was still less than a quarter of the size of the older Western hosts, such as the Don Cossacks. However, it did include some genuine Mongols. Around 12 per cent of the Transbaikal Cossacks were Buriat Mongols, small, round-faced men, Buddhist in faith and with strong links to their cousins back home. Ordinary Buriats often returned to Mongolia for pilgrimage or trade, married Mongolian women, and had political links with the Mongolian nobility. The tsarist regime recognised and even funded the Buriat Buddhist hierarchy, which had ties to both Tibet and Mongolia; their loyalty to Tsar Nikolas was strong. Ungern found the company of the Cossacks pleasing. He was closer to them than to his fellow Russians, and he took a particular interest in the Buriat. Already an accomplished linguist, he picked up their language and studied their customs. Perhaps, as he did during the war, he lived and slept among them. He found their way of life simple, appealing and pure, especially in contrast to the complexity of Western culture, and developed a deep liking for the region and its peoples.

— ◆ ◄◆► ◆ —

The nominal duty of the Argun Regiment was the defence of the borders of the empire. The Transbaikal Host was named after the great Lake Baikal, in the middle of Siberia, and their territory ran along both the Mongolian and Manchurian borders. In the nineteenth century they had spawned two other Siberian hosts, the Amur and the Ussuri, and together their territory included the whole border zone. If Japan or China started trouble across the frontier, the Transbaikal would be the first line of defence. It was a duty to which Ungern was deeply committed. The Russian Empire was sacred to him, but it was an idea of empire formed around the 'combination of the peoples'.[14] Buriat, German, Russian, Cossack – all of them could come together in unity and strength, under a monarchy blessed by God.

His was a romantic version of what was, in fact, an entirely pragmatic approach towards the Russian borderlands. Like most imperial peoples, the Russians soon realised that it was easier to co-opt than coerce. They lacked the numbers to try the Chinese or American approach to dealing with areas dominated by minority ethnic groups; open up the borders, encourage (or coerce) hundreds of thousands of your own people to settle the region and outnumber the locals within a generation or two. With the borderlands so strategically crucial, they had to be secured another way. Membership in the Russian Empire had to be made attractive, particularly to the local elites. Old tribal structures and religious hierarchies were maintained, but were incorporated into the imperial bureaucracy. As a result Russian officials found themselves deciding obscure questions of tribal inheritance, or determining whether a new visionary religion among the Oirat Mongols threatened imperial stability, or funding the construction of Buddhist temples. Local leaders or priests were paid off with lucrative government jobs or posts in the army. If these tactics failed, though, imperial policy could demonstrate a Roman ruthlessness, crushing rebellious tribes and salting their fields.

The Buriat provide a good example of the ambiguous attitude of the Russian Empire towards its ethnic minorities. On the one hand, it had

35

conquered and (theoretically) subjugated them, and the majority of ethnic Russians maintained profoundly racist attitudes towards the various Asian peoples. Russian settlement had driven some, particularly the various Siberian tribes, away from their traditional territories, brought disease and stripped them of their traditional independence. On the other hand, the empire had a vested interest in keeping the Buriat and other large groups happy. In many ways they had more rights than the average Russian – they paid less tax, they were exempt from conscription,[15] they were able to keep their traditional leadership. Many of the Asiatic minorities were actually more privileged than the Ukrainians and Poles, who were forbidden even from using their own languages. The Asiatic minorities benefited from their very foreignness. The Western minorities were seen as a plausible target for Russification, but the Mongol-descended peoples, far more ethnically and religiously distant, were left to their own devices.

The empire remained focused around its Great Russian and religiously Orthodox core, but at the same time was able to embrace numerous diverse groups at its edges. Sometimes members of these groups could be the most ardent proponents of imperial expansion. For instance, the Buriats' place within the empire was made even more secure by the rise to power and influence of one of their compatriots, Piotr Badmaev. A convert to Orthodoxy and practitioner of Tibetan medicine, he had the ear of both Alexandr III and Nikolas II, and considered himself the protector of the Buriats. He also pushed for plans, never realised, to expand the empire yet further, annexing Tibet and parts of western China.

With the exception of his time in St Petersburg, Ungern's whole life was spent on the fringes of the empire. They would come to define the Russian Empire for him, even when its core was abandoned, but his idealistic vision of it didn't make the mundane work of guarding its frontiers any less boring. Ungern was stationed in Dauria, a town which existed only because of the nearby border and the railways (it sat on the main line to Manchuria); all it had were barracks, a station and a smattering of camp followers, and the tedium of life was enlivened only by traders occasionally passing through.

It was the kind of place where younger sons gambled away the family fortune for lack of anything better to do. The historian Willard Sunderland sums life there up as drills, patrols, escort duties (of convicts and settlers), raids (against Chinese bandits), and more drills, punctuated with gambling, drinking, and horse races, in the midst of mostly wilderness and overwhelmingly male company. The officers' libraries had few books. Towns with shops, playhouses, or bordellos could be days away.[16]

The nearest settlement that even resembled a real city was the large town of Chita, two hundred miles down the railway. The surrounding countryside was beautiful but bare, a dry plain broken only by small clusters of hills. It was sparsely populated, with scattered villages of poor illiterate peasants eking out a living.

The broken landscape and lack of roads meant that horses were the only practical way to patrol the border, and this was good horse country, which pleased Ungern. He had chosen to join a cavalry division not only for its glamour but also because he loved horses. The Buriat, like their Mongolian cousins, were excellent riders and good judges of horseflesh. Ungern was already a talented rider, but under the tutelage of more experienced officers his skills improved further. He soon mastered the art of mounted combat and became respected in the regiment for his riding skills. Warfare on horseback has a romanticism which has not quite disappeared from the Western consciousness,[17] and Ungern would remain eternally enthusiastic, to his later tactical disadvantage, about the possibilities of the cavalry charge and the lightning raid. He had other diversions too; one report mentions his interest in 'general' as well as 'military' literature and European philosophy.

Ungern would make an extraordinary claim about his time in Dauria:

> In Transbaikalia I tried to form the Order of Military Buddhists for an uncompromising fight against the depravity of revolution [. . .] For what? For the protection of the processes of evolution of humanity and for the struggle against revolution, because I am certain that evolution leads to the Divinity and revolution to bestiality.[18]

The Order apparently had strict rules, which Ungern's companions were unable to live up to. In response,

> I introduced the condition of celibacy, the entire negation of woman, of the comforts of life, of superfluities, according to the teachings of the Yellow Faith; and in order that the Russian might be able to live down his physical nature, I introduced the limitless use of alcohol,

hasheesh, and opium. Now for alcohol I hang my officers and soldiers; then we drank to the 'white fever', delirium tremens. I could
not organise the Order but I gathered round me and developed three
hundred men wholly bold and entirely ferocious.[19]

A bunch of supposedly Buddhist officers wandering around the
Transbaikal, drunk and stoned and preaching the 'Yellow Faith' is a
wonderful picture, but that Ungern actually organised such an Order
seems unlikely. One would expect somebody else to mention it, for one
thing. The witness to this speech of Ungern's, Ferdinand Ossendowski,
was not always the most reliable of storytellers. The account is repeated
in one other memoir, where 'Nikolay looked at me with the wide, staring
eyes of a fanatic. I knew he was a Buddhist, as were Baron Ungern and
some three hundred of the others around them,'[20] but this in turn is
probably culled from Ossendowski.

It may be that Ossendowski made up the story himself, but it seems
more likely that it was a later fantasy of Ungern's, perhaps rooted in
some drunken scheme. The language is distinctly Theosophical, with
its talk of 'the evolution of humanity', and perhaps it reflected his
thinking and reading at the time – or perhaps it reflected Ossendowski's
own esoteric interests. The close connection of war and religion was
certainly part of Ungern's later thinking; perhaps he was considering,
even then, how Buddhism could be harnessed to raise an army for a
holy war.

One trait that certainly wasn't fictional was drunkenness. Alcohol was
a staple of garrison life everywhere, and Ungern developed a ferocious
love of it. The toast to the 'white fever' sounds worryingly plausible for
a group of young, bored soldiers. Ungern was not a gentle drunk, and his
drinking led to his departure from the Transbaikal Host. The circum-
stances are unclear, but he got into a duel with another officer, which
resulted in no serious harm to either party – it may not have actually
been fought at all – as a result of drunken insults, most probably at a
'wine party'. As a result he felt obliged or was pressured to resign from
the regiment so as not to serve with the man he had fought. That it was
Ungern who resigned, and not his opponent, suggests where the fault lay.
Using family influence, he found a new posting easily enough with the
1st Amur Regiment of the Amur Cossack Host, in the extremes of the
Russian Far East near Blagoveshchensk. It was another bleak garrison

town, even further from civilisation than Dauria. The Chinese border was close by, and raids by Chinese bandits commonplace.

Before Ungern set out from Dauria, he made a wager with the local officers that he could 'travel the more than 400 versts [around 270 miles] to Blagoveshchensk, where the Amur camp was located, only on horseback, eating what could be found along the way.'[21] This kind of long solitary ride was a common form of macho display among soldiers and travellers in the region. Ungern's was relatively short, but an excellent chance to show off his riding skills and toughness, and to make an impression upon his new comrades in the Amur Regiment. It also deepened his familiarity with the region. It is unclear how long Ungern took to make the journey, but he won his bet. Some writers suggested that he veered into Mongolia, and even served with the Russian Consulate Guard there, but he would not have had the time to do so before taking up his new posting.

◆━◆━ ≡◆≡ ━◆━◆

Ungern found the Amur posting even more tedious than his life in Dauria, despite the fact that during his time there he was posted to the machine-gun division, served as head of the intelligence division and led patrols along the Manchurian border. His record mentions various 'incidents', for which read quarrels, fights and duels. He took a six-month leave in 1911, returning home to see his family. Once back at Blagoveshchensk he continued quarrelsome as ever, and soon found himself in another duel. This was probably the source of his famous forehead scar, inflicted by a sabre-wielding opponent. Partly because of this incident, partly because of his own dissatisfaction, he sent a letter to Petersburg on 4 July, 1913 requesting a discharge from active service and a transfer to the reserve.

This was the second time he had left a regiment because of a duel, and the fourth time he had been effectively expelled from an institution following a breach of discipline. In some ways Ungern's antics harked back to the traditions of the archetypal eighteenth-century officer, Russian or Prussian: an exaggerated sense of honour, a disdain for inferiors and, above all, a propensity to use force to make one's point. At that time throwing a merchant out of a window for having the effrontery to present a bill, or slapping a peasant down the street with the flat of a sword had been fairly regular occurrences. For a Russian officer in the twentieth century, the occasional beating, or even drunken duel, might remain acceptable, but getting roaring drunk and firing at random at the patrons of cafes and taverns to prove your marksmanship, as Ungern is alleged to have done, was now considered excessive.

The Russian army had a long tradition of institutionalised violence, too, especially towards recruits, and had abolished flogging only with the reforms of 1864, decades after other European armies. The documented evidence of Ungern's attacks probably excludes numerous assaults against servants, enlisted men, peasants and other such lowly specimens. By the standards of both the Baltic aristocracy and the Russian army, these were effectively non-people, and violence against them left no mark on the record. It is reasonable to assume that the reports of assaults on fellow cadets at school and outbursts against officers represent only a small fraction of Ungern's thuggery.

Many who knew him later were forever seeking the root cause of Ungern's wild rages. One theory was that his wounded forehead, injured either in his duel of 1913 or while fighting in the Caucasus in the Great War, sometimes flared up painfully and prompted Ungern's wrath. Such a simple and organic explanation seems unlikely. Perhaps it was genetic, for his great-great-grandfather, his father, and Ungern himself were all prone to outbursts of rage. Privilege certainly had something to do with it; despite all his expulsions, there had always been a way back in for Ungern. Now, however, even the army was unwilling to offer a welcoming home. The combination of bureaucracy, tedium and alcohol finally became too much for him. His spirit was better suited to a land of magic and adventure.

THREE

Suspended Between Heaven and Hell

By the time the letter releasing him from duty arrived at Blagoveshchensk, Ungern was well into Mongolia, 'in search of bold accomplishments', as the letter he carried with him from his commander attested. Hermann Keyserling, a fellow Baltic noble, thought that Mongolia was a natural destination for him. He had a strong impression of Ungern:

> certainly the most remarkable person I have ever had the good fortune to meet. One day I said to his grandmother, Baroness Wimpfen, 'He is a creature whom one might call suspended between Heaven and Hell, without the least understanding of the laws of this world.' He presented a really extraordinary mixture of the most profound aptitude for metaphysics and of cruelty. So he was positively predestined for Mongolia (where such discord in a man is the rule), and there, in fact, his fate led him. [. . .] He was not of this world, and I cannot help thinking that on this earth he was only a passing guest.[1]

As Ungern passed into Mongolia he was riding through an otherworldly environment. Sometimes on the grasslands he could look in any direction and see no human sign all the way to the horizon, the blue of the sky like a vast ocean above him, broken only by the flicker of a bird of prey. Unless he ran across herders, or saw a marmot scurrying briefly above ground, the world would seem entirely devoid of life. The empty landscape was similar to that of Siberia. Perhaps he even found comfort in being only a speck on a vast expanse of nothingness – he never had great need of any company other than his own.

Not all of Mongolia is flat, particularly in the north-east, and much of the time he would have been travelling through long stretches of hills, rising sometimes into mountains, across swamps, or between thick forests where humans rarely intruded. Small clusters of rocky hills broke up the open countryside, as though the earth had been punched from beneath. Ungern regarded the landscape with a tactician's trained eye, looking for routes that a cavalry army could take; he could still remember them a decade later. Such terrain was also attractive to the builders of monasteries, the only permanent structures in most parts of Mongolia, the steep slopes and commanding views being excellent defensive features. Here travellers could find rest and safety; the monks were often trained fighters and the monastery walls thickly reinforced. Ungern would have been made welcome, for the monks paid little heed to race or religion and usually accepted Chinese, Russian and Mongolian visitors alike – a laudable generosity given the fact that the preceding few hundred years had seen several Chinese invasions of Mongolia, and many monastery-fortresses, which had been centres of resistance, had been either burnt down or stuffed with gunpowder and blown up. Destroyed monasteries were not the only ruins Ungern would have encountered; he might have stumbled upon remnants of pre-Mongol civilisations, perhaps the Ozymandian palace of a long-forgotten Turkic king. In the summer heat herds of horses pressed themselves against the old walls, or gathered under the rare bridges, desperate for shade.

Ungern could not have carried enough food and water to survive the entire journey self-sufficiently, so must have relied upon the everyday hospitality of the Mongolians. Mongolia's harsh terrain and climate, particularly in the winter, meant that feeding and housing travellers was considered a duty by every household. Even a foreigner would be given shelter for the night unquestioningly, and food for the next day. Ungern must have spent many nights in the cramped and dark interior of a Mongolian tent, with a barrel of fermented mare's milk by the door and the family sleeping on cushions inside. He must also have seen the regular devotions of the Mongols, sprinkling offerings to the spirits and praying to the gods and Buddhas.

As a foreigner travelling alone he would have drawn special attention from the locals. Many European visitors to Asia liked to wear traditional dress, often writing self-flatteringly that they were indistinguishable from the locals. This seems hard to believe. Even today, any European male in rural China, regardless of dress, draws a crowd of open-mouthed children, middle-aged women cheerfully assessing his looks and young men shouting '*Hello!*' There were only a few hundred Europeans in the whole country at the time, among perhaps a million Mongolians; apart from the small Russian settlement around the consulate in Urga, which was the sole foreign enclave, they were guaranteed to attract attention from the locals, curious as to what exotic items or powerful magic they might possess. (Europeans were seen by many Mongols as being potentially powerful sorcerers. The explorer Henning Haslund described how a young woman had come to him and begged him to symbolically 'adopt' her sick baby, since his powerful 'white man's magic' would be able to drive away the spirits that plagued the child. He went through the ritual, and the child promptly recovered.) A traveller would never be without company, however unwelcome.

Ungern would certainly have stood out among the Mongolians, with his bullet-shaped head, stage-villain moustache and tufts of reddish-blond hair. He was in first-rate physical condition, lean and hard, but when he spoke his voice varied wildly in pitch, like that of a teenager, although he was almost thirty. Aleksei Burdukov, a Russian merchant, fell in with Ungern for a while. He left an unforgettable picture of him: 'a scrawny, ragged, droopy man; on his face had grown a wispy blond beard, he had faded, blank blue eyes, and he looked about thirty years old. His military uniform was in abnormally poor condition, the trousers being considerably worn and torn at the knees. He carried a sword by his hip and a gun at his belt.'[2] Ungern rode alongside Burdukov's coaches, a skilled, tireless horseman, shouting at the coachmen when he felt they were slacking and striking them with his whip. When the group stumbled into a swamp, Ungern 'laid on the ground and refused to move, listening'. Then, going forward and ordering the others to follow, he led them from patch to patch through the bog, 'finding the most convenient solid places with surprising dexterity and often getting into knee-deep water'. Eventually he sniffed at the air, 'seeking the smell of smoke to find nearby settlements. At last he told us one was nearby. We followed him, and he was right – in the distance we heard the bark of dogs. This unusual persistence, cruelty, instinctive feelings amazed me.' Burdukov despaired of the quality of young Russian officers in the country, if Ungern's bad manners and cruelty were typical of the breed.

―•― ≡✦≣ ―•―

The first thing Ungern would have noticed about Urga, Mongolia's most populous settlement, was the smell. Sewers were as unheard of as electricity, and human waste was simply thrown into the streets to be devoured by the packs of scavenging dogs that roamed the city. Anybody venturing outdoors at night took a stick to beat off the animals, but their main enemies were the hordes of beggars, mostly old women no longer able to bear the rigours of steppe life, driven to the town to live a few last miserable years fighting with the dogs for scraps. To add to the stench, the Mongolians were a notoriously unwashed people, believing the rare springs and streams in the country were home to territorial spirits who would inflict dreadful illness on trespassers.

Ungern arrived there in the autumn of 1913, but it was a strangely timeless city; apart from the rifles sometimes carried by hunters and soldiers, and the very occasional European motor car, it would have been hard to tell whether it was 1913 or 1193. Merchants rode in on camel or horse from China, bearing silks, drugs and teas; trappers hawked furs that would eventually be sold for a thousand times their initial price when they reached Moscow or London; fortune-tellers cast oracle bones on the street to determine the fates of young nobles.

It was a trading city, where Mongols, Chinese and Russians met to exchange goods worth over a million dollars a year. Its Chinese and Russian enclaves were well established, almost entirely separate from the Mongolian one. Urga lay at the centre of the Tea Road, the overland route to Russia, and originally the local currency had been bricks of tea, but now most traders preferred the brass cash of the Chinese, or even Mexican dollars (a common trading currency at the time). The markets were full of livestock, enlivened by the occasional Western wonder such as a gramophone or a camera, normally brought for the amusement of the Jebtsundamba Khutuktu, also known as the Bogd Gegen, Holy Shining One, Holy King or Living Buddha: the ever-reincarnating head of the Mongolian Buddhist orders and one of the very few Mongols

44

who could afford such toys.[3] It was the closest that Mongolia had to a capital, being the nominal centre of the most dominant Mongolian group, the Khalkha,[4] but the real power lay in foreign hands. Mongolia had been under Chinese control for three centuries, and the Chinese administration, including a small garrison, was based in Urga.

Primarily, it was a city of religion. Out of the roughly twenty-five thousand permanent Mongolian residents, an estimated ten thousand were either monks or had some sort of affiliation with the monasteries. There were a hundred and three reincarnated lamas in Mongolia, returning life after life, and many of them lived there. Urga had been founded in the seventeenth century as the Ikh Khuree, or 'great monastery', to serve as the residence of the Bogd Gegen, and that remained its Mongolian name; 'Urga' was used only by Russians and other foreigners. Temples were everywhere, dark and smoky, statues of their gods concealed in numerous alcoves. The gods were usually depicted in a warlike stance, brandishing weapons and trampling on corpses, but some were joined together in elaborate and implausibly athletic couplings, no doubt to the ribald amusement of the more elderly and worldly-wise female pilgrims.[5] The statues were dressed by the temple's monks, some of whom would climb, agile as monkeys, over the larger examples, sometimes twenty metres tall, in order to change a goddess's scarf or repaint a cracked face. Most of the monks wore the conventional saffron robes of Buddhism, but some wore heavy wooden masks depicting the angry or ecstatic faces of the gods, dancing and singing in their honour. Yellow silk banners fluttered in the breeze outside the temples, emblazoned with the swastika, an ancient symbol of Buddhism and one particularly venerated by the Mongolians.

Being a monk was a relatively good life, compared with that of herder, scratching out a bare subsistence and ever fearful of a bad *zud*, a peculiar local combination of hard winter and quick-melting frost that could kill a quarter of the country's livestock. The vast majority of Mongolians lived as nomads, moving between camps according to the seasons and relying on their animals to survive. Monks were certain of a full bowl and a comfortable place to sleep, if nothing else, and the temples were major money makers, storing most of what wealth there was in Mongolia. The temples were visible for miles, since they were the only large buildings in Urga; most of the population lived in gers (felt tents). Important gers were surrounded by walled compounds, marking an uneasy compromise between settled and nomadic life. Only in the Russian compound and the Chinese trading town of Maimaichen, a few miles from the main city, were permanent buildings common.

Throughout the year the population of the city would be bolstered by pious pilgrims, bringing offerings of food, money and incense. By local standards, Urga was a major site of religious tourism, sometimes drawing Buddhists from China and Tibet as well as from all the Mongol tribes. The Gandan Temple, the residence of the chief Mongolian oracles, was the most visited location, a steep and shadowy building designed to induce a suitable degree of fear and trembling in the approaching supplicant. The Bogd Khan's own palace, a couple of miles away, was a two-storeyed European-style affair, painted in lurid shades of green and yellow and greatly venerated. Today it seems a modest building, on the same scale as a decent sized English farmhouse, but it was the first building in Mongolia to have more than one floor, and pilgrims would come to see the miracle of its staircase, treading gingerly upon each step.

Religion was not the only amusement. The 'three manly sports' of wrestling, horse-riding and archery, the foundations of the Mongolian's old military might, were hugely popular. Men of all ages would come to compete against each other at tournaments, and informal matches were common; travellers reported young men racing on horseback through the city, or two bear-like amateur wrestlers grunting and shoving against each other in the street as their wives watched and cheered. The 'three manly sports' were really five; drinking and boasting were considered equally important.[6] The Mongolian assertion that 'every man is Genghis Khan in his own tent' was surely heard as widely then as today, and if all the drunken claims of beasts slain, Chinese humiliated and women wooed were true, Mongolia was a nation of heroes.

Religious ceremonies, frequent and extravagant, were at the core of life in the city. At festival times the perimeter could expand to four or five times its normal size, acquiring a huge outer ring of gers and becoming a great campground with the city at its centre. New buildings would be hastily constructed to bear enormous statues or prayer-flags; rows of lamas danced through the streets; crowds cheered and clapped and prayed. Festivals were times of masks: skull-masks for the dancers of death, demon-masks stuck on poles to grin eerily in the sunlight like disembodied heads, the great ox-mask of Erlik Kam, a legendary monk-turned-demon, curling horns dipped in blood and crown adorned with five skulls as eight terrible demons dance attendance around him.[7] The smallpox god, his face red with buboes, and the blue-skinned, four-armed Yamantaka, God of Death, accompanied him. The heavy masks and robes turned the dancers into living marionettes, their strings pulled by the gods. Buddhist passion-plays, half spiritual metaphor and half kung-fu drama, were enacted before vast crowds, who would cheer and shout as the monk-actors fought battles of lama versus demon on stage, or wrestled with the temptations of the flesh – normally shown as a young woman, or at least a good-looking novice dressed as such. Despite the grand menace of the gathered demon-gods, and the awestruck respect shown to the great lamas, these were clearly crowd-pleasing events, a welcome respite from the daily grind of Mongolian life. The German traveller Rudolf Strasser describes one festival:

> The crowd, ever increasing, surged round like a moving rainbow on a waterfall. Two men could be seen mounted on one pony and cling-ing to each other, people on foot talking and laughing, children on the shoulders of men and women. All the wonderful pomp of Mongolia lay spread out in the sun in a blaze of colours impossible to describe, running up and down a full scale of orgiastic notes in gleaming silks – salmon pink, milky green, and pale blue; stiff gold brocades all patterned in brown and emerald green; rows of red lamas like the crimson flesh of a pomegranate; others in robes of cit-ron and amber – with blue cuffs and black velvet hems that curved around the neck and breast like a note of interrogation; helmet-shaped hats in citron and saffron with black brims turned high and trimmed with blue bows; caps of clipped woolly fur; clean-shaven heads of priests like pale tulips.[8]

When Ungern arrived, Mongolia had been independent for just two years, and was still fighting to secure itself. After three centuries of Chinese rule a small coterie of nobles, combined with the theocratic power of the Buddhist temples, had come together to free the country from Chinese control, and proudly proclaimed Mongolia free, strong and Buddhist.

The revolution had been a painful affair. In China, the Qing dynasty was finally collapsing after a drawn-out agony of more than a century during which China's rulers had proven woefully unprepared to deal with Western guns, opium or ideas. The few Chinese remaining in Mongolia, mostly officials and merchants, had no stomach for a fight, especially in the name of a foreign dynasty. There were just over a hundred Chinese troops in Urga facing four thousand Mongolian soldiers and perhaps a thousand Russians. The worst fighting had been in the west, around the city of Khobdo, where Mongol forces stormed the Chinese compounds and slaughtered the garrison. Other resistance leaders led small bands against the Chinese elsewhere in the country; one of the most successful was formed by Togtokh, a Mongolian prince and long-standing opponent of the Chinese, who headed a group of warriors equipped with Russian rifles.

The Qing themselves were not Chinese but Manchu. A nomadic and warlike group of northern clans unified under the charismatic leadership of Nurhaci, much as the Mongols had been under Genghis Khan, they had conquered China in 1644, driving out the reigning Ming dynasty. The Mongol leaders loathed the Ming, who were descended from the leaders of the original Chinese rebellion against the Mongols, and were only too happy to see the Qing take the throne, swiftly sealing deals whereby the leaders of each Mongol clan effectively accepted Manchu rule. (So happy, in fact, that the southern Mongol tribes of modern Inner Mongolia acknowledged the first Qing emperor as the 'great khan' in 1636, eight years before the final conquest of China, although it took another sixty years for the northern Mongols to accept Qing leadership.) The early Qing emperors took wives from among the Mongols, particularly those who could prove direct descent from Genghis, in order both to strengthen their ties to Mongolia and bolster their claim to be the true heirs of the Mongol Yuan dynasty, and so the legitimate rulers of China. They also spread rumours that they had discovered the legendary Great Seal of Genghis Khan, legitimising their reign through prophecy.[9]

The greatest challenge to the Qing came from the Zunghar kingdom of western Mongolia, led by the powerful and charismatic leader Galdan Khan, who also made claims to legitimacy through descent from Genghis. Its power was destroyed by a century of Qing campaigns, combined with outbreaks of smallpox which killed 40 per cent of the population. Continued Mongolian resistance resulted in the Chinese adopting a policy of genocide in the 1750s, effected by starvation tactics and an imperial order 'to take the young and strong and massacre them'. Siberian governors reported refugees' stories of Manchu troops massacring entire settlements. Roughly one hundred and eighty thousand people were killed, and the survivors fled to join the Kazakhs and Buriats in Russia. 'For several thousand *li* [around 600 miles],' reported one historian, 'there was not one single Zungharian tent'.[10]

Despite the devastation wrought by the Qing in the west, many Mongolians were content to live under Manchu rule. The Manchu were determined to keep their original homelands in the north free from corrupting Chinese influence, and so banned all settlement in both Manchuria and northern Mongolia. They issued a series of decrees in the nineteenth century which forbade Mongols from learning the Chinese language, taking Chinese names, adopting Chinese clothing and habits, or even eating Chinese food. Population pressures resulted in widespread settlement by Han Chinese in southern Mongolia, which had effectively been absorbed into China by the beginning of the twentieth century and today is the modern-day province of Inner Mongolia. The breakdown of the non-settlement policy, combined with incompetent administration and the stranglehold that Chinese traders had on the Mongolian economy, kindled anti-Qing feelings among the Mongols. By 1911 demonstrations, rebellions and attacks on Qing officials were becoming increasingly common. Debt and natural disaster drove a growing number of former nomads into a pitiful life as beggars on the edge of the towns.

The communist regime was later to claim the 1911 rebellion as a precursor to Mongolia's glorious Marxist uprising. That the Mongols had petitioned Russia for support in their revolution made good communist propaganda, and it has been called Asia's first modern revolution. In truth there was very little modern about it. Democratic ideals were current among a tiny fraction of the Mongolian population, mostly those lucky few who had worked or been educated in Russia or China and who had picked up ideas from reformers there. The instigators of the petition to Moscow comprised a small circle of young hereditary nobles, determined to regain some measure of their ancient power. The heads of each Mongol tribe had been obliged, under the Qing, to visit Peking to make obeisance to the emperor, and any who failed to do so were forced to pay tribute in sheep to his representatives in Mongolia.

This rankled the nobles, whose ancestral memories of the mighty Yuan dynasty of Genghis Khan were still vivid. Back then the 'proper' order of things had been established and the Chinese had paid tribute to the Mongols, not the other way round. Life had at least been tolerable so long as the Qing had maintained their distinctly Manchu, nomadic identity, but resentment against them increased as they became more Sinicised. The Manchu language, which bore some similarity to Mongolian, had been almost completely abandoned by the Qing except for ceremonial purposes and they had become virtually indistinguishable from the Han Chinese. Even their hairstyles were identical, for the Han had been forced to adopt the pigtail among several other Manchu customs.

The rebellion mustered considerable popular support, not so much from any great liking for the nobles as from distaste for the Chinese. In order to placate dissenters at home and defend against Russian expansionism, the Chinese authorities had begun allowing much greater colonisation in Mongolia. They stationed two regiments in Inner Mongolia in 1906 and began the construction of a railway to compete directly with the Russian line. Over twenty thousand square miles of land had been taken away from the Mongols for the Chinese settlers to farm, and three hundred and fifty thousand Chinese settlers had moved into Inner Mongolia.

All these measures were resented by the Mongols, especially Chinese colonisation. The Mongolians, still almost entirely herders and nomads, valued their land and their space more than anything else, and saw urban life as essentially soft, fit only for beggars and monks. The Chinese merchants and bankers were resented most of all; the Mongols, increasingly impoverished by colonisation and Qing taxation, were forced to buy on credit, often at crippling rates of interest. Chinese merchants were the main target of the outbreaks of violence during the revolution; over three hundred of them were murdered and their debt records burned in ceremonial pyres on the streets.

Anti-Chinese feelings were even more intense in Inner Mongolia, where the call for Mongolian independence was eagerly taken up by the eight Mongol clans there, all of whom were suffering badly from Chinese expansionism. One of the largest groups was the Chahars – so prominent, in fact, that one province, which encompassed much of modern Inner Mongolia, was named after them. They held territory around the Chinese city of Chengde and were particularly fierce in their opposition to Chinese rule, but Han settlers outnumbered them by a ratio of nearly 19 to 1 and many Mongols were driven over the border into northern Mongolia or Russia.

The superior attitude of the Chinese towards the Mongolians didn't help matters. In the Chinese suburb of Urga, Maimaichen, the people lived in wooden buildings instead of gers and kept their distance from the Mongolian city. Mongolia was the edge of the Chinese Empire, and the colonists harboured the usual prejudices against the natives. Themselves stereotyped by the British and Japanese as lazy, backward, cruel and ignorant, the Han Chinese applied their own sets of prejudices to the northern barbarians. Nineteenth- and early twentieth-century Chinese accounts consistently portray the Mongols as scurrilous, lazy and drunken – sometimes accurately, especially in respect of the town-dwelling Mongols they encountered most often – and this attitude seems to have carried over into everyday dealings between the two groupings.

The Mongolian reputation for cruelty, insensibility and stupidity, a legacy of the ruthless conquests of the hordes, still survived in both Asia and Europe. Chinese popular dramas featured Mongolian henchmen, often Oddjob to Japanese Blofeld, who habitually threatened the hero or heroine with sadistic torture.[11] A later but telling example comes from the Second World War, where one French doctor, witnessing the execution of a Mongolian prisoner, a member of a German repression unit (perhaps lent by the Japanese; perhaps drafted by the Russians, then captured and drafted again[12]) spoke of how 'he had no thoughts at all about what was happening to him. He had died as an animal does'.[13] Medically speaking, Down's syndrome children were 'mongoloid', a term originally intended to reference not only their epicanthic eyes, but also their diminished mental capacity. Western visitors remarked upon the Mongolians' 'remarkable naivety' or 'child-like attitudes'. The Chinese mocked them as dumb, smelly barbarians, and took remorseless advantage of their (quite genuine) gullibility in matters of trade. One Briton commentated sniffily, 'Ch'ou

Ta-tzu ("foul Tartars") is a Chinese term of contempt hundreds of years old, and the justice of this approach in the mouth of a race whose notions of sanitation are still rudimentary, is not at first apparent. At Urga a comparison is possible, and it is in favour of the Chinese.'[14] In many ways the situation paralleled American and Amerindian relations in the nineteenth century; an expansionist colonising power against a nomadic and defensive group of natives.

The difference here was that, thanks to the collapse of the Qing and the aid of Russia, the natives stood a good chance of winning. This didn't make the Chinese happy. To be beaten by Western devils was hard enough on national pride; to be beaten by a bunch of northern barbarians, even if their ancestors had had delusions of grandeur, was too much to take. For added insult, the ceremonial trappings and nomenclature adopted by the new Mongolian court mimicked the customs of the Chinese emperors; not only an unprecedented impertinence but a clear sign, in the language of dynastic mandate understood by both courts, of an assertion of sovereignty over Mongolia and all the previous Mongolian territories of the Chinese Empire.

━━━ ⅸ◊Ⅺ ━━━

The new ruler of Mongolia, de facto head of the rebellion, was the Bogd Khan (Holy Emperor), the head of Mongolian Buddhism and a figure of great importance in Ungern's later life. Previously he had been known as the Bogd Gegen (Holy Shining One). He was the third most important 'Yellow Hat' in the Gelugpa tradition of Tibetan Buddhism, below only the Dalai and Panchen Lamas. Like the Dalai Lama, he was a living bodhisattva, one who had chosen upon reaching enlightenment not to achieve the blissful state of nirvana but rather to reincarnate himself constantly in order to help enlighten other souls. These figures were often known as 'living Buddhas' to Westerners, and by the Tibetan term *trulku* among Mongolians.

His present incarnation, his eighth, offered an unusual perspective on the Buddhist notion of enlightenment, a man bloated through overeating and binge drinking. The cruelty and carnal appetites of the Bogd were legendary in Mongolia. The communist regime was later to claim in its propaganda that he violated children of both sexes while performing Buddhist rites. He was certainly an enthusiastic whoremonger.

52

European and Tibetan travellers commented disapprovingly on his apparent penchant for young boys, but it was considered an entirely acceptable vice among Mongolian monks. (The Japanese spy Hideo Tasuki was told in the 1940s that 'Mongolian [monks] prefer boys front-side up, Tibetans from behind.'[15]) It was widely believed that he had had a homosexual relationship with at least one of the monks at his court, Legtseg, who eventually fell out of favour and was exiled, then, on the Bogd's orders, executed. Almost inevitably he contracted syphilis, endemic in Mongolia at the time, and it was slowly blinding him, a condition charitably blamed by his contemporaries on his drinking rather than his sexual adventures. That his cabinet meetings invariably turned into night-long drinking binges added plausibility to the claim.

Whatever the cause, disease had affected his eyes, but by no means his mind. Though of noble Tibetan stock, the Bogd Khan was a fervent advocate of Mongolian independence, chiefly for self-serving ends. In the eighteenth century one of his predecessors had supported Mongol rebels against the Qing dynasty in China, and as a result the Qing had declared that future incarnations of the line could be discovered only in Tibet. However, after the rebellious clans had been subdued by the Qing armies, native Mongolian political power shifted largely to the Buddhist theocracy. As the head of the Mongolian Buddhist hierarchy and a figure of immense spiritual importance, he knew that any increase in Mongolian autonomy would inevitably lead to an increase in his own power and wealth. At the same time, he was a canny political operator, unwilling to commit to any cause unless certain of its success. Although not a leader of the initial independence movement, he was more than willing to support the declaration of independence after it flatteringly declared him 'radiant as the sun, myriad aged, the Great Khan of Mongolia'. His presumably long-suffering wife, the Ekh Dagina, an incarnation of the important Buddhist goddess Tara in her own right, was simultaneously declared 'the Great Mother of the Country'.

In the 1890s, he had a new palace built for himself. At first, this aroused considerable resentment in Mongolia, causing him to write petulantly in an encyclical letter,

The rumours saying that in order to house the image of the seventh Bogd Gegen I had built a new two-storeyed house adorned on all sides with glass windows and painted inside as well as outside with pure gold, and put up the statues of the protective deities on the four sides, and that such a beautiful house was built in which I live alone happily rejoicing myself, are not true. I only took the opportunity when the good omens coincided, and prepared a peaceful place to call people together in the North.[16]

He was lying; it was for himself, and he filled it with magazines and toys from the West.

At first the stories about the Bogd seem suspiciously lurid, the product of the considerable effort by Soviet authorities to smear his memory after his death, or the Fu Manchu-like fantasies of Western travellers. Some of the legends are certainly exaggerated, such as the claim that he fed his enemies to his collection of exotic animals. However, both contemporary Mongolian and foreign witnesses, including prominent lamas and anti-communists, have testified to his ruthlessness, alcoholism and greed. Only one Western writer, the Danish-American Erik Larson, thought well of him, and even he tells stories that, stripped of Larson's general good nature and love of all things Mongolian, seem petty and sadistic, such as his habit of dangling an electrified rope over the wall of his palace so that innocent pilgrims would touch it, receive a shock and believe themselves to have received a spiritual blessing. A pair of guns presented to him by a Russian visitor gave him particular joy, and were often fired at random targets when he was bored. They still survive, little eight-pounder cannon, unmounted and lying on his palace lawn.

His political policies often extended to murder, notably of his opponents, and he acquired a notorious reputation as a poisoner. Some laid the blame on his wife, but this seems to stem from a combination of misogyny and an understandable reluctance to admit that the spiritual leader of the country was an assassin. His own theology preached a twofold path to enlightenment, one road of asceticism and meditation and another, reserved for particularly wise individuals such as himself, upon which the traveller was free to indulge in whatever debauchery he chose as he 'strolled along the mantra path'. Fool-saints who stood outside conventional morality, such as the notorious but beloved Sixth Dalai Lama, a flamboyant bisexual poet, were part of the Buddhist tradition, but the Bogd Khan's eminently materialistic concern with power and influence put him firmly beyond the pale.

Monks who preached against him rarely survived their dinner invitations. According to Ossendowski, 'The Bogd Khan knows every thought, every movement of the Princes and Khans, the slightest conspiracy against himself, and the offender is usually kindly invited to Urga, from where he does not return alive.'[17] Those who declined were usually later found strangled. One notable banquet, given for a group of Tibetan emissaries from the Thirteenth Dalai Lama, who, no political slouch himself, was uncomfortable with his supposed underling's debauchery and independence, ended with all the representatives perishing that very night. He could be more direct: a monk who drunkenly wondered aloud, 'Is that miserable old blind Tibetan still alive? What do we call him our king for? I don't care a fig for his orders and admonitions' was executed for blasphemy.[18] To us it might seem that the spirit of an especially degenerate Borgia had entered the Bogd in some kind of terrible metaphysical mix-up, but in fact such murderous tactics were hardly unusual in the cut-throat politics of Buddhism.

The Bogd was the son of a monastic Tibetan administrator in Mongolia. Recognised at four as the new incarnation of the Bogd Khan, he would have been all too aware of being surrounded by enemies. Reincarnated lamas retained their possessions between lives, but until they came of age these were in the hands of their regents. Consequently, many met with fatal accidents before they reached adulthood – the Thirteenth Dalai Lama, the Bogd Khan's contemporary, was the first to make it to his thirties in nearly a century.

Those who did survive faced a lethal combination of Buddhist theological and temporal politics. The history of Tibetan Buddhism is a corrupt and Byzantine affair, seemingly tailor made to suit old-fashioned anti-clericalism. It is like *I, Claudius* with silk scarves: in every scene somebody is either poisoned, stabbed, caught *in flagrante* or shoved over a cliff. The Fifth, or Great, Dalai Lama established himself as the ruler of Tibet chiefly through the exile, disgrace or murder of most of his opponents, and some of the Bogd Khan's previous selves had shown a similarly direct approach to their opposition.

His paranoia and taste for power went along with a desire to add to the material possessions he had accumulated over the course of several lives. In this incarnation they were frequently supplemented by expensive imports from America, Britain and China. 'Motorcars, gramophones, telephones, crystals, porcelains, pictures, perfumes, musical instruments, rare animals and birds; elephants, Himalayan bears, monkeys, Indian snakes and parrots – all these were in the palace of "the god" but all were soon cast aside and forgotten.'[19] His macabre collection of stuffed animals; puffer-fish and penguins and elephant seals may still be viewed, laid out in a back room of his palace. Sadly, the mirrors with 'intricate drawings of a most grossly obscene character'[20] have been removed. His zoo was particularly infamous, including giraffes, tigers and chimpanzees preserved in a miserable half-life of cruel teasing and desperate cold. One unfortunate elephant had to walk to Urga from the Russian border, a three-month tramp. He valued human oddities, too; the elephant was looked after by Gongor, a seven foot six inch giant from northern Mongolia.

Despite the Bogd's dubious ethics and repellent appearance, most European visitors were rather charmed by him. Some claimed to find in him a true example of the duality of Buddhism, embracing both good and evil. Others found him an amusing and witty conversationalist, knowledgeable about political dealings in China and Russia. Ungern's relationship with him would be half-wary, half-worshipful, although in 1913 he had no inkling that his path would eventually bring him into the closest contact with the 'great, good Buddha'.

⸙

Soviet accounts would later claim that after Ungern was 'cashiered from the army' he was driven to a life of crime, forming a group of brigands that preyed on Russian and Chinese alike. This was certainly not the case – apart from the lack of any evidence, it was the kind of thing Ungern would have boasted about, or at least used to enhance his credibility with the Mongols. Among the Russians, claims of Ungern's achievements became equally exaggerated. He was 'the commander of the whole cavalry force of Mongolia',[21] claimed one of his later superiors. In fact, his journey in 1913 left little trace in the historical record. And he was not the only Russian interested in the country.

The Russian government was only too happy to provide aid to the new Mongolian government, which had approached them as early as July 1911, six months before the actual expulsion of the Chinese. By December 1912 there were treaties of mutual aid and support in place. The humiliation of the Russo-Japanese war still smarted, and Korea and Manchuria were, at least for the moment, outside the Russian sphere of influence, but Mongolia was a perfectly plausible option. China, weak and backward, was a much easier target than Japan, and Mongolia, while neither rich nor populous, was a perfect location for a base to exert further influence on the region. Relations between China and Russia were customarily peaceful, thanks to the Treaty of Nerchinsk in 1687, which had ended twenty years of border conflicts and neatly divvied up north-east Asia between them. Yet the opportunities for expansion as China's border territories started to fall apart had been too good to miss, and Russia had extorted considerable land concessions in the nineteenth century. Mongolia was merely an extension of this policy.

Consequently Mongolian independence, while given no outright backing from Moscow, was tacitly encouraged from 1905 onwards. The Russians began to compete in earnest against the Chinese, building their own railway through Mongolia and dropping none-too-subtle hints to the nascent independence movement that they might find Russian aid in their time of need. A small-scale trade war began between Russian and Chinese merchants, both competing to offer the most favourable terms to their Mongolian suppliers. Although they rejected an initial approach by the Mongolians, their policy soon changed when it became apparent that the Chinese had neither the power nor the troops to keep control of Mongolia.

In the long run, the Russians had no interest in Mongolian independence. Aleksei Kuropatkin, the general responsible for the farce of the Russo-Japanese war and leader of a clique at court dedicated to Asian expansion, wrote that 'in the future, a major global war could flare up between the yellow race and the white. [. . .] For this purpose, Russia must occupy north Manchuria and Mongolia [. . .] Only then will Mongolia be harmless.'[22]

Kuropatkin's words perhaps indicate another source of Russian anxiety about Mongolia; a deep-rooted memory of the Mongol conquests that gave this otherwise minor country a greater importance. His real worry, though, concerned the waves of Chinese immigration into Manchuria and Inner Mongolia, which he and other military and political leaders saw as 'the first blow of the yellow race against the white' – the 'Yellow Peril' feared throughout Europe. Indeed, in European eyes the Mongols often stood in for the whole of Asia, over-breeding and posing a constant threat to Western civilisation. In the pseudo-science of racial hierarchies, 'Mongol' was used for the whole of East Asia, and the spectre of Genghis Khan was raised time and time again during the early twentieth century, especially as Japan began its rise to power; convenient shorthand for the 'Yellow Peril' as a whole.

One party in the Russian government seriously considered annexing Mongolia outright in 1912, but more cautious voices prevailed. Instead they would arm and train the new regime as a buffer against China. In the summer of 1912, then, the Russians dispatched a small group of military advisers to train the Mongolian army, some twenty thousand strong but completely unskilled in modern warfare. Many of the troops didn't even have guns, preferring the composite bow, taut and powerful, that dated back to Genghis Khan's mounted archers, and military discipline had become a foreign concept. Under Genghis and his immediate successors, the Mongolians had been a more streamlined, disciplined and deadly war machine than any army until the Second World War, but nothing of this remained; now the emphasis was on individual glory, outdoing rival clans, and plunder. They needed to be licked into shape, and the Russians had the men for the job.

Ungern latched on to them, attempting to get himself a post with the Russian garrisons in Urga and the western city of Khobdo, both of which contained members of his former regiments. He was refused, but found himself attached to the Khobdo guard as a supernumerary captain. With few actual duties, he spent his time studying the language (he would scribble down new words he came across), practising his riding and talking to the lamas and monks who dominated the Mongolian cities. The other officers found him strange and off-putting, and effectively excluded him from their society. One witness remembered him sitting alone in silence much of the time, and on other occasions being seized by a strange spirit and leading whooping Cossacks in wild charges across the plains.

He may have had some contact with one of the most legendary lamas, Dambijantsan, also known as the Ja Lama. This mysterious figure had been fighting against the Chinese for over thirty years; he claimed to be the great-grandson, and later the reincarnation, of Amursana, a famous eighteenth-century fighter against the Manchus who was in turn a purported incarnation of Mahakala, the Great Black God, a ferocious deity who, like the other 'dharma protectors', shielded

Buddhists from the enemies of the faith. Popular memory maintained a series of classic 'hidden king' legends around him, and his eventual return to liberate the Western Mongols (the Oirats) from Chinese domination. In reality Amursana had been, at times, a collaborator of the Manchus, but this was conveniently forgotten. Critically, Amursana's place of magical concealment, from which he would soon emerge, was in Russia – the ever-mystical north, where he had died while under Russian protection in 1757. By making his claims, then, Dambijantsan sought to legitimise himself dynastically, through Amursana's nobility, politically, by assuming the mantle of anti-Chinese resistance, and theologically, by claiming the magical inheritance of Amursana and the incarnated power of Mahakala. As an epic poem written in his voice put it:

> I am a mendicant monk from the Russian Tsar's kingdom, but I am born of the great Mongols. My herds are on the Volga river, my water source is the Irtysh. There are many hero warriors with me. I have many riches. Now I have come to meet with you beggars, you remnants of the Oirats, in the time when the war for power begins. Will you support the enemy? My homeland is Altai, Irtysh, Khobuk-sari, Emil, Bortala, Ili, and Alatai. This is the Oirat mother country. By descent, I am the great-grandson of Amursana, the reincarnation of Mahakala, owning the horse Maralbashi. I am he whom they call the hero Dambijantsan. I came to move my pastures back to my own land, to collect my subject households and bondservants, to give favour, and to move freely.[23]

These were grand claims for a squat, ugly monk, but his charisma and his military success gathered many followers. Ungern had learnt about him from Russian and Chinese newspapers, and probably from the travelogues of the Russian ethnologist and political agent Aleksei Pozdneiev, who collected stories of him in the 1890s, and hoped to join him to fight against the Chinese, but was forbidden from doing so by his superiors. Khobdo had seen fierce fighting only that year between Mongolian fighters and the Chinese garrison, and the Chinese fortress had fallen in a scene of bloody revenge.

The Ja Lama had been at the forefront, politically and militarily, of these battles; he was, as Ungern aspired to be, a near-legendary figure of militant Buddhism. After he seized western Mongolia, although he claimed to still be loyal to the Bogd Khan, he ruled autocratically for more than two years. The atrocities at Khobdo were typical of his regime. There were plausible accounts, both from his enemies and, later, from former allies, that he conducted a ritual, upon taking the fortress, in which the hearts of two Chinese victims were literally ripped from their chests, like victims of an Aztec sacrifice.[24] The rumour that his ger was lined with the skins of his enemies was probably false, but other lamas reported that he used terror ruthlessly. If Ungern met the Ja Lama, he found him a disappointment – he had sung his praises before his arrival in Mongolia, but referred to him only in disparaging terms afterwards – though he must also have drawn many lessons from him.

Throughout his later career in Mongolia, Ungern professed nothing but respect for Buddhism and 'the destiny of the Buddhist peoples'.[25] It was on this trip that he learnt the importance of these beliefs among the Mongolians. It was a strikingly, almost fanatically, Buddhist country, hence the power of the Bogd Khan. No matter what his sins, the Bogd's theological status – and his political clout – were beyond question. What we observe so often, and what seems so strange at first, is the fear and awe that the Mongolian temples created, both in ordinary Mongolians and even in those, like Ungern, raised in an utterly foreign tradition.

Mongolian Buddhism hinged on sacrifice. The Mongolian gods were demanding, and unmoved by anything except offerings. Although the merciful bodhisattvas did feature in Mongolian religion, they could be overshadowed by the more uncaring deities. Offerings were made for the usual reasons: relief of illness, fertility of crops, cursing of enemies. Averting disaster also loomed large as a pious motive. Tibetan Buddhism makes very specific distinctions between offerings for worship, which honour the enlightened gods, and offerings of propitiation, made to keep the unenlightened gods from getting angry. Many Mongolian offerings fell into this second category; payoffs to various malevolent spirits in a divine protection racket.

A cynic might say that this protection racket benefited corporeal lamas more than spiritual gods. Every year, a significant part of the national income drained into the coffers of monasteries already stuffed with the wealth of centuries. Another goodly portion went, quite literally, up in smoke, for holocausts were an integral to Mongolian ritual. Animal sacrifice was common, hecatombs of livestock being offered to the blood-hungry gods. The meat, as with most offerings, ended up feeding the monks – or sometimes the poor.

The lamas were greatly concerned with sacrifice themselves. The Bogd Khan's failing eyesight was a particular worry; ten thousand statues of the Buddha were ordered from Poland, and a gigantic statue of the Buddha brought from Inner Mongolia and placed in a newly built temple. Together these two offerings, both made in 1912, cost some 400,000 Chinese silver taels, a vast sum of money. They had no effect on the Bogd's vision.

And behind all this there was always the whiff of something older and perhaps more frightening. Mongolian Buddhism, like Tibetan, drew heavily on older religions, particularly shamanism. The Chinese had their shamanic traditions too, but they were largely corralled and suppressed, surviving only in a few figures such as the ancient Mother Goddess of the West and the shape-shifting heroes of primordial Chinese mythology. They are uncomfortable figures, standing somewhat outside the comfortable domesticity or light bureaucratic satire of most Chinese gods. Even today they have an unnerving power. In Hong Kong I once handled a statue of a snake-god who, in ancient Chinese mythology, shaped the formless chaos of the newly created universe.[26] It caught my attention because they are so rarely depicted directly, but it was long and thin and sinuous and seemed to twist oddly in the half-light.

Western writers have been fascinated by shamanism, in Asia and elsewhere, seeing in it the dawn of religion. In Mongolia, it seemed, one barely had to scratch the surface of Buddhism to uncover essentially shamanic beliefs. Indeed, some of the more remote tribal groups still had shamans of their own. In shamanic cosmologies, the spirit world is ever-present, and the rituals and sacrifices needed to deal with it a mainstay of everyday life. The shaman stands between two worlds, pleading or bargaining with the spirits for power for himself and his community. Much of the Mongolian relationship with their gods seemed to be drawn from this worldview, and the gods themselves were, in many cases, of pre-Buddhist origin. The range of gods and spirits was highly varied; broad distinctions could be made between the *lu* or *nagas*, spirits of water, the *savdag*, spirits of land, and *dashgid*, the Wrathful Ones, spirits of air, but within these there were numerous subcategories – nagas, for instance, could be categorised by colour, origin, caste, intention and sex – and only the lama or shaman could be expected to have the nous to deal with them properly.

Tibetan Buddhism made this explicit in its legends, telling of how early Buddhist saints had wrestled, argued, or, in a few notable cases, seduced the demons of the land into becoming good Buddhists. The myths weren't as explicit in Mongolia, but the links were clear. Some gods were even regarded as having not yet found the true path of Buddhism, and so could not be worshipped, but merely propitiated with offerings, kept sated in order to avoid their vengeance. The bloody iconography of Mongolian deities grew out of this ancient legacy. Buddhist theologians, particularly those trying to promote the religion in the West, have manfully tried to co-opt the corpses and skulls and bloodstained weapons into images of peace and salvation. Their efforts – 'The corpse being trampled beneath his feet represents the death of the material world' – are unconvincing.

Gods were frequently taken from Hinduism and turned into demons, a folk memory of old, and often extremely violent, conflicts between Hinduism and Buddhism in India.[27] The pleasantly domestic elephant-headed Indian deity Ganesha is depicted in Mongolian art as a hook-tusked, ferociously red demon, often shown crushed beneath the feet of Buddhist warrior deities.

Even the enlightened gods had their dark sides. The gentle female deity Tara had her wrathful aspect of Black Tara, benevolent smile turned to gnashing fangs, long fingernails turned to claws. Even more terrible was Palden Llamo, one of the divine protectors of Buddhism but also a devouring mother who sacrificed her own children. She rode upon a lake of entrails and blood, clutching a cup made from the skull of a child born from incest, her thunderbolt staff ready to smash the unbelievers and her teeth gnawing on a corpse. Her horse's saddle was made from the flayed skin of her own child, who had become an enemy of the faith, and snakes wound through her hair. Like many gods, she bore a crown of five skulls and a necklace of severed heads. Her ostensible purpose was to defend Buddhism against its enemies, and in particular to guard the Dalai Lama, but she must have terrified many true believers as well. The Tibetans considered Queen Victoria to be one of her incarnations.

One consequence of this pre-Buddhist legacy was an intense sense of place. Buddhism, in common with most of the major faiths, is a universalist, evangelical religion, intended to be heard and practised worldwide. In Mongolia, however, religious practice was deeply tied to locality, and to a semi-nationalistic, semi-mystical notion of the country. Mongolian rituals were often linked with binding or controlling the spirits of the land, keeping them simultaneously imprisoned and appeased. A typical example could be seen in the scattered *ovoos*, stone cairns which both paid homage to the spirits of a place and signified the Mongolians' connection to their land. Mongolians travelling abroad, particularly those going on pilgrimage to other holy sites in Tibet or Nepal, would tie blue ribbons or scarves to the *ovoos*, remembering themselves to their country before leaving. Certain places were to be avoided altogether, for fear of offending the spirits. *Lu*, the river spirits, were particularly given to entering trespassing swimmers through their urine, poisoning their bodies.

There was a constant sense of the fragility of humanity. The spiritual world was in a state of conflict between malevolent and benevolent spirits, in which humanity played only a small part. Regular intervention with the spirits and gods was necessary in order to ward off catastrophe. The lamas played an intercessory role they had inherited from the shamans, praying to, pleading with, and sometimes commanding other-worldly figures. The difference between the lamas and the beings they interacted with sometimes became blurred; during rituals they could appear to be possessed by the gods themselves, and some of the semi-secret mystical paths involved the merging – or spiritual consumption – of the initiate and his patron deity. In Mongolian popular legend, then, the lamas were sometimes sharpsters and cheats, sometimes wise men, and sometimes threatening, powerful figures in their own right.

In reality, then as now, lamas were equally varied. Mongolian lamas did not reach the same extremes as their Tibetan counterparts, where some monasteries were notorious bandit centres and others famous for their charity and wisdom, but some Mongolian monks were clearly in it for everything they could get, some were just happy to have a relatively secure berth, and some were saintly, generous figures who used their wealth to help the poor.

For ordinary Mongolians, the terrors of the spiritual world were offset by the security it offered. Living on the hard steppe and at the mercy of plague, weather and bandits, any form of control, no matter how illusory, was comforting. For the destitute widows and scavengers who made up so much of the population of Urga, the possibility of spiritual salvation was perhaps the only hope left. It could also assert humanity and happiness; the rituals, no matter how menacing, contained an element of celebration and glamour.

It is likely that most Mongolians did not live in the state of spiritual paranoia that a cold reading of their belief system might indicate. Today, after all, we live in a world of invisible, intangible life forms that can, if we fail to observe the proper rites and taboos, strike us down with uncomfortable, agonising or even fatal results. A few people are obsessed and terrified by these beings, but most of us merely make sure we wash our hands and then forget about them most of the time. The Mongolian attitude towards the spirit world was, perhaps, often the same as ours towards bacteria: a fixation for some, a living for others, just part of everyday life for most.

The terrifying nature of some of the images was also somewhat diluted by their entertainment value. The fear they inspired was part of the thrill, and even the most serious rituals could also be an excuse to party. There was aesthetic pleasure there, too; virtually all Mongolian art was religious and much of the more transitory art, such as banners and paper hangings for poles, was produced communally. Although it was usually more vivid than beautiful, it gave people an opportunity to express and enjoy values that didn't otherwise feature on the steppe.

Some of the enjoyment was a little more prurient; the religious art occasionally strayed into outright pornography, and even the most devoutly depicted female deities were often remarkably nubile. The temple of the Mongolian state oracle contained a private building full of images of divine couplings, where, according to the temple records, it was possible to 'meditate upon the secret Tantra'.[28]

Such comforting, reassuring, occasionally erotic aspects of Mongolian religion were unfathomable to most Western observers. European visitors to Mongolia regarded its religious medley and semi-theocratic society with a mixture of contempt and fear. On the one hand Mongolians were superstitious, priest-ridden, ignorant, fanatical, classically heathen. Those travellers who had some knowledge of Buddhism tended to look down on the Mongolians as practising a debased version of what they saw as a philosophical and refined religion. On the other hand, Mongolian religion was seen by outsiders as both frightening and powerful. Certain phrases recur in the European accounts: 'hidden powers', 'strange and dreadful things', 'demon-haunted land', 'mysterious abilities' and so on.

These occult fantasies were related to the fear of the rise of the East expressed by so many thinkers of the time. The mirror image of these nightmares of oriental domination was the utopian hope that ran through Tibetan and Mongolian folk legend, focused around the hidden kingdom of Shambhala. Familiar to us as the peaceful retreat of Shangri-La, Shambhala was, to the Mongolians, the hidden kingdom of the Pure Land, containing the unknown King of the World. The myth came from the Tibetan *Kalachakra Tantra*, traditionally (but falsely) dated to the ninth century BC. Traditional Buddhist interpretations saw it as a metaphorical text, and Shambhala as a state of being rather than an actual location, but many Mongolians were having none of that.

Ideas of Shambhala were common among the Russian occultist intelligentsia. Theosophy drew heavily from second- or third-hand notions of Tibetan theology, especially the mystical Kalachakra scriptures, so the Shambhala legend featured heavily in Blavatsky's writings as one of the Hidden Masters' bases of operation. Importantly, Shambhala was traditionally associated with the north, and so with Russia. The Russians were aware of this, and in the 1900s the Russian secret agent Agvan Dorjiev, a Buriat monk with strong political links to Tibet, attempted to spread the belief among the Tibetans and Mongols that the Romanovs were the descendants of the rulers of Shambhala. Dorjiev claimed that the 'White Tsar' Nicolas II was a reincarnation of Tsongkapa, the founder of the dominant Tibetan Gelugpa tradition, pointing to the tsarist patronage of Buddhism among the Buriats and Kalmyks as evidence. He managed to get a Kalachakra Tibetan temple opened in St Petersburg in 1913, which was inaugurated with a celebration of the Romanovs' 300th anniversary.

One day, according to the legends, the King of the World would burst forth from Shambhala at the head of a conquering army, bringing the world to the true faith – through the sword. Mandalas depicting Shambhala inevitably included scenes of the last King, Rudrachakrin, spearing the barbarian enemies of the faith. The idea of the righteous crusading army was a familiar one in Tibetan Buddhism, where the Indian emperor Ashoka, who is viewed by most Buddhists as heroic for his *renunciation* of war, was instead lauded for conquering in the name of the Buddha. Provided war helped spread the word of the Buddha, it was deemed entirely acceptable by many Buddhist thinkers.

The mystical Russian artist and orientalist Nicolas Roerich, travelling through Mongolia in 1926–27, heard legends of Shambhala wherever he went. Of course, he was listening for – and occasionally inventing – them, but so was Ungern. The two were connected; Roerich's brother, Vladimir Konstantinovich, had been a supply officer in Ungern's army.[29] Roerich drew images of the warrior kings riding forth from Shambhala, modelled on the statues of the Mongolian war gods. He recorded war songs, sung by Buddhist revolutionaries:

> We raise the yellow flag
> For the greatness of Buddhism
> We, the pupils of the Living Buddha,
> Go to battle for Shambhala

And another:

> The War of Northern Shambhala!
> Let us die in this war
> To be reborn again
> As Knights of the Ruler of Shambhala

Prophecy was central to Mongolian political activity. There was a long tradition, known as *lungdeng*, of prophecies being discovered, invented, or reinterpreted as needed. To drive away the 'yellow Chinese population', the Bogd Khan had called for Mongolians to 'read the *Mani Megjim* [a mystical text] for the sake of supporting the good and make it your protector. Place wind-horses at the door. Women should tie their hair into two tails and wear white on the breast – it is good. Do not eat goat meat, chicken meat, and eggs. Do not buy Chinese tobacco!'[30] This combination of magical and economic warfare – goats, chickens and eggs were usually brought from Chinese merchants – was typical of the confusion of political and religious-apocalyptic vision in the period. The Russians had tried to foster these beliefs to their own ends through Dorjiev and others, and the Thirteenth Dalai Lama had fled from the British to Mongolia at the beginning of the century, trying to whip up military support through the myth of Shambhala. None of these had worked; the messiah-King had not yet come.

Imagine, then, Ungern, head bent in supplication, in the Choijin Temple in Urga, contemplating the lurid images of the gods. Above him are severed heads and flayed skins, desecrated corpses blossoming into gardens of blood, eyeballs dangling from sockets, bones poking from mangled limbs. This is only wood and cloth, but in the smoke and the darkness it seems all too real. There are images of the many Buddhist hells, too, pink naked bodies of sinners speared by pendulous-breasted demonesses, frozen in icy lakes, consumed by scorpions.

He is duly afraid, as are the pilgrims milling around him, of the awful forms of the divine. It is frightening and alien to him, but also attractive, the hint of mysterious powers, the echoes of the peasant beliefs of his homeland, the skulls and swords and corpses that call to his urge to battle and the twisted and mangled bodies that tantalise his sadism. They would have reminded him, too, of the scenes of the Apocalypse that traditionally decorated the entrances of Orthodox churches; grislier, certainly, but in the same spirit. There is a cannier, more pragmatic side to his observations; perhaps he senses the power of this faith, the potential for devotion, contained in the crowds around him. They have just cast off one empire and they built one of their own in the past. He sees the potency of the 'militant Buddhism' that he will speak of so often in the future, and, perhaps, he senses the longing for a messiah, for a saviour from a foreign land.

He will remake Urga in the image of hell; every one of the tortures shown in miniature in the temple's paintings will be enacted in reality. And it is in this temple that, ten years later, Ungern will learn of his doom – and will do his best to take the rest of the country with him.

FOUR

Things Fall Apart

Despite his earlier hopes of great accomplishments, Ungern left Mongolia without having achieved much. He had familiarised himself with the country, the faith and the people, but he had accomplished no significant feats, and his future looked equally unpromising. At the beginning of 1914 he was kicking his heels in Reval, without employment or money, living off his savings and handouts from his family. It seemed as though his career had ground to a halt, brought down by his reckless violence. The Great War saved him. Before it broke out he was a hopeless drunk, expelled from school, academy and two regiments in turn. He was a loser – albeit an upper-class one who would always be sheltered from the consequences of his own actions – but a loser none the less. By the time it finished he was a hero; the character traits that had hampered his pre-war career – brutality, impulsiveness, coarseness – had become his greatest assets.

Ungern was mobilised on 19 July, 1914 and returned to the embrace of the Transbaikal host. His new home was the Nerchinsk Regiment, which would have the dubious distinction of fighting in some of the most stupid and bloody actions of the Eastern Front. Among the officers, the casualty rate was 170 per cent. Among ordinary soldiers, it was 200 per cent. (In other words, almost the entire regiment was killed or crippled, and so were most or all of their replacements.) It was a rate three to four times greater than that for the entire Russian army, never noted for being especially protective of the lives of its men. The chances were that Ungern's contribution to history would be as part of a casualty list or the recipient of a posthumous medal.

For the Russians the war began, like the Russo-Japanese conflict, disastrously. Ungern's regiment was part of the infamous march into East Prussia, where General Alexandr Samsonov led a hundred and fifty thousand men to ignominious defeat. Although the initial Russian advance panicked the Germans, and raiding by advance guards of Cossacks was depicted in the German press as heralding a new invasion of barbarians from the East, the entire column was quickly caught in a pincer movement and destroyed.

The final confrontation took place at Tannenberg, the site of a famous defeat of Ungern's ancestors the Teutonic Knights by Polish–Lithuanian forces, whose name was 'pregnant with painful recollections for German chivalry, a Slav cry of triumph',[1] according to Paul von Hindenburg, one of two German generals jointly commanding the operation. (Erich Ludendorff was the other.) Now it was the Germans who were triumphant. Thirty thousand Russians were killed, including a cousin of Ungern's, Friedrich Ungern-Sternberg, who died charging the enemy machine guns. A hundred thousand more were captured. Of those who took part only ten thousand, one in fifteen, made it back to Russian territory; Ungern was among them.

Ungern's survival was due partly to blind luck, partly to an almost suicidal absence of fear. As he was to show in winning his medals, he could do things so madly heroic that his enemies would often pause in sheer astonishment. Perhaps it was this very visibility that let him live; among the mass slaughter, it may have been harder, psychologically, to fire at a man who was so determined *not* to be anonymous.

Ungern loved the war. Finally, he had found something at which he excelled: 'an exemplar to the other officers and soldiers', as one of his superiors put it.[2] He was in the forefront of every charge, constantly encouraged his soldiers and eagerly accepted the most dangerous missions. Living rough with his men, moving from front to front, battle to battle, his life was fulfilled. His letters home, now lost, were, according to his cousin Arvid, full of descriptions of action and adventure. Among the slaughter of his comrades, he thrived. There were tens of thousands like him on all sides, men for whom the war was a release from tedium and a grand advance of the national spirit. For them, peace meant only decadence and sloth, whereas war was dynamic, thrilling, unifying.

For others the issues were less clear cut. As the German forces pushed into the Baltic in 1915, many of the Baltic Germans collaborated with the occupiers and were often rewarded with positions of power in the new administration. Among the Central Powers, the descendants of the Baltic Germans who had fled Russification in the 1860s were among the most vocal in advocating reclamation of the Baltic lands for Germany. Ungern appears to have felt no divided loyalties, despite his own family links to Germany and Austria. He had sworn allegiance to the tsar and he would keep that pledge. Ungern thoroughly approved of the German system; it was authoritarian, militaristic and monarchist, qualities all dear to his heart. Frederick the Great was one of his heroes. The only thing Germany lacked was the *spirit* of Russia, her connection to the East.

Ungern's later battles – against Bolshevism, for example – were matters of black and white, good against evil. This war was less idealistic, simply an upthrusting of each side's energy. 'Life', he declared later, 'is the result of war, and society is the instrument of war. [. . .] To refuse war means to refuse an epic life.'[3] For him war brought out the true essence of things, sweeping away the clutter of civilian existence – such as a poor military record, alcoholism and social failure.

Not everyone was as enthusiastic about the war as Ungern, least of all the civilians caught up in it. While the Western Front was becoming an enclosed killing-field, the horror mainly limited to the combatants of both sides, the relative openness and vast scale of the Eastern Front inevitably meant that the violence spilled into civilian life. On the German side a relentless programme of cultural colonisation began, bringing Kultur to the new citizens of the German Empire whether they liked it or not. It was matched by the imposition of German military law, with draconian penalties for anyone suspected of aiding the enemy. In the Russian borderlands the military authorities cleared the area of any elements they deemed politically or culturally unreliable. Russian Jews, suspect both for their religion and for their German-derived Yiddish language, were the most obvious target. Tens of thousands were forcibly deported from the border areas, rounded up with casual violence by the army, sometimes on as little as a day's notice, and bundled on to east-bound trains. Ungern presumably approved; at the same time, though, his Lutheran co-religionists were suffering similar treatment, paying the price for following a 'foreign' religion by being shipped off from the borderlands in trainloads. Russian and German soldiers alike 'requisitioned' goods with worthless credit notes, dismissing complaints with the offhand comment 'War is war.' Bandit groups, hiding in dense forests, impenetrable to the regular army, thrived, as locals fled to avoid deportation or labour battalions, and were joined by deserting soldiers.

This absence of people added to the eeriness of the war in the east. Three million men fought over an empty landscape, nothingness behind them and death ahead. The vast spaces, like the Mongolian steppe, dwarfed the troops moving over them, making them feel as though the landscape itself was swallowing them up. Faced with the elemental weather, the primeval forests, humanity became an irrelevance. The land seemed untouched by human hand; bison, long extinct in the rest of Europe, still roamed in the forests. In battle the enemy was a ghost, barely glimpsed among the fires and smoke. As a German soldier put it during one encounter, 'Countless farms and entire villages are in flames. One sees not a single human creature in the wide plain, spreading up to most distant eastern heights. And yet, in this frightful vacuum which is only filled with the noise of rumbling artillery and the rattle of machine guns, thousands lie in battle.'[4]

Ungern was a born horse soldier, but this was the war in which the obsolescence of cavalry was brutally driven home to all except the most pig-headed of generals. On a battlefield of wire and machine-guns, a cavalry charge was suicidal. Horses were as fragile as men, and the Russians lost half or more of their painstakingly trained mounts in the first three months of the war; one of the grimmest duties of the cavalry was to go round after a battle and shoot their former steeds, lying on the ground with broken legs or stumbling over their own torn-out guts, snorting and whinnying in pain. In practice, the Russian cavalry was reduced to fighting as dragoons; riding to battle and then dismounting. Even their much-vaunted mobility was belittled by the sheer scale of the war theatre; a train could outrun any horse, but it took four times as much space and effort to transport a cavalry regiment and their horses as the same number of infantry.

Nevertheless Ungern remained convinced to the end of his life of the virtues of cavalry. Perhaps this was because he discovered one of the few remaining practical uses for horsemen: as guerrilla fighters. He was often assigned to special raiding parties, striking deep inside enemy lines. This sometimes required cunning as well as speed; if need be, he had no trouble posing as a German officer. Such raids were commonplace on the Eastern Front, where the shape of battle was more flexible and there were often openings in enemy lines. During such operations there was no time to take prisoners, and little distinction was made between enemy civilians and soldiers. Ungern would always favour this kind of warfare: swift, precise and brutal. He developed an expert eye for exploiting the terrain, and learnt how to lead a party of horsemen on little-used paths to evade an overwhelming army.

In trench battles, Ungern was known for leading parties into no-man's-land to scout and sabotage the enemy's trenches. He won the Cross of St George, one of the most prestigious Russian military medals – although his was only fourth class – for scouting enemy positions on 22 September, 1914 'only four or five hundred steps from the enemy positions, under fierce rifle and artillery fire'.[5] He would sit in trees above the enemy, watching the German soldiers and spotting for the Russian artillery. He earned four other lesser medals in his first two years of war, including the St Anne's Cross, but the Cross of St George had a special place for him. After he received it, he wore it almost always.

For millions of Germans and Russians alike the war was a brutalising experience, creating the hard generation of the Freikorps, the right-wing militia groups of post-war Germany, and the fighters of the Russian Civil War.[6] The old values of peacetime no longer applied. On the haunted battlefields, they learnt cruelty, contempt for ordinary life, casual violence. Ungern was already brutal, but the war undoubtedly worsened him. There was always something fractured in him; the war just widened the breaches. It refined and affirmed his tendencies to violence, even legitimised them as heroic. In military-controlled territory on both sides he saw his dismissive attitude towards his inferiors confirmed, watched the rounding-up of the undesirable Jews and learnt that the civilian world existed merely to provide the resources for war.

From 1914 to 1916 he again fought in East Prussia, and then in Galicia and the Carpathian mountains. It was in the Carpathians that, it was often claimed, he received one of the most visible of his wounds, his long forehead scar. More probably this was a legacy of the pre-war duel referred to earlier, but he was certainly wounded while at the front. Five times in two years, in fact, but his injuries barely seem to have slowed him down, and he was absent from active service for only brief periods. He sent home a coat riddled with bullet holes and stained with blood; an odd present, but one that demonstrated his sacrifices for his country and king. For once, his family had reason to be proud of him.

In 1916 he was assigned to the command of General Petr Nikolaievich Vrangel, a tall, aristocratic man also from a Baltic German family, who had come to soldiering late in life. He would become one of the last White leaders in the Russian Civil War, holding the Crimea to the end and denigrated by the Bolsheviks as the 'Black Baron'. He had met Ungern socially on occasion, and his opinion of him was distinctly mixed:

> War was his natural element. He was not an officer in the elementary sense, he knew nothing of system, turned up his nose at discipline, and was ignorant of the rudiments of decency and decorum. He was not an officer but a hero out of one of Mayne Reid's novels.[7] He was dirty and dressed untidily, slept on the floor with his Cossacks and messed with them. When he was promoted to a civilised environment, his lack of outward refinement made him conspicuous. I tried in vain to awaken his conscience to the need for adopting at least the external appearance of an officer. He was a man of queer contrasts. He had an angular, penetrating mind, but at the same time an astonishing lack of culture, an extremely narrow outlook, the shyness of the savage, a foolish swagger and an unbridled temper.[8]

Vrangel's doubts concerning Ungern's refinement might perhaps account for his rather slow rate of promotion. Despite his medals, the loyalty of his men and his undoubted skill in battle, it was not until September 1916 that he was promoted to *pod'esaul*, junior captain, with command over a *sotnia*, a group of a hundred men. Sadly his behaviour did not improve with his rank. On 22 October, 1916 Ungern and another officer, who was named Artamonov, were on regimental leave in the city of Chernivtsi, in the Ukraine. They spent the afternoon getting drunk and then went to the Black Eagle hotel, where Ungern demanded a room. Wartime procedure required that Ungern have a certificate from the commander of the city to do so, which he didn't have, and the desk clerk told him so. Ungern tried to take a swipe at the desk clerk. He missed, breaking some glass instead, and Artamonov and he made their unsteady way to the office of Commandant Treshev, the city's governor. Once there they confronted his junior aide-de-camp, a man named Zagorsk. According to Zagorsk's report, Artamonov insisted that Zagorsk telephone Treshev and attempt to get the two of them permission to stay in the hotel, but Treshev refused. At this point Ungern ran into the room and began to make trouble, shouting, 'Whose face do I have to mess up?!'[9] Stymied by bureaucracy, his instinct was to find somebody to beat up. Zagorsk explained that no permit was available and attempted to pacify Ungern, at which point Ungern called him a swine – one of his favourite insults – and swiped at him with his sabre, giving him a nasty cut to the head. The terrified Zagorsk ran to get help; eventually the senior aide-de-camp appeared, found Ungern dozing drunkenly in an armchair and arrested him.

This was not the first time Ungern had been drunk on duty, and Wrangel is reported to have disciplined him frequently for the offence. The incident at Chernivtsi sounds plausible, though others may have been embellished in the telling; for example it was later alleged by the Soviets that he entered a café and drunkenly fired into the ceiling, killed fellow officers during drinking bouts and so on. Even the Russian army was not sufficiently desperate to keep a drunken murderer on its staff. (Another unproven Soviet claim was that Ungern had been imprisoned for beating up a lower-ranking officer and was released only as a result of the Revolution.)

Following the Chernivtsi episode, Ungern was able to escape serious punishment, sentenced to only two months' imprisonment by the 8th Army's Staff Court. His superb record on the battlefield made a good impression upon the military authorities, as did the intervention of Wrangel and other former commanders. Ungern probably couldn't understand what all the fuss was about.

After his release from military prison in January 1917, Ungern was transferred to the army reserves. Being away from the front was not to his taste, and he soon negiotiated a transfer to Vladivostok, from where he managed to return to the fighting on a different front: the Caucasus. Here Ungern linked up with the man who was to shape the rest of his life. Captain Grigori Michaelovich Semenov was half-Buriat, half-Cossack, like Ungern a product of the fringes of the tsarist empire. Clever and charming, he was a voracious reader and fluent in several languages, including Buriat, Mongolian and Kalmyk. He was

> a man of medium height, with square broad shoulders, an enormous head, the size of which is greatly enhanced by the flat, Mongol face, from which gleam two clear, brilliant eyes that rather belong to an animal than a man. The whole pose of the man is at first suspicious, alert, determined, like a tiger ready to spring, to rend and tear, but in repose the change is remarkable, and with a quiet smile upon the brown face the body relaxes.[10]

It was unusual for an officer in a Cossack regiment to be a Cossack himself, let alone have 'Asiatic' ancestry, and Semenov suffered a certain amount of snubbing from his peers. Undeterred, he had already earned a considerable reputation as an up-and-coming officer.

Like Ungern, he had spent time in Mongolia, but he had achieved rather more while he was there. He surveyed the country from end to end after the declaration of independence in 1911, and was then sent to Urga as part of the consular guard, where, thanks to his fluent Mongolian, he was able to befriend the Bogd Khan and other prominent leaders. He rescued the Chinese *amban* (the former colonial administrator) from an enraged mob and disarmed, on his own initiative, the Chinese garrison to prevent the situation worsening. These qualities – bravery, decisiveness, leadership – would remain constant, and so would another side of him that showed itself for the first time in Urga: corruptibility. Various politicians showered him with gifts, as did the directors of a Chinese bank after he foiled an armed robbery there. By his own account he donated the gifts to his unit; if this is true he showed scruples then that were absent in later life.

Recalled from Mongolia for exceeding the limits of his command, he rode the 232 miles from Urga to Kiatkha, on the Russian–Mongolian border, in twenty-six hours, setting a new record. Desperate to get back to Mongolia, where he had been offered a high rank in the national army by his political friends, he instead found himself on the fringe of the empire, hunting bandits and rebels. When the Great War broke out he showed the same courage as Ungern, raiding the enemy's rear and penetrating deep into German-held territory. He won the Cross of St George twice (fourth class, the same as Ungern's), and these exploits built up his reputation as a daring and cunning leader. He was as skilled at throwing grenades or leading charges as he was at inspiring his men, although by Vrangel's cynical account, he 'knew how to make himself popular with Cossacks and officers alike, but he had his weaknesses – a love of intrigue and indifference to the means by which he achieved his ends'.[11]

It was almost inevitable that he and Ungern would become friends. They had much in common, including a desire for military success, a love of Mongolia and a keen interest in the peoples of central Asia. Perhaps most of all, they were both outsiders in their own regiment, although Semenov was isolated by race and Ungern by choice and temperament. With such similar careers, they must have met before, but it was under Vrangel's command in Poland that they became solid friends. Semenov was five years younger than Ungern, but he was very much the senior partner. They fell into a common pattern of close friendship; Semenov was the talker and charmer, Ungern the thinker, in the shadow of his charismatic friend. Ungern was, perhaps, a little overwhelmed by Semenov's Mongolian achievements. Later accounts would sometimes attribute Semenov's adventures in Urga to Ungern, a mistake which could be explained by their closeness to each other, but one wonders if Ungern didn't occasionally take the credit for his friend's exploits.

Now they were stationed together on one of the forgotten flanks of the First World War: the Turko-Russian conflict in Persia. Both were assigned to the mountains around Lake Urmia in what is now north-west Iran, and found themselves caught up in one of the war's worst horrors. Since August 1915 the Turks and their Kurdish auxiliaries had been engaged in the systematic genocide of the Christian Assyrian population in the area, on the excuse that some of them had allowed themselves to be drafted into Russian service when the Russians first invaded.

Thousands of Assyrians were massacred in the region around Lake Urmia alone and up to a quarter of a million elsewhere, a slaughter which has the unhappy distinction of being one of the least remembered genocides of the twentieth century, eclipsed by the slaughter of the Armenians elsewhere in the Ottoman Empire and obscured by continued government denial. It was carried out using the most primitive methods. Assyrian villagers were roped together and pushed off cliffs, hacked to death, shot en masse, sent on death marches. If their Muslim neighbours tried to protect them, they suffered the same fate. Mass starvation and disease helped finish off those Assyrians who escaped the Turkish troops. Signs of the massacres were visible everywhere, and the few survivors, gaunt and traumatised, appealed to the Cossacks for aid.

Ungern saw them as potential military material. He dreamt up a scheme to recruit another Assyrian regiment, which would be motivated by revenge against the Turks and help alleviate Russia's increasingly desperate shortage of manpower. He rounded up some men, but his plan never came to fruition. The Assyrians ended up abandoned after the revolution, left with eight cannon and a few machine guns to face the murderous Turkish army. However, the idea inspired Semenov, who conceived of an all-Buriat regiment, fired with the fighting spirit of the steppe. Both soldiers became convinced that the salvation of the Russian state lay in recruitment among the native peoples of the East.

That state, however, was already on its last legs. Appalling casualties on the front, shortages at home and growing revolutionary sentiment combined to spark countrywide protests in February 1917. The brutal incompetence of the tsarist system, especially its inability to cope with the slow transformation of Russia from agricultural serfdom into a modern industrial power, had been increasingly obvious for over a decade. Then the Cossacks had been used to repress the uprisings; now mounted Cossack policemen were among the first to refuse orders and turn against the government. The old regime lost its authority in a matter of weeks. All over the empire soldiers turned against officers, workers against bosses, peasants against landowners. For Ungern and other natural reactionaries, it was the world turned upside down, the natural order perverted. The nightmarish visions of 1905 had returned.

By March Nikolas II had been forced to abdicate, and a democratic government was established. Led by the bantamweight figure of Alexandr Kerenskii, a young nobleman with dreams of being a new Napoleon, the Provisional Government re-established a veneer of order, but its authority was extremely weak. Badgered by generals, and still hoping for a German collapse, the government refused to accept the reality of Russian military defeat in the West, souring its chances with ordinary soldiers as a result. Some optimistic liberals hoped that Russia had finally thrown off the shackles of her feudal past, and could now become a modern state. Meanwhile, more fanatical or realistic revolutionaries began to plan the seizure of power.

The collapse of the old order, especially the tsar's abdication, struck Ungern hard. Unlike Semenov, who was more phlegmatic about his political allegiance, and whose loyalty was to empire rather than tsar, Ungern was a pronounced monarchist. For him, the monarch was the fount of all honour, the 'first person in the state'.[12] Around him he saw mass desertion from the army, which in his eyes was a kind of treason. The Kerenskii government, in his opinion, was a 'total mess', but for the moment he respected its authority. Ungern and Semenov continued to work to recruit Assyrians, but Semenov also submitted a petition to the new government, hoping to receive permission to begin recruiting among the Buriat. The fragile Petersburg government was desperate for any measures that could boost manpower and strengthen the commitment of the border tribes to a crumbling empire. Semenov received the authority to begin recruiting for his Mongol-Buriat Regiment. Travelling to the Transbaikal, he found the going tough. He sought to bolster the thin ranks of his new force by opening recruitment to all, and by contacting friends across the border in Mongolia.

Between March and November 1917 Ungern's whereabouts are hard to place. He travelled with Semenov in the Transbaikal, but may have also returned to Estonia to visit his family. It's possible he was involved in the abortive coup in St Petersburg that August, led by the Cossack general Lavr Kornilov. One of Kornilov's grievances, the Provisional Government's abolition of capital punishment in the military, was a cause particularly dear to Ungern's heart. If he did visit Reval, his leaving was a final break with his homeland, and with his family. His real father died in St Petersburg four years later, while the rest of his family fled abroad, either to America or to Germany. He made no subsequent effort to contact them. Meanwhile, Estonia declared her independence in a brief period between Russian retreat and German occupation in 1918, and reasserted it again after the German collapse in November. The fledgling state faced two threats; the Red Army and German freebooters. The Baltikumer, groups of fighters made up of former German soldiers, characterised their rampages through the region as a new *Ritt gen Osten*, the Ride Against the East of the Teutonic Knights.

If Ungern had remained in the region, perhaps he would have found his place among these hard, wild men. Many of them ended up fighting alongside White forces during the Russian Civil War, wearing a combination of Russian and German insignia and dreaming of a restored Russian Empire, 'to be reconstructed and administered by a ruling class of German nobility'.[13] Their eventual defeat meant, it seemed, a final end to German power in the region, just as the throwing back of the Red Army promised a future separate from the Russian Empire. Most of his relatives eventually made their way to Germany, where many Baltic Germans schemed for revenge against the Soviets. Both Ungern's aristocratic and his imperial roots in the region had been torn up; he had no reason to return there. Later, asked whether he had wealth and property, he said, 'Yes, in Estland I used to, but now, really, no.'[14]

In early November came the Bolshevik coup in St Petersburg.[15] The Winter Palace, symbolic heart of government, was seized by a tiny band of revolutionaries, led by Lenin, freshly returned from German exile. The new Soviet order was established by bluff and chutzpah, and solidified by the revolutionaries' determination to use any means to hold on to power. Bolshevik ruthlessness disturbed many leftists, but reactionaries such as Ungern were more troubled by the prevalence of Jews among the revolutionary leaders. Jewish traditions of education and social justice, combined with the indignities heaped upon Jews by Nikolas's government, resulted in them being over-represented among the leaders of revolutionary groups. Anti-Semites came to regard Bolshevism and Judaism as identical. In the anti-revolutionary press, Trotskii was usually referred to by his original, distinctly Jewish name of 'Bronstein', and even the non-Jewish revolutionary leaders were claimed to possess Jewish blood. Lenin's Mongol ancestry gave him distinctly Asiatic features, which were often cited as evidence of his 'oriental' Judaism.

＊＊ ☧ ＊＊

Wherever Ungern was when the St Petersburg coup took place, his feelings about the Bolsheviks were clear. Anti-religious, anti-monarchist, riddled, in Ungern's view, with Jews, extolling the peasants and seizing land from the aristocracy; they were the antithesis of everything

Ungern held dear. Their worst betrayal was the treaty of Bresk-Livotsk, a shameful peace signed with the Germans that ceded great swathes of western Russia to their rule, invalidating everything Ungern had fought for during the last four years. Now he had a new and greater battle to fight. The Germans had been merely the enemy of Russia; the Bolsheviks were the enemy of good. To Ungern the revolution was a kind of apocalypse, the end of the world as he knew it. Out of apocalypse, though, could come utopia, Christ's return after Satan's reign, the opening of the pure land of Shambhala after the defeat of the enemies of the faith. But before that could happen the world had to be purged. Only the most stalwart crusader could stand against the black curse of revolution, holding the banner of imperialism, divine religion and absolute monarchy. This would be Ungern's role.

For the moment, however, he was playing second fiddle to Semenov. He made his way across Siberia to join him at his old station posting, Dauria, and found himself swept up in his friend's plans to turn Siberia into a centre of anti-Bolshevik resistance. The Bolsheviks had already begun to raise a military force of their own: the Red Army. Inspired by Trotskii's skills at recruiting and propaganda, and drawing upon a generation of soldiers embittered by the war, it was already the most powerful army in Russia. Although at times during 1918–19 the total number of anti-Bolshevik fighters outnumbered the Reds, Bolshevik control of the central portion of Russia and its opponents' vast range of political views, from anarchists to conservative monarchists, meant that the anti-revolutionary forces remained scattered and divided. The Bolsheviks also inherited most of the materiel of the old army, and the industrial capacities of St Petersburg and Moscow, leaving their opponents reliant upon provincial arms stocks and supplies from abroad. Much of the military opposition to the Reds came from the officers of the old tsarist army; they became known, in contrast to the 'Red' Bolsheviks, as the 'Whites'.

Ungern and Semenov were in some ways typical of this officer caste, but most of the White leaders were former generals and admirals. Their plan to raise a regiment was a hugely ambitious scheme for two junior officers, but the scale of it deterred neither man. Their resources, however, were limited; they had no money, no troops, and only six other men with them. After months of effort, Semenov had at last achieved some success with his Mongol-Buriat recruitment, persuading Buriat elders to go along with his scheme and recruiting, on paper, around six hundred men, but he had left the few troops he had back in the west of the country. As a result, the counter-revolution in Siberia began with eight men and a colossal bluff.

Close to Dauria, just across the Chinese border in Manchuria, was the important junction of Manchzhuriya, commonly known as Manchuli or, confusingly, Manchuria. It was a nothing town, a 'small, wind-swept village, lying in a vast, but naturally not less wind-swept plain'.[16] The Russian garrison there was in open mutiny; they were already setting up revolutionary tribunals to try their officers and the local railway officials. The Chinese commander there, Major-General Gan, had been ordered to disarm them, but quailed at the diplomatic consequences and felt he had insufficient men. Semenov caught a train down, invited the commander and other Chinese officials to dinner and proposed that he, as a Russian officer, should disarm the troops without bloodshed. Believing he had a substantial number of soldiers to back him up, Gan gratefully agreed and offered to help if necessary. It was a sign of the total breakdown of Russian military authority that Semenov needed a *Chinese* officer to give him permission to disarm a mutiny.

Semenov now had a mandate to act, but no men to back up his plan. He told the station master to put together a troop train and send it to Dauria to retrieve his imaginary regiment. Along with the train he sent one of his Cossacks with a message for Ungern; grab whoever he could in Dauria, light up the train as though there were soldiers on it, and come back to Manchuli. Ungern's first recorded action in Siberia was simple and brutal. With a single Cossack assistant, he was sent to ensure the co-operation of Captain Stepanov, chief of the railway militia, in disarming the mutinous troops. When Ungern declared that the three of them together were going to take on two armed companies, Stepanov laughed in his face and said he was going home. According to Semenov's memoirs, Ungern promptly smacked him in the gut with the scabbard of his sabre and told him he was going nowhere.

Stepanov was to become a notoriously ruthless White leader; the ease with which the Baron cowed him shows how terrifying the slightly built Ungern could be. He emanated danger, ready for violence at any moment and to any extreme. Even battle-hardened Russian soldiers at Manchuli were easily intimidated and, with Stepanov's help, Ungern disarmed hundreds of men in a few hours. Eventually the tiny group had succeeded in packing fifteen hundred men into the train to be shipped back to Bolshevik territory; a remarkable achievement diminished only a little by the fact that most of the homesick revolutionaries were desperate to get back to Russia anyway.

The neutralisation of the Manchuli garrison won the small White group the approval of the Chinese, and by the beginning of the New Year Semenov's success had attracted more men to his cause. Nearly half were Buriats, the rest mostly Cossacks and Mongolians, led by Russian officers. The Buriat, like other minorities, were used to special status. Like the Cossacks they enjoyed unusual dispensations; they were exempt from conscription, adept at eluding taxation and, despite imperial efforts to transform them into more compliant citizens, managed to maintain the traditional rule of their elders. The new regime threatened to strip them of their privileges and turn them into good little Russian sheep. While some Buriats fought with the Bolsheviks, most often those dissatisfied with or excluded by the complex Buriat webs of kinship and patronage, the majority were committed reactionaries. The newly formed Soviet secret police, the Cheka, began to establish control points throughout the Russian far east to filter out potential Semenovite recruits.

Semenov and Ungern's troops still numbered only in the hundreds, but they were one of the few organised armies in the Transbaikal region. Although there were numerous Bolshevik soviets and units, few had mobilised effectively and there was very little coordination between their units, nor any clear chain of command. The battle lines of the civil war were only just being drawn up, and many people were unclear where they stood. Semenov and Ungern had three clear advantages: they were unambiguously anti-Bolshevik, well organised and had a simple plan of action. They asked only three questions of their recruits – 'Do you believe in God? Do you refuse to recognise the Bolsheviks? Will you fight them?' The new army was named the Special Manchurian Division, after the place of its formation.

Semenov's army crossed the border back into Russia on New Year's Day 1918. Ungern was at the forefront of this advance. He knew this territory, the woods and rivers and small, neat towns along the tracks; after all, he had served here for over three years. On 12 January, 1918 he pushed up another sixty miles into Russia to take the small settlement of Oloviannaia, stealing what munitions he could before being driven out of town by Red Guards. This was scrappy, low-key fighting; the number of troops involved on either side rarely exceeded a hundred and fifty, and both were quick to retreat if things seemed to be going badly. The Buriat were experts at this kind of skirmishing, disappearing into the forests loaded with as much ammunition as they could carry. The revolutionary units rarely put up much of a fight, instead melting away as the Whites approached. It was the depths of winter, and fighting was draining for all concerned; battles often petered out in desultory exchanges of rifle fire, neither side willing to push forward. Surrender was still an option. For the moment, both sides were treating their prisoners with a modicum of decency.

By mid-January the Semenovites held two hundred miles of the railway, but they were running out of supplies and were having difficulties in their rear. Fortunately, Ungern had become something of an expert in managing mutinous garrisons; early in 1918, in the Russian quarter of the Manchurian city of Hailar, he disarmed a group of revolutionary soldiers who outnumbered him three to one. He captured them while their leaders were immersed in a series of ideological discussions – amazingly, they remained oblivious for two hours – and then sent them, stripped of weapons, back to Red territory. That he let them live, even sent them back to fight for the other side, is an indication of his relative magnanimity at this point. Not all his prisoners would be so lucky.

Desperate for manpower, Semenov turned once more to the tradition of recruiting from an ethnic minority, in this case a small group of Mongols, the Bargut, who had settled in Manchuria. The Bargut had briefly declared independence from China in 1912, with Russian assistance, but their dreams of autonomy had been comprehensively shattered by the Chinese. At present, things were complicated by the presence of another anti-Chinese Mongol group, the Karachen, who had come to Bargut territory from Inner Mongolia to escape the Chinese army. Inner Mongolia was still firmly under Chinese control, and many of the Mongols there had been pursuing a long, and ultimately futile, guerrilla struggle against the Chinese authorities for over forty years.

The Karachen were no happier in Bargut territory. Tension between the two tribes had grown, and they were practically at war. Semenov had made contacts there during his recruitment efforts in 1917 and, with Ungern's help, not only negotiated peace between the two groups and an amnesty from the Chinese, but also managed to get them to contribute men to his new army. Both distrusted the Bolsheviks almost as much as their fellow minorities in Siberia, and they had also traditionally looked to the tsarist regime as a potential foreign patron against the hated Chinese. Since the Karachen were experienced guerrilla fighters in a region where soldiering frequently blurred into banditry, the chance to make a fortune through plunder was also appealing.

Ungern was given command of a detachment of these new Mongol soldiers, around two hundred and fifty Bargut horsemen. After helping to put down the mutiny in Hailar, they went on to occupy another station in Bargut territory, Bukhedu. The Chinese authorities, who were becoming increasingly nervous of the Semenovites, sprung a trap. Ungern was invited to lunch by the commander of the Chinese garrison. He accepted, but in a table-turning reversal of his usual practice, was himself held prisoner while his Mongols were disarmed. A furious Semenov responded quickly, constructing a fake armoured train using a dummy howitzer placed on a platform car and half-covered with a tarpaulin, which he then used to bluff the Chinese commander into releasing Ungern and his men.

***

Such a simple deception would not be sufficient to secure them the Transbaikal. By February, the Soviets had rallied, holding a pan-Siberian Congress which appointed a young, charismatic leader, Sergei Lazo, to drive the Semenovites out of the Transbaikal. They had more men and better arms than Semenov's forces, and they easily forced them out of the towns they had taken in January. By March the Special Manchurian Division was trapped and beaten. The only thing that saved the Whites was the intervention of the Chinese army, which, not wanting the conflict to spill over their border, enforced an armistice that allowed the Semenovites a breathing space.

Semenov and Ungern both moved into the province of Manchuria to begin looking for help and support. It was difficult work for Ungern, given his almost complete absence of social skills. On the other hand, he could speak the language, poor as his Chinese was, and he was always more comfortable dealing with 'Orientals' than his fellow Russians. He spent the early months of 1918 shuttling back and forth along the Manchurian railway. His work was concentrated in Harbin, the great northern city of Manchuria which had been virtually a Russian colony for many years.

He was required to act as go-between to different White factions, shame armchair generals into making real contributions, negotiate with the Japanese, and ensure that the Chinese officials stayed at least neutral, if not friendly, towards the Whites. He had to deal with bank transfers and arms shipments, hire mercenaries and hear false promises from all sides. From his letters to Semenov and others, it is clear that he found the work frustrating, and it left him exhausted, annoyed and cursing Mongol and Chinese leaders as 'scoundrels'. There were petty intrigues and rivalries; other Russians, even professed Whites, were often not to be trusted, although the Mongols were a little more more reliable. Ungern was working closely with the leader of the Karachen Mongols, Fushenge, training and advising the Karachen and Bargut troops. Several Mongol leaders supported the restoration of the Qing dynasty, for much the same reasons as they supported the restoration of the tsar: the old imperial order had given them greater protection than the new, populist one ever would. It was an idea that stuck with Ungern.

Meanwhile, Semenov was casting around desperately for a patron who could supply the Special Manchurian Division with the arms and supplies he needed to take on the Reds. He found one in the Japanese. Not only were they deeply concerned about the possibility of Bolshevik revolution spreading to Japan, they also saw the fighting in Siberia as a golden opportunity to extend Japanese power in the region. Eventually over a quarter of a million Japanese soldiers would be sent there.

Japanese ambitions overseas had grown stronger since the Russo-Japanese war, and elements within the Japanese military, nobility and political establishment increasingly saw Manchuria, Mongolia and eastern Siberia as their natural territory. Ultra-nationalist secret societies were formed to promote Japanese expansion overseas, some of which had strong ties to mystical forms of Buddhism. They had close links to the messy world of Japanese intelligence, dominated by nobles who ran private spy networks only loosely affiliated with the government. Several of these were based in Harbin. The Japanese needed a Russian proxy, however, and were eager to find a White leader they could back. Semenov impressed them with his usual charm and vigour, and they began supplying him with money, arms and numerous military and political advisers. He was also able to secure guns and funds from the British and French, though on a much more limited scale. He used his fresh resources to hire and arm Chinese mercenaries, merging them with his Mongol troops under Russian leadership.

Semenov was still, in theory, a mere captain, and his brash manner and overreaching ambition made him unpopular with many in the White hierarchy, several of whom regarded him as little more than a puppet of the Japanese. The worst breach was with Admiral Kolchak, who became leader of the Whites in western Siberia, eventually establishing a military dictatorship based at Omsk. He was older and more renowned than Semenov, and the quarrel between them started when Semenov insolently failed to meet his train as promised. From that point on there was a permanent rift between Kolchak's followers and Semenov's. It was representative of a deeper division within the White movement. Kolchak's followers tended to be more liberal, more committed to democratic ideals, supporters of the February constitutional revolution but not the Bolshevik coup. Many had been involved in socialist movements themselves. The Semenovites, on the other hand, were mostly deep-dyed reactionaries who regretted the fall of the old regime. Kolchak began to work to block Semenov's funding, while Semenov denounced the admiral as an elderly idiot.

In March 1918, newly invigorated by foreign aid, the Special Manchurian Division began to push back into the Transbaikal region. By early June they were some two hundred miles across the border, but were still being pressed hard by the Red forces. The Bolsheviks brought thousands of men to bear against Semenov's ragtag collection of Cossack and Buriat cavalry. It seemed as though their efforts were doomed once again, until salvation appeared from another unlikely source. During the First World War the Russians had captured many Czech and Slovak soldiers who had no love for the Austro-Hungarian Empire, and had tried to form them into a unit to fight for their country's liberation. After the Bolsheviks came to power, the 'Czechoslovakian Legion' decided to attempt to return to the Western Front to fight. Since the Germans blocked the way west, the only route was east – along the Trans-Siberian Railway to Vladivostok, and from there round the world to home.

They had an uneasy relationship with the Bolsheviks, especially since the latter made peace with the Germans in March 1918. The Bolshevik leaders vacillated over whether they should be allowed to leave, and the Czechs became increasingly frustrated. On 17 May, a fight between a Czech and a Hungarian internationalist escalated into a series of violent clashes between the Legion and Bolshevik troops, which culminated eight days later in Trotskii ordering the Legion to disarm. This was the last straw, and fifty thousand Czechoslovakian soldiers erupted against the Soviets. Their main target was the Trans-Siberian Railway, their only way back to Europe, and they seized stations and rolling stock across the country. White sympathisers joined them, and the Bolsheviks were driven out of cities across Siberia and the Urals.

The Special Manchurian Division attempted to help the Czechs on 13 July, throwing themselves against Red-held towns in a desperate outnumbered assault. After days of savage fighting, they were yet again forced back across the border at Manchuli, where the Bolsheviks, despite Chinese promises, were this time able to pursue them. The division was almost wiped out, not least because one of Semenov's commanders defected to the Reds. Only a heroic charge by a battalion of Japanese 'volunteers' repelled the Bolshevik assault. During a brief ceasefire negotiated by Ungern's Chinese contacts, Semenov was able to evacuate his troops deeper into Manchuria. Eventually they regrouped in Hailar. Ungern and Semenov began to put the force back together, benefiting from increasing Bolshevik cruelty, which drove over ten thousand refugees to Manchuria and provided them with a steady stream of recruits.

In August 1918 they returned to the Transbaikal yet again. This time, with Czech and Japanese assistance, they were finally able to drive the Reds out of the region altogether. By September Semenov was installed in Chita as de facto dictator of the entire Transbaikal. With him came the Japanese army, raising the flag of the Rising Sun across the railways and placing tens of thousands of troops in the region. Along with the Japanese were other foreign soldiers, the

Siberian Expeditionary Force, comprising mostly American troops, which had been sent by the Allies to help retrieve the Czech Legion and with the secondary aim of frustrating Bolshevik ambitions without being drawn into open warfare. It was a farce; the troops froze and grumbled and fought with their supposed Russian comrades, and the foreign intervention or 'imperialist invasion' gave Soviet apologists an excuse for the atrocious Bolshevik policies of the civil war era for decades afterwards.

For now, Semenov's court became stuffed with Japanese 'advisers' and Allied observers. He assumed the Cossack rank of *ataman,* 'chief', but true power lay with the Japanese. His foreign policy, his attitudes towards other White leaders, even the movements of his armies, were all directed from Tokyo. Ungern, in turn, became commander of Dauria. Along with the post went a new rank, granted by Semenov; he was now a major-general, a title of which he was inordinately proud. Semenov's new slogan was *For Law and Order!* The residents of the Transbaikal, and especially of Ungern's new fiefdom, would soon find only grim irony in this motto.

FIVE

Carrion Country

Siberia was wolf-haunted that year. They followed close on the scene of battles, feasting on the dead. Both sides strung enemy corpses on trees alongside the roads and the wolves gnawed off their feet. Perhaps it was these images that Ungern remembered when he spoke later of leaving 'an avenue of corpses' from Urga to Moscow. Sometimes, emboldened by the abundance of human flesh, the wolves grew bold enough to attack men, even – barely known before – men in groups.

The whispers of war said that Ungern and the wolves had an affinity. He certainly kept some 'in an attic in his house in Dauria, for an unknown purpose',[1] reported a friend who often stayed there. A legend arose that he fed his tame pack on prisoners and mutinous soldiers. Sometimes, the stories had it, he would harness them to his sleigh and ride through town, whipping them on as they howled in terror. He was supposed to walk out in the hills on his own in the evening, striding like a grim pagan god through a landscape of wolf-gnawed bones. He suited this carrion country all too well.

His new base at Dauria was not a prepossessing site. One White officer, Dmitri Alioshin, wrote that he

had gone through it several times before without paying it the slightest attention, so hopelessly flat and miserable it had seemed. Situated in a dead plain, it is surrounded by small sandy hills, and consists of a score of dirty huts spread over the naked hills. A small church rears its spire, and in the middle of the valley sprawls a fort. The fort is constructed of red bricks, and from the distance looks like a dirty slaughterhouse painted with blood. This was the head-quarters of Baron Ungern.[2]

Here Ungern began to build his own regime. He was to remain at Dauria for nearly two years, and made it and the surrounding region unquestionably his personal domain. It was a near-medieval polity, like one of his knightly ancestors establishing a border fortress six hundred years earlier. Virtually every witness used the word 'feudal' to describe his rule, and Ungern would have approved. Power revolved around him. He had been stationed here before, and it had been the scene of one of his many disgraces. There must have been a certain satisfaction in being master in this place, barren as it was. Semenov had become the *ataman*; now Ungern became the Baron. There was no shortage of titled nobility on the White side, but everyone in Siberia knew who 'the Black Baron', 'the Bloody Baron', 'the Mad Baron' or simply 'the Baron' was.[3]

Here, as elsewhere in Russia during the civil war, social norms had broken down entirely. Violence, or the threat of violence, became the stuff of everyday life. Even between groups supposedly allied with each other, confrontations were common, as when a drunken American infantry unit beat up a trainload of Whites. Some tried to keep a semblance of normality, to maintain shops or stations or hospitals, but they were always vulnerable.

Semenov's soldiers became particularly infamous for casual thuggery. They assaulted railway workers, harassed refugees and pressed men into service. The foreigners working with them were often shocked by their brutality; one noted how the Russian officers, in particular, 'remarked almost daily that it was necessary for them to whip, punish, or kill someone every day in order that people know who was protecting them from the Bolsheviks'.[4] Even in this atmosphere Ungern stood out. Beforehand there had always been restraints on his rages, or at least consequences following them. Now he had his own fiefdom, and was part of a movement where extreme violence, especially against acceptable targets, was applauded rather than condemned.

Something about Ungern's rule at Dauria naturally attracted myth-making. Elsewhere in the Russian Far East, another of Semenov's protégés, Ataman Kalmikov, was managing a regime of unbelievable cruelty. His prisoners were reduced to flayed meat by days of torture, then finally disposed of by having a live grenade forced into their mouth or anus. Yet Kalmikov's actions didn't result in even a fraction of the stories that arose around Ungern. This was due partly to his sheer strangeness, and perhaps his aristocratic heritage, but his territory was also well positioned. Dauria sat on one of the main railway lines to Manchuria – it can still be seen, red-brick and miserable, from the train – and refugees trying to reach relative safety in China had to run the Baron's gauntlet. Anybody with useful skills, especially trained soldiers and medical staff, were liable to be commandeered on the spot. Elsewhere in Siberia, refugees and travellers warned others not to fall into the hands of the Baron. Rumour spread fast. By the time the young White officer Dmitri Alioshin arrived in Dauria, he had already heard 'fantastic stories of the Baron's mad bravery, of his justice to horses and cruelty to his own officers'.[5]

Kalmikov also alienated his own men; hundreds of his Cossacks fled from him. In contrast, Ungern seems to have been extremely popular among many of his troops. His sharing of their lifestyle, which had made him an outsider as an officer, his distaste for bureaucracy and his concern for their wellbeing led them to overlook his eccentricities and cruelties. Among them he was known as the 'stern grandfather', despite being barely in his thirties. There was no doubt of his ability to inspire loyalty; many of them were to follow him for the next three years, until his fanatical ambitions stretched even the most committed of them to breaking point. Although a relatively late arrival at Dauria, and, he claimed later, a constant sceptic about Ungern, Alioshin remarked repeatedly on the devotion of Ungern's troops, particularly the ordinary soldiers.

One benefit of Ungern's rule for his men was the chance to rob the travellers, mostly refugees, who passed through Dauria. They took particular delight in targeting Chinese merchants, who even in the chaos of the civil war made heroic trading runs through Siberia. Most of those unfortunate enough to pass through Dauria were stripped of their possessions, usually on the pretext that they were communist agitators. One typical case was reported in the *Peking and Tientsin Times* on 25 January, 1919, when six Chinese, innocent traders returning from Irkutsk, were accused of being 'the first batch of Bolshevik emissaries' and were stripped of six and a half million roubles. Not wanting to be cheated of plunder, Ungern's men sometimes chopped off fingers in order to remove tight-fitting rings. Rank was no protection; a former governor of the Urals had his money seized and, for protesting, was sentenced to fifty strokes of the whip.

These 'requisitions' were actively encouraged by Ungern, since they were his main source of funding. Plundered goods would be sent to an agent in Harbin, who would sell them on and use the profits to buy supplies for Dauria. The diamonds or gold that some refugee families hoped would fund their new lives thus became converted into oats, flour, tobacco, boots and mustard for Ungern's men – and on one occasion, coconuts, suggesting some odd craving on Ungern's part. Unlike most of Semenov's cronies, Ungern never took the opportunity to enrich himself; everything went to the division, while he went about in ragged trousers and old overcoats.

Ungern sometimes made inspections of the trains himself, especially when an important personage or suspected spy was passing through. If someone displeased him, he hauled them on to the platform and administered a beating himself. One traveller described how, when Ungern fixed an obnoxious travelling companion with the 'steel, steady gaze of his grey eyes' and questioned him about his credentials, 'the arrogance and importance of yesterday's boor disappeared! Entirely disappeared! – and before the iron baron there was a pitiful, cringing coward.'[6]

While the rest of Semenov's administration attempted to keep up at least a façade of civil order, maintaining courts, paying officials and issuing new laws, Ungern scorned such affairs. He had a dislike of paperwork, and regularly used to heave staff documents into locomotive furnaces when he felt they were no longer useful, but his feelings went beyond mere administrative frustration. He gave his orders orally, rather than go through the bother of writing them down. When asked to acknowledge receipt of one document he sneeringly replied, 'Paper? You need paper? I'll send you the whole desk.' He ordered one bureaucrat sent from Chita to inspect his paperwork to be flogged and drafted into the army. His short-temperedness with officials became part of his legend; he was supposed to have discovered one day that 'the salt fish, given every day to the soldiers, was not of the best quality', and so 'the officer in charge was sent to a military prison where he was fed upon that spoiled fish, and nothing else, for three days. And at no time was he given a single drop of water.'[7]

Ungern, who had been such an unruly subordinate himself, tolerated no slacking in his men. His own offences were against staff officers and the inconveniences of military red tape; his men, on the other hand, were at war, and as such had to operate under wartime discipline. Slips caused him to break into terrible rages. They had to spend their days drilling and training. Study of Mongolian was compulsory for officers, with examinations supervised by Ungern himself. Like a frustrated schoolmaster, Ungern complained in January 1919 that 'only two officers had attended the last class' and that missing lessons was tantamount to 'evasion of duty'.[8] There was time off, however. Provided they gave notice, soldiers could specify which national and religious holidays they wished to observe; an incongruously enlightened touch in Ungern's medieval regime. In the evening prayers were held, in which each man could pray to the god or gods he preferred.

Indeed, Ungern was both racially and religiously tolerant. What mattered was the system that men lived under, the way they ordered their lives. He remained a Lutheran himself, at least nominally, but he was also a self-admitted mystic. In practice, Russian mystics of the period tended to fall into one of two camps. Either they became crazy-Orthodox, and all other religions, including other branches of Christianity, were the devil's tools, or they became universalists, looking for a shared core to all religions. Ungern was undoubtedly in the latter camp. Although his view of religion was apocalyptic and fundamentalist, it was also inclusive. The Russian imperial mindset he had worked in was equally expansive; capable of embracing a Muslim-Buddhist fringe around a Russian-Orthodox core.

The great exception to this was Judaism. As with Theosophy, even the most expansive visions of religious unity still seemed to find a special place for the Jews, and not a good one. Both religiously and ethnically they were a fly in the ointment. Ungern had been raised with the normal prejudices of his class and time, which were perhaps heightened by his esoteric studies. He had plenty of reading material to help him clarify his thoughts. Anti-Semitic literature circulated widely among the White armies, often printed and distributed by the leadership. Chief among them was the 'Protocols of the Elders of

Zion'. This was claimed to be an outline of the Jewish plan for world domination, which would work by spreading such diabolical forces as republicanism, liberalism and social tolerance. Now rightly infamous as one of the cornerstones of Nazi anti-Semitism, its distribution among White émigrés helped kickstart its international popularity.

Ungern almost certainly read it; one of his letters includes a brief precis of how 'the principles of Talmud, preaching the tolerance of all and any means for the attainment of the goal afford the Jews a plan and method of activities in the destruction of nations and states',[9] ideas straight from the 'Protocols'. Their popularity received a considerable boost when the news came that Tsarina Alexandra had been reading a book by the anti-Semitic apocalyptic writer Sergius Nilus, which included the 'Protocols', while in captivity. She had also etched a swastika, already recognised as an anti-Semitic symbol, on her window. This came as a 'testament from on high' to many Whites. The tsarina's use of this Buddhist, esoteric and anti-Semitic symbol, which was also very common in Mongolia, would have thrilled Ungern.

The 'Protocols' meshed well with Ungern's interest in esoteric Eastern religion. There are some striking examples of the two mirroring each other, such as the following two passages. The first is from the introduction to the original 1905 edition of the 'Protocols', working imaginatively within both apocalyptic and conspiratorial traditions:

> There is no room left for doubt. With all the might and terror of Satan, the reign of the triumphant King of Israel is approaching our unregenerate world; the King born of the blood of Zion – the Antichrist – is near to the throne of universal power. Events in the world are rushing with stupendous rapidity; dissensions, wars, rumours, famines, epidemics, and earthquakes – what was yesterday impossible has today become an accomplished fact.[10]

The second is from Ferdinand Ossendowski, a companion of Ungern in Mongolia, describing one of the Hidden Masters in Shambhala:

> Now it is a large kingdom, millions of men with the King of the World as their ruler. He knows all the forces of the world and reads all the souls of humankind and the great book of their destiny. Invisibly he rules eight hundred million men on the surface of the earth and they will accomplish his every order. [. . .] The crowns of

kings, great and small, will fall . . . one, two, three, four, five, six, seven, eight . . . There will be a terrible battle among all the peoples. The seas will become red . . . the earth and the bottom of the seas will be strewn with bones . . . kingdoms will be scattered . . . whole peoples will die . . . hunger, disease, crimes unknown to the law, never before seen in the world.[11]

In the West, the malevolent power of the hidden Jewish king caused apocalyptic devastation; in the East, the benevolent power of the hidden Buddhist king plucked the world from the fires. It was not such a stretch to meld the two worldviews into a Manichean whole, the two hidden forces, light and dark, materialist and spiritual, clashing with each other behind the visible world as it lurched towards apocalypse. This image of a cosmic struggle, a battle between good and evil, would become the core of Ungern's beliefs.

Another anti-Semitic piece, the 'Zunder Document', never achieved the same popularity as the 'Protocols', but was even more widely distributed in Russia in 1919. It was a regular feature of White newspapers, and was alleged to have been taken from the body of a dead Jewish revolutionary leader named Zunder. The letter was a gloating testament to how 'the Sons of Israel [. . .] stand on the threshold of leadership of the world' and that the Russian people were now 'under the yoke of Jewish power'. Now the Jews had finally seized power, they should 'show neither pity nor mercy' to the Russian people, a sentiment stressed throughout the letter.

The logical conclusion for many Whites was that the Jews should be shown no mercy in return. Such materials built on anti-Semitic feelings which were common among the Russian officer caste in particular, who saw Jews as soft, city-dwelling, and unmanly.[12] It was this kind of propaganda, combined with the traditional anti-Semitism of the region, which caused the horrors of the White retreat across the Ukraine in late 1919. There, tens of thousands of Jews were slaughtered by vengeful White soldiers, especially by the Ukrainian Cossacks. Many of the most vehement anti-Semites came out of the Ukraine with the German armies, and went on to help drip the poison of Jew-hatred all over Europe. Ungern's Baltic German compatriots were particularly prominent among this new wave of anti-Semites, such as Fyodor Vinberg, who published lists of Jews supposedly involved in the Bolshevik revolution, Max von Scheuber-Richter, an early financial backer of the Nazis, and the Nazi theorist Alfred Rosenberg, a veteran of the *Baltikum*.

Broadly speaking, traditional Russian thought about the Jews had been focused on exclusion, not extermination. It was based on Christian principles. The Jews had refused to accept Christ, and had killed him; they were therefore tainted as a people, and had to be kept away from good Christians, and reminded of their sin. Yet at the same time their existence was necessary for the fulfilment of biblical prophecy; they had to continue existing, persecuted and isolated, until Judgement Day. Traditional Russian imperial thinking followed these lines. The Jews' continued existence as a people had not been seriously threatened, but they were subject to literally hundreds of rules and restrictions, particularly concerning their settlement in Russian lands and their contact with ordinary Russians. These petty discriminations grew worse in the last years of the tsarist system, especially under the highly anti-Semitic Nikolas II. They could never be part of the wider Russian world, but remained eternally foreign.

For Ungern, however, the Jews were not merely tainted, but actively evil. Like many others, he was convinced that the driving force behind the Bolsheviks was essentially Jewish. They were constantly striving to corrupt society. Their evil could not be contained, but had to be eradicated, down to the roots. The revolution had been caused not only by their actions, but by their mere corrupting presence; they were the 'sinners of the revolution'.[13] He discussed this 'important question' with another anti-Semitic White leader, Lieutenant-General Molchanov, in a heartfelt conversation during a downpour in Dauria. They, or at least Ungern, came to the conclusion that it was necessary to 'exterminate Jews, so that neither men nor women, nor even the seed of this people remain'.[14] The seeping poison of the 'snake' of Jewish influence had been the downfall of the old regime. With the Jews eliminated, the Russian Empire could be redeemed, and a new imperial utopia emerge.

As a result, Jews passing through Dauria were in great danger. One man recalled decades later how his father, who ran a medical train along the route for over two years, had given the Jewish doctors on his staff 'small crosses to wear on little chains around their necks, so that they could pass superficial checks by the Baron's men'. When Ungern's men went out checking for partisans, any Jew they found was liable to be murdered. A Red Cross official who visited Dauria heard a story that Ungern saw a particularly pretty Jewish girl in a village and offered a thousand roubles to whichever of his men brought him her head. The tale seems unlikely, but only because it has a sexual-sadistic element that is uncharacteristic of Ungern; it would be far more in character simply to have hung or shot the girl out of hand.

◆━◆══◆━◆

Ungern had other hobbies beside planning genocide, however. An 'interesting conversationalist',[15] he would often sit and discuss philosophy, world affairs, and religion with visitors from Chita. Semenov remembered his 'ability to delve with feeling into philosophical deliberation on questions of religion, literature, and military science'.[16] Mongolia, and Mongolian affairs, remained on his mind. He spent most of his time with his Mongol troops, and often dressed in Mongolian style. One foreign correspondent visiting Dauria found him wearing

> a silk Mongolian hat and sitting in Mongolian national dress [. . .] He turned to me and said, 'My dress seems unusual to you? There's nothing surprising in it; most of my horsemen are Buriats and Mongols, and it pleases them that I wear their clothing. I highly appreciate the Mongolian people and over several years had the opportunity to be convinced of their honesty and fidelity.'[17]

Ungern showed 'great knowledge in the field of Mongolian customs and religion'.

He dwelt on superstition and magic, too, with particular reference to Mongolia. Another interviewer found him bent over a table, playing with a pack of cards, and was forced into a truly awkward conversation:

> 'Spades,' he said, 'always spades. And the ace of hearts. You'd think there were fifty-one spades in the pack. You don't know,' he asked me suddenly, 'what the ace of hearts means?'
>
> 'No, Your Excellency.'
>
> 'Then you ought to.' The Baron brooded for a moment or two. 'The Mongols,' he went on, 'believe that the heart is a triangle

situated in the middle of the chest, and that its apex points to the right in men and to the left in women. Of course, you think that's nonsense, don't you?'

He stared at me in no friendly fashion. I murmured:

'I'm bound to say, Your Excellency . . .'

I didn't feel very comfortable.

'You may be right,' said Ungern, 'Or you may be wrong.' He brooded again for a minute or two. Then he went on, sharply:

'How do you explain the fact that the Mongols manage to cure diseases which we Europeans regard as incurable?'

I preferred to make no reply.

'I'd give a good deal to know what the ace of hearts means,' said the Baron, as though he were talking to himself. 'Do you think it's a good sign or a bad sign?'[18]

This was the first sign of an interest in fortune-telling, but not the last. There were stories that he consulted with Buriat soothsayers even in Siberia. He described himself as 'a fatalist' and someone who 'strongly trusts in destiny'.[19] Later, in a psychological report, the Soviets would characterise Ungern as being obsessed with military authority, and with the receiving and carrying out of orders. This was only half true. Military authority, for Ungern, was always secondary to the authority of fate. His wilfulness, his growing conviction of his own destiny, would not admit a lesser master. He looked for confirmation in stars, oracle bones and tea leaves. His obsession with prophecy and fate would only grow; the fate of thousands would depend upon it.

These beliefs may have been fuelled by a new habit. At some point he had given up drinking entirely. Indeed, he began to disapprove of his men doing so, warning early in 1919 that drunken soldiers 'would in future be charged with all the severity of wartime law'.[20] Perhaps the shock of the revolution had made him determined to remain clear-headed. If so, he appears to have failed, for, according to several accounts, he merely replaced one dependency with another: opium. (He refers at one point to an 'opium-smoking party' in his letters.) He could easily have become addicted during his diplomatic trips into Manchuria, where opium-smoking was common among the officials and nobles with whom he was dealing. There would have been no difficulty ensuring a regular supply with so many Chinese in the region.

His officers believed that he saw visions in the opium haze, visions which reinforced the prophecies he read.

＊＋＝◆＝＋＊

Apart from his opium habit, Ungern lived simply, exhibiting a lack of ostentation and a complete disregard for material possessions. His rigorous honesty, especially with regard to his own division's finances, made him almost unique among the Semenovites. He even devoted his personal salary, and the sale of some property he owned in China, presumably brought on earlier trips to Peking, to the division. Ungern's ascetic lifestyle stood in stark contrast to Semenov's life in Chita. The *ataman* was indulging in a whirlpool of pleasures, from theatre to champagne dinners to extravagant balls. Chita's nightlife was notorious: cocaine-addicted Russian whores, officers pimping their wives, exotic oriental hostesses imported across the Manchurian border. Semenov's own appetite for women was insatiable, and he had at least a dozen known mistresses. He maintained a private railway carriage entirely devoted to his harem, known as 'the Summer Car', which contained 'thirty of the most beautiful women I ever saw',[21] according to one American visitor, as well as an orchestra made up of Austrian-Hungarian prisoners and a copious stock of champagne. He was siphoning off money from both foreign aid and general plunder, and reportedly depositing it in foreign accounts. Literally trainloads of gold were sent by him to China, for eventual deposit in Japanese banks. Despite his public statements that the Bolsheviks would never take Siberia, an aeroplane was always kept handy in case he needed to flee with his loot.

Semenov rewarded Ungern in March 1919 with another Cross of St George, fourth class, for his disarming of the garrison at Hailar; he also promoted him to lieutenant-general. Ungern was proud of these awards, although there was something of an excess of generals among the Whites. Nevertheless, he disapproved of his old friend's growing corruption, of the extravagance of his lifestyle and of his tolerant attitude towards Jews. Semenov had expressly forbidden pogroms under his command, kept a Yiddish theatre and a synagogue running in Chita and had a favourite mistress who was strongly rumoured to be Jewish, upon whom he lavished plundered jewellery. (Perhaps

Ungern didn't believe the rumours, since he asked after his friend's mistress in terms that implied some kind of private joke between them – 'How is your Masha? Do not fall asleep again.'[22] He named a white mare given to him by Semenov Masha, too, which could be either an affectionate tribute or an insult.) Semenov even attempted to raise a Jewish Cossack division, reviving the short-lived and bizarrely titled Sons of Israel regiment formed by Potemkin in 1787 to help liberate Jerusalem from the Turks.

Ungern and he were drifting apart. On 17 September, 1918 Ungern thanked a Russian friend in Manchuria for his previous two letters, which had 'breathed faith in success. I lost this faith myself on my last trip to Chita. It is a shame to admit it, but be assured that when we last talked I did not think that this would be an uphill battle. Now it is time to change colours. The passivity and apathy of some people have ruined everything.'[23]

He also disagreed with Semenov on the nature of the government they were fighting for. Semenov advocated the restoration of the Romanovs, but he envisioned a constitutional monarchy with limited powers, a semi-democratic system with a parliament and a cabinet, such as had existed, at least in theory, before the revolution. Ungern, however, was a committed monarchist. Since the murder of the imperial family, he had pinned his hopes on the tsar's younger brother, the amiable but dim Prince Michael. Unknown to Ungern, the man he was championing had been murdered in secret by the Bolsheviks in 1918, but rumours of his supposed whereabouts circulated throughout Russia and Ungern was determined to put him back on the throne.

Of all the great vanished ideologies, monarchism, especially religious monarchism, often seems to be the most ridiculous. It is hard to imagine that anybody could regard the deeply stupid Nikolas II or the drooling, retarded Taisho emperor, for example, as the representative of God's will on earth. For Ungern, though, this was the natural order of things; the monarch, however flawed, was 'the first person in the state'.[24] He could stand apart from all the classes, and as such treat them all equally. Nevertheless, he would be supported by the advice of aristocrats such as Ungern. Aristocrats had to be loyal, since 'history showed that they were the class that had the power to destroy the monarchs'.[25]

Beneath them would be a solid base of faithful peasantry who would labour to support the monarchy and defend it with their lives. This ideal system of rule had been in decline for a long time before the revolution, in Ungern's view. Liberalism and capitalism, which was 'only good for exploiting the blood of the people', had weakened the natural order, allowing the final triumph of revolution. The workers had been spoilt, become lazy, and had spent 'the last fifteen years just sitting around'. Behind it all, of course, was the diabolical hand of the Jews, who had worked throughout the nineteenth century to cause 'revolutions, rebellions, and the overthrowing of monarchy and authority'.[26] In Russia, only the power of the foreign aristocracy, such as the Baltic Germans, had prevented the corruption of the country by the perverse talents of the Jews. After the revolution Ungern was firmly convinced that 'aristocracy will pass to the Jews, since the Slavs are not capable of building a state, and the only capable people in Russia are the Jews'.[27] Ungern was never shy of acknowledging Jewish 'cleverness', especially in contrast to the idiotic nature of peasants and workers left without guidance; he just believed it was always put to evil ends.

Ungern's faith in Prince Michael's eventual return echoed old peasant stories of the 'tsar-deliverer', an idealised version of the tsar who would, it was often believed, miraculously appear to smite corrupt local officials, give the peasants back their land and generally put the world to rights. Among the peasants it was an extreme form of the common belief in the 'good tsar', kept from knowing the people's true state by his corrupt officials. The tsar-deliverer was often believed to be hiding in some secret place until the time was right. Then he would return to destroy his enemies and a golden age of peace and harmony would follow.

It was a powerful myth; Lenin saw it as the major obstacle to peasant rebellion. Until the events of Bloody Sunday in 1905 destroyed trust in the tsar for good, he believed that peasants 'have been able naively and blindly to believe in the Tsar-Deliverer [. . .] *Peasants could not rise in rebellion, they were only able to petition and to pray.*'[28] For reactionaries like Ungern, such legends were evidence of the peasants' ultimate faith in the tsar and the imperial system. In fact, the legend of the tsar-deliverer had inspired far more rebellions than it had restrained; it empowered peasants to act 'in the name of the Tsar' while really asserting their own rights. As the situation worsened for the Whites, many of them developed a naive faith of their own in the peasants, who, so Ungern and others believed, would ultimately rise up against the Bolshevik usurpers and restore the monarchy they clearly longed for.

＊━ ☰◈☲ ━＊

Before monarchy could be restored, however, the war had to be won. The Siberian front was both highly mobile and deeply constrained. The territory was so vast that scouts, raiding parties, even entire battalions, could move undetected through land theoretically controlled by the enemy, but at the same time the strategically important areas were incredibly narrow. The rail tracks and stations were the lifeblood of the region, and their sabotage, capture or protection the daily work of the war.

Thousands of people lived on the railway, travelling from station to station without a fixed home. Whole communities became mobile, and great trains of carriages bore generals from place to place. Amazingly the employees of the old Trans-Siberian, often coerced and bullied by Semenov's men, still made up the majority of those who kept the network running. The railway was a mobile city: there were hospital cars, headquarters, brothels, travelling theatres, dining cars appointed like opulent Moscow restaurants, libraries, motor workshops, churches, mobile electric generators, printing shops, offices, and torture chambers. White generals especially liked to travel in style, recapturing some of the glory of the good old days.

Armoured trains were the dreadnoughts of this war. Huge and expensive, they could bring a devastating amount of firepower to bear – albeit upon a necessarily limited area. Three standard types of armoured train had been manufactured during the war, but in Siberia many of them were unique, improvised creations; engineers took an ordinary train and bolted great slabs of steel to its sides as armour, then took whatever guns could be found and attached them to the roof of the carriage. Some were merely semi-armoured, their wooden carriages reinforced only with bricks or sandbags – enough to deflect rifle bullets, but useless against serious artillery.

Most comprised eight to ten carriages, but they could be much longer. Their modular nature made for both flexibility of purpose and ease of replacement; damaged rolling stock could be cannibalised for spares. Some of these snaky juggernauts were painted in camouflage colours, greens and browns, while others were liveried in menacing black. Churchill wrote of armoured trains that 'the very name seems strange; a locomotive disguised as a knight-errant, the agent of civilisation in the habiliments of chivalry', but there was nothing either civilised or chivalrous about their use in the Transbaikal. Semenov's trains had no effective opposition, and to be the commander of one was like being captain of a pirate vessel; one could simply roll into a small town and demand that the locals either hand over whatever they had or be blown to smithereens. The Reds strove to set up their armoured train crews as a trained, organised force, and tried to use them as massed artillery. In contrast, Semenov's captains recruited or press-ganged their own men, often acting on their own initiative rather than any higher orders. Crew sizes ranged from forty to nearly two hundred, sometimes with an auxiliary infantry force of two or three hundred men. Many were armed with naval artillery, stripped from the gunboats of the Siberian lakes. They were given names fit for machines of mass destruction; the Reds had the ideological *Death to Parasites, Ruin of the Counter-revolution, Liberty or Death,* while among the White trains in Siberia were the *Valiant, Swift* and *Just,* along with the more aptly named *Master, Avenger, Destroyer, Terrible* and *Merciless.*

Behind them followed the death trains. Both sides rarely took prisoners, and neither wanted the burden of looking after them. The repatriations of the first tentative stage of the war, when Red troops could simply be disarmed and sent back to Bolshevik territory, were a thing of the past. Now prisoners of war taken by the Whites were simply herded into railcars, stuffed fifty or so to a wagon, and carried aimlessly from station to station with neither food nor water. Their guards had no idea what they were supposed to be doing with the prisoners, and when the trains ran out of fuel they were often just shunted into a siding and abandoned. Local people were forbidden from giving the desperate prisoners food. Often 30 or 40 per cent of the prisoners on a single train perished in the weeks spent chugging aimlessly back and forth; the eventual fate of the rest was to be secretly executed in some nameless patch of Siberia.

Although the Transbaikal was under the nominal control of Semenov and his lieutenants, their grip on the area was weak, especially outside the zone of the railway. They terrorised the railway workers, causing many to become Bolshevik sympathisers. Red partisans began to infiltrate into White-held territory, sometimes in groups several hundred strong. Their object was to do as much damage and cause as much mayhem as possible and then disappear; the goal of their opponents was to exterminate them like vermin. The partisans tried to terrorise the peasants into giving them food, the Whites tried to terrorise the peasants into not supporting the partisans.

The partisans were helped by the many Bolshevik sympathisers who had gone underground when Semenov took control of the region. Chita was the centre of Semenov's regime, but it was also the lynchpin of the underground; officers going out at night had to be careful of wandering into dark alleys, or of getting sniped at from a high building. Semenov and Ungern both acquired Mongol bodyguards to protect themselves from would-be martyr-assassins. Some of the partisans hid among ordinary villagers and townsfolk, but most made their bases in the great dense forests. The railway lines, the backbone of the regular armies, were their primary targets. They tore up track, sabotaged repair facilities, ambushed trains and placed rocks and logs across the tracks.

Ungern's men were often called out to deal with the aftermath of partisan attacks, or to sweep the forests for their hideouts. Villages would be combed for signs of partisan support, an exercise which invariably turned into another opportunity to steal from the locals. Such operations were similar to those his regiment had carried out in Dauria before the war, when suppressing banditry had been a regular part of their routine. Here, cultural differences exacerbated the situation; Ungern's Mongol troops looked down upon the ethnically Russian villagers with the age-old contempt of the nomad for the soft, settled farmer, an attitude that Ungern encouraged. He received occasional notes of congratulation from other commanders for the successful 'cleansing' of villages.

Partisans were not the only threat. The very nature of the civil war and the divided factionalism of the anti-Bolshevik movement fomented constant suspicion about political loyalties. Counter-intelligence was an obsession of most of the Semenovites, who often devoted more time to sniffing out supposed traitors than to fighting the Bolsheviks. A series of torture chambers was established across the Transbaikal,

choked with Red prisoners and suspected traitors. One was established at Dauria. Many of Ungern's soldiers were veterans of these
grisly institutions, which deeply shocked foreign observers. One of the
most infamous was at Makkaveevo, where over five thousand victims
were murdered. After the war visitors recalled seeing 'dried slices of
human flesh dangling from nails. Blood had so saturated the ground
under the building that the soil was discoloured and befouled.'[29]

Ungern's ties to Mongolia inevitably involved him in one of Semenov's
grandest schemes, the plans for 'pan-Mongolia'. This was an idea that
had been popular among some Mongol intellectuals since the beginning of the century, particularly among the Buriat. It was a scheme for
unification of the Mongol peoples, creating a new state that would
unite Outer and Inner Mongolia with the Buriat and Bargut territories.
Semenov was keen on this plan, seeing in it an opportunity to become
'King Gregorii I', as the sardonic White diarist Baron Budberg put it.

Some among Semenov's Japanese backers were also eager to test
pan-Mongolia's feasibility; a Japanese-backed puppet state would
immeasurably strengthen Japan's power in the region, giving her a base
for future assaults on Russia and China. They had already created a
pan-Buddhist society in 1918 as a front to promote pan-Mongolian
ambitions, hoping to foment anti-Chinese feeling in Inner Mongolia in
particular. It tied into the popularity in Japan of pan-Asiatic thinkers,
who saw Asian unity as a spiritual and political necessity for Japan. All
the peoples of Asia, linked by faith, ethnicity and culture, could come
together – under suitable Japanese guidance.[30]

Under Semenov's sponsorship, and with Japanese observers, two
congresses were called; one in Dauria in early February and a later
one in Chita on 25 March. Representatives from Inner Mongolia,
Bargut and Buriatia attended, though the Buriats dominated. A grand
state was sketched, with Hailar, in Bargut territory, as the capital of
the new country, though the provisional capital was to be Dauria. The
delegates proclaimed a respected Inner Mongolian lama, the Niis
Gegen, prime minister of the nascent state, and sent a representative
to the Paris Peace Conference, then seeking to reorder the post-war
world.

Although he arranged the initial conference, Ungern was opposed to the idea. The thrust behind it was a modernising one, an attempt to create an organised state from disparate peoples, with a federal government and an elected parliament. It was the antithesis of all that Ungern valued in the Mongols: tradition, leadership, the preservation of values that had been lost in the West. Nor were the delegates his kind of people. He disliked European intellectuals quite enough; to have to deal with Mongolian ones, polluting the purity of his beloved nomads, must have been even more irritating. His relationship with Fushenge, the Inner Mongolian prince and enthusiastic pan-Mongolist to whom he had been providing military advice for over a year, was also deteriorating. He wrote about the conference with indifference, even bitterness, and noted to a friend that he had forgotten to ask him for help to send the delegates to Paris. Later he spoke of the plan as a 'soap bubble' and its proponents as 'empty-headed'. Its main virtue to him was as a recruiting tool to amass more Mongol troops.

Fortunately for Ungern, the idea was stillborn. The meetings were attended by only sixteen representatives, and none from Outer Mongolia. Three delegates, including Fushenge, were sent to Urga to try to raise support for the idea among the Bogd's court and the nobles. They were snubbed; not only was the Bogd, like Ungern, opposed to the idea of a modern state but he could see the risk of threatening China with further loss of territory and a new, hostile power, and knew that the chances of his having any real power in a Semenov-led, Japanese-backed puppet state were exceedingly small. The pan-Mongolian delegates were forced to return to Dauria, where they proposed an attack on Urga to drive out the Chinese and act as a spark for pan-Mongolian feeling. It was a bluff; with the Japanese backers gone, funding was limited and barely three thousand troops could be raised for the threatened assault.

In Paris, Kolchak's representatives and the Chinese both manoeuvred to prevent the pan-Mongols from being represented at the conference, and nobody was anyway in much of a mood to listen to idealists from the backwaters of the world. Optimistic telegrams seeking recognition were dispatched to world leaders, without result. After the meeting at Dauria was reported in the Chinese newspapers, the Japanese cabinet grew nervous of the risk of alienating the other great powers, who had guaranteed the integrity of Chinese territory. On 16 March Japan forbade its citizens, military and civilian, from participating in the pan-Mongolian movement in any way. It was to be another decade before Tokyo took up the idea again.

Like many pan-national movements before and since, the main cause of its disintegration was disagreement about who was the most truly 'national'. Outer Mongolians had no interest in a Buriat-led movement, and considered themselves the largest and most important group; Inner Mongolians believed that they represented an older and purer form of Mongol culture; and the Buriats argued that, as the most advanced and modern group, and as the originators of the idea, they should obviously take the lead.

Tensions between the Buriats and Fushenge's Inner Mongolian fighters grew. In anticipation of the threatened attack on Urga, both had been stationed at Dauria, where they were being trained by Russian officers under Ungern's command. On 3 September, 1919, under Fushenge's leadership, fifteen hundred Inner Mongolians mutinied, killing their Russian officers, disarming their Buriat comrades and seizing an armoured train. The exact cause of the revolt is unclear, but there were stories of plots and counter-plots, and rumours that the Karachen were planning to defect to the Chinese side. The cause may have been more mundane; it had been a long time since most of the soldiers had been paid. Whatever the catalyst, Dauria became a battlefield for two solid days, as more armoured trains were rushed down to pound the rebels into submission, and the Cossack and Buriat troops fought against their former comrades. All the revolt's leaders were killed, including Fushenge, and the remnants escaped into Mongolia, where they were captured and executed by the Chinese army. Pan-Mongolism had been a political farce that ended with Mongol killing Mongol, but to Ungern's fertile imagination it suggested unfulfilled possibilities.

——◆——

Conspicuously absent from records of Ungern's life is any mention of either love or sex. A common story circulating during the 1920s ascribed to him a wife and children in Estonia who had been brutally murdered by the Bolsheviks, but this was a complete fabrication, an attempt to put a reason to his fanatical hatred of revolutionaries.

It was not unusual for members of the Baltic aristocracy to marry relatively late, but there is no trace of any courtship, infatuation, mistress, or even casual affair. Unlike other officers, he never frequented the many brothels in Chita. When he spoke of women it was either in terms of concern for their morals or the danger posed to them by revolution.

He found the company of women uncomfortable; a friend recalled how 'It often happened that he would sit with me until my wife or another lady came. At their arrival he would immediately try to leave and say goodbye; he could not stand the company of women.'[31] Celibacy was clearly part of his generally ascetic lifestyle; he referred later to 'the comforts of celibacy, the entire negation of woman, of the comforts of life'.[32] He was brutally sarcastic about women's rights, suggesting to a friend that his wife should take up the mock-revolutionary slogan 'Women of the world, unite!' and that that 'stupid woman Pankhurst',[33] referring to the famous British suffragette, should be forced to come to Siberia.

His passion for military life, his desire to stay close to his men and an indifference to women bordering on misogyny all suggest that Ungern may have been homosexual.[34] Perhaps there was even an element of sexual attraction in his close relationship with the young, handsome Semenov. One unverified report of a conversation attributes to him disgust at 'Those dirty workers who've never had any servants of their own, but still think they can command; those Jews who started the revolution to be revenged on us; those women who lie in wait for you everywhere, in the streets, in drawing-rooms, with their legs spread out – we've got to get rid of all that.'[35] Whatever his preference, he seems to have repressed it deeply, for nowhere in the literature is there concrete evidence of any sexual encounter.

The record of his marriage in Harbin on 16 August, 1919 therefore comes as something of a surprise. The bride was an aristocratic Chinese lady, just nineteen years old, with the Russian name of Elena Pavlovna. She must have been from an educated and modern family, since she apparently conversed with Ungern in English. She was supposed by some Whites to have been a daughter of the famous Chinese republican leader Dr Sun Yat-Sen. She was certainly not one of his acknowledged daughters, but he was a notorious womaniser and had numerous illegitimate children, so there is a bare outside chance the claim was true. Far more likely is that the rumour started simply because Sun Yat-Sen was the only Chinese leader the troops knew of. The marriage was almost certainly a purely political one arranged by Semenov, since the bride was related to an influential Chinese general. Ungern was on a long trip away from Dauria, nearly seven months, meeting with Chinese and Russian leaders in China, which is presumably when the arrangements were made. He returned to Dauria shortly after the wedding. In all likelihood the marriage was never consummated before the bride returned to her parents' house, although Ungern sent money regularly to a bank account in Manchuli set up in her name. Most usefully, it gave Ungern a Manchurian title to match his German one, something he rarely failed to mention when dealing with Chinese or Mongolian officials.

One reason Semenov was eager to encourage closer links with the Chinese and Japanese was that his relationships with the wider White movement were becoming increasingly strained. His old enemy, Admiral Kolchak, found himself reluctantly thrust into leadership of the Whites in Siberia after an officers' coup overthrew the Directory, the supreme body of the provisional Siberian government. Semenov responded immediately, cutting off communications and blocking supplies from the Far East intended for Kolchak's base at Omsk. After protests by railway workers, he stationed troops at every station and began a programme of ruthless intimidation to ensure that they bent to his will. Like rival medieval popes, the feuding leaders began an exchange of ever-more insulting letters, culminating in a public disavowal of the validity of each other's governments in early December.

The schism brought to the forefront already existing dissensions within the White movement. The Japanese backed Semenov, and hinted that if Kolchak attempted to remove him by force, the Japanese army would stand in the way. The Czechs began to distance themselves from both sides. All along the railways, men who found themselves on the wrong side of the quarrel were beaten up or arrested. Kolchak attempted to have the *ataman* arrested 'for disobedience and infringement of the telegraphic service in the rear of the Army, which is an act of high treason',[36] but the punitive expedition he assembled ended up in a tense stand-off with Semenov's men, which broke down only when the White soldiers on either side started chatting and drinking together. Troop movement and supplies snarled to a halt as crucial railway officials were seized for being pro-Kolchak. In the end the squabble was resolved by the Japanese negotiation of an uneasy peace between the two leaders, who mutually, if reluctantly, recognised each other's authority. The rift, however, remained. Ungern and his men were solid Semenovites; for them the quarrel only established Kolchak's followers as weaklings and traitors. They would mete out their own kind of punishment to them in due course.

Ungern's own links to Semenov were growing weaker. The *ataman*'s control of his lieutenants was always dubious, and bit by bit Dauria began to act as an entirely separate force from the rest of the Special Manchurian Division. In February 1920 they were formally organised as an entirely separate unit, the Asian Cavalry Division. Ungern was still in regular contact with Semenov in Chita, but there was little doubt in anybody's mind that he was now an autonomous power in his own right. Semenov publicly recognised that Ungern's forces equalled his own in importance. Soldiers whispered to each other of how 'Ataman Semenov is afraid of Baron von Ungern-Sternberg, for he possesses the only real military power upon which that adventurer can build his career as a sovereign ruler.'[37]

For a while the White-held territories to the west had provided the Transbaikal with a measure of insulation against Red attacks. Now, as the Bolshevik assaults tore ever bigger holes in the White defences, it became easier for large groups of Red partisans to enter Semenov's territory. Sometimes they did things on a grand scale, as on the morning of 31 October, 1919, when two thousand men took over six miles of railway near Khada-Bulak, up the line from Dauria, and spent the day systematically destroying track, telegraph lines and bridges. By the time a furious Ungern arrived, along with his Cossacks, they had melted away into the landscape, and although Ungern and his men spent the night searching for them, they found not a single partisan.

Entire towns were taken over by partisans, an experience that was often less painful than being scourged by the Whites afterwards. One notorious example of this was in the small station of Zilovo, which was occupied by the Reds for eight days in September 1919. When the armoured train *Avenger* arrived in response, captained by Colonel Popov, one of Semenov's cronies, it lived up to its name. The Reds had all left, so Popov shot the village elders who turned up to welcome him, then proceeded to shoot a dozen more villagers at random and rape two local girls.

Such behaviour prompted the formation of a growing number of partisan groups with no connection to the Bolsheviks; they were simply peasants who, tired of having their daughters raped, their houses burnt and their stores confiscated, had taken to the forest to fight the Semenovites. By the end of 1919 there were around a hundred thousand anti-White partisans operating in Siberia, and approximately thirty thousand in the Transbaikal alone. Many of Semenov's soldiers, sick of the random cruelty of their superiors, deserted to join the partisans.

Despite his growing distance from Semenov, Ungern's base at Dauria still played a crucial, gruesome part in the White infrastructure; it was the execution camp. Prisoners were sent there in trainloads to be disposed of by Ungern's killers. As with the 'death trains', frontline soldiers were often too squeamish to dispose outright of men who, only a year or two before, had been their compatriots. At Dauria, Ungern's men had no such compunction about executing the Red captives who arrived there. Many of the White leaders in the west believed – or claimed to believe – that a system of prisoner-of-war camps still existed in Siberia, and that the men they sent there would be treated humanely. Some prisoners had been 'processed' through the torture chambers beforehand; others were civilians, suspected Bolshevik sympathisers put through a quick and farcical trial before being sent to Dauria for execution. Men were hanged or shot in batches of seventy or eighty at a time. The bodies were left in the open to rot, and surrounding hills came to resemble the aftermath of a battle. Body dumping, unhygienic as it was, was standard practice around Semenov's execution and torture centres. At Makkaveevo, so many bodies were dumped into the nearby river that it became polluted, and after local peasants complained Semenov ordered that the bodies be burnt instead.

Ungern, one of his officers claimed, found the macabre atmosphere relaxing. 'On these hills, where everywhere were rolling skulls, skeletons, and decaying body parts, Baron Ungern used to like to go to rest.'[38] Perhaps it reminded him of the Mongolian temples. The killings reached a peak in the spring of 1920, as the Red tide threatened to wash over Siberia and the Semenovites became more desperate and vicious in response. In April 1920 an American report noted that two thousand Chinese prisoners had been dispatched in two weeks, and that Dauria was known as 'the gallows of Siberia'.

This grisly work was managed by Colonel Sipailov, one of the many petty sadists among the Semenovites. A former mechanic, he suffered what appears to have been Tourette's syndrome: 'He was always nervously jerking and wriggling his body and talking ceaselessly, making most unattractive sounds in his throat and sputtering with saliva all over his lips, his whole face often contorted with spasms.'[39] He had 'cold colourless eyes under dense brows' and the 'strange undulating line of his skull' made his head look like a saddle. He was despised for his 'scandalous meanness and cunning, his bloodthirstiness and cowardice' by Ungern's other officers. He was supposed to have been tortured by the Bolsheviks, and his family murdered by them, though this was a common excuse used to explain the excesses of White torturers. He had been involved in an infamous massacre on Lake Baikal on 6 January, 1919, where Bolshevik hostages had been herded on to a ship and then, after being promised freedom, brought up on deck one by one to have their heads smashed in by a Cossack with a ice-breaking mallet on the top of the gangway.

He did similar work at Dauria, after Ungern ordered one of his first executions, that of Lieutenant-Colonel Laurent, shot on suspicion of treason. Dmitri Alioshin was informed that

> tonight the soldiers of Commandant Sipailov will go into the prison, tie the prisoners, load them one on top of the other, like cargo, into wagons, and haul them into the mountains. According to the playful humour of the soldiers, they will be killed, either by shooting in the back or by being spitted upon bayonets and swords.[40]

Dauria's grim reputation was made worse by rumours of Ungern's policies during the typhus and cholera outbreaks which swept through Siberia in 1919–20. He ordered those unlikely to recover to be shot in the hospital in order to prevent further infection, a policy he continued during his later campaigns. The atrocities at Dauria outraged American observers. One, Major Flanagan, was able to intervene to have forty prisoners – a drop in the ocean – released, telegraphing Semenov and imploring the Japanese. Ungern was furious with him, and when

Flanagan suffered a nervous breakdown three weeks later, his friends, according to American reports, suspected 'Mongolian poison' administered by Ungern's agents. It seems highly unlikely, especially since the sights in Siberia were enough to inspire nightmares in anybody, but it was an indication of how powerful the Baron's legend was becoming, and of how closely he was associated with Mongolia.

By the summer of 1920 there was little hope left for Semenov's men. White resistance in Western Siberia had collapsed the previous winter, and Omsk had been evacuated. Kolchak fled to Irkutsk, but it had been taken over by a leftist faction, who handed him over to the Bolsheviks in January. After a brief 'investigation', but not even a show trial, he was shot on 7 February. Before his death he had written an order handing over control of his remaining troops to Semenov, since, however much he disliked the *ataman*, he was the only effective White leader remaining in Siberia. The White position in Crimea was also untenable, and Wrangel evacuated the last of his men in November 1919. The White cause was obviously doomed. Semenov's control over the Transbaikal could last a little longer, but only because of the huge distances involved, the chaos throughout Soviet Russia and the support of the Japanese. There was no future in it, and Ungern knew it. He needed a way out.

Ungern met Semenov for one last time, in the tiny station of Olovyan. Later, Semenov would take credit for planning the whole Mongolian expedition, claiming that the Asian Cavalry Division was intended to be the core of a new Mongolian army which would liberate the country from Chinese imperialism, a cause that had been close to his heart since his time there in 1911. It was probably true that his pan-Mongolian schemes were part of Ungern's inspiration, but the true plan was different. Ungern was directed by Semenov to take the town of Aksha, on the Mongolian border, as part of a scheme for the Asian Cavalry Division to operate as a guerrilla force against the Bolsheviks. The ultimate aim of the original plan was probably to work their way up through Siberia, living off the land and mobilising the peasantry against the Bolsheviks, and meet up with one of Ungern's old comrades, Colonel Rezuhin. Rezuhin was a small, dapper man, known for his loyalty to Ungern and his brutality; his name meant 'cutter' in Russian, and he lived up to it. On 15 August, with very little warning, Ungern gathered his men and rode for Aksha, where they skirmished with Bolshevik fighters. Some of his Chinese troops deserted, perhaps sickened by his rule. From Aksha, Ungern's army crossed the border into Mongolia.

Before he left, he sent a note to his wife, divorcing her. Their marriage had, at least theoretically, been made under Chinese law, and only the husband's will was necessary for a divorce. Perhaps she was grateful enough to be rid of a politically burdensome husband, and to be free to make a real marriage. He gave his wedding ring to a friend for safe keeping. Of his wife, we hear no more. His marriage was behind him, his service to Semenov was at an end and he had had no contact with his family for nearly two years. There was nothing left to tie him to his old life.

Ungern claimed that the move to enter Mongolia was a spontaneous one, after some of his Chinese units had revolted and after he realised that Semenov was not going to complete his part of the plan. It was a disingenuous claim. Others believed that he had been driven over the border by Bolshevik forces and had simply fled to the only refuge left to him, though if driven by pure pragmatism the Far Eastern provinces under the protection of the Japanese army would have been a more likely destination. Later the Soviets would accuse Ungern of being in the pay of the Japanese when he invaded Mongolia. Japan's interest in pan-Mongolian schemes had been very real, but they had no involvement in Ungern's plans – Tokyo had called a halt to pan-Mongolian activities months beforehand. Although there were Japanese officers attached to his army they were not on active service, but mercenaries and drifters of the type that adventurers such as Ungern always attract.

More probably, he had planned to take the division into Mongolia from the start. Mongolia had been in his thoughts for many years, and more powerful than any order was the call of fate. It was fate that 'was always making my decisions' whereas 'orders were merely pieces of paper'.[41] Ungern had always felt his destiny was wrapped up in Mongolia, 'the land of great conquerors'. Now his path was even more certain. Everything had been stripped away from him. The empire whose boundaries he had struggled to defend and define had been fragmented by a civil war in which the forces of evil were triumphing.

His closest friend had become a degenerate tool of a foreign power. His childhood homeland had been taken over by peasants. The only thing that was constant, unchanged, was the purity of the Mongolian peoples, who had 'not forgotten their ancient faiths and customs'.[42]

He had striven to save the empire he had been raised in, but it was almost irretrievably corrupted. Russia's core had been lost to the Bolsheviks. A new empire would have to be created, and he had the model for it in the empire of Genghis Khan, which had once stretched 'from the Amur Mountains to the Caspian Sea'.[43] Ungern did not believe himself, as some later claimed, to be the reincarnation of Genghis Khan;[44] instead, he saw himself as restoring his legacy. He dwelt on Genghis on occasion in conversation, referring to him as 'the Great Leader'[45] and claiming, later, that his army was 'the equal of Genghis Khan's'.[46] Like the steppe tribes before Genghis who had once fought to recreate the empire of the Huns, Ungern would recreate the empire of the Mongols.

Attempts to claim the legacy of Genghis were common in Mongolian political culture, as Ungern would have known from his interest in Dambijantsan. This was not a complete fantasy, although it was supported by Mongolian religious beliefs, such as the prophecies he heard from Mongolian travellers, and from his Buriat troops. Variants of the ever-fresh Shambhala legend, they spoke of a saviour from the north who would save the Mongolian people in their time of crisis. Transmitted orally, only scraps and hints of these prophecies survive. Like the oracles circulated around the time of the first Mongolian declaration of independence, these prophecies were rooted in political reality. Mongolian independence was threatened once again by the Chinese, and so they naturally looked towards the other great regional power, divided as it was, for protection. Ungern took these prophecies and exploited them, claiming to be the saviour the stories spoke of.

Asked later how he could claim to be 'sent by God for the salvation of Mongolia' he replied, 'I wrote it because it sounded good.'[47] But Ungern at least half-believed in the legends himself. He was particularly taken with one that spoke of how 'Ivan from the North would come to save Mongolia'. Prophecies could be unclear on the details, but they pointed the way nevertheless. Mongolia longed for a foreign saviour, and from there the restoration of the world could begin.

SIX

Ragged Crusade

The sudden departure of Ungern's forces from Dauria sparked rumours from Paris to Tokyo. This mobile, piratical force could strike anywhere, at any time. In Moscow, some of the Soviet newspapers reported that Ungern's forces had been engaged and destroyed, but the Bolshevik leadership knew better and displayed great nervousness as to where he might attack next. The Soviet-run *Far East Review* commentated, 'If it were announced to-morrow that Ungern was in sight of Irkutsk or at the gates of Peking, we could merely confess our ignorance about where he was, and admit that anything is possible with this devil of a man.'[1]

The Mongolian rumour mill was better informed. Lacking grapevines, the Mongolians say that news spreads through the countryside like 'a crack in the ice'. Especially in the summer, life was constantly mobile; trading, visiting, courting were all done on horseback. If your mount was tired or sick, it was perfectly usual to leave it with the family you were staying with and ask to borrow one of theirs in 'much the same way as a European will turn to a passer-by for a match'. It was a distant echo of the old Mongolian postal system, and Mongolians could travel hundreds of miles in a few days as a result.

News travelled with them. In less than a couple of weeks, virtually all the country knew about the entry of the White forces, and most people were eager for their arrival. Upon crossing the border Ungern was supposed to have made three promises – 'We will place the Bogd upon the throne, and restore the autonomous government,' 'We will free the Mongols from the Chinese,' and 'We will build Greater Mongolia.'

━━┈━━┈━━ ⊯◆⊱ ┈━┈━

Mention Mongolia to most Chinese and the inevitable response is, 'Ah, you know that Mongolia used to be part of China.' A little more drink, and more imperial ambitions begin to emerge; now the Russians are gone, China should take back Mongolia – well, after the persistent canker of Taiwan is dealt with, at least. The Mongolians look on their immensely richer and stronger neighbour nervously. One Mongolian might be worth eight Chinese,[2] but there are five hundred Chinese for every Mongolian. They only have to look at Inner Mongolia, where ethnic Mongols, once the majority, now make up less than 5 per cent of the population, to see their likely fate if swallowed by the new Chinese imperium: reduced to a colourful sideshow in dancing displays staged to demonstrate the wonderful diversity of China while their children study Mandarin in school.

The origin of these tensions lies in the years between Mongolian independence and Ungern's invasion. When Ungern visited Mongolia in 1913 it was a sovereign state, albeit one under heavy Russian pressure, newly free of its Chinese overlords and anticipating an independent future. By 1920 it was yet again occupied by Chinese forces. After the collapse of the Qing dynasty in 1911 China had fragmented into a cracked mess of feuding warlords. At first, something of a centralised government remained in Peking, under the leadership of General Yuan Shikai, and was able to conduct diplomatic relationships with other states. China still had considerable territorial ambitions, and the reclamation of Mongolia was an important foreign policy aim.

The weakness of the Chinese government, and the counterbalancing influence of Russia, made this impossible. The Mongolians were even able to win a minor conflict, more a series of skirmishes than an actual war, when they sent troops to support Inner Mongolia's attempt to also break away from China in 1912. Instead, China tried to claim at least symbolic suzerainty over Mongolia at the bargaining table. A tripartite conference was held in 1914 between Russia, China and Mongolia. It dragged on for months, and only the Russians emerged satisfied. The Mongolians, who had been hoping for an acknowledgement of their full independence, and even harboured ambitions of taking back Inner Mongolia, found themselves forced to accept the dubious status of an 'autonomous' region of China. The Bogd Khan was made to abandon the title 'king', thought inappropriate to the new Chinese republic, and to assume the less exalted status of *povelitel*, 'ruler'. On the other hand, the Chinese agreed not to station large numbers of troops in Mongolia, or settle Chinese there. Mongolia's status was now deeply ambivalent; in theory the country remained part of China, but in practice China had no way of enforcing its authority.

The Bogd Khan was left de facto ruler of Mongolia. His government was not a shining example of civic responsibility. A Western-style government was formed, with two houses of parliament, a prime minister, and a cabinet, but it was a cargo-cult semblance, imitative in form but not in content. Real power lay with the ecclesiastical court and the monasteries. Prominent secular politicians were frequently assassinated, and the business of government conducted in all-night binges at the Bogd's palace.

A couple of the more competent members of the government were assassinated. Others qualified themselves to serve on the Bogd's cabinet by accompanying him in his legendary drinking sessions. The theocrats and aristocrats in the government were primarily interested in enriching themselves, and both their foreign and domestic policies were wasteful, aimless and costly. Taxation, a perennial source of complaint under Manchu rule, was increased under the new government, and entire regions were impoverished. Five million silver taels, a huge amount of money, was borrowed from Chinese banking houses, and to have even a chance of paying the interest the government had to squeeze ordinary Mongolians dry.

The regime did begin to reconcile itself with China, perhaps out of the Bogd Khan's natural inclination to hedge his political bets. The careful diplomacy of the new Chinese commissioner, Chen Lu, admired by all sides for his charm and intelligence, undoubtedly helped, as did the relative unpopularity of the Russian representative. Chinese traders had started drifting back into Urga in 1914, and their domination of Mongolian trade was, if anything, stronger than ever. Much of the reconciliation was accomplished through the use of symbolic politics which deliberately echoed the tributary status of Manchu times: gifts of horses and camels, the investiture of the Mongolian leaders with

Chinese decorations, regular audiences between Chen and the Bogd Khan. The Chinese even agreed to modify some diplomatic ceremonies for the Bogd, since his bulk made bowing and kneeling difficult.

Chinese opportunity came with the Russian revolution. Chinese troops began to infiltrate the region, initially on the pretext of being consular guards. They played on Mongolian fears of post-revolutionary chaos in Russia, using at different times the threat of both Red and White invasion as an excuse to move soldiers into the country. Ordinary Mongolians began to feel threatened by the number of Chinese troops in Urga, especially as they became increasingly arrogant. The revolution also caused a financial crisis. The Russians had always exercised a degree of oversight over Mongolian financial affairs; with their agents gone, there was now almost nobody in Urga with the slightest idea how to manage an economy. The post-revolution collapse of the rouble, now the base currency of Mongolia, further wrecked trade; prices soared, activity in the Urga markets collapsed and the Chinese merchants began calling in debts. Freedom from China suddenly seemed much less attractive.

In truth, the financial situation in China was hardly more stable, nor the government less corrupt. Nevertheless, the Mongolian nobles began pushing for a full reconciliation with China, the prospect of financial security overcoming patriotic feeling. Getting rid of theocratic rule appealed to the nobles; while they were mostly devout Buddhists, they had no great love for the Bogd's court or for the burdens that maintaining the monasteries placed on their finances and manpower.

During August and September 1919 Chen Yi, the new Chinese commissioner, successfully negotiated with the nobility for the abolition of autonomy. Sixty-three conditions were agreed, and sent to Peking on 1 October. They were reasonably accommodating of Mongolian demands, symbolically and politically tactful, and, much to the horror of the ecclesiastical court, removed them from power and instituted the Mongolian nobles as the effective leaders of the region, with Chinese administrative aid. The Bogd's court did everything it could to frustrate them, but to no avail.

Everything seemed to be going smoothly, but the ambitions of one man were to put a much more decisive end to Mongolian autonomy. Xu

Shuzheng, generally known as Xiao Xu, 'Little Xu', was a major member of the Anfu clique, a group of largely pro-Japanese Chinese leaders. In his late thirties, he was the main aide of Duan Qirui, a key player in Chinese politics and the head of the War Participation Office, a body initially founded to train and manage the Chinese contribution to the war in Europe. The Peking government had been supplying the British and French with enormous amounts of coolie labour – nearly three hundred thousand men in total – to build the trenches on the Western Front. They had also been planning an expeditionary force of trained soldiers in order to curry favour with the post-war Allies. The leaders of the War Participation Office were more concerned, however, with producing a well-trained and well-equipped army for themselves. Their funding came mostly from the Japanese, who wanted to build up military forces sympathetic to them in the north of China, similar to the Manchurian militias they had used in 1904.

When the European war ended, Duan Qirui and Xu Shuzheng were left in an embarrassing situation. Without the excuse of the war, they had no cover for the raising of their forces, and their political opponents were threatening to fold their men into the main bulk of the Chinese army. They dealt with this through the simple expedient of renaming themselves the Bureau of Frontier Defence. This required making at least some token effort to defend the frontier, but fortunately this fitted in well with Xu's ambitions. The end of the war had also meant the end of the funding from Japan, and Xu badly needed a new source of income. He had seen how Zhang Zuolin, a warlord known as the King of the North-East, had built up a regional power base in Manchuria, and Xu was ambitious to become the King of the North-West. Mongolia was a potential source of both men and money. He also seems to have been genuinely concerned with national unity, and eager to bring Mongolia back into the Chinese fold – but only on his terms. The new treaty agreed by Chen Yi threatened his plans, and he had to act fast.

On 23 October, 1919 Xu left for Mongolia, taking with him a substantial number of troops. Together with the forces sent previously, during the invasion scares, this placed over two thousand Chinese soldiers in the country. His unit was supposed to be motorised, having purchased over a hundred vehicles in Peking, but most of the vehicles gave out somewhere on the long hard route from China to Mongolia. Horses and camels proved more reliable.

When Xu arrived he initially attempted to persuade the Mongolian parliament to relinquish autonomy voluntarily. When this failed he resorted to less subtle methods, posting soldiers outside the prime minister's offices and threatening to deport the Bogd Khan to Peking. The Mongolians caved in, and the country became, in theory, a part of China again. The old Mongolian army was disbanded and its weapons turned over to the Chinese.

If Xu had exercised even the slightest amount of tact towards Mongolian feeling, he might well have gained considerable public support. Instead he behaved with arrogance and crudity. After the humiliations of the 'unequal treaties' that had been forced upon them by the Western powers, the Chinese nationalists were keen to regain face by reasserting traditional Chinese dominance in the region. On 20 February, 1920, the Chinese New Year, Xu forced the Bogd and other prominent Mongolians to repeat the traditional gesture of submission; kowtowing before the Chinese emperor or his image. Unfortunately there was no longer a Chinese emperor, so a portrait of the new Chinese President, Xu Shicheng was substituted.[3] At this farcical imperial-republican ceremony, Xu stood by the side of the picture. It was clear that the true point of the exercise was the acknowledgement of his lordship of Mongolia, not the suzerainty of a distant and fading government in Peking.

Xu was genuinely concerned with improving the Mongolian economy, planning an extensive programme of reforms and attempting grandiose building projects, such as the construction of a large radio station to ensure regular communications with Peking. He was also a classical Chinese warlord, however, and the Mongolians found themselves presented with demands for back tax, forced to pay a duty on all exports and impressed into service with Xu's army. Xu's bullying of the Mongolian aristocracy was mirrored by the bullying of his soldiers. Everyday brutality by the Chinese hurt Mongolian pride, and risked reprisal. American intelligence reported that 'it is no uncommon sight to see a Chinese policeman-soldier beating a Mongol child on the streets here, although you can bet that they let the grown ones alone unless they are in force'.[4] The Mongolian nobility began to put out tentative feelers for foreign support, and to make discreet enquiries as to where a new arsenal might be obtained.

There was also tension between the Chinese soldiers and the monasteries. Tibetan Buddhism made some inroads into China, but had a poor reputation. Popular stories often associated it with sexual rituals, human sacrifice, corruption, and a host of other evils. Buddhism as a whole was often stuck with this reputation, but the Tibetan branch got it worst. Most of this was due to religious jealousy, prurience, and xenophobia; the equivalent of English anti-Catholic fantasies of the lurid *Maria Monk* type. (I heard a few examples of such prejudice even today in China; a nice modern touch was added by the supposedly high percentage of ex-convicts – or ex-soldiers, to Chinese thinking almost as bad – among Buddhist monks, ever ready, according to the Chinese, to slip back into their old ways.) Xu's soldiers frequently harassed monks and pilgrims and stole from the temples.

Xu was suspicious of the foreigners in Urga, particularly the European merchants. Only the Japanese found it easy to do business, and the rest of the foreign community in Urga, swollen with Russian refugees, was also regularly squeezed for money. Families who had fled the Bolsheviks with whatever they could carry found themselves stripped of their few remaining possessions by the Chinese soldiers. Even the Chinese merchants suffered from the high-handed manner of their compatriots, organising a self-defence group to protect their own property. Buddhist ritual, the lifeblood of Urga, was curtailed, causing great resentment. It reminded the Mongols of centuries-old stories of seventeenth-century Chinese punitive expeditions, when temples had been burnt and ransacked across the country, leaving still-visible ruins.[5] The Bogd Khan complained that Chinese greediness had 'become unbearable day by day, hurting our land, people, and wealth'. He was no longer allowed to drive his beloved cars during festivals and had to heave himself through the crowds of pilgrims on foot.

Resentment was growing day by day, but the military stranglehold of the Chinese army was too tight for the Mongolians to take action by themselves. Ungern offered the possibility of freedom. He contacted the Bogd by secret messenger, asking for entrance to Urga and declaring that 'I, Baron Ungern, of the Russian imperial lineage, intend to enter Khuree (Urga) according to the Mongolian customs of friendship, accompanied by soldiers, to provide assistance to the Bogd Khan, to protect Mongolia, and to set it free from ruthless Chinese oppression.'[6] His ambitions were grander than that, though, after 'providing to the Mongolians seven cannons and four thousand rifles' he and his men would become the nucleus of a new Mongolia, which would bring together 'an army made up of all the nations formerly under the rule of Genghis Khan.'[7]

The Bogd responded eagerly, requesting that Ungern come to Urga as quickly as possible. A cannier and more realistic political operative than Ungern, he hoped for independence but the dream-talk of a revived Mongolian Empire probably meant little to him. Perhaps he thought that it was just bluster, the empty boasts of a man desperate to impress a potential ally.

For Ungern, though, it was deadly serious. And among ordinary Mongolians, too, old prophecies of a foreign saviour were being spread once more, dreams of white kings, Shambhala, liberation from the enemies of the faith. Some parts of the prophecies seemed to have already come to pass. As one prophecy circulated twenty years earlier had put it, the Mongolians were being 'tortured by enemy armies [. . .] the arms of the enemy will be in the city [. . .] the people of the great Khan will be killed'.[8] But they would have to endure worse before the liberation, and the heavenly kingdom which followed, could come. The prophecies said so – fire, torture and blood.

Armies have a pleasing look on military charts, neat little boxes that suggest orderliness, discipline, drill. Ungern's army was a straggling, ungainly mess, a long way from this image. Nobody even seemed to be clear how many soldiers there were. Ungern's habit of burning paperwork and his hatred of red tape made things unclear even to him. Later legends spoke of a tiny band of brothers, thirty-five men dedicated to Ungern-Sternberg, but this was wild fantasy – probably, as with some other stories about Ungern, a confusion of his career with Semenov, who had started the Siberian counter-revolution with just a handful of officers. Even before Ungern arrived there were White forces roaming the further reaches of Mongolia, clusters of renegade soldiers barely surviving on the charity provided by the locals, or who had turned to banditry in order to survive.

One of the largest, with two hundred or so men, was led by Colonel Kazagrandi, a 'decent and honourable man' who had led his group of refugees since spring 1920, when they had escaped from the Red conquest of Irkutsk and practised guerrilla warfare against the Bolsheviks from the taiga. When this became too dangerous, they had fled from place to place, scraping a living and surviving in terrible conditions, eventually ending up in Mongolia. Now Ungern, whom Kazagrandi had never met, represented a new, faint hope for the White cause. Despite hearing disturbing stories of the Baron's 'wild temper and improbable cruelty', he reluctantly sent messengers to Ungern and accepted his command, hoping that the rumours were exaggerated or untrue. His hopes were to be proved sadly wrong.

Imagine a nomad family, somewhere in the plains of northern Mongolia in the autumn of 1920, making their autumn camp. There are probably seven or eight people in the family, and their nearest neighbours are an hour's ride away.[9] Over the course of the last year they have seen, at the most, a hundred people; their nomadic neighbours, some traders visiting to buy furs, a wandering fortune-teller, travellers stopping to spend the night, a refugee Russian family grateful for the freely offered shelter and food. If they were particularly unlucky, maybe a group of Chinese soldiers, passing to garrison duty on the new frontier, stopped to seize some of their livestock. Perhaps a couple of them once made a pilgrimage to the capital, saw the great gatherings there, but it is hard for them to imagine such a crowd in the stark isolation of the steppe.

Away from the herds and the ger, the landscape is dead silent, only the occasional cry of a falcon breaking the stillness. But not today. Now they can hear the familiar sound of horses approaching, but in numbers never before conceived; a thunderous storm of hooves beating the ground, audible well before the first riders can be seen. At first only a few scouts break the horizon, then dozens of horsemen, then hundreds, riding two abreast so that their numbers seem even greater than they are. As they canter they leave the ground marked with the imprint of thousands of hooves. This is the great army the family have heard spoken of for weeks, the holy northern force that will liberate the country for Buddhism.

By the standards of the day, Ungern's army was not particularly large. When he crossed the border into Mongolia, Ungern had only fifteen hundred or so men with him. A couple of months later his forces had grown, but by how much is hard to judge. He probably had around two and a half thousand men, but intelligence reports were prone to exaggeration, particularly those of the Chinese, who were always unwilling to admit how small the forces opposing them were. Insignificant by the standards of the civil war, it was a stunning sight for Mongolia. There had not been such a cavalry army in Mongolia since the wars of the great western Mongolian leader Galdan Khan in the seventeenth century, when the Mongolians had challenged China and Russia for dominance in central Asia. Just the sight of it, even though many of the soldiers were non-Mongols, stirred Mongolian pride.

It was still, in theory, the Asian Cavalry Division, and one thing that was never in short supply was horses. Even an impoverished Mongolian family kept two or three horses for every adult, and better-off nomads had herds of hundreds. It's hard to conceive of the horse as a herd animal before witnessing a cluster of them moving together, turning and running with some collective will. They gave Ungern's army its chief advantage, mobility; the Chinese, few of whom were skilled horsemen, had no chance of catching them. Even the machine-guns and artillery were moved by horsepower, placed on an odd wooden construction slung between two horses.

The core of the army was still the Asian Cavalry Division, which was split into three separate regiments; Cossack, Mongol-Buriat and Tatar. Ungern was exceptionally close to the Buriats, pitching his tent in the middle of their encampment. He had some Japanese with him, about sixty men, mostly artillery officers, commanded by Colonel Hiro Yama. They were almost certainly adventurers rather than a formal contingent from the Japanese army, but they had received professional training, and were among his most efficient troops. His machine-gun and artillery sections comprised some of his best men, reflecting the Russian army's traditionally strong emphasis on fire support.

Despite the impression the army made, initial support for Ungern among the local Mongolians was surprisingly lacking. According to his own account only two hundred signed up, although he received the backing of several prominent nobles. For the moment, though, most Mongolians seemed to be hedging their bets until Ungern could demonstrate that he wasn't simply another wandering marauder.

Ungern's army was even joined by a Mongolian delegation freshly returned from the Soviet Union, suggesting that the Mongolian commitment to his force was far more pragmatic than ideological. If the two great powers, China and Russia, could be encouraged to fight each other, Mongolian independence might be possible after all.

The banners under which the army rode were nearly as varied as the soldiers themselves, but two symbols were particularly prominent. One was a curly capital M, with II below it and a crown above. This stood for Michael II, the missing but, Ungern hoped, future monarch of Russia. He was, we now know, nearly three years dead, and even the most optimistic monarchists were having doubts by this point, but a vanished prince, who might then return like a fairy-tale king, was a fitting symbol for Ungern's dreams of Russian revival. One surviving banner shows this symbol on one side and the face of Christ on the other; the colour, however, was Buddhist yellow, thus appealing to both aspects of Ungern's beliefs. The other popular symbol was the swastika, often matched with the Mongolian *soyombo*. This was, of course, an old and valued Buddhist motif, but Ungern would also have been aware of its anti-Semitic interpretation, as would most of the Whites.

⊶ ⊰◈⊱ ⊷

In mid-September, Ungern received unusual reinforcements. Mongolia and Tibet have a long shared history, both religious and political. The Mongolian religious hierarchy was dominated by Tibetans, and both had also been subjugated by the Qing, although the Tibetans had been able to maintain considerably more political autonomy. As the Chinese Empire collapsed in 1911, Mongolia and Tibet simultaneously recognised each other's independence. Article 4 of their 1913 treaty pledged mutual defence, promising that if one state were threatened – implicitly by China – the other would send military aid.

In addition, the Thirteenth Dalai Lama, Thubten Gyatso, had an unusually strong relationship with Mongolia. He was something of a tragic figure. For over a century the Dalai Lamas had been powerless figureheads, subordinate to the Chinese and to their own minders. Reincarnated lamas inherited their property from life to life, and until they reached maturity their often unscrupulous regents administered their considerable estates for them. Gyatso's six predecessors had died of unknown causes while still young, while their regents lived to a happy and prosperous old age.

With the crumbling of the Qing empire Gyatso had been able to take power in his own country. Playing nobles and monks against each other, he had begun to restore discipline and centralised order. This was disrupted by the British invasion of 1904, when a military expedition was sent on a bizarre attempt to forestall a supposed Russian invasion of Tibet that was probably never coming.[10] The British expedition was met by Tibetan soldiers determined to halt the foreign invaders, and one of the most one-sided massacres of imperial history ensued as the Tibetans, armed with swords and antique muskets, were mown down by the British Maxim guns. Tibet's isolation was shattered and, terrified of the foreigners' intentions, the Dalai Lama fled from Lhasa and took refuge in Mongolia under the protection of the Bogd Khan. The two incarnations of the god of compassion found it very hard to get on. They were politico-theological equals, which neither of them was used to, and the Dalai Lama was reported to be disgusted by the Bogd's excesses. Chinese accounts claimed that the Dalai was becoming more popular than the Bogd among the Mongolian people, and the Bogd was refusing to talk to him as a result. The Dalai was also nearly bankrupting his host. The British Legation in Peking reported that his visit was 'ruining the [. . .] Bogdo Lama both in revenues and reputation'.[11] Both sides breathed a sigh of relief when he left for China, and eventually returned to Tibet, but the Dalai Lama retained a special interest in the fate of the Mongolian people, and, despite their personal differences, a certain concern for his fellow theocrat.

He was also a convinced anti-communist, paranoid about the spread of revolutionary sentiment into Tibet. His dislike of communism was to lead him into some unpleasant company in the early thirties, when the Nazis were showing a peculiar interest in Tibet, and it pushed him into aiding Ungern now. The White expedition seemed tailor-made to his needs, and he sent several hundred men. Quite how the two forces found each other is unknown. It must have been a formidable task, the Tibetans coming down from the plateau into the vastness of the steppe, but the grapevine of nomads, lamas and merchants was surprisingly effective, even in a landscape where there was often two hundred miles between settlements. Ungern was always fascinated by Tibet and by the Dalai, and would have been only too eager to accept help. These were not token forces, though. After the expedition of 1906 the British had begun training the Tibetan army, and they were a cut above the Mongol forces. Ungern was to make great use of the elite Tibetan cavalry, employing them on the most dangerous missions. Expert warriors with a fierce hatred of the Chinese, they were soon to have a chance to put their killing skills to use in the defence of Buddhism.

— — ☷◈☰ — —

Ungern gloried in his visibility in battle. In Siberia he had worn a bright red Chinese jacket and blue trousers, but after the army moved into Mongolia he wore an elaborate yellow silk *deel*, a long robe, with the markings of noble rank, so 'as to be visible to [my] troops'.[12] It reminded his Russian troops of a dressing gown. Many thought he went into battle drugged, or high on mystical exhilaration; he had the disconcerting habit of skipping in battle on the rare occasions when he dismounted. He usually rode a pure white mare, presented to him by Semenov. The general on the white horse traditionally represented Bonapartism and military dictatorship, an image Ungern deliberately evoked. White horses were the traditional bearers of triumphal generals – but also a symbol of doom.[13] In Russian artistic symbolism, horses stood for war, tyranny and the Apocalypse.

Omens were on his mind as the army moved towards Urga. He had acquired several soothsayers – a wandering Buddhist fortune-teller here, a Buriat shaman there. As ever, he was intrigued by oracles, predictions, any way in which he might interpret the grand patterns of fate. As in Mongolia and China today, fortune-tellers were often destitute vagrants who had turned to predicting fate as a way of scraping a living, and they made a poor impression upon his Russian officers, who described them as 'impudent, dirty, ignorant and bandy-legged'. Among the Cossacks and Mongolians, however, the prophets were more respected. Soldiers are often superstitious, the Mongolian soldiers very much so, and his appeals to prophecy reassured his troops. Ungern trusted them implicitly, and often made strategic decisions based upon their predictions. Very few of these turned out well.

One of the most popular fortune-telling methods was to heat the shoulder bones of sheep and interpret the resulting cracks, and Ungern heeded the oracular bones when time came for the attack, choosing what was supposed to be a 'propitious day', 26 October. He split his forces into two groups, one under his command and one under Rezuhin, but both aiming for the same target, Upper Maimaichen (the name means 'buy-sell town'), the Chinese settlement down the valley just west of the main city of Urga. Unlike central Urga, with its felt gers and high temples, this was a proper, walled town, built with the crooked streets and courtyard buildings of China. The main Chinese garrison was here, though another group occupied the Russian buildings and central barracks down the road. Urga was surrounded by wooded hills, which concealed approaching troops but which rose and fell confusingly, with many gorges, sudden cliffs, and dead ends. Even from the top of the hills it was impossible to see which way the city lay, since there were few lights at night. The plan was to attack from the south, but the troops got lost in the moonless dark. Ungern mistook the location of Maimaichen, they spent the night stumbling around uselessly, and the only engagement was a skirmish with the Chinese in the early dawn. Several of the artillery pieces had to be abandoned in the night, and were taken by the Chinese.

Ungern delayed, waiting for another auspicious day, and then five days later charged forward with his men again, this time from the north-east, only to be beaten off once more. He had been confident enough to leave a large proportion of his troops, along with most of the army's supplies, at a base near the Onon river only twenty miles from the city, but the troops he took with him proved grievously inadequate. The attack was ill thought-out and poorly planned, and the dug-in Chinese were in strong positions.

It was close, though. The Chinese had only a couple of thousand men in the city, slightly fewer than Ungern's force, and Ungern's soldiers fought with the desperation of a homeless army on the brink of winter, and the outer defence of Upper Maimaichen was an archaic, crumbling wall, built in the preceding century from larch logs, earth and brick. Ungern was always behind his men, beating them on the back with his bamboo stick when they faltered in the face of machine-gun fire, yelling shrill encouragement. The initial attacks broke the Chinese perimeter, driving them back to the temples on the edge of Maimaichen, but they were rallied by some brave but nameless young officer and forced Ungern's men back from the city.

There followed two days of close-quarters fighting in the hills, with Ungern urging his tired men on to attack after attack. His cavalry made probing lunges around the city's perimeter, looking for some weak spot in the defences, but finding none. The Chinese hated the berserk rushes by Ungern's followers. These dirty, half-starved men fought with a deadly seriousness that was completely unlike the bullying and skirmishing the Chinese soldiers were used to, and killed with an ease that terrified them. With no medical facilities or supplies, wounded men were left to die where they lay. The Russians began to run short of bullets, and the Cossacks made increasing use of their sabres. When the Chinese, never very competent with their artillery, finally managed to range the Russian positions, it was too much, and Ungern called off the attacks.

There were rumours that they had succeeded, though. On 30 October Lenin and the other Bolshevik leaders received a panicked telegram from Irkutsk, drawing upon Bolshevik spies in China and Mongolia, which stated that 'after the rout of the Chinese armies, Ungern has taken Urga with three thousand fighters, and around 3000–6000 of Semenov's men expelled from Chita are hastening to him'.[14] The Russian leadership began to take the threat of Ungern seriously, and to consider a move against Mongolia in the future, though for the moment they had no plans to force a confrontation with China over the country. They even wrote to the Chinese government in Peking, urging them to consider a joint military expedition against Ungern, after which Russian forces would leave Mongolia. The Chinese haughtily declined, maintaining that they were capable of dealing with Ungern on their own.

The attacks caused a wave of anti-foreign feeling among the Chinese in Urga. After Ungern's first attacks on the city, the Chinese soldiers began to suspect every foreigner of collusion with the invaders, and to treat them with increasing contempt and aggression. Under pressure from the American consulate, the Peking government guaranteed the safety of foreigners, but this had little effect in practice. Chinese soldiers began looting houses on the pretext that they were searching for weapons. Soon enough they ceased using even this excuse and began simply to take whatever they fancied from the non-Chinese. Russians were particularly targeted, and many were summarily executed or imprisoned. It was luridly claimed by an American officer that 'scarcely a day passed without one or more cases of rape by Chinese soldiers upon white women and girls'.[15]

One witness of the soldiers' harassment was Dmitri Petrovich Pershin, the humane, ironic director of a Russian-Mongolian bank, formerly an ethnographer and journalist. He had lived in Urga for some years, spoke Chinese and Mongolian, and had friends among every community in the city. A regretful Chinese friend, a bank employee, explained to him that 'nails aren't made of good iron, soldiers aren't made from kind people'. Pershin described how the Chinese leaders were 'skilled and practical' in evaluating which foreigners were worth squeezing for money. The Mongols suffered even more than the Russians. Around Urga, their barns and shelters were burnt on the grounds that they might give cover to an attacking army. The Chinese soldiers stole hundreds of animals from herders accused of having aided Ungern's soldiers. For a people dependent upon livestock, this was a deep wound. Martial law was declared throughout Urga and a curfew imposed. The powerful monastery of Dambadarjaa, just outside of Urga, was attacked by soldiers amid accusations that the monks had harboured Ungern, and several lamas were shot on the spot. At least fifty Mongolians were killed in Urga, more or less at random.

Most critically, the Bogd Khan and several other prominent Mongolian nobles were arrested. After being imprisoned in a Chinese house for some weeks – for his own protection, according to the Chinese – the Bogd was placed under humiliating house arrest in his palace; the others remained in a Chinese prison, along with dozens of other Mongolians and Russians. He began to plot revenge against his captors, through both mundane and supernatural methods. With the help of divination he discovered that the source of his misfortune was presents given to him by a Chinese-friendly Mongol leader. He ordered them ceremonially burnt, along with the hair of a Chinese soldier, obtained with some difficulty, and declared that this would free him within fifty days of the ritual.

Ungern had made an indelible impression upon the Chinese, and an equally strong one upon the Mongols. To the Chinese he was a mysterious and terrifying enemy. They had been used to the sporadic raids of other White bandits, but this fierce attack seemed to come out of nowhere. To the Mongols he was now the chief symbol of anti-Chinese resistance. Beyond that, though, he was near-invulnerable.

He had seemed to be everywhere during the battle, but had never been wounded. Mongolians saw the marks of karma everywhere and somebody with such formidable luck was clearly not entirely of this world. He started to wear charms and amulets around his neck. It was said that he was bulletproof, protected by his talismans. The legends of a foreign saviour began to carry more weight.

· — · ⛤ · — ·

For now, though, Ungern had been beaten. The army retreated to Zam Kuren, a hundred and sixty miles east of Urga, and made camp. The worst result of the failure to take Urga was that the army was left exposed to the fierce Mongol winter. Up until then it had been a cool, dry autumn, but now the serious cold had come. Temperatures some-times dropped below minus 40 °C, and normally hovered around minus 20 to minus 30. The European soldiers copied their Mongolian neighbours, sleeping in insulated gers, wrapping themselves in several layers of clothing and huddling around the central stove for warmth. Most of them came from countries with similarly awful conditions, and many had already survived at least one Siberian winter. There was little spare clothing, though, and they had to make do with whatever bizarre array of rags was available. Comradeship was a forgotten virtue, and the strong preyed upon the weak and old, especially those hapless villagers Ungern had mobilised from the Russian borders. Stripped of clothes by their fellow soldiers, many died of the cold. A favoured item of footwear was the 'eternal boot', whereby a soldier took the fresh skin of a slaughtered sheep or cow, wrapped it round his foot and let it harden. By the end of the winter the soldiers had been wearing the same clothes for three or four months, without changing or washing, and must have stunk to high heaven.

In such conditions reserves of body heat ran down quickly and almost all activity stopped as a result. The army could move, en masse, only a few miles each day. Men slept as much as they could, passing the short days with the normal amusements of soldiers: gambling, fighting and lewdness. With no outside support, they survived mostly by plunder. One small expedition went three hundred and fifty miles out of their way to raid Lamyn Gegen Dedlen Khid, the third largest monastic settlement in the country. It had around ten thousand monks and their considerable provisions for the winter, which the Russians stole. Any settlement they encountered, especially the farms of Russian refugees, was ransacked. Along the way they commandeered hundreds of sheep and cows, which were herded by the Buriat soldiers. As a result meat, at least, was always in good supply.

What was missing, fatally for some, were vegetables and fruit. The Mongolian word for vegetables – all vegetables – was the same as that for grass. As a result of the lack of greens many of the soldiers, particularly the Russians, developed scurvy and similar diseases. The general state of health of the army was poor. There were even been minor outbreaks of bubonic plague, caused by eating the flea-infested marmots that were common in the Mongolian hills and perhaps related to a major outbreak of the disease in Manchuria that same year. The field hospital set up by the Baron soon became full – but not for long. It was run by Dr Klingenberg, who had joined the camp in the winter, a fellow Baltic German who was keen on ideas of fitness, evolution and survival. As a matter of both practicality and ideology he suggested to Ungern that those men who were so sick as to be worthless for any future fighting be poisoned, continuing the policy instituted in Dauria during the typhus outbreak. Dozens were murdered by him as a result.

The healthy were not much safer than the sick. Ungern's obsession with sadistic discipline, already well nurtured in Dauria, had grown even stronger. He would stalk around the camp looking for offenders to punish, and the terrified soldiers would hide from him 'like mice from a mean cat'.[16] Alioshin wrote:

> To maintain discipline, he invented penalties that only his insanity could have invented. Those penalties began by whipping with bamboo lashes. A hundred strokes was considered a mild reminder. Saltanov was given fifty bamboo strokes every day for ten days, until his flesh was cut through to the bone. He was taken to the hospital to be cured so that more bamboo could be administered.[17] He was beaten for two months and finally went insane, and the executioners shot him.[18]

Ungern spoke of the necessity of the 'discipline of the rod' which had served his military heroes, Frederick the Great and Nikolas I. Nobody was immune from being seized and beaten; Rezuhin,

Klingenberg, Sipailov – all of them were publicly and humiliatingly beaten by Ungern at one time or another. These beatings, interspersed with sporadic praise, seemed only to increase their loyalty to him.

Flogging was the most straightforward of Ungern's punishment techniques. His cruelty took on much more varied forms, such as a peculiar fascination with torments involving trees. One punishment involved forcing the offender up to the top of a tall tree and making him remain there all night. Those who faltered in this 'acrobatic farce' and fell broke their arms or legs and were shot as useless mouths. For executions, he sometimes ordered his men to bend back a tree, then bound the victim to it to be ripped apart by the branches when it was released. He also employed execution by fire, particularly of deserters or recalcitrant recruits. They were tied to a tree, or herded into barns or houses, then burnt alive.

Some of the stories are so extreme that they have sometimes been attributed to Red propaganda. However, many contemporary accounts, whatever their writers' feelings about Ungern, agree on the range and inventiveness of his sadistic discipline. Red propaganda about Ungern inevitably concentrated on the atrocities committed against loyal Soviet citizens, not reactionary Whites. Nor did Ungern, when questioned, ever deny any of these cruelties. He was not the only perpetuator by any means, but he was the prime mover.

A culture of cruelty evolved around Ungern whereby officers, both fascinated by and terrified of him, would attempt to imitate and impress him by devising increasingly horrific punishments. Rezuhin, Ungern's shadow, was particularly keen to copy his master. The physical and cultural isolation of being in the wilderness, surrounded by strange 'Asiatics', made the Russians behave even more badly than their contemporaries in the civil war back home. After the war Russian memoirists preferred to blame the majority of the horrors either on the dead or on the 'Mongolian cruelty' of Ungern's non-Russian troops. When they did admit to their own involvement in murder and torture, they found excuses in the madness of war, pressure from their comrades or an understandable terror of Ungern. 'It was kill or be killed in those days,' wrote Alioshin, 'and we fought like demons from hell.'

Ungern used a small group of executioners to enforce his punishments. These were hated by even his most dedicated followers, and all witnesses write about them in dramatic and unflattering terms. One particularly loathed figure was Evgenie Burdokovskii, his Cossack ensign. He was

> tall and of a powerful physique. He had a huge body with a high and broad chest, and the thick arms and legs of an elephant. A little curly blond head rested on his wide shoulders. Small, colourless eyes looked straight and without any expression whatever from under a narrow forehead. The small nose was almost lost on his flat face. His mouth was wide, still and stiff. He spoke through his teeth, and the words came from the corner of his fleshy lips, which quivered in contempt.[19]

Another witness wrote of his 'wide mouth, capable of swallowing ten cutlets and a quart of vodka at a time, his Mongolian yellow peaked cap with hanging flaps [. . .] and an enormous cane in his hand'.[20] He was known as 'Teapot', since in private audiences pouring tea was the sign Ungern would give him to seize a victim from behind and choke him to death. He seemed to live only to obey Ungern's orders, and could knock a man unconscious with only five blows of his light bamboo cane. He had been with Ungern since the disarming of the mutinous troops in Manchuli, where he had specialised in clubbing revolutionaries with his rifle. Another favoured executioner was Captain Veselovskii, Rezuhin's adjutant, a young man with 'long curly red hair and an unusually white face, though heavy and stolid, with large, steel-cold eyes and with beautiful, tender, almost girlish lips. But in his eyes there was such cold cruelty that it was quite unpleasant to look at his otherwise fine face.'[21]

Casualties from the attacks on Urga had been heavy, and the army was shaken. Desertions began to increase, particularly among the Russian officers. Ungern showed a growing fixation with desertion and treachery. It was revolution, weakness, caused by infiltrating Bolshevik agents. He used his most loyal troops, most often Inner Mongolian Chahars, to chase down those who deserted, hanging them on the spot or ordering them lashed to death. One of the things he scribbled most commonly as a postscript to letters was 'Do not trust . . .', followed by the names of various faithless officers. Alioshin described how he learnt of the terrible death of a friend of mine, Captain Rujansky. He and his sixty-eight men deserted the Baron one night, being unable to stand his atrocities any longer. Ferocious Chahars were sent after them and returned with a sack filled with sixty-nine human ears, as evidence that the Baron's orders had been carried out. Rujansky's beautiful wife was given to the Chahars as a reward. She went insane and died in agony.[22]

The Mongolian regiments were often quick to desert, though Ungern seems to have treated them with considerably more forbearance than he did European or Japanese deserters.

Siberian political divisions carried over into the new army. A split developed between the new Russian troops, the majority of whom had been followers of Admiral Kolchak, and those who had been with Ungern at Dauria. One of the former, dragooned into Ungern's army after the fall of Urga, wrote,

The attitude of the Baron to everyone who was not connected with Semenov during the Civil War, and who had not been linked to the Transbaikalian torture chambers, was one of offensive suspicion and distrust. Among the gang of criminals, degenerates and bastards which Ungern brought from Dauria to take part in his Mongolian adventure, the word *kolchakovec* was a pejorative nickname, a curse.[23]

There was a good deal of self-protection in such comments. After the war, Ungern's reputation was so infamous that anybody who had been in Mongolia during his reign had to excuse themselves from any association with him. Dozens of 'decent' Whites who successfully escaped persecution in Ungern's Mongolia berated him from exile in the Harbin and Peking press. Ungern remarked dryly that 'the White newspapers write worse things about me than the Reds'.

The Russian officers were certainly the most wretched members of the army, particularly the former officers of the regular army, and were treated roughly by the other soldiers. Alioshin, one of this caste himself, described them as being 'dressed in rags, with pieces of leather tied to the soles of their feet. Unshaven and dirty, cynical and cunningly cruel, they were lost to the world. Death was always welcome to them, and they fought like devils.'[24] Ungern spoke of them as 'rotten through and through, demoralised, sunk into the depths'.[25]

Apart from the White officers, numerous ordinary Russian refugees and émigrés, some of them with no military training whatsoever, were drafted into the army. Both groups were under a cloud of suspicion as potential revolutionaries or even Jews, and they became the focus of Ungern's growing paranoia. There was a political reason for their low status, too; Ungern could obviously not treat the new Mongolian troops with anything like the same contempt without risking losing the support of the Mongolian leaders. Maintaining ethnic divisions within the army also strengthened the loyalty of various favoured groups, such as the Buriats. As Alioshin bitterly put it, 'What the Baron dared not do to his Orientals he did all too readily to his own countrymen.' Given half a chance they deserted, fleeing to Manchuria or even to Bolshevik territory; one of them remarked when informing Alioshin and others of his plan to escape: 'Even death is better than the Baron!' He was caught and hanged.

Now sober, if drug addled, Ungern was particularly intolerant of drunkenness in others. Mongolians have an astonishing ability to produce alcohol from the most unlikely ingredients, and vodka and *airag* (fermented mares' milk) was often brought into the camp. Anyone drinking to excess risked one of Ungern's favourite punishments: a night on a frozen river or lake without shelter. Sometimes they were stripped naked first and, if Ungern was feeling especially vindictive, left to shiver for several days on a diet of raw meat. On one particularly gruesome occasion an entire group of men who had been forced to the centre of the frozen Tula river attracted the attention of a pack of wolves. Naked and unarmed, the soldiers tried to fight off the animals with their bare hands. Only half the men survived. Even being hung-over was dangerous. One group of officers who missed roll-call were forced to stand to attention through an entire night, ceaselessly repeating their names and ranks.

The Baron's punishment tariff was denounced by European officers as 'insane', 'inhuman' and 'incomprehensible'. To the Baron, however, it made perfect sense. Sadism exists in all cultures, and is given its opportunity in all wars, but its practice is infinitely various. During the Russian Civil War the regalia of White officers provided great sport for their captors; they replaced the pips on their captives' ornate epaulettes with nails driven into their flesh, and boiled the skin off their hands in imitation of gloves. Other Bolshevik tortures were derived from the practices of the Okhrana, the old Russian secret police; the Cheka, their revolutionary successors, quite literally used their manuals as examples. White violence was that of an outraged upper class, often – like the Ku Klux Klan in America – holding mock trials in kangaroo courts and carrying out mass hangings. Other communist prisoners were crucified, nailed to trees with railway spikes. Peasant armies buried their Red victims alive, entombed in the earth they had tried to take from the villagers.

Ungern's formalised sadism was of a different order. It was appalling and inexcusable, but also explicable. The obsession with lashing and whipping was an exaggerated version of the discipline of the old Russian imperial army, where fifty lashes were considered a light punishment. Ungern favoured 'a hundred blows to each part of the body' as an average punishment, which left men staggered and blinded by blood. Ungern's excesses sometimes surprised even him. 'Did you know,' he mused, 'that men can still walk when the flesh and bone are separated?'[26] The rest of his ideas come straight from the Buddhist hells, of which there are a great variety, with numerous punishments for each sin. Popular literature in both China and Mongolia included compendiums of these; the worst sin, according to one, was murdering your grandmother and feeding her to Buddhist monks, thus simultaneously violating filial piety, insulting the aged, promoting cannibalism and transgressing against vegetarianism.

It seems unlikely that this particular offence was rife, but even relatively small sins mandated a grim range of soul-purging retribution. Hammering home the point to the illiterate were the hell scrolls: lurid depictions of the fates awaiting the sinful deceased. These were sometimes given three-dimensional form in the hell galleries, annexes of Buddhist monasteries that contained realistic sculptures of demons gleefully torturing sinners. All of Ungern's favourite tortures were prominent in the hell scrolls of the Mongolian monasteries: exposure on the ice, burning alive, rending by wild beasts.

There was clearly a strong sensational aspect to these displays and also, since a majority of the victims were naked and female, a pornographic one. The various Christian depictions of hell and judgement that the young Ungern had been raised with, including the portrayals of the Last Judgement he must often have seen on the porticoes of Orthodox churches, also showed the torments of the damned, writhing in flame or speared on pitchforks by demons. However, in the Christian tradition the emphasis was on terrifying the sinner into obedience. While this was one of the goals of the Buddhist images, there was also a more mystical purpose. Just as the souls in torment were ultimately undergoing a redemptive journey, so contemplating their fate could effect the same process of soul-cleansing in those still living – a purifying experience rather than a terrifying one.

Ungern's worldview combined both. His cruelty kept his troops in line, but it was also a necessary part of the spiritual purification of the degenerate, revolutionary world. Deserters and revolutionaries were not just human criminals, they were on the wrong side of a Manichean struggle between good and evil. He wrote of revolutionaries as though they were demons, 'Evil spirits in human shape who destroy kings, turn brother against brother, son against father, and bring forth great trouble in life.'[27]

Such language was not necessarily meant literally. The *Mitteilungen für die Truppe,* a German army newsletter for the Eastern Front in the Second World War, described the 'mostly Jewish' commissars in similar terms, 'the embodiment of the Satanic and insane hatred against the whole of noble humanity [who] would have brought an end to all meaningful life [through manipulating the masses], had this eruption not been dammed at the last moment'.[28] Only a tiny minority of Nazis, however, would have believed that Jews and revolutionaries were *actually* demons in human form. For Ungern, such words carried more weight. He was, after all, living in a culture which regarded evil spirits as a very serious problem. Certainly he believed that the Communist International was just the latest representative of an ancient spiritual evil. When asked where he thought it was founded, he replied, 'In ancient Babylon [. . .] All history shows it.'[29]

Despite all this, the army was growing every day. Troops were arriving from all over Mongolia. For the Russian troops who arrived, it was a trap. Often initially sceptical of the stories they'd heard about Ungern, they found the truth worse, and desertion often fatal. For the Mongolians, though, it was an opportunity. They were relatively safe from Ungern's disciplinary zeal and eager to join so great a warrior. Ungern took full advantage of the Mongolian rumour mill and issued declarations that he had come to liberate the Mongols from Chinese oppression and rescue the Bogd Khan from his captors. All the old

Mongolian resentment of Chinese rule came bubbling up. Combined with the fresh humiliations inflicted by Xu's men, it was enough to recruit many to Ungern's forces.

The support of the nobility was vital. The Mongolian aristocracy was organised under the same militaristic banner system as the Manchurians in China, so that nobles could mobilise hundreds or thousands of men with relatively little difficulty. Most of these men were not trained soldiers, but every Mongolian man knew how to ride, hunt and shoot. Recruitment was particularly strong among refugees from Inner Mongolia, where Mongol tribes, their traditional lands taken over by settlers, had been skirmishing with the Chinese for decades. Particularly prominent was an Inner Mongolian contingent under the command of two princes, Bayar and Togtokh, both heroes of the 1911 revolution. The 'Determined Hero' Togtokh, in particular, was famous throughout Mongolia; a chivalrous and charismatic man now in his fifties from an impoverished noble family, he had fought the Chinese since the beginnings of major Han settlement thirty years beforehand. He was also a strong supporter of pan-Mongolian ideas. Immensely popular among the ordinary people, his support gave a major boost to Ungern. Another prince, Sundui Gun, also a well-known anti-Chinese guerrilla, was to join later.

Not every Mongolian was a volunteer, or even conscripted through the banner system. Many, particularly young men, were simply drafted into the army, snatched from their homes and families. Ungern had a high opinion of the fighting quality of Mongolians, but many of his draftees were deeply unhappy. Villages, Mongolian and Russian, had little choice but to turn over their sons to Ungern's army; one Russian came across the 'smoking ruins of the settlement of Mandalas, whose inhabitants had been exterminated only because they had not wished to turn over volunteers for the Baron's army'.[30]

As ever, the exact strength of the army was almost impossible to evaluate, since there were so many separate contingents, and recruitment and desertion were continuous. Ungern's own staff recorded them only to the nearest hundred. At most, Ungern had something between five and six thousand troops, with probably about half of them Mongolians. It was a colourful force, with no common uniform or doctrine. Ungern's Cossacks wore long blue coats while the Mongols and Tibetans wore 'red coats with yellow epaulettes bearing the swastika of

Genghis Khan and the initials of the Living Buddha'. Most of the army were equipped with Japanese rifles, accumulated during Ungern's reign at Dauria, but Ungern had also acquired Italian machine-guns, originally purchased during the Great War by the Mongolian military. However, many of the Mongolian troops had no guns, but brandished pikes and lances.

⊷ ≡◆≡ ⊶

According to contemporary Russian accounts, the Mongolians believed that Ungern was considerably more than just a general. They called him the God of War, and some temples even began to dedicate services to him. How widespread this belief was, and exactly what it meant, is still unclear. It was, of course, perfectly normal for human beings to be recognised as the incarnations of the gods in Mongolia. Most of the *khutukhu* lineages, the reincarnated lamas such as the Bogd Khan, were considered to be the manifestations of one god or another, particularly of the bodhisattvas, the compassionate souls who turned back from the brink of enlightenment themselves to save others. Mongolian Buddhism was also fairly flexible about its objects of worship; great leaders could easily be assimilated into the pantheon while still alive, or formally acknowledged by the Buddhist hierarchy as a reincarnation of a past khan or the avatar of a god.

There was no official Mongolian recognition of Ungern as an incarnate god, despite all the other titles that would be heaped on him. The belief probably sprang up spontaneously: a mysterious figure from the north, riding a white horse, ignoring bullets and claiming to fulfil ancient prophecies – it was only logical to think him a god. Even the Russians often ascribed a quasi-supernatural element to the myths around Ungern, such as his affinity with the wolves and his fondness for surrounding himself with the bones of his victims. Ungern or his Mongolian allies may have paid lamas to spread the word further; bribing monks for political ends was standard Mongolian practice. As Ungern had seen with the Ja Lama, claiming to be the reincarnation of a past hero, who in turn would often have claimed to be the incarnation of a god, made good political currency in Mongolia.

Quite *which* god they thought he was is unclear. Looking for a 'god of war' in the eclectic Mongolian pantheon is like looking for a virgin martyr among the Catholic saints. There was the fat, fiery Begtse, with his goat-skin cloak, high boots, drawn bow and garland of fifty freshly severed heads, or Pehar, an old regional war god bound by monks to serve the faith, who rode wolves, bears and elephants to battle. Or there was the Red Horseman, who trampled and speared the enemies of the faith, Geser Khan, a hero who became a god, had his own stupendously gory epic, Mahakala, a tame demon who carried a cleaver to chop up those who strayed from the righteous way, and a skull bowl to mix their remains, and an infinity of other possibilities. To confuse things further, all the great spiritual and martial leaders of the Mongols had had their own tutelary deities, any one of which could reasonably be described as a war god. One witness confidently identified the name of the god that Ungern supposedly incarnated as Tsagan Burkhan. Unfortunately, *tsagan burkhan* is simply the Mongolian for 'white god' or 'white Buddha', an obvious name for the white-skinned, White-leading Ungern.

Whichever god or gods were manifest through Ungern, they undoubtedly fell into the category of *dharmapala* ('defenders of the faith'), the wrathful protectors. This was a general term for the ferocious gods, particularly prominent in Tibet and Mongolia, who defended monasteries, fought off hostile spirits and struck down the enemies of Buddhism. Many of the *dharmapala* were tamed demons, bound into service by the spiritual-magical powers of great lamas. Only a minority of them were considered enlightened beings them-selves. They protected the faithful, but they were depicted in the most terrible fashion, festooned with weapons and skulls and claws. They were a good match for Ungern, who professed to be the defender of Buddhism and Mongolia, and who was clearly prepared to do anything, no matter how terrible, to achieve this end. It was a way of saying, 'This man is a blood-soaked monster – who happens to be on our side.'

There is also a definite possibility that the Russian officers merely misheard, or misunderstood, the Mongolians' references to Ungern. *Bogd*, one of the Mongolian words for 'sacred' or 'holy', is easily con-fusible with *bog*, the Russian word for god. What Russian officers translated as *bog voiny*, 'God of War', may have been closer, in

Mongolian, to 'holy warrior' or 'sacred warrior'. It would have been commensurate with how Ungern saw himself, as a 'crusader'.

There is another intriguing possibility, though. Among the Oirat Mongols of Russia, now dwelling in the Altai region near the south of Mongolia, a bizarre cult had arisen fifteen years beforehand around the visions of a simple shepherd and his daughter. They saw a rider dressed in white, riding a white horse. They referred to him as the Ak-Burkhan, which also meant 'white god'. He was a herald who signalled the return of ancient messianic heroes such as Amursana, an eighteenth-century opponent of Manchu power. The Ja Lama in the west, Ungern's erstwhile hero, already claimed to be his reincarnation. The new faith founded as a result was violently anti-Christian and anti-Russian. Partly because of the colour association, but mostly due to commonplace minority fears of forced assimilation and loss of privileges, the Burkhanists fought on the White side in the civil war, waging a vicious guerrilla fight in the mountains. Another White officer, Captain Satunin, had deliberately assumed aspects of the Ak-Burkhan in order to raise support among the Oirat. Perhaps these myths had passed from the Oirat to their Khalkha cousins in northern Mongolia. Ungern, a 'white' fighter who was famous for his white horse, and who fought both the Russians and the Chinese, would have been the perfect fulfilment of such messianic expectations.

⸻ ⚎ ⸻

The God of War, meanwhile, was planning his next move. By the New Year there were enough soldiers to make another attack on Urga viable. Ungern had kept up reconnaissance and skirmishing throughout the winter; the American representative of the Mongolian Trading Company reported that the edge of town was harassed by 'strange patrols of Cossacks and Mongols' who cut the telegraph lines. Ungern's men had been setting night-fires on top of Bogd Uhl, Holy Mountain, for two months. Blazing high in the darkness, they looked unearthly, and the Mongolians whispered that Ungern was making sacrifices to the mountain spirits, the *savdag*, to curse those who had brought evil upon the Bogd. The Chinese soldiers were nervous of the wrath of the mountain gods[31] – also common in Daoism and Chinese Buddhism – and refused to aim their artillery at the mountain. The Mongolians delighted in telling the Chinese tall stories about the extent of the Baron's army, his supernatural powers, and the fierceness of his soldiers.

Frightened of spies, the Chinese tried to seal off the town as best they could, but Ungern remained in communication with the Bogd Khan, and also with spies in the city. On 18 January, 1921 he moved his army to a site on the Tula river, only twenty-six miles from the city. He sent a large group of men to engage a Chinese detachment to the north, resulting in a short battle and convincing the Chinese that the main attack would come from that direction of the Tula. In truth, Ungern planned to attack from the south and east, this time decisively, but he still faced some formidable obstacles.

Urga was not a naturally defensible site. Before the coming of foreigners it had been more or less unwalled. Respect for its holy status had dissuaded most would-be attackers and there were no fortifications around the Mongol section. Traditionally, the Mongolians had regarded city walls and strong defences as anathema to their way of life and of warfare. Although during their campaigns they had rapidly developed great skill at siege warfare, adopting the methods of the Chinese artillery and sappers, they still thought of hiding behind walls as somehow cowardly. They had no respect for cowards and most of their worst atrocities were committed after taking fortified cities.

In contrast, the Chinese have something of a reputation for walls, both national and domestic. The Great Wall itself functioned more as customs border and cultural marker than fortification, but nevertheless represented the fundamental Chinese attitude towards the northern barbarians. Chinese city walls were used as major defensive points during the war against Japan, many of them blasted into rubble by Japanese artillery – and the surviving masonry torn down by the communists as a symbol of the feudal past. In Beijing today, middle-class apartment blocks are insulated from the slums around them by two or three layers of wall topped with glass and a platoon of guards and barbed wire in the bushes.

Unsurprisingly, then, almost the first thing the Chinese forces in Urga did was build some walls. The Mongolian centre of the city was composed of gers surrounded by fences, with the occasional temple, and so was entirely unprotected. As before, the Chinese were forced to concentrate their troops in the Chinese suburbs, Upper and Lower

Maimaichen. They formed a kind of crescent around the southern part of Urga, with the old Russian consulate area sandwiched between them. From Upper Maimaichen ran

> a broad road, lighted by lamps on little wooden posts, and the first house of importance met with is the 'Mongolore', the offices of the gold-mining concern of that name. This building is in direct contrasts to the Russian consulate, almost opposite to it, the consulate being a poor, old-fashioned building, protected by trenches and barbed wire entanglements.[32]

Matters weren't helped by Urga's topography, nestled in a valley with hills overlooking each side and having no natural barriers to deter an attack. In summer the Tula river (then a fierce current; nowadays, thanks to drainage, a slow stream) would have provided some natural protection, but this was winter and it was solidly frozen; a slippery inconvenience rather than a major obstacle. The outer defences of Upper Maimaichen had been poor when Ungern had first attacked, but now the Chinese were better prepared, and had enclosed Upper Maimaichen in a network of trenches, fences, barricades and wire. Beyond this outer layer of defence lay an inner fortress, the solid stone buildings of the Russian consulate and gold-mining company. The Russians had fortified these a decade earlier during the revolution of 1911, and the Chinese repaired and reinforced them.

The quality of the defences may have been sound, but the quality of the soldiers was not. The Chinese soldiers were typical of their time; they had been recruited from the displaced peasantry or the urban poor by one warlord or another, given a modicum of training and, if they were lucky, a working rifle, and sent off to fight in one of China's seemingly endless civil struggles. They were used to changing sides when defeat threatened, and, with no co-ordinated system of supply, lived off the land like locusts, robbing and bullying the local villages. The difference between a soldier and a bandit was no more than a uniform, and sometimes the 'soldiers' lacked even that. They had no expectation of victory. Twenty hard years later the war correspondent Theodore White remarked, looking at Chinese troops, how 'the men walked quietly, with the curious bitterness of Chinese soldiers who expected nothing but disaster at the end of the trip. They were wiry and brown but thin; their guns were old; their yellow-and-brown uniforms threadbare.'[33]

Fortunately for the Chinese, the balance of firepower was massively in their favour. They had heavy artillery, thousands of rifles and numerous machine-guns, which they positioned around their new defences. However, they didn't have much of an idea how to use them. To us, familiar with the machine-gun as the deadly reaper of the Western Front, the position of the Chinese forces might seem virtually unassailable, covered as it was by heavy machine-gun points on all sides. Chinese soldiers, however, were notoriously inept at the use of such weaponry. As its name implies, the machine-gun is not a weapon that can be used in isolation, but the lethal outcrop of an entire industrial society. Chinese troops, dragooned from a peasantry still living a medieval lifestyle and with no proper military training, had no idea how to set the bullets on their intended course, nor how to clear a jam efficiently, nor how to keep a barrel from rusting. The extreme cold must have contributed to frequent mechanical failure.

Foreign observers also noted how untrained Chinese officers positioned the weapons poorly, narrowing their scope of fire. Most importantly, their soldiers made no adjustment for the inevitable upward rise of their weapons, jerked up by the sheer force of their fire, and tended to aim high – for power, as with a bow. As a result, the machine-gun fire was usually directed well above the heads of the assaulting soldiers, so that spent casings dropped like hailstones around the edges of the city, and only the unfortunate or the foolish were caught in the Chinese soldier's 'unsystematic and mad shooting'.

The garrison in Urga had received no pay from Peking for months, although they had been promised settlement in full after their initial success in repulsing Ungern, and were surviving as best they could. Mongolia was almost as exotic a location to them as to the Europeans, perhaps more so since they considered themselves the superiors of the Mongolians and very rarely made any effort to learn their language or conform to local customs. The Chinese soldiers disrupted the Buddhist festivals, bullying pilgrims into handing over their sacrifices. After Ungern's first attack, they began to close down the ceremonies altogether, fearing that the lamas would take the opportunity to invoke malignant spirits against them. Sometimes they would burst into temples and begin shooting randomly into the air to clear out the lamas. The Bogd Khan complained how they 'caused devastation until the end, some of them used all manner of tricks, and others viciously threatened us'.[34]

The Chinese soldiers were scared, undisciplined and untrained. On the other hand, the Baron's soldiers were outnumbered, attacking fortified positions and fighting in winter conditions with only the barest of shelter, unlike their well-billeted opponents. The temperature that February was around minus 20 °C; the sustained effort required for combat in such conditions could rapidly exhaust even the fittest and best-insulated soldier. All they had on their side was military training, desperation and the manic inspiration of their leader. The promise of food and housing if they did capture Urga was also a spur; this was a last-chance attack.

This time they had reconnoitred Urga's defences well, making use of information given to them by refugees fleeing a lawless city. Ungern was rumoured to have made a survey of Urga himself, in disguise and accompanied by only one man, presumably drawing upon his experience of sorties behind enemy lines a few years earlier. For good measure, he was supposed to have killed three Chinese soldiers, including an officer, on his way back – using only his bamboo stick.

Dmitri Pershin, the local bank director, heard an even more incredible account. Ungern had gone in to scout the town at night, for some reason choosing to ride his white horse and wearing a favourite cherry-red jacket. Riding back to his troops, he saw a Chinese sentry asleep on duty by the prison. This slacking, even by an enemy, so disgusted him that he dismounted and began to smack the unfortunate man with his cane, yelling at him in pidgin Chinese that he had neglected his duties as a soldier, and that he, Baron Ungern, was taking the time to punish him personally. The soldier was so disconcerted that he failed to raise the alarm immediately, and Ungern galloped off. Pershin recognised the improbability of the story, and took pains to emphasise that the whole thing had been seen by Mongolian prisoners through a gap in the prison fence, and that he had personally tracked them down to confirm that the story was true.

Seeking to give the impression of an attacking horde, Ungern ordered fires to be lit in the hills all around Urga, three for every soldier. The Chinese, who consistently overestimated Ungern's force, were fooled, and became even more nervous. Meanwhile a loose plan was formed; one party would block off the caravan road, preventing the Chinese from receiving reinforcements, and cover it with machine-guns. A main group would attempt to steal up on the Chinese trenches from the east, ready for an attack in the morning. A third group would cross the mountain and rescue the Bogd Khan. Four Mongolian regiments were kept in reserve, but many of them, seeing the odds and having experienced Ungern's notion of discipline, deserted overnight.

The main party of soldiers, around five hundred men in all, quietly closed in on the Chinese positions around Maimaichen. The hills were gentler here, allowing them a relatively easy passage, save for the freezing cold and the bitter wind, blowing from the north and pinning them against the hillside. The first Chinese barricade was along the embankment of the frozen river, which curved up to the north and marked the boundary of the suburb. By eleven at night they had reached positions on the nearby hills, and were waiting for their few artillery pieces to come up. While they were waiting they were discovered by the Chinese, and came under heavy, though inaccurate, fire. They had no choice but to attack, advancing like a swinging chain. One group would stay behind and hold their position while another moved forward to attack. Once their new position was secured, the forward group would stay put while the others went ahead to seize another position. In this way, they eventually penetrated Maimaichen.

Here the attacking soldiers found themselves under attack from the Chinese trenches. The noise was terrible; the constant racket of machine-gun fire interspersed with Chinese and Mongolian war cries and the shouts of wounded men in a dozen different languages. Both sides possessed rockets, still inaccurate and on the whole useless weapons that were little more than glorified fireworks, and occasionally one would explode high in the sky, providing a pyrotechnic element. The terrified animals of the Bogd Khan's zoo added their yelps and howls to the cacophony. His elephant was so frightened it broke free from its cage and charged trumpeting through the lines of battle. It was discovered a week later nearly a hundred miles away, grazing peacefully among a herd of camels.

⟶ ⇥◈⇤ ⟶

Rescuing the Bogd Khan was one of Ungern's top priorities, but his palace was deep within the Chinese defences. Only one approach was left unguarded, for the Chinese were confident that no attacker could strike from that direction. Behind the palace was Bogd Uhl, a sacred preserve, covered in virgin forest, created by the Buddhist monks three hundred years beforehand. Animals roamed there free from fear of the normally rapacious Mongolian hunters, since the penalty for trespass was execution. They included some strange creatures; the Bogd had a liking for exotic animals and the tranquillity of the forest was sometimes disturbed by tigers, cheetahs, even the Bogd's pet elephant. So strong was the prohibition that the wolves on the mountain had learnt to exploit it, streaming out of the forest to attack the locals' herds. When chased by the shepherds, they would retreat back over the line of sanctuary, regarding, according to the shepherds, their frustrated pursuers with a look of distinct smugness. For three centuries the mountain had remained inviolate.

The Chinese guards had no desire to risk supernatural wrath, especially after the mysterious night-fires of the winter, or to provoke further Mongolian anger, and they made no patrols on the mountainside. On that clear, cold winter morning they had no idea what was coming, although even Pershin saw the Tibetan cavalry moving down the mountainside, 'like little black dots against the snow'.[35] The Bogd was imprisoned inside his European-style house, which was in the centre of a complex of temples surrounded by a flimsy wall. When the horsemen burst through the gates, the Chinese didn't have a moment's warning. The outer sentries were either shot silently with arrows, or murdered by Tibetan infiltrators disguised as Mongolians bringing food and supplies. Some of the attackers seemed to gleam unnaturally and to have distorted, terrifying faces; the Chinese must have been uncertain, in their last moments, whether their assailants were men or gods. In truth, they were *dobdobs*, Tibetan monk-enforcers, their clothes lightly smeared with butter and their faces painted with soot to strike fear into the enemies of the faith. Although the attackers were outnumbered two or three to one, the terrified Chinese barely resisted. Of a hundred and fifty men, ninety-seven were dead within minutes, and the remainder were running for the main Chinese lines.

The liberators had brought spare horses for the Bogd Khan and his entourage, planning to take them to safety in a nearby hill monastery, but there was a small hitch. During his months of captivity the Bogd's already formidable bulk had grown to the point where he could no longer sit on a horse without overbalancing. After a couple of panicked minutes, a solution was found. Two muscular Tibetans hauled him on to the horse and rode either side of him, balancing his weight between them. Ten Tibetans remained behind to cover their escape, exchanging sporadic fire with the Chinese before making their own getaway. An American merchant, A. M. Guptill, witnessed the whole attack and commentated that 'the entire action consumed exactly one half-hour and was the prettiest piece of cavalry work that one could desire to witness'.[36] When Ungern heard the news, he yelled exuberantly, 'Now Urga is ours!' His Mongolian ally Togtokh was able to raise a two-hundred-strong personal bodyguard for the Bogd to ensure that he would not fall back into the clutches of the Chinese.

The fighting at the eastern end of the city had reached a temporary stalemate. The plan was gradually to squeeze the Chinese inwards from both sides. Japanese artillerists had brought their guns up to the hills in the north-east that the Whites had seized the previous day, and had begun to pound the Chinese positions. But the Chinese had consolidated their forces in their trenches and, although fighting continued throughout the day, neither side made any significant advance.

The Russians and other foreigners sealed up their homes, barricading their doors and arming themselves with whatever weapons they could find. They stored food and organised twenty-four-hour watches, praying that Ungern would take the city before the Chinese could begin a fresh wave of persecution. They need not have worried; the Chinese were too panicked to make reprisals. They had dreaded the attack all winter, and the seizure of the Bogd Khan was almost the final straw. On the morning of 1 February, the day following the Bogd's liberation, the Chinese officers grabbed all the motor vehicles and fuel they could find and roared north out of town, heading for Kiatkha and safety and leaving their men to cope as best they could. An American observer wrote contemptuously, 'They left at daybreak, just in time to save their skins in the most approved Chinese manner, and will probably be made Field Marshals for their bravery and skill in retreating.'[37] Years later the locals still sang 'a Mongolian battle song whose text, dealing with Chinese Generals riding in *Muhor teleg* (motor-cars), bore witness to its modern origin'.[38]

The following night a soldier on the Russian side accidentally shot a rocket into the sky, causing the Chinese rump to open up with all the firepower it had. Seized by some collective impulse, the main force of European soldiers rushed the Chinese positions. The Baron was equally carried away by the fervour of the attack, riding on his white horse between the trenches and pressing his troops forward over the wire. He inspired others to take suicidal risks; perhaps their fear of him outweighed their fear of the enemy.

At the same time some of the Mongolian cavalry had reached the Chinese rear, where fire was already being directed onto their enemies from the positions seized at the Bogd Khan's palace. Maimaichen was blazing; Alioshin claims that the fires were lit by sympathisers in the city, but this would have been unnecessary, given the artillery on both sides and the easy combustibility of old Chinese wooden buildings. The fighting became a series of running battles through the crooked, smoke-filled streets. There were no gutters worthy of the name, and the alleys quickly filled with slippery filth. It was impossible for either side to maintain any kind of order, but in the noisome, lethal scramble the attackers prevailed. The Chinese abandoned their trenches in disarray. A mass of them fled Maimaichen altogether, running for the relative safety of the old fortified Russian compound, but Ungern's men had set up machine-gun nests in the hills and woods on either side of the route. The fleeing Chinese were enfiladed and slaughtered.

The survivors of the Maimaichen garrison retreated into the Russian buildings, which occupied a substantial area, situated near the river on a slight rise. As ever, the Baron was omnipresent during the battle, riding among his men and leading them in insanely brave attacks on the walls. They used whatever they could to force the gates: battering-rams improvised from fence posts, mass charges, explosives.

Once the gates were breached, the fighting turned into a general killing spree. The main work was done with bayonets, but an extraordinary variety of knives, swords, and even cleavers were wielded by both sides. The Chinese made their last stand in three solid wooden buildings: the Russian barracks, the consulate, and the gold-mining company. These had been heavily fortified over the years, and had become a mass of trenches and barbed wire, but the Chinese had no time to set up their defences properly. The Baron's troops rushed the Chinese positions, using grenades to break through the windows and doors. When their ammunition ran out, the Chinese fired arrows and hurled stones at the attackers. In the chaos, groups of soldiers on the same side sometimes fought each other, unable to understand the language of their allies. Neither side was taking prisoners, but many of the Chinese were stripping off their uniforms and hoping to pass as Mongolian.

By now Chinese morale had completely collapsed. Over two thousand fled the city, taking whatever they could carry into the bleak, cold hills. Of the three thousand Chinese soldiers left inside, barely eight hundred survived. Urga had been laid bare to the untender mercies of the war god's soldiers.

A couple of days later, one of the city's markets was burning. Nobody knew who had started the blaze, and nobody seemed to care. It became a bonfire, fresh fuel piled on by Ungern's men: paper money, tea, furs, hair, bone, flesh. A boy had been roasted alive in a baker's oven the day before, suspected of being 'Red'. The Bolsheviks were being dealt with in Ungern's habitual fashion.

Maimaichen had descended into chaos and terror. To the Mongolian cavalry, pillaging and wrecking Chinese towns came naturally, and they took to it with enthusiasm. The atrocities committed by the Europeans, however, were worse. The Baron's soldiers had spent a desperate winter struggling to live off an alien landscape, and the last time any of them had been in a city was a year or more ago. They were veterans of two of the most brutalising wars in history, they were led by a madman, and they had very little prospect for the future. They went berserk, indulging in orgies of rape, torture and murder.

The Baron, always keen to gain the support of the local population, tried to limit the victims of the atrocities to the Europeans and Chinese. He failed. As one observer noted, 'One wished to avert one's gaze from the hangings, all over the place, of the poor, lamas, men and women, old and young, even children,'[39] although any soldier Ungern caught attacking Mongolians was summarily punished, sometimes executed. Suspected Bolshevik sympathisers were murdered on the spot, but no great excuse was needed for any killing. One Russian soldier reportedly made a speciality of strangling old women, seizing them off the street and choking them to death from behind. His fellows did nothing to stop him, nor, at first, to stop the Cossack soldier who decided that his own comrades were equally valid targets and began firing at them at random. Only after he had killed several did someone casually repay the compliment.

After three days Ungern ordered that the looting should cease, a command he enforced with iron rigidity. An American observer noted that 'Baron Ungern is strictly prohibiting looting and is heavily punishing the slightest disobedience.'[40] He even applied it to civilians; a Mongolian woman he caught rifling through looted Chinese stores was hanged on the spot by Ungern's own hand. The looting stopped. Ungern was keen to reinstate the rule of law and order.

The law, however, did not apply to all. Ungern ordered the harassment of civilians to stop, save for that of the Jews, because, 'in my opinion, the Jews are not protected by any law'.[41] An eternally foreign element, always working to undermine the rule of empire and true religion, they could not expect the protection that accompanied that rule. A systematic purge of Jews began. The capture of Urga was the first triumph in the building of Ungern's Holy Asian Empire, and Jews had no place in it. The murder of commissars and Jews had been a standard part of Ungern's military practice for the last year, but this victory gave him an unprecedented cluster of victims.

There were still a few hundred Jews left in the city, and Mongolia must have been the last place they expected a Cossack pogrom. Many of the Mongolians, who had no native tradition of anti-Semitism, were just as shocked by the Whites' behaviour, as were most other foreigners in the city. Mongolian friends of a kindly baker named Moshkovich asked vainly, 'What harm has he done, this good old man?' as he was taken away. Extreme violence has a shocking playfulness, and the Cossack pogroms had always had a festive quality about them, a mixture of drunken indulgence and wilful murder; now, among the looting and the flames, the game was on again. Jews were hunted on horseback through the streets of Urga, lynched in their homes, tortured for amusement. Afterwards, the murderers took their property. The repulsive Dr Klingenberg, who had been responsible for the 'mercy' killings of his own patients during the winter, led several of the mobs and took eager possession of much of the loot. He deliberately targeted one (non-Jewish) doctor, an American named Olay, so that he could seize his medical supplies.

The soldiers made no distinction of age or sex. Ungern had spoken, back in Dauria, of how 'neither men, nor women, nor their seed should remain'.[42] Now he had a chance to put theory into practice. Gang rape had always been part of pogroms, although traditionally the women's lives were spared, not from mercy but to gain additional amusement when they became pregnant with Cossack children.[43] That was not the case here. The best to be hoped for were bizarre spasms of chivalry such as that shown by the Russian officer who allowed one young Jewish girl to commit suicide before the soldiers could have her. One Russian émigré returned to Urga a few days later to find 'dozens of raped and mutilated women, slaughtered children, the bodies of old men'.[44]

There was little use in protesting. Togtokh, the Mongolian prince and anti-Chinese fighter who had been one of Ungern's strongest supporters, tried to hide some Jews in his own property, but they were discovered,[45] wrenched out of their hiding places, and beaten to death on the street. Togtokh protested this violation of the sacred laws of Mongolian hospitality, and barely avoided being hanged himself. A Danish missionary named Olsen, who had lived in Mongolia for several years, also protested the atrocities. He was tied to a horse and dragged to his death through the city. A carload of Jews trying to flee was ridden down by the Cossacks and lynched.

A few Jews were saved. Pershin concealed several in his house, bluffing the Baron's men into not searching his basement, and smuggled them out of the city later. One baby who survived was hastily baptised at the Orthodox church at the former consulate, brought there by a heroic Mongolian nurse. The Cossacks would have killed the child regardless, but the priest, Father Parnjakov, well-known as a philanthropist, forced them to back down. Cheated of their prey, they murdered the nurse instead. Ungern regarded the massacre as a positive benefit for the new country, not only spiritually but financially. Writing on the 'regrettable losses' of the Chinese merchants during his men's excesses, he remarked, 'At least with the Jews gone, Chinese business will be freed from their stranglehold.'[46]

The struggle against the Chinese was by no means over, but now, deprived of their main camp and scattered throughout the country, the

Chinese forces were pathetically easy for the Baron's men to catch. Many were hunted down by the Cossacks, with the help of the Tibetans. Some of the Chinese had not even stopped to put their boots on, and were running barefoot through thick snow. Great mounds of dead Chinese, horses and camels could be seen for miles along the Tula river. In their desperation to escape the pursuing horsemen, the Chinese had discarded anything that might weigh them down, even those items most necessary for survival in the Mongolian winter. As a result 'the road was strewn with overcoats, shirts, boots, caps and kettles'.[47]

Other survivors of Ungern's assault joined up with another group of Chinese soldiers, numbering somewhere from four to six thousand. They had come from the Chinese settlement opposite Kiatkha, on the Russian border, another trading town also called Maimaichen. Their original intent had been to reinforce or relieve Urga from the Baron's assault, but they were far too late. Tired, demoralised and disorganised, they were ambushed by Cossack and Tibetan soldiers under the command of Rezuhin, at Ude, twenty or so miles north of Urga. Living up to his name of 'the Cutter', Rezuhin charged them from all sides, resulting in a general slaughter. Hundreds of bodies, covered in 'terrible sword wounds', were left unburied, preserved for weeks by the cold. The local herders deserted the spot entirely, leaving the bodies to be eaten by packs of winter-hungry wolves.

After this battle nearly two thousand Chinese surrendered, upon which Ungern promptly ordered that they be formed into a new division. The prospect of a revived Chinese Empire was never far from his mind, and these troops, whose uniforms he ordered emblazoned with an imperial dragon, were the beginning. A force so used to changing sides at a moment's notice might be expected to take this in their stride, but Ungern's army was clearly too much even for them. That very night they deserted, breaking out en masse – but they were on foot, and the Cossacks and Tatars soon caught up to them. Relatively merciful for once, the Cossacks killed only a couple of hundred, surrounded the rest and herded them back to Urga, where they were put under tight watch. Some of the remainder enlisted with Ungern, others were hanged as suspected revolutionaries or managed to desert and drift back to the safety of Chinese territory.

Meanwhile, more thousands of Chinese soldiers were reported to be advancing from the south, but the slaughter and capture of the garrison in Urga had been so complete that they had no idea of the disaster that had befallen their comrades. Simultaneously the cavalry sent north from Urga turned back to try to relieve the city. Both groups were easily overwhelmed over the course of the next few weeks, encircled by the superior White cavalry and killed or scattered. The Mongolian cavalry were all-terrain riders: when they pursued one group of Chinese into the desert they happily swapped their horses for camels.

The Danish explorer Henning Haslund stood, two years later, at the site of one of these final massacres:

> We saw a large Mongolian monastery not far from the road, [and] we at once steered our course thither, glad of the chance to encounter living beings. But within the whitewashed walls with their gay red edgings all lay desolate and abandoned. On the steppe in front we had seen numerous Chinese uniforms, felt boots and sheepskins lying widely scattered around, and within the cloister lay the many-coloured remnants of lamaistic robes, red togas, and rusty yellow hats, and many of the red cloaks contained bleached fragments of skeletons.
>
> A last remnant of General Hsu's [Xu's] ten thousand soldiers had halted there in their flight from the avenging Mongols, and all this silence and death was the last achievement of the Chinese soldiery in the 'Grass Country.' But in that very place the Chinese troops had been overtaken by a dreaded Kalka General with his mounted Mongols, and not one of the ten thousand invaders had found his way home to China.
>
> The wild dogs of the steppe now nosing round the ruined buildings indicated the fate that had overtaken both lamas and soldiers after death.[48]

SEVEN

Lord of the Steppe

For the Bogd Khan, Ungern's triumph was also his own. Safe in the hill monastery of Manzshir, where he had been spirited away by the Tibetans, he planned his glorious return to a newly liberated city. Before he might achieve this, however, there was some cleaning up to be done. A sacred peace had traditionally held in Urga, and its violation was all too clear in the aftermath of Ungern's conquest. The horrific depictions in the temples were now a reality on the streets. Maimaichen, in particular, was strewn with dead Chinese. Elsewhere in the city Ungern's soldiers' penchant for mutilating their victims had left the streets littered with hacked-up bodies. The ever-present dogs were growing fat off the remains.

For the Mongols, this was more or less business as usual. Corpses were traditionally disposed of through exposure on the steppe, eaten by wild dogs and birds, but even those of Ungern's men who had experienced the charnel fields around Dauria became uncomfortable spectators as packs of 'growling and yapping creatures drew and tore at long bloodstained strings of entrails, and under the whirl of their many trampling feet the pale soles of the dead Mongol's boots shifted about as the corpse was dragged to and fro upon the ground'.[1]

Ungern's soldiers went to work cleaning up the city, burying the bodies and, disregarding Mongolian tradition, killing any dog they saw eating human flesh. Hardened soldiers spent the days sweeping streets and washing blood off doorsteps. Bloodletting ceased for a week, or was at least curtailed. The Bogd consulted his brother the state oracle, and determined that the most auspicious day for his restoration as Khan of Mongolia would be 22 February, which was also the Lunar New Year. The Mongolian nobles were summoned to witness the coronation, and thousands of Mongols poured in from the countryside to celebrate their triumph over foreign oppression.

Ungern was determined to make a proper occasion of it. He had the textile factory in Urga whip up new uniforms for some of his men: dark blue hooded Mongolian coats, lined with silk. His interest in distinctions of race and status perhaps led him to pay close attention to the uniforms' accessories, for the hats, belts and epaulettes he stipulated differed in colour according to the rank and nationality of the wearer. A place of honour was taken by the Bogd's Tibetan rescuers, dressed in a fetching green. The Bogd had awarded noble Mongolian rank to their Buriat leader in appreciation.

Ungern himself was declared to be a reincarnation of the Fifth Bogd Gegen, the Bogd Khan's predecessor, a rather dull figure of the early nineteenth century. It was an odd choice, and exactly how both the Bogd and Ungern could be reincarnations of the same person simultaneously was a spiritual mystery (although multiple incarnations were not unknown in Tibetan Buddhism), but it suggested an unusual affinity between the two. He was also made a *khan*, as well as being granted a hereditary double princedom and the splendid title of Outstanding Prosperous-State Hero. There were rewards, too, for Ungern's fellow Russians and his Mongolian allies, most of whom became Heroes of some variety – roughly equivalent to the European 'knight'.

Ungern's new title conferred sartorial benefits as well; he was now entitled to wear, according to the decree proclaiming his rank, 'a green sleeveless jacket, a red and yellow coat, a yellow silk thread in his hat, and three peacock feathers'. The Bogd lavished praise upon him, declaring that he was

> a meritorious person for restoring our independence and the State of Mongolia. Since he mobilised his army in this land, he has never been frightened, has never hurt our people, and has seized Khuree [Urga] in the blink of an eye, a meritorious deed. He destroyed evil and, if we consider his army regime and command, it is truly rigorous.[2]

Ungern must have been especially pleased by the last sentence, confirming a religious sanction of his disciplinary methods.

Before the coronation there was a procession from the Bogd's palace to the central temple where the ceremony was to take place. Crowds lined the route even before dawn, fighting for a good view and scrabbling up onto roofs and fences to witness the restoration of their old king. The procession began at about ten o'clock with Mongolian heralds riding out to announce the coming of the king. When they blew their horns, the crowd froze, and it was 'as though a thousand people turned to stone sculptures'.[3] Behind them came a procession of monks, chanting hymns of praise. In their centre was a horse-drawn wooden pyramid on a cart, from which a huge flag rose. On it, woven in gold thread, was the *soyombo*, a national symbol of Mongolia created by the first Bogd Gegen. It was a complicated fusion of images, chief among them a burning flame over the moon and the Chinese yin/yang symbol, but to the crowd it meant only one thing: independence.

At last came the Bogd himself, accompanied by his wife. He was huge and motionless, incongruously wearing dark glasses to shield his eyes against the low winter sun. He rode in a Chinese carriage, with guards to his left and right. Only one man rode behind the Bogd, in the place of honour; Baron Ungern, on his familiar white mare. Much to the shock of his men, their usually scruffy leader wore the full uniform of his new rank, peacock feathers bobbing slightly as he rode. His red Mongolian coat was still glossy; he had pinned on it his Cross of St George, and tightened his sword belt. It was a moment of pure, happy triumph. He had restored a king, and captured a country.

For Ungern, the restoration of the Bogd was no mere political act. In Dauria he had recreated medieval feudalism, but for the feudal order to work it had to be headed by a king, and a king blessed by the heavens. It was the first blow in the grand campaign of monarchy and good against revolution and evil. The revolutions sparked by the First World War had been disastrous, the people had lost belief in the truth, and he believed that there had been only two monarchies left: England and Japan.[4] But 'now Heaven has taken pity on the guilty, and there are kings in Bulgaria, Greece and Hungary again, and on the third of February the Bogd Khan was restored'.[5] He saw the restoration of the Bogd as a turning point for Asia, writing that the news 'was quickly carried to every part of the Middle Kingdom [China], and has caused the hearts of all good people to tremble joyfully and see in it a new display of heavenly blessings'. Even towards the end of his life he fervently maintained that 'until now everything had been in decline, and now everything is becoming better, and everywhere there will be monarchy, monarchy, monarchy'.[6] There was still much work to be done, however, for the 'restoration of the sacred Bogd' demanded 'vigorous and self-denying work from all true monarchists of the East'.[7]

Monarchs were the ultimate bulwark against revolution and chaos, only they could keep 'truth, kindness, honour and tradition from being trampled from impious people'. A state could no more exist without a king than 'the earth exist without the sky'. Without the monarch the apocalyptic End Time would come when, as he wrote to one Mongol leader, 'there was no happiness and even those looking for death could not find it'. (This letter, with its oblique reference to Revelation 9 : 6 – 'And in those days shall men seek death, and shall not find it; and shall desire to die, and death shall flee from them.' – must have left its Buddhist recipient somewhat confused.)

Ungern's faith in monarchy drew upon many Russian ideas, though typically went beyond them. The God-given nature of the tsarist system was taken for granted by many of its supporters, and it was deeply tied into the Russian Orthodox Church. Russia claimed to inherit the divine and imperial destiny of both Rome and Byzantium, and the tsar, according to the Church, was 'God's viceroy on earth'. Disobedience to the tsar was rebellion against God; as the school catechism taught, it was every subject's religious duty 'to obey from the inmost recess of the heart every authority, and particularly the Tsar'. These were stronger claims of divine favour than those of any other contemporary European monarchy, and were sustained right up to the revolution – if anything, Nikolas II demanded more ridiculously sycophantic praise from the Church than his predecessors, and in turn rigorously supported Orthodox dominance.

For Ungern, of course, monarchical authority went far beyond a single dynasty, or even a single religion. He saw heaven's stamp on all emperors, regardless of their faith. He showed even more enthusiasm for the (quasi-)Buddhist Qing dynasty or the Shinto-rooted Japanese monarchy than for the Orthodox monarchy in Russia, and was always keen to get in touch with the Chinese Muslims, believing them to be possible supporters of the restoration of the Mongolian Empire. His belief in cross-cultural aristocracy was not unique. In Europe, even at the height of imperialism, there had always been a tendency to suspend the rules of race for the nobility, no matter how 'savage' or 'primitive'. One of the attractions of foreign empire for many was the preservation of hierarchies abroad that seemed to be threatened at home. The vast masses of the East were not so different from the vast masses of peasants and workers in Russia, and there was a natural sympathy among those 'appointed to rule' in both cases. There could be a surprising egalitarianism, regardless of race, among those who believed in the inherent inequality of most of their compatriots. For Ungern there was far more intrinsic difference between a noble and a peasant than between a Russian and a Chinese.

Indeed, his conception of divine monarchy seemed to owe much to the Chinese and Japanese empires. He rarely wrote of 'God' when talking about monarchy, instead preferring a more ecumenical 'Heaven' which seemed closer to East Asian concepts of a generalised divine authority and certainly accommodated the possibility of polytheism. He wrote that 'the highest embodiment of the idea of monarchy, this connection of a deity with human authority, was the Bogd Khan in Mongolia [. . .] and in the old times the Russian tsars'.[8] Not only was the 'deity' unspecific, but the Russian tsars were roughly shunted into the past. When Ungern spoke of the restoration of kings being 'predicted in the Scriptures', he was as likely to mean Buddhist prophecies as the Book of Revelation. The closest contemporary example to Ungern's essentially medieval ideas of heaven-blessed kingship was the Yamato dynasty in Japan, with an emperor considered by many to be, quite literally, a living god and the descendant of the Sun. Ungern had fought the Japanese as a young man, consulted with them in Siberia, and had Japanese officers with him, and it seems likely that he had picked up some ideas from them. Their system seemed to have all the symbolic and political force that Ungern wished to impart to the monarchy he had 'restored'.

However, the Japanese imperial system in its current form was itself a recent creation. The emperors had been powerless, largely meaningless puppets until the Meiji restoration, barely twenty years before Ungern's birth, and even now they were surrounded and controlled by political and military cliques. Even among true believers, the emperor's divinity was always tempered by political reality. It was particularly hard to see the heavens at work in the ruling Taisho emperor. As a result of childhood meningitis, he was a mental and physical cripple kept locked away from the public and utterly incapable of ruling the country, but the sacred nature of the monarch as the ultimate expression of Japan transcended his human frailties. In a few years this would evolve into the principle of 'double loyalty' invented by the Japanese right-wing, whereby a truly loyal follower could take actions that, while seeming to go against the emperor's will, were in fact fulfilling Japan's destiny.

In the same way Ungern's respect for the Bogd as 'the perfect embodiment of divine authority' co-existed with an appreciation of his many flaws and a willingness to engage him in political struggle if need be. Ungern was well aware that the Bogd was an alcoholic, and spoke disapprovingly of his drinking binges and secret stores of champagne. He was important, but he was also, ultimately, secondary to Ungern's wider schemes of divine restoration. Ungern claimed later that the Bogd was 'petty, and unable to understand wide ideas'.

The Bogd Khan was also hedging his bets. He remained an astute politician, and his main goal, as ever, was to secure a comfortable living for himself and his entourage. Only a few days after being rescued he was writing to both the Bolshevik government in Moscow and the Republican government in Peking. He maintained his willingness to work with both regimes, protesting to Moscow that he had nothing against revolutionaries and to Peking that he had nothing against Chinese rule, and claiming that he had been 'abducted by force' by Ungern's men. Meanwhile, the two strange and wary bedfellows turned their mind to the business of government.

Later, when he was trying to ingratiate himself with the new Red regime, the Bogd Khan would vigorously protest that he had had no real political role under Ungern, but had been sidelined and powerless, used as a symbolic figurehead. Ungern would counter-claim that all power had been concentrated in the hands of the Bogd Khan, and that he had 'no political influence' in Mongolia and was valued by the Bogd only as the head of an army.

The truth was that both of them tried to maximise their personal political power and, while rarely at loggerheads, each followed his own agenda. Ungern protested that he 'tried to stay out of Mongolian affairs, but my soldiers were Mongolian, so it was necessary to get involved',[9] but his ambitions went far beyond the military. Initially at least, he effectively controlled the government, running taxation, administration and his own peculiar version of law and order. He re-established the five ministries of the old autonomous government – Foreign Affairs, Finance, Defence, Justice and the General Command of the Armed Forces – and placed Mongolian nobles, chiefly those who had helped him in the initial stages of the campaign, in charge. Ungern insisted that, at first, 'I just made suggestions, because the politicians were very slow in deciding their own affairs. Even when they see something good for them, they still can't decide what to do.'[10] However, from the start each department also had White Russian 'advisers' attached to it, and it was clear where the real power lay.

A telling example of the peculiar relationship between the Bogd Khan and the Baron was the paper bills issued by the Bogd Khan on behalf of Ungern, $250,000 worth in total, which entered circulation on 20 April, 1920. They were wood-block printed, hand-coloured and rather flimsy, and with no gold in the treasury to back the new currency, the Bogd was forced to guarantee them in an authentically Mongolian way; against his personal herds of livestock. Perhaps in recognition of this odd arrangement, each denomination had a picture of a different animal; a sheep on the ten-dollar bill, a cow (in the auspicious and unusual colours of red and white) on the twenty-five, a horse on the fifty, and a camel on the hundred. They carried a long explanation in Mongolian as to their value, and, in English, the words MONGOLIAN GOVERNMENT'S TREASURE and their nominal interest rate, 6 per cent per annum. Although issued by the Bogd Khan's government, with no mention of Ungern on them, they were universally known as 'Barons' among the Mongolians. Linked to the Mexican dollar, a key international currency of the time, at first they were accepted at close to their face value, but as Ungern's fortunes declined, so did their worth.

Although he was now both a Russian and a Mongolian noble, a lieutenant-general and, to all intents and purposes, the dictator of Mongolia, Ungern kept to his old ascetic habits. Not wanting to be softened by city life, he slept in a ger set in the courtyard of a Chinese manor, and conducted business in a small two-room house in Maimaichen, 'without a hint of any comfort', taken from a ordinary Chinese merchant. It was cold and bare, with paper strips covering holes in the windows, a smoky stove and a couple of wooden benches. Ungern was as slovenly as ever, and the house was 'intolerably dirty'. In the room referred to as Ungern's 'cabinet', he had only a single chair and desk, and forced visitors to stand. He wore a Mongolian *deel*, the long robe often mistaken for a dressing gown by his Russian officers, but now it bore some of the decorations of his new Mongolian rank: alongside his Cross of St George he also wore a swastika-emblazoned ruby ring he had been given from the Bogd's personal treasury. He left the peacock feathers in his wardrobe.

In contemporary photographs of him wearing Mongol costume he sits awkwardly, hair combed back, staring at the camera, his arms folded and the Cross of St George prominent on his chest. His gaze has a mad intensity that stands in stark contrast to his nervous glances at the camera in his photos as a young man. In one picture his moustache is overgrown and lopsided, his hair wild; this was clearly remarked upon, for in others apparently taken later the same day both are trimmed. His self-confidence carries through, and even in these exotic conditions he retained traces of his aristocratic upbringing. Another picture shows him striding out of the doorway of his house, giving orders to his underlings. Pershin, visiting him immediately after the fall of Urga, remarked dryly, 'If the Baron had been dressed in a good fashionable suit, his chin shaved and his hair brushed, [. . .] he would have been quite at home in any luxurious drawing room among polite society.'[11]

Much of the business of the new state was conducted from Ungern's two small rooms, or in private meetings in his ger. He roamed about the city and the outlying territory, making surprise inspections at all hours of the day and night. He had commandeered a swift motor car, a Fiat, and was driven around at terrifying speeds, the horn blaring out to alert passers-by. His every waking moment seemed to be taken up with meetings, consultations or drill, and his attention to detail amazed his staff; he demanded reports on every aspect of state affairs, but particularly on military matters, and devoured them at night. They wondered when he slept.

The liberation of Urga made Ungern extremely popular among the Mongolians. Widely viewed as a saviour and Buddhist hero, his reputation as a living god spread throughout Mongolia. He had addressed the gathered crowds at the Bogd Khan's coronation personally, reminding them of the glory of the moment, to great applause. The Bogd Khan's grant of noble rank and his recognition as a reincarnation of an earlier leader added greatly to his kudos, and as he rode or drove through Urga, mutters of 'God of War!' half-respectful, halffearful, could be heard among the crowds. He was particularly popular among the Buriats, who were highly sympathetic to both his pan-Mongolism and his anti-Russian and anti-Chinese sentiments. As Mongols living outside the country's borders, they were seeking to forge their place in the new state. Many had fled to Mongolia after 1917 from the Transbaikal and almost every Buriat in Urga volunteered for Ungern's forces, probably around a thousand or more.

The injection of Ungern's mongrel army brought new life to the city. The Russians already there remarked on the multitude of races among his men, mixtures of Buriat, Mongol, Siberian, Turkish and others. For many of them it was the closest they had come to normal life in four years. They billeted themselves in Chinese houses, took Mongol girls to the Chinese brothels or set up gers around the city. When not dashing to fulfil Ungern's orders they traded with the locals or consulted the Mongolian soothsayers. Recognising that the Chinese merchants, however disliked, were vital to the city's commercial life, Ungern did his best to protect and reassure them, succeeding, at least at first, to the extent that the Chinese banking community held a banquet – which he declined to attend – to praise the 'saviour and defender from the arbitrariness of the Chinese authorities'.[12]

For a time the city became busier than ever:

lively coloured groups of men buying, selling and shouting their wares, the bright streamers of Chinese cloth, the strings of pearls, the earrings and bracelets gave an air of endless festivity; while on another side buyers were feeling live sheep to see whether they were fat or not, the butcher was cutting great pieces of mutton from the hanging carcasses and everywhere these sons of the plain were laughing and joking. The Mongolian women in their huge black coiffures and heavy silver caps like saucers on their heads [. . .] a skinny, quick black Tibetan [. . .] and everywhere Buriats in their long red coats and small red caps embroidered with gold helped the Tartars in black overcoats and black velvet caps on the back of their heads to weave the pattern of this Oriental human tapestry. [. . .] Occasionally one saw the soldiers of Baron Ungern rushing about in long blue coats; Mongols and Tibetans in red coats with yellow epaulettes bearing the swastika of the Living Buddha; and Chinese soldiers from their detachment in the Mongolian army.[13]

Ungern was keenly aware of the polyglot nature of his new domain, and established a multilingual group of scribes, nearly a dozen in all, who worked to translate his pronouncements into four languages: Mongolian, Chinese, Tibetan and Manchurian. By this stage he spoke reasonable Mongolian, and pidgin Chinese, but conducted most of his personal business in Russian. The first few weeks of his rule were, in some ways, surprisingly constructive, going far beyond anything he had done at Dauria. He bucked his normal reactionary and archaic tendencies, and attempted to modernise the city. The retired British army official who had originally helped set up the power station, Major S. T. Dockray, greatly approved of the reopening of the electric station, allowing 'splendid great arc lights' to illuminate the city for the first time, which, for a people who had been quite literally shocked by the Bogd's car battery, must have seemed almost miraculous. Dockray himself agreed with Ungern to repair the wireless station built by the Chinese.

Having no tolerance for what he saw as idleness, Ungern ordered his men to 'clean and disinfect the city which had probably not felt the broom since the days of Genghis Khan'. In early March we find him writing letters demanding that expert engineers be sent to the city as soon as possible and he tried to put the city back to work, reopening the mines previously run by Mongolore, a Russian mining company, and even a textile factory, which was kept busy producing uniforms and flags. At the same time he began a series of construction projects, ranging from new river bridges to veterinary laboratories, hospitals and schools. His actions seem to have been motivated primarily by a desire to win Mongolian popular support and most of the projects never saw completion, not least because within a couple of months the staff required to run them had often either died or fled.

Maintaining his principled dislike for bureaucracy and codified law, he made no effort to establish a regular police force, judiciary or any kind of formal legal system. Instead, law and order were maintained through on-the-spot penalties. Although not quite as ferociously harsh as the discipline he imposed on his army, Ungern's idea of justice remained arbitrary and sadistic. Minor offenders were punished by banishment to the rooftops for up to a month at a time, where they lived precarious, bird-like existences, relying on food passed up by their friends. It was a version of the familiar tree punishment, only longer and less lethal. Discipline for the Baron, as ever, was all about display, and the unfortunate roof-dwellers served as an example for others, as did the corpses strung up at gates. Merchants protested that the bodies hung above their doors drove away business.

⚬⚬ ⚎◆⚏ ⚬⚬

Terrifying potential thieves was only a small part of Ungern's plan to purify Mongolia. Before monarchy and order could be restored in full, the impure elements had to be cleansed from Mongolian society. To Ungern, the defeat of the Chinese had been merely the first stage in this. The Chinese garrison had, in truth, exhibited no discernible trace of communism, though undoubtedly there were a few soldiers who were vaguely sympathetic to the cause. In Chinese the occupiers had been called *ge-ming*, in Mongolian *gamin*, both meaning 'revolutionary' soldiers, but this was a misnomer. Since the revolution of 1911 in China, any soldier associated with the central nationalist government, as opposed to the 'counter-revolutionary' forces of some provincial warlords, had been known thus.[14] The 1911 revolution in China had no Bolshevik involvement at all, and the Chinese Communist Party hadn't even been founded then, but Ungern understood Chinese politics only in the context of his own country's civil war, and the wider struggle against revolution. He claimed that the dead Chinese soldiers were Bolsheviks, corrupted by the insidious evil of foreign agitators, who had to be purged root and branch. 'Bolshevik passports' were said to have been found on the bodies of dead Chinese officers.

The arrival of the Whites also brought about the release of the many Mongolians and Russians who had been prisoners of the Chinese, one of Ungern's most popular achievements. The prison dungeons were soon refilled; revolutionaries, traitors and Bolshevik infiltrators were everywhere, and they had to be dealt with. A Bureau of Political Intelligence was duly established and soon set to the grim business of the political purge. The whole operation was run by Colonel Sipailov, the spasming psychopath who had been with Ungern since 1918. It was the same kind of work he had done as part of the White counter-intelligence network in Chita, but now he was completely unsupervised. Ungern gave him free rein to conduct his operations, and turned a blind eye to the resultant excesses. Unlike Ungern, he was sexually sadistic, personally greedy and derived great pleasure from the suffering of his victims. As with Ungern, other Whites blamed his cruelty partly on Mongolian influence, claiming that he had studied under Mongolian executioners. He was an alcoholic, and was often half-drunk while doing his work. Ungern had whipped him for it before, but some Russian observers thought that Sipailov must have a special hold over him to get away with such behaviour.

With the logic of the witch-hunt, victims were tortured to reveal other sympathisers and gave up random names in desperation, so providing the torturers with new victims. The process was observed nervously by other foreigners; an American commentator noted that one victim had surrendered twenty-eight names before being 'cut in pieces' himself. They concentrated on the Russian refugees in the city, who were most likely to have been infected with the virus of revolution, but Mongolians suspected of collaborating with revolutionaries were butchered as well. There were genuine revolutionary sympathisers in Urga, and there had been attempts to organise a soviet. Knowing what awaited them, many of the would-be communists attempted to volunteer for Ungern's forces, but were found out and executed. A few escaped; one Buriat revolutionary, Ajushi, managed to get a job as a supplier of hay to Ungern's army, used his credentials to get to revolutionary-held territory in northern Mongolia and ended up returning to Urga with the Russians months later.

White terror had been common enough elsewhere in Russia, but the persecutions in Urga exceeded most of the others in viciousness and scope, especially given the small size of the Russian population in the city. With Ungern and Sipailov supervising, and no foreign observers or political masters to restrain it, the Bureau of Political Intelligence operated effectively without limits. The similarity to the Bolshevik political police, the Cheka, was noted by the more moderate Whites in the city. Sipailov's power was made greater by the lack of reliable intelligence. Urga's isolation and the chaos of the last few years meant that rumour, slander and guesswork were all that Ungern's 'counter-intelligence' efforts had to go on. New arrivals were constantly coming in from Siberia, or returning from China, and any one of them, to Ungern's mind, could be a potential Red infiltrator. Even having the same family name as a known Bolshevik could be enough to condemn somebody.

In addition there was the division between Ungern's soldiers, among the most reactionary of the Whites, and the ordinary Russians in the city, who were mostly *kolchakovec*, refugees unaffiliated with any White faction, or stranded pre-revolutionary expatriates. Many therefore had moderate socialist or radical connections in their past histories, more fuel for political paranoia. People were targeted for the pettiest reasons. One intellectual and philanthropist, a man named Cybiktarov, was beheaded in a Maimaichen courtyard because of a leftist speech he had given three years beforehand. Father Parnjakov, the Orthodox priest whose baptism of a Jewish baby had saved it from the Cossacks, was one of the first victims. The charge was that he had a son who was associated with the Bolsheviks in Irkutsk.

The most powerful motivation was greed. Ungern had declared that after a political execution, a third of the deceased's property should go to the informer on whose word he had been convicted and the rest to the government. As a result Sipailov's depredations rapidly lost even a trace of political motivation, and became blatant murder. A typical, but unusually well-recorded, case was that of a successful young Dane named Olufsen, who was working for Andersen and Meyer, a Chinese-based Danish-American import–export company. He had wisely also exported his Russian Jewish wife from the city before Ungern's arrival, but stayed behind himself to dispose of the firm's property. He was 'one of those people who, if they think a fellow is a cad, positively have to go straight up to him and tell him so to his face with due emphasis. [. . .] He found himself obliged to rout round the town until he got hold of Ungern and could hiss the truth in his face.'[15]

Sipailov became convinced that Olufsen had some hidden treasure, and so claimed that he wanted to buy the firm's herds, thus inducing Olufsen

> to go by car to the place where the herd was, in order to have the beasts valued. [. . .] When they were well outside Urga, the chauffeur announced that there was something wrong with the back wheel. He got out and called to Olufsen to come and help him. Olufsen got out and was standing forward [sic] when the car [. . .] suddenly began to move forward at the same time that the chauffeur threw a running noose, fastened to the car, around Olufsen's neck. While he was slowly dragged along the ground Olufsen was interrogated about the hiding-place of the treasure, and since he had no information to give, he was dragged to death in a barbarous way by these white bandits.[16]

In total somewhere between two hundred and fifty and three hundred people were murdered by the Bureau, around 10 per cent of the expatriate community. The survivors were seized by fear, and most of those who could flee the city did so, even if they had previously sympathised with the Whites. Anybody in possession of money or property stood a good chance of having it requisitioned by Ungern's men, and probably being killed to prevent them complaining. Word spread fast, and the exodus of foreigners from Urga caused thousands living elsewhere in Mongolia to do likewise. Ungern soon put measures in place to prevent anyone recruited into the army from 'deserting', but civilians, at least at first, were free to leave. Nearly thirteen hundred took the railway to Mukden in Manchuria, and over fifteen thousand eventually made their way to China or the Far Eastern Republic. Few ever returned to Mongolia.

Even Ungern was sometimes troubled by Sipailov's excesses. He would hasten his pace when passing the interrogation centre from where tortured screams emanated constantly, and never visited the dungeons in which the suspects were held. He later admitted that he knew about Sipailov's 'executions, murders, and confiscations'[17] as well as his drunkenness – he had beaten Sipailov for drunkenness before, in fact – but he was unwilling to acknowledge Sipailov's sexual sadism, which he considered only 'false rumour'. Corruption and murder were within the possible scope of a purifying army, but to the Baron sex was beyond the pale. Even those sympathetic to Ungern found it hard to understand how he could tolerate Sipailov. There were widespread rumours that Sipailov had found a Transbaikalian shaman who, like the legendary and canny court soothsayer, had told Ungern that he would die shortly after Sipailov did. The truth was simpler; Ungern needed Sipailov in the same way as he did the Bogd Khan. He was a useful tool, especially since he brought in, despite his own corruption, considerable sums of money from those he targeted.

Ungern did take a more personal interest in certain political killings, especially of anybody who might threaten his position as leader. He probably had General Evtina, an ageing and popular officer who had arrived in Mongolia a few months beforehand, disposed of by the reliable Dr Klingenberg under the guise of treatment. Fear of poisoning was common in Urga; perhaps inspired by the Bogd's own record, both Sipailov and Ungern are widely presumed to have used it against political enemies. There was a certain amount of score-settling, too, as in the execution of one old colonel who had criticised Ungern's reign in Dauria.

His own methods of detecting revolutionaries were more direct than the Bureau's. Bolshevik scout parties were becoming increasingly common, and he liked to deal with them personally. He claimed to be able to discern commissars by sight, a kind of mystic vision which allowed him to see the traces of evil. Perhaps he believed Keyserling's claim that he had 'peculiar clairvoyant gifts'. After the capture of six Red soldiers,

> the Baron stopped and glared sharply at them for several minutes. [. . .] Afterwards he turned away from them, sat down on the doorstep of the Chinese house and for a long time was buried in thought. Then he rose, walked over to them and, with an evident show of decisiveness in his movements, touched all the prisoners on the shoulder with his *tashur* [bamboo cane] and said, 'You to the left and you to the right!' [sending] four on the right and two on the left.[18]

He identified the two as commissars, and passports were found marking them as such. 'Beat them to death with sticks,' he ordered. The others were 'peasants mobilised by the Bolsheviki' and were enlisted into his army. His perceptions were rarely so accurate. To most witnesses, Ungern's screening process was a random absurdity, life and death hanging on what resembled a medieval priest witch-sniffing for evil, yet the techniques he employed to screen out those undeserving of life would be taken to far greater extremes a couple of months later.

Ungern often interrogated people personally to determine their sympathies. N.M. Ribo, an émigré doctor working with other White forces, was interrogated by Ungern personally. Throughout their dialogue Ungern fixed him with his 'inflamed stare' as if 'he wished to glare directly at my soul'.

'Is it true that you are a committed socialist?'
'No, Your Excellency, it is a lie.'
'Then you can confirm it?'
'Some of my fellow countrymen, the Orenburg Cossacks who have known me for a long time, serve in your division. They know that I was in the Ural mountains after returning from the front, and what my attitude is to extreme parties and to Bolshevism. The fact that I was the personal doctor of Ataman Dutova and the head physician of the staff of General Bakicha after he was interned in Chinese Turkestan also shows my political views well enough. I arrived in Urga on the official sanction of General Bakicha, and I accompanied the aged and sick General Komarovsky, who is well known to you, and can inform you of the character of my political beliefs.'[19]

This impressive listing of Ribo's anti-revolutionary credentials was not quite enough for Ungern, however, who went on to ask accusingly why he had tried to intervene to prevent the executions of two other Russians, 'known socialists whom I had ordered to be finished off'. Ribo knew his life hung on the answer, but decided to be direct, firmly answering that, having known the accused in Urga before Ungern's conquest, he was 'confident that both of them were enemies of Bolshevism and sincerely loved Russia' and so it was natural for him to protest their arrest. He was reluctantly accepted as a genuine White – for the moment – but Ungern shrieked at him in his shrill voice, 'I shall not suffer any criminal criticism or propagation in my armies! Remember this and know, my eyes and ears are everywhere!'

Ungern used terror not only in Urga, but in order to bring White groups into line elsewhere in Mongolia. The other White groups, in Ungern's opinion, were doomed unless they had a single leader, and harsh measures were justified in order to unify them. He ordered, by his own estimate, the execution of one or two hundred people, sending out executioners and death warrants for any leader he perceived as disloyal, potentially revolutionary, or a challenge to his own power. The threat of execution hung over every other White in Mongolia. The machine guns and artillery he sent them from his stocks in Urga can hardly have been adequate consolation.

＋·＝◆＝·＋

Despite Ungern's paranoia and Sipailov's greed, there were real revolutionaries in Mongolia. In 1919, with the abolition of autonomy, several groups had formed which espoused socialist views mixed with nationalism. They comprised mostly young officials and army officers, intellectuals by the standards of Mongolia at the time, with a smattering of foreign education and a vague ideology. They had established contact with the Bolsheviks in 1920, talking up their strength in an effort to secure aid against the Chinese – claiming, for instance, that they had thousands of members and hundreds of rifles, when the real numbers of both were in the dozens – and had formally organised the Mongolian People's Party on broadly Leninist principles.

Sensibly, most had left the city long before Ungern arrived, not least because the Chinese liked them no better than the Whites did. The few that remained went into hiding, while their colleagues embarked on their own mission of liberation – with the help of the Soviets. Two of their leaders, both in their twenties and from poor backgrounds who were to become Soviet-era heroes in Mongolia, were Damdin Suhbaatar and Khorloogiin Choibalsan. Suhbaatar (the name means 'axe hero') was a young, passionate former officer, who had served against the Chinese in border skirmishes in 1917. Choibalsan was a former Buddhist novice who had managed to get himself sent to Russia for formal education, but had been recalled by the Mongolian government after the outbreak of the Russian revolution.

In mid-1920 they both travelled to Irkutsk, where they joined representatives of many other ethnic minorities seeking Soviet help in their struggle for freedom. Unsurprisingly, both of them became more doctrinally Marxist-Leninist, but their quest for aid was at first largely futile. They lived on the margins of the new order, constantly trying to raise awareness of Mongolia's plight. While some Soviet authorities, particularly in the Comintern, remained enthralled by the romance of igniting revolution in far-flung states, central foreign policy was more pragmatic. Still nervous about the risk of conflict with China, and struggling hard to maintain the pieces of the former Russian Empire they had left, they saw Mongolia as a step too far. Marxist doctrine held that the oriental nations were centuries behind Europe in their development. Rustic, underdeveloped and monk-ridden, the country was considered a long way from ready for the proletarian revolution.

All that changed with Ungern's arrival. The risk of Mongolia becoming a permanent base for further White incursions into Soviet territory, combined with the brutal reputation Ungern had acquired in Siberia, prompted a shift in policy. Although the Red Army was clearly on the brink of total victory in Russia, with the few remaining Whites contained in the Maritime Province in the Far East, the threat of counter-revolution still haunted many of the Bolshevik leadership. There remained an eagerness to work with the Chinese if possible – and, indeed, the Peking government was making cautious overtures to Moscow for help against Ungern – but Mongolia had become a clear strategic objective. The Red Army began to be readied as soon as the first false reports of Ungern's capture of Urga were received in Moscow in November 1919. The Fifth Red Army was ordered to prepare the 104th Brigade on the border in order eventually to 'cross the Mongolian border and attack the detachment of Baron Ungern with the aim of smashing and destroying it',[20] though the terrible condition of the Trans-Siberian Railway and food shortages throughout the region left the Red Army in no position to launch an immediate offensive. Things were made worse in February 1921 when, in preparation for the Russian attack on Poland, all available resources were shifted from the Eastern to the Western Front. For the moment, there could be no invasion – but the Mongolian revolutionaries looked like a playable alternative.

For Suhbaatar and Choibalsan, who had spent months writing importuning letters requesting 'mercy on the suffering of our people', all this meant that the Soviet government was finally coming through with arms and money. Ungern's taking of Urga clinched the deal, and they returned to Mongolia and began to gather the nucleus of a revolutionary army. Their first unit, formed on 17 February, consisted of twenty horsemen riding under two yellow-and-red banners. The red was for communism, the yellow for Buddhism. The Mongolian People's Party was not so revolutionary as to give up the faith, or the Bogd. For all their Marxist education, the leaders were almost certainly still believers themselves. They claimed that the Bogd had been forced to become Ungern's puppet, and that they, not the White forces, were the true warriors of the faith and liberators of Mongolia. Still undermanned and mostly unarmed, they relied on a paltry supply of Russian weapons and captured guns from dead Chinese.

After fighting a series of skirmishes and recruiting more men, they decided to target Kiatkha, a trading city on the northern border, conveniently near their lines of supply from the Soviets. The Chinese garrison there, some two and a half thousand soldiers, was partly made up of men who had fled from Urga, had no winter clothing and little ammunition, and were completely demoralised. They had carried out a bloody purge of Russians and Mongols over the winter, killing several dozen as revenge for Ungern's actions, and the locals were keen to see them go. With only a few hundred men, the Mongol revolutionaries successfully took the city on 18 March, a military success on a par with Ungern's capture of Urga.

Renaming the city Altan Bulag (Golden Spring) to symbolise the rebirth of Mongolian hopes, a rival government to the Urga-based regime was rapidly established. Although they controlled only a small part of Mongolia, eighteen hundred square miles or so, stories of their success soon spread through the whole country. They had achieved less than Ungern had against the Chinese, but they had done so using only Mongolians, and without Ungern's excesses. While they still claimed that they were setting out to liberate the Bogd Khan, the Bogd began to issue encyclicals against them, describing them as criminals, Bolsheviks, bearers of 'a disease worse than the plague', and revolutionaries who would tear down the very foundations of Mongolian life. They represented a direct challenge to Ungern's rule, and they spread the word of White atrocities wherever they could.

＋・ ☒◈☲ ・＋

For the moment, Ungern had other worries. What the Mongolians valued most about their new state was their independence from China.

Revered though the Bogd was, it was the sight of the routed and shamed Chinese, hated both as usurers and looters, that really solidified the popularity of the new regime. Ungern, however, was deeply concerned about keeping up relations with the Chinese. Although the Chinese in the country were scattered and defeated, there was still the risk of another expeditionary force. With the Bolsheviks in control of most of Siberia, the main line of trade and supply ran from Peking to Urga. The only other possible route was through eastern Mongolia to the territories still held by the Whites and Japanese in the Maritime Province on the edge of the Pacific, but the route was dangerous and bandit-ridden, and it was unlikely that the beleaguered Whites there could spare men or supplies.

A central government still existed, at least nominally, in Peking, but Ungern had no great interest in dealing with it. Centralised power had more or less collapsed, and a series of provincial leaders were vying for control. The key figure in northern China was Zhang Zuolin, the 'Old Marshal' of the north. A veteran of the Qing armies and an ethnic Manchu, he had begun building a power base in the north as early as 1904, when he had used his troops to aid the Japanese in the war against Russia. Now in moderately firm control of most of Manchuria, he continued to receive orders from the 'central' government, which he ignored. He was exactly the kind of figure who had risen in the past, after a period of chaos, to found a new dynasty.

Right now, in the swirl of alliances, Zhang was temporarily against the Anfu clique who had sent Little Xu to Mongolia. He also controlled the main line of possible supply for the White forces in Mongolia, coming from the Russian exiles in Manchuria and arms dealers in Peking and other parts of China. His men were thoroughly bribable and most of the rural areas of Manchuria were barely policed, so his approval was not absolutely necessary for supplies to get through, but it was helpful. Beyond the practical reasons for buttering up Zhang lay a deeper-rooted ideological sympathy on Ungern's part. Zhang was anti-republican, pro-Japanese and supported the restoration of the imperial family – so long as it remained under his thumb. For Ungern, the collapse of the old Qing empire had been a calamity, part of the wave of 'revolutionary death' which had swept over Asia and Europe. The Qing had preserved the Mongolians in their isolated purity, they had 'covered themselves with undying glory', and, most importantly of all, they had been a divinely appointed monarchy. The new Chinese Republic, on the other hand, was nothing but a pack of revolutionaries.

Ungern tried to make diplomatic contact with Zhang through a White Russian agent, Andrei Pogodaiev, who was living in Manchuli, Zhang's headquarters. Before a proper relationship could be established there was the small obstacle of the Chinese forces that Ungern had just routed and massacred. Pogodaiev somewhat stretched the truth when he wrote to Zhang, claiming that the Chinese garrison in Urga had been penetrated by 'about 200 Russian communists, after which it was not difficult and did not take them long to corrupt the Chinese Garrison with the assiduous help of their Chinese adherents'.[21] This demonic communist influence caused 'robbery and murder' until Ungern's intervention meant that the 'rioters were driven out of the precincts of Urga' with the aid of loyal Chinese troops. Although actual fighting against the communists was years away in China, most of the new warlords were paranoid about the possibility of Bolshevik infiltration, and this picture of insidious corruption may have struck a chord with the Marshal. Pogodaiev threw in a little appeal to his regional pride, claiming that the uncorrupted Chinese troops had been '[mostly] of North China origin'. Ungern also opened another correspondence with a Chinese general attached to Zhang's forces, Lu Zhang-Ku. They had known each other since 1918 and, according to Ungern, his memories of these years were 'always associated with your encouragement and sympathy', and he seems to have helped Ungern get in touch with Zhang, or at least those closer to him.

Zhang responded to Ungern's communications with cautious enthusiasm. He had no particular wish to expand his territory into Mongolia, and while he sent no aid himself, he permitted supplies and a small number of men to reach Urga. Replying to him in late March, Ungern felt he could 'rejoice in the knowledge of your continued favour and good will to in regard to myself' and that 'it is still more gratifying to me because of the heartfelt affection, which animates me towards you, and because I appreciate your partiality and the ample trust which Your Excellency is placing with me'.[22] The Peking government had finally got round to calling a conference on what to do about Mongolia in April, and had ordered Zhang to move against Ungern, but he was in no evident hurry to do so. It was widely rumoured that he had met with representatives of both the Japanese and Semenov at Mukden in March, where there had been mutual agreement to recognise Zhang's control over Manchuria and the Whites' over Mongolia. For now, a stand-off suited both sides perfectly well.

⚜

It was at this point that one of the most entertaining, but also one of the most frustrating, witnesses of Ungern's regime arrived in Mongolia. Ferdinand Antoni Ossendowski was a Polish geologist, writer and nationalist. He was forty-five, but he looked older, grey-haired and slightly stooped, with a soft voice and gentle manners. Educated in St Petersburg, he had travelled throughout Asia as a young man, and published numerous travel and scientific writings. He was interested in Eastern religion and Theosophy, moved in spiritualist and occult circles and was a friend of the Christian mystic, anti-Semite and Romanov adviser Father John of Kronstadt. His later books would show an obsession with religion, superstition, and the occult, but particularly with 'the gloomy shadows of the East'.

He had also been involved in revolutionary activities. He was part of a left-leaning group that tried to seize power in Manchuria during the revolutions of 1905 – something he wisely failed to mention to the Baron – and had been imprisoned and sentenced to death for protesting against the brutal Russian repression in Poland after the 1905 revolution. His sentence commuted, he managed to leave prison in 1907 on a wolf's ticket, a kind of parole for dissidents which consigned them to a shadowy existence, forbidden to reside in many areas or to obtain regular employment. Out of work and poverty stricken, he wrote *In Human Dust*, a widely praised account of his time in jail, and joined the Russian literati. It was a career that would support him all his life; by his death he had published over seventy books and his overseas sales were the second highest of any Polish author.

When the First World War broke out he was a surprisingly strong supporter of the Russian cause, writing anti-German propaganda novels and brochures. His time with Ungern was to produce his greatest success, a book called *Beasts, Men, and Gods*. Published in 1922, only a year after he left Mongolia, it went through ten editions in its first year. It is a minor classic of a popular twenties form, the Russian émigré escape story. Like most of the genre, it begins *in media res*. After briefly telling us that he was 'suddenly caught up in the whirling storm of mad revolution raging all over Russia' the third paragraph begins: 'One morning, when I had gone out to see a friend, I suddenly received the news that twenty Red soldiers had surrounded my house to arrest me and that I must escape.'[23] He fails to mention why they had come; since 1917 he had been a prominent figure in Kolchak's government, acting, at various times, as emissary to the American intervention force, an intelligence officer, and as an assistant to the Polish corps.

After fleeing from Russia he eventually arrived in Mongolia, whereupon he was ordered to the Baron's ger. He entered fearfully, forewarned by both the prophecy of a shaman that 'death from the White Man will stand behind you' and the more down-to-earth fears of fellow White officers.

> At the entrance, my eyes were struck with the sight of a pool of blood that had not yet had time to drain down into the ground – an ominous greeting that seemed to carry the very voice of one just gone before me. I knocked.
>
> 'Come in!' was the answer in a high tenor. As I passed the threshold, a figure in a red silk Mongolian coat rushed at me with the spring of a tiger, grabbed and shook my hand as though in flight across my path and then fell prone on the bed at the side of the tent.
>
> 'Tell me who you are! Hereabouts are many spies and agitators,' he cried out in a hysterical voice, as he fixed his eyes upon me. In one moment I perceived his appearance and psychology. A small head on wide shoulders; blond hair in disorder; a reddish bristling moustache; a skinny, exhausted face, like those on the old Byzantine ikons. Then everything else faded from view save a big, protruding forehead overhanging steely sharp eyes. Those eyes were fixed upon me like those of an animal from a cage.[24]

His life was spared, while a colonel summoned to Ungern's presence alongside him was executed after 'secret Bolshevik codes' were, according to Ungern, found in the lining of his coat. He seems to have been one of the very few people with whom Ungern established some kind of genuine friendship. For all his expressed contempt for the intelligentsia, Ungern occasionally took to older, better educated men with whom he could discuss serious issues of philosophy, mysticism and history. They talked about grimmer things, too; according to another Polish émigré in Mongolia, Ossendowski, with his training in chemistry, offered to teach Ungern's men how to make poison gas. Ungern jokingly referred to him as 'the professor', and he in turn painted Ungern as a kind of romantic hero, passionate and intense but also deeply flawed, who cries, 'I am not simply a man, I am a leader of great forces and have in my head so much care, sorrow, and woe!'[25] He omitted Ungern's anti-Semitism from his account entirely, instead having him say, totally implausibly, that 'my agents [. . .] are all Jews, very skilled and very bold men, friends of mine all.'[26]

Ossendowski was a tremendous storyteller in every sense. *Beasts, Men, and Gods* is thrilling, from his account of hiding from the Bolsheviks in the woods, accompanied by a jovial axe murderer, to gunfights on the Seybi river, avalanches in Tibet and finally his arrival in Mongolia.

Unfortunately, chunks of it seem to be outright fiction. Sven Hedin, the famous explorer of Asia, wrote a short book, *Ossendowski und die Wahrheit* [*Ossendowski and the Truth*], in which he proved that the entire section dealing with Ossendowski's travels in Tibet was a fabrication. Another writer more tactfully commented that he hoped Ossendowski would 'forgive him if I say that [upon meeting him in Mongolia] I cannot remember a single word about his attempts to get into Tibet, about which he has written so colourfully and in such detail in his book'.[27]

He was also prone to mixing up Mongolian legends and Western fantasies. Most prominently, the last few chapters of *Beasts, Men, and Gods* describe a hidden kingdom beneath the earth, ruled by 'the King of all the World', who secretly 'was in contact with the thoughts of all the men who influence the lot and life of all humankind; with Kings, Czars, Khans, warlike leaders, High Priests, scientists and other strong men'.[28] Ossendowski portrayed this as genuine Mongolian legend, and it did, indeed, seem to have traces of the myths of Shambhala. Unfortunately, it was also a virtual word-for-word precis of the mystical fantasies of the French occultist Saint-Yves d'Alveydre, in his self-published book of 1886 *Mission de l'Inde*. Confronted about this later, Ossendowski denied it indignantly, claiming never to have read the book, but the similarities are so close – with the exception of a few minor changes in spelling – that his protests seem ridiculous.

━━ ☰◈☰ ━━

According to Ossendowski, Ungern was a devout Buddhist, who had devoted his life to 'war or the study and learning of Buddhism'.[29] He gives us some of Ungern's best mystical speeches but, sadly, his desire to tell a good story and his own occult leanings cast doubt on much of what he says. It was undoubtedly true that Ungern was deeply curious about Buddhism, in a half-superstitious, half-philosophical way. He asked Pershin one day, 'I hear you have studied Buddhism and are friends with the lamas; could you tell me something interesting about it? I am very much interested in it, and want to know . . .' He trailed off, but Pershin assumed, probably rightly, that he was talking about the more esoteric practices of Buddhism, and told him that 'I know very little about the occult part of Buddhism. Really, I am interested only in the ethnography of the religion.'[30] His offer to show Ungern more temples and introduce him to some Buddhist philosophers was never taken up.

Despite this interest, Ungern maintained that he was 'a believer in God and the Gospels, and practised prayer'.[31] There is no record of him attending church, but he certainly prayed, though those around him were often uncertain to which deity or deities. He sometimes led the ecumenical evening prayer sessions of the Asian Cavalry Division. He seemed to feel that modern Christianity was a long way from the divine principles which had originally driven it. When addressing his Russian troops he unhesitatingly employed Christian references, but when talking to lamas and philosophers he was equally willing to engage in discussion of Buddhist principles. He was a believer in protective charms, divinations, the efficiency of alternative medicine and, possibly, reincarnation, but considered it perfectly feasible to hold all those beliefs and still think of oneself as Christian, if some way outside the mainstream.

So, what did Ungern actually believe? Was he a Christian or a Buddhist? He would, I think, have dismissed the question as irrelevant; he saw the two – indeed, he seems to have seen all religions – as essentially compatible. Surprisingly tolerant in some ways, doctrine and creed didn't matter to him. This was a common enough trend in esoteric Western circles, where all religions were often seen as fragments of a greater truth. Ungern believed in this ultimate truth, and what mattered for him was where a person stood in the great battle of ordered good versus revolutionary evil. To be 'called to struggle for the truth and the Gospels' was the same as fighting for the truth of Buddhism; he could combine the roles of Christian crusader and Buddhist wrathful protector without difficulty. Although it seldom arose, he was similarly tolerant of Islam, since many of the Mongolian-descended ethnic groups were Muslim. His religious points of reference were always ecumenical, and very similar to the language of other Russian occultists: 'Heaven', 'the Divine', and particularly 'truth'.

As we saw earlier, such universalising language was common in the Western esoteric tradition in the early twentieth century. The next step of Ungern's thought was more unusual. Socialism was blasphemous not only because it went against divinely ordained order, but because it was a false religion. Communism was, according to Ungern, 'a kind of religion. It is not obligatory for a religion to have a god. If you are familiar with Eastern religions, they present the rules of how to order your life and the state. Ordering your life based on Lenin is also a religion.' The issue of true and false religion was far more important than nationality; people did not go to war for their 'tormented homeland' – you can almost hear the sneer in his voice there – but for religion, the only thing that 'made war possible!' To us this might sound like a criticism of religion, but for Ungern, still as enthusiastic about the vital qualities of war as ever after seven grim years of slaughter, it simply meant that religion was an essential part of a serious life.

All this said, his knowledge of both Christianity and Buddhism was rudimentary. He had never formally abandoned his family's Lutheran faith, but his thinking was clearly far more Orthodox, drawing upon traditions of hierarchy, stability and monarchy that were deeply rooted in Russian religion. Although he constantly made reference to 'the Scriptures', he barely knew the Bible at all, with the exception of the great, awful images of Revelation and portions of the Old Testament prophets. When he was asked for the specifics of a supposedly biblical prophecy to which he attributed such authority, his response was that it was 'somewhere in the Scriptures' and that although he had looked, he had been unable to locate it. Perhaps he found it easier to believe in their truth if he only engaged them at second hand, like a fundamentalist churchgoer who never reads the Bible in full. He maintained that all his cruelty and terror in no way 'contradicted the doctrine of the Gospel'.

⊹≡⟡≡⊹

He certainly doesn't seem ever to have attained any deep understanding of Buddhism. It was the surface trappings that appealed to him: ritual, order, ceremony. Most of all he valued its purity, the preservation of the old and correct order of things. This applied not only to Buddhism but to all the beliefs and practices of Asia. The restoration of divine monarchy would come not from the 'rotten West, which is under the influence of mad revolution and the decline of morality in all its manifestations, both physical and spiritual',[32] but from the 'yellow Eastern culture, which was formed three thousand years ago and has been kept inviolable'.[33] It was 'impossible to aspire for the restoration of European Monarchs, owing to the deterioration of public mind and science which has driven the nations out of their minds'. The East would rise, and replace the irretrievably corrupt West, from which 'no deliverance could be expected'[34] and which brought 'corruption to mankind'. There was no 'Yellow Peril', but instead, in Ungern's mind, a deadly 'white peril'. He considered 'the yellow race more vital and more capable of state-building, and the victory of the yellow over the white both desirable and inevitable'.[35] He had taken the old Russian and German fears of Asia and reversed them, seeing in the 'Yellow Peril' the triumph of righteousness rather than a wave of barbarians.

All this was, apparently, predicted in the Bible. Ungern was uncertain exactly where, but he assured anyone who would listen that, according to biblical prophecy, 'The yellow race will move against the white, both in ships and in fiery chariots. The yellow race will gather together and fight the white; eventually the yellow will be the masters.' This was probably a confused memory of Ezekiel, which is full of foreign armies descending in 'chariots, wagons and wheels' to punish the faithless and also features the famous 'chariots of fire' which bore Ezekiel to heaven, and which have fascinated wacky biblical theorists from William Blake to UFO cultists ever since. Ungern also drew upon Buddhist prophecies to bolster his assertions, saying, according to

187

Ossendowski, that 'in the Buddhistic and ancient Christian books we read stern predictions about the time when the war between the good and evil spirits must begin. Then there must come the unknown "Curse" which will conquer the world, blot out culture, kill morality and destroy all the people.'[36]

Russia existed half-way between the pure East and the corrupt West. It was still redeemable, but its 'future, crushed morally, mentally and economically, is terrible and can not be imagined'. However, Russia could 'rise unanimously against the revolutionary spirit' which 'cannot be expected of the Western Powers now'. The monarchy could be restored, but only 'on the condition that the Russian people would regain their common sense, otherwise they would be subjugated to acknowledge such necessity'.[37] Ungern, and others like him, would whip the country into shape, but first it had to undergo a cleansing period to rid itself of corrupt Western influence, particularly that of the Jews.

Against Asia's preservation of the truth stood the lie of Jewish Bolshevism. 'Eastern culture' had been founded three thousand years ago; so had Judaism and the International, in ancient Babylon. The Communist Party was 'a secret Jewish party which arose 3000 years ago for the capture of authority in all countries, and its purpose now is being carried out'.[38] This was the climax of a long war. Hidden oriental wisdom contrasted with hidden Jewish evil. Knowledge of their true purposes was another hidden secret, 'known only by a few people', while 'all the Jewish states have followed their plan'. The Jewish hand could be seen in more than just revolution, however. Like many anti-Semites, Ungern believed the Jews were sufficiently cunning as to be simultaneously behind both capitalism and revolutionary socialism. As he outlined in a letter to a friend in Peking, the West was fundamentally corrupted by Jewish capitalists, an 'omnipotent, though very often undetected, enemy'. The Western Powers cared

for only one thing – to protect their capital and property against the usurpation of the revolutionary forces by simple methods, not attributing to those methods any moral value. The conclusion is one – the revolution will triumph, the culture of the highest product will fall under the assault of the rough, greedy and ignorant mob, possessed by the madness of revolution and extermination, leading to international Judaism.[39]

Judaism, socialism, capitalism – all were fundamentally corrupt.

The plan was simple. The first stage had already been accomplished; the restoration of the Bogd Khan and the creation of a new Mongolian state. This state, especially when reunified with Inner Mongolia, would provide 'military and moral defence against the rotten West, which is under the influence of mad revolution and the decline of morality in all its manifestations, both physical and spiritual'. Now the other tribes of central Asia, those 'of the Mongol root', could be united under the banner of Ungern's state. As he wrote, 'The next stage in the revolutionary movement in Asia, the movement carried on under the watchword of "Asia for the Asians", means the formation of the Central Mongolian Kingdom which must unite all the Mongolian tribes.'[40]

The Tibetans, the Kirghiz and the 'Chinese Mohammedans' – the Uighur of Xinjiang, then Chinese Turkestan – would, Ungern presumed, all join this alliance, along with the various Mongol and Turkic-descended peoples of the former Russian Empire:

> Into this State must come the Chinese, Mongols, Tibetans, Afghans, the Mongol tribes of Turkestan, Tartars, Buriats, Kirghiz and Kalmucks. This State must be strong, physically and morally, and must erect a barrier against revolution and carefully preserve its own spirit, philosophy and individual policy. If humanity, mad and corrupted, continues to threaten the Divine Spirit in mankind, to spread blood and to obstruct moral development, the Asiatic State must terminate this movement decisively and establish a permanent, firm peace.[41]

An essential part of this was the restoration of the Qing dynasty, so bringing about a resurgent monarchist China. Like the old Russian union, the new empire needed a central core, and 'the salvation of the world should start from China'.[42] After that, Japan and the other Asian countries would naturally join this happy yellow union, and the full power of the yellow race could be brought to bear against the degenerate whites.

There were a few holes in this plan. The most obvious was that Ungern had only the vaguest idea how each stage was to be carried out. He had conquered Mongolia through sheer energy and desperation, but had no clear idea what to do next. His first step towards broadening his pan-Asian alliance was to send letters to a swathe of prominent regional figures and hope for a favourable response. The targets included Buriat and Altai leaders, Chinese warlords and politicians, the Dalai Lama and the deposed Qing boy-emperor Pu Yi. They were strange communications, a mixture of lecture and sycophancy, with an easy assumption that the recipient shared Ungern's views about monarchy, revolution, the Apocalypse and Judaism. They mirrored, ironically enough, the naive enthusiasm of the International Comintern, which fired off a similar series of letters to a different set of foreign parties and figures. Few of Ungern's letters ever reached their intended recipients, most of their carriers taking the opportunity to desert if they were not intercepted by the Bolsheviks, and those that did were disregarded. In any event, he received no replies.

He placed a heavy burden upon his agents in China and Manchuria, asking them to 'address your activities to Tibet, Chinese Turkestan, and in the first place in Sin-tsan. You must find influential persons in the mentioned regions to whom you can address yourselves personally.'[43] His agents, who were living an impoverished existence on the edges of the White refugee community, did not manage to spin the web of influence Ungern was hoping for. Yet he remained optimistic about his prospects and continued to canvass support for his crusade from visiting foreigners; understandably reluctant to upset him, their response was more often diplomatic than truthful.

The next problem was Ungern's splendid ignorance of the region's politics. He was familiar only with Mongolia and Manchuria, had never ventured further south than Peking, and his grasp of reality about the rest of Asia was tenuous in the extreme. His vision of China, and especially of the popularity of the Qing dynasty, was a mixture of wishful thinking, projection and fantasy. The Han Chinese had no love for their former rulers, who had not only been corrupt, incompetent and arrogant, but had compounded these typical failings of Chinese government by being foreign as well. Ungern maintained a naive faith that, like the Russians, the Chinese people had been led astray by revolutionaries, and that they remained essentially monarchist. Most of the other groups he was so keen to bring together wanted nothing more than autonomy; the Tibetans and the Uighur, in particular, were pushing hard to keep their independence from China. Ungern, however, believed that the 'majority of the peoples of

Northern China and Manchuria are monarchists, and that the western Mohammedans [the Uighur] will not lag behind in the business of the restoration of the rightful heir to the Chinese throne'. Equally, a resurgent China, free from Japanese control, was Japan's worst nightmare. When he talked with people about his plans, they 'considered it inconvenient to object to the optimistic hopes of the Baron'.[44]

But it was precisely Ungern's ignorance of the realities of most of Asia which let him dream of creating an ideal empire there. There is a tremendous sense of fantasy about his plans. They smack of the oriental dreams of European mystics; the preservation of hidden secrets and pure kingdoms. It was also the ultimate exertion of his own sense of will; he could be, if not emperor of China, at least a kingmaker on a grand scale. The pan-Mongolian movement had been distasteful to him because it looked to establish an essentially modern idea of a state, because of the obvious corruption of those involved, and because it was all too clearly a plan to create a Japanese puppet. Nevertheless, it provided the kernel of his own scheme, though Ungern's proposed state would not be a modern country but a revived empire, a re-creation of the legacy of Genghis Khan. It was also a mirror image of the most cosmopolitan dreams of imperial Russia. A single overarching kingdom could take in a multitude of peoples, languages and religions, united by one monarchy and a belief in 'truth and honour'. Having lost his place in one empire, he could regain it in another. He would be a preserver of the things that had been good and righteous about the old imperial Russia; a carrier of the truth from one race to the next, like the hidden masters of occult tradition.

As ever with Ungern, such ambitions unnervingly portend something much worse. One of the elements of Ungern's plan that is most striking with hindsight is how close it was to the Japanese blueprint for expansion into Asia during the 1930s and 40s. The kick-starting of conquest from the north-east of China, the restoration of the Qing dynasty – albeit by the installation of the hapless puppet Pu Yi as 'emperor' of Manchukuo – the unity of pure and uncorrupted Asian peoples against the degeneration of the West, the attempt to instil worshipful respect of a dynasty that linked heaven and earth; all this would come to fruition under the Greater Asian Co-Prosperity Sphere. As Ungern did, the Japanese tried to reach out to the Tibetans and Uighur, sending secret agents to propose treaties guaranteeing independence in return for support against the Chinese.

There was clearly a measure of disgust with his own side here, too. The rest of the White movement had repeatedly proven weak, cowardly, corrupt, demoralised. Perhaps the separation from Semenov had stung more than he admitted. Not just the Whites, but all Russia had proved unworthy. They were more redeemable than decadent Europe, but they had turned away from the truth none the less. He would never see his yellow empire built, but he would bring his fevered vision back into Russia. Soon, as they had been seven hundred years earlier, the Mongols would be the scourge of God to punish a sinful people.

EIGHT

A Hundred and Thirty Days

I was nosing around a small Mongolian town, looking for traces of Ungern, when I came across a man who knew about a battlefield. A detachment of Ungern's men had destroyed a group of Mongolian soldiers there eighty years ago, riding over a hill with the sun at their backs and charging down on a blinded enemy. His grandfather had told him about it. To reach it entailed a bumpy ride over the grasslands, and a nervous one, because our car had broken down the evening before. Nobody had stopped to help, which surprised me. My driver explained that this was how roadside bandits got people nowadays, fake breakdowns in the night, preying on the Mongolian instinct to aid unlucky travellers. He was full of bandit stories, as were the Mongolian tabloids; highway robbery was on the rise again that year. There were a lot of places where people could just disappear out in the steppe.

On the way to the battle site, our guide reconsidered. It might not have been Ungern's men who did the killing there, he thought. Perhaps it was them who were killed, ambushed by revolutionary soldiers or just angry locals. Or maybe the revolutionaries ambushed the Chinese. Or the Russians ambushed the Chinese. It was a long time ago, and it was hard to tell, but there had definitely been bloodshed; that was part of the landscape now, and you didn't forget it. You didn't graze your herds there, either. Unlucky, grass fertilised by the dead. There was nothing much to the site itself when we arrived; just a low hill and a natural ditch where the soldiers, whoever they were, had been killed. It was probably an illusion, but the grass seemed brighter and greener there.

There were dozens of incidents like that over Mongolia during the spring of 1921, miniature battles that left the faintest mark on the collective memory. Here and there were clusters of Chinese soldiers who had escaped from the collapse of their garrisons, desperate to make their way back home. Bands of Russians were everywhere, either trying to join Ungern's forces or looking to escape to exile in China. The revolutionaries in the north were gradually expanding their territory, calling upon their fellow Mongolians to join them in throwing out the Russians. Various local leaders had mobilised their men, and plenty of Mongolians were practising simple banditry without any ideological excuse. All of them were living off the locals. There were no supplies coming into Mongolia from abroad, nor any large stores of food, so every army was accompanied by stolen herds, meals on the hoof. The Whites were among the worst of the pillagers. They were all over the country and, although the main groups had tentatively accepted Ungern's leadership after his seizure of Urga, many still operated autonomously. By now many of them had abandoned any hopes of a return to Russia, and were taking whatever valuables they could in order to fund a new life abroad.

Chinese merchants and Russian businesses, the main sources of wealth in the country, were particularly vulnerable to looting, though after a while it must have been hard to find one that hadn't already been targeted. The monasteries were the greatest potential treasure-houses, but, while some were pillaged, many were protected by Mongolian reverence and White caution. All sides practised gunpoint conscription, and it was a lucky young Mongolian who wasn't drafted into one army or another. Some escaped their abductors only to be captured by others, and found themselves fighting for yesterday's enemies.

Ungern needed men and arms as desperately as anyone else. Mongolia was hardly an industrial powerhouse, and Ungern's army was still badly under-equipped, especially with heavy weaponry. Fortunately, the Chinese leadership had been so desperate to flee that they had left behind the entire war chest for their expedition; over nine million Mexican dollars. The army was also able to scavenge four thousand rifles, but ammunition remained a worry. His letters fret about calibre, manufacture, quality.

The Mongolian banner system provided a quick and easy way to mobilise more men for the planned army. The Bogd ordered the conscription of a thousand men from each of three different districts. Ungern, meanwhile, wrote an ultimatum to the Russian Buriats in Mongolia, a major force among his men, ordering them to 'join the army within three days; those who don't come will be arrested'.[1] Ungern had roughly four thousand local soldiers under his command, about two-thirds of them Khalkha Mongols and the rest mostly Buriats, with a smattering of other Mongol-descended groups. Their leaders were also Mongols, mainly nobles, and several of them were veterans of the skirmishes in Inner Mongolia against the Chinese. In Urga, he also had about fifteen hundred foreign troops. Elsewhere in the country, around three thousand Russian soldiers were now nominally attached to Ungern's forces.

By April it had become evident that the only way for Ungern to sustain his new army was by wholesale plunder and seizure of assets. Ungern had a deep-rooted distrust of trade and merchants; they were too close to Jewish-capitalist ideals. Better than Jewish-revolutionary, but only just. There were to be no fripperies in a society at war, and trade should be directed purely towards military goals. He fixed the prices of goods in Urga, a move which would have been welcomed by ordinary Mongolians except that he set them so low that businesses were forced to operate at horrendous losses. Unsurprisingly, the flow of Chinese imports into Urga soon slowed to a trickle. White commentators noticed the bizarre similarity between Ungern's ideas and those of his communist opponents; collectivisation, terror, torture and the sustaining vision of a utopia, monarchist or proletarian, seemed to drive them both.

Baron Witte, the finance minister, was ordered to find three million taels of silver in order to support Ungern's military plans. The Chinese banks had their treasuries plundered, yielding an enormous sum of money, and every business that could be stripped, was. Russian enterprises were no less vulnerable. One of the murders that most shocked the Russian expatriate community was that of the head of the Mongolore mining company, the popular and friendly Dr Gay, along with his wife, mother-in-law and three small children. The usual excuses were given, and Ungern later claimed, without the slightest justification, that Gay was an 'adventurer'. The truth was simply that Ungern wanted the company's assets. Within a month he accumulated an enormous pile of currency: Soviet and old tsarist roubles, Mexican dollars, credit notes. In those days of spiralling inflation, it was hard to judge exactly how much any of it was worth; the value of the gold and silver pillaged from the Chinese was far more certain.

Mongolian humour runs along predictable lines. The central figure is usually a sly guest, one of the class of professional itinerants living off the country's code of hospitality, like the old Yiddish jokes about *schnorrer*. He either successfully cheats a mean host, or his cheating leads to disaster.[2] They're very, very tedious, but they highlight one of the great Mongolian social dilemmas: a guest overstaying his welcome. This was the problem facing the Mongolian government in April and May 1921. The stresses of supplying Ungern were beginning to tell; after the revolutionary seizure of Kiatkha and the final driving out of the Chinese Ungern's appeal as a liberator was seriously eroded, and there were increasing conflicts between his men and the Mongolian officials. Ungern later spoke bitterly about their pettiness and corruption – though that was his opinion of all bureaucrats. The turning point came when Mongolian officials began to ask openly, 'Until when will the Russians live off us?'

The crowds had lost their old affection for him. If his depredations had been limited to the Chinese and Russians, his popularity among ordinary Mongolians might only have risen. Increasingly, though, he ordered the seizure of livestock and goods from locals, taking, according to one ridiculously precise tally, 4,635 camels, 40,174 horses, 26,407 head of cattle and 100,729 sheep and goats. By any standards these so-called 'requisitions' represented a small fortune; for the Mongolians it was seized from, it was their entire living. If Ungern was a god, his demands for sacrifice were distinctly out of proportion to the protection he was giving.

The areas around Urga and other White-held settlements became more and more desolate as the Mongolian herders retreated further into the steppe to avoid the attentions of Ungern's men. Families were devastated not only by the loss of their animals, but by the drafting of the young men who did the heavy work necessary for survival. Young Mongolians who had arrived in Urga on pilgrimage, or to try to sell furs, or to gawp at the Bogd Khan's coronation, were drafted;

any who tried to flee were hanged, their bodies left on display as an example to others.

Most of all, the army needed feeding. Pay was optional, as it had been for the last four years, but food was not, and the lack of it was increasingly telling upon the soldier's morale. Thinking it over later, Ungern reflected, 'To be fed is necessary . . . it is difficult to express . . . if only I could just have put on a cap and vanished!'[3] It was a problem facing any army that stayed too long in one place, when, according to Ungern, 'the signs of corruption would inevitably set in – drunkenness, robberies . . .' Ungern also knew the solution. In the north, the Bolsheviks and their Mongolian allies had violated the territory of Mongolia itself. It was time to take the fight to them. War would lift the spirits of the army, for 'a soldier at work cannot be demoralised'.[4]

It was an odd choice, for there were other ways out. In the Transbaikal, facing the complete collapse of his forces, Semenov was already planning his final evacuation to Manchuria, which was fast becoming virtually a White colony. Harbin was crawling with White refugees, and from the Chinese ports a man with money – and Ungern had plenty of that now – could make his way anywhere in the world. Even in China there was no shortage of opportunities for a man with a taste for killing; warlords needed lieutenants, gangsters needed bodyguards. The civil war had not yet taken on the clear outline of nationalists against communists – and Ungern anyway still branded most of the Chinese leaders as 'revolutionaries' for overthrowing the Qing – but there were leaders out there who shared at least some of Ungern's worldview. It was rumoured that Zhang Zuolin, with whom he had been corresponding, even offered him a job as commander of his cavalry.

So why head north? There was no rational way to believe that invading Russia again would prove anything but disastrous. Ungern's total force was less than half the size of the Soviet forces along the Mongolian border alone, and a minnow compared to the shark-like reserve forces in the Far Eastern Republic. He had devoted minimal resources to intelligence, believing it to be a military irrelevance, but he must have had some inkling of the disparity between the two sides.

His strategy was not quite so insane as it must have appeared to many around him. At least at first, Ungern had no plan to try to conquer Russia with the handful of men at his disposal. He was convinced that he could 'destroy any Soviet division' on its own,[5] but knew that his supplies were not sufficient to sustain a long war. Instead, he would strike a blow at the Bolsheviks which would 'strengthen his position in Urga' and improve his reputation. After this grand raid, and the elimination of revolutionary forces in Mongolia, he could return to Urga and begin the work of building the grand Asian empire he envisaged, or, if things went right, liberate the Transbaikal and transform it into a renewed centre of counter-revolutionary resistance, reinforced by White and Japanese forces from the eastern provinces. There were twice as many soldiers on the other side, true, but hadn't he beaten the Chinese when fighting against similar odds? If he could lure the Soviet forces deeper into Mongolia, then surround and destroy them, it would be a blow to Soviet prestige in the region and a great boon to his own.

⊷ ⊷ ⊫◈⊒ ⊷ ⊷

It may be that Ungern had other reasons for striking against Russia, motives tied up with his ever-present obsession with prophecy. According to Ossendowski, he had an exact sense of his own doom. He went to fortune-tellers and oracles, looking for guidance on what to do next. At the 'old Shrine of Prophecies [. . .] a small building, blackened with age and resembling a tower with a plain round roof', he consulted two monks and said, 'Cast the dice for the number of my days!' The priests rolled the dice and 'the Baron looked and reckoned with them the sum before he spoke "One hundred thirty! Again one hundred thirty!"' Later he went with Ossendowski to an audience with the Bogd Khan and was told, 'You will not die, but you will be incarnated in the highest form of being. Remember that, Incarnated God of War, Khan of grateful Mongolia.'[6]

The most ominous prophecy, though, was given in consultation with a Buriat fortune-teller in the ger of Ungern's Buriat friend Djambolon. Ossendowski was with him again, and turns it into a long and dramatic set piece. He describes the fortune-teller as

a little woman of middle years, who squatted down eastern style before the brazier, bowed low and began to stare at Baron Ungern. Her face was white, narrower and thinner than that of a Mongol woman. Her eyes were black and sharp. Her dress resembled that of a gypsy woman. Afterwards I learned that she was a famous fortune-teller and prophet among the Buriats, the daughter of a gypsy woman and a Buriat. She drew a small bag very slowly from her girdle, took from it some small bird bones and a handful of dry grass. She began whispering at intervals unintelligible words, as she threw occasional handfuls of the grass into the fire, which gradually filled the tent with a soft fragrance. I felt a distinct palpitation of my heart and a swimming in my head. After the fortune-teller had burned all her grass, she placed the bird bones on the charcoal and turned them over again and again with a small pair of bronze pincers. As the bones blackened, she began to examine them and then suddenly her face took on an expression of fear and pain. She nervously tore off the kerchief which bound her head and, contracted with convulsions, began snapping out short, sharp phrases.

'I see . . . I see the God of War . . . His life runs out . . . horribly . . . After it a shadow . . . black like the night . . . Shadow . . . One hundred thirty steps remain . . . Beyond darkness . . . Northing . . . I see nothing . . . the God of War has disappeared.'

Baron Ungern dropped his head. The woman fell over on her back with her arms stretched out. She had fainted, but it seemed to me that I noticed once a bright pupil of one of her eyes showing from under the closed lashes. Two Buriats carried out the lifeless form, after which a long silence reigned in the yurta of the Buriat Prince. Baron Ungern finally got up and began to walk around the brazier, whispering to himself. Afterwards he stopped and began speaking rapidly:

'I shall die! I shall die! . . . but no matter, no matter . . . the cause has been launched and will not die . . . I know the roads this cause will travel. The tribes of Jenghiz Khan's successors are awakened. Nobody will extinguish the fire in the heart of the Mongols! In Asia there will be a great State from the Pacific and Indian Oceans to the shores of the Volga. The wise religion of Buddha shall run to the north and the west. It will be the victory of the spirit. A conqueror and leader will appear stronger and more stalwart than Jenghiz Khan and Ugadai. He will be more clever and more merciful than Sultan Baber and he will keep power in his hands until the happy day when, from his subterranean capital, shall emerge the King of the World. Why, why shall I not be in the first ranks of the warriors of Buddhism! Why has Karma decided so? But so it must be! And Russia must first wash herself from the insult of revolution, purifying herself with blood and death; and all people accepting Communism must perish with their families in order that all their offspring may be rooted out!'

The Baron raised his hand above his head and shook it, as though he was giving his orders and bequests to some invisible person.

Day was dawning.

'My time has come!' said the General. 'In a little while I shall leave Urga.'

He quickly and firmly shook hands with us and said:

'Good-bye for all time! I shall die a horrible death but the world has never seen such a terror and such a sea of blood as it shall now see . . .'

The door of the yurta slammed shut and he was gone. I never saw him again.'[7]

Ossendowski, meanwhile, managed to get himself assigned to a dubious 'diplomatic mission' to Japan, taking him conveniently out of the upcoming war. As ever with Ossendowski, it's hard to know how seriously to take his account of Ungern. Ungern was certainly obsessed with his own fate, and convinced that biblical prophecy sanctioned his expedition; it would be entirely in character for him to consult with Mongolian oracles, as he did with the fortune-tellers who travelled with him. Elsewhere, though, he seems confident in his mission, not overshadowed by doom. It's possible that the Mongolians played Ungern's own superstitions against him. Eager to see the city rid of his men, it would have been relatively simple – and with some precedent – to influence the oracles to push him in a certain direction.

＊ ・ ⇥◆⇤ ・ ＊

Whether motivated by oracles or logistics, the army began to move north. It was still the same ragtag mixture of nationalities – sixteen in total, according to Ungern – but bolstered with substantial contingents both of Mongolians and of former Chinese prisoners-of-war. Supplies were drawn by cart or carried by columns of camels, a favourite Mongolian beast of burden. Before they rode out, Ungern issued a proclamation to the whole army, sending it by horse messenger to each White group. The Urga presses ran off hundreds of copies, and it was distributed not only in Mongolia, but among Whites elsewhere in Asia. It was the first such order he had made, but it was titled Order No. 15 for both political and superstitious reasons. It gave the impression of previous orders, and so of a more sizeable and organised force than actually existed. His fortune-tellers had also advised him that fifteen was his lucky number; the Bogd Khan had been crowned on the fifteenth day of the lunar month, after all.

It had a long, strangely academic opening, describing how

> Russia was formed gradually out of various elements, few in number, which were welded together by unity in faith, by racial relationship, and, later, by similarity in government. So long as she was untouched by the principles of revolutionary thought, which are inapplicable to her owing to her composition and her character, Russia remained a powerful, indissoluble empire. The revolutionary storm in the West profoundly undermined the mechanism of the State by detaching the intellectuals from the mainstream of national ideas and aspirations. Led by the intelligentsia, both politico-social and liberal-bureaucratic, the people – though in the depths of their hearts they remained loyal to Tsar, Faith and Fatherland – started straying from the narrow path laid down by the whole development of national thought and life.[8]

The opening text was not composed directly by Ungern, but written by Ossendowski. This was reflected in the historical-analytical language of the passage, some way removed from Ungern's own style. The ideas, however, were Ungern's, albeit tempered somewhat by Ossendowski's more moderate views. There was the appeal to the unity of nation and empire, the locating of the source of degeneration and chaos – the 'revolutionary storm' – in the West, and the disdain for the intelligentsia. The view of the ordinary Russian people was pure Ungern; their hearts remained pure, but they had been corrupted by revolutionary influence.

The Order went on to explain how 'revolutionary thought flattered the vanity of the mob, but it did not teach the people the first principles of freedom or construction'. Peasants, as Ungern had stressed before, were not capable of doing anything without higher leadership. It echoed, too, a statement in the Russian edition of the 'Protocols of the Elders of Zion' that 'the crowd is a barbarian, and acts as such on every occasion. As soon as the mob has secured freedom it speedily turns it into anarchy, in itself the height of barbarism.' It continued, 'First the year 1905, and afterwards 1916–1917, witnessed the criminal, horrible harvest of the seed sown by the revolutionaries. [. . .] Three months of revolutionary licence sufficed to destroy what many centuries had achieved.' The emphasis on 1905 was straight from Ungern, remembering his wrecked home and ruined estates; Ossendowski, after all, had been involved in revolutionary activity himself at the time. It also reasserted Ungern's place among the most reactionary White faction for whom 1905 had been the beginning of the end, rather than an aborted opportunity for reform. Tradition and unity, preserved over generations, had been destroyed by the black forces of revolution.

There was still hope, though. 'The people feel the need of a man whose name is familiar to them, whom they can love and respect. Only one such man exists; the man who is by right lord of the Russian earth, THE EMPEROR OF ALL THE RUSSIAS, MICHAEL ALEXAN-DEROVICH.' The capitals give the pronouncement a cranky edge, like a letter written in green ink. Prince Michael had been missing, presumed dead for three years, and most of the Russian people didn't give a damn about him, but that no more dissuaded Ungern than the lack of support for the Qing among the ordinary Chinese had. Monarchy was the only right way to order the people, and they ought to long for it. If they didn't, they had been corrupted and would have to be punished.

The next few passages dealt with matters of logistics, organisation and movement, detailing how the various White groups should coordinate their assault. They outlined a tightly controlled partisan war, striking at the railways and using 'Poles and foreigners who have suffered from the Bolsheviks' to replace Bolshevik leadership, rather than trusting to local authority. Most of them were composed by Ungern's chief of staff. The most important of them was the fourth statement, that 'I recognise the authority of Ataman Semenov.' Asked about this, Ungern commented that 'he did not consider himself Semenov's subordinate, but recognised Semenov only in order to favourably influence the armies'.

Mixed in with the instructions to other White units was a typically obsessive interest in the maintenance of discipline. The order regretfully stated that 'because of the distances involved, I am deprived of the opportunity to administer punishment in person' and so order had to be upheld instead by each individual commander. 'Future generations would bless or damn their names', depending on how well they performed. Everyone must 'submit implicitly to discipline without which, as before, everything will collapse'.

So far, the Order could have been issued by many White commanders; there was nothing particularly unusual in it. The next passages, however, were entirely Ungern's:

9. Commissars, Communists, and Jews, together with their families, must be exterminated. Their property must be confiscated.

10. In the course of the struggle against the criminals who have destroyed and profaned Russia, it must be remembered that, on account of the complete depravation of morals and the absolute licentiousness, intellectual and physical, which now prevail in Russia, it is not possible to retain our old standard of values. 'Truth and mercy' are no longer admissible. Henceforth there can only be 'truth and merciless hardness'. The evil which has fallen upon the land, with the object of destroying the divine principle in the human soul, must be extirpated root and branch. Fury against the heads of the revolution, its devoted followers, must know no boundaries.

This was the ultimate expression of Ungern's belief in the counter-revolutionary struggle as essentially a metaphysical one. Evil, as represented by Judaeo-communism, threatened everything. To oppose these evils, 'mercy' had to be replaced with 'hardness'. This was Nietzschean language, showing some of the same contempt for the old Christian values of softness and mercy. For Nietzsche, though, hardness was attained by discarding the old religious falsehoods and finding a new sense of values, a personal integrity. In Ungern's thought, the new moral values were still drawn from an ultimate divine authority, the 'truth' that, for Ungern, represented divine revelation. The old values were not false; they were just no longer admissible in a time of such struggle. Facing a merciless enemy, it was necessary to be merciless in return. Ungern had praised war for scouring away weakness; now, souls fired and hard, he and his followers could become the scourge of God. Only when Judaism and communism were removed would 'Peace – the greatest gift of Heaven' be restored to earth.

The same principles would be preached a generation later, in another order given before an invasion of Russia:

> In the battle against Bolshevism, the adherence of the enemy to the principles of humanity or international law is not to be relied upon. [. . .] The originators of barbaric, Asiatic methods of warfare are the political commissars. So *immediate* and unhesitatingly severe measures must be undertaken against them. They are therefore [. . .] as a matter of routine to be dispatched by firearms.[9]

Hitler's infamous Commissar Order, however, did not include the dramatic prophecy of Ungern's peroration:

> The Holy Prophet Daniel foretold of the cruel time when the corrupt and the unclean would be defeated and the days of peace would come: 'And at that time shall Michael stand up, the great prince which standeth for the children of thy people: and there shall be a time of trouble, such as never was since there was a nation even to that same time: and at that time thy people shall be delivered, every one that shall be found written in the book. Many shall be purified, and made white, and tried; but the wicked shall do wickedly: and none of the wicked shall understand; but the wise shall understand. And from the time that the daily sacrifice shall be taken away, and the abomination that maketh desolate set up, there shall be a thousand two hundred and ninety days. Blessed is he that waiteth, and cometh to the thousand three hundred and five and thirty days.'

This was a direct quotation from the opening and closing verses of the twelfth chapter of Daniel, a famously strange and ambiguous prophecy. It was often strongly associated with the purported wrongdoing of the Jews, whose refusal to recognise Christ was taken to be the sign that 'none of the wicked shall understand', and used to justify anti-Semitism. There is a sense of mystery about the prophecy, too, a suggestion of hidden wisdom and secrets revealed only to the initiate, which appealed to Ungern's esoteric sensibilities. His own interpretation of the text was that the abomination of desolation referred to was the Bolshevik decree of 20 January, 1918, which had closed the churches and thus removed the 'daily sacrifice' of communion. One thousand two hundred and ninety days had passed from then to the beginning of his attack on the Bolsheviks. Actually, it was one thousand two hundred and sixteen, but it was close enough, and figures were never Ungern's strong suit. Some kind of blessed relief, then, would come forty-five days after the struggle began. A month and a half was hardly a long time to endure.

⊷ ⇇⬥⇉ ⊶

The Order was not a success. The *kolchakovec* saw it, reasonably enough, as 'the product of someone [. . .] suffering from megalomania and a thirst for human blood'.[10] Over-long and complicated, it confused even Ungern's most loyal supporters. Few people shared Ungern's wild, prophecy-seeking optimism as his men rode out from Urga on 21 May. Most expected only to inflict a local defeat to the Red Army, perhaps to liberate part of the Transbaikal and inspire further resistance. Many of the Russians, particularly those recruited in the last few months, knew the expedition was doomed and remained with the army only for fear of execution as a deserter. For a large number of the soldiers, particularly the Chinese, it was just another assignment in an essentially meaningless martial career, in which all that mattered was survival and loot. There was not much promise of either in this campaign.

Ungern's main force moved towards Kiatkha, the city the Mongolian revolutionaries had seized in March. Kiatkha itself was a border town, a sprawling mess that was essentially one city with its twin on the Russian side of the border, Troitskosavsk. The Kiatkha river supposedly separated the two, but it was a mere trickle. The Russian town was in Buriat territory anyway, and they were close to their cousins across the border. Although Russian Orthodox churches stood on one side and Buddhist temples on the other, both towns shared the same architecture: low-slung wooden Siberian cabins and tea-trading warehouses. It had been wealthy in the past, when it had been the only funnel for trade between the Manchurian and Russian empires; the magnificent Church of the Resurrection, built by Russian merchants close to the border, had been the second-richest in the empire, with altar doors of solid silver. By now, these had been long-ago stripped, melted down for funds by one side or another, as had the rest of the town's riches. Like Urga, it had a Chinese section known as Maimaichen, walled and isolated. A trading centre for two hundred years, a place where Chinese and Russian and Mongol could mix and do deals, it was a fitting target for Ungern's Russian-Mongol army.

They were facing a similar mix of Russian and Mongolian soldiers, assembled around Kiatkha in the last couple of months. The core was the 35th Division of the Fifth Red Army, experienced fighters tough-ened, like so many of Ungern's men, by seven years of continuous fight-ing. They were under the command of the Latvian soldier Konstantin Neumann, a skilful veteran of both the Imperial and Red armies, with a small auxiliary cavalry force led by Konstantin Rokossovskii, later one of the great generals of the Second World War. They had been in the most tumultuous battles of the civil war, taking on the vast White armies which had come close to crushing the Bolsheviks entirely in 1919. Now, with the Whites defeated and exiled, and Soviet power hardening across the country, this was mopping-up work for them; bandit-crushing, not battle. Many of them were reservists, who had been called up when the division was reactivated in March. The soon-er this was finished, the sooner they could go home.

There were around eight thousand of them, outnumbering Ungern's main force by two to one, in defensive positions, with better artillery and considerably more machine-guns. They were supplemented by around two thousand Mongolians. The Russian soldiers had been ordered to hang back for the moment and engage Ungern's men only when they actually crossed the border. This thwarted Ungern's best chance of success; he had hoped for a major Red incursion, which would have given him the opportunity to use his superior knowledge of the terrain and the mobility of his cavalry to harass, encircle and destroy the enemy. Now the fight was on the enemy's terms.

The battle began with an impulsive disaster. The forces of Bayar Gun, a noted Inner Mongolian prince and anti-Chinese guerrilla fighter, were ahead of the main body of troops, eager to clash with their treacherous countrymen. On the morning of 1 June, they destroyed themselves in a heroic, spontaneous charge against the fortified revolutionary positions; Bayar Gun himself was mortally wounded and died in hospital the next day. Both Ribo and Alioshin recorded that the news sent Ungern into a wild rage; he seized, beat and tied up Dr Klingenberg, presumably blaming him for Bayar Gun's death. He replaced Bayar with another Mongolian prince, who was foolish enough to express doubts about whether the operation could succeed. Ungern had him buried alive.

Ungern's men called, according to their memoirs, for him to move immediately upon the city, but he tarried. The omens were not yet right, and the artillery and machine-guns were kept behind. (One sometimes wonders whether Ungern's fortune-tellers weren't deliberately trying to sabotage his efforts.) He was confident; according to him his army was well-fed, supplied with ammunition (two hundred bullets a man), and 'as strong as the army of Genghis Khan'.[11] The delay gave the Reds time to plan their attack, moving men and artillery up into position. Around Kiatkha were low hills, covered with woods, some of the most beautiful territory in the region, but also ideal ambush country. The heat was sweltering; Mongolia turns from freezer in the winter to oven in the summer. In these bucolic surroundings, Ungern brought his army against his true enemy for the first time – and was shattered.

After some skirmishing, fighting began in earnest on 11 June. Ironically, the Red cavalry used the oldest of Mongolian tactics, engaging Ungern's forces in battle for six hours, then staging a mock retreat. Ungern's soldiers rushed after them only to find themselves trapped in a ravine, whereupon they were pounded with artillery and enfiladed by machine-gun fire from all sides. They 'were swept from their feet like grass before a scythe. Men and horses were piled together in bloody heaps.'[12] Two days of chaotic fighting ensued. Ungern's army was caught in the woods, surrounded and forced into a panicked retreat. Their own heavy equipment, with the exception of a couple of guns, was abandoned as they dashed back through the hills, seeking safety beyond the river.

They could have been annihilated then, but the Red commanders were relying on forty-year-old maps of no great accuracy, and misread the course of the Iro river. Ungern brought the remnants of his force together there, and drove them across. Even today many Mongolians not only cannot swim, but are distinctly afraid of water. Back then, when fear of vengeful water spirits was far more potent, the idea of plunging into the raging river on horseback must have terrified Ungern's Mongolians. Fortunately, some of the Chinese soldiers found boats, but

Ungern disapproved of this slow and unmanly method, which would also mean abandoning good horses. He discouraged them in the only way he knew; anyone who took the boat was to receive ten strokes on the back when they reached the other side. Some troops were lost in the river, but most made it across.

— · ⟩⟨◆⟩⟨ · —

As Ungern tried to regroup his scattered forces, the Soviets openly entered Mongolia on 28 June. The decision to 'liberate' the country had formally been made on 14 June, and confirmed by Lenin and the Politburo two days later, but it was an inevitable consequence of the decision to mobilise the troops and support the Mongolian revolutionaries months beforehand. The official reason was to pursue and destroy Ungern, 'the common enemy of both the Russian and the Chinese people', but there were other motivations. Control of Mongolia would prevent it falling into permanent warlord-anarchy, becoming a borderland state from which White guerrillas could raid into Soviet territory. It would give Russia a buffer zone against Chinese chaos and Japanese expansionism. It was part of the final chapter of the civil war, the last stomping-out of territory controlled by the enemies of the people – but it was also the completion of an age-old imperial dream.

There was nobody left to stand in the way of the Red Army. Ten thousand men marched slowly across the hills to Urga, wilting in the summer heat. They were preceded by armoured cars and reconnaissance planes, sending a shock wave of alarm through the country. The Bogd Khan's court panicked, alternately threatening the revolutionaries and pleading with them to retreat. They turned to prayer and sorcery, invoking the wrath of Mongolia's divine protectors against the Red plague. The last god they had called upon, however, was currently hiding in the hills. There would be no more saviours from the north.

There was only a paltry garrison left in the city, under the command of Sipailov. It put up a token resistance, easily brushed aside by the advancing enemy, and then fled, escaping to Manchuria. A few messengers rode north to find Ungern. The revolutionaries and their Russian comrades entered the capital in triumph, greeted by rapturous crowds. Despite the imprecations of the lamas, the Reds still declared their commitment to Buddhism. 'Everything, except religion, must be subject to gradual change,'[13] they stated in a letter given to the Bogd's court. The chief sin of the old regime, the invaders claimed, had been its wounding of the spirit of the faith. The Bogd had only been an unwitting tool of evil forces, and bore no blame for what had occurred, either during the White occupation or during the calamitous years of independence, when he had been beguiled and misguided by wicked aristocratic advisers. He, of course, was only too eager to embrace this version of events. He might have lost his political power, but his life of privilege remained untouched.

Public opinion was squarely in favour of the new rulers, for the moment. The corruption and incompetence of the old regime had been clear to see for the last decade, and Ungern's tyranny had permanently discredited the White cause. His enemies could only be good. There was the exciting possibility of real change, but with the reassuring continuity of Buddhism and the Bogd. The new state would be a people's republic, but the Bogd would remain the ceremonial monarch, and Buddhism the state religion. The presence of the Russians was a worry, but not a huge one; Mongolians were used to surviving with foreign patronage from one or another of their great neighbours. They had no way of knowing that within the next two decades the monasteries would be burnt, the statues melted down, the lamas murdered and the rituals proscribed, all under the auspices of their new comrades.

✦

When I visited Ulaanbaatar in 2005 I found the buildings covered with pictures of a portly, genial-looking Russian actor in imperial dress. He was clearly trying to act 'mad' but came across more as an eccentric grandfather. Across the posters were the words 'BARON UNGERN! WHERE DID YOU HIDE YOUR GOLD?' This was a reference to what remains in Mongolia the most enduring aspect of Ungern's legend. After his defeat at Kiatkha, Ungern had retreated deep into the Mongolian hills, eventually gathering his forces near Karakorum, which had once been the great capital of Genghis Khan's empire. It had been a city of gers, like old Urga, but all that remained now were two giant stone turtles, glumly facing the desert. The magnificent monastery of Erdene Zuu, one of the largest in Mongolia, was close by, and his beleaguered army had received food and succour there.

Not wanting his personal treasure to fall into Soviet hands, Ungern ordered it to be thrown into the nearby Orkhon river. Stories claim the treasure-bearers were then disposed of, like the coffin-bearers of Genghis Khan. This was untrue, but the exact location of his loot remains unknown, creating a mystery that puzzles acquisitive Mongolian fortune-hunters to this day. This was the message behind the posters; they reassured their readers that Ungern's gold would not have been lost had he invested it in Ulaanbaatar Savings and Loan.

From Erdene Zuu the army moved up to the Selenge river, huddling in the hills to evade the Red Army. They had retreated into a particularly vile part of the countryside, covered in stinking bogs and swarming with poisonous serpents. The horses proved more vulnerable than the soldiers; snake venom left men suffering from inflammations and fever, but it was fatal to horses. On the prompting of his fortune-tellers, Ungern prohibited the soldiers from killing the snakes, since it would bring bad luck. Trapped in mud, running from the enemy and hundreds of miles from home, most of them reasoned that their luck could hardly be any worse, and began a campaign of 'ruthless extermination' against their reptilian enemy. At least they could kill the snakes. Enemy planes buzzed them from the air, scouting their positions and occasionally dropping bombs by hand on the hapless troops. They were only ancient reconnaissance aircraft, borrowed from the Far Eastern Republic, but there was nothing the men on the ground could do against them.

They were joined by other White forces, some of whom had successfully penetrated the border and terrorised the Russian inhabitants. Dr Ribo, who had been threatened with death as a possible socialist when he returned to Urga a couple of months beforehand, had been travelling with Ungern's secondary regiment, led by the notorious 'Cutter' Rezuhin. They had sliced over the border, taking tiny towns and looking for communists to lynch. Upon learning in one village that every local Bolshevik had taken off on hearing of his coming, he was furious and ordered a randomly chosen old man to be hanged instead. The only communist left in town was the village schoolmistress, who was raped by the counter-intelligence officers and then shot. Ribo observed in horror as Rezuhin did his best to imitate Ungern, torturing and executing seemingly at random and copying Ungern's lunatic disciplinary techniques. After fierce battles with the Reds, in which they had some success, they received word of Ungern's defeat and returned to reinforce him, carrying with them over a hundred wounded men.

Another force of mostly Buriat Cossacks had been sent to Urianhai in western Mongolia; they had had little luck, and on 21 July many were beaten to death by their Mongolian comrades during the evening prayers. Many of the Mongolian auxiliary units, in the meantime, had surrendered to the Red Army, seeing no reason to stay with Ungern's doomed crusade. Around this time Ungern decided that Colonel Kazagrandi, who was leading a group of three or four hundred Whites elsewhere, was a 'robber', and dispatched another Cossack leader, Suharev, and a few dozen men with orders to find Kazagrandi's group, kill him and any officers loyal to him and take command. Suharev disobeyed and instead, along with Kazagrandi, tried to lead the group to China, but most of the men, along with Suharev and Kazagrandi, were lost in fighting with the Reds or the Chinese army.

On 15 July they received word of the fall of Urga. Many men had homes and families there; when they asked Urgen to discover the fate of their relatives they were brutally informed that 'a good soldier should have no family', because worrying about them would sap their own courage. Ungern wrote a letter to the Bogd Khan four days after he heard the news, addressing him in the deferential third person, and saying that Urga's fall made him feel 'ashamed not only before the Bogd Khan, but before every last simple Mongol, and it would be better if the ground swallows me up'.[14] Deferentially, emphasising that he 'was only a man, and it is not given to me to know the behaviour of a god [such as the Bogd]', he stated that 'thinking with a simple mind' he could see that the Reds would 'plunder everything and leave only beggars behind. So they have done not only in Russia, but also in other states. That is why it would be better, in my opinion, if the Bogd Khan would move to Uliassutai for a while.' Uliassutai was a region of western Mongolia not yet in Soviet hands, where Dambijantsan had previously held power. From there the Bogd could, in Ungern's view, direct resistance against the Red invaders and wait for Ungern to rescue him. In the meantime, he should trust to prophecy, and remember that this was all the fault of 'the secret Jewish party'. As long as the Mongolian people 'kept their beliefs and customs, God will take pity on them and not allow violence and robberies by the Reds'.

The Bogd probably never received the letter, unless Ungern sent multiple copies, since it was intercepted by the Reds. Even if he did, he was canny enough to know that Ungern's cause was sinking fast. The capture of Urga by the Reds finally extinguished Ungern's dreams of empire. He now had no territory, few allies and was facing massively overwhelming Soviet forces. Now, more than ever, the only thing left to do was to run to Manchuria. Yet he resolved that he 'could not approach the Chinese. Though I was at war with the Chinese revolutionaries, all the same I could not do it, and without the consent of Zhang Zuolin it would be impossible. The Chinese were arresting everyone who came across.'[15] There was a certain truth in this; the Chinese authorities were making some attempts to prosecute various White arrivals, particularly Semenovites, for their actions in Siberia. Given the breakdown of law and order elsewhere in China, this effort to punish crimes committed abroad was strange. It reflected the political clout of the White exiles in Manchuria and elsewhere, many of whom were outraged at the misdeeds of Semenov's men. After the mass Russian exodus from Mongolia, reports of the atrocities had caused Ungern's property in Harbin and Khailar to be seized and auctioned, with the profits being distributed among the families of his victims. There was a serious risk of his facing trial and jail if he returned to Manchuria, no matter how good his previous connections among the Chinese officials.

More than that, though, becoming a skulking exile was not his vision of his own destiny. Even in the swamps word was still filtering in of the wider world, transmitted by messengers from the other scattered White groups. False rumour and wild hopes were endemic among the Whites in the Far East, beaten and despairing as they were. Ungern became convinced that the Japanese had launched a new counter-attack on the Far Eastern Republic, which had been so successful that they had retaken Chita, along with Semenov's men, and were even now pressing further into Russian territory. He probably believed this was the 'blessing' that would come with the 'thousand three hundred and five and thirty days'. The timing was about right, after all, and Ungern's interpretation of prophecy was always flexible. It was a sign that 'God will hear the tortures and sufferings of the people and break the head of this poisonous snake. It will happen in the third month of this winter.'[16] His path was clear; he would lead his men into Russia again, where he could link up with the Japanese and Semenov and begin the struggle once more. Or, as he claimed to the Bogd, 'the Reds [in Urga], being afraid of being cut off, will return back. The government of Suhbaatar and others will be easily liquidated without help from the Reds.'

Despite being beaten and pursued, he still believed he held the military advantage. Ungern's faith in the mobility of cavalry, who could 'strike from any direction and at any time',[17] remained unshaken. He was convinced that no infantry force could ever match or surround cavalry, and envisaged himself striking into Soviet territory yet again, terrifying and impossible to capture. 'Cavalry is not afraid of infantry,' he declared later, 'even of a million infantry!' His strategy also included that mainstay of disastrous military expeditions from Harpers Ferry to the Bay of Pigs: 'The people will rise and join us!' He still trusted in the essential fealty of the Russian peasantry to the monarch, and believed that with his arrival the people would rise up against the Bolsheviks as though at the return of some prophesied king, sparking a counter-revolutionary wave; the uncorrupted Asian heart of Russia throwing off the decadence of the West. He based this upon the information he received from Russian refugees, the babblings of tortured Red prisoners, telegrams from the remaining White forces, and émigré rumour. Russia, he declared, was 'a powder keg'.

His men were not as optimistic about their chances, nor happy about this plan. Ribo reported that 'the mood in the regiment was suppressed and embittered. Everywhere grumbles were heard, threats to finish with "this unbearable experience" were distributed. Everyone who still had self-respect and the ability to protest gathered near my hospital tent for confidential conversations.'[18] Only a few close lieutenants among the Russians, like Rezuhin, remained constant. Ungern's Mongol troops, particularly the Buriat, were still loyal, and the soldiers were still paralysed with fear. Horsemen patrolled the edges of the camp each night, hunting for deserters.

Punishments were as rigidly insane as ever; men were perched in the trees overnight, flogged to death, forced to run miles in full gear. As before, Ungern's followers from Dauria received kinder treatment than the *kolchakovec*; they were merely beaten for an offence that would normally warrant execution. The paranoia about revolutionary spies continued; a young medic sent from Urga by Sipailov was burnt alive because Sipailov included a letter noting that he had allegedly been a Soviet public health commissioner. The few men who did escape still had to travel hundreds of miles across country, dodging revolutionary horsemen and vengeful Mongolians, until they arrived at safety in Manchuria.

*   *

According to Ungern there were 'no signs of collapse' in the army and, indeed, it held together well enough as Ungern brought it across the border, evading the Red patrols by taking the narrow paths through the mountains. He was proud of this achievement, claiming that there were 'tracks everywhere in Mongolia. Nowhere is impossible to pass, all it takes is energy', and that he had been able to lead his men despite 'only having ever seen the area from a steamship' before.[19] He had lost many men, but he still had around two thousand troops; enough, he hoped, to link up with his imagined Japanese expedition. He was striking for Verkhne-Udinsk (modern day Ulan-Ude), the capital of the Far Eastern Republic, but also the heartland of the Buriats. The army roughly followed the route of the Selenge river, which flows from the Mongolian mountains to Lake Baikal. This was the area where the 'true Cossacks' lived, who, Ungern thought, would already be chomping at the bit of Soviet oppression.

The vast Russian–Mongol border was littered with *ovoos*, Mongolian cairns. Passers-by considered it brought good luck to add a stone or tie a scarf; the oldest had been marked by thousands of cross-border travellers. In the borderlands were dozens of scattered villages, tiny Russian outcrops with a couple of hundred souls at most, scrabbling to eke out a living from the hard Siberian landscape. It was upon these isolated communities that Ungern fell. Hearing of his coming, most of the villagers had already fled. In any village he thought might be 'Red', which was most of them, he ordered the buildings to be set alight. There was the normal run of wholesale slaughter, directed by Ungern. A typical instance was at Novodmitrievka, where he murdered two whole families, including the children. Asked why he ordered the killing of children, he replied, 'To leave no tails . . .'[20] – the children, he thought, would otherwise grow up seeking revenge. The families of commissars were 'superfluous ballast'. In another village he locked the villagers in a barn and ordered it to be burned, standing and chanting prayers while he watched it blaze.

On 31 July, he came upon the 7th Special Detachment of the Red Army, quartered near the great Buriat Buddhist monastery of Guzino Ozero, situated on the lake of the same name. To many of Ungern's men this was an important sacred site, and its occupation by the Bolsheviks a kind of sacrilege. Taking it would be a boost to morale. The enemy had artillery, and Ungern callously sent the transports and the wounded along the main road to attract the Red artillery fire, while the rest of the men moved in to surround them. They rushed fiercely upon the Reds, battling among the outlying temples of the monastery and the Buriat yurts. Many of the Reds fought to the last. Ungern admired them. 'Clever,' he remarked, 'to shoot up to the last moment, and then to shoot yourself.' It was probably his own ideal of death; fighting to the last moment, and then an honourable suicide. It was 'clever' in another way; captured Red officers and commissars were inevitably tortured to death. In this case Ungern lined up the four hundred prisoners taken during the battle and, using his magic communist-detecting powers, ran his eyes over them and picked out a hundred as either commissars or Jews. They were killed; their comrades were reluctantly mobilised into Ungern's army. The local monks, meanwhile, attempted to steal from Ungern's transports, upon which he had them all flogged. Monastic sanctity, for Ungern, took second place to all-important military discipline.

When word of Ungern's reappearance reached the Soviet commanders they were nonplussed. They had thought his force entirely destroyed during the battles at Kiatkha; now he was raiding Russian soil. Thousands of men were mobilised by train or horse to track and surround Ungern's force. In the early weeks of late July, as Ungern came close to Verkhne-Udinsk, he found himself hemmed in by Soviet forces. There was no final battle, no clash of good and evil, just a series of blockings, skirmishes and retreats, and, for Ungern, the slow, painful realisation that his plans had been based on fantasy. His forces were harassed by Soviet regiments with armoured cars, but were able to evade them by riding through terrain too rough for the vehicles to follow. The worst moment came when his men saw planes in the sky, and rode joyfully towards them, believing them to be Japanese.

Then the bombs started falling, accompanied by rains of sharp nails, shaken out of the planes in boxes by the Soviet aviators.

On 4 August Ungern reluctantly concluded that the people would not rise, and that the Japanese invasion was a fiction. He began to head back towards Mongolia, slipping between the Soviet divisions, despite the pursuing aircraft. They could move only slowly, since both horses and men were worn out. Most of the men who had lost their mounts were left behind, but it still took ten days to ride the hundred miles back to the border, a trip that cavalry would normally expect to do in four. On the 14th he brought his exhausted, tattered force back across the border into Mongolia. Only around five hundred of them were left; the rest had been killed, abandoned or captured, or had deserted. It had been roughly a year since he had first brought his army here to find safe haven from the Bolshevik advance. Now this last bastion was taken, but Ungern was not defeated yet. With Mongolia gone, he would seek a new land of Buddhist purity – whether his men liked it or not.

NINE

The Last Adventurer

With this final defeat, Ungern shed any trace of civilisation. He 'rode silently with bowed head in front of the column. [He] had lost his hat and most of his clothes. On his naked chest numerous Mongolian talismans and charms hung on a bright yellow cord. He looked like the reincarnation of a prehistoric ape man. People were afraid to look at him.'[1] He had been literally stripped of his German and Russian heritage; now only the holy warrior remained. The rest of the division was equally battered; over a hundred were wounded and they had not had rest or proper food in days. Even Ungern now acknowledged that they could not confront the Red Army by themselves. Flight was the only choice.

In the soldiers' view there were just two rational alternatives; they could strike out north-east, attempting to rejoin the remnants of Semenov's forces and the shelter of the Japanese army, or they could head to Manchuria. Predictably, Ungern scorned such tediously rational options and declared instead that they were going to Tibet. There were some minor logistical problems: crossing the Gobi Desert without food or water supplies; the fact that the Reds held much of the territory through which the route passed; the formidable barrier of the Tibetan mountains in winter. There was also no guarantee of a friendly welcome if they reached their destination. When Rezuhin cautiously pointed out that if they attempted to cross the desert, 'they would be doomed from lack of water and rations', Ungern cynically answered that 'the loss of human material did not frighten him, and that his decision was final'.[2]

Ungern's Tibetan soldiers had been among the most loyal and skilled of his followers, and he seems to have had some tentative contact with the Dalai Lama, so the plan might not have been utterly lunatic, but the decision to go to Tibet was nevertheless rooted not in logic, but in Ungern's vision of the mystical East. More importantly, Tibet was a holy country, a place of pilgrimage for Mongolian Buddhists, and in the West it was the ultimate land of mystery. Sealed to foreigners and more or less completely uncharted until the British expedition of 1904, it was a perfect blank slate on which Ungern could project his mystical fantasies. Mongolia had failed and been corrupted; Tibet was his last hope that there still existed a place where the old 'beliefs and customs' had been preserved.

Few of the Baron's men shared his fantasies. Tibet was a country of which they knew nothing apart from travellers' tales; it was famously inhospitable to foreigners and offered no easy prospect of escape to the wider world. They might make a new home in Vladivostok or Harbin, but never in Lhasa. Ungern's decision was the final straw. Dissent among the men turned to talk of mutiny and it soon became clear that their predicament had but one practical solution: Ungern had to die.

The extent of the conspiracy to murder Ungern is unclear, but it involved a minimum of fifteen officers, probably more, who acted with the tacit support of most of the Russian soldiers, at least. Among the ringleaders were several high-ranking staff officers including two Russian colonels, Ostrovskii and Evfaritskii, and Ungern's physician, Dr Ribo. Several of the prime movers were, like Ribo, fellow country-men from Orenberg who had joined Ungern en bloc in Mongolia and so trusted each other, but others, including Makeev, Ungern's ensign, had been with him since Dauria. Success, fear and greed had so far kept them on side – those who had become sick of Ungern's cruelty or madness had simply tried to desert – but with the mood of the division so embittered, they now resolved to demand that the division change direction, and to kill Ungern if he refused.

On 19 August the division camped in a wooded valley, some dis-tance into Mongolia, near the monastery of Khalkkhanzyn Khuree. Makeev wrote of it lyrically: 'Among the hills, by a cold stream, in a wide green valley, the famous Asian Cavalry Division of Baron Ungern lived out its last hours.'³ Ungern had planned to hold hostage some of the Mongolian nobles still with him in order to buy safe passage through the country, but they wisely disappeared before he could do so, taking off into the countryside along with some of their men. Russians, particularly those drafted in the last few months, were also fleeing; the rigorous patrols against deserters could no longer be kept up. Hoping to nip the rebellion in the bud, an outraged Ungern seized Colonel Ostrovskii, and forced him to sit overnight in a tree. Ribo found him the next morning, shaking and exhausted. Many of the conspirators suffered similar punishments, or the threat of them, which both steeled their desire to kill Ungern and increased their terror of the risks of failure. Rezuhin's regiment had been separated from the main group, and Ungern was becoming increasingly concerned that no word from them had been received. He spent the following day in nervous consultation with his fortune-tellers, and sent out messengers to contact Rezuhin.

In fact, the Cutter was already dead. His column had been trailing Ungern's, guarding the rear from the Reds. He had been approached by some in his regiment who supported the conspiracy, but had refused to turn against his old master. Riding before his assembled men, he ordered his counter-intelligence unit to round up the conspirators. In response, several of the soldiers opened fire on him. He fell from the horse, wounded in the leg, and called on anyone still loyal to him to help. No one stepped forward, though nor did anyone else shoot at him. He hobbled over to a Chinese unit, demanding aid. A medical attendant bound his wound, but also his hands.

A crowd of soldiers gathered. With the strange passivity that was to persist throughout the mutiny, they did nothing other than stare at their former tormentor, wounded and bound. Perhaps they were afraid of reprisals from those still loyal to Rezuhin, or perhaps their will had been so broken by his sadistic authority that its sudden disappearance was too much to take in. It was 'a simple Cossack' who finally took action. He pushed his way through the crowd around the fallen colonel, berating them for their disloyalty, their cowardice, their betrayal, calling out, 'Oh, what have you done? What have you done to our little father-general?' His apparent concern was either sarcasm, or a ruse to fool loyalists. When he came close to Rezuhin he pulled out a Mauser from his tunic and shouted, 'You would drink our blood? Drink this instead!' and emptied the pistol into Rezuhin's head. The mood of the crowd changed from apathy to panic, and half the brigade was on horseback and preparing to ride away into the night, terrified of Ungern's vengeance, before another officer calmed the crowd and took control. They decided to ford the Selenge and head back towards Manchuria as quickly as possible, though not before Rezuhin had been given a shallow grave.

Two messengers were sent to warn the conspirators in the forward brigade to either finish off Ungern as soon as possible, or desert and join the escape to Manchuria. The first, a Tatar, was caught and interrogated by Ungern, but the second, a Cossack officer named Kalinin, made it to Ribo's medical tent and told the conspirators what had happened. They decided that they needed to act that evening, and adopted a plan proposed by Evfaritskii that he and four others would go to Ungern's tent, lure him out and shoot him. If they were successful, they would fire four cannon shots to let the others know. Whatever happened, they would break away from any remaining Ungern loyalists and lead the group to safety.

Evfaritskii and his companions duly made their way to Ungern's tent and waited in ambush outside. They called to their general, and levelled their guns on the opening of the tent. Much to their surprise, however, the head that poked out was Colonel Ostrovskii's. Ungern had forced him to move to his tent earlier that day, probably sensing the mood of the division and fearing that there might be an attempt on his life. Ungern emerged from a tent nearby, where he had been consulting his fortune-tellers. The assassins turned and fired, but he dropped to the ground with razor-sharp reflexes before taking cover in a thicket. Things became confused and chaotic. The assassins continued to fire randomly into the bushes while Ungern crawled around in the scrub like a hunted animal, unsure in the dark who was stalking him and believing that the camp was under attack from the Reds. The fortune-tellers, who presumably knew what was coming, disappeared from the scene.

Meanwhile, Ungern's soldiers were huddled together in small groups, wet, filthy and hungry. They had gathered wood from the forest to start small fires. Their only food for the last two weeks had been whatever they could seize from the locals during days of desperate riding through the hills, Red soldiers hot on their trail, which had left them mentally and physically exhausted. Even so, many could not sleep, still gripped by fear. It was hard to know which was the greater terror; the Bolsheviks or Ungern's random sadism. At least the Bolsheviks took prisoners. When they heard the shots they gathered in confusion and panic, not knowing what was happening. Whatever was going on, it was bound to be bad.

The conspirators seized command, rallying the other soldiers around them. They rounded up Ungern's two chief executioners, Burdokovskii and Veselovskii. Accounts are confused, but it seems they were led off on the pretext that they had been summoned by Ostrovskii, the chief of staff, before being summarily executed with their former comrades' swords. They must have guessed their fate when Burdokovskii shouted to Ribo, 'Doctor, where are you taking us?' and heard in reply, 'To the place where you have sent so many others!' Still, the Teapot managed a final moment of defiance, sneering, 'Me? How dare you!' before his head was cut clean from his shoulders by way of reply. Veselovskii was indignant when arrested: 'Only "the grandfather" has the power to arrest me!' he protested.[4] Makeev dealt with Veselovskii himself, remembering how afterwards he 'glared with hatred, watching the blood spurt from his head, and wiped the blade on the grass'. The remaining men began to move through the hills, but found the night-going too rough, and so stopped and waited for dawn.

Meanwhile, Ungern had found his horse but lost his division. He rode back, looking for his men, still thinking, he said later, that the camp was under attack by the Bolsheviks. When they 'were not in the same place' it began to dawn on him that something was afoot. Seeing the chief of the artillery, Dmitriev, he asked, 'Who ordered the regiment to move?' Told it was 'an order from your staff', he asked who the messenger was, but Dmitriev claimed not to know. Ungern cursed him as 'an old fool', ordered the artillery to stop and rode on after his straying division.

The three hundred or so men who had been at the camp were now strung out through the hills in three or four large groups, although with stragglers all around. They were almost all Russians, with a smattering of Chinese; the Mongol troops had mostly broken away and were making their own way through the hills, or disappearing among the locals. The conspirators were clustered together, like children huddling against a monster, when they heard the sound of hooves and the hushed whisper of 'The Baron! The Baron!' They had gathered in a low valley, leaving a cordon of a hundred men and several machine-guns at their rear to guard against Ungern's approach. He had ridden round it, unseen in the darkness, and emerged in their midst. Ribo described how 'the officers surrounding me hastily rushed aside, snatching out revolvers as they ran and clicking the shutters of their carbines'.[5] He 'pulled out his old Colt, having resolved to blow my brains out rather than undergo the tortures which we all expected if we fell into the hands of the Baron'. Several of the officers, including Evfaritskii, were so frightened they disappeared on horseback into the night, where all but two of them were captured or killed by the Bolsheviks.

Ungern shouted in the darkness, 'Who are you! What group!' but nobody answered. He called out for Burdokovskii, asking where he had gone, and somebody replied sarcastically, 'He has gone to see the chief of staff . . .' At last he recognised one of his commanders, a man named Ochirov. 'Where are you going?' he screamed. 'What have you started? I order you to return the regiments back to the camp!' Ochirov answered firmly, 'We shall not go back. We wish to go to the East and save ourselves. We want nothing to do with Tibet.'

Weapons drawn, the conspirators faced their lone target. There were other soldiers present, a few dozen in total, including several machine-gunners, positioned on the hillside by the valley. The mutineers were now undoubtedly in charge, and few, if any, of the men had any sympathy left for Ungern, but yet they did nothing. Ungern was only one man but, despite their previous murderous intentions, his presence was still overwhelming. Everyone save Ungern was paralysed by fear. Ungern began to harangue the troops in his high-pitched voice, riding from group to group as they stood silent and frozen. By his own account he told them that 'to go east was impossible, that there would be a famine, that they must go to the west'. According to others, his language was apocalyptic, drawing upon the texts he knew best. 'Alternating threats with terrible curses, he told them that they would gnaw each other's bones in famine, and that tomorrow the Reds would exterminate them one by one. The answer was all the same; obstinate, terrible silence.'[6] Nobody moved.

Ungern's adjutant, Makeev, was the first to act, the spell conjured up by his own fear, the Baron's curses and the night-time darkness broken only after Ungern's mare accidentally nudged him. He saw him suddenly illuminated as the moon broke through the clouds. 'It was terrible. His mad eyes were shining, shining [. . .] the Baron sat on the saddle without a cushion, his horse beat its hoof upon the ground.'[7] He drew his Mauser and fired at his master, but missed. The crack of the shot snapped the others back into the world and they opened up with everything they had, including the machine-guns. Somehow, no bullet so much as grazed him. Perhaps no one could quite bring himself to shoot straight at the man who had alternately led and terrorised them all for the last three years, or perhaps Ungern's superb instinct for survival saved him again. He saw 'bullets all around me. Then I realised what business was afoot.'

Ungern spurred on his faithful white mare, who 'with one bound flew up on to the top of the hill and carried [him] away from the pursuing fire of the machine-guns'. As he left his soldiers shaking in the dark, he gave one final cry: 'Bastards!' Then he continued into the night, looking for his Mongol soldiers, who had been acting as outriders for the main force. They, at least, would be true to him. He got lost in the darkness, for they lit no fires, but found them in the new dawn, just a few miles from the main camp. Greeting their leader, Sundui Gun, the only Mongolian prince remaining in the division, he told them that 'the army had gone bad'. The prince replied – and we can imagine Ungern shaking his head in weary agreement – 'Russians, in general, are all bad people.'[8]

The Mongolians would prove no more faithful to Ungern than the Russians. The next day, Sundui Gun asked Ungern for a match to light his pipe. Ungern reached into his pockets and Sundui grabbed him by the elbows as other Mongols tackled him from behind. Binding his hands, they sat him on the luggage train. Ungern had no idea why they turned against him; perhaps they had been in on the plot from the start, or perhaps they had spontaneously decided to make a deal with the Reds; by now, after all, many of their former comrades had turned themselves over to the Bolsheviks and even started fighting for them.

Mongols who switched sides had been treated with more mercy, for the moment, than Ungern ever showed deserters.

What happened next was the source of many legends. According to several of Ungern's Russian officers, who claimed to have got the story from two other officers who had been attached to Sundai Gun's Mongolians, he was simply abandoned, left on the steppe. Most claimed that he had been given a tent, from which his Mongols had departed 'with respectful bows'. The Russians considered it unlikely that the superstitious Mongols would simply have handed over a god incarnate to the Reds for fear of divine vengeance. Taking imaginary revenge on his tormentor twenty years later, Alioshin pictured him, after being wounded by Makeev and falling from the saddle, being discovered by the Mongolian soldiers, and then tied up and left to be tormented by ants and the sun. He hoped that 'he fell into delirium again and again, and it felt to him as though he was being burnt alive in a haystack, as he had ordered to do to so many people'.[9] There was a touch of wistfulness in the less-gruesome Russian accounts; abandonment on the steppe gave Ungern a final grandeur, as the simple Mongolians bent to their Russian superior, terrible even in defeat. Alioshin believed that even the Red Mongolian cavalry, upon discovering him and hearing his name, ran away in terror.

The truth was less dignified, though less sadistic than Alioshin's. The Mongolian soldiers continued to ride and, according to him, Ungern 'noticed that they were going the wrong way, and told the Mongols that they could come across the Reds'.[10] If his rantings at his Russian troops were anything to go by, his tone was probably less calm that he claimed. They took no notice, nor did they attempt to fight back when they were rushed by Red cavalry, 'like lava, with shouts of "Hurrah!" and calls to throw their weapons down'. It may have been simple exhaustion, or they may have been looking to surrender from the start. Sundui Gun certainly claimed credit for it afterwards, but by that stage it was obviously sensible for him to curry favour with the Soviets. Among the Mongolians, an even less dignified version of his capture spread; he had been tackled, it was claimed, bodily off his horse in a flying leap by Sundui Gun, who was well known for his wrestling skills. The story arose at the height of Russian oppression, when it must have given the Mongolians some pleasure to think of a Russian leader, even a White one, brought low by a Mongol hero.

The Reds milled around, inspecting their new captives and their baggage. One of them found Ungern sitting despondently, his arms bound. Every Red soldier knew his name, had spent the last few months reading or hearing about his mythical cruelty and ferocity, and had been told that his capture was of the utmost importance. But this beaten, unshaven man in a Mongolian robe hardly resembled the bogeyman of legend. 'And who are you?' asked the soldier, expecting the name of a minor White, or a fellow Bolshevik, captured by the local reactionaries. Perhaps Ungern could have brought himself a chance to escape by lying, but he was not going to deny his own heritage or rank. 'I am Baron Ungern von Sternberg, commander of the Asian Cavalry Division,' he replied. Amazed and disbelieving, the soldier called to the others, and soon the whole group was jostling for a glimpse of the captive before he was marched off to the army commander.

⚊⚊ ⚌◆⚌ ⚊⚊

Ungern had sought a heroic death in battle, but he had made contingency plans in case of capture. An ampoule of poison was always attached to a button of his robe, and he had planned to commit suicide as soon as he was taken. After 'a minute in captivity, he put his hand into the bosom of his robe where he kept poison, but it had gone'.[11] It had been shaken out at some point during his mad night ride. He tried to commit suicide twice on the journey back to Russia, but was frustrated by his guards on both occasions.

In Moscow, the Soviet leadership received news of his capture gleefully. Trotskii announced it in a typically gloating, sarcastic speech at the Moscow Soviet a week later, on 30 August. Denigrating émigré newspapers, he spoke of

> a report concerning Siberia, which the White-Guard press fills with endless revolts and coups d'etat, although complete calm reigns there. This is what the Paris paper has to say: 'A Havas [a well-known news agency] telegram from Tokyo reports the capture of Chita by Baron Ungern and the fall of Soviet power in Irkutsk.' News, as you see, of high importance! Baron Ungern was a major card in the intervention in the Far East. He invaded Mongolia and threatened the Far Eastern Republic. Now they tell us that he has taken Chita and overthrown Soviet power in Irkutsk.

I must admit that in this report, unlike the others, there really is a grain of truth. Baron Ungern is now indeed west of Chita. I have recent official dispatches from our Siberian command which, while confirming in this respect the telegram from Tokyo, on the other hand correct what it says to a very substantial degree. I will allow myself to read out one of these dispatches: "On August 22, at 12 o'clock, Shchetinkin's combined force (then follows a list of units) captured General Ungern with his bodyguard of 90 Mongols, led by a Mongol prince. General Ungern was brought to headquarters at 10 o'clock on August 23 and interrogated. General Ungern readily answered all questions, on the grounds that it was all up with him anyway. There is no fresh information about some small, scattered units of General Ungern's force." Thus, Baron Ungern was taken prisoner and taken under escort westward of Chita. His army has been destroyed. Consequently, this card, too, of the intervention in the Far East has been covered.[12]

As Trotskii said, Ungern had become more or less reconciled to his captivity. He knew that there was no hope left, and that his death was a few weeks away at best. He began to regard his interrogators, who included the Red commanders who had defeated him, as military equals, complimenting them on the Red Army, which he had once thought to be a 'degenerative rabble'. Meeting them in battle had changed his opinion, however, and he now found them to be 'very well-organised, operating under very strict rules'. Military discipline, even on the side of evil, was to be respected. They, in turn, questioned him over his war decisions, the routes he had taken, the order and strength of his army. When they asked him about his disciplinary methods, he 'spoke easily about executions, murders, punishments of every kind and degree'.[13] He insisted that everything he did had been intended as punishment, not torture.

A Soviet report wrote that he was

very tall, very thin, and when he speaks it is very direct. His head is not big, but his forehead is high. He has an overgrown light red beard, grey eyes, on his forehead is a scar, received in duels on the East, light sparse hair. He is dressed in a shabby yellow-red Mongolian gown with a very loose belt, the Cross of St George around his neck, and a Mongolian decoration on his shoulder.[14]

He was sent to the major Siberian city of Novonikolaevsk for trial. It still had its embarrassingly imperial name, 'New Nikolasville', but in a couple of years it would become Novosibirsk. The journey took him back along his old fighting route on the Trans-Siberian; he stared out at stations he had spilled his men's blood to capture and hold, now firmly in the grasp of Red power.

Ungern was treated well; certainly better than the prisoners he had taken. He was a high-profile item, the first major White leader to be captured alive since Admiral Kolchak. The Bolsheviks had been nervous around the time of Kolchak's capture, and had disposed of him straightaway; Ungern could be dealt with at greater leisure. Along the way he was displayed to selected journalists; crowds came to gawp at the train bearing him. Interrogations continued at each stop: What was his family background? Was he psychologically healthy? Had he had help from any other enemies of the revolution? He gave the same clear, peaceful answers; there were endless repetitions of favourite phrases. 'Hanging, shooting, flogging.' 'About the children – one should not leave a tail behind.' 'The rule of the rod.' Unlike a later generation of murderers, he made no attempt to make excuses or deny his actions. There was no hiding behind soldier's oaths or higher orders; for Ungern his atrocities had been divinely sanctioned.

The Soviet journalist Vladimir Zazubrin interviewed him, finding him 'sitting in a low soft armchair, one leg thrown over the other. He smokes cigarettes, kindly given to him by his enemies,' which he reached for with 'a thin dry skeletal hand'. He had a 'mild, guilty smile', and seemed to be 'a tiger turned into a lamb', but 'his claws, though receded, were still sharp'. When the train stopped in Irkutsk, his captors took him on a brief tour of Soviet achievement, showing him 'a number of offices where their bureaucratic machine ran at full speed'. He sniffed ostentatiously and sneered, 'It smells strongly of garlic. Why do you employ so many Jews?'[15] He looked curiously at everything, like a man who knew these sights would be among his last.

⊷ ⧫ ⊶

As Ungern's train chugged slowly towards his trial, the beaten and weary men of his division made their way towards Manchuria. The former conspirators took control of the troops, abolishing corporal punishments. They outdistanced the Reds and crossed the Selenge, pausing to regroup on a large island in the centre of the river. There they held a short 'trial' and shot eleven of Ungern's enforcers. Ironically, discipline collapsed almost immediately; without the constant fear of Ungern's whip there was nothing holding the division together. Dozens of men, particularly the Cossacks, deserted, riding back north to surrender to the Red Army. The division began to implode, fighting over food and water. After appeals to their better nature – 'Shame upon shame! In these times when everyone should think as one, friend to friend, you turn traitor?'[16] – corporal punishment was reinstated, providing a modicum of discipline.

Some few men chose to stay behind and continue the futile struggle against the Bolsheviks; the core of persistent survivors, after skirmishes with Red cavalry and Mongolian bandits, finally made their way to Manchuria. There were only six hundred of them left. They were helped by a secret order of the Bogd Khan that they should be given food, supplies and directions. Locals warned them of the approach of the Red forces and showed them which paths to take through the hills. On 6 October they arrived at Khailar in Manchuria, where they were able to use Ungern's old contacts to negotiate the surrender of their weapons to the Chinese army in return for food, money and transport to the last bastion of White resistance in Vladivostok. Taken there by train, the Asian Cavalry Division finally disintegrated, its members making their separate ways among the great White diaspora. The other White groups in Mongolia either did the same, often after killing their leaders, fell victim to the Red Army, or were wiped out by former Mongolian allies who decided their best chance lay with the revolution.

━━◄◆►━━

Ungern's train arrived in Novonikolaevsk on the first day of September, whereupon he was taken for yet more interrogation and examination. His captors concluded that he 'was by no means psychologically healthy' and, rather crushingly, that he 'certainly did not have the capacity to run a whole country'.[17] He was 'pathologically impulsive', and the only rule he could imagine was a totalitarian military order. He had been 'infected by mysticism'.[18]

His trial was held two weeks later, on 15 September, 1921. There was never any question as to the verdict; Lenin had sent a telegram with clear directions: the tribunal should proceed with all due speed, and pronounce a sentence of death by shooting if the evidence against him was valid, 'of which, apparently, there can be no doubt'. The London *Times* was so confident that it jumped the gun, reporting his execution on 13 September, two days before the trial started, and the New York Times *four* days beforehand – both of them apparently working off a Soviet news bulletin.

The Soviet authorities had no time for legal niceties. Unlike later show trials, this was no drawn-out, months-long affair but a brief display of revolutionary triumph over aristocratic decadence. There was, however, a considerable element of display in bringing him such a long distance from his point of capture, unlike other White leaders, such as Kolchak, who had been shot more or less on the spot. The trial of Ungern, a freakish sadist, would provide a splendid example of the horrors of the old regime. Appropriately enough for a staged trial, it took place in the Sovnoska Garden Theatre, in the centre of the city. The crowds were eager to see Ungern, gawping at him like a freak at the fair, jostling for places in the overcrowded theatre and grumbling when they couldn't get in. According to the official report, several thousand people were present. In a dramatic touch, Ungern's yellow coat was hung above the stage. From beginning to end, the trial lasted five hours and twenty minutes. Witnesses were deemed unnecessary, since Ungern freely admitted his guilt. There were five judges, all stalwart members of the communist hierarchy, and led by the old Bolshevik Oparin. One had been a renowned partisan leader in Siberia, fighting the Semenovites. The prosecutor, Eme'lian Iaroslavskii, was a Siberian Jew, which must have given Ungern a certain resigned satisfaction.

Ungern faced the tribunal and the crowd with cold resignation, sitting on a bench on the theatre's proscenium, eyes downcast much of the time, and his hands wrapped in the sleeves of his new robe. The onlookers wondered if this stiff, odd man could really have been such a horror, but occasionally he would look up and there would be a glimpse of something fierce in him, like 'a fire covered with ashes'. Many of his answers were melancholy. Iaroslavskii, trying to set a final stamp on the White movement, asked him, 'Do you consider the end of your campaign to be the last of all the adventures of the past few years and do you not believe that it was the last attempt to bring about the ideas which you profess?' Ungern replied, 'Yes, the last. I suppose I am the last.'

Proceedings opened with Ungern being asked which political party he belonged to. 'None,' he replied.[19] There were three charges: treason, in collusion with Japan; attempting to overthrow the revolution and restore the Romanovs; and perpetuating terror and atrocities. The meat of the trial was over in seconds, when he was asked, 'Do you admit the crimes you have committed?' 'Yes, but there is one point. I had no connection with the Japanese.' With a typical Soviet interest in class background, Iaroslavskii proceeded to question him about his family. Ungern perked up at this point, and gave proud answers. Seventy-two of his family had died serving Russia! They had been around for a thousand years! Moving on to his crimes, Iaroslavskii asked, 'Do you often beat people?' Ungern dryly answered, 'Not enough – but it happened.'

His atrocities were related for the court, focusing particularly on the murder of Jews and commissars. His time in Russia and his attempt to rouse the people there naturally interested them more than his Mongolian activities. Determined to demonstrate the decadent nature of the aristocracy, Iaroslavskii dwelt at some length on his drunken beating of an aide-de-camp, using it as an example of typical upper-class violence against the lower orders. Ungern made no real effort to defend himself, except that he protested that he had never ordered violence against women. Occasionally he tried to claim that his punishments had been administered only to soldiers, not civilians. When the prosecution produced evidence, he admitted that it had occurred in at least one instance. His memory failed him at several points; he could not remember the name of the priest he had ordered killed in Urga, and thought that it was because he, not his son, had been involved in revolutionary activities.

As befitted a future leader of the League of Militant Atheists, Iaroslavskii zeroed in on religion. 'Why, if you are a Christian, and you believe Christianity was the basis for your actions, did you do so many cruel things, including killing children?' 'Because they were all sinners.' Ungern was given little chance to expound upon his odder beliefs, apart from some brief, incredulous questioning as to whether he really believed that communism had been founded three thousand years ago by the Jews in Babylon. All of Ungern's horrors, Iaroslavskii pronounced, 'were done in the name of God and religion!' Ungern also gave his unrepentantly reactionary views on the stupidity and laziness of the working classes, and the need to stomp down hard on them, allowing Iaroslavskii to conclude that the sentence 'should be a verdict against all noblemen who try to lift a hand against the authority of workers and peasants!' The judgment 'would be a judgement on an entire social class [. . .] which cannot give up its power and wants to keep it for ever, even if were to mean the extermination of half of humanity!'

Ungern's defender, Bogoliubov, a former tsarist barrister, seems to have made at least a token effort to mount a defence for his obviously doomed client. He argued, reasonably enough, that there was no evidence that Ungern had actually co-operated with the Japanese, and that his psychological disorder meant that he had not been responsible for his actions as such. Rather than being executed, he should be put in solitary confinement, where he would have time to reflect upon his crimes. Ungern was in no mood to co-operate. Asked by Bogoliubov if a history of mental illness ran in his family, he bluntly lied, 'No.'

The final verdict was unsurprising. He was guilty on all charges, and the only possible punishment was execution. The court accepted that Ungern was mentally ill, but saw it as no excuse. Oparin's final judgment stated that, 'for such a one as Ungern, execution, an instant death, will be the most easy end of its tortures. It will be similar to the compassion we show to a sick animal in finishing it off. In this respect, Baron Ungern will accept our mercy with pleasure.' Ungern received the news stoically; he can have expected nothing else. Finally, Oparin turned to the man he had just sentenced to death:

'Citizen Ungern, you may have the last word.'

'I have nothing to say.'

Sentence was passed at a quarter past five, and the execution was carried out the same evening. It was a cleaner death than most of those Ungern had overseen himself; just him and the firing squad. He faced them with stoic courage. Before the shooting he posed for two final photographs with his executioners. In one, he stands straight and tall, as though he were on parade. In the other, his hands seem to be folded together in prayer. When he learnt of his death, the Bogd Khan ordered prayers for his soul to be read throughout Mongolia. They were undoubtedly needed.

Various legends arose around his last moments, spread among the Whites as they brooded in exile. Pieces of his Cross of St George were supposed to have splintered as the bullets hit, striking his executioners. 'When told he could buy freedom by singing the first verse of the "International", he asked his judge first to sing the Russian National Anthem!'[20] He was so fearsome that he had been executed in secret, shot in the back of the head by the local Cheka commander. Or he had escaped death altogether, breaking out of prison and vanishing into the forests to continue his war against Bolshevik evil.

Even in death, Ungern disappeared into myth.

Epilogue

In the Zanabazar Art Museum in Ulaanbaatar, named after the first Bogd Gegen, there is a remarkable picture. Drawn in the simple, colourful style of Mongolian popular art, it seems at first to be a hell scroll like those in the temples. Monasteries and monks perish in flame. Men kneel for execution. Women throw themselves in rivers, or have babies torn from their arms. Lamas are decapitated. Horsemen drag victims by their hair. This is no fantasy, but a depiction of Mongolian life in the late twenties and early thirties. It is a kind of parody of two famous paintings showing pre-revolutionary life, grand canvases full of everyday Mongolian vignettes, trading, bartering, lovemaking, laughing. In this picture, though, everything good and human about ordinary life has been replaced with nightmare.

Nearby, in an undistinguished building just off Suhbaatar Square, there is a collection of skulls on a table. Each skull has a single bullet hole in the crown. They were dug up after the collapse of communism; there are thousands upon thousands of others scattered in graves around the country. Their new home is the Memorial Museum for the Victims of Political Repression. It has six rooms, in which it makes a heroic attempt to commemorate somewhere between one and two hundred thousand victims. The Bogd Khan's court had been thoroughly self-serving when they spoke of the revolutionaries as a poison, a plague, the enemies of religion, destroyers of the faith. In the event, they were also right. Organised Buddhism was almost completely eradicated in Mongolia, but this was only part of a series of terrible purges directed from Moscow. For all the chaos and horror he had brought, the Soviets, operating on a scale he could never manage, made Ungern look like an amateur piker when it came to mass murder.

From a Mongolian point of view, Soviet rule was at first not so bad. Certainly it was not an auspicious sign when the Soviet Union ripped away a chunk of western Mongolia – the same part claimed by the tsarist regime in 1911 – and declared it a new, 'independent' republic, Tanna Tuva. Tuva's only notable achievement was the production of extremely beautiful stamps during the 1930s, and it was subsequently absorbed outright into the Soviet Union. To the Mongols it was all too reminiscent of the chipping away at Mongolian territory by the Chinese. Although the country was nominally governed by the Mongolian People's Revolutionary Party, everyone knew who held the ultimate authority. However, until the mid-1920s, the actual Russian population in the country remained relatively small. Only a few hundred Russian soldiers and officers were sent to train the new Mongolian army, and life continued much as it had in the past. There was little persecution at first, either of political or religious figures. Western travellers could still witness prayers and dances, the gods were still appeased, and new novices even joined the ranks of the monasteries, despite official discouragement. One of the first leaders declared, after Lenin's death, that there had been 'two great geniuses on earth – Buddha and Lenin'.[1] There was the normal spurt of idealism among the early communists, with attempts made to improve literacy, reduce the horrendous child mortality rate and introduce foreign culture to Mongolia.[2]

The Bogd Khan was allowed to live out his life in peace, still nominally the head of state. He, and many of the other nobles and officials who had worked with Ungern, initially suffered no persecution. Notable exceptions included Togtokh and Dambijantsan, both of whom refused to co-operate with the new regime and were killed in skirmishes in 1922. Their widespread popularity made them far too dangerous to be allowed to live. Dambijantsan's death, like Ungern's, rapidly acquired the characteristics of legend: shot by a Mongol betrayer who infiltrated his camp and then, according to the stories, ripped out his heart and displayed it to his followers.

After the Bogd died in 1924, the Party declared that he was not returning. Ironically, they did so by turning to Buddhist tradition and visions, stating that as there is a tradition that after the Eighth Incarnation he will not be reincarnated again, but will be reborn as the Great General Hanamand in the realm of Shambhala, there is no question of installing his Ninth Incarnation. Nevertheless, many of his unenlightened disciples, with their fleshy eyes and stupid understanding, are unwilling to grasp this, so it is decreed that the Central Committee to be newly elected shall take charge of reporting this and clearing it with the Dalai Lama.[3]

Later in the twenties, there was a systematic campaign to smear the Bogd's memory and turn people against Buddhism. However, until the beginning of 1930, the temples still controlled large amounts of land and livestock, although the number of lamas had decreased by a third. Party congresses had resolved that the nature of religion was 'reactionary' and the lamas 'parasitic', but anti-religious measures were cautious and restricted in scope. As Stalinist oppression got into full swing in Russia, Mongolia, Russia's only satellite state, began to imitate it. Unlike Russia, where persecution of Orthodoxy was secondary to purging the party itself, in Mongolia Buddhism was one of the main targets. 'The most aggressive methods' had to be applied in the 'struggle against religion'.[4]

First to suffer, though, was the traditionally nomadic Mongol way of life. Under the tsars, Russian nomadic groups had managed to evade the gaze of the state but there was no hiding from the Soviets. As among the nomadic tribes of Siberia, the Mongolians were forced off the steppe and into more 'progressive' collective farms, regulated and controlled. Rich herdsmen were condemned as *nodargan*, the Mongolian equivalent of the Russian *kulak*, and particularly persecuted. Collectivisation destroyed a third of Mongolian livestock, since the new collective farms were disastrously badly handled. Many nomads slaughtered their herds to eat the meat rather than handing them over to collective authority. Alongside the forced confiscation of private herds went the seizure of the property and livestock of the temples. Not everything was confiscated; young Mongolians were encouraged to treat the religion of their fathers with contempt, which no teenager ever needs great encouragement to do, and were formed, like the Red Guards into China and Tibet just over a generation later, into an 'Anti-Religious Brigade'. They smashed statues, vandalised frescoes and burnt paintings, banners and masks. The Mongolians fought back as best they could. The easiest form of resistance for a nomadic people was flight; over thirty thousand people crossed the border into China.

The most direct forms of resistance were directly inspired by prophecy. Belief in Shambhala, in some foreign saviour, had not lost its power since Ungern's time. Rumours and prophecies began to circulate that a great Buddhist army was coming, led by the Panchen Lama of Tibet, the second most important figure in Tibetan Buddhism. The then Panchen Lama, Thubten Choekyi Nyima, was working with the Chinese nationalists at the time, having fled Tibet after quarrelling with the Dalai Lama. The nationalists had given him a guard of soldiers, which sparked the original rumour. It was an obvious retelling of the Shambhala myth, fastened on to a convenient theological-political figure of the time. As before, political grievances and anger at foreign repression were transformed by prophecy into sacred war.

In early 1932 the rebellion erupted. The partisans fought for the Buddhist cause with a cruelty that would have made Ungern proud. It is hard to know how plausible accounts of the revolution are, since most were derived from torture-tainted interrogations, but revolution-aries confessed to ripping the hearts from captured enemy soldiers and carving holy swastikas into their chests. Certainly anyone associated with the regime was in danger, and the revolutionaries murdered both communist cadres and their families. Symbols of Russian power were burnt; co-operative farms in particular were a favourite target. Many of the fighters were Buriats. They had fled collectivisation in the Soviet Union en masse, only to find the situation no better among their Mongol kin. They had had enough of running, and were determined to fight. The rebels had almost no modern weaponry; many fought with bows, arrows and swords. There was no holy army coming to aid them. They were crushed by the Red one, with the help of Russian air power and a special detachment of the NKVD, the Soviet secret police. By October the rebellion was over. Although hundreds were shot, the rebels were treated with greater leniency than usual, since the Soviets blamed Japanese pan-Mongolian agitation for the revolt.

There would be no mercy in 1936, though. Then the Mongolian purges began, carried out with a thoroughgoing brutality by Marshal Choibalsan. He had accompanied Suhbaatar on his visit to Russia and was now one of Stalin's most toadying lackeys. He bent with the winds from Moscow; as the Soviet party was purged, so was the Mongolian. After the execution of the previous Mongolian prime minister, Genden, who had tried to stand up to Stalin, Choibalsan became the unquestioned leader of the People's Revolutionary Party in 1935. A fat, vulgar man, he switched from wearing traditional Mongolian dress to a Russian army uniform, lined with medals in traditional tinpot-dictatorial style.

Now the killing began in earnest. Any old grievance could be used as an excuse for political murder, including having worked with Ungern. Sundui, who had captured Ungern, was executed, despite his protests that he had intended to hand over the Baron. Thousands upon thousands were killed. The Buriats, particularly hated by the Russians for having fled from the collective paradise of the Soviet Union, were targeted with a special intensity, as were the monks, sixteen and a half thousand of whom were shot in one year, and tens of thousands more forcibly laicised. Bizarre conspiracies were invented; monks were accused of sending secret telegrams to Japanese conspirators, or of flying private aeroplanes to meet German fascists. By the end almost nothing remained of the country's religion. A report to Moscow in 1938 stated, 'The top ecclesiastics have been eliminated. By 29 July, out of 771 temples and monasteries, 615 have become ash heaps. Today only 26 are functioning. Out of a total of 85,000 lamas, only 17,338 remain. Those who were not arrested have decided to turn lay.'[5] Religion and learning had been closely linked, so Mongolia's system of education was also devastated. There was more in it for the Russians than mere ideological satisfaction; the Mongolian temples contained the accumulated wealth of centuries, and trucks loaded with gold and silver, produced from melted-down statues, rolled across the borders.

Similar happenings in Tibet following the Chinese invasion of 1950 shocked the world, but Mongolia never caught the attention of the West. It was too early in the century, and too far away, and a large proportion of the Western intelligentsia was still in thrall to utopian lies. Tibet did not truly become a cause, after all, until communism was cracked and failing all over the world, and the cult of Mao had almost entirely disappeared in the West. The massacres in Tibet had initially taken place as a result of an outside agency; in Mongolia, while the

Russians had been the instigators, young Mongolians themselves had enthusiastically participated in the destruction of their own culture, foreshadowing the later barbarities of student mobs in the Cultural Revolution in China and Tibet. Most crucially, though, many Tibetans escaped to form the large and vigorous exile community in India. In Mongolia, nobody made it out.

Part of this is simply victim chic; the invasion of Tibet and the persecution of Tibetan Buddhism naturally garners sympathy. It is the perfect cause: intriguingly exotic and appealingly distant, with a convenient and clearly defined villain in the Chinese and a highly visible and likeable spokesman in the Dalai Lama. Tibet has also has a long history as a land of mystery, concealed by mountains and sealed from Western intrusion, a reputation enhanced in the 1920s by books such as James Hilton's *Lost Horizon* and the subsequent popularisation of Tibet as a utopian Shangri-La. In the light of this reputation, the Chinese invasion of 1950 was akin to a violation of Eden. In the 1930s communist idealism still formed a sufficiently protective veneer for the very few stories that did emerge from Mongolia to be ignored or dismissed. As with the Chinese and the Whites, Mongolia had been devastated by those who claimed to be her protectors.

※◆≋◆※

Neither China nor Japan had given up on its ambition to rule Mongolia, despite the Russian occupation. The 1920s saw a series of skirmishes along the Mongolian border, mostly minor but including a fierce clash between the Chinese and Russian armies in November 1929 around Semenov's former base at Manchuli. White exiles, serving with the Chinese military, instigated many of them, and raiding parties of Russian exiles struck into Soviet territory, terrorising and looting villages, just as they had done under Ungern eight years before. When the Soviets struck in force, the White and Chinese forces collapsed in days, leaving the humiliated Chinese to sue for peace.

Although their intervention in the Russian Civil War had been a mistimed waste of men and resources, Japan's ambitions in the region were far from thwarted. Their influence and military strength in Manchuria only grew until, after openly invading in 1931, in 1932 they established a new state, Manchukuo, under the former boy-emperor of China, Pu

Yi. It was the fulfilment of one of Ungern's imperial dreams, the restoration of the Qing and the beginnings of a new nomad empire, even if the Great Manchu Empire was never more than a Japanese puppet.

Alongside Manchukuo, the Japanese carved the territory of Mengjiang, or the Mongol Border Territory, out of Inner Mongolia. It was officially a new country, but received even less international recognition than Manchukuo. The Japanese attempted to draw upon pan-Mongolian ideas to bolster support for Mengjiang, and to attract Mongol volunteers for the army, but the attempt was crippled by the fact that the population of the new state, after the settlements of the last sixty years, was now three-quarters Han Chinese. The nominal head of state was Demchugdongrub, a Chahar prince who claimed, like most Mongolian leaders, descent from Genghis. He was a political opportunist, siding first with the government in Peking, then with Zhang Zuolin and his son, then with the Japanese before ending up, like his much better-known counterpart Henry Pu Yi, the 'Last Emperor' of China, 'rehabilitated' by the communists and working in a museum. For the moment, though, he and his Japanese handlers envisaged his accession to the throne of a Greater Mongolia seized back from the Soviets, using the same motley combination of forces – Buriats, Inner Mongolians, Chinese, exiled White Russians – that had made up Ungern's army.

—◆—

After a particularly bloody skirmish around Lake Khasan, near Vladivostok, in 1938, with three thousand dead on the Japanese side and about half that for the Russians, the two armies clashed in open, large-scale battle in 1939. The ostensible cause of the fighting was whether the border lay on the Khalkin river, as the Japanese claimed, or just past the village of Nomonhan, ten miles east, as the Soviets argued. Strategically, it made only a marginal difference – in the event of an invasion, the Soviet placement would save the Russians from having to strike over the river – but there were much wider implications.

Among the Japanese high command, the impending battle was seen as an opportunity to test the strength of the Soviet Union. Opinion was still divided as to whether imperial expansion should eventually be directed north, into Siberia, or south, against the Dutch and British. For the

Soviets, it was a chance to stem Japanese expansion and secure their eastern borders. Neither side wanted an open war and so the battle remained, in theory, a 'border conflict'. To the sixteen thousand men who died, it made little difference. Fighting started when Mongolian cavalry wandered across the border to graze their horses, followed by a series of small conflicts until both sides began to build up their armies properly. The Soviets were commanded by an up-and-coming young lieutenant-general, Georgy Zhukov, soon to be one of the greatest commanders of the Second World War.

After months of stalemate the Japanese pushed forward in July, throwing a pontoon bridge across the river and taking the Baintsagan Heights, a strategic hill position on the other side of the river. Zhukov responded with a three-pronged tank attack, striking the Japanese from all sides. The encircled Japanese had neither experience of fighting armour nor the equipment to do so, and resorted to desperate massed attacks, hurling satchel charges against the oncoming tanks. The Soviets suffered more casualties, but they had more men, and soon the Japanese had lost both the Baintsagan Heights and their one bridge across the river. The battle was a long way from both sides' main bases, and supplies became crucial. Here the difference between the military-industrial might of the Soviets and the essentially nineteenth-century logistics of the Japanese became clear, as the Russians used a fleet of sixteen hundred trucks to keep their men in food and ammunition while the Japanese remained dependent on mules and foot porters. Typhus and dysentery swept the Japanese army as a result of tainted water and lack of food, leaving many men incapacitated.

By August, Zhukov was following up his initial success with a massed assault across the river. Using the tactics that he would perfect against the Germans, he co-ordinated air strikes, artillery bombardment and tank assaults. Foreshadowing the American tactics that would be developed against the Japanese later in the war, Soviet flame-thrower tanks burnt out Japanese strongpoints, while two hundred bombers wreaked havoc from high in the sky, above the range of the Japanese fighters. A hundred thousand Russians and Mongolians decisively crushed the sixty thousand Japanese, forty-five thousand of whom died, many committing suicide when surrounded. One of the battalion commanders sacrificed himself in a single-handed charge against a tank, while another took his own life in a more traditional fashion, disembowelling himself as the Soviets moved on his position. A further three thousand were taken prisoner, of whom only two hundred ever returned to Japan; the others either committed suicide or settled in the Soviet Union or Mongolia, fearful and shamed.[6]

Tokyo's ambitions towards Mongolia and Siberia were in ruins, and the Japanese high command acquired a new respect for the power of the Red Army – leading them to turn away from plans to strike the Soviet Union in conjunction with Germany, and to look to a fresh enemy instead, the United States. While they never entirely gave up hope of occupying Soviet territory – they ran training schools for the children of exiled Whites in China at the height of the war, looking to train them as translators and guides for the planned invasion of the Soviet Union – the wartime truce between the two countries held. The Mongolians went on to provide both men and materials for the Soviets during the war.[7] Their most crucial role, though, was as a jumping-off point for the stunning Soviet invasion of Manchuria in 1945, just after Hiroshima, when the whole of the territory was conquered in barely two weeks.

Many of Ungern's former comrades ended up working for the Japanese. This was one of the most viable options for those who, facing a bleak exile from their homeland, wished to remain in Asia. Others eked out an existence in China, or migrated overseas to start new lives. Pershin fled to China, where he scraped a living as a translator and tutor, and died in poverty in 1936. Alioshin settled in London and published his memoirs during the Second World War. Makeev served as a bodyguard in Shanghai, while Ribo emigrated to the US, continued to work as a doctor and lived until the 1970s. Sipailov fled to China, where he was arrested for the murder of the young Dane, Olufsen. Somehow he engineered his release, and was last heard of in 1932 when, greedy as ever, he led sixteen other exiled Russians in a secret expedition from Manchuria into Mongolia to search for Ungern's gold. Rousted by an NKVD officer and his Mongolian cavalry, he was arrested and handed over to the Japanese.

Of all Ungern's old comrades, it was the flamboyant Ataman Semenov who had the most dramatic post-war career. After fleeing

Chita with the Japanese, he wandered around Korea and Japan for a few months before ending up in Shanghai. After a Bolshevik assassination attempt, he decided China was too dangerous and headed for the United States, intending to make his way to France. In the US he decided to apply for political asylum and found himself caught up in a legal imbroglio concerning his conduct in Siberia. The opposition to his application was led by General W. S. Graves, the former head of the American forces, who loathed him. Numerous witnesses testified to the atrocities committed by Semenov's forces. Accused of presiding over robbery, banditry, bigamy, murder, torture, rape and pillage, he ended up in jail in New York. After his bail was raised by White organisations he was almost lynched by a crowd of three thousand Russians, mostly Jews who blamed him for White anti-Semitism. Eventually he fled the country and returned to Japan, and from there to Manchuria.

In Manchuria he became the godfather of the more reactionary Whites, working with Japanese intelligence and Chinese and Russian gangsters, and overseeing the Cossack overseas union. By the outbreak of the Second World War he was working for the Japanese directly, living in 'a ninety-thousand yen villa which contains offices, residential quarters, an air raid shelter, and a small arsenal, including stores of ammunition. The residence is carefully guarded by Japanese secret agents.'[8] He grew very fat in the face, and extremely ugly. To his credit, he opposed the growing Russian Fascist Union, calling instead, as he always had, for the restoration of a 'semi-democratic monarchy'. However, when the captured Soviet general Andrei Vlasov formed his Russian Liberation Army, a group of former Russian POWs who fought (reluctantly) for the Nazis, Semenov was quick to declare his friendship. The enemy of the Bolsheviks was still his ally, however unpleasant the company kept.

In 1945, as the Red Army ripped through Manchuria, Semenov planned to flee to China, but the speed of the Soviet advance caught him unprepared. According to White legend, he offered a formal dinner to his captors at his villa, at the end of which the Soviet commander rose, toasted their host, and then placed him under arrest. He was taken back to Russian soil for the first time in twenty-two years and, in a highly publicised trial, sentenced to death as an 'enemy of the Soviet people' and 'active accomplice of the Japanese aggressors'. He was hanged on 30 August, 1946. In the thorough Stalinist manner, his son had already been murdered, and his daughters sent to the Gulag. Like Ungern, the Soviets left no tail.

Ossendowski's career was also dramatic. After escaping to Japan he moved to America and published his memoir of his escape from the Bolsheviks and his time with Ungern, *Beasts, Men, and Gods*. A massive bestseller, the proceeds set him up for life, but he continued to travel and write, maintaining a consistently anti-Soviet line. He returned to his native Poland in 1923 and, when the Nazis invaded, served heroically, despite his age, in the Polish underground. He died of natural causes in January 1945. It was rumoured that just before the end he was visited by a great-nephew of Ungern's who was serving in the Wehrmacht. His death was well timed – he was already on an NKVD list as an enemy of the people.

Ungern's legacy emerged in odd ways in the West. In the murky world of post-war rightist occultism he was remembered as a precursor figure of the weirder fringes of Nazism. They were right, but only indirectly. Ungern's mixture of esoteric beliefs and anti-Semitism shared some common roots with the Thule Society and other minor occult groups involved in the early days of the Nazi Party, and the eccentric obsessions of Himmler and others sprang from the same sources. His particular brand of eliminationist anti-Semitism, transferred to Germany by his former White comrades, and especially by the Baltic Germans, was also a major influence on the German right in the 1920s. As ever with Ungern, he foreshadowed a worse madness. He was even the subject of a trashy novel published in Germany in 1938, *I Order! The Struggle and Tragedy of Baron Ungern-Sternberg*,[9] which portrayed him as a heroic precursor of the Führer, struggling against Judaism, communism and betrayal within his own ranks. Meanwhile, he remains, along with Ossendowski's fantasies of hidden underground realms, a minor part of the mythology of the modern extreme right, still given to occult conspiracies.

Ungern did better in literature, where the bizarre nature of his legend attracted Russian and Western writers alike. He turns up in everything from serious philosophical novels to comic books. (My own favourite

Ungern cameo is in *Corto Maltese in Siberia*, a graphic novel by the Italian writer Hugo Pratt.) The surrealist modern Russian writer Victor Pelevin includes him in several books, most notably in *Buddha's Little Finger,* which contains a brilliant, haunting scene in which Ungern and his companions are gathered around a campfire, seemingly together but separated by aeons of space-time. He crops up in other places; the Spanish thriller writer Arturo Pérez-Reverte squeezes a reference to him into several of his books, and an entire (and rather mediocre) computer game, *Iron Storm*, featured an Ungern avatar as the villain.

Many of these depictions draw on the most popular and enduring book about Ungern, Ossendowski's *Beasts, Men, and Gods.* Ossendowski wrote one of Ungern's better epitaphs, towards the end of that book:

> In the Mongol *yurtas* and at the fires of Buriat, Mongol, Djungar, Kirkhiz, Kalmuck and Tibetan shepherds still speak the legend born of this son of crusaders and privateers:
>
> From the north a white warrior came and called on the Mongols to break their chains of slavery, which fell upon our freed soil. This white warrior was the incarnated Jenghiz Khan and he predicted the coming of the greatest of all Mongols who will spread the fair faith of Buddha and the glory and the power of the offspring of Jenghiz, Ugadai and Kublai Khan. So it shall be![10]

Quite how Ossendowski could have known this, given that he left Mongolia before Ungern's death, he never revealed. New York was clearly very well connected to the Mongolian campfire grapevine. It was typical hyperbolic Ossendowski – but he had tapped into something real nevertheless. As the revolt showed in the 1930s, the hope of a foreign messiah remained vibrant for a decade or more after Ungern's death. There were rumours of the return of the Bogd Khan, the Panchen Lama and other messianic figures recorded as recently as the early 1960s, although they never reached the same pitch of apocalyptic intensity.

And in a typically perverse way, Ungern did, indeed, prove to be Mongolia's saviour. Even after being driven out, the Chinese never gave up their ambitions towards Mongolia. The Republic of China, on Taiwan, despite nominally recognising Mongolia in 1946, soon changed its tune and refused to acknowledge Mongolia as a separate country until 2002, drawing it as part of China on official maps. They maintained the post of provincial governor of Mongolia for eighty years after the territory was lost, which must have been one of the great sinecures of all time. Taiwan still nominally claims both Mongolia and the formerly Soviet territory of Tuva, and has not yet established any diplomatic relations with the country. The post-war communist government in Beijing, meanwhile, reluctantly acquiesced in their Soviet patrons' takeover of Mongolia, although Mao's private rhetoric inevitably included Mongolia in his listing of Chinese territory,[11] and the Sino-Soviet split ended all diplomatic relations between the two nations, which were not renewed until 1997. Tellingly, the Chinese state firewall continues to block many internet sites related to Mongolian culture and identity, even those related chiefly to Mongols in Russia.[12]

Without Ungern, the Chinese would have remained in Mongolia, the Soviets would never have taken over the country, and it would have remained a part of Chinese territory. From the point of view of anybody in Mongolia in the 1930s, Chinese oppression, however petty and brutal, would have been infinitely superior to the Soviet version. In the long run, though, Mongolia would have gone through exactly the same collectivisation, cultural destruction and mass homicide, only twenty years delayed. Both Inner Mongolia and Tibet, respectively inherited and invaded by the Chinese communists, suffered terribly in the 1950s. In Inner Mongolia, Mao first promised independence and then betrayed and brutally murdered Mongol leaders, including fighters against the Japanese, when he came to power. And finally, with the fall of the USSR, Mongolia experienced a new freedom. It kept its own culture and its own religion, however damaged by seventy years of Russian occupation. The People's Republic would have flooded Mongolia with Han settlers, as happened in the other non-Chinese provinces of the new communist empire, leaving the Mongolians a minority in their own lands, culturally and economically marginalised.[13]

As it was, after the collapse of communism, Mongolian traditions returned. It was a formidable task. An entire world of belief had been wiped out in a single generation, leaving only oral tradition and a few determined individuals to help rebuild it. The old world was just about within living memory, but reconstructing it, lacking the religious ceremonies, buildings and lineages of the pre-communist era, was never going to be easy. Scraps survived – boxes of artefacts, books of herbal medicine – but their uses had been lost.

Although everything was stripped away from them, right down to their own Mongolian names, the people still strive to remember their past. Family names traditionally had Buddhist connotations, so under communism they were banned, and only a personal name permitted. By the 1990s most families had forgotten their original names, so chose new ones from a list of possible Buddhist alternatives, or else named themselves after their professions; Mongolia's only astronaut, for example, rejoices in the name of Kosmos.

Yet even under the worst of communist oppression, Mongolian religion survived. The oldest Mongolian I met was a 102-year-old woman, lost in a blissful religious senility, who spent her days turning a prayer wheel. She had kept the faith throughout the years of persecution; she, and many others, had hidden holy books, preserved statues in caves in the hills, and maintained in secret the worship of the gods. Veneration of popular figures of the Bogd Khan era survived, including of the Bogd himself, despite all the vilification heaped on him by communist propaganda. Worship continued in less obvious ways. For instance, even in the 1970s people in Ulaanbaatar 'remembered a certain freshwater spring where the Bogd's wife, the Ekh Dagina, used to go to worship. A visit to this spring, which officially could be described as "medicinal", could also be privately interpreted as a commemoration of the Eke Dagini.'[14] The vagaries and sins of the real person could be forgotten this way, as they became increasingly depersonalised, remembered instead as incarnations of gods or as local spirits.

I wondered whether the same process had transformed folk memory of Ungern. Personally, I thought there was little chance that any trace of such worship had survived, until I attended a dinner at a friend's home in Ulaanbaatar. My friend was a product of bizarre regional politics himself, an ethnic Tibetan who had been brought to Japan as a teenager in the 1950s as part of a programme set up by former members of the Japanese government guilty about their involvement with Tibet during the war, and wanting to do something for the country. Now he worked to strengthen Japanese–Mongolian relations, and was in the country buttering up various Mongolian university deans. I was sitting next to his translator, a charming multilingual Mongolian woman in her thirties, chatting in slightly broken English and occasionally very broken Russian. I mentioned that I was working on a book about Baron Ungern, and she said words I almost didn't believe at first. 'Oh, Baron Ungern? In my family, he is a god.'

I asked her for details. Her grandfather had been a prominent lama at the time of the Bogd Khan government, and he had spent time with Ungern – enough to ensure he was persecuted in the 1930s, and eventually shot. Before he died, however, he had given her grandmother a box containing pieces of Ungern's clothing and hair, which was supposed to have magical powers. Buried in a piece of barren land near Karakorum, where Ungern had regrouped his forces after his first defeat by the Soviets, it had caused the land to spring up green and fertile, good for grazing. The family had worshipped Ungern himself as a personal protector, naming him in prayers even when she was a child in the 1970s.

In at least one family, then, Ungern was more than just a man. Two generations had preserved his memory; there must have been others, scraps of tradition, that remembered him in the same way. It would have pleased him to be known as a protector of Buddhism, deified among those bloody-handed gods.

Notes

INTRODUCTION

1 Technically, the Whites – never a formal movement – were only one
   faction among many opposed to the Bolsheviks, and tended to represent
   the most reactionary of their opponents, but the term was often used to
   cover all anti-Bolshevik opposition.
2 Transliteration from Mongolian and Tibetan is not standardised, and
   spellings, especially of pre-modern figures, are extremely varied; when a
   name, such as Genghis, has a familiar Western form, I have therefore
   preferred to use that.
3 The Bolshevik revolutionary Nikolai Bukharin applied a similar
   description to Stalin in the 1930s, describing him as 'Genghis Khan
   with the telephone'.
4 The Lama Temple, damaged in the Cultural Revolution, stripped of
   monks and now with bright electric lights, is a very different experience
   nowadays. It feels like a tamed, Sinified, acceptable version of Lamaism;
   noticeably, the more gory or sexually explicit statues are now covered up.
5 Vladimir Pozner, *Bloody Baron: The Story of Ungern-Sternberg*, trans.
   Warre Bradley Wells (London, 1938), p. 7.
6 My first Chinese girlfriend's family exemplified this. Her grandmother
   had a mincing and useless walk thanks to her feet being bound as a child,
   and her mother was four inches shorter than she should have been,
   thanks to malnutrition suffered as a child during the famines caused by
   Mao's Great Leap Forward.

ONE – A SON OF CRUSADERS AND PRIVATEERS

1 Ferdinand Ossendowski, *Beasts, Men, and Gods* (New York, 1922),
   p. 248.

2 The long-term success of which is dubious, given that the Estonians took the first opportunity to break away from Russia after the 1917 revolution. After being snapped up by Stalin again in 1940 (in an agreement concluded in, literally, about five minutes just before lunch) most of the population welcomed the 'liberators' of the Wehrmacht with much enthusiasm. The Germans were the happiest; they had been evacuated by Hitler just before the Soviet takeover and were restored as soon as the Wehrmacht rolled in again. Even the Baltic peasantry initially preferred the Nazis to the Soviets, not least because the Germans gave them an opportunity to express bloodily their long-standing anti-Semitism. The Nazis handled the situation with their typical lack of grace, looking to banish the Slavic population and 'turn the Baltic into a German lake'. The Germans were driven out again in 1945, part of the great forced exodus from the newly Russian territories.

3 Isaiah Berlin, *Against the Current* (London, 1980), p. 258.

4 *Sovetskaya Sibir* (Novonikolaevsk), no. 200 (560), 17 September, 1921.

5 A simple practical experiment to demonstrate this: go to a typical Wiccan coven and see how long it is before somebody tells you how they were initiated into the Craft by their grandmother, who was part of an ancient line of witches.

6 Eesti Ajalooarhiiv [Estonian National Archives], f. 860, n. 1, s. 1672, leht [list], 1.

7 Rossiiskii Gosudarstvennyi Arkhiv Voenno-Morskogo Flota [State Archive of the Russian Navy] (RGAVMF), f. 432, op. 1, d. 2162, 11.

8 The combination of word elements to express compound ideas.

9 Pozner, *Bloody Baron*, p. 58.

10 RGAVMF, f. 432, op. 5, d. 8586, p. 1.

11 RGAVMF, f. 432, op. 1, d. 2162.

TWO – THE ENDS OF THE WORLD

1 Pozner, *Bloody Baron*, p. 43.

2 This was only slightly higher than the percentage of manor houses destroyed across Russia – about 15 per cent. What was unusual in Estonia was how far the destruction extended into towns and cities, where German-owned businesses were singled out by rioters.

3 Ossendowski, *Beasts, Men, and Gods*, p. 245.

4 Ossendowski, *Beasts, Men, and Gods*, p. 241.

5 Gosudarstvennyi arkhiv Rossiiskoi Federatsii [State Archive of the Russian Federation] (GARF), f. 5431, op. 1, d. 40, 11. 1–3 (b).

6 Though there's still plenty of room for right-wing esotericism, as Nicholas Goodrick-Clarke demonstrates in his examination of post-war Nazi occultism, *Black Sun* (New York, 2003). Even the relatively cuddly world of English paganism occasionally has some nasty racist overtones, with its emphasis on 'native' religion.

7 George Orwell, 'W. B. Yeats' (first published in *Horizon*, London, 1943).

8 Cited in Maria Carlson, *No Religion But Truth* (Princeton, 1993), p. 4.

9 This interest in the occult has revived in post-Soviet Russia. Even popular booksellers – the Russian equivalents of W. H. Smith – commonly carry a substantial 'esoteric' selection.

10 Hermann Keyserling, *Reise durch die Zeit* [*A Journey through Time*], vol. II (Vaduz, 1948), p. 53, n. 1.

11 Helena Blavatsky, *The Secret Doctrine* (Pasadena, 1988), vol. II, pp. 106, 470.

12 Available in *The World War I Document Archive: The Willy–Nicky Letters*, at http://www.lib.byu.edu/~rdh/wwi/, accessed 6 March 2007, originally published New York, 1920.

13 John Keegan, *A History of Warfare* (New York, 1993).

14 Rossiiskii gosudarstvennyi voennyi arkhiv [Russian State Military Archive] (RGVA), f. 39454, op. 1, d. 9, 1. 53 (b).

15 Especially important, given that conscription was one of the dreads of the ordinary Russian peasant. The chances of ever making it back to home and family were so low that funerals were held when the draftee left the village.

16 Willard Sunderland, 'Baron Ungern, Toxic Cosmopolitan', *Ab Imperio*, Spring 2006.

17 Think of two recent Hollywood epics, for instance, *The Last Samurai* and *The Return of the King*, both of which featured spectacular cavalry charges against hopeless odds. The Rohirrim in *Return*, Anglo-Saxons of the steppe, even wore the white horsetails of Mongols and Huns.

18 Ossendowski, *Beasts, Men, and Gods*, pp. 240, 245.

19 Ossendowski, *Beasts, Men, and Gods*, p. 246.

20 Dmitri Alioshin, *Asian Odyssey* (London, 1941).

21 N. Khisight, 'Baron Ungern's Mongolian Connection', *Journal of the Institute of Social Sciences, National University of Mongolia*, no. 188 (14), 2002.

THREE – SUSPENDED BETWEEN HEAVEN AND HELL

1 Pozner, *Bloody Baron*, p. 82.

2 A. V. Burdukov, *V staroi i novoi Mongolii: vospominaniia, pis'ma* [*Old and New Mongolia: Memoirs, Letters*] (Moscow, 1969), pp. 100–102.

3 'Living Buddha' is a general term for any reincarnating lama – *trulku* in Tibetan – of which there were some 250 in Mongolia in 1911. Western travellers often used it simply to refer to the most senior of them. Throughout I refer to him as the 'Bogd Khan', or 'Holy King', his most commonly used title in Mongolia, although technically the epithet applied only during the period during which he held secular, as well as religious, power.

4 Within Mongolia there are at least fifteen different Mongol groups, of which the Khalkha make up around 85 per cent of the population. 'Mongolian' in this volume usually means Khalkha and other small Mongol groups within the borders of Mongolia, while I use 'Mongol' with respect to the wider ethnic and cultural group.

5 At least, if the behaviour of their modern counterparts is anything to go by. Most temples, particularly in China, now cover up the more luridly sexual scenes, such as the *yab-yum*, or 'divine coupling'.

6 Alcoholism is even more common in modern Mongolia than it was a century ago, with rates among men reaching 50 per cent or higher. Foreign businesses generally employ Chinese immigrant workers, because too many of the Mongolians will vanish after the first month to drink their pay.

7 Kam's is one of those head-swapping stories that so often crop up in Hindu and Buddhist mythology. In this case Erlik, a pious monk, was meditating in a cave, an hour away from enlightenment, when two bandits entered to behead a stolen ox. Not men to miss an opportunity, they beheaded Erlik too. His body promptly grabbed the ox-head, put it on and slaughtered the bandits.

8 Rudolf Strasser, *The Mongolian Horde* (New York, 1930), p. 174.

9 The reverse process is taking place today as the Chinese attempt to legitimise their claims to Inner and Outer Mongolia by appropriating the image of Genghis Khan. At a convivial dinner in Inner Mongolia in 2003 I asked a couple of the diners about a portrait of Genghis and was told, 'Genghis Khan! Yes, he is a great Chinese hero!' There was nodding and general approval round the table, and some toasting of Genghis's spirit. We were in Inner Mongolia, but every one of the diners save me were Han Chinese, for all their downing of Mongolian spirits and singing of sentimental songs about the steppe, bows and the deep love between a man and his horse. One of them, a local Communist Party boss, grasped my arm sincerely. 'Genghis was *born* in Mongolia,' he said, 'but he was Chinese. He loved China, like we love China.' Genghis loved the Chinese so much that he killed around ten million of them, and seriously considered burning every city in northern China to the ground to create a vast grassland for his horses.

10 Peter Perdue, *China Marches West* (London, 2005), pp. 283, 185.

11 The idea of Mongolian cruelty crops up frequently elsewhere; the mute Mongolian human-skinner in Haruki Murakami's novel *The Wind-Up Bird Chronicle* (New York, 1997), for instance, or Lenin's cold cruelty being attributed to his 'Mongol blood' – he was a quarter Kalmyk.

12 A remarkable number of Mongols seem to have ended up on the Western Front, though surely many of them were other central Asians, misidentified. Eric Newby, imprisoned in Italy, remarked on his guards that 'they were Mongols, apostates from the Russian Army, dressed in German uniform, hideously cruel descendants of Genghis Khan's wild horsemen who, in Italy, had already established a similar reputation to that enjoyed by the Goums, the Moroccans in the Free French army' (*A Traveller's Life*, London, 1982, p. 130). Central Asian and Mongolian soldiers were also widely blamed by other Russian soldiers for the rapes committed by the Red Army in 1945, in supposed contrast to the heroic – and ethnically Russian – front-line soldiers.

13 Glenn Gray, *The Warriors: Reflections on Men at War* (Lincoln, NE, 1959), p. 98.

14 C. W. Campbell, *Travels in Mongolia* (London, 1902), p. 9.

15 Hideo Tasuki, *A Japanese Agent in Tibet* (London, 1990).

16 University Bibliotheca, Oslo, Ethnographical Museum, manuscript 38416, quoted in Alice Sárközi, *Political Prophecies in Mongolia in the 17th–20th Centuries* (Wiesbaden, 1992), p. 120.

17 Ossendowski, *Beasts, Men, and Gods*, p. 293.

18 Caroline Humphrey, 'Remembering an "Enemy"', in Rubie S. Watson (ed.), *Memory, History and Opposition Under State Socialism* (Santa Fe, 1994), p. 31.

19 Ossendowski, *Beasts, Men, and Gods*, p. 291.

20 Ladislaus Forbath and Joseph Geleta, *The New Mongolia* (London, 1936), p. 261.

21 Karl Gustav Vrangel, *The Memoirs of Count Vrangel: The Last Commander-in-Chief of the Russian National Army,* trans. Sophie Goulston (London, 1929), p. 7.

22 Quoted in Baabar, *History of Mongolia* (Ulaanbaatar, 1999), p. 144, originally from Aleksei Kuropatkin, *What's to be Done with Mongolia and Manchuria* (1913).

23 Quoted in Perdue, *China Marches West,* p. 493.

24 Ripping out the heart of an enemy, however, is a scene occasionally depicted in Mongolian Buddhist art and literature, and there were numerous reports of it from foreign travellers, but always second-hand. It certainly became one of the standard Russian tropes of writing about the Mongols, but may have been actually performed on occasion.

25 GARF, f. 9427, op. 1, d. 392, p. 48.

26 Almost all shape-shifters in primal mythologies turn into either bears or snakes, which suggests all manner of wonderful but incredibly speculative connections; the bear cult so strikingly preserved in the Swiss caves, the temptation in Eden, the immortal snakes in Babylonian mythology, the bear-heraldry of King Arthur (whose name in itself means 'bear'), dragons, etc. It crops up in odd places; there is a strong suggestion in *Beowulf* that the hero can transform himself into the 'bee-wolf'; the bear – picked up by Tolkien and used for Beorn in *The Hobbit*. I suspect that bears are so striking because they seem so human, and snakes because they are so alien.

27 Something which neither community likes to discuss nowadays, but which is strikingly preserved in images found in many northern Indian temples of an elephant, symbolising Hinduism, crushing a deer, symbolising Buddhism, beneath its foot. Conversely, Mongolian and Tibetan gods are sometimes depicted crushing an elephant.

28 Quoted from the temple's notice to visitors.

29 Which makes it strange that Roerich doesn't mention Ungern at any point in his books. Perhaps he found the similarity between Ungern's mystical beliefs and his own disturbing, given that he was a leftist pacifist.

30 Sárközi, *Political Prophecies*, p. 131.

FOUR – THINGS FALL APART

1 Quoted from http://www.firstworldwar.com/source/tannenberg_hindenburg.htm.

2 S. L. Kuzmin (comp.), *Baron Ungern v dokumentakh i memuarakh* [*Baron Ungern in Documents and Memoirs*] (Moscow, 2004), p. 10.

3 Kuzmin, *Baron Ungern*, p. 293.

4 Bernhard von der Marwitz, *Stirb und Werde* [*Dying and Becoming*] (Breslau, 1931), p. 82.

5 Kuzmin, *Baron Ungern*, p. 10.

6 If there had been no revolution, presumably this violent generation would have been bled off into the frontiers of empire, as were so many of the young French and British men traumatised by war.

7 Mayne Reid was a Irish-American cavalry officer and writer of American adventure stories, largely forgotten in the West but persistently popular in Russia. Exactly what 'a Mayne Reid' hero denotes is well summarised by Jess Nevins in the *Encyclopaedia of Fantastic Victoriana* (New York, 2005): 'gallant, skillful at arms, far more at ease around men than around women, has lots of time for trappers and soldiers but little for the

upper classes or intellectuals, and is much happier hunting and killing than thinking'.

8 Vrangel, *Memoirs of Count Vrangel*, p. 4.

9 Kuzmin, *Baron Ungern*, p. 64. Literally, Ungern shouted, 'Whose muzzle do I have to beat?'

10 Colonel John Ward, *With the Die-Hards in Siberia* (London, 1920), p. 238.

11 Vrangel, *Memoirs of Count Vrangel*, p. 6.

12 GARF, f. 9427, op. 1, d. 392.

13 Vejas Gabriel Liulevicius, *War Land on the Eastern Front* (Cambridge, 2000), p. 238.

14 *Sovetskaya Sibir*, no. 200 (560), 17 September, 1921, s. 4.

15 Confusingly known as the October Revolution since it took place on 25 October under the old Julian calendar, but in November according to the modern Gregorian version adopted after the revolution.

16 Peter Fleming, *One's Company* (London, 1931), p. 21.

FIVE – CARRION COUNTRY

1 V. A. Kislitsin, *V ogne grazhdanskoi voiny* [*In the Fire of the Civil War*] (Harbin, 1936), p. 101.

2 Alioshin, *Asian Odyssey*, p. 17.

3 General Vrangel, Ungern's old commander, also acquired this sobriquet in the Crimea, but it was more common to refer to him by his full name rather than just his title. One of the most popular Red Army songs began mockingly: 'White Army, Black Baron, prepare for us a Tsarist throne . . .' Probably referring to Vrangel, it was sung about Ungern as well.

4 US Senate Committee on Education and Labor, *Deportation of Gregorie Semenoff: Hearings Relative to the Deporting of Undesirable Aliens* (Washington, DC, 1922), pp. 21–2.

5 Alioshin, *Asian Odyssey*, p. 14.

6 Kuzmin, *Baron Ungern*, p. 274.

7 Alioshin, *Asian Odyssey*, p. 14.

8 Kuzmin, *Baron Ungern*, pp. 72–3.

9 Special Delegation of the Far Eastern Republic, *Letters Captured from Baron Ungern in Mongolia* (Washington, DC, 1921), p. 4.

10 Norman Cohn, *Warrant for Genocide* (Harmondsworth, 1970).

11 Ossendowski, *Beasts, Men, and Gods*, pp. 313–14.

12 In the whole of the nineteenth century there was only one Jewish officer in the Russian army, Captain Herzl Yankl Tsam, and he was made a captain only after forty-one years' service.

13 GARF, f. 9427, op. 1, d. 392, p. 38.

14 *Sovetskaya Sibir*, no. 201 (561), 18 September, 1921, s. 4.

15 Kislitsin, *V ogne grazhdanskoi voiny*, p. 101.

16 Grigori Semenov, *O Sebe [About Myself]* (Harbin, 1938), p. 119.

17 Quoted in Leonid Ieuzefovich, *Samoderzhets pustyni: fenomen sud'by barona RF. Ungern-Shternberga [Autocrat of the Desert: The Phenomenon of Baron R. F. Ungern-Sternberg]* (Moscow, 1993).

18 Pozner, *Bloody Baron*, p. 39.

19 RGVA, f. 16, op. 1, d. 37, p. 298.

20 Kuzmin, *Baron Ungern*, p. 71.

21 *Deportation of Gregorie Semenoff*, pp. 100–101.

22 Kuzmin, *Baron Ungern*, p. 69.

23 Kuzmin, *Baron Ungern*, p. 70.

24 GARF, f. 9427, op. 1, d. 392, p. 60.

25 GARF, f. 9427, op. 1, d. 392, p. 59.

26 *Sovetskaya Sibir*, no. 202 (562), 20 September, 1921, s. 2.

27 GARF, f. 9427, op. 1, d. 392, p. 59.

28 Quoted in Daniel Field, *Rebels in the Name of the Tsar* (Boston, 1976), p. 2.

29 Jamie Bisher, *White Terror* (London, 2005), p. 185.

30 Pan-Asiatic ideas of the period in Japan lacked much of the aggressive and extreme right-wing tone of the movement in the 1930s and 40s. Instead, they often envisaged bringing liberal, anti-imperialist thought to the rest of Asia, envisaging a federation rather than an empire, albeit one in which the Japanese would be the clear leaders, treating other Asians in a paternalistic fashion.

31 Kislitsin, *V ogne grazhdanskoi voiny*, p. 102.

32 Ossendowski, *Beasts, Men, and Gods*, p. 246.

33 Kuzmin, *Baron Ungern*, p. 70. Immersed as I had become in Ungern's world while researching his life, this reference to Pankhurst came as a jarring reminder that alongside Ungern's Siberia of feudalism and constant war there existed another world, a relatively peaceful one in which the modern struggle for women's rights was taking place.

34 Konstantin Leontiev, the ultra-conservative Russian writer who influenced Ungern, was not unique among Russian writers and explorers in his liking for virile Asian men.

35 Pozner, *Bloody Baron*, p. 42.

36 Quoted in Bisher, *White Terror*, p. 128.

37 Alioshin, *Asian Odyssey*, pp. 18–19.

38 Quoted in Evgenii Belov, *Baron Ungern fon Shternberg: biografiia, ideologiia, voennye pokhody 1920–1921 [Baron Ungern von Sternberg:*

Biography, Ideology, Military Campaigns 1920–1921] (Moscow, 2003), p. 28.

39 Ossendowski, *Beasts, Men, and Gods*, pp. 233–4.

40 Alioshin, *Asian Odyssey*, p. 19.

41 RGVA, f. 16, op. 3, d. 222, p. 14.

42 Ossendowski, *Beasts, Men, and Gods*, p. 247.

43 GARF, f. 9427, op. 1, d. 392, p. 47.

44 The widespread notion that Ungern believed himself to be Genghis's direct reincarnation seems to have stemmed from a passage in Ossendowski, *Beasts, Men, and Gods*, where Ungern reportedly told the Mongolians that '[Genghis's] soul still lives and calls upon the Mongols to become anew a powerful people and reunite again into one great Mid-Asiatic State all the Asian kingdoms he had ruled' (p. 253). Even here, there is no direct claim to Genghis's soul, only his imperial inheritance.

45 Pozner, *Bloody Baron*, p. 43.

46 GARF, f. 9427, op. 1, d. 392, p. 56.

47 *Sovetskaya Sibir*, no. 200 (560), 17 September, 1921, s. 4.

SIX – RAGGED CRUSADE

1 Pozner, *Bloody Baron*, p. 40.

2 The formula, commonly used in Mongolia and explained to me by the president's nephew, was very exact. One Mongolian is worth two Japanese is worth four Koreans is worth eight Chinese. Notice that the Mongolians are just about the only people in Asia who *actually like* the Japanese – and even then they rank them as distinctively inferior to themselves. I wasn't told where the English fitted in.

3 'Big Xu' to Xu Shuzheng's 'Little Xu'. China has always been short on surnames. A much older statesman, but often confused with Little Xu in Western accounts.

4 Bisher, *White Terror*, p. 269.

5 If you come across a ruined monastery in Mongolia, it's just as likely to have been burnt by the Chinese in the 1600s as by the Russians in the 1930s.

6 Kuzmin, *Baron Ungern*, p. 90.

7 Kuzmin, *Baron Ungern*, p. 75.

8 Sárközi, *Political Prophecies*, p. 110.

9 Visiting friends in the countryside near Ulaanbaatar in 2004, I was told that the area was suffering from dangerous overcrowding; it was now possible, with a good eye, for a man to see his neighbour's camp.

10 Led by Sir Francis Younghusband, a famous British explorer who, although a far better man, shared some interests with Ungern, such as his concern for martial virtues and his deep, eclectic interest in Eastern mysticism.

11 Peter Fleming, *Bayonets to Lhasa* (London, 1962), p. 302.

12 Kuzmin, *Baron Ungern*, p. 206.

13 At the victory parade after the end of the Second World War, Stalin was due to ride a white horse in triumph, but it threw him on a practice run and Zhukov was given the honour instead.

14 Kuzmin, *Baron Ungern*, p. 82.

15 US National Archives and Records Administration (NARA), MID report no. 212 (RH165, file 2657-I-158/3), 30 March, 1921.

16 A. S. Makeev, *Bog voiny* [*God of War*] (Shanghai, 1934), p. 23.

17 Alioshin presumably means 'to heal' here. Horrible as this is, this type of punishment was not unique to Ungern. Cyclical flogging, where the flesh was allowed to heal and was then scourged again, was common in convict-era Australia, where sentences of five hundred or a thousand lashes were sometimes carried out over months at a time.

18 Alioshin, *Asian Odyssey*, p. 188.

19 Alioshin, *Asian Odyssey*, p. 223.

20 Kuzmin, *Baron Ungern*, p. 430.

21 Ossendowski, *Beasts, Men, and Gods*, p. 219.

22 Alioshin, *Asian Odyssey*, p. 168.

23 N. M. Ribo, 'The Story of Baron Ungern Told by His Staff Physician', Hoover Institution, Stanford University, CSUZXX697-A, p. 4.

24 Alioshin, *Asian Odyssey*, p. 222.

25 Ossendowski, *Beasts, Men, and Gods*, p. 251.

26 GARF, f. 9427, op. 1. d. 392, pp. 35–46.

27 *Letters Captured from Baron Ungern in Mongolia*, p. 8.

28 Omar Bartov, *Hitler's Army: Soldiers, Nazis and War in the Third Reich* (New York, 1992), p. 126.

29 *Sovetskaya Sibir*, no. 197 (557), 14 September, 1921, s. 1.

30 Ribo, 'The Story of Baron Ungern', p. 6.

31 The Chinese mountain gods, it must be said, were a little less ferocious than the Mongolian *savdags*, being more petty and bureaucratic than vengeful. I was once involved in building a temple on the minor holy mountain of Taibaishan. Half-way through the process the Daoist leaders declared that the building needed to be widened, because the three gods of the mountain required five bays. We asked why, and it was explained that the gods didn't get on, and so needed an empty space between them, or they would fight and bring disharmony.

When we asked why a fairly small mountain needed three gods anyway, we were told, 'Each god will only work eight hours on, sixteen hours off.' Divinity clearly remains a unionised business.

32 Captain R. B. Otter-Barry and Perry Ayscough, *With the Russians in Mongolia* (London, 1914), p. 105.

33 Theodore White and Annalee Jacoby, *Thunder Out of China* (New York, 1946), p. 187.

34 National State Archives of Mongolia, a. 5, g. 7, n. 288.

35 D. P. Pershin, *Baron Ungern, Urga i Altan-Bulak* (Stanford, 1933), quoted in Kuzmin, *Baron Ungern*, p. 370.

36 NARA, MID Report no. 212 (RG59), 30 March, 1921.

37 NARA, MID Report no. 212 (RG59), 30 March, 1921.

38 Henning Haslund, *Tents in Mongolia: Adventures and Experiences Among the Nomads of Central Asia* (London, 1934), p. 306.

39 Khisight, 'Baron Ungern's Mongolian Connection', p. 6.

40 NARA, MID Report Di-JI/BMM-SS (RH165, file no. 2657-1-159/1).

41 *Sovetskaya Sibir*, no. 200 (560), 17 September, 1921, s. 4.

42 *Sovetskaya Sibir*, no. 201 (561), 18 September, 1921, s. 3.

43 The Jewish matrilineal tradition is sometimes – very probably mistakenly – held to have arisen as a result of rape, ordained by the rabbis so that no prejudice would be shown to the children; a heartbreakingly humane response to an evil practice.

44 Ribo, 'The Story of Baron Ungern', p. 1.

45 Surreally, they were betrayed by a Korean doctor who was accompanying the mummified body of his three-year-old daughter, a typhus victim, out of the city. The Jews had given him letters to take with him, but he was caught and confessed all to his captors in an attempt to save his own life. He failed.

46 *Letters Captured from Baron Ungern in Mongolia*, p. 6.

47 Ossendowski, *Beasts, Men, and Gods*, p. 229.

48 Haslund, *Tents in Mongolia*, p. 54.

SEVEN – LORD OF THE STEPPE

1 Strasser, *The Mongolian Horde*, p. 273.

2 National State Archives of Mongolia, a. 4, g. 7, n. 1321.

3 Makeev, *Bog voiny*, p. 52.

4 Had Ungern forgotten about Denmark, Sweden, Norway, Italy, Belgium, etc., or did they not have the age and tradition to count? Or did he, deprived of news, believe that the revolutionary tide that had swept away the Romanovs, Habsburgs and Hohenzollerns must inevitably have taken the others with it?

5 RGVA, f. 39454, op. 1, d. 9, p. 84.

6 RGVA, f. 16, op. 3, d. 222, p. 123.

7 Kuzmin, *Baron Ungern*, p. 126.

8 Kuzmin, *Baron Ungern*, p. 126.

9 Kuzmin, *Baron Ungern*, p. 207.

10 Kuzmin, *Baron Ungern*, p. 207.

11 Kuzmin, *Baron Ungern*, p. 370.

12 Kuzmin, *Baron Ungern*, p. 436.

13 Ossendowski, *Beasts, Men, and Gods*, pp. 235–6.

14 Though the literal meaning in Chinese was 'change the mandate', and implied more a shift of dynasty than what we would think of as revolution.

15 Haslund, *Tents in Mongolia*, p. 67.

16 Haslund, *Tents in Mongolia*, p. 68.

17 *Sovetskaya Sibir*, no. 201 (561), 18 September, 1921, s. 3.

18 Ossendowski, *Beasts, Men, and Gods*, p. 242.

19 Ribo, 'The Story of Baron Ungern', p. 2.

20 Thomas Ewing, *Between the Hammer and the Anvil: Chinese and Russian Policies in Outer Mongolia, 1911–1921* (Bloomington, IN, 1980), p. 208.

21 *Letters Captured from Baron Ungern in Mongolia*, p. 2.

22 *Letters Captured from Baron Ungern in Mongolia*, p. 3.

23 Ossendowski, *Beasts, Men, and Gods*, pp. 2–3.

24 Ossendowski, *Beasts, Men, and Gods*, pp. 222–3.

25 Ossendowski, *Beasts, Men, and Gods*, p. 224.

26 Ossendowski, *Beasts, Men, and Gods*, p. 246.

27 Ribo, 'The Story of Baron Ungern', p. 2.

28 Ossendowski, *Beasts, Men, and Gods*, p. 309.

29 Ossendowski, *Beasts, Men, and Gods*, p. 240.

30 Kuzmin, *Baron Ungern*, p. 393.

31 GARF, f. 9427, op. 1, d. 392, p. 48.

32 *Letters Captured from Baron Ungern in Mongolia*, p. 3.

33 Kuzmin, *Baron Ungern*, p. 201.

34 *Letters Captured from Baron Ungern in Mongolia*, p. 5.

35 GARF, f. 9427, op. 1, d. 392, p. 49.

36 Ossendowski, *Beasts, Men, and Gods*, p. 240.

37 *Letters Captured from Baron Ungern in Mongolia*, p. 4.

38 Kuzmin, *Baron Ungern*, p. 183.

39 *Letters Captured from Baron Ungern in Mongolia*, p. 4.

40 *Letters Captured from Baron Ungern in Mongolia*, p. 3.

41 Ossendowski, *Beasts, Men, and Gods*, p. 247.

42 RGVA, p. 16, op. 3, d. 222, p. 125.

43 *Letters Captured from Baron Ungern in Mongolia*, p. 4.
44 Kuzmin, *Baron Ungern*, pp. 126, 393.

EIGHT – A HUNDRED AND THIRTY DAYS

1   Uradyn Bulag, *Nationality and Hybridity in Mongolia* (Oxford, 1998), p. 82.
2   There is often some overlap between them and the wandering monks who service the spiritual needs of outlying herders, as evidenced by, for instance, a rare example of an excellent and dry Mongol joke, recorded among the Buriat. One monk was travelling deep in the steppe, and at twilight came across a solitary ger, with a young woman living there alone. When he asked to stay the night, she insisted that he perform one of three tasks: drink alcohol, sleep with her, or sacrifice a goat, the last an act done only by shamans. Since all of them were sins, he chose the least harmful, and drank the alcohol. While he was drunk he killed the goat, and when he woke up the next day he was on the couch with the woman. He thus learned that drinking alcohol is only a small sin, but it can easily make a man do wicked things.
3   RGVA, f. 16, op. 3, d. 222, p. 4.
4   RGVA, f. 16, op. 3, d. 222, p. 1.
5   Kuzmin, *Baron Ungern*, p. 208.
6   Ossendowski, *Beasts, Men, and Gods*, pp. 261, 263.
7   Ossendowski, *Beasts, Men, and Gods*, pp. 264–6.
8   The full text of Order No. 15 is in GARF, f. Varia, d. 392, pp. 1–6; also Kuzmin, pp. 169–73.
9   Commissar order, 6 June, 1941. Available at http://www.jewishvirtuallibrary.org/jsource/Holocaust/commissar.html, accessed 28 December, 2006.
10 Ribo, 'The Story of Baron Ungern', p. 4.
11 GARF, f. 9427, op. 1, d. 392, p. 55.
12 Alioshin, *Asian Odyssey*, p. 250.
13 Ewing, *Between the Hammer and the Anvil*, p. 255.
14 Kuzmin, *Baron Ungern*, p. 183.
15 GARF, f. 16, op. 3, d. 222, p. 4.
16 Kuzmin, *Baron Ungern*, p. 183.
17 GARF, f. 16, op. 3, d. 222, p. 8.
18 Ribo, 'The Story of Baron Ungern', p. 12.
19 GARF, f. 16, op. 3, d. 222, p. 8.
20 GARF, f. 9427, op. 1, d. 392, p. 13; also *Sovetskaya Sibir*, no. 201 (561), 18 September, 1921, s. 3.

NINE – THE LAST ADVENTURER

1 Alioshin, *Asian Odyssey*, p. 270.
2 Ribo, 'The Story of Baron Ungern', p. 39.
3 Kuzmin, *Baron Ungern*, p. 471.
4 Kuzmin, *Baron Ungern*, p. 474.
5 Ribo, 'The Story of Baron Ungern', p. 41.
6 Ribo, 'The Story of Baron Ungern', p. 41.
7 Kuzmin, *Baron Ungern*, p. 470.
8 Kuzmin, *Baron Ungern*, p. 208.
9 Alioshin, *Asian Odyssey*, p. 232.
10 Kuzmin, *Baron Ungern*, p. 200.
11 Kuzmin, *Baron Ungern*, p. 201.
12 *Military Writings of Leon Trotsky*, vol. IV (London, 1981), available at http://www.marxists.org/archive/trotsky/works/1921-mil/ch64.htm.
13 Kuzmin, *Baron Ungern*, p. 205.
14 GARF, f. 9427, op. 1, d. 392, p. 47.
15 Kuzmin, *Baron Ungern*, pp. 557, 408.
16 Kuzmin, *Baron Ungern*, p. 480.
17 GARF, f. 9427, op. 1, d. 392, p. 36.
18 Kuzmin, *Baron Ungern*, p. 210.
19 The trial account, and all the following quotes, are in *Sovetskaya Sibir*, no. 200 (560), 17 September, 1921, s. 4, no. 201 (561), 18 September, 1921, s. 3, and no. 202 (562), 20 September, 1921, ss. 2–4.
20 Strasser, *The Mongolian Horde*, p. 106.

EPILOGUE

1 C. R. Bawden, *The Modern History of Mongolia* (London, 1968), p. 260.
2 This idealism did not entirely die out with the purges. There is a passage in Peter Fleming's travel memoir, *One's Company*, which is both hysterically funny and, in context, very sad. On a train through Russia, he meets a young intellectual from Baku, Assorgim, 'extremely intelligent [with] an understanding of the theatre and a feeling for it', who, at twenty-two, has been sent by the Soviet regime to 'found a National Theatre in Outer Mongolia', where he intends to put on the plays of Shakespeare to improve the Mongolians' cultural level.
3 Bawden, *Modern History of Mongolia*, pp. 262–3.
4 Baabar, *History of Mongolia*, p. 293.
5 Baabar, *History of Mongolia*, p. 363.

6 Alvin Coox, *Japan Against Russia* (Stanford, 1985), features various heartbreaking stories of these exiled Japanese soldiers, pp. 940–50.

7 Mongolia's importance could be exaggerated, as in one historian's claim: 'If I say that Mongolia was as important as the United States [as an ally for the Soviet Union], there is no need to laugh or tease' (Baabar, *History of Mongolia*, p. 394, quoting Victor Suvorov, *The Last Republic,* Moscow, 1995), referring to its provision of sheepskin for the Red Army's winter clothes.

8 Bisher, *White Terror*, p. 366.

9 Berndt Krauthoff, *Ich befehle! Kampf und Tragödie des Barons Ungern-Sternberg* (Bremen, 1938).

10 Ossendowski, *Beasts, Men, and Gods*, p. 270.

11 Along with Nepal, which is even more optimistic.

12 For instance, www.buryatmongol.com and www.doncroner.com/Mongolia/, as of December 2006, were both firewalled. Several online library and academic publication services, such as Questia.com, are also forced to limit access of Chinese subscribers to books about Mongolia.

13 In Hohhot, the capital of Inner Mongolia, I saw an old robe-wearing herder come into a 'Mr Lee's Taiwanese Noodles', full of noisy Chinese. He shuffled up to the counter and asked the price of a bowl of noodles. Shocked at what he heard, he stumbled out again, muttering under his breath, 'Four yuan! Four yuan for a bowl of noodles!' Four yuan is around 24p or 50¢.

14 Humphrey, 'Remembering an "Enemy"', p. 26.

Bibliography

ARCHIVES

Eesti Ajalooarhiiv [Estonian National Archives]
Gosudarstvennyi arkhiv Rossiiskoi Federatsii [State Archive of the Russian
    Federation]
National State Archives of Mongolia
Rossiiskii Gosudarstvennyi Arkhiv Voenno-Morskogo Flota [State Archive
    of the Russian Navy]
Rossiiskii gosudarstvennyi voennyi arkhiv [Russian State Military Archive]
US National Archives and Records Administration
The World War I Document Archive: The Willy–Nicky Letters, at
    http://www.lib.byu.edu/~rdh/wwi/

JOURNALS AND PERIODICALS

Sovetskaya Sibir (Novonikolaevsk)
The Times (London)
The New York Times
Peking and Tientsin Times
Pravda

PUBLISHED SOURCES

Alioshin, Dmitri, *Asian Odyssey* (London, 1941)
Baabar, *History of Mongolia* (Ulaanbaatar, 1999)
Bartov, Omar, *Hitler's Army: Soldiers, Nazis and War in the Third Reich*
    (New York, 1992)
Bawden, C. R., *The Modern History of Mongolia* (London, 1968)
Belov, Evgenii, *Baron Ungern fon Shternberg: biografiia, ideologiia, voennye*

pokhody 1920–1921 [Baron Ungern von Sternberg: Biography, Ideology, Military Campaigns 1920–1921] (Moscow, 2003)

Berlin, Isaiah, Against the Current (London, 1980)

Bisher, Jamie, White Terror (London, 2005)

Blavatsky, Helena, The Secret Doctrine (Pasadena, 1988)

Bulag, Uradyn, Nationality and Hybridity in Mongolia (Oxford, 1998)

Burdukov, A. V., V staroi i novoi Mongolii: vospominaniia, pis'ma [Old and New Mongolia: Memoirs, Letters] (Moscow, 1969)

Campbell, C. W., Travels in Mongolia (London, 1902)

Carlson, Maria, No Religion But Truth (Princeton, 1993)

Cohn, Norman, Warrant for Genocide (Harmondsworth, 1970)

Coox, Alvin, Japan Against Russia (Stanford, 1985)

du Quenoy, Paul, 'Warlordism à la russe: Baron von Ungern-Sternberg's Anti-Bolshevik Crusade, 1917–1921', Revolutionary Russia, vol. 16, no. 2 (2003)

du Quenoy, Paul, 'Perfecting the Show Trial: The Case of Baron von Ungern-Sternberg', Revolutionary Russia, vol. 19, no. 1 (2006)

Ewing, Thomas, Between the Hammer and the Anvil: Chinese and Russian Policies in Outer Mongolia, 1911–1921 (Bloomington, IN, 1980)

Field, Daniel, Rebels in the Name of the Tsar (Boston, 1976)

Fleming, Peter, Bayonets to Lhasa (London, 1962)

Fleming, Peter, One's Company (London, 1931)

Forbath, Ladislaus and Joseph Geleta, The New Mongolia (London, 1936)

Goodrick-Clarke, Nicholas, Black Sun (New York, 2003)

Goodrick-Clarke, Nicholas, The Occult Roots of Nazism (New York, 1993)

Gray, Glenn, The Warriors: Reflections on Men at War (Lincoln, NE, 1959)

Haslund, Henning, Tents in Mongolia: Adventures and Experiences Among the Nomads of Central Asia (London, 1934)

Hopkirk, Peter, Setting the East Ablaze (Oxford, 1984)

Humphrey, Caroline, 'Remembering an "Enemy"', in Rubie S. Watson (ed.), Memory, History and Opposition Under State Socialism (Santa Fe, 1994)

Iuzefovich, Leonid, Samoderzhets pustyni: fenomen sud'by barona RF. Ungern-Shternberga [Autocrat of the Desert: The Phenomenon of Baron R. F. Ungern-Sternberg] (Moscow, 1993)

Keegan, John, A History of Warfare (New York, 1993)

Keyserling, Hermann, Reise durch die Zeit [A Journey through Time], vol. II (Vaduz, 1948)

Khisight, N., 'Baron Ungern's Mongolian Connection', Journal of the Institute of Social Sciences, National University of Mongolia, vol. 14, no. 188 (2002)

Kislitsin, V. A., V ogne grazhdanskoi voiny [In the Fire of the Civil War] (Harbin, 1936)

Krauthoff, Berndt, *Ich befehle! Kampf und Tragödie des Barons Ungern-Sternberg* [*I Order! The Struggle and Tragedy of Baron Ungern-Sternberg*] (Bremen, 1938)

Kuzmin, S. L. (comp.), *Baron Ungern v dokumentakh i memuarakh* [*Baron Ungern in Documents and Memoirs*] (Moscow, 2004)

Kuzmin, S. L. (comp.), *Legendarnyi baron: neizvestnye stranitsy grazhdanskoi voiny* [*Legendary Baron: Unknown Pages of the Civil War*] (Moscow, 2004)

Liulevicius, Vejas Gabriel, *War Land on the Eastern Front* (Cambridge, 2000)

Mabire, Jean, *Ungern, le dieu de la guerre: la chevauchée du général-baron Roman Feodorovitch von Ungern-Sternberg, du Golfe de Finlande au désert de Gobi* [*Ungern, God of War: the Chevauchée of General Baron Roman Feodorovitch von Ungern-Sternberg, from the Gulf of Finland to the Gobi Desert*] (Paris, 1887)

Makeev, A. S., *Bog voiny* [*God of War*] (Shanghai, 1934)

Marwitz, Bernhard von der, *Stirb und Werde* [*Dying and Becoming*] (Breslau, 1931)

Murakami, Haruki, *The Wind-Up Bird Chronicle* (New York, 1997)

Nevins, Jess, *Encyclopaedia of Fantastic Victoriana* (New York, 2005)

Newby, Eric, *A Traveller's Life* (London, 1982)

Orwell, George, 'W. B. Yeats' (first published in *Horizon*, London, 1943)

Ossendowski, Ferdinand, *Beasts, Men, and Gods* (New York, 1922)

Otter-Barry, Captain R. B. and Perry Ayscough, *With the Russians in Mongolia* (London, 1914)

Perdue, Peter, *China Marches West* (London, 2005)

Pershin, D. P., *Baron Ungern, Urga i Altan-Bulak* (Stanford, 1933)

Pozner, Vladimir, *Bloody Baron: The Story of Ungern-Sternberg*, trans. Warre Bradley Wells (London, 1938)

Ribo, N. M., 'The Story of Baron Ungern Told by His Staff Physician', Hoover Institution, Stanford University, CSUZXX697-A

Sárközi, Alice, *Political Prophecies in Mongolia in the 17th–20th Centuries* (Wiesbaden, 1992)

Semenov, Grigori, *O Sebe* [*About Myself*] (Harbin, 1938)

Special Delegation of the Far Eastern Republic, *Letters Captured from Baron Ungern in Mongolia* (Washington, DC, 1921)

Strasser, Rudolf, *The Mongolian Horde* (New York, 1930)

Sunderland, Willard, 'Baron Ungern, Toxic Cosmopolitan', *Ab Imperio*, Spring 2006

Suvorov, Victor, *The Last Republic* (Moscow, 1995)

Tasuki, Hideo, *A Japanese Agent in Tibet* (London, 1990)

BIBLIOGRAPHY

Military Writings of Leon Trotsky, vol. IV (London, 1981)

US Senate Committee on Education and Labor, *Deportation of Gregorie Semenoff: Hearings Relative to the Deporting of Undesirable Aliens* (Washington, DC, 1922)

Vrangel, Karl Gustav, *The Memoirs of Count Vrangel: The Last Commander-in-Chief of the Russian National Army,* trans. Sophie Goulston (London, 1929)

Ward, Colonel John, *With the Die-Hards in Siberia* (London, 1920)

White, Theodore and Annalee Jacoby, *Thunder Out of China* (New York, 1946)

Index

Jost Schillemeit

Bonaventura. Der Verfasser der ‹Nachtwachen›

JOST SCHILLEMEIT

Bonaventura
Der Verfasser der ‹Nachtwachen›

VERLAG C. H. BECK MÜNCHEN

ISBN 3 406 04972 9
© C. H. Beck'sche Verlagsbuchhandlung (Oscar Beck) München 1973
Umschlagentwurf: Walter Kraus, München
Gesamtherstellung: Passavia Passau
Printed in Germany

Vorwort

Die Aufgabe, die sich die folgende Untersuchung gestellt hat, ist mit wenigen Worten angedeutet: es geht um die Bestimmung der Verfasserschaft eines Buches: ‹Nachtwachen. Von Bonaventura›, erschienen «Penig 1805 bey F. Dienemann und Comp.», wie es auf dem Titelblatt der Erstausgabe heißt. Ein Vorsatzblatt gibt zusätzlich Auskunft über den Rahmen, innerhalb dessen das Buch erschien, und zugleich eine gewisse Präzisierung zum Erscheinungsdatum: «Journal / von / neuen deutschen Original Romanen / in 8 Lieferungen jährlich / Dritter Jahrgang. 1804 / Siebente Lieferung.» Eine Charakteristik des Buches, über das inzwischen eine umfangreiche Sekundärliteratur vorliegt, erübrigt sich hier, wäre auch innerhalb eines Vorwortes nicht gut möglich; einzelne Beiträge dazu finden sich verstreut im Verlauf der folgenden Darstellung. Über die wichtigsten Hypothesen, die zur Frage der Verfasserschaft bisher vorgetragen wurden, versucht – innerhalb einer entdeckungs- und wirkungsgeschichtlichen Einleitung – das erste Kapitel einen knappen Überblick zu geben. Als Verfasser des Buches galten u. a. Schelling, Caroline, E. T. A. Hoffmann, Brentano und schließlich Friedrich Gottlob Wetzel, der in den meisten heutigen Nachschlagewerken als zumindest mutmaßlicher Verfasser angegeben wird, oft allerdings mit dem Zusatz, die Autorschaftsfrage sei «immer noch kontrovers» (so J. Körner in seinem ‹Bibliographischen Handbuch des deutschen Schrifttums›).

Auch die Methode der folgenden Verfasserbestimmung bedarf kaum einer ausführlichen Erläuterung, da sie, wie ich hoffe, sich selbst erläutert. Es ist im wesentlichen die des Indizienbeweises, ergänzt durch den Nachweis ‹innerer› Gemeinsamkeiten, also durch den Nachweis von Homogeneitäten allgemeinerer, gehaltlicher, kunsttheoretischer und ‹weltanschaulicher› Art. Das Gerüst der Darstellung wird durch die Indizien gegeben. Vor allem um der Lesbarkeit der Darstellung willen sind sie im wesentlichen (d. h. insbesondere: was die untersuchten Quellenbereiche: die ‹Zeitung für die elegante Welt› etc. betrifft) in der Reihenfolge mitgeteilt, in der sie sich mir im Lauf der eigenen Nachforschungen ergeben haben. Die Indizien selbst sind verschiedener Art. Viele von ihnen ließen sich unter der Überschrift ‹Prinzip der aufschlußreichen Detailkenntnis›, andere unter der Rubrik ‹Prinzip der aufschlußreichen Abweichung› zusammenstellen. Um das erste dieser Prinzipien kurz durch ein Beispiel zu verdeutlichen: in der antiken kunstgeschichtlichen Überlieferung und der auf sie zurückgreifenden archäologischen Fachliteratur der Moderne ist gelegentlich von einem Bild eines griechischen Malers die Rede, das die Opferung der Iphigenia zum Gegenstand hatte und auf dem Agamemnon mit verhülltem Haupt dargestellt war. Angenommen nun, ein belletristi-

scher Autor der hier in Betracht kommenden Zeit kannte diese Überlieferung, kannte auch den Namen des Malers, und angenommen ferner,
er habe von diesem Wissen zweimal Gebrauch gemacht, einmal in einer
pseudonym erschienenen, das andere Mal in einer etwa gleichzeitig unter
eigenem Namen erschienenen Veröffentlichung, so ergibt sich daraus
offenbar ein gewisses Indiz für die Identität der beiden Verfasser (kein
sehr starkes, wie zugegeben sei, aber doch auch kein ganz schwaches,
denn nicht jeder damals schreibende belletristische Autor kannte den
Namen jenes griechischen Malers, wie wir sehen werden). Will man ein
Beispiel für das zweite ‹Prinzip›, so mag man sich etwa vorstellen, ein
Autor verwende ein bestimmtes Substantiv, das gemeinhin als Neutrum
gebraucht wird, als Maskulinum: auch dies kann offenbar, bei entspre-
chendem Niederschlag in verschiedenen Publikationen, ein gewisses Indiz
ergeben. Weniger Wert gelegt habe ich auf ‹freischwebende› Strukturparallelen wie das wiederholte Auftreten bestimmter Motive bei der Ausgestaltung von Roman- oder Novellensituationen oder die Wiederkehr
ähnlicher Phantasiemotive; Parallelen dieser Art wurden nicht gänzlich
beiseite gelassen, aber doch nur in besonders frappanten und zugleich für
die Charakteristik des Autors wichtigen Fällen aufgeführt. (So gut wie
ganz dagegen fehlen im Folgenden Äußerungen über den ‹Stil› des ‹Nachtwachen›-Verfassers – dies deshalb, weil es mir, zurückhaltend formuliert,
außerordentlich schwierig scheint, unter den Stilzügen eines Werks diejenigen herauszufinden und kenntlich zu machen, die einzig und allein
dem Autor eigentümlich sind, und zwar so eigentümlich, daß sie auch in
anderen Werken desselben Autors wiederkehren: wieviel scheinbar ‹Indi-
viduelles› kann nicht auf das Konto der literarischen Gattung gehen, wie
vieles kann dem Autor mit anderen Autoren gemeinsam, vielleicht auch
von anderen Autoren übernommen sein!) Im übrigen habe ich mich bemüht, nicht nur Indizien auszubreiten, sondern zugleich eine Vorstellung
von den Zusammenhängen zu geben, in denen sie stehen, also vor allem
von den Werken, in denen sie vorkommen, ihrer Eigenart, ihrer historischen Situation und ihren historischen Voraussetzungen. Auch dies einer
der Gründe für die im Folgenden gewählte Gliederung nach Werken statt
nach irgendwelchen systematischen Gesichtspunkten.

Zum Schluß möchte ich vor allem den Mitarbeiterinnen der Braunschweiger Stadtbibliothek und den Damen von der Fernleihstelle der
Universitätsbibliothek Braunschweig für viel Hilfsbereitschaft und Geduld
danken. Mein Dank gilt ferner, insbesondere für die Erlaubnis zur Einsicht in Handschriften, dem Stadtarchiv und dem Landesmuseum Braunschweig, der Herzog-August-Bibliothek und dem Niedersächsischen
Staatsarchiv zu Wolfenbüttel sowie den Handschriftenabteilungen der
Stiftung Preußischer Kulturbesitz, der Deutschen Staatsbibliothek Unter
den Linden und der Staats- und Universitätsbibliothek Hamburg.   J. S.

INHALT

I. Einleitendes zur Geschichte des Buchs und des Problems

Das Buch, um dessen Ursprung es im Folgenden geht, ist lange Zeit fast unbeachtet, ja so gut wie unbekannt geblieben. Der einzige unter den uns bekannten Zeitgenossen, der es erwähnt – oder um genau zu sein: der es in einer uns erhaltenen Äußerung erwähnt – ist Jean Paul, der sich hier auf eine Weise nachgeahmt sah, die ihn eher zwiespältig berührte. «Lesen Sie doch», schreibt er am 14. Januar 1805, kurz nach dem Erscheinen des Buchs, an einen Freund, «die Nachtwachen von Bonaventura, d. h. von Schelling. Es ist eine treffliche Nachahmung meines Gianozzo; doch mit zu viel Reminiszenzen und Lizenzen zugleich. Es verräth und benimmt viele Kraft dem Leser. – Selten les' ich in neueren Zeiten etwas sehr Gutes oder sehr Schlechtes, ohne daß mir meine Bescheidenheit sagt: hier bist du denn wieder nachgeahmt. Am Ende glaub' ich, haben die Alten mich fliegend durchblättert und mir Sachen gestohlen, die ich lieber nicht hätte schreiben sollen nachher.»[1] Der nächste uns bekannte Leser, der sich durch eine auf uns gekommene Wiedergabe seines Eindrucks als solcher bezeugt, ist – fast vier Jahrzehnte später – Varnhagen von Ense, der in seinem Tagebuch unter dem 17. August 1843[2] die Lektüre der ‹Nachtwachen› verzeichnet und einige charakterisierende Bemerkungen hinzufügt. Auch er hält, aus Gründen, über die gleich zu sprechen sein wird, das Buch für ein Werk Schellings, was ihn nicht hindert, es ein «unglaublich schwaches Erzeugniß, und für Schelling allzu gering» zu nennen. Es scheint ihm «eben so unreif, willkürlich, unorganisch», als lese er «ein Buch des jungen Deutschlands», freilich auch «eben so talentvoll, auf-

---

[1] An P. E. Thieriot in Offenbach. Hist.-krit. Ausgabe, 3. Abt., 5. Bd. – Briefe 1804–1808. Hrsg. v. Eduard Berend. Berlin 1961, S. 20.

[2] Tagebücher von K. A. Varnhagen von Ense. 2. Bd. Leipzig 1861, S. 206. – Die genaue Geschichte des Exemplars, aus dem Varnhagen die ‹Nachtwachen› kennenlernte, findet sich verzeichnet im Nachwort von Raimund Steinerts Neuausgabe des Werks (Weimar 1914). Danach stammte es aus der Bibiliothek Rahels; 1858 war es von Varnhagen an den Leipziger Professor Ch. H. Weiße ausgeliehen worden, der auch bereits seinen Freund Rudolf Seydel beauftragt hatte, es Varnhagen zurückzugeben, als dieser die Nachricht von Varnhagens Tod (10. 10. 1858) erhielt; das Buch blieb dann bei Weiße, gelangte nach seinem Tode in die Bibliothek Rudolf Seydels und von dort in die eines seiner Söhne; dort wurde es von R. Steinert endeckt und seiner Neuausgabe der ‹Nachtwachen› zugrunde gelegt.

blitzend und versprechend»; auch an «Keckheit» fehle es nicht. Er spricht auch von einem Exemplar, das bei der Versteigerung von Friedrich Schlegels Bücherei aufgetaucht sei (die allerdings schon sehr viel früher stattgefunden hatte), das Schelling diesem «geschenkt» und in das er «sich als Verfasser eingeschrieben» habe, und schließt seine Tagebuchnotiz mit der Feststellung: «Auch in früherer Zeit hab' ich nie von dem Dasein eines solchen Buches gehört» – einer Feststellung, der einiges Gewicht zukommt, da sie von einem Manne stammt, der die deutsche Literatur, mit Einschluß der Romantik, kannte wie wenige.

Nun waren die Beziehungen zwischen Friedrich Schlegel und Schelling bekanntlich von Anfang an kühl und seit dem Scheitern von Friedrich Schlegels philosophischer Universitätskarriere im Winter 1800/1801 mehr als kühl, und die Vorstellung, daß einer dem andern um die hier in Frage kommende Zeit ein eigenes Werk, noch dazu ein pseudonym erschienenes, mit handschriftlicher Widmung zugeschickt haben sollte, ist entsprechend unwahrscheinlich. Aber es gab in der Tat einen Grund – und einen triftigeren als jenes von Varnhagen tradierte Gerücht von einem handschriftlich dedizierten Exemplar in Friedrich Schlegels Besitz –, der es innerhalb eines gewissen Kreises von ‹Eingeweihten› zumindest nahelegte, hinter dem Pseudonym «Bonaventura» Schelling zu vermuten. Dieses Pseudonym war nämlich, drei Jahre vor Erscheinen der ‹Nachtwachen›, schon einmal benutzt worden, und zwar in einer zu ihrer Zeit vielbeachteten gemeinschaftlichen Publikation der ‹romantischen Schule›, dem von A. W. Schlegel und Ludwig Tieck herausgegebenen Musenalmanach für 1802, und in diesem Falle war es jedenfalls im engeren Kreise der beiden Herausgeber bekannt, daß die so unterzeichneten Gedichte von keinem anderen als von Schelling stammten[3]. Hinzu kam, daß das eindrucksvollste dieser Gedichte, ‹Die letzten Worte des Pfarrers zu Drottning auf Seeland› überschrieben, eine nächtlich-schauerliche Begebenheit zum Inhalt hatte, an die man sich durch die ‹Nachtwachen›, auch wenn man nicht viel mehr als ihren Namen kannte, erinnert fühlen mochte. Wo immer man also in den ersten Jahrzehnten nach Erscheinen dieses Buchs auf eine Einreihung unter Schellings Werke stößt, wird man mit einer gewissen Wahrscheinlichkeit ein Mit-Hineinspielen jener ersten Bonaventura-Publikationen im romantischen Musenalmanach von 1802 zumindest vermuten können. So etwa in Friedrich Raßmanns ‹Kurzgefaßtem

---

[3] Daß sie von ihm stammen, wird unbezweifelbar bezeugt u. a. durch Briefe A. W. Schlegels an Tieck (14. 9. 1800: «Schelling giebt uns gewiß manches, für's erste die letzten Worte des Pfarrers [...]», ähnlich am 23. 11. 1800; vgl. H. Lüdecke: L. Tieck und die Brüder Schlegel, Frankfurt a. M. 1930, S. 55 ff.) und einen Brief Carolines an Schelling, in dem der ‹Pfarrer› «Dein Werk» genannt wird (Afg. 1801; vgl. E. Schmidt: Caroline, 2. Bd., Leipzig 1913, S. 25).

Lexikon pseudonymer Schriftsteller› von 1830 oder in Meusels ‹Gelehr-
tem Teutschland› (20. Bd., 1825), wo die Einwirkung des romantischen
Musenalmanachs nicht nur zu vermuten, sondern offensichtlich ist, denn
es heißt dort (unter ‹Schelling›), «unter dem Namen Bonaventura» stün-
den von Schelling «zwey Gedichte: ‹Nachtwachen› und ‹Letzte Worte des
Pfarrers auf [sic] Drottning› in A. W. Schlegels und L. Tiecks Musenalmanach»: offenbar allein unter dem Eindruck desselben Pseudonyms
sind hier die ‹Nachtwachen›, ein Buch von immerhin fast 300 Seiten im
Erstdruck, kurzerhand zum «Gedicht» erklärt und in den Musenalmanach für 1802 verwiesen worden; auch dies zugleich ein neues Zeugnis
für die Unbekanntheit des Buches während der ersten Jahrzehnte des
19. Jahrhunderts.

Die eigentliche Entdeckungsgeschichte des Buches beginnt in den siebziger Jahren des Jahrhunderts, im Zusammenhang mit der historischen
Erforschung der Literatur und Kultur der Romantik. 1870 erscheint Rudolf Hayms Werk ‹Die romantische Schule›, wo in einer Fußnote auch
die ‹Nachtwachen› kurz besprochen und zu den «geistreichsten Produc-
tionen der Romantik»[4] gerechnet werden – ein Hinweis, der trotz seiner
Knappheit und seiner unauffälligen Stelle, bei der Bedeutung des Haymschen Buches für alle spätere Romantikforschung, beträchtlich gewirkt
haben dürfte. Zur Frage der Verfasserschaft äußerte Haym sich vorsichtig: «Ob die im Jahre 1805 in dem ‹Journal von neuen deutschen Origi-
nalromanen› (Penig 1802–1805) erschienenen ‹Nachtwachen von Bonaventura› wirklich ein Werk Schelling's sind, wage ich nicht zu entscheiden.»
Unter den Argumenten, die er aufführt, werden die Argumente pro
Schelling – «einzelne naturphilosophische Anspielungen und ein Über-
gewicht ernster und tiefsinniger Reflexion» – überwogen von den gegen
Schelling sprechenden: «Die Einmischung Jean-Paul'scher Töne indeß,
das Grelle mancher Erfindung, wie z. B. die Auftritte im Narrenhaus und
auf dem Kirchhof, deuten mehr auf die spätere romantische Schule, auf
einen Dichter, halb in der Weise Arnim's und Brentano's, halb in der
Weise T. A. Hoffmann's.» Überdies wird ihm die Schellingsche Autorschaft auch «durch die Ehebruchsgeschichte des dritten Abschnitts, deren
Heldin eine Caroline ist, endlich auch dadurch unwahrscheinlich, daß der
vornehme Schelling sich schwerlich in die Gesellschaft solcher Autoren
wie Franz Horn, Küchelbecker, K. Nicolai, Jul. Werden, Vulpius usw.» –
Autoren von Trivialromanen, die sämtlich auch in Dienemanns ‹Roma-
nenjournal› aufgetreten waren – «begeben haben dürfte».

Neues Material brachten 1872 die Lebenserinnerungen des Kirchen-
historikers Karl von Hase[5] und 1875 die ‹Festschrift› von Hubert Beckers

---

[4] Berlin 1870 (photomechanischer Nachdruck: Darmstadt 1961), S. 636.
[5] Ideale und Irrtümer. Leipzig 1872.

zum hundertsten Geburtstag Schellings[6]. Es betraf im wesentlichen den
Verlag, in dem die ‹Nachtwachen› erschienen waren. Karl von Hase (1800
bis 1890), der in seiner Jugend eine Zeitlang als Pflegekind im Hause des
«Generalakzisinspektors» und Advokaten Karl Dienemann in Penig, des
Vaters des Verlegers, gelebt hatte, berichtete von der Gründung der
Buchhandlung durch den Vater Dienemann und von ihrem baldigen Un-
tergang durch eine Polizeiaffäre in Petersburg, wo «ein reiches Lager aufgestellt» und eine offenbar nicht unbedeutende Niederlassung des Ver-
lags entstanden war: wegen einiger nach Petersburg verbrachten Exem-
plare eines dort verbotenen Buches – «Bülows Feldzug von 1805» – sei
Ferdinand Dienemann, der junge Verleger, am 20. November 1806 in
Petersburg «zum Polizeiminister beschieden» und ihm der «sofortige
Transport zur Grenze angekündigt» worden. Ein Offizier der Polizei habe
ihn zur finnisch-schwedischen Grenze gebracht, wo ein Nervenfieber ihn
überfiel; das Geschäft sei bald darauf durch die Polizei geschlossen worden, und «nach Jahren» sei nichts übrig geblieben, «als die Vorräte zu-
gunsten der Gläubigen unter den ungünstigsten Verhältnissen loszuschla-
gen», wodurch der Vater sein ganzes Vermögen verloren habe, sogar auf
Veranlassung der Firma Breitkopf und Härtel mit Wechselarrest belegt
worden sei. (Ein Bericht, durch den vieles von den Schwierigkeiten späterer Bonaventura-Forscher erklärlich wird.)

Hubert Beckers teilte vor allem einen Brief Varnhagens aus dem Jahre
1856 mit, in dem Varnhagen, über siebzigjährig, zwei Jahre vor seinem
Tode, über die näheren Umstände bei der Entstehung der ‹Nachtwachen›
berichtete. Auch hier nennt er Schelling als ihren Verfasser. Über Dienemann schreibt er, er sei der Verleger einer «Gruppe» geworden, die nach
der Entfernung der Schlegels aus Deutschland «das Schlegel'sche Wesen
fast blindlings auf die Spitze treiben wollte». Er nennt «Friedrich Mann
(nachmals Superintendent in Charlottenburg) und Adolph Winzer (Ju-
stizcommissarius in Berlin, aber schon 1809 spurlos verschwunden)», die
sich als Julius und Adolph Werden «verbrüderten»; zu ihnen habe sich
Wilhelm Schneider aus Dessau gesellt. Eine Zeitschrift ‹Apollo› (ihr genauer Titel lautete: ‹Apollon›) sei erschienen, ebenso wie Romane von
Julius und Adolph Werden, ein Journal für Romane «versprach jährlich 8 Lieferungen». Aber bald hätten sich die Kräfte jener Verbrüderten
als nicht ausreichend gezeigt, «um ein so starkes Versprechen zu erfül-
len». In dieser Not habe Dienemann gewagt, «an einige ihm dem Namen
nach bekannte Anhänger der neuen Schule zu schreiben und sie dringend
um Beiträge zu bitten, die er stracks und gut bezahlen wollte. Er schrieb

---

[6] Schelling's Geistesentwicklung in ihrem inneren Zusammenhang. Festschrift zu Friedrich Wilhelm Joseph Schelling's hundertjährigem Geburtstag
am 27. Januar 1875. München 1875.

in diesem Sinne», fährt Varnhagen fort, «an Schelver in Jena, an Bernhardi in Berlin, an Koreff nach Paris und besonders auch an S c h e l l i n g,
der damals, glaub' ich, in Würzburg lebte. Dieser letztere soll sich damals
in peinlicher Geldverlegenheit befunden haben, und ging daher willig
auf das unverhoffte Anerbieten ein. Sein Buch ist wahrscheinlich binnen
wenigen Wochen in guter Laune verfaßt worden. Gleich den anderen
Bänden der Sammlung blieb es fast unbeachtet.» Es folgen noch einige
Worte über das Unglück des Verlages im Jahre 1806 und das «Erlöschen»
der literarischen Tätigkeit seiner Mitarbeiter. Hitzig, der Berliner Buchhändler, habe ein «scherzhaftes Sonett auf diese Geschichte» gemacht,
von dem Varnhagen noch zwei Zeilen erinnerlich sind, nämlich «der sehr
glückliche Anfang:

‹Der Dienemann will nicht dem Mann mehr dienen›

und dann

‹Weil sie nichts sind, so können sie sich werden.›»[7]

Beckers selbst erklärt, er habe ungeachtet aller «dafür sprechenden
Umstände und Gründe, daß Schelling der Verfasser des Romans» sei,
«doch nach der ersten Lectüre desselben keine hinlängliche Überzeu-
gung hievon gewinnen» können und sei «lange – bis zu seiner wiederhol-
ten aufmerksameren Durchlesung – der gegentheiligen Ansicht» gewesen.
Zu dieser erneuten Lektüre sei er veranlaßt worden durch die Mitteilung seines Freundes, des Pfarrers Friedrich Köstlin (der an Schellings
Verfasserschaft glaubte), daß auch «der mit ihm eng befreundete
Sohn Schelling's, der verstorbene Herausgeber der Werke seines Vaters,
unter Aufgebung der früher entgegengesetzten Ansicht, sich zuletzt gleichfalls der seinigen angeschlossen». Was ihn selbst, Beckers, bei der ersten
Lektüre an der Schellingschen Autorschaft irre machte, sei «die auch von
H a s e hervorgehobene Formlosigkeit» gewesen, die er «mit dieses Den-
kers ganzer Geistesart und seinem steten Streben nach möglichst vollendeter Form in Composition und Darstellung nicht zu vereinigen» gewußt
habe: «Das ist nicht Schelling's durchgängig classischer Styl, konnten wir
nicht umhin zu sagen, so tritt er uns in seinen Schriften nirgends gegenüber.» Aber man dürfe «nicht vergessen, daß uns hier ein Geistesprodukt
ganz eigenthümlicher Art geboten ist», fährt er in seinem altväterischen
Festschrift-Deutsch fort: in Schelling habe zu jener Zeit seiner «ersten ge-

---

[7] Op. cit., S. 91 f. (innerhalb des ‹Anhangs› der Festschrift). Die Stelle «so
können sie sich werden» ist offenbar verderbt; in dem Bericht R. Seydels (s. u.)
über die von ihm eingesehene Varnhagensche Niederschrift heißt es statt dessen: «so nennen sie sich W e r d e n.»

waltigen speculativen Conceptionen und der heftigen Angriffe, die er darob zu erdulden hatte, zugleich ein unbändiger Drang» gelegen, «sich auch wieder von der Speculation los zu machen und auf dem Gebiet der Dichtung in ungehemmter und – seinen Gegnern gegenüber – trotzigster Weise sich auszulassen». Im «epikurischen Glaubensbekenntnis Heinz Widerporstens» habe dieser Drang seinen ersten Ausdruck gefunden, in den ‹Nachtwachen› seinen zweiten. Beckers teilt auch – außer den verschiedenen, eben kurz referierten Ansichten zum Problem der Verfasserschaft – eine Äußerung mit, die Schelling selbst, auf eine Frage des klassischen Philologen und Ästhetikers Ernst von Lasaulx, getan habe. Es ist allerdings eine wahrhaft sibyllinische Äußerung: Lasaulx habe – so berichtet Hubert Beckers, der es «aus dessen eigenem Munde» erfahren hat – «auf seine an Schelling einst gerichtete Frage über die ‹Nachtwachen› von diesem die Antwort erhalten: ‹Reden Sie mir nicht davon!›»

Eine gewisse Präzisierung der bisherigen Informationen erfolgte 1879 durch eine Miszelle in der ‹Zeitschrift für deutsches Altertum›[8], in der sich einer der wenigen Besitzer eines Exemplars der Erstausgabe der ‹Nachtwachen›, der Leipziger Philosoph Rudolf Seydel[9], zu Wort meldete und mitteilte, was er von dessen Vorbesitzer, seinem Leipziger Lehrer C. H. Weiße, zur Frage der Verfasserschaft erfahren hatte. Er berichtet zunächst von einer Niederschrift Varnhagens, die Weiße ihm gezeigt habe und die dem Seydelschen Referat zufolge im wesentlichen denselben Inhalt hatte wie die oben erwähnte, von Beckers 1875 mitgeteilte, und gibt dann auszugsweise einen Brief wieder, den Schellings Sohn Friedrich, der Herausgeber der Werke des Philosophen, am 30. April 1858 an Immanuel Hermann Fichte im Zusammenhang mit der Verfasserschaftsfrage der ‹Nachtwachen› schrieb: Friedrich Schelling habe, «nachdem er das motiv der geldverlegenheit als sehr unwahrscheinlich beseitigt, wie folgt» geschrieben: «Bis jetzt habe ich keine spur gefunden, welche Schellings autorschaft jenes romans anzeige. – – Hat mein seliger vater jene Nachtwachen Bonaventuras verfaßt, so verdanken sie ihren ursprung sicher nur Schellings humor (...)»[10] Ohne die Autorschaft seines Vaters schlecht-

---

[8] Rudolf Seydel: Schellings Nachtwachen. ZfdA., 23. Bd. (1879), S. 203–205.

[9] Siehe oben Anm. 2. Seydel war 1867, nach dem Tode Ch. H. Weißes, in den Besitz des ehemals Varnhagenschen Exemplars gelangt.

[10] ZfdA., 23. Bd. (1879), S. 204. Der volle Wortlaut des F. Schellingschen Briefs vom 30. 4. 1858 ist später im Anhang von R. Steinerts Ausgabe (1914) publiziert worden; dort liest man genauer, wie und warum Schellings Sohn und Herausgeber «das motiv der geldverlegenheit als sehr unwahrscheinlich beseitigt» hat: «Ich bearbeite gegenwärtig für den Druck Schellings Philosophie der Kunst (...). Diese Schrift ist nach Inhalt und Form von der Art, d. h. so merkwürdig, daß, wenn Schelling, wie der Verf. jener Angaben über die Entstehung des Romans supponirt, damals sich ‹in ziemlicher Geldverlegenheit› befunden

hin auszuschließen, äußert er sich im ganzen doch zögernd, hat denn auch die ‹Nachtwachen› bekanntlich nicht aufgenommen in die Werkausgabe (im Gegensatz zu den im Schlegel-Tieckschen Almanach erschienenen Gedichten und anderen poetischen Versuchen Schellings), wobei er freilich – auch dies zeigt der von Seydel im Auszug publizierte Brief F. Schellings – ‹interessiert› ist: es wäre ihm offensichtlich lieber, das Büchlein von 1804 n i c h t aufnehmen zu müssen, mit Rücksicht auf das, was Varnhagen seine «Keckheit» nannte, und wohl auch auf das, was bei Beckers und ähnlich bei Karl von Hase als die «Formlosigkeit» dieses Buches beschrieben wird.

So also standen die Dinge in den siebziger Jahren des 19. Jahrhunderts: Schelling oder etwa nicht Schelling, lautete die Frage, wobei das Schwergewicht auf der Seite Schellings lag, wenn man einmal absieht von dem Votum, das Rudolf Haym in der vorhin angeführten Anmerkung in der ‹Romantischen Schule› abgegeben hatte. Überzeugt von der Autorschaft Schellings war auch der Herausgeber des ersten Neudrucks der ‹Nachtwachen›[11], der vor allem aus der Biographie Heines bekannte Schriftsteller Alfred Meißner. «Über den Ursprung des vorliegenden Buches ist unter Literaturkundigen kein Zweifel mehr», schrieb er in seinem Vorwort, das datiert ist: «Lindau im September 1876»: «Es ist ein dichterischer Versuch J. v. Schellings»; es folgt ein nicht ganz exakter Hinweis auf das unter demselben Pseudonym «in A. W. v. Schlegel's Musenalmanach auf 1802» erschienene «erzählende Gedicht ‹Letzte Worte des Pfarrers auf [!] Drottning›» und eine ebenfalls ungenaue Wiedergabe des Varnhagenschen Berichts, den wir schon kennen. Meißner behauptet auch, ein Exemplar des Buches, «mit einer Widmung von Schelling's Hand», sei «aus A. W. Schlegel's Bibliothek in die Varnhagen's» gekommen, was völlig ausgeschlossen ist, da nicht nur in den Tagebüchern Varnhagens nicht das Geringste über ein derartiges Exemplar verlautet, sondern auch über Varnhagens eigenes Exemplar seit seiner Entdeckung und Beschreibung durch Steinert[12] alle nur wünschbare Klarheit besteht, insbeson-

---

hätte, man nicht einsieht, warum er nicht damals diese Philosophie d. K. herausgab, wodurch er sich zweifelsohne viel mehr Geld gemacht hätte, als indem er den Roman, wie Varnhagen voraussetzt, um Geld zu bekommen für Dienemann schrieb.»

[11] In: Bibliothek deutscher Kuriosa. Lindau und Leipzig 1877. – 2. Aufl. Berlin 1881.

[12] Siehe oben Anm. 2. Höchstwahrscheinlich handelt es sich bei Meißners Behauptung über jenes aus A. W. Schlegels Bibliothek stammende Exemplar um eine nach dem Prinzip der ‹stillen Post› entstandene Variation der Varnhagenschen Tagebuchnotiz über das Exemplar, das bei der Versteigerung von Friedrich Schlegels Büchern aufgetaucht sein soll, wobei dieses Exemplar zu Varnhagens eigenem und Friedrich zu August Wilhelm Schlegel geworden ist.

dere auch darüber, daß es keine «Widmung», geschweige denn eine von
Schellings Hand, enthielt. Unangetastet durch derartige Unzuverlässig-
keiten, die auch Meißners sonstige Angaben zur Autorschaftsfrage so
gut wie wertlos machen, bleibt die Tatsache, daß das Werk selbst durch
seine Edition überhaupt erst über den kleinen Kreis der Besitzer und
Benutzer von Erstdrucken hinaus bekannt werden konnte. Es scheint
denn auch, der schon 1881 erschienenen zweiten Auflage nach zu urteilen, auf ein gewisses Interesse gestoßen zu sein.

Eine neue Phase der Geschichte unseres Problems beginnt im ersten
Jahrzehnt des 20. Jahrhunderts damit, daß zum erstenmal mit derselben
Entschiedenheit, mit der bisher die Autorschaft Schellings behauptet wor-
den war, während die Einwände gegen sie immer nur auf den Ton des
Zweifels gestimmt waren, die Atheierung vertreten wurde. Das erste
Votum dieser Art, das bekannt wurde, war eine Äußerung Diltheys,
keine schriftliche, sondern eine mündliche, im Gespräch mit einem Berliner Kollegen getane, über die der Gesprächspartner, der Germanist
Richard M. Meyer, im Euphorion, Jahrgang 1903, berichtete: auch er,
R. M. Meyer, habe «früher die Nachricht von Schellings Verfasserschaft
der ‹Nachtwachen› einfach hingenommen», doch sei vor kurzer Zeit
«plötzlich die Notwendigkeit der Revision dieser Frage» an ihn heran-
getreten: «Der beste lebende Kenner der romantischen Philosophie, Wilhelm Dilthey, erklärte mir im Gespräch, daß das von ihm neuerdings
gelesene Werkchen unmöglich von Schelling herrühren könne. Er führte
dabei drei Gründe an, von denen mindestens zwei mir allerdings zwingend erscheinen: In dem ganzen Buch sei keine Spur von Schelling's doch
so stark ausgeprägter Eigenart, die sich sonst auch in kleinen Stücken
nie verleugne; es finden sich darin so triviale Partien, wie sie bei ihm
überhaupt undenkbar seien; es wehe darin eine Stimmung, von der der
Philosoph 1805 sich so energisch abgewandt hatte, daß auch nur eine
nachträgliche Veröffentlichung eines in diesem Sinne gehaltenen Bekennt-
nisses ausgeschlossen sei.»[13] Letzteres zielt zweifellos auf die düsteren,
wild-satirischen, ‹nihilistischen› Züge des Buches – auch von ‹Pessimis-
mus› hat man gesprochen – die auch Schellings Sohn und den Schelling-
Forscher Beckers schon irritiert hatten und auf die unten noch in verschiedener Hinsicht näher einzugehen sein wird: Züge, wie sie etwa in dem wie-
derholten «Nichts!» am Schluß des letzten Kapitels besonders auffällig
entgegentraten. Das Argument, dem R. M. Meyer nicht glaubt beipflich-
ten zu können, ist das zweite: das die «trivialen Partien» betreffende.
Meyer sucht ihm zu begegnen, indem er zunächst das Urteil Rudolf
Hayms zustimmend zitiert, die ‹Nachtwachen› gehörten «zu den geist-

---

[13] Richard M. Meyer: ‹Nachtwachen von Bonaventura.› Euph. 10. Bd. (1903),
S. 578–588. Das Zitat S. 578 f.

reichsten Produktionen der Romantik», und dann zu bedenken gibt, daß wir ja «bei diesen» «fast stets auf eine Ungleichheit der Stücke, auf das Vorkommen ganz öder Partien neben bedeutenden gefaßt» seien, er «erinnere nur an die ‹Lucinde›». Eine Entgegnung, die schon rein logisch auf schwachen Füßen steht, ja auf eine petitio principii hinausläuft, indem sie von einem Allgemeinbegriff ‹Romantik› ausgeht, von dem erst noch zu beweisen wäre, ob Schelling als Dichter unter ihn fällt (was Meyer offenbar stillschweigend voraussetzt). Schwach ist Meyers Entgegnung aber auch insofern, als sie sich auf ein argumentum ex auctoritate stützt, das vielleicht nicht einmal so gemeint war, wie Meyer es versteht: nämlich die Einordnung der ‹Nachtwachen› unter die «Produktionen der Romantik». Die Frage: wie weit sind die ‹Nachtwachen› «romantisch»? wird von Meyer nicht gestellt, ebensowenig wie die sich sofort anschließende: in welchem Sinne des Wortes wären sie so zu nennen? Etwa in einem Sinne, der ein Vorkommen «trivialer Partien» einschlösse? Aber was wäre das für ein Romantikbegriff? Wie gelangt man zu ihm? Und – womit wir wieder bei der ersten Gegenfrage wären – wie weit kommt Schelling in Betracht als praktisch-poetischer Beiträger zu einem solchen, gelegentliche Trivialität nicht ausschließenden Romantikbegriff?

Ich habe bei dieser Differenz zwischen Dilthey und R. M. Meyer auch deshalb etwas verweilt, weil sie prototypisch ist für eine Differenz, die fortan in der Bonaventura-Forschung immer wieder aufgetreten ist: die Differenz in der Einschätzung des Werks, mit anderen Worten: in der Bestimmung seine literarischen Werts. Selten sind die Urteile weiter auseinandergegangen als gegenüber diesem Buch, wobei vermutlich zu den höchsten Einstufungen nicht selten auch das Dunkel um den Namen Bonaventura, das Rätsel der Verfasserschaft, die Ungreifbarkeit des Autors einiges beigetragen hat. Die Ausschlagweite der Urteile reicht von Varnhagens Verdikt «unglaublich schwaches Erzeugniß» über gemäßigte Äußerungen wie «geistreich», «anziehend», «interessant» bis zum Prädikat des «Genialen» oder allgemeineren Thesen superlativischer Art, in denen sich das jeweilige Wertsystem des Beurteilers mehr oder weniger deutlich aussprach, Thesen wie etwa der vom «Beweis für die illusionslose Existenznähe bis an die Schwelle des mit menschlichen Mitteln überhaupt noch Faßbaren»[14]. Strittig wurde in diesem Zusammenhang besonders die Frage der Originalität des ‹Nachtwachen›-Dichters – um so strittiger, je mehr der schon von Rudolf Haym gegebene Hinweis auf die «Einmischung Jean-Paul'scher Töne» präzisiert und ergänzt wurde, worüber sogleich zu reden sein wird. Zuvor aber ist noch, mit einigen Worten wenigstens, von der eigentlichen These, besser: Hypothese des R. M.

---

[14] Joachim Müller: Die Nachtwachen des Bonaventura. In: Neue Jahrbücher für Wissenschaft und Jugendbildung, XII (1936), S. 443.

Meyerschen Aufsatzes zu berichten: auch sie gehört zum Anfang der angedeuteten neuen ‹Phase›, insofern mit ihr die Reihe der Versuche beginnt, einen anderen Verfasser als Schelling namhaft und, soweit wie
möglich, dingfest zu machen. R. M. Meyer schlägt E. T. A. Hoffmann
vor, fügt allerdings nach Darlegung seiner Beweggründe abschließend
hinzu, es liege ihm «fern, in all dem eine zwingende Beweisführung zu
sehen oder etwa die Sicherheit zur Schau zu tragen, mit der man beliebige
Lustspiele Heinrich von Kleist zugeschrieben hat». Seine Beweisführung
wird vor allem dadurch stark beeinträchtigt, daß aus der fraglichen Zeit
sehr wenig an schriftlichen und fast gar nichts an literarischen Äußerungen Hoffmanns vorliegt: «Seit dem kleinen Artikel im ‹Freimüthigen› von 1803 (Schreiben eines Klostergeistlichen ‹Ueber die Chöre in
Schillers Braut von Messina›) hat Hoffmann» – nach der Mitteilung E. v.
Grisebachs, die R. M. Meyer ohne Widerspruch zitiert – «nichts Literarisches drucken lassen bis zum 15. Februar 1809, wo sein ‹Ritter Gluck› in
der Allgemeinen Musikalischen Zeitung erschien.» Dies ‹Schreiben eines
Klostergeistlichen› ist denn auch die Hauptstütze der Meyerschen Argumentation: er setzt es in Beziehung zum Marionettenspiel von den zwei
Brüdern in den ‹Nachtwachen›, das er versuchsweise als Parodie auf
Schillers ‹Braut von Messina› deutet, und kommt so – da doch auch jenes Hoffmannsche ‹Schreiben› im ‹Freimüthigen› von 1803 eine «mit
herbstem Spott» vorgetragene Kritik an den Chören in der ‹Braut von
Messina› enthalte – zu der allerdings im coniunctivus potentialis vorgetragenen Folgerung: «Da wäre es für seine Autorschaft der ‹Nachtwachen› doch kein geringes Indizium, wenn diese Schrift über dasselbe
Drama in Form einer grausamen Parodie urteilen würde!» Die Schwä-
chen dieses Arguments, die Meyer offensichtlich selbst bewußt waren,
brauchen kaum ausdrücklich dargelegt zu werden, ebensowenig wie die
Problematik der übrigen von Meyer angeführten Argumente, unter denen so unglaublich schwache sind wie der Hinweis darauf, daß der
Name ‹Bonaventura› «stark an den ‹Benfatto› des Berganza erinnert»[15],
also an einen Namen aus einer Novelle E. T. A. Hoffmanns von 1811.

Es liegt nicht in der Absicht der vorliegenden Studie, sämtliche Argumente sämtlicher bisher vorgetragener Verfasserschaftshypothesen vor-
zuführen und auf ihre Stärke oder Schwäche hin zu prüfen, was ein sehr
langwieriges und wohl auch, mit Verlaub zu sagen, sehr langweiliges
Geschäft wäre. Eine solche Musterung ist auch – der Zielsetzung dieser
Arbeit nach – gar nicht notwendig, da sie nicht auf Darstellung und Kritik der bisherigen Beweisführungen, sondern auf die Darlegung eines
neuen, diese an Stringenz übertreffenden Beweisganges abzielt, wobei sie
es dem Leser überlassen muß, wie weit er bereit ist, die einzelnen Schritte

---

[15] A. a. O., S. 586.

dieses Beweisganges und schließlich die Ergebnisse zu akzeptieren. Auch den Vergleich mit den früher vorgetragenen Beweisführungen, den Vergleich also im Hinblick auf Stringenz und Evidenz, kann sie (und will sie) dem Leser nicht abnehmen. Wenn hier also von früheren Beiträgen zum ‹Bonaventura›-Problem, in diesem Kapitel oder auch an einzelnen Stellen der folgenden, die Rede ist, so lediglich im Sinne einer Nennung der wichtigsten Stationen innerhalb der Geschichte unseres Buchs, seiner allmählichen Entdeckung und seiner Wirkungen, zu denen ja auch die Mutmaßungen über seinen Verfasser gehören, und allenfalls noch im Sinne einer knappen Andeutung über Inhalt, Methode und Niveau des betreffenden Beitrags. Was die Vermutung R. M. Meyers angeht, so ist sie im übrigen sehr bald schon, ja bereits im Augenblick ihrer Veröffentlichung, auf ein äußerstes Maß von Unglaubwürdigkeit reduziert worden durch eine im selben ‹Euphorion›-Heft erschienene Mitteilung des E. T. A. Hoffmann-Forschers Hans von Müller über ein kürzlich aufgefundenes Manuskript E. T. A. Hoffmanns von 121 Blättern, dessen erster Teil eine Buchführung über die Produktion des Schreibers enthält, von ihm selbst betitelt als «Miscellaneen / die litterarische und künstlerische / Laufbahn betreffend. / Angefangen im Exil und zwar im August / 1803», nach dem Kommentar Hans von Müllers «unschätzbar als o f f e n b a r v o l l s t ä n d i g e s Repertorium aller vorbambergischen Versuche Hoffmanns, als Komponist oder Schriftsteller an die Öffentlichkeit zu kommen» (d. h. aller Versuche vor September 1808). Man dürfe «hier sagen: quod non est in actis, non est in mundo». Von den ‹Nachtwachen› aber ist darin nicht die Rede, ebensowenig wie von irgendeiner ihnen auch nur entfernt vergleichbaren Produktion[16].

1904 erschien dann der Neudruck der ‹Nachtwachen› innerhalb der Reihe ‹Deutsche Literaturdenkmale des 18. und 19. Jahrhunderts› (als No. 133), mit einer langen Einleitung und gemäß den wissenschaftlichen Prinzipien dieser Reihe herausgegeben von Hermann Michel. Der Text ist der der Erstausgabe, unter Wahrung von Orthographie und Interpunktion, beigegeben ist ein außerordentlich sorgfältiger und gehaltvoller Kommentar, die Quelle für unzählige spätere Beiträge innerhalb einer, hier wie anderswo, immer maßloser anschwellenden Sekundärliteratur. Die Einleitung gibt zunächst ein Bild von der Verlagstätigkeit des Hauses Dienemann, mit genauen Auskünften insbesondere über die Romanserie, in der das Werk erschien, darunter zum erstenmal, aus Meßkatalogen und dergleichen ermittelt, eine Aufstellung sämtlicher Titel die-

---

[16] Hans von Müller: Nachträgliches zu E. T. A. Hoffmann. Euph. 10. Bd. (1903), S. 589–592. Merkwürdigerweise ist trotzdem immer wieder die Verfasserschaft E. T. A. Hoffmanns zur Diskussion gestellt und sein Werk entsprechenden Untersuchungen, neuerdings auch mit sprachstatistischen Methoden, unterworfen worden.

ses ‹Journals von neuen deutschen Original Romanen›, eine Aufstellung, die in der Tat eine – wie Michel schreibt – «wunderlich gemischte Gesellschaft» beieinander zeigt, von Sophie Brentano, deren (sicherlich mit Clemens gemeinsam übersetzte) ‹Spanische und italienische Novellen› hier 1804–05 in zwei Bänden erschienen, über Franz Horn, den später als Literarhistoriker bekanntgewordenen, bis zum «Verfasser des Rinaldini», also Christian Vulpius, und dem berüchtigten Trivialromanschreiber Karl Nicolai. (Die Namen der Autoren waren zu einem großen Teil schon in der oben zitierten Haymschen Fußnote genannt.) Es folgt eine vortreffliche Charakteristik des Werkes selbst, die unter anderem, ebenfalls zum erstenmal, den ganzen Umfang der von Haym bereits bemerkten «Einmischung Jean-Paul'scher Töne» sichtbar macht, durch eine Fülle von Nachweisen auf allen denkbaren Ebenen, der gehaltlich-motivischen wie der grammatischen und lexikalischen, und schließlich eine Erörterung der Verfasserschaftsfrage, mit einer detailierten Bestandsaufnahme des bisher dazu Bekanntgewordenen und manchen neuen Hinweisen – auf die zurückzukommen sein wird – und einem vorsichtigen Fazit: «Nach alledem ist es doch wohl verfrüht, einen anderen Verfasser der Nachtwachen als Schelling anzunehmen»[17]. R. M. Meyers Zuschreibungsversuch betreffend, erinnert er nur an den Hinweis H. v. Müllers auf das erwähnte Hoffmannsche Tagebuch, durch den er bereits «widerlegt» sei. Im übrigen geht es ihm weniger darum, Schelling als Autor der ‹Nachtwachen› zu erweisen, als darum, zu zeigen, daß er es gewesen sein k a n n, trotz aller inzwischen angehäufter Gegenargumente; wozu er nochmals, wie schon Beckers, auf den ‹Heinz Widerporst› als eine ähnliche Mischung aus Ernst und Scherz hinweist, auf die ‹Letzten Worte des Pfarrers›, aber auch auf die «deprimierende Wirkung» der ersten Würzburger Erfahrungen Schellings, freilich auch die Gegenargumente ernst genug nimmt, am ernstesten die von ihm selbst am wesentlichsten geförderten: die Beziehungen der ‹Nachtwachen› zu Jean Paul: «Hier aber stocken wir. Der Name Jean Pauls erinnert uns daran, wieviel Bonaventura ihm verdankt. Kein Zweifel, daß er über eine vortreffliche Kenntnis dieses Autors verfügte. Läßt sich nun eine solche bei Schelling nachweisen?» So fragt er, um mit der lapidaren, den Stil wie den Mann kennzeichnenden Antwort fortzufahren: «Nein. Seine Briefe sprechen selten und immer nur beiläufig von Jean Paul. Seine philosophischen Schriften verraten weder nach Inhalt noch Form die Einwirkung Jean Pauls. Seine Vorlesungen über Philosophie der Kunst, die so viele Namen nennen, gedenken Jean Pauls mit keiner Silbe.»[18] Anschließend geht er, um zu zeigen, daß jenes Dilemma vielleicht doch nicht unauflösbar sei, auf

---

[17] Op. cit., S. LXV.
[18] A. a. O., S. LXI.

Schellings Eigenart ein, sich gern von ungenannten Vorbildern anregen zu lassen, sowie auf die große Beliebtheit von Jean Pauls Romanen zu jener Zeit, erwägt auch, ob nicht Caroline ihrem Mann «geholfen» haben könne. Gleichwohl bleiben die Bedenken auch zuletzt, in der Formulierung seines Fazits, unverhohlen: «Eine Reihe von Argumenten konnten wir zu Gunsten Schellings anführen. Weniges, aber Gewichtiges sprach gegen ihn; wir versuchten es zu entkräften, ohne doch die Schwierigkeiten zu verkennen.»[19]

Den Michelschen Resultaten in mancher Hinsicht verpflichtet ist auch die Bonaventura-Arbeit, von der die meisten Wirkungen ausgehen sollten und die zugleich die heftigste Polemik gegen Michel enthielt: das Buch von Franz Schultz: ‹Der Verfasser der Nachtwachen von Bonaventura› (Leipzig 1909), das gleichzeitig mit einer ‹Nachtwachen›-Neuedition desselben Autors[20] erschien. Michel hatte unter den Titeln der Dienemannschen Romanserie auch ein Werk des Dresdener Romantikers, Naturphilosophen und Schelling-Schülers Gotthilf Heinrich Schubert (1780 bis 1860) nachgewiesen: ‹Die Kirche und die Götter›, anonym erschienen im Jahr 1804. Ein Freund Schuberts war der bis dahin wenig bekannte Karl Friedrich Gottlob Wetzel (1779–1819), mit Schubert bekannt seit ihren gemeinsamen Universitätstagen in Leipzig, wo sie beide Medizin studiert hatten, promoviert zum Dr. med. in Erfurt (1805), seit 1802 als Verfasser von Publikationen verschiedenster Art nachweisbar – als Verfasser von Gedichten, Romanen, Dramen, Satiren, aber auch medizinischen Schriften – zeitweise Mitarbeiter der ‹Dresdner Abendzeitung› (1806), seit 1810 in Bamberg, wo er die Redaktion des ‹Fränkischen Merkur› übernahm. Beide, Schubert und Wetzel, bilden den Gegenstand des ersten Kapitels des zweiten, ‹Der Verfasser› überschriebenen Teils in Franz Schultz' Buch, nachdem im ersten Teil die bisher bekanntgewordenen Zeugnisse zur Dienemannschen Verlagsgeschichte und zur ersten Wirkungsgeschichte des Buches sowie die bisherigen Verfasserschaftshypothesen behandelt wurden, mit scharfer und gelegentlich unnötiger Polemik nicht nur gegen Michel, freilich gegen diesen ganz besonders[21], sondern auch gegen die ebenfalls bereits vorgetragene Hypothese von Carolines Verfasserschaft[22] und die in der Tat, wie wir sahen,

---

[19] Op. cit., S. LXIV f.
[20] Die Nachtwachen des Bonaventura. Hrsg. v. Franz Schultz. Leipzig 1909.
[21] Er glaubt z. B. bei Michel eine «mit dem Scheine philologischer Akribie» aufgebotene «Dialektik und Sophistik» feststellen zu müssen (op. cit., S. 87).
[22] Sie war vertreten worden von Erich Eckertz in: Zs. f. Bücherfreunde, 9. Jg. (1905/06), Heft 6, S. 234–249 (‹Nachtwachen von Bonaventura. Ein Spiel mit Schelling und Goethe gegen die Schlegels von Caroline›), nachdem schon Michel, wie erwähnt, die Möglichkeit einer Mitbeteiligung Carolines erwogen hatte (S. LXIII–LXV seiner Einleitung).

überaus unwahrscheinliche E. T. A. Hoffmann-Hypothese. In seinem
eigenen Versuch, die Verfasserfrage zu lösen, geht Schultz zunächst ausführlich auf Schubert und seine naturphilosophischen Anschauungen ein,
um erst von hier aus überzuleiten zu dem in vielem ähnlich denkenden
Wetzel und, zum Beweis seiner Autorschaft, von der er fest überzeugt
ist, eine Fülle von Material aus Wetzels Schriften, vor allem den humoristisch-satirischen und dem Roman ‹Kleon der letzte Grieche›, aber auch
aus den ‹Briefen über Brown's System der Heilkunde› und anderen
Schriften, auszubreiten: Parallelstellen zu einzelnen ‹Nachtwachen›-Pas-
sagen, gewisse Motive, die ähnlich auch in diesen nachzuweisen sind,
stilistische Eigentümlichkeiten, «Einflüsse» anderer Autoren, die auch in
den ‹Nachtwachen› erkennbar sind (Jean Paul, Shakespeare, Tieck, No-
valis) und Philosophisch-Gedankliches. Der Evidenzgrad der einzelnen
Argumente ist sehr ungleich, die Auswahl, die der Verfasser unter den
Parallelstellen getroffen hat, die ihm aufgefallen waren, sehr großzügig
– wofür im Folgenden einige Beispiele gegeben werden –, aber der Ge-
samteindruck der von Schultz gegebenen Nachweise war doch so stark,
daß viele Leser seines Buches sich für überzeugt erklärten, darunter übrigens auch Richard M. Meyer, der die Rezension für den ‹Euphorion›
schrieb und in ihr, nach einigen kritischen Bemerkungen über die «Ma-
nieren» des Verfassers, abschließend erklärte: «Das Ergebnis scheint mir
beinahe so unwiderleglich wie (S. 326) dem Verfasser.»[23]

Fortan lassen sich die Beiträge zur Bonaventura-Frage, seien es Lexi-
konartikel, Vor- oder Nachworte zu Editionen, Untersuchungen, Interpretationen oder Erwähnungen in größeren Zusammenhängen, etwa in
Literaturgeschichten, im wesentlichen in zwei große Gruppen aufteilen:
solche, in denen die Verfasserschaft Wetzels als gesichert betrachtet wird,
und solche, in denen die Schultzsche These zwar erwähnt, aber gleichzeitig mit mehr oder weniger starkem Akzent angezweifelt wird. Eine
Gegenthese, die nicht nur als schiere Behauptung, sondern mit einem
ernstzunehmenden Versuch einer Begründung auftrat, ist nur noch einmal, schon drei Jahre nach dem Buch von Franz Schultz, vorgelegt worden, freilich nicht von einem Germanisten, sondern von einem ‹Außen-
seiter›, einem Philosophiehistoriker: 1912 erschien gleichzeitig eine Neuausgabe der ‹Nachtwachen› mit dem kühnen Titel: ‹Clemens Brentano /
Nachtwachen von Bonaventura› und ein Aufsatz ihres Herausgebers
Erich Frank: ‹Clemens Brentano der Verfasser der Nachtwachen von
Bonaventura›[24]. Erich Frank, der von der Heidelberger Akademie der
Wissenschaften den Auftrag erhalten hatte, «Schellings Beziehungen zur

---

[23] Euph. 16. Bd. (1909), S. 800.
[24] Germanisch-Romanische Monatsschrift, 4. Jg. (1912), S. 417–440.

Literatur festzustellen»[25], waren besonders gewisse sprachliche Eigentümlichkeiten im Text der ‹Nachtwachen› aufgefallen, Eigentümlichkeiten wie etwa eine besondere Konsequenz in der Setzung des Dativ-‹e›, und er meinte, ähnliche Züge, zusammen mit gewissen inhaltlichen Entsprechungen, auch bei Brentano feststellen zu können, von dem er vornehmlich den ‹Godwi› heranzog. Die Sicherheit, mit der er von der Autorschaft Brentanos überzeugt war, zeigt schon dessen Name auf dem Titelblatt der Frankschen Neuedition. Ihm entgegnete Eduard Berend in einer noch im selben Jahr erschienenen, sehr gehaltvollen und gründlichen Rezension[26], in der er die Frankschen Argumente teils als nicht zwingend, teils als selbst nicht genügend begründet erwies. Die «allerdings auffallende Häufigkeit des Dativ-e der starken Maskulina und Neutra in den Nachtwachen» betreffend, teilte er die Ergebnisse seiner eigenen Nachprüfungen an mehreren Brentanoschen Werken mit, die ein den Frankschen Behauptungen keineswegs entsprechendes Bild boten. Er wies auch auf die Schwierigkeit hin, bei den Gepflogenheiten damaliger Setzer wie Autoren aus orthographischen Spezialitäten, wie etwa der Schreibung ‹z› oder ‹zz› für heutiges ‹tz›, irgendwelche Rückschlüsse auf die Identität des Autors zu ziehen, wie Frank das versucht hatte, und erinnerte vor allem an ein Zeugnis, das in der Tat ein sehr starkes Argument gegen die Autorschaft Brentanos ist: an einen Brief Brentanos an Arnim vom 3. Oktober 1804, in dem Brentano u. a. schreibt, es sei nun «ein Jahr», daß er «keine Zeile gedichtet». Josef Körner, selbst einer der hervorragendsten Kenner der Romantik, faßte in seinem ‹Bibliographischen Handbuch des deutschen Schrifttums› (1948), bei Erwähnung der Frankschen Edition, dessen These zur Verfasserschaft und die Berendsche Entgegnung in dem einen knappen Satz zusammen: «den hier unternommenen Versuch, das Werk C. Brentano zu vindizieren, erledigte E. Berend in Euph. 19, S. 796 ff.» Körners Urteil über die Schultzsche These gehört zur zweiten der eben genannten Gruppen: das Buch von Schultz wird aufgeführt, sein Inhalt durch den Zusatz «[Friedrich Gottlob Wetzel?]» angedeutet und nach einigen weiteren Angaben zur späteren Sekundärliteratur schließt Körner den Artikel ‹Nachtwachen von Bonaventura› mit dem (schon einmal zitierten) Satz: «Die Autorschaftsfrage ist immer noch kontrovers.» Die folgende Zeit ist freilich nicht gerade durch ein Austragen dieser Kontroverse gekennzeichnet, sondern eher durch eine gewisse Resignation im Hinblick auf die Verfasserschaftsfrage. Sie schloß übrigens nicht aus, daß das Werk als solches immer wieder Interesse fand, wie nicht nur eine Reihe von z. T. sehr eindringlichen Interpretationen, sondern auch die Reihe der Neudrucke zeigt, die seit dem von

---

[25] A. a. O., S. 417.
[26] Euph. 19. Bd. (1912), S. 796–813.

E. Frank herausgegebenen erschienen sind, von der eingangs erwähnten Raimund Steinertschen Edition bis zu den Ausgaben der zweiten Nachkriegszeit, unter denen besonders die vier dicht aufeinanderfolgenden auffallen, die unmittelbar nach dem Krieg von Walter Widmer (1945), Renate Riemeck (1946), Franz Schultz (1947) und Wolfgang Pfeiffer-Belli (1947) besorgt wurden.

II. Die ‹Zeitung für die elegante Welt› und einer ihrer Mitarbeiter

1. Erste Indizien

Es ist das Verdienst Hermann Michels – eines der Verdienste, die sich Michel um die Bonaventura-Forschung erworben hat – auf zwei Veröffentlichungen hingewiesen zu haben, die beide in unmittelbarem Zusammenhang mit dem hier erörterten Problem stehen und beide, um dieselbe Zeit, in einem der damals führenden deutschen belletristischen Journale erschienen sind: der ‹Zeitung für die elegante Welt›. Am 21. Juli 1804 erschien hier, mit der Anmerkung «Fragment aus einem noch ungedruckten Roman: N a c h t w a c h e n von Bonaventura, der zur Michaelismesse herauskommen wird», und unter dem Titel «Prolog des Hanswurstes zu einer Tragödie: d e r M e n s c h», ein Prosastück von rund vier Textspalten, das bis auf wenige geringfügige Abweichungen identisch ist mit dem dritten und letzten Teil der achten Nachtwache (also des Kapitels, das in seinen beiden ersten Teilen den Tod des Tragödiendichters oder, wie es im originalen Inhaltsverzeichnis heißt, die «Himmelfahrt des Dichters» beschreibt und dessen «Absagebrief an das Leben» wiedergibt). Und in derselben Zeitung erschien am 26. März 1805 ein etwa zweispaltiges Prosastück mit dem Titel «Des Teufels Taschenbuch. Einleitung» und der wiederum in Fußnotenform gegebenen Erläuterung: «Man hat sich in den Taschenbüchern bereits dergestalt erschöpft, indem es außer den historischen, poetischen und dergleichen schlechthin, noch eine Menge für das weibliche Geschlecht, für die elegante Welt u.s.w. u.s.w. gibt, daß es in der That nothwendig scheint, mit dem Publikum zu wechseln, weshalb denn diesem Teufels Taschenbuche, welches zur Ostermesse erscheinen wird, hier eine flüchtige Erwähnung eingeräumt ist. B o n a v e n t u r a.» Sowohl der Name am Schluß der Erläuterung als auch der Text dieser «Einleitung» zu einem Teufels-Taschenbuch[1], der direkt an die «Teufelsphantasien»[2] der «Nachtwachen» anknüpft, sprechen eine so eindeutige Sprache, daß in der Tat an der Identität d i e s e s Bonaventura mit dem der ‹Nachtwachen› «kein Zweifel herrschen»[2] kann und bisher auch von niemandem gezweifelt worden ist. Damit aber ist eine Beziehung – wie auch immer sie geartet sein mag

---

[1] Abgedruckt im Anhang zu Michels Ausgabe (DLD Nr. 133, Berlin 1904).
[2] Michel, S. XLVIII.

– zwischen dem ‹Nachtwachen›-Verfasser und der ‹Zeitung für die elegante Welt› gegeben, deren Herausgeber damals, bis zu seinem Tode am 19. 1. 1805, der Hofrat Spazier war, ein Schwager Jean Pauls.

Michel hat daraus keine sehr erheblichen Schlüsse gezogen. Er versuchte lediglich, aus dieser Beziehung ein (nicht sonderlich starkes) Argument für seine Schelling-Hypothese zu gewinnen, indem er auf die Beziehungen des ebenfalls an Schelling glaubenden Jean Paul zu Spazier und die Bekanntschaft Schellings mit Spazier hinwies sowie darauf, daß «er selbst und Caroline mindestens je einen Artikel für die ‹Elegante Zeitung› geschrieben haben»[3]. Das bezieht sich auf die Artikel über A. W. Schlegels ‹Ion› vom 16. 1. 1802 und 29./31. 7. 1802, die Haym, mit den A. W. Schlegelschen Einsendungen an dieselbe Zeitung, als «höchst ergötzliches kritisches Nachspiel»[4] zur Erstaufführung des ‹Ion› geschildert hat. Aber diese Artikel liegen gegenüber dem Erscheinungsdatum der ‹Nachtwachen› und den beiden Einsendungen an die ‹Elegante Welt› um mehr als zwei Jahre zurück, und Anzeichen für spätere Kontakte Schellings mit dieser Zeitung hat auch Michel nicht gefunden. Es erhebt sich die Frage, ob irgendein anderer, etwa jemand, der nachweislich in den Jahren 1804–05 in Beziehung zur ‹Eleganten Welt› stand, und der vielleicht auch sonst, gelegentlich oder öfter, Beiträge zur ‹Eleganten› geliefert hat, die beiden genannten Prosastücke, den Trauerspiel-Prolog und die Ankündigung des Teufels-Taschenbuchs, in die Zeitung hat einrücken lassen. Und setzt man einmal voraus, was vorauszusetzen jedenfalls nicht von vornherein verboten ist: nämlich daß der, der sie einrücken ließ, zugleich ihr Verfasser war (und nicht etwa sein Verleger), so steht man vor der Frage, ob dieser unbekannte Verfasser sich etwa auf anderen Blättern derselben Zeitung – sei es in einer Rezension, einer Abhandlung oder was für einer Art von Beitrag auch immer – durch irgendwelche Anzeichen verrät; wobei die Beweiskraft und die Bedeutung solcher Anzeichen zunächst noch dahingestellt bleiben mögen. Ich habe die in Frage kommenden Jahrgänge der Zeitung in diesem Sinne, also durchaus im Sinne einer Frage oder, wenn man so will, eines Experiments, durchgesehen, meine auch, eine beträchtliche Anzahl solcher «Anzeichen» gefunden zu haben, die allerdings erst im Verein mit den entsprechenden Ergebnissen späterer und weiterreichender Nachforschungen, über die im folgenden Kapitel berichtet wird, zu einem Grad von Evidenz führten, der mir hinreichend erscheint. Die Anzeichen, von denen dabei zu reden sein wird, liegen auf der Ebene des Wortlauts ebenso wie auf der der Motive und der des «Gehalts», wenn es erlaubt ist, mit diesem Terminus einmal all das zusammenzufassen, was man mit «geistiger Welt», «geistiger Hal-

---

[3] Michel, S. XLVII.
[4] Haym, op. cit., S. 706 ff.

tung», «weltanschaulicher Position» usw. zu bezeichnen pflegt. Ich beginne mit einigen Beispielen für Indizien auf der Ebene des Wortlauts und lasse insbesondere die auf der Ebene des Gehalts, die für sich allein am wenigsten besagen (vestigia terrent), zunächst beiseite.

Erstes Beispiel: im ersten Teil der achten *Nachtwache* – der eben schon erwähnten *Himmelfahrt des Dichters* – liest man, wie der Erzähler den *Stadtpoeten* in seinem *Dachkämmerchen* erhängt findet – offenbar aus Verzweiflung über die Ablehnung seines Stückes – was mit dem jeanpaulisierend-zeugmatischen Wortspiel ausgedrückt wird, der Erzähler habe *statt eines Trauerspiels,* das er *nicht erwartet hatte,* ihrer zwei gefunden: *das rükgehende vom Verleger, und den Tragiker selbst der das zweite aus dem Stegereife zugleich gedichtet und als* **Protagonist** *aufgeführt hatte*[5]. Zu **Protagonist** ist in der Fußnote die Erläuterung gegeben: *So hieß der e i n e Akteur der zu Tespis*[6] *Zeit mit dem* **Chore** *die ganze Tragödie ausmachte.* Eine fast gleichlautende Belehrung zur altgriechischen Theatergeschichte aber wird in einem Artikel gegeben, der am 7. 6. 1804 in der ‹Zeitung für die elegante Welt› erschien, also rund sechs Wochen vor dem Vorabdruck aus demselben Kapitel der ‹Nachtwachen›. Der Artikel – der erste einer Reihe von «Briefen über die neuesten Werke der deutschen schönen Literatur» – handelt zuerst von J e a n P a u l s ‹Flegeljahren›, vergleicht sie mit dem ‹Titan› – im ‹Titan› «glühet und brennt alles», «ja ist das Leben oft bis zum Vernichten groß und gewaltig», hier dagegen herrsche ein «milderes Klima» – erkennt in der Figur des Vult einen alten Bekannten wieder, der, wenn er noch einige Jahre fortwachse «in dem Buche», sich auch Siebenkäs oder Leibgeber oder Graul nennen könne («bei denen wir den Namentauschhandel schon gewohnt sind») und der «das eigentliche Ich im Ganzen» sei. Danach kommt er auf «etwas dramatisches», das ‹Wilhelm Tell›-Drama eines gewissen Veit Weber, zu sprechen: «Ich sage Etwas, denn viel werden Sie nicht finden, es ist kaum hinlänglich, um das Dramatische vom Rhetorischen zu unterscheiden, ja man könnte fast die vielen Personen in einen einzigen **Protagonisten** zusammenschmelzen, **der zu Thespis Zeiten mit dem Chore die ganze Tragödie ausmachte**».

Die Übereinstimmung im Wortlaut, die bis in das Dativ-‹e› hineingeht («Chore»), das Erich Frank als charakteristisch für den Sprachge-

---

[5] Zitat nach Michel (S. 68), ebenso wie alle folgenden Zitate aus den ‹Nachtwachen› und der Ankündigung des Teufelstaschenbuchs. Für diese Zitate und n u r für diese Zitate wird grundsätzlich *Kursivdruck* verwendet. Wörtliche Übereinstimmungen werden gelegentlich durch **Fettdruck** hervorgehoben.

[6] Daß die Fehlschreibung für «Thespis» nicht zu Lasten des Verfassers gehen muß, braucht kaum erinnert zu werden. Vgl. dazu auch die oben erwähnten allgemeinen Ausführungen E. Berends in seiner Rezension von E. Franks Ausgabe (Euph. Bd. 19, Jg. 1912, bes. S. 800 ff.).

brauch des ‹Nachtwachen›-Dichters überhaupt erkannte, mag als solche auf einen ‹Zufall› zurückführbar sein. Es ist freilich ein schon ziemlich unwahrscheinlicher Zufall, an den dabei zu denken wäre – umso unwahrscheinlicher, als es sich nicht nur um eine Übereinstimmung des Wortlauts, sondern zugleich um eine solche der Gedankenverbindung handelt: beide Male geht es nicht nur um eine Worterklärung, sondern zugleich darum, einen bestimmten Sachverhalt, das Zusammenschmelzen der Figuren eines Dramas in eine einzige, zu beschreiben, wozu beide Male zum Mittel jener theatergeschichtlichen Parallele gegriffen wird. Mit anderen Worten: nicht nur die Folge der Wörter stimmt überein, sondern auch die Art ihrer Verklammerung mit dem Kontext; nicht nur die Formulierung als solche, sondern auch die Art, in der sie aus dem ganzen Gedankengang hervorgeht.[7]

Ich schließe, alle Folgerungen zunächst zurückstellend, einige weitere, z. T. ebenfalls ins Theaterfach einschlagende Textparallelen an, die sich

---

[7] Derselbe Artikel bietet noch einige weitere, freilich erheblich schwächere Anklänge an die ‹Nachtwachen›, die hier wenigstens angemerkt sein sollen: 1.) (mit bezug auf den «Hauptkarakter W a l t» in den ‹Flegeljahren›:) er «ist höchst liebenswürdig, durch seine herzliche Ungeschicklichkeit im Leben und Lieben; er wird mit dem Leser so vertraut, daß man ihn aus dem Buche heraus in die Wirklichkeit zaubern möchte.» (Zu vergleichen mit den Worten der Ophelia in der 14. Nw., S. 123: *Gottlob, daß ich aus dem Stücke herauskomme und meinen angenommenen Namen ablegen kann,* sowie denen des starrsüchtigen Unbekannten in der 4. Nw., S. 38: *O schon seit vielen Menschenaltern habe ich mich bestrebt aus dem Stücke herauszuspringen (...)* und ähnlichen Beispielen für ein oszillierendes Hin und Her zwischen Fiktions- und Wirklichkeitszusammenhang, auf das später zurückzukommen sein wird.) 2.) (Fortsetzung der Ausführungen über Walt:) «Seine Gefühle für Freundschaft müssen indeß Männern, besonders eleganten, fast unverständlich erscheinen (...); manchem möchten sie gar anstößig erscheinen, weil der ächte reine Idealismus, blos durch rasches Umkehren als Realismus da steht.» (Wozu zu vergleichen: a) in der *Himmelfahrt des Dichters* die Stelle: *Der Stadtpoet auf seinem Dachkämmerchen gehörte auch zu den Idealisten, die man mit Gewalt durch Hunger, Gläubiger, Gerichtsfrohne usw. zu Realisten bekehrt hatte (...)* (8. Nw.; S. 66); b) in der letzten Nw. die Frage an den Wurm: *Den Idealismus wie vieler Philosophen hast du auf diesen deinen Realismus zurückgeführt?* (16. Nw.; S. 141); c) *No. 2 und 3 sind philosophische Gegenfüßler, ein Idealist und ein Realist (...)* (9. Nw.; S. 79).) 3.) Die polemische Besprechung eines autobiographischen Buches von Kotzebue, gegen den bekanntlich auch in den ‹Nachtwachen› polemisiert wird, am Ende des Artikels sowie 4.) die dabei fallenden abschätzigen Worte über den «Karakter der Zeit»: «Hr. v. K. setzt den Grund des Beifalls seiner literarischen Produkte in die Wahrheit der Empfindung, die, nach ihm selbst, darin herrschen soll, und die er über alle Kunst der Darstellung erhebt. Ich hingegen in den bloßen Dilettantismus, der in jeder Rücksicht den Karakter der Zeit

in Artikeln desselben Verfassers finden, die eine in einem Artikel über den «Chor in der Tragödie; besonders in Beziehung auf Schillers Braut von Messina» vom 12./14. 5. 1803, die anderen in einem Aufsatz über Schillers ‹Wilhelm Tell›, der als «Achter Brief» der schon genannten Reihe am 29. 11. 1804 erschien. In dem Artikel über den «Chor in der Tragödie» findet sich nicht nur der Bezug auf die ‹Braut von Messina›, den die Bonaventura-Forschung seit R. M. Meyer[8] immer wieder aus dem Text der ‹Nachtwachen› herausgehört hat. Es findet sich dort nicht nur, expressis verbis, die «Hindeutung auf Masken und Kothurn», die auch am Schluß des Hanswurst-Prologs und d. h. zugleich: der achten Nachtwache erscheint[9]. Man findet dort nicht nur die uns schon bekannte Polemik gegen Kotzebue wieder, hier mit einer Wendung gegen den Mangel an «wahrhaft poetischer Erhebung»[10], die sehr an eine Stelle in den ‹Nachtwachen› anklingt, auf die noch öfter zurückzukommen sein wird: Die kleinen Wizbolde und gutmüthigen Komödienverfasser dagegen, die sich

---

ausmacht, und den er sich aufs vortheilhafteste, und, wie er gezeigt, besonders zu seinem eigenen Vortheile angeeignet hat.» (Wozu man in den ‹Nachtwachen› vergleichen mag: Der Zeitkarakter ist zusammengeflikt und gestoppelt wie eine Narrenjakke (3. Nw.; S. 18) und zahllose ähnliche Ausfälle gegen die Zeit und ihren Karakter, aber auch den Grimm des Erzählers über das Betragen des kleinen Dilettanten im Antiken-Museum: Mich ergrimmte es, weil ich in dieser herzlosen Zeit nichts weniger ausstehen kann, als die Frazze der Begeisterung (13. Nw.; S. 109).) Schließlich könnte man noch 5.) die Selbstcharakteristik hinzunehmen, die am Anfang dieses ersten ‹Literaturbriefs› steht: «Ich hoffe aber doch auf Ihre Nachsicht, wenn mich meine Unart, Händel zu suchen, dann und wann unerwartet überraschen sollte», und in ihr einen Anklang des bärbeißigen Tons hören, auf den die ‹Nachtwachen› fast durchweg gestimmt sind (Ein Kerl wie ich, der aus Haß und Grimm zusammengesetzt ist (14. Nw.; S. 114) und ähnliche Selbstdarstellungen wären hier zu vergleichen.)

8 Euph. Bd. 10, Jg. 1903, S. 583 ff.; vgl. auch Michel, S. XXXIII.

9 Gegen die Maskeneinführung habe ich mich nicht gesperrt, heißt es dort (8. Nw.; S. 76), und weiter: Auch gegen die Verse habe ich nichts einwenden wollen, sie sind nur eine komischere Lüge, so wie der Kothurn nur eine komischere Aufgeblasenheit (ebd.). Und in dem ‹Elegante Welt›-Artikel über den «Chor in der Tragödie» anläßlich der ‹Braut von Messina›, z. T. wieder mit wörtlichem Gleichklang: «Schon der Wiedereinführung des R h y t h m u s widersetzte man sich von allen Seiten; die Hindeutung auf M a s k e n und K o t h u r n fand man im höchsten Grade lächerlich (...)». (‹El. Welt› v. 12. 5. 1803).

10 «Es ist undeutlich, ob er [der Verfasser einer Kritik im ‹Freimüthigen›, der die Statthaftigkeit der Chöre für «unsere Bühne» bestritten hatte; J. S.] unter dem Ausdruck u n s e r die Kotzebuesche Bühne versteht, worauf es nie eine wahrhaft poetische Erhebung gegeben hat, und wo Alles auf einer einseitigen und unrichtigen Ansicht der Natur beruht; – oder ob er dieses Wort auf die äußere Einrichtung der neuern Bühne überhaupt bezieht. Im ersten Falle hat er

nur blos in den Familien umhertreiben, und nicht, wie Aristophanes, selbst über die Götter sich lustig zu machen wagen, sind mir herzlich zuwider, eben so wie jene schwachen gerührten Seelen, die, statt ein ganzes Menschenleben zu zertrümmern, um den Menschen selbst darüber zu erheben, sich nur mit der kleinen Quälerei beschäftigen (4. Nw.; S. 29), wobei offensichtlich eine berühmte Schillersche Formulierung Pate gestanden hat[11]. Es findet sich dort überdies eine Erklärung des Chors in der «ächten Tragödie», die der in der achten *Nachtwache* gegebenen sehr nahesteht und in einem zentalen Terminus[12] sogar wörtlich mit ihr übereinstimmt: «Der Chor ist der ächten Trogödie, die auch das Schmerzlichste nicht scheuen darf» – heißt es in dem ‹Elegante Welt›-Artikel – «durch seinen festen lyrischen Schwung, und dadurch, daß er die Gefühle des erschütterten Zuschauers **besänftigt** und gleichsam sogleich als eine zweite höhere Poesie ausspricht, unentbehrlich». Und in der achten *Nachtwache*, kurz vor dem Beginn des Hanswurst-Prologs: *Die alten Griechen hatten einen Chorus in ihren Trauerspielen angebracht, der durch die allgemeinen Betrachtungen die er anstellte, den Blick von der einzelnen schrecklichen Handlung abwendete und so die Gemüther* **besänftigte**. (S. 72)

Auch in der wichtigsten Parallele des Artikels vom 29. 11. 1804, des Briefes über Schillers ‹Wilhelm Tell›, geht es um Antikes. Diesmal ist es ein Faktum oder besser wohl: eine Anekdote aus der Geschichte der bildenden Kunst, die vergleichsweise herangezogen wird, zur Verdeutlichung eines heiklen dramaturgischen Problems: «Ob es übrigens besser gethan gewesen wäre, in dem Momente, als Tell nach dem Haupte des Kindes zielt, diese That selbst mehr in den Vordergrund zu stellen, statt das Auge durch die dazwischen fallenden Reden des Rudenz von ihr abzuwenden? das möchte ich erst, nachdem ich einer Aufführung des Stücks beigewohnt, entscheiden. Offenbar handelte Schiller hier nach dem Muster des **Timanthes**, der, als er den **Agamemnon** mahlte, den tiefen

---

vollkommen Recht (…)». Vgl. auch die Fortsetzung: «Wir lieben die Natur, d. h· nicht die alles schaffende, sondern eine konventionelle Wirklichkeit; in u n s er e r sogenannten Tragödie zerstörte dies besonders jeden Aufschwung, und statt tragischer Erhebung, gab es hier nichts als Heulen und Wehklagen.» (‹El. Welt› v. 12. 5. 1803).

[11] ‹Shakespeares Schatten›, Vers 35 f.: «Woher nehmt ihr denn aber das große, gigantische Schicksal, / Welches den Menschen erhebt, wenn es den Menschen zermalmt?»

[12] Es sei ausdrücklich vermerkt, daß eine gemeinsame Abhängigkeit von Schillers Aufsatz ‹Über den Gebrauch des Chors in der Tragödie› nicht in Frage kommt: nicht nur weil der genannte Terminus in Schillers Abhandlung nicht vorkommt, sondern auch weil diese selbst damals noch nicht vorlag. (Sie wurde erst am 7. 6. 1803 an den Verleger abgesandt.)

Schmerz des Vaters auf seinem Gesichte **verhüllte.**» Damit vergleiche man
in den ‹Nachtwachen›, in der Schilderung des Besuchs im Antikenkabinett, die beiden Sätze: *Diese Minerva ohne Kopf erregt überhaupt noch
in weit größerem Maaße meine Aufmerksamkeit, als der* **Agamemnon** *mit*
verhülltem Haupte, in dem bekannten Gemälde des **Timanthes.** *So wie
dieser nämlich den Künstlern die Regel gegeben hat, den höchsten un-
endlichen* **Schmerz** *nur errathen zu lassen, so scheint jene dasselbe in Hinsicht auf die Urschönheit anzudeuten.* (13. Nw.; S. 111[13].)
   Nun ist die Überlieferung von dem Gemälde des Timanthes, das die
Opferung Iphigeniens darstellte, in damaliger Zeit, zumindest innerhalb
eines gewissen Kreises von Autoren, durchaus nicht unbekannt. Lessing
etwa hatte im ‹Laokoon› von ihr gehandelt und auch die wichtigsten ein-
schlägigen Textstellen bei Plinius und Valerius Maximus zitiert. Aber
daß sie keineswegs Gemeingut der um 1800 Schreibenden war, zeigt eine
Stelle in Wetzels Roman ‹Kleon›, die zugleich ein sehr starkes Indiz gegen Wetzels Identität mit dem Verfasser der ‹Nachtwachen› ist: eine
Stelle, an der Wetzel Timanthes, den Maler, mit dem Bildhauer Phidias
verwechselt: «Als Phidias das Opfer der Iphigenie malen sollte, aber ver-
zweifelte, den Schmerz des alten Vaters darzustellen im Bilde; so verhüllte
er ihm das Gesichte...»[14]. Die Stelle verrät eine doch recht erhebliche
Unkenntnis in bezug auf alte Kunstgeschichte und Alte Geschichte überhaupt, und die Vorstellung (zu der die an Wetzel Glaubenden gezwungen sind), daß Wetzel im Laufe der zwei Jahre zwischen ‹Kleon› und
‹Nachtwachen› den Kenntnisstand des ‹Nachtwachen›-Dichters, der mit
der Timanthes-Überlieferung ebenso wie mit anderen Details aus der
antiken Überlieferung (siehe oben) immerhin recht geläufig umgeht, erreicht habe – diese Vorstellung ist zumindest nicht sehr wahrscheinlich.[15]
   Aber der Artikel über Schillers ‹Wilhelm Tell› vom 29. 11. 1804 bietet
noch einige weitere, wiederum zugleich gedankliche und verbale Parallelen, z. B.:
den musikalischen Vergleich für den vierten Akt des ‹Wilhelm Tell›:
«(...) er gleicht einem großen **Konzerte,** das **durch chromatische Gänge**
läuft, und **endet in einer kühnen** – ich möchte sagen h a r m o n i s c h e n

---

[13] Dasselbe Bild erscheint noch einmal, in verkürzter Form, in der 14. Nw.,
in der Rede an den Mond: *(...) ja verhüllst du nicht gar, wenn dich die Rührung überwältigt, dein Gesicht wie der weinende Agamemnon (...)* (S. 116).
[14] Kleon der letzte Grieche oder der Bund der Mainotten. Nach dem Neu-
griechischen von F. G. Wezel. Ronneburg und Leipzig 1802, S. 374.
[15] Gleichwohl hat Franz Schultz keinen Anstand genommen, eben diese
Stelle aus dem ‹Kleon›, zusammen mit dem Thimanthes-Bild in den ‹Nachtwachen›, in die Reihe seiner Argumente für Wetzels Verfasserschaft aufzunehmen (a. a. O., S. 319).

– Dissonanz» – der an den *Lauf durch die Skala* erinnert, als den der Nachtwächter die eigenen Empfindungen beim Anblick des Begräbniszugs der Nonnen in der zehnten *Nachtwache* beschreibt: *Mein Gemüth indeß, (das einem mit Vorsatz widersinnig gestimmten Saitenspiele gleicht, auf dem daher niemals in einer reinen Tonart gespielt werden kann, wenn nicht anders der Teufel einmal ein* **Konzert** *darauf ankündigt) wurde wenig ergriffen, und es kam im Grunde nichts weiter als ein toller* **Lauf** *durch die Skala zuwege, der ohngefähr durch die folgenden Töne ging und in einer* **Disharmonie** *stehen blieb (...)* (S. 92) [16];

die sonderbare Wendung von der «Poesie», die im ‹Wallenstein› «eng von der Geschichte umstellt erscheint, und **sich gewaltig Luft machen** möchte», was an die in den ‹Nachtwachen› mehrfach anklingende Vorstellung von dem *eingesperrten*, ja *eingemauerten* Riesen erinnert, der *sich ausdehnen und aufrichten will, ohne es im Stande zu sein,* nicht als *poetische Leuchtkugeln* hervorbringt, mit den Titanen verglichen wird, über welche *Berge geworfen sind: (...) und nur selten gelingt's ihnen* sich **Luft** *zu* machen, *und ihr Feuer zornig aus dem Vulkane gen Himmel zu schleudern* (7. Nw.; S. 60) [17];

schließlich auch die ziemlich respektlose Bemerkung über Schiller ganz zu Anfang des Artikels: «Rafael lies, nachdem er seine Verklärung [18] vollendet, den Pinsel ruhen und arbeitete nicht mehr. Schiller hat nach seiner Verklärung mehrere Werke geliefert, und das neueste ist: W i l h e l m T e l l. Ich läugne es nicht, ich wünschte jetzt er hätte Johanna von Orleans noch nicht geschrieben, denn der Tell übertrift sie nicht.» Derselbe Vorwurf, nicht wie Raffael gehandelt zu haben, wird ja auch, freilich in ganz allgemeiner Form und auch ohne Nennung des Raffaelschen Vorbilds, lediglich als satirische Marginalie, am Anfang der zwölften *Nachtwache* ausgesprochen: *Es geht nun einmal höchst unregelmäßig in der Welt zu, deshalb unterbreche ich den Unbekannten im Mantel hier mitten in seiner Erzählung, und es wäre nicht übel zu wünschen daß mancher große*

---

[16] Vgl. auch dasselbe Bild, in noch ähnlicher Formulierung, im ‹siebenten Brief› derselben Reihe (‹El. Welt› v. 23. 10. 1804), an einer Stelle, auf die später noch einzugehen sein wird: «(...) die Geschichte ist gewissermaßen in einem Schrei von **Dissonanzen** stehen geblieben».

[17] Dieselbe Grundvorstellung in der 16. Nw. (S. 143), mit bezug auf sitzende Götter, die, sich aufrichtend, sich die Köpfe an der zu niedrigen Decke zerstoßen würden, und in der Novelle von den zwei Brüdern, hier mit wörtlicher Übereinstimmung: Juan *stand ganz in Flammen wie ein Vulkan, durch dessen tausendjährige Schichten das innere Feuer sich mit einemmale* **Luft** machte *(...)* (5. Nw.; S. 44).

[18] Gemeint ist natürlich das die Verklärung Christi darstellende Bild Raffaels, das dann mit Schillers ‹Jungfrau von Orleans› in Parallele gesetzt wird.

*Dichter und Schriftsteller sich selbst zur rechten Zeit unterbrechen
möchte (...) (S. 99 [19]).*

2. Vorstellung eines vergessenen Autors

Alle eben herangezogenen Artikel aus der ‹Zeitung für die elegante Welt›
sind mit dem Namen ihres Verfassers gezeichnet. Sie stammen von August
Klingemann. Der Name des Mannes, der damit, durch die bisher beigebrachten Indizien, um vorsichtig zu reden, mindestens in eine beträchtliche Nähe zum Verfasser der ‹Nachtwachen› gerückt wird, war damals
nicht unbekannt, jedenfalls bekannter als heute. Jean Paul nennt ihn in
der ‹Vorschule der Ästhetik›, in der Vorrede zur zweiten Auflage, in einer
Reihe mit den beiden Schlegels, Bouterwek und Franz Horn (der übrigens
ein Schulfreund Klingemanns war) und stellt ihnen die Reihe der «Sulzer,
Eberhard, Krug etc. etc.» gegenüber mit der Behauptung, man könne,
wenn man «ästhetische Aussprüche» der einen wie der anderen Partei
lese, «leicht erraten, welche Partei nie gedichtet». In der Tat hatte auch
Klingemann, und zwar schon zu der Zeit, mit der wir es hier zu tun
haben, nicht nur «ästhetische Aussprüche» von sich gegeben, sondern
auch «gedichtet», unter anderem einen Roman in der Nachfolge des
‹Sternbald›, der im nächsten Kapitel dieser Studie genauer betrachtet werden soll: ‹Romano› (Braunschweig 1800/01); ein Trauerspiel ‹Die Maske›,
das Goethe 1797 in Rudolstadt durch die Weimarer Truppe hatte auf-
führen lassen und das im Juli 1800 auf der Liebhaberbühne des Hauses
Schütz in Jena gespielt wurde; ein als «Karaktergemählde» bezeichnetes
Drama mit dem eigenwilligen Titel ‹Selbstgefühl› und einer an Schillers
‹Luise Millerin› angelehnten Handlungs- und Dialogführung (Braunschweig 1800); dazu einiges, was kaum sehr viele Leser gefunden haben
dürfte: die zwei Ritterstücke, mit denen der noch sehr jugendliche Autor
debütierte: ‹Wildgraf Eckart von der Wölpe› (Braunschweig 1795) und
‹Die Asseburg› (Braunschweig 1796/97), den Schauerroman ‹Die Ruinen
im Schwarzwalde› (Braunschweig 1798/99) [20] und die lyrisch getönte
Abenteuergeschichte ‹Albano der Lautenspieler›, 1802 in Leipzig in zwei
Bänden erschienen, jeder Band «mit 1 Kupfer und Musik für die Guitarre
von Bornhard». Das witzigste Produkt des jungen Autors, ein anonym

---

[19] Auf die Fortsetzung dieser «Glosse an den Text des Zeitalters», die viel-
diskutierte Äußerung über den *Sonnenadler*, der *durch die neuere Geschichte
schwebt*, wird in anderem Zusammenhang einzugehen sein.

[20] Es ist das Buch, über dessen allzu viele Gedankenstriche sich Brentano im
‹Godwi› lustig macht. Vgl. Clemens Brentano: Werke, 2. Bd., München 1963.
Hrsg. v. F. Kemp, S. 65.

erschienenes satirisches Possenspiel mit einem Hanswurst, der auch den Prolog und den Epilog spricht, ebenfalls den meisten Zeitgenossen unbekannt und erst recht nicht – bis auf den heutigen Tag – als Werk Klingemanns erkannt, wird uns gleichfalls im nächsten Kapitel beschäftigen. Was Klingemann jedoch bekannt, wenn auch nicht berühmt, gemacht hatte, das waren seine ästhetischen, dramaturgischen und kritischen Beiträge. Es war vor allem die Zeitschrift ‹Memnon›, die er 1800 herausgegeben hatte, die allerdings über des «Ersten Bandes Erstes Stück» nicht hinausgediehen war, ferner die Schrift ‹Über Schillers Tragödie: Die Jungfrau von Orleans› (Leipzig 1802) und nicht zuletzt die Artikel, Rezensionen und Theaterberichte, die er seit 1802 ziemlich regelmäßig zur ‹Zeitung für die elegante Welt› beisteuerte. Außerdem waren an verschiedenen, z. T. entlegenen Orten, kleinere Schriften zum Theater erschienen: ‹Briefe über Menschendarstellung›[21], ein Aufsatz über Klingers ‹Zwillinge›, in dem diese mit Leisewitzens ‹Julius von Tarent› verglichen werden[22], eine dramaturgische Programmschrift mit dem Titel: ‹Was für Grundsätze müssen eine Theaterdirektion bei der Auswahl der aufzuführenden Stücke leiten?›[23]

Was bei Betrachtung dieser Liste von Publikationen zunächst auffällt, ist die starke und sehr früh entschiedene Hinneigung zum Theater. Es ist das Gebiet, auf dem sich Klingemann mehr und mehr zum Fachmann entwickelte und das dann sein eigentliches Metier werden sollte: 1813 übernahm er die Leitung des Braunschweiger Theaters[24], für das er schon vorher als Dramaturg, Textdichter und journalistischer Berichterstatter

---

[21] Neues Journal für Theater und andere schöne Künste. Herausgegeben von D. Schmieder, 3. Bd., Hamburg 1800, S. 10–30.

[22] Journal für Theater und andere schöne Künste. Herausgegeben von Dr. Schmieder. Zweiten Bandes erstes Heft, Hamburg 1797, S. 44–60.

[23] Leipzig 1802. Die Schrift entstand offenbar aus Anlaß einer Bewerbung um den Frankfurter Theaterdirektorsposten, zu der Brentano den einstigen Jenaer Studienfreund hatte auffordern lassen, die jedoch ohne Erfolg blieb. (Vgl. Bentanos Brief an Winkelmann von Anfang November 1801 in: Das unsterbliche Leben. Unbekannte Briefe von Clemens Brentano. Hrsg. v. W. Schellberg und F. Fuchs. Jena 1939, besonders S. 238, wo es heißt: «Er kann auch schnell einen Bogen über Theaterführung schreiben und beilegen, aber sehr iffland-kotzebuisch und schillerisch, auch ökonomisch.»)

[24] Vgl. zur Biographie: Joseph Kürschner in ADB (16. Bd., S. 187–189), Paul Zimmermann: Aus den Briefschaften August Klingemanns. Braunschw. Magazin 1923, Sp. 17–28, und 1924, Sp. 7–11, 21–26 und Hugo Burath: August Klingemann und die deutsche Romantik. Branschweig 1948. – Die Lebensdaten Klingemanns: 31. 8. 1777 Braunschweig – 25. 1. 1831 ebda. Das erhaltene Brief- und Handschriftenmaterial ist übrigens außerordentlich spärlich; Klingemanns Nachlaß ist «nicht zusammengehalten» und, soweit nicht der Vernichtung anheimgefallen, «in alle Winde zerstreut» (Zimmermann).

gewirkt hatte, und ist später einer der namhaftesten deutschen Theater-
direktoren geworden. (Berühmtestes Ereignis seiner Theaterlaufbahn war
1829, zwei Jahre vor seinem Tode, die Erstaufführung von Goethes
‹Faust› auf dem Braunschweiger Theater, das unter seiner Leitung zu einer
der führenden Bühnen Deutschlands geworden war. Sechs Jahre vorher
hatte er die erste und, abgesehen von einer Festaufführung im Jahre 1899,
wohl bisher einzige Aufführung von Heines ‹Almansor› gewagt, die zu
einem Mißerfolg und einem unerfreulichen Eklat führte, über dessen
Hintergründe Ernst Elster in seiner Heine-Ausgabe das Nötige berichtet[25].)
Aber auch in den Ausführungen über die ‹Braut von Messina›, den
Schillerschen ‹Tell› und den von Veit Weber, die eben betrachtet wurden,
und ähnlichen Äußerungen zur damaligen Dramenproduktion fällt bereits
die Sprache des Mannes vom ‹Fach› auf, die Sprache des Mannes, der erst
«entscheiden» möchte, wenn er «einer Aufführung des Stücks beigewohnt»,
der den «Karakter des Tell etwas zu zweideutig ausgefallen» findet, der
dem Schauspieler des Tell den Rat geben möchte, gewisse Stellen «ironisch
zu nehmen»[26]. Es liegt nahe, von hier aus auf das oft schon bemerkte
Durchsetzt-Sein der Sprache der ‹Nachtwachen› mit Theatermotiven einzugehen, das über den üblichen Gebrauch des alten theatrum-mundi-
Topos weit hinausgeht, auf die zahllosen Theatermetaphern und -ver-
gleiche, auf den Einsatz von Vokabeln wie *Maske, Kothurn, Chor, Tragödie, comédie larmoyante, Marionettenspiel, Marionettendirekteur* und
Theatermeister, Hanswurst und *Arlequin, Skaramuz* und *Kolombine,
Monolog, Prolog, Prologist, Rolle* und *Karakter*, letzteres vor allem in
Verbindungen wie *Teufelsrolle*[27], *Karakter des Teufels*[28] und *sich in den
Karakter eines Selbstmörders versetzen*[29]. Doch lassen wir es bei diesen
lexikalischen Hinweisen bewenden und bleiben wir zunächst bei der
Biographie Klingemanns bis zum Jahre 1804.

Ihr wichtigster, ja entscheidender Abschnitt waren die Jahre, die er um
1800 in Jena, in unmittelbarer Nähe der beiden Schlegels, Fichtes, Schel-

---

[25] Heinrich Heine, Sämtliche Werke. Hrsg. v. E. Elster, 2. Bd., Leipzig und
Wien o. J., S. 247.

[26] Alle Formulierungen im oben zitierten ‹Wilhelm Tell›-Artikel in der ‹Eleganten Welt› vom 29. 11. 1804.

[27] *Der Pfaff seiner Teufelsrolle getreu* (...) (1. Nw.; S. 8).

[28] (...) *was sich indeß mit dem Karakter des Teufels sehr wohl verträgt*
(Des Teufels Taschenbuch, S. 148, Michel).

[29] (...) *und ich suchte mich nur hier am Grabe durch mäßiges Rasen in den
Karakter eines Selbstmörders zu versetzen, den ich morgen darzustellen habe*
(12. Nw.; S. 105). Siehe auch 3. Nw.; S. 18: *Er verschwur jezt nacheinander in
zehn Karaktern aus den neusten Dramen und Tragödien seine Seele, wenn er
jemals treulos; zulezt redete er gar noch in der Manier des Don Juan, dem er
diesen Abend beigewohnt hatte* (...).

lings, Ritters, Brentanos und August Winkelmanns, seines Braunschweiger Landsmannes und Freundes, verbracht hatte – als studiosus iuris, was
freilich wieder zu einem Seitenblick auf den ‹Nachtwachen›-Text nötigt.
Denn w e n n sich hier die Spuren einer Bekanntschaft mit einer der damaligen Fakultätswissenschaften finden – einer Bekanntschaft, die über
das Normalmaß eines belesenen und selber schreibenden Zeitgenossen
hinausgeht – so sind es Spuren einer Bekanntschaft mit der Jurisprudenz[30].
Am 14. 5. 1798 wurde er an der Jenaer Universität immatrikuliert; «Ende
1801 kam er», wie Burath[31] schreibt, «von Jena als Rechtskandidat heim,
ohne Examen, mit dem offenbaren Plan, sich als freier Schriftsteller
durchzuschlagen». An Lebenszeugnissen hat sich aus diesen dreieinhalb
Jahren sehr wenig erhalten. Interessant ist ein Brief Brentanos[32], der um
dieselbe Zeit nach Jena gekommen war (immatr. 5. 6. 1798), an Klingemann, offenbar aus der ersten Zeit ihrer Bekanntschaft: eine etwas ver-
worrene Klage darüber, falsch verstanden worden zu sein, aus der jedenfalls das «Bemühen» Brentanos hervorgeht, mit dem andern «bekannt zu
werden, und dadurch zu gewinnen, waß mir in einer bestimmteren
Form nötig ist, weil ich es nicht besize, den Umgang eines Menschen, der
mich übersieht ohne auf mich herabzusehen» (was Klingemann offenbar
getan hatte: «um keine zu große Idee von sich zu haben», heißt es weiter,
«haben sie eine erbärmliche von mir gefaßt.»)
Wichtiger für unser Thema ist dann, um die Mitte des Jahres 1800, die

---

[30] Vgl. darüber zuletzt W. Paulsen – gegen Schultz, der mit Wetzels Medizin-
studium als Argument operiert hatte – in Jb. Schiller (1965), S. 467: «Mir will
absolut nicht eingehen, daß Bonaventura Arzt gewesen sein soll (...). Kreuz-
gang [der Name, den der Nachtwächter einmal als den eigenen nennt] operiert doch ungleich mehr und präziser mit juristischen als mit medizinischen
Argumenten, ja seine Freude an juristischen Spitzfindigkeiten scheint mir geradezu ein Merkmal für seinen Witz zu sein. Die medizinischen Hinweise dagegen (auf Brown, Haller) bleiben doch ganz allgemeiner Natur und gehen
über Jean Paulsche Dicta kaum hinaus.» Im Text der ‹Nw.› selbst wäre vor allem
zu vergleichen: der Hinweis auf *Weber über Injurien im ersten Abschnitte pag.*
29 (7. Nw.; S. 65) (dazu Michels Kommentar zur Stelle mit dem exakten Nachweis des Fachbuchs und des Zitats: Adolph Dietrich Weber: ‹Über Injurien und
Schmähschriften› 1, Schwerin und Weimar 1793, S. 27, was einen Fehler von
immerhin nur 2 Seiten bedeutet, der noch dazu vom Setzer verursacht sein kann),
überhaupt die ganze Verteidigungsrede gegen die Anklage wegen Verstoßes
gegen die Gesetze *de iniuriis* mit ihren Fachausdrücken und Abkürzungen
(7. Nw.; S. 62 ff.), das mäßige, an Studentenulk erinnernde Wortspiel mit
Carolina (im Sinne der Halsgerichtsordnung Karls V. (3. Nw.; S. 23)) und der
juristisch-quellenkritische Terminus technicus ›lex cruciata‹ (7. Nw.; S. 57).
[31] A. a. O., S. 83.
[32] Braunschweiger Stadtarchiv; abgedruckt bei Zimmermann a. a. O. (1923),
Sp. 20–21.

Publikation, in der sie beide – und mit ihnen ihr gemeinsamer Freund August Winkelmann – zusammen auftraten: ‹Memnon. Eine Zeitschrift›, von Goethe, ähnlich wie später der Kleistsche ‹Amphitryon›, zu «den merkwürdigen Erscheinungen und Zeichen der Zeit» gerechnet, von Schiller, der Goethe die Zeitschrift geschickt hatte, mit weit weniger gemessenen Worten kommentiert: «Ich lege ein neues Journal bei, das mir zugeschickt worden, woraus Sie den Einfluß Schlegelischer Ideen auf die neueste Kunsturteile zu Ihrer Verwunderung ersehen werden. Es ist nicht abzusehen, was aus diesem Wesen werden soll, aber weder für die Hervorbringung selbst, noch für das Kunstgefühl kann dieses hohle, leere Fratzenwesen ersprießlich ausfallen.»[33] Man kann dasselbe auch mythologisch und ohne Polemik sagen: die Sonne, von der diese Memnonssäule tönt, ist das ‹Athenäum›. Vor allem die Aufsätze, die der Herausgeber, Klingemann also, beigesteuert hat – ‹An Julius›, ‹Religion›, ‹Poesie (Fragmente, an Louise)› und ‹Briefe über Wallenstein› – sind in einer Weise von den im ‹Athenäum› erschienenen Schriften, namentlich den Friedrich Schlegelschen, abhängig, die erstaunlich ist und gelegentlich bis an die Grenzen der Parodie geht (obwohl eine solche zweifellos nicht beabsichtigt ist). Was man hier findet, ist ein Widerhall nicht nur der Ideen, die Friedrich Schlegel in den ‹Fragmenten›, dem Brief ‹Über die Philosophie› (‹An Dorothea›), im ‹Gespräch über die Poesie› entwickelt hatte, sondern auch der Form, in der sie vorgetragen wurden, eine Nachahmung in Sprache und Stil, die bis in Einzelheiten des Satzbaus und des Tonfalls hineingeht. Man betrachte nur etwa den Anfang des Aufsatzes ‹Poesie› (der schon in seinem Untertitel gleich zwei, übrigens schlecht zusammen passende Anknüpfungen enthält: eine an die ‹Fragmente› im ‹Athenäum› und eine an den Schlegelschen Brief an Dorothea ‹Über die Philosophie›): «Du liebst die Astronomie – es hat mir Freude gemacht, als ich es hörte, da ich weiß, daß Du zuviel Poesie hast, um es je bis zur endlichen Zahlenbestimmung und mathematischen Berechnung zu treiben» – und vergleiche ihn mit dem Anfang des Schlegelschen Briefs ‹An Dorothea› (obwohl man eigentlich sehr viel mehr von ihm zum Vergleich lesen müßte): «Was ich Dir von Spinosa erzählte, hast Du nicht ohne Religion angehört; Hemsterhuys hat Dir viel Freude gemacht; und sogar die Übersetzungen haben Dich vom Plato nicht abschrecken können (...). Ich freue mich, daß es Dir so Ernst ist. Wie sollte es auch anders seyn? Eitle Neugier ist Dein Hang zur Philosophie gewiß nicht (...)».

Es ist hier nicht nötig, alles aufzuzählen, was im einzelnen an Schlegelschen[34] Gedanken übernommen ist. Das Wesentlichste ist der neue Begriff

---

[33] An Goethe 26. 7. 1800; Goethes Formulierung in dessen Antwortbrief vom 29. 7. 1800.

[34] Schlegel selbst war wenig beeindruckt von dieser Schülerschaft: «Klinge-

der Poesie als einer mit Religion, Philosophie und Mythus verwandten
«universellen Sprache der Menschheit»[35], dazu die Grundbegriffe einer
«historischen Bestimmung des Zeitkarakters»[36], besonders die Auffassung
der eigenen Gegenwart als einer Epoche, in der eine neue Synthese der
Lebens- und Wissensgebiete «an der Zeit» sei, deren Grundlage eine neue
Mythologie[37] bilden werde, wobei als Wahrzeichen für die «Morgenröte»
zwei Namen genannt werden: Jakob Böhme und Goethe. Die
«Morgenröthe im Aufgang, von Jakob Böhm» wird erwähnt:
«wenn wir den Tag ahnen; so ist es Zeit, auf die Morgenröthe hinzudeu-
ten», sein Name ein «heiliger» genannt und die Empfängerin des Briefes
an den Abend erinnert, «als wir ihn zusammen lasen»[38]. Und von Goethe
heißt es in etwas anderem Zusammenhang: «(...) mit ihm beginnt die
Morgenröte der deutschen Dichtkunst, und eine neue herrliche Bildung
steigt mit dem schönen Lichte empor.»[39] Erwähnen wir schließlich
noch die – für einen damals in Jena Lebenden ohnehin nicht verwun-
derlichen – Reflexe der Begriffssprache des transzendentalen Idealismus: «Der Realismus ist gestürzt, Spinoza ist todt», heißt es etwa,
mit deutlichem Anklang an eine Stelle aus der ‹Rede über die Mythologie›[40], «aber auf seinem Grabhügel ist sein Geist erschienen und weis-

---

mann und Brentano haben unterdessen auch den Memnon und Wasa an mich
eingesandt. Da man aber nicht darüber lachen kann, wenn man nicht schon
sehr aufgelegt dazu ist, schicke ich sie nicht», schreibt er im Juli 1800 an den
Bruder (Walzel, S. 429) und dieser an Tieck: «Mit dem Memnon ist es auch
eine schlechte Freude.» (23. 11. 1800; in H. Lüdeke (Hrsg.): Ludwig Tieck und
die Brüder Schlegel. Frankfurt am Main 1930, S. 61. Voraus geht die allgemeine
Feststellung: «Das Elend mit den Nachahmern wird nun erst noch recht an-
gehn.»)

[35] ‹An Julius›. In: Memnon, S. 11.

[36] Ebda, S. 13.

[37] ‹Poesie (Fragmente, an Louise)›, a. a. O., S. 62 f.; vgl. dazu die ‹Rede über
die Mythologie› in Friedrich Schlegels ‹Gespräch über die Poesie›.

[38] Ebda, S. 59, 62; es ist dasselbe Buch, in dem man auch den Helden der
‹Nachtwachen› lesen sieht, nämlich in der Beschreibung des Dritten Holz-
schnitts: Das Buch worauf ich sitze, enthält Hans Sachsens Fastnachtsspiele,
das woraus ich lese ist Jakob Böhmens Morgenröthe (...) (4. Nw.; S. 26)!
(Vgl. auch die Erwähnung Böhmes am Ende der 1. Nw., S. 9).

[39] ‹Briefe über Wallenstein›; a. a. O., S. 81. Vgl. diesmal den ‹Studium›-
Aufsatz Friedrich Schlegels: «Der Charakter der aesthetischen Bildung unsres
Zeitalters und unsrer Nazion verräth sich selbst durch ein merkwürdiges und
großes Symptom. Göthens Poesie ist die Morgenröthe echter Kunst und
reiner Schönheit.» (Pros. Jugendschriften, hrsg. v. J. Minor, 1. Bd., Wien 1906,
S. 114). Auch Hinweise auf Böhme konnte man bei Friedrich Schlegel finden,
aber natürlich nicht nur bei ihm.

[40] Kritische Friedrich-Schlegel-Ausgabe, Bd. 2, München usw. 1967, S. 316.

sagt die Geheimnisse einer höhern Welt. Der Transcendentalismus, dieser g ö t t l i c h e Atheismus, der, indem er uns alles zu nehmen scheint, das Leben erst einweihet für die Ewigkeit und für die Götter, hat jetzt seine höchste Kraft erreicht, und ist kühn genug gewesen, bis zu seinem eigenen Tode hinauszublicken; – aber nur Wenige haben den Muth, alles um sich her niederzureißen, die Welt aus sich selbst hinzustellen, und aus dem Tode selbst das Leben hervorzuführen.»[41]

Ein ähnliches Bild bieten die kunsttheoretischen und geschichtsphilosophischen Einlagen im ‹Romano› und die umfangreichste kritische Schrift dieser Jahre: ‹Über Schillers Tragödie: Die Jungfrau von Orleans›. Letztere zeigt besonders in der Abhebung der modernen Poesie von der antiken, die ein in sich «geschlossenes» Ganzes und «in dieser Rücksicht als ein einziges Gedicht anzusehen» sei, ihrer Bildungsart nach einer «Pflanze» vergleichbar, die «aus dem mütterlichen Boden sich natürlich entfaltete»[42], die engsten Berührungen mit Schlegels Aufsatz ‹Über das Studium der griechischen Poesie›, während es im ‹Romano› vor allem die chiliastisch-prophetischen Töne der späteren ‹Athenäum›-Stücke sind, die man aufgenommen und reproduziert findet, besonders im letzten Kapitel des Romans – ‹Camillos Vision› betitelt – wo in der Form eines Visionsberichtes und schließlich in einer langen Folge von Sonetten der Anbruch eines neuen goldenen Zeitalters der Kunst verkündet wird: geführt von einem würdigen Alten, wie einst Dante von Vergil, schreitet der Visionär, der Maler Camillo, von einer Offenbarung zur anderen, Stimmen ertönen aus dem Dunkel – unter ihnen die des alten Jakob Böhme, des «ehrlichen Sehers»: «Die Morgenröthe ist im Aufgehen!» und eine andere, «ernste», die «wie aus der Tiefe herauf» ruft: «Die Zeit ist da!» – ein «Heiligthum» öffnet sich und wölbt sich um die beiden Wanderer «wie eine unermeßliche Welt», Göttergestalten erheben sich auf ihren Fußgestellen «mit freundlichem Ernste» – sie bilden den «mythischen Cyklus einer neuen Religion», erläutert der Führer[43] – und dann folgt der Kranz von

---

[41] ‹An Julius›, a. a. O., S. 6. Auch letzteres offensichtlich ein Reflex Schlegelscher und natürlich auch Fichtescher Gedanken, insbesondere der These Friedrich Schlegels, daß so, wie es «das Wesen des Geistes ist, sich selbst zu bestimmen und im ewigen Wechsel aus sich heraus zu gehn und in sich selbst zurückzukehren; wie jeder Gedanke nichts anders ist, als das Resultat einer solchen Tätigkeit», auch der Idealismus selbst «im ganzen und großen» «auf ein oder die andre Art aus sich herausgehn» müsse und werde, «um in sich zurückkehren zu können, und zu bleiben was er ist» (a. a. O., S. 314 f.).

[42] Über Schillers Tragödie: Die Jungfrau von Orleans; Leipzig 1802, S. 24 f.

[43] Als der Künstler, der sie erschuf, wird «Spinosa» genannt, entsprechend der Lehre Friedrich Schlegels im ‹Gespräch über die Poesie›, daß der «Anfang und das Ende aller Fantasie» und also auch der «neuen Mythologie» im Spinoza zu finden sei (a. a. O., S. 315 ff.).

onetten, in dem nun den Chorführern einer neuen Poesie gehuldigt wird, on der es schon in einer vorhergehenden Prophezeiung geheißen hatte, daß Deutschland der Ort ihres Aufganges sein werde. Den Anfang macht ein Sonett ‹Lucinde›, es folgen, ganz in der Art der Kunstsonette im ‹Athenäum›, Huldigungsgedichte an Tiecks ‹Genovefa›, an die Dramen Schillers seit dem ‹Don Carlos› und schließlich ein eigener, umfangreicher Zyklus von Sonetten an Dichtungen Goethes.

Kaum weniger charakteristisch aber als alle diese Anleihen ist das Faktum und die Art der Übernahmen selbst, die erstaunliche Assimilations- und Verwandlungsfähigkeit, die sich in ihnen bekundet, das histrionische Element, das die besondere Begabung, aber auch die Gefahr und offenbar auch das Problem dieses Autors war. Denn es begegnet in seinen Schriften durchaus auch als Gegenstand der Reflexion und der Kritik – so vor allem in einem Bekenntnis, das der Held des ‹Romano› in einem langen Brief an den Mönch Augustin ablegt und in dem es heißt:

«Ich suche mich selbst, und fliehe ewig vor mir; was ich eben noch war höre ich schon auf zu seyn wenn ich mich nach mir erkundige und wie ein wandelbarer Proteus entwinde ich mich meinen eigenen Armen. Glaub mir, es ängstigt mich oft daß ich in mir selbst so wenig einheimisch bin und mir so fremd erscheine – wie werde ich mir je vertrauen und mich lieben können bei diesem Wechsel meiner selbst! Nur die Gestalt ist's die ich festhalte und worin ich mich wiedererkenne und ich flieh zu den Sinnen wenn die fremden wunderbaren Töne im Herzen zu mir sprechen. Oft indeß geht dieses seltsame Spiel so weit, daß ich mich auch hier verdoppele und eine andere Gestalt aus dem klaren Gewässer mir zunikt und mein Lächeln mit Ernst erwiedert.

Ich glaube, daß die Menschen mit minderer Empfänglichkeit fester da stehen, und ich fange schon an sie mit ihrem Phlegma und ihrer kalten Ruhe wegen zu beneiden. – Überall ist es doch das Originale das hervorspringt und Aufsehn macht in der Welt, und dieses besteht nur in der innern Abgeschlossenheit und der selbstständigen Kraft des Geistes, der sich durch nichts irre machen lässt, auf sich selbst sich gründet und dem Fremden nicht huldigt. Bei mir hingegen gehen die fremden Geister wunderbar durch mein Leben und sie antworten mir, wenn ich mich frage; ja diese fürchterliche Empfänglichkeit geht so weit, daß ich mich oft aus mir selbst verliere und in einem andern Wesen wiederfinde. Es ist mir als schwebte ich oben über dem Ganzen und stellte chemische Prozesse in der Geisterwelt an; ich trenne und vereinige, bald burlesk, bald groß und kühn wie es mir die Laune eingiebt und bin Meister in der Kunst des Amalgamirens; aber mein eigenes Selbst geht dabei zu Grunde und verliert sich in die Allgemeinheit meiner Geschicklichkeit.»[44]

Schließlich aber ist, bevor wir zu den Artikeln Klingemanns in der ‹Zeitung für die elegante Welt› zurückkehren, noch ein Wort über die Kontro-

---

[44] Romano [1. Bd.], Braunschweig 1800, S. 135–137.

versen vonnöten, die in den fraglichen Jahren eine nicht unbedeutende
Rolle in seiner literarischen Biographie spielen. Klingemann hatte sich –
schon durch die Herausgabe des ‹Memnon› und seine Beiträge zu dieser
Zeitschrift – entschieden auf die Seite der Romantiker gestellt, konnte
also des Mißtrauens, wenn nicht der Feindschaft der antiromantischen
Fronde gewiß sein. Deren prominenteste Wortführer in den ersten Jahren
des neuen Jahrhunderts waren bekanntlich Kotzebue und der in Berlin
lebende Lette Garlieb Merkel, ihre beiden wichtigsten Publikationsorgane
Merkels ‹Briefe an ein Frauenzimmer über die wichtigsten Produkte der
schönen Literatur› und die zuerst von Kotzebue allein, ab Herbst 1803
mit Merkel gemeinsam herausgegebene Zeitung ‹Der Freimüthige›. Mit
beiden Antiromantikern geriet Klingemann in Streit, besonders mit Merkel, mit dem es allerdings schwer war, nicht in Streit zu geraten. Man
findet die Niederschläge dieser Auseinandersetzung, was die Klingemannschen Beiträge betrifft, nicht nur in den Spalten der ‹Eleganten Welt›, sondern auch in seiner Schrift über Schillers ‹Jungfrau von Orleans›, wo er
die Merkelsche Kritik an den gereimten Partien in der ‹Maria Stuart›[45]
zum Ausgangspunkt seiner eigenen Darlegungen über Schillers «romantische Tragödie» macht, um dann zu zeigen, wie sich hier «nicht allein diese
Unnatürlichkeit (nach M.)», sondern noch ganz andere finden, angefangen von der Verwendung von ottave rime bis zur Erhebung des Haupt-
charakters ins Übernatürliche, Wunderbare. Damit ist auch bereits der
Hauptstreitpunkt angedeutet: es ist das von Kotzebue und Merkel ver-
tretene Prinzip der «Natürlichkeit» im Drama samt seinen Folgen, gegen
das wir Klingemann schon einmal polemisieren sahen: in seinem Artikel
über den Chor in der Tragödie anläßlich der ‹Braut von Messina›. Was
Merkel und Kotzebue ‹Natur› nannten und als Instanz gegen gereimte
Verspartien im Drama oder auch die Chöre in der ‹Braut von Messina›
ins Feld führten, das nannte Klingemann «konventionelle Wirklichkeit»,
wie wir sahen, und wo Kotzebue von «Wahrheit der Empfindung» als der
Ursache des Erfolgs seiner Stücke sprach, da sprach er von «Dilettantismus».

Der persönliche Ton, der in den Äußerungen gegen Kotzebue hörbar
wird, ist noch auffälliger in der Auseinandersetzung mit Merkel. Dieser
replizierte zunächst auf die Angriffe in Klingemanns ‹Jungfrau von
Orleans›-Schrift, indem er sich besonders auf die Ansichten vom reinen
«Schönen» und seiner Autonomie auch gegenüber dem «Sittlichen» bezog, die Klingemann dort entwickelt hatte, und erklärte, ebensogut, «mit
denselben rhachitischen Schlüssen», könne man beweisen, daß es «nichts
Uebelriechendes in der Natur» gebe: so wie dieses eben dasjenige sei, was
«die Geruchswerkzeuge widerlich afficirt», so sei das «Unsittliche» das,

---

[45] Im 35. seiner ‹Briefe an ein Frauenzimmer› (Mai 1801).

was «das sittliche Gefühl beleidigt»; freilich gebe es Leute, die «einen Sinn zu wenig» hätten...[46]. Klingemann antwortete darauf mit einer «Oeffentlichen Erklärung an den Herrn Garlieb Merkel»[47], in der er sich über die «komische» Wirkung ausspricht, die Merkels ‹Briefe› von jeher auf ihn ausgeübt hätten, und ihm «öffentlich seiner Schriftsteller-Ehre wegen, und um ihn gänzlich zu besänftigen», erklärt, daß er ihn «für den ersten A e s t h e t i k e r (der Grundbedeutung des Wortes nach) in der Welt» halte; besonders seitdem er ihn «über die Wichtigkeit des Geruchs in Hinsicht auf die Poesie, so originell als gründlich belehrt» habe. Noch gröber ist dann der «Brief an den Herrn Garlieb Merkel» im Intelligenzblatt der ‹Eleganten Welt› vom 22. 1. 1803, mit dem er auf dessen angebliche Aufforderung antwortet, den «Beweis über die Lächerlichkeit» seiner «literarischen Existenz zu führen»; der Briefschreiber deutet u. a. die Möglichkeit an, aus Merkels eigenen Äußerungen zu beweisen, wie es «nicht möglich sei in einem edlen Style» mit ihm zu reden. Worauf Merkel seinerseits an einen seiner Frauenzimmer-Briefe – den hundertsten und letzten der ersten Folge – ein ‹Intelligenzblatt› anhängt, in dem er gleichzeitig gegen Spaziers Herausgeberpraxis und die «pöbelhaften und schiefwitzelnden Briefe an mich, von H. Klingemann» protestiert.

Merkels wütend-ironisches ‹Intelligenzblatt› zeigt zugleich, wie die Fehde zwischen ihm und Klingemann hineingehört in den Zusammenhang jener größeren Auseinandersetzung, die damals die literarische, vor allem die journalistische Szene beherrschte, deren Hauptlager eine Zeitlang die ‹Elegante Welt› – mit ihrem vielverspotteten Namen – auf der einen, der ‹Freimüthige› auf der andern Seite waren und in der sich die verschiedenartigsten Privatfehden miteinander verquickt hatten, die zwischen Merkel und Spazier ebenso wie die Differenzen Klingemanns mit Kotzebue und Merkel, auch z. B. die weit bekanntere Fehde zwischen Kotzebue und A. W. Schlegel. In einem Artikel über die von Kotzebue veröffentlichte Probe einer eigenen Molière-Übersetzung[48] spricht Klingemann von einem «Krieg, der in diesen Tagen in unserer schönen Literatur ausgebrochen ist» und der «allerdings heilsam» sei, «wie jeder Krieg

---

[46] ‹Bemerkungen›, in: Briefe an ein Frauenzimmer, 5. Bd. (Berlin 1802), S. 381 f. (im Anschluß an den 74. Brief).

[47] Intelligenzblatt der Zeitung für die elegante Welt v. 18. 9. 1802.

[48] ‹Moliere im neuen Gewande. Etwas auf Veranlassung der Ecole des femmes, auf dem franz. Theater in Braunschweig›. (‹El. Welt› v. 21./23. 4. 1803). Kernstelle des Artikels: «Derbe kräftige Gesundheit und durchgeführte komische Treue ist der wahrhafte Karakter Molieres, den uns leider Hr. v. K. durch nach modernen Grundsätzen unternommene Beraubung des Derben zu verderben versucht. Die einzige Szene, die ich vor mir liegen habe, zeigt dieses leider nur zu deutlich, und dieser Moliere wird jedem, der den alten Moliere wahrhaft liebte, unerträglich seyn.»

überhaupt»; nur müsse der Mann – fügt er mahnend hinzu, offenbar aus gegebenem Anlaß – «mit dem Schwerdte für die Fahne kämpfen, nicht aber aus persönlicher Rachgier den Dolch zükken».

3. Motivparallelen

Nach diesem biographischen Zwischenspiel ist es Zeit, den Faden der im ersten Abschnitt begonnenen Untersuchung wieder aufzunehmen. Mit den dort beigebrachten Nachweisen war ja erst ein kleiner Teil der Artikel in der ‹Eleganten Welt› ausgeschöpft; sie stammten aus insgesamt drei Artikeln: dem über den Chor in der Tragödie (12./14. 5. 1803), dem über Jean Pauls ‹Flegeljahre›, Veit Webers ‹Tell› und Kotzebues ‹Erinnerungen› (7. 6. 1804; erster der ‹Briefe über die neuesten Werke der deutschen schönen Literatur›) und dem über Schillers ‹Tell› (29. 11. 1804; achter ‹Brief›). Ich habe nicht die Absicht, alle in den andern Artikeln nachweisbaren Indizien hier auszubreiten – schon um die Darstellung nicht allzu atomistisch werden zu lassen – will aber wenigstens einiges hier vorlegen, was zur Abrundung des eben Gesagten beitragen kann; anderes wird später, in Verbindung mit anderen Argumentationsschritten, nachzutragen sein. Dabei gehe ich im Unterschied zum Verfahren des ersten Abschnitts nicht von der Ebene des Wortlauts, sondern von der des Motiv-, insbesondere des Themenbestandes aus und knüpfe unmittelbar an das Thema der letzten Ausführungen an: das Thema Kotzebue.

(1) Kotzebue, die *schwache Manier des modernen Teufels*
    und Verwandtes

Auch in den ‹Nachtwachen› wird der Name Kotzebues genannt, sogar verhältnismäßig oft, insgesamt viermal (kein Name kommt öfter vor; wenn man Nennungen des Autornamens, Nennungen von Werken und von Gestalten aus Werken jeweils zusammenzählt, so liegt nur ein Autor über Kotzebue, nämlich Shakespeare). Zusammenhang und Tonlage sind jedesmal satirisch-polemisch. Verspottet wird Kotzebues *ephemerische* (4. Nw.; S. 31) Vielschreiberei und vor allem die Rührseligkeit seiner Stücke. *Weinen wie Kotzebue und niesen wie Tiek* hat der in der zwölften *Nachtwache* vorgestellte *berühmte Dichter* gelernt (S. 100), *mechanisches Lesen Kotzebuescher Dramen* wird an anderer Stelle (15. Nw.; S. 126) als probates Mittel für das Zutage-Fördern von Tränen empfohlen. Dieser Spott liegt freilich auf der Linie des Üblichen, abgesehen höchstens von der Gegenüberstellung mit Tieck und mit dem Motiv des Niesens (über diese weiter unten). Aparter ist dagegen die Nennung Kotzebues im Zusammenhang mit dem Teufelsmotiv (3. Nw.; S. 17 f.), also mit d e m Motiv, das wie kein anderes – von den Teufelsszenen der

beiden ersten *Nachtwachen* bis zur Erzählung von der Teufelsbeschwö-
rung und der eigentümlichen Teufels-Patenschaft in der letzten – durch
das ganze Buch hindurchgeht. Hier in der dritten *Nachtwache* handelt es
sich um die Vorfälle nach dem Tode des Freigeistes: den Kampf des (an
Valentin im ‹Faust› erinnernden) Soldaten mit den drei Teufeln und das
am nächsten Tag aufgefundene Teufelshaupt:

*Die Geschichte ging mir während meiner Nachtwache sehr im Kopfe
herum, denn ich hatte bis jezt nur an einen poetischen Teufel geglaubt,
keinesweges aber an den wirklichen. Was den poetischen anbetrifft, so ist
es gewiß sehr schade, daß man ihn jezt so äußerst vernachlässiget, und
statt eines absolut bösen Prinzips, lieber die tugendhaften Bösewichter, in
Ifland und Kotzebuescher Manier, vorzieht, in denen der Teufel ver-
menschlicht, und der Mensch verteufelt erscheint. In einem schwankenden
Zeitalter scheut man alles Absolute und Selbstständige; deshalb mögen
wir denn auch weder ächten Spaß, noch ächten Ernst, weder ächte Tugend
noch ächte Bosheit mehr leiden. Der Zeitkarakter ist zusammengeflikt
und gestoppelt wie eine Narrenjakke, und was das Aergste dabei ist – der
Narr, der darin stekt, mögte ernsthaft scheinen.* – (3. Nw.; S. 17 f.) Auf
dieselbe Vernachlässigung des Teufels als Symptom des *Zeitkarakters*
kommt der Erzähler auch schon in der ersten *Nachtwache* zu sprechen,
anläßlich des um die Seele des Freigeists kämpfenden Pfaffen, der, um
stärker zu wirken, *in der Person des Teufels* spricht: *Er drückte sich wie
ein Meister darin aus, ächt teufelisch im kühnsten Style, und fern von der
schwachen Manier des modernen Teufels* (1. Nw.; S. 8).

Hierzu gibt es eine ganze Reihe von Parallelen bei Klingemann; am
nächsten steht die folgende aus einem Artikel über das ‹Faust›-Drama
eines gewissen Johann Schink, der am 19. Juni 1804 (einen Monat vor
dem Vorabdruck aus den ‹Nachtwachen›) in der ‹Eleganten Welt› erschien, übrigens als zweiter ‹Brief über die neuesten Werke der schönen
Literatur›: «Der Teufel nun gar spielt eine besonders traurige Figur. Wagt
man sich einmal an den Teufel, so denke ich muß man es auch mit ihm
aufnehmen. Der Verfasser hat aber in der That die ganze Hölle, die doch
sonst in einiger Achtung stand, durch diesen Teufel aus ihr beschimpft,
denn er ist wirklich nicht viel teufelischer als irgendein unglücklicher Böse-
wicht in einem modernen Drama. Wie ganz anders stellt ihn dagegen
G ö t h e dar! –: still, schleichend, ohne viel höllischen Aufwand, fast gebildet und gefällig, aber tief in sich seiner Bosheit gewiß. – Vor d e m
Rothrocke fürchtet man sich wahrlich!» (Eine Passage, die ihrerseits zurückweist auf eine Reihe von Äußerungen Bonaventuras, u. a. auf eine
Stelle in der Ankündigung des Teufelstaschenbuchs: *Gesteht es, meine
Brüder, wir sind im Ganzen ziemlich zurück, weshalb uns die Menschen
denn auch nicht sonderlich mehr fürchten oder achten und selbst auf
unsere Kosten Sprüchwörter einzuführen wagen – als dummer Teufel!*

armer Teufel! u. dgl. (S. 148). Aber auch in den ‹Nachtwachen› geht es ja mehrmals um die Abnahme des Glaubens an den Teufel in neueren Zeiten, u. a. an der zuerst zitierten Stelle.) Im übrigen enthält der Artikel über das ‹Faust›-Drama von Schink noch einige weitere Parallelen zu unserem Ausgangszitat, insbesondere ein gewisses Insistieren auf der Kategorie der «Selbstständigkeit»[49], das auch sonst für Klingemann typisch ist, sich übrigens auch auf Friedrich Schlegel zurückführen ließe, ferner die Antithese von «Scherz» und «Ernst» als der zwei «Pole» der Poesie[50] und die generelle Feststellung, es sei «erfreulich, wenn beide selbstständig nebeneinander erscheinen». Klingemann ist auch sonst mit Nachdruck für die eigenen Rechte des Komischen – ebenso wie des Tragischen – eingetreten, z. B. in dem vorhin schon herangezogenen Artikel anläßlich der Kotzebueschen Übersetzungsprobe aus dem Molière[51], in dem er die «derbe kräftige Gesundheit und durchgeführte komische

---

[49] «Derjenige, der die poetische Travestie durchaus verwirft, macht es nicht viel besser als der Orthodoxe, der einem Heterodoxen Stillschweigen auflegen will – beide fürchten etwas für die Selbstständigkeit desjenigen, was sie in Schutz nehmen. (...) ja er [der Dichter jenes ‹Faust› nämlich, der als sein eigener Kommentator auftritt; J. S.] behauptet, daß Faust's moralische Selbstständigkeit nirgends beschränkt, und er auf keine Weise das Werkzeug übersinnlicher Mächte würde. – Das ist nun freilich als Spiegelfechterei ganz gut; der Leser indeß sieht diese Selbstständigkeit durchaus nicht im Innern begründet (...)». (›El. Welt‹ v. 19. 6. 1804).

[50] «Alles wahrhaft Vortrefliche hat zwei Pole, den Scherz und Ernst, so wie überhaupt die ganze Poesie in den zwei großen Entgegensetzungen des T r a g i s c h e n und K o m i s c h e n besteht.» (Ebda.)

[51] ‹El. Welt› v. 21./23. 4. 1803, vgl. auch oben, S. 42, und die dort mitgeteilte Textprobe (Anm. 48). – Charakteristisch auch die Klage, daß sich auch im wirklichen Leben das Komische «unter uns verlohren» habe, in einem «Postskript» in der ‹El. Welt› vom 23. 10. 1804; Klingemann spricht dort von den «im Gehege des Freimüthigen» versteckten, «von Gott und Poesie verlassenen Schülern» (selbst dieses Wort sei allerdings «noch zu edel») als «unwillkührlichen Beiträgen zur grotesk komischen Literatur unsers Zeitalters» und von seinem Vorsatz, «von Zeit zu Zeit in einem und dem andern Postskripte, zur Abwechselung darauf reflektiren» zu wollen, «da das Komische sich so sehr unter uns verlohren hat, daß selbst Herr von Kotzebue es nicht durch einen Preis von 100 Friedrich-d'oren wiederzufinden vermogte, und wir deswegen die etwanigen Reste aus allen Winkeln zusammensuchen müssen». Vgl. dazu in der 4. Nw. (S. 33 f.) den Bericht über die Äußerungen des Hanswursts: *Ueber das Leben und den Zeitkarakter macht er die höchst albernen Bemerkungen, daß beide jezt mehr rührend als komisch seyen, und daß man jezt weniger über die Menschen lachen als weinen könne, weshalb er denn auch selbst ein moralischer und ernsthafter Narr geworden, und immer nur im edlen Genre sich zeige, wo er vielen Applaus bekäme.*

Treue» des alten Franzosen in Schutz nimmt gegen seinen modernisierenden Übersetzer und dessen «heillose Arroganz», den «d e r b e n gesunden Moliere per Augustum Kotzebue, d. h. hier s e h r s t a r k per Johannem Balhorn, verbessern und entkräften» zu wollen. Abschließend heißt
es in diesem Artikel vom 21./23. April 1803 – und auch zu diesem Satz
gibt es eine Stelle in den ‹Nachtwachen›, die an ihn anklingt –: «Durch
dieses Alles habe ich übrigens einen allgemein beliebten Schriftsteller, wie
er sich bescheiden von sich selbst ausdrückt, nicht vor dem Publikum
unanständig behandeln, sondern nur eine höchst unanständige Arroganz
gebührend rügen wollen.» Was hier und dort, im ‹Elegante Welt›-Artikel
vom 21./23. April 1803 und in den ‹Nachtwachen›, anklingt, ist das Stichwort «beliebt»: «O besäßen doch», heißt es an der oben schon genannten
Stelle über die *ephemerischen* Schriftsteller (4. Nw.; S. 31), «*dieses dein
Talent manche von unsern beliebten Schriftstellern!*» *rief ich aus,* «*Ihre
Werke könnten dann immerhin Ephemeren bleiben, wären sie selbst doch
unsterblich, und könnten ihre ephemerische Schriftstellerei ewig fortsetzen, und bis zum jüngsten Tage beliebt bleiben.*»

(2) Der sterbende Freigeist

Ich schließe zwei Parallelen zu dem Handlungsmotiv an, das die Betrachtungen des Nachtwächters über den wirklichen und den poetischen Teufel
auslöst: dem Tod des *Freigeists* in der ersten *Nachtwache*. Über diese
Szene ist viel geschrieben worden. Michel hatte auf vergleichbare Vorgänge in der Schein-Sterbeszene im ‹Siebenkäs› hingewiesen – zu Recht,
wie mir scheint – spätere, namentlich neuere Interpreten haben demgegenüber das Eigene, «Abgründige» der Gestaltung bei Bonaventura nachzuweisen versucht. Michel hat aber auch bereits auf den Vergleich aufmerksam gemacht, der in der Erzählung selbst gezogen wird, und zwar
gleich zu Anfang, und der den erdichteten Vorfall in Beziehung setzt zu
einem historischen, zumindest als historisch überlieferten: *Der Mann war
ein Freigeist von jeher, und er hält sich stark in seiner letzten Stunde, wie
Voltaire.* So die Erzählung selbst (1. Nw.; S. 6), an der Stelle, wo die neue
Figur eingeführt wird. Michel verweist dazu in seinem Kommentar auf
die betreffende Stelle in Condorcets Voltaire-Biographie. Daß sie die
‹Quelle› des Verfassers war, ist wenig wahrscheinlich, wird auch von
Michel nicht behauptet. Die Stelle klingt ja eher so, als handle es sich um
etwas allgemein Bekanntes, was man nicht durch Lektüre historischer
Schriften aufnehmen mußte. Wie auch immer – auf jeden Fall wird man
annehmen dürfen, daß dem Verfasser i r g e n d e i n e Überlieferung vom
Tode Voltaires, des berühmtesten aller Freigeister, und der Art, wie er
«sich gehalten» habe, zu Ohren gekommen ist und daß zumindest er
selbst sie als nicht ganz unbekannt beim Publikum voraussetzte.

Dasselbe historische Paradigma begegnet aber auch, nur etwas ausführlicher, in einem Artikel Klingemanns vom 19. Oktober 1805, der überschrieben ist: ‹Einige Worte über Schillers Uebersetzung der Phedra von Racine›. Es geht um die Frage, wie gerade Schiller dazu gekommen sei, eine französische Tragödie zu übersetzen, da doch vielleicht niemand «einen größern Widerwillen gegen die französische Tragödie im Allgemeinen» gehabt habe als er: «Man dürfte in Verlegenheit gesetzt werden, wenn man den Grund dieser Uebersetzungslaune in etwas anderm, als der bloßen L a u n e , aufsuchen sollte; ja Schwachköpfe könnten dabei leicht auf die Vermuthung kommen, daß Schiller sein poetisches Glaubensbekenntniß noch kurz vor seinem Tode verläugnet habe, im Gegensatze von Voltaire, dessen ne parles pas de cet homme! in Hinsicht auf sein christliches, weltbekannt ist.»[52] Zu dieser Parallelstelle, die für sich allein natürlich, wie alle diese Parallelen, wenig besagt, stellt sich eine andere, die immerhin zeigt, daß der Verfasser eine gewisse eigene und anhaltende Beziehung zu dem Motiv des «Sich-Haltens» in der Todesstunde hatte. Der Aufsatz, in dem sie steht, einer der merkwürdigsten unter den literarischen Artikeln Klingemanns, im selben Jahrgang 1805 der ‹Eleganten Welt› erschienen, behandelt eine Frage, auf die auch schon die mehrfach genannte Schiller-Schrift von 1802 eingegangen war: «Wer ist der schwarze Ritter in der Jungfrau von Orleans?»[53] «Die Kunstrichter haben es sich sehr angelegen seyn lassen, ihm nahe zu kommen», heißt es hier zunächst in einer Art Vorgeplänkel, «ja einige glauben wirklich etwas von der verborgenen Physiognomie abgelauscht zu haben, das dem Teufel nicht unähnlich sehen soll; nur sind sie noch darüber uneinig, was d e r denn da eigentlich zu thun hat; denn ohne einen Zweck pflegt der Teufel so wenig, wie der Dichter, etwas anzulegen.» (Man beachte auch das besondere, hier nicht zum erstenmal begegnende Verhältnis zum Teufel, vor allem den angeschlagenen Ton persönlicher Vertrautheit mit seinen Gepflogenheiten!) Aber die These, auf die der Verfasser zusteuert, die er auch schon in der Schrift von 1802 vertreten hatte, zielt in eine andere Richtung, auf eine der dramatis personae, die der Zuschauer schon vor der Szene mit dem Schwarzen Ritter hat kennenlernen können: auf Talbot. Sein Ausgangspunkt ist der Hauptcharakterzug des englischen Heerführers, den er als «Nüchternheit» bestimmt und zu dessen Illustration er die Verse zitiert, die Schiller ihn im Augenblick seines Todes sprechen läßt (Verse, die sehr an die Worte erinnern, mit denen die ‹Nachtwachen› schließen). Talbot ist für ihn ein Mann, der «sein Daseyn bis auf das Atom begriffen» hat, «das er sterbend der Erde wiedergibt». Was darauf

---

[52] Ein Zitat aus Voltaires Werken steht übrigens als Motto vor dem ersten Abschnitt von Klingemanns ‹Ruinen im Schwarzwalde› (1798).
[53] Dies zugleich der Titel des Aufsatzes. (›El. Welt‹ v. 7. 5. 1805).

folgt, sei vollständig wiedergegeben, da es mehr als e i n Schlaglicht auf unseren Haupttext wirft:

«Ein Materialist, der sich selbst im Tode getreu bleibt, und der sein nüchternes Leben mit den Worten abschließt:

> die einzige
> Ausbeute, die wir aus dem Kampf des Lebens
> Wegtragen, ist die Einsicht in das Nichts,
> Und herzliche Verachtung alles dessen,
> Was uns erhaben schien und wünschenswerth.

Unstreitig derjenige Karakter, der im schneidendsten Gegensatze mit dem poetisch religiösen Theile des Gedichtes steht, und dessen Tod noch dazu durch die kräftigste und in sich vollendetste Darstellung um so schwerer auf das Ganze eindrückt.

Nun aber schwebt über dieser Tragödie der glänzende Himmel einer höhern Welt, gleichsam wie die in das Unermeßliche emporsteigende Kuppel eines Pantheons, und das zweite Leben schaut hell und leuchtend in das Irdische hinein, und umstralt die darin wandelnden Gestalten. Ein solcher Stral fällt denn auch durch die Worte der Jungfrau:

> Hätt' ich
> Den kriegerischen Talbot in der Schlacht
> Nicht fallen sehn, so sagt' ich Du wärst Talbot!

auf diesen und auf den schwarzen Ritter. Aber es durfte nur ein rasches Schlaglicht seyn, gleichsam ein Blitz, den derselbe Moment gebiert und vernichtet, eben weil durch eine anhaltendere grelle Beleuchtung der Zweck der Erscheinung auf eine harte und prosaische Weise sich offenbart hätte. Aus diesem Grunde wandelt der Geist des Talbot mit fest geschlossenem Visire, das er nimmer öffnet, und er verrät sich nur durch den selbst in ein zweites Leben hinübergetragenen Haß, der in dem Blute seiner ganzen Nation seinen Ursprung findet, und sich durch die ganze Geschichte beider Nachbarvölker forterbt. Noch im Tode führt dieser Hartnäckige den Krieg mit dem Heere der Jungfrau (...)»[54].

Der Passus bietet eine solche Fülle von Berührungen verschiedenster Art mit dem Text der ‹Nachtwachen›, daß man sich zu bereits ziemlich unwahrscheinlichen Annahmen gezwungen sieht, wenn man n i c h t an die Identität der beiden Verfasser glauben will. Es findet sich hier nicht nur das oben erörterte Freigeist-Motiv, sondern auch das der Fortdauer gerade des starken (im Sinne von ‹esprit fort›), «nüchternen» Geistes[55], nicht nur

---

der Gedanke der *Vernichtung*, der der freie und starke Geist ruhig ins Auge schaut, sondern auch der komplementäre einer «höheren», «zweiten» Welt, der auch in den ‹Nachtwachen› so auffällig und oft bemerkt worden ist, ja der ganze vielerörterte Dualismus von «erster» und «zweiter» Welt, der in den ‹Nachtwachen› mehrfach und auf nicht immer ganz klare Weise angedeutet ist, findet hier seine Entsprechung; eine Entsprechung, von der man sogar sagen könnte, daß sie so etwas wie einen Kommentar zu den entsprechenden ‹Nachtwachen›-Stellen darstelle. Auch in den ‹Nachtwachen›, auch in der Sterbeszene, von der wir ausgingen, ist ja nicht nur von *starker* Haltung und Gleichgültigkeit gegenüber dem *Donnern* des Pfaffen die Rede, sondern auch von einer höheren, unirdischen Welt, die *auf einen Augenblick* – man weiß nicht recht, für wen eigentlich – sichtbar wird:

Ich schauderte, der Kranke blickte plötzlich kräftig um sich, als gesundete er rasch durch ein Wunder und fühlte neues höheres Leben. Dieses schnelle leuchtende Auflodern der schon verlöschenden Flamme, der sichere Vorbote des nahen Todes, wirft zugleich ein glänzendes Licht in das vor dem Sterbenden aufgestellte Nachtstück, und leuchtet rasch und auf einen Augenblick in die dichterische Frühlingswelt des Glaubens und der Poesie. Sie ist die doppelte Beleuchtung in der Correggios Nacht, und verschmilzt den irdischen und himmlischen Strahl zu Einem wunderbaren Glanze. (1. Nw.; S. 7).

So wie hier dem Sterben des *Freigeistes* die *dichterische Frühlingswelt des Glaubens und der Poesie* gegenübergestellt ist, so dort, im ‹Jungfrau von Orleans›-Artikel, dem Sterben des Talbot der «glänzende Himmel einer höhern Welt»[56]. So wie hier, in der ‹Nachtwachen›-Szene, ein *glänzendes Licht* in das *vor dem Sterbenden aufgestellte Nachtstück* fällt, eine *doppelte Beleuchtung* erzeugend, die mit der in Correggios «Heili-

---

Geist nicht vor ihr zittert (...) (S. 8). Über diese Stelle und ihre «Paradoxie» ausführlich W. Paulsen, a. a. O., S. 475 ff..

[56] Und an der entsprechenden Stelle der ›Jungfrau von Orleans‹-Schrift von 1802, die in mancher Beziehung noch näher steht, das Begriffspaar von «Poesie und Glaube» und, als «glänzendes Gegenstück», der Tod der Jungfrau (op. cit., S. 64). (Der entscheidende Passus in der ‹Jungfrau›-Schrift lautet: «Talbot [...] stirbt für die Vernunft, da er nicht für sie siegen kann. [...] Fallend ruft er noch: Erhabene Vernunft [folgt Zitat bis: «Gehört die Welt –»] Sein Ende rückt heran – und sterbend noch bleibt er der Vernunft getreu; Poesie und Glaube nahen sich ihm nicht, und seine letzte Einsicht ist – in das N i c h t s. [Es folgt ausführliches Zitat der entsprechenden Verse.] Wahrlich es schaudert uns, diesen kühnen Mann sterben zu sehen; – aber erinnern Sie Sich, welches glänzende Gegenstück zu diesem finstern Gemälde [!] der Tod der Jungfrau dagegen abgiebt.» [Über Schillers Tragödie: Die Jungfrau von Orleans. Von August Klingemann, Leipzig 1802, S. 63 f.])

ger Nacht»⁵⁷ verglichen wird, so schaut dort, in völlig ähnlicher Lichtmetaphorik, das «zweite Leben» «hell und leuchtend in das Irdische hinein, und umstralt die darin wandelnden Gestalten»⁵⁸. Und so wie hier
jenes *glänzende Licht* nur *rasch und auf einen Augenblick* auftritt,
so ist es auch dort nur ein «rasches Schlaglicht», das in die irdische Welt
hinabfällt, «gleichsam ein Blitz, den derselbe Moment gebiert und vernichtet». Hinzu aber kommt, hier wie dort, die Verknüpfung mit dem
eigentümlich paradoxen Motiv der «Fortdauer» eines Geistes, der selbst
nicht glaubt⁵⁹, sich vielmehr noch in der Sterbestunde als «Materialist»
erweist und dem «Nichts» (wie es im ‹Jungfrau›-Aufsatz heißt), der
Vernichtung (wie es in den ‹Nachtwachen› heißt) ruhig ins Auge blickt:
alles in allem eine Konformität nicht nur des Motivs, sondern der ganzen
Motivkonstellation, die sich kaum anders erklären läßt als damit, daß
sie sich dem Verfasser, will sagen: einem und demselben Verfasser,
irgendwann einmal, am wahrscheinlichsten bei Betrachtung der bewußten ‹Jungfrau von Orleans›-Szene (III, 9), so «tief in den Sinn drückte»
(um eine Formulierung Goethes⁶⁰ zu gebrauchen), daß er im Laufe von
drei Jahren dreimal darauf zurückkam.

(3) Das *Pantheon*-Motiv

Der eben herangezogene Passus aus dem Aufsatz Klingemanns über den
«Schwarzen Ritter» bietet aber nicht nur das eben betrachtete Indizien-
material, er bietet zugleich die Möglichkeit des Übergangs zu einem weiteren Motivkomplex, der in den ‹Nachtwachen› ebenfalls eine nicht un-
wichtige Rolle spielt.

Sieht man sich die Gestaltung der Vorstellung von den zwei «Welten»
innerhalb dieses Aufsatzes genauer an, so bemerkt man: es sind im wesentlichen zwei Metaphern, mit denen sie sprachlich realisiert wird: einmal die Lichtmetaphorik, von der eben die Rede war, zum andern die
eigentümliche Gebäudemetapher, mit der das Motiv der höheren Welt
dort eingeführt wird, in entschiedener Antithese zur vorausgehenden
Charakteristik des «nüchternen» Talbot:

«Nun aber schwebt über dieser Tragödie der glänzende Himmel einer

---

⁵⁷ Das Bild, in der Dresdner Galerie hängend, ist bekanntlich oft und gern
zum Gegenstand literarischer Würdigung gemacht worden, unter anderem in
den Kunstsonetten im ‹Athenäum›.
⁵⁸ Ein anderer Reflex derselben Vorstellung in den ‹Nachtwachen›: *Ein Poet
meinte, die zweite Welt lausche in die untenliegende herunter (...)* (16. Nw.;
S. 133).
⁵⁹ Siehe o. Anm. 55.
⁶⁰ Im Aufsatz «Bedeutende Fördernis durch ein einziges geistreiches Wort»
(Artemis-Gedenkausgabe, 16. Bd., S. 880).

höhern Welt, gleichsam wie die in das Unermeßliche emporsteigende Kuppel eines Pantheons (...)».

Dies Bild findet in der Todesszene der ersten *Nachtwache* keine Entsprechung, wohl aber in der letzten *Nachtwache*, in der Rede des Nachtwächters auf dem Kirchhof, die mit der *zornigen* Frage beginnt, warum man den Vater auf dem Grabmal betend dargestellt habe, und dann gewaltig anschwillt zu einer mit grimmigem Pathos vorgetragenen Exposition materialistischer Doktrinen, sich bis zu den Sternen erhebend – *diese Myriaden von Welten saußen in allen ihren Himmeln nur durch eine gigantische Naturkraft* – um dann ebenfalls eine antithetische Wendung zu nehmen:

Der alte Schwarzkünstler scheint zu meiner Rede zu lachen! Weißt du es etwa besser, Teufelsbanner – und steigt über diesem zertrümmerten Pantheon ein neues herrlicheres auf, das in die Wolken reicht, und in dem sich die kolossalen ringsumher dasizenden Götter wirklich aufrichten können, ohne sich an der niedern Decke die Köpfe zu zerstoßen – – wenn es wahr wäre, so möchte es zu rühmen sein, und es dürfte schon die Mühe verlohnen zu zu schauen, wie mancher unermeßliche Geist auch seinen unermeßlichen Spielraum erhielte (...) (16. Nw.; S. 142 f.).

Identisch auf beiden Seiten ist nicht nur das Bild, sondern auch sein Sinn: die Andeutung einer über der materiellen, der Vergänglichkeit preisgegebenen Welt sich erhebenden Sphäre des Geistes und der Unsterblichkeit, der *Selbstständigkeit des Geistes*, wie es in derselben *Nachtwache* kurz vorher heißt, ebenfalls in sprachlicher Verbindung mit dem *Pantheon*-Bild, nur daß dort wieder der negative, skeptische, der Talbotsche oder auch: Hamletsche Ton, um im Bilde zu sprechen: der düstere Aspekt der *Corregios Nacht*, vorherrscht: *Was sind die Phantasieen der Erde, der Frühling und die Blumen, wenn die Phantasie in diesem kleinen Rund verweht, wenn hier im innern Pantheon alle Götter von ihren Fußgestellen stürzen, und Würmer und Verwesung einziehen. O rühmt mir nichts von der Selbstständigkeit des Geistes – hier liegt seine zerschlagene Werkstatt (...)* (S. 141).

In alledem ist wenig ‹Originales›, dagegen sehr viel Toposartiges, allgemein Verfügbares und, zumindest damals, allgemein Bekanntes, von Voltaires «weltbekanntem» Bonmot auf dem Totenbett bis zur *doppelten Beleuchtung* der «Heiligen Nacht» des Correggio, von den Totenschädels-Betrachtungen à la Yorick bis zum Pathos des Schauders angesichts der *gigantischen Naturkraft*, das man etwa bei Schiller, in seinen Gedichten wie in seinen Dramen, finden konnte. Ein gewisses Maß von Eigentümlichkeit, von ‹Apartheit›, zeigt allenfalls die Gebäude-Metapher, die im letzten Kapitel auftritt und wesentlich zum feierlichen Charakter der ‹Schlußapotheose› beiträgt: das Bild des Pantheons, genauer: des *neuen herrlicheren Pantheons*, das über einem anderen, darniederliegenden aufsteigt und einen *unermeßlichen Spielraum* bietet. Gerade dieses Bild aber findet sich bei Klingemann, d. h. in den unter seinem Namen veröffentlichten Schriften, nicht nur in dem zuletzt besprochenen Aufsatz aus der ‹Eleganten Welt›, sondern auch in ganz anderen, auch untereinander sehr verschiedenen Kontexten. Die beiden Hauptstellen seien der Übersichtlichkeit halber hier schon vorweggenommen, obwohl sie eigentlich erst ins nächste Kapitel hineingehörten, in dem die übrigen Schriften Klingemanns auf Indizien hin untersucht werden sollen. Der eine Kontext ist uns in früherem Zusammenhang bereits begegnet: es ist der feierliche Schluß des ‹Romano› (1801), «Camillos Vision» betitelt, der andere steht im ersten Band einer sehr viel späteren, nicht-fiktionalen Veröffentlichung Klingemanns: ‹Kunst und Natur; Blätter aus meinem Reisetagebuche›; sie erschien in drei Bänden, der erste 1818[61].

«Camillos Vision»[62] hat, wie schon angedeutet, die Form einer Wanderung, die ihrerseits im Sinne einer Klimax angelegt ist. Als Stationen werden zunächst ein «Hain», darauf eine Reihe von immer riesenhafteren Tempeln erkennbar, jeder von ihnen mit einer allegorischen Bedeutung versehen, die zu erraten dem Leser überlassen bleibt. Der Name «Pantheon» fällt nicht, dafür aber begegnen von Anfang an, schon in der Schilderung des Hains, immer wieder dieselben charakteristischen Merkmale: die «unermessliche»[63] Kuppel, Lichteinfall von oben und die «ringsum» verteilten Götterbilder:

«Die Götterbilder, die ringsum den Hain auszierten, blikten mit ernsten Mienen zu mir her (…) Wir waren jezt näher gekommen, und ich sah daß der Glanz durch die hohen Hallen eines unermesslichen Tempels fiel (…) es wird eine Zeit kommen, wo diese gewaltigen Kräfte sich vollenden und reifen; dann werden die Säulen ihre lebendigen Zweige in einander schlingen, und der Himmel wird seine unermessliche Kuppel über ihnen wölben (…) Vor uns öfnete sich das Heiligthum, und wölbte sich wie eine unermessliche Welt rund um uns her (…) Ein weiter Kreis nahm uns jetzt auf (…) Darauf befand ich mich in einer unermesslichen Halle, die Kuppel erhob sich bis in die Wolken und um die mäch-

---

[61] Zum Vergleich mögen hier auch die beiden Stellen stehen, die F. Schultz – ebenfalls zum Pantheon-Motiv – aus den Schriften F. G. Wetzels herangezogen hat: 1) «Ja selbst, wie Kepler sie erkennt, sind sie doch nur Gerüst, hinter welchem der Größere das Pantheon erbaut» (Brief v. 3. 2. 1807, mit bezug auf den Naturphilosophen Schubert; «sie» sind die Gravitationsgesetze); 2) «Wie mag er Grund und Eckstein des Pantheon seyn, welches in unverwelklicher Schönheit und Herrlichkeit dasteht, frey und erhaben über alle Stürme flüchtiger Zeit?» (Briefe über Browns System der Heilkunde. von F. G. Wezel (…). Leipzig 1806, S. 47) (Zitate nach F. Schultz, op. cit., S. 319 f.).

[62] Romano. Zweiter Theil. Braunschweig 1801, S. 245 ff.

[63] Vgl. im Text der ‹Nw.›, a. a. O.: (…) *wie mancher unermeßliche Geist auch seinen unermeßlichen Spielraum erhielte* (…).

tigen Säulen schlangen sich hohe Lieder wie ewige Gebete (...) Da öfnete sich über meinem Haupte die hohe Kuppel, und von einer lichten Wolke umgeben erschien mir Beatrice (...)».

Die andere Stelle bietet Parallelen nicht nur zu der Gebäudephantasie am Schluß der ‹Nachtwachen›, sondern auch zu einem anderen, uns bereits bekannten Bonaventura-Motiv, das ebendort – freilich nicht nur dort – auftritt. Ausgangspunkt ist die neuerbaute evangelische Kirche in Karlsruhe, die «ganz im römischen Style ausgeführt» ist, was den Reisebeschreiber zu einem kunstgeschichtlich-ästhetischen Exkurs veranlaßt:

Gegen die edle Ausführung des Ganzen wird Niemand etwas einwenden können; indeß verschweige ich meine Ansicht nicht, daß mir der antike Styl in dem Baue christlicher Kirchen mit dem Grundcharacter der bestimmten Religion selbst, welche darin gleichsam ihren Wohnsitz aufgeschlagen hat, im Widerspruch zu stehen scheint. Der antike Tempel umschloß den ganzen s i c h t - b a r e n Olymp, und vom hoch erhabenen, donnernden Jupiter an, bis zur süß lächelnden, anmuthsvollen Cypris, erschien alles Göttliche in ihm in klarer Vollendung und unmittelbarem Dasein für die Anschauung selbst; dieser mythischen Sculptur, welche die Götterbilder in den nächsten Gesichtskreis zu stellen wagte, mußte sich, (wenn ich mich so ausdrücken darf,) auch die mythische Architectur anschließen und jenen sichtbaren Olymp mit einem klaren und edel ausgeführten Raume umgeben, in dem die Deutlichkeit und Bestimmtheit der Verhältnisse sich in ihrer harmonischen Verbindung bis zur Schönheit selbst verklärte. – Anders dagegen aber in dem christlichen Tempel und ganz besonders in der evangelischen Kirche: so wie nämlich der alte Mythus seine Götter vom Himmel zur Erde herunterführte, so ließ der christliche dagegen das Göttliche umgekehrt, und gleichsam in einer Rafaels-Verklärung von der Erde zu dem Himmel emporsteigen, hob die Grenzen des Raums, welcher das Unendliche nicht in sich einzuschließen vermogte, völlig auf, und ließ, in Beziehung auf dasselbe, die Welt der Erscheinungen vor der höhern Ideenwelt zurücktreten. Der alte sitzende Olympische Jupiter richtete sich so gleichsam in höchster Allgewalt empor, und hob die Kuppel über seinem Haupte aus ihren Fugen; die Horazische «magna manus» streckte sich, wie in der Klopstockschen Messiade, durch die Unendlichkeit aus, und die sichtbare kolossale Größe verschwand vor der unsichtbaren geistigen, in Nichts.»[64]

---

[64] Kunst und Natur. 1. Bd., Braunschweig 1818, S. 126 f.. Innerhalb des zitierten Textes fallen außer den oben behandelten noch zwei Entsprechungen auf, die hier wenigstens angemerkt seien: 1) die Genitivfügung innerhalb der metaphorischen Wendung «gleichsam in einer Rafaels-Verklärung» (vgl. dazu in den ‹Nw.›: *die doppelte Beleuchtung in der Correggios Nacht* (S. 7), *wie wenn ein blutiger Bankos Geist sich daraus erheben sollte* (S. 43) u.a.m. sowie Michel, S. XXI, über das Jean-Paulsche dieser Fügungen); 2) der Dualismus von «sichtbarer kolossaler Größe» und «unsichtbarer geistiger», wozu das oben über Dualismus Ausgeführte zu vergleichen ist.

Die kunstgeschichtliche Überlieferung, auf die der letzte Passus zurückgeht – die vom Zeus des Phidias in Olympia, der bekanntlich sitzend
dargestellt war, und zwar so groß, daß man den Eindruck gewann, als
würde der Gott «den Tempel abdecken, wenn er sich erhöbe»[65] – findet
auch im Text der ‹Nachtwachen›, wie schon angedeutet, an mehr als
einer Stelle ihren Niederschlag: vor allem in der schon angeführten in unmittelbarer Umgebung des Pantheon-Bildes: *(...) steigt über diesem
zertrümmerten Pantheon ein neues herrlicheres auf, das in die Wolken
reicht, und in dem sich die kolossalen ringsumher dasizenden Götter
wirklich aufrichten können, ohne sich an der niedern Decke die Köpfe
zu zerstoßen (...)* (S. 143), aber auch an der Stelle über den *Riesen, den
man als Kind in einen niedrigen Raum eingemauert* (7. Nw.; S. 60), und
in der Vision im Antikensaal, in der *bei dem täuschenden Fackelglanze*
sich der *ganze verstümmelte Olymp umher plötzlich zu beleben* scheint:
(...) der zürnende Jupiter wollte sich aufrichten von seinem Sitze (...)
(13. Nw.; S. 112).

---

[65] Strabon VIII, 353.

III. Weitere Schriften und Indizien

1. Frühe kritische und erzählende Schriften

Dem Anfang dieses Kapitels ist in gewisser Weise bereits vorgearbeitet durch die knappe Charakteristik des Klingemannschen Frühwerks, die im biographischen Abriß gegeben wurde. Besonders bei der Besprechung des ‹Romano› und der Zeitschrift ‹Memnon› ist bereits ein Zug berührt worden, der auf die ‹Nachtwachen› vorauswies: die wichtige Rolle, die Jakob Böhme, der «ehrliche Seher», der Autor der «Morgenröthe», in beiden Veröffentlichungen spielt und die im Text der ‹Nachtwachen› ihr Pendant findet, vor allem in der Beschreibung des *Dritten Holzschnittes* (4. Nw.; S. 26 ff.)[1]. Es liegt nahe, hier anzuknüpfen und zunächst einige weitere Indizien derselben Art folgen zu lassen, also Indizien, die sich durch gemeinsame Bezugnahmen auf bestimmte Autoren oder Werke der Literaturgeschichte oder ähnliche Daten ergeben. Die Bedeutung dieser Indizien – ‹Referenz-Indizien›[2] könnte man sie nennen – liegt auf der Hand, wenn man bedenkt, daß durch die in einem Werk vorkommenden Bezugnahmen dieser Art, die man möglichst noch mit ihrem jeweiligen ‹Gewicht› zusammennehmen muß, so etwas wie eine Ortsbestimmung seines Autors – bei der die ‹Daten› als Koordinaten fungieren – mindestens aber eine gewisse Aussage über seine ‹Position› möglich wird. (Letztere Einschränkung ist notwendig, weil selbstverständlich nicht unbedingt in e i n e m Werk a l l e historischen oder auch nur literarhistorischen ‹Daten› anvisiert werden müssen, zu denen der Autor selbst eine Beziehung hat, vielmehr allein schon durch die Gattung, in der das Werk steht, bestimmte ‹Daten› bevorzugt, andere vielleicht völlig ausgeschlossen werden.) Was die ‹Nachtwachen› betrifft, so sind Bezugnahmen auf derartige ‹Daten› in ihnen nicht allzu häufig, weshalb denn auch jede Bezugnahme, von den wenigen spärlichen Erwähnungen Dantes bis zu der Bemerkung über die *Nachtuhren* des Samuel Day, von den Forschern mit entsprechender Aufmerksamkeit bedacht und umrätselt worden ist, seit den Tagen Hermann Michels, der aus derartigen Erwägungen seiner Edition auch ein Verzeichnis der im Text genannten Namen beigab, in dem man den Erfinder jener *Nachtuhren* ebenso findet

---

[1] Siehe oben S. 38, auch Anm. 38 ebda.
[2] In diesem Sinne wäre also z. B. auch die oben behandelte Erwähnung des Timanthes und seines Agamemnon-Bildes ein ‹Referenz-Indiz›.

wie Dante und den Naturforscher Erasmus Darwin. Einer der am häufigsten genannten Namen ist, wie gesagt, derjenige Kotzebues: darüber und
über die entsprechenden, auch dem ‹Gewicht› nach entsprechenden Bezugnahmen bei Klingemann ist im vorigen Kapitel das Notwendigste gesagt worden. Zwei weitere, ebenfalls relativ häufig genannte Autoren
(bzw. deren Reflexe in den hier zu behandelnden Werken) sollen nun
folgen: Hans Sachs[3] und Dante[4]; darauf einige weitere ‹Referenz-Indizien›
aus dem Bereich der Schriften um 1800, schließlich noch einige Parallelen
anderer, nicht ‹referentieller› Art (reine ‹Strukturparallelen› also): Übereinstimmungen in der Gestaltung novellistischer Situationen, mit Gleich-
klängen auch im Wortlaut, trotz einer vergleichsweise großen zeitlichen
Distanz.

(1) Hans Sachs

Was das Auftreten des Hans Sachs in den ‹Nachtwachen› angeht, so ist
uns eine der beiden wichtigsten Stellen, zugleich die Stelle seiner Einführung, bereits begegnet: es ist die Beschreibung des Holzschnittes, auf
dem der Held, ein Buch lesend, auf einem anderen sitzend, dargestellt
ist: *Das Buch worauf ich sitze, enthält Hans Sachsens Fastnachtsspiele, das
woraus ich lese, ist Jakob Böhmens Morgenröthe, sie sind der Kern
aus unserer Hausbibliothek, weil beide Verfasser zunftfähige Schuhmacher
und Poeten waren.* (4. Nw.; S. 26). Auf zwei weitere, ziemlich knappe
Nennungen in derselben und in der siebenten *Nachtwache*, in denen es
sich ebenfalls um Hans Sachsens Doppeleigenschaft als Schuhmacher und
Poet handelt, folgt als vierte und letzte eine Erwähnung, die eine Beziehung zur gegenwärtigen deutschen Literatur herstellt: *Göthe, der den
Hans Sachs, die Romantiker und Griechen in sich vereinigt*, wird als
Beispiel für die Bedeutung des *Essens* auch im Reich des Geistes angeführt
(12. Nw.; S. 104 f.).

Auch hierzu lassen sich, ganz wie im Falle Jakob Böhmes, Analogien
im Frühwerk Klingemanns nachweisen, vor allem im ‹Romano›, wo
einem «der alte Hans Sachs» in der «Eingangs-Halle» (dies der Titel der
Vorrede) zum zweiten Band des Romans begegnet – dem Band also, dessen Hauptinhalt die Verkündigung einer von Deutschland ausgehenden
Erneuerung der Kunst ist, worauf schon das Motto, ein Zitat aus Friedrich
Schlegels Terzinen «An die Deutschen», hinweist. Und was kaum weniger

---

[3] Mit vier Nennungen seines Namens der neben Kotzebue am häufigsten
genannte Autor.

[4] Sein Name wird ausschließlich in Verbindung mit dem ‹Inferno› genannt,
dieses selbst insgesamt dreimal in den ‹Nw.›, einmal in der Ankündigung des
Teufelstaschenbuches. (Michels Register ist hier unvollständig.)

bemerkenswert ist: auch hier wird eine Beziehung zu Goethe hergestellt, wenn auch, der anderen Gattung entsprechend, in anderer, nicht satirisch-komischer Tonart. Denn e r , Goethe, ist der «Meister», dessen «Bildniß» der Leser am Ende des Buchs «auf dem Altare», im letzten, heiligsten Tempelbezirk, erblicken wird und auf den schon die Vorrede geheimnis-voll hindeutet:

«Bis jezt bist Du mit mir durch lange Vorhöfe gewandelt; an den Säulen erbliktest Du mancherlei Symbole und Gemälde; deren Bedeutung Dir noch dunkel blieb, auch sahest Du die Zurichtungen zu einem Opfer, ohne daß ich Dich zum Altare selbst geleitete. Jezt aber trete ich zurück, und überlasse Dich einer höhern Führung, als die meinige sein konnte; der Tempel liegt vor Dir, die Flügel sind geöfnet und am Eingange erwartet Dich der alte Hans Sachs und bietet Dir traulich die Hand. Rede freundlich mit ihm und spotte seiner Treuherzigkeit nicht, Du hast Dich seiner Bekanntschaft nicht zu schämen; selbst der Meister, dessen Bildniß Du auf dem Altare erblikken wirst, lächelt ihm zu und plaudert gern mit ihm.»[5]

Auch Beziehungen zu den *Romantikern* und den *Griechen* sind zu-mindest nicht allzu fern: auf den vorangehenden Seiten wurden, als «Führer» in andere Gegenden der Poesie, Dante, Ariost und Petrarca genannt, also die Hauptautoren der romantischen Poesie im Schlegelschen Sinn, nachdem eine dem ersten Band vorangestellte literarhistorische Skizze, ‹Ein Fragment› betitelt, von der Antike als dem «goldenen Zeit-alter» der Kunst ausgegangen war und ihr, nach berühmten, nicht mehr ausdrücklich hervorzuhebenden Mustern, den «beständigen Progressus» der modernen Poesie gegenübergestellt hatte; als Repräsentanten der drei Hauptgattungen, der drei «schönen Blüthen der Poesie im klassischen Zeitalter», waren Homer, Pindar und Sophokles genannt worden. Zu allen diesen Namen gesellt sich also hier, in der «Eingangshalle» zum zweiten Teil, der des «alten Hans Sachs», vorausdeutend auf Goethe: nicht der Ton, aber die Konfiguration ist durchaus vergleichbar derjeni-gen, in der er an der zuletzt zitierten ‹Nachtwachen›-Stelle auftritt.

Sein Name taucht dann auch innerhalb des Romans selbst auf: ein «alter Mann», selbst mit «sehr kräftigen» Zügen, die «den treuherzigen graden Karakter» nicht verkennen lassen, wird vor einem großen auf-geschlagenen Buch angetroffen und erklärt dem Hinzukommenden: «Das ist ein Schaz, den ich über alles hochhalte; es ist ein kluges und verständi-ges Buch, und der alte Meistersänger der es schrieb, kannte das Leben wol genau.» Es folgt eine längere Auslassung darüber, was «der alte

---

5 Romano. Zweiter Theil. Braunschweig 1801, S. 8 f.

S a c h s verstanden» habe, wie er «mit hellen Augen in die Welt hinein»[6]
sehe, wie er das «Einzelne gar zierlich» figuriere, es «gehörig einander gegenüber» setze, und sich «selbst nicht vor dem Teufel» (!) fürchte, «ihn zu
citiren, wenn er da sein muß; dadurch wird seine Geschichte ergözlich
zugleich und erbaulich»[7].

Von den übrigen Erwähnungen des Hans Sachs will ich nur noch eine
hier anführen, weil sie gleichzeitig einen anderen Namen ins Spiel bringt,
der uns ebenfalls noch wichtig werden wird: den Namen Ludwig Tieck.
Im September 1804 veröffentlichte Klingemann, der ja schon im ‹Romano›
für Tieck eingetreten war, einem seiner Stücke, der ‹Genovefa›, sogar ein
Denkmal in Sonettform errichtet hatte, «Einige Worte über L u d w i g
T i e c k. Auf Veranlassung seines Lustspiels: O k t a v i a n u s», in denen
er der Frage nachgeht, auf welche Weise Tieck es mit dem größten Teil
des Publikums «verdarb», und zugleich den Weg andeutet, auf dem Tieck
versucht habe, «der Poesie wieder Muth einzusprechen, und ihr die ge-
bundenen Fittige zu lösen»[8]. Einer der Schritte auf diesem Wege, zugleich
einer der Gründe für das Mißfallen des Publikums: Tieck betrug «sich
nicht als Landsmann, vernachlässigte sein verständiges deutsches Vater-
land, und floh hin nach dem fantastischen Süden, oder besprach sich mit
dem gigantischen englischen Abentheurer (Shakspeare). Da, wo man ihn
ja noch als einen Deutschen betrachten konnte, ging er tief in die Vorzeit
zurück zu dem alten verstorbenen Hans Sachs und der verschollenen
Minne.»

---

[6] Formulierungen, die ziemlich deutlich auf Goethes Gedicht ‹Erklärung eines
alten Holzschnittes, vorstellend Hans Sachsens poetische Sendung› zurückwei-
sen, das auch bei der vorher besprochenen gemeinsamen Nennung von Hans
Sachs und Goethe in der Vorrede mitgewirkt haben dürfte – ebenso wie, zweifellos, bei der eingangs erwähnten ‹Nachtwachen›-Stelle, wo der Erzähler sich als
Kommentator jenes Holzschnittes betätigt, der ihn selbst, auf Hans Sachsens
Fastnachtspielen sitzend, zeigt.

[7] A. a. O., S. 91 ff.; vgl. auch S. 176 f., wo die Erzählung nochmals auf Hans
Sachs zurückkommt.

[8] ‹El. Welt› v. 6./8. 9. 1804. Der Anfang dieses Artikels enthält übrigens gleich
zwei eindrucksvolle Verbalparallelen, die bei dieser Gelegenheit mitgeteilt seien:
«Das neueste Werk eines Dichters, wie Tieck, der von dem größten Theile der
Lesenden herabgewürdigt, von einem geringern geduldet, und nur von einem
ganz kleinen Häuflein b e w u n d e r t wird, möchte man nur mit den Fingerspitzen anzugreifen wagen, wenn man darüber etwas mittheilen soll. Ich will die
Sache umgehen, und vom Eie anfangen.» Zu vergleichen mit: *Ich will etwas*
ausholen! sagen die Schriftsteller, wenn sie vom Eie einer Sache anheben wol-
len (...) (14. Nw.; S. 113; man beachte das Dativ-‹e›!) und: *Zu guter letzt ver-*
spreche ich (...) meine Wahrheiten (...) möglichst mit spitzen Fingern anzu-
greifen (...) (Des Teufels Taschenbuch, S. 149).

(2) Dante

Der Name Dantes erscheint in den kritischen und erzählenden Schriften Klingemanns mit einer gewissen Regelmäßigkeit dort, wo er in literar-historischen Exkursen oder Ausblicken auf die «gährende» Zwischenzeit zwischen Antike und Moderne zu sprechen kommt, so z. B. in dem gerade zitierten Artikel über Tieck: «B e g r i f f e herrschten in diesem Zeitpunkte nur wenige, und die Kulturgeschichte jener Epoche hat, was dies betrifft, nur leere Blätter aufzuweisen; daher denn auch der wenige Antheil, den der V e r s t a n d an den früheren romantischen Gedichten hat. Belege mögen Sie in dem Riesenwerke des Vaters der romantischen Poesie, D a n t e , aufsuchen.» Die Äußerung ist typisch für das Dante-Bild dieses Autors, das er mit den meisten seiner Zeitgenossen teilte: Dante ist vor allem der Dicher eines «Riesenwerkes» – fast gleichlautend heißt es schon im ‹Romano›, in ganz ähnlichem Zusammenhang: «(...) ich nenne hier nur das Riesenwerk des D a n t e »[9] – das, voll von Unverständlichkeiten und ohne erkennbaren Plan, «für die Theoretiker unauflösbare Auf-gaben»[10] stellt. Im Vordergrund steht das ‹Inferno›. Aus ihm stammt das einzige Dante-Zitat im ‹Romano›: die Inschrift auf dem Höllentor (per me si va nella città dolente...), wiedergegeben bis zum neunten Vers des dritten Gesanges, und was als Hauptvorstellung, mit deutlichem und ein-seitigem Bezug auf das ‹Inferno›, vorschwebte, zeigt etwa eine allgemeine Äußerung wie die des schon erwähnten Camillo[11], «alle die Riesengestal-ten, die Dantes düstre Phantasie erblickte», seien «in fürchterlicher Wirk-lichkeit» vor ihm erschienen[12]. Aus dem ‹Inferno› wird auch eine Hand-lungsepisode, die Geschichte der Francesca da Rimini, direkt übernom-men und als «Novelle» ausgestaltet[13]. Nur selten einmal erscheint ein Reflex der anderen Teile der ‹Divina Commedia›, der Name der Beatrice etwa, oder es wird eine knappe, bildhafte Andeutung vom Gang des gan-zen Gedichts, vom ‹Inferno› bis zum ‹Paradiso›, gegeben: «Liebst Du die Natur» – so wird der Leser in der Partie vor der Einführung des Hans

---

[9] 1. Bd., S. 25.

[10] Ebda.

[11] 2. Bd., S. 51; unmittelbar darauf das Zitat von Inf. III, 1–9.

[12] Zur Popularität dieses Dante-Bildes und der Rolle, die Gerstenbergs ‹Ugolino› dabei spielte, vgl. Erich Auerbach, in: Entdeckung Dantes in der Roman-tik (wiederabgedruckt in: Ges. Aufsätze zur roman. Philologie, Bern 1967, S. 176–183): «Durch die Berühmtheit dieser Tragödie wurde die populäre Dante-Vorstellung in Deutschland geschaffen, die sich also ganz auf die grauen-vollen Stellen des Inferno gründet.» (A. a. O., S. 178). Einer der vielen Belege hierfür, gerade was den Ugolino betrifft, ist dessen Erwähnung in der 8. Nw. (S. 71).

[13] «Franceska da Polenta [,] eine Novelle.» (Romano, 2. Bd., S. 54–72).

Sachs angeredet – «in ihrer Hoheit und verweilst Du gern bei ihren großen Schauspielen – wohlan, so nimm den D a n t e zu Deinem Führer;
sein Gesang braust wie ein Katarakt von himmelhohen Felsen herab, und
stürzt sich aus der Nacht hervor, bis ihn das stille Ufer umfängt, und die
heilige Morgenröthe sanft aus ihm wiederscheint.»[14]

Zu alledem paßt nun zunächst, daß sich auch die ‹Nachtwachen› an
keiner Stelle über die angedeutete populäre Dante-Vorstellung erheben
(was allein schon Grund genug hätte sein können, an Schellings Autorschaft ernsthaft zu zweifeln). Auch hier ist Dante in erster Linie der Dichter des ‹Inferno›, und sein Name steht, fast in der Art einer obligaten
Redefigur, für das Grauenvolle und Düstere. So malt der Pfaffe dem sterbenden Freigeist, ihm das Jenseits vor Augen stellend, *nicht das schöne
Morgenroth des neuen Tages und die aufblühenden Lauben und Engel,
sondern, wie ein wilder Höllenbreugel, die Flammen und die ganze schaudervolle Unterwelt des Dante* (1. Nw.; S. 7), oder es heißt von einem der
Wahnsinnigen in der neunten *Nachtwache*, als *Radikalkur* solle ihm die
Hölle des Dante dienen *(durch die ich ihn jezt alle Tage führe,* wie der
Redner hinzusetzt) (S. 79). Nur an einer Stelle wird über den ersten Teil
des Danteschen Gedichts hinausgeblickt – einer Stelle, die schon öfter die
Aufmerksamkeit der Forschung auf sich gezogen hat, da sie eine sprachliche Eigentümlichkeit enthält: den Gebrauch von ‹Inferno› als Maskulinum, der auch damals nicht gerade das Übliche war[15]. Die ‹Divina Commedia› wird hier als Metapher benutzt, innerhalb der Scheltrede über die
gegenwärtigen Schauspieldichter, die *statt ein ganzes Menschenleben zu
zertrümmern (. . .), sich nur mit der kleinen Quälerei beschäftigen (. . .),
damit der arme Schelm, obgleich geradebrecht, doch mit dem Leben zulezt noch davon gehen kann; als ob das Leben das Höchste wäre, und
nicht vielmehr der Mensch, der doch weiter geht als das Leben, das gerade
nur den ersten Akt und den inferno in der divina comedia, durch die er,
um sein Ideal zu suchen, hinwandelt, ausmacht* (4. Nw.; S. 29).

Um das Material vollständig auszubreiten, füge ich noch die betreffende
Stelle in der Ankündigung des Teufelstaschenbuchs hinzu: es ist eine
Danksagung des Teufels an Jean Paul – dafür, daß er *auch für uns ein
Uebriges in seiner poetischen Schatzkammer niedergelegt hat, und neben
dem goldführenden Strome, den er durch das Paradies zieht, wie* D a n t e

---

[14] A. a. O., S. 6 f..

[15] A. W. Schlegel in seinen Berliner Vorlesungen (wo Dante im dritten Zyklus
– Winter 1803/04 – behandelt wird) sagt «das Inferno», Schelling in der ‹Philo-
sophie der Kunst› (vorgetragen zuerst in Jena, Winter 1802/03, wiederholt in
Würzburg, Winter 1804/05) «das Infernum»; am gebräuchlichsten sind die voll-
ständigen Eindeutschungen wie «die Hölle des Dante», «die Unterwelt des
Dante».

auch einen siedenden schwarzen Styx und Phlegeton in die Unterwelt hinabbrausen läßt (S. 148).

Soweit die Erwähnungen Dantes bei Bonaventura. Vergleicht man sie genauer mit denen im ‹Romano›, so fallen mehrere, z. T. sogar wörtliche Korrespondenzen auf, von denen zumindest eine verdient, festgehalten zu werden: auch der Verfasser des ‹Romano› verwendet «Inferno» als M a s k u l i n u m :

«Ich erwachte noch im Grabe – da riß mich eine unsichtbare Hand auf, und führte mich hinab in den Inferno, und alle die Riesengestalten, die Dantes düstre Phantasie erblickte, erschienen hier in fürchterlicher Wirklichkeit vor mir.»[16]

Hinzu kommen einige schwächere Anklänge von entsprechend geringerer Beweiskraft, die hier aber doch, als Appendix, mitgeteilt seien: einmal die gemeinsame Metapher vom herabbrausenden Strom[17], zum andern die Vorstellung vom Verlauf des Danteschen Gesanges als einer Bewegung, die in der Finsternis der Unterwelt beginnt, dann aber über sie hinaus- und einer Sphäre des *Ideals* oder der «heiligen Morgenröthe» entgegengeht, schließlich auch die nicht ganz alltägliche Antithese von Unterwelt und Morgenröte, die sowohl im Stromgleichnis des ‹Romano› als auch in der Schilderung der Rede des Pfaffen begegnet[18] und die zugleich an Einsichten, die früher schon zum Bild der «Morgenröthe» gewonnen wurden, erinnert.

(3) Antikes

Mustert man den Text der ‹Nachtwachen› auf Bezüge zur Antike hin, so fallen, abgesehen von den oben schon berührten Details (Thespis, Timanthes, Chor und Protagonist), vor allem einige Anspielungen auf die griechischen Tragiker sowie auf die griechische bildende Kunst auf. Ich stelle das Wichtigste kurz zusammen:

---

[16] Romano [2. Bd.], S. 51. Ebenso an der einzigen anderen Stelle, die einen Unterschied gegenüber dem Neutrum erkennen läßt: «Hier hielt Camillo einige Zeit inne; dann aber fuhr er fort den übrigen Theil seiner Reise durch den Inferno zu erzählen.» (a. a. O., S. 72.)

[17] «(...) sein Gesang braust wie ein Katarakt von himmelhohen Felsen herab» (Romano, II, 6); (...) *wie Dante auch einen siedenden schwarzen Styx und Phlegeton in die Unterwelt hinabbrausen läßt* (Teufels Tb., S. 148).

[18] «(...) und stürzt sich aus der Nacht hervor, bis ihn das stille Ufer umfängt, und die heilige Morgenröthe sanft aus ihm wiederscheint» (Romano, a. a. O.); (...) *und er mahlt das Jenseits in kühnen Bildern; aber nicht das schöne Morgenroth des neuen Tages und die aufblühenden Lauben und Engel, sondern wie ein wilder Höllenbreugel, die Flammen und die ganze schaudervolle Unterwelt des Dante* (1. Nw.; S. 7).

1. *Ich habe mich jezt so ziemlich angekündigt, und kann das Trauerspiel nun allenfalls selbst auftreten lassen mit seinen drei Einheiten, der
Z e i t – auf die ich streng halten werde, damit der Mensch sich gar nicht
etwa in die Ewigkeit verirrt, – des O r t s – der immer im Raume bleiben
soll – und der H a n d l u n g – die ich so viel als möglich beschränken
werde, damit der Oedipus, der Mensch, nur bis zur Blindheit, nicht aber
in einer zweiten Handlung zur Verklärung fortschreite.* (8. Nw.; S. 76)

2. *(. . .) denn es ist doch spaßhaft und der Mühe werth, dieser großen
Tragikomödie der Weltgeschichte bis zum lezten Akte als Zuschauer
beizuwohnen, und du kannst dir zulezt das ganz eigne Vergnügen
machen, wenn du am Ende aller Dinge über der allgemeinen Sündfluth
auf dem lezten hervorragenden Berggipfel als einzig Uebriggebliebener
stehst, das ganze Stück, auf deine eigene Hand, auszupfeifen, und dich
dann wild und zornig, ein zweiter Prometheus, in den Abgrund zu stürzen*
(4. Nw.; S. 32).

3. *Ich hoffe indeß das alte Schicksal, unter dem bei den Griechen selbst
die Götter standen, darin abzugeben (. . .)* (8. Nw.; S. 75 f.).

4. *In der einen Sekunde, die sie das goldene Zeitalter nannte, schnizte
sie Figuren lieblich anzuschauen und baute Häuserchen darüber, deren
Trümmer man in der andern Sekunde anstaunte und als die Wohnung
der Götter betrachtete.* (9. Nw.; S. 81).

5. *O Freund, was die Kunstärzte der neuern Periode auch immer heilen
und flicken mögen, sie bringen doch die von der tückischen Zeit verstümmelten Götter, wie z. B. diesen daliegenden Torso, nicht wieder auf die
Beine, und sie werden immer nur als Invaliden und emeriti hier in Ruhe
gesezt verbleiben müssen. Einst, als sie noch aufrecht standen, und Arme
und Schenkel und Häupter hatten, lag ein ganzes großes Heldengeschlecht
vor ihnen im Staube; jezt ist das umgekehrt, und sie liegen im Boden,
während unser aufgeklärtes Jahrhundert aufrecht steht, und wir selbst
uns bemühen leidliche Götter abzugeben.* (13. Nw.; S. 110).

Zu allen diesen Stellen gibt es – stärkere und schwächere – Entsprechungen in den erzählenden und kritischen Schriften Klingemanns, vor
allem in den ‹Memnon›-Aufsätzen und im ‹Romano›; ich versuche sie
ebenfalls so knapp wie möglich darzustellen und zu kommentieren:

1. Die als erste aufgeführte ‹Nachtwachen›-Stelle, die im *Prolog des
Hanswurstes zu der Tragödie: der Mensch,* kurz vor dessen Ende, steht,
spielt offenbar auf die beiden Ödipus-Dramen des Sophokles an, also
nicht nur auf den ‹König Ödipus›, sondern auch auf den weit weniger
berühmten ‹Ödipus auf Kolonos›: er ist die *zweite Handlung,* in der der
Held, der in der ersten am Ende erblindete, zur *Verklärung* fortschreitet.
Bemerkenswert auch die metaphorische Beziehung, die zwischen Ödipus
und dem *Menschen* überhaupt hergestellt wird (der ja gleichzeitig die
Titelfigur des hier bevorworteten Trauerspiels ist). Dazu stellt sich in

Klingemanns «Briefen über Schillers Wallenstein» im ‹Memnon› der Passus, wo der Verfasser, in einem typischen literarhistorischen Exkurs, auf die griechische Tragödie und besonders auf Sophokles zu sprechen kommt, von dessen Stücken wieder weitaus am ausführlichsten die beiden Ödipus-Dramen gewürdigt werden, mit besonderem Akzent auf dem zweiten Ödipus und der «Verklärung», mit der er endet; aus ihm, also dem ‹Ödipus auf Kolonos›, stammt auch das einzige Zitat, das überhaupt aus einer griechischen Tragödie gegeben wird. Es heißt dort:

«Wo soll ich ihn finden, der den O e d i p erschuf, dieses hohe, göttliche Werk, das das ganze vollendete Leben in seinen heiligen Gesängen ausspricht? Der ganze Kreis der Menschheit ist in diesen beiden Tragödien durchlaufen, die beide unzertrennlich zusammen gehören, und gleichsam eine Weltgeschichte enthalten; alles darin ist kühne Offenbahrung, und ein höherer Geist schreitet durch das ganze Werk, und verkündet nie enthüllte Wunder. So gründet der Mensch kühn sein erstes Dasein, und trotzt den geheimnißvollen Mächten, wie der stolze Frevler Oedipos; aber das dunkle Räthsel löset sich, über ihm rollt ein höheres Fatum, er erkennt es, und der Fluch trifft ihn; – aber sein Haupt beugt der Kühne nicht, sein eigner Rächer wird er an sich selbst, und beraubt sich des schönen Lichts auf ewig. So erhebt er sich auch im Sturze noch über das Schicksal, und steht auf sich selbst gegründet. – Sehe ich dagegen auf das zweite Gemälde: so hat sich alles verändert, und wenn in dem ersten die höchste menschliche Kraft und Kühnheit mich entzückte: so erblicke ich hier alles göttlich vollendet, und in himmlischer Verklärung. – Die Menschheit, mit dem Schicksale versöhnt, ist ein überirdisches Schauspiel. Vom Gotte geweiht weissagt der blinde Seher, und sein prophetischer Gesang verkündigt die dunkelen Geheimnisse des Schicksals, bis seine Verklärung nahet, und das Sterbliche von ihm niedergesunken ist.»[19]

Hierauf folgt aus dem Bericht des Boten am Ende des Dramas die Stelle über die Entrückung des Ödipus (insgesamt 14 Verse) und eine abschließende Bemerkung: «Dies ist das Gemälde seines Todes und seiner Verklärung. – Der Gesang des Dichters schwebt hier über der Erde, und die Schönheit ist beinahe göttlich, und kaum noch kann das sterbliche Auge ihren reinen Lichtglanz ertragen.» – Außer den Übereinstimmungen in den zentralen Begriffen und in der Akzentsetzung fällt auch hier die Vergleichsbeziehung auf, die zwischen Ödipus und dem «Menschen» überhaupt hergestellt wird: Ödipus s t e h t geradezu – auch hier – für den Menschen: «So gründet der Mensch kühn sein erstes Dasein, und trotzt den geheimnißvollen Mächten, wie der stolze Frevler Oedipos; aber das dunkle Räthsel löset sich (...)». Auch zu dieser letzten Formulierung übrigens gibt es eine Parallelstelle in den ‹Nachtwachen›: es ist die andere der (insgesamt zwei) Erwähnungen des Ödipus; sie steht in der fünften

---

[19] Memnon, S. 92 f.

Nachtwache, in der Geschichte von den zwei Brüdern, und lautet: *Juan stand starr und eingewurzelt, die finstere Ahnung stieg rasch vor seinem Geiste auf und verschwand nicht wieder, und wurde furchtbar deutlich, wie das sich plözlich auflösende Rätsel des Oedipus.»* (5. Nw.; S. 44).

2. Zu vergleichen ist hier die sehr viel kürzere Charakteristik des Aischylos, die den Worten über Sophokles in den ‹Wallenstein›-Briefen vorausgeht und in der als einziges Beispiel der ‹Prometheus› angeführt wird: «A e s c h y l u s ist durchgehends nicht schön, aber die Schönheit ist in ihm angekündigt; er ist groß und kühn bis zum Zerreißenden, alles hohe Erhabenheit und vollendete männliche Kraft; die Umrisse seiner Gestalten sind groß, und gehen ins Kolossale; aber nirgends ist Anmuth und stille ruhige Vollendung. Im P r o m e t h e u s hat er sich selbst vollkommen ausgesprochen, und wie dieser kühne Frevler, so endigt das ganze Leben – mit Erdbeben und Untergang.»[20] Auch hier liegt der Akzent auf dem Untergang des Prometheus am Ende des Stücks und der ihn begleitenden, gleichsam umrahmenden Weltkatastrophe[21].

3. Zu vergleichen ist hier alles, was über das «furchtbare Schicksal» in den ‹Wallenstein›-Briefen gesagt wird, besonders der Satz: «Bei den Alten war das S c h i c k s a l die dunkle unbezwingliche Macht, der kein Sterblicher entfliehen konnte, und der sogar die Götter sich unterwerfen mußten; der Glaube daran war allgemein herrschend, und die antike Tragödie bekam dadurch einen ernsten und großen Gang.»[22]

4. Die Stelle steht im *Monolog des wahnsinnigen Weltschöpfers* und zielt offensichtlich auf die Antike als goldenes Zeitalter der Kunst. – Nicht nur das Bild des goldenen Zeitalters, sondern auch seine Anwendung auf die Antike begegnet mehrfach in den kunsttheoretischen Äußerungen Klingemanns, so in der Einleitung zum ersten Band des ‹Romano›, nach der Erwähnung von Homer, Pindar und Sophokles: «Die Kunst ruhete in diesem goldenen Zeitalter noch an dem mütterlichen Busen der Natur, leicht entfaltete sie sich und strebte dann mächtig durch eigene Kraft empor. Doch als die Bildung den höchsten Gipfel erreicht hatte und vollendet war, sank sie wieder in sich zurück und nur die heiligen Monumente der Künstler bezeugen daß diese Periode einst war.»[23] Und im ersten einer Reihe von «Fragmenten» von 1805, hier in etwas weniger hoher Stillage, der komisch-satirischen des ‹Nachtwachen›-Zitats etwas näher: «In dem goldenen Zeitalter der Welt steht die Poesie noch in dem Leben selbst, und erst nach dessen Verschwinden geht sie als Archimimus hinter der Königlichen Leiche her – ein Miltonsches verlornes Para-

---

[20] Memnon, S. 91.
[21] Vgl. Prom., Vers 1043 ff.
[22] Memnon, S. 103.
[23] Romano, 1. Bd., S. 13 f.

dies hinter dem verlornen wirklichen.»[24] Es ist jedesmal derselbe Gedanke, jedesmal mit demselben Element elegischen Rückblicks, nur in jeweils verschiedener Brechung im Medium verschiedener literarischer
Gattungen.

5. Die Stelle, selbst unmittelbar in den eben erörterten Zusammenhang hineingehörig (die Antike als Ruine), ein neuer, wiederum satiri-
scher Niederschlag desselben Grundgedankens mit scharfer Wendung
gegen das gegenwärtige Zeitalter, findet eine nicht-satirische Entsprechung u. a. in einem Brief Romanos: «Ist denn die Erde nicht mehr die
vorige, und haben wir sie entweihet, daß alles Schöne zum Himmel ent-
flohen ist? Die alten Götter liegen zertrümmert in dem unheiligen Boden, und ihre Geister blikken nur noch aus den Gestirnen zu uns nieder.»[25]

(4) Novellistisches

Auffällige Parallelen in der Anlage und Ausgestaltung rein erzählerischer,
‹fiktionaler› Partien finden sich besonders in der schon erwähnten Novelle «Franceska da Polenta», die der Francesca da Rimini-Episode in der
‹Divina Commedia› nacherzählt und in den ‹Romano› eingelegt ist[26]. Die
entsprechenden Vergleichspunkte innerhalb der ‹Nachtwachen› liegen in
der Geschichte von den zwei Brüdern (5. Nw.; S. 45), die ja ebenfalls das
Hauptmotiv der Francesca da Rimini-Episode wiederholt: das Motiv
einer heimlichen ehebrecherischen Liebe, wobei der Liebende – und Wie-
dergeliebte – zugleich der Bruder des betrogenen Ehemanns ist.

Aber nicht nur in dieser motivischen Grundstruktur gibt es Übereinstimmungen zwischen den beiden erzählerischen Einlagen: der im ‹Romano› und derjenigen in den ‹Nachtwachen› (*Die Brüder* wird sie im
Inhaltsverzeichnis des Erstdrucks genannt), sondern auch in der Ausführung, in der Inszenierung, in der eigentlichen sprachlichen Realisierung.
So vor allem in der Art, wie der Erzähler es zur ersten Annäherung der

---

[24] ‹El. Welt› v. 15. 6. 1805. (Man beachte auch das Jeanpaulisierende der
Formulierung im Einzelnen wie in der ganzen Anlage des Aphorismus.)

[25] Romano, 1. Bd., S. 280. (Eine weitere Parallelstelle in anderem Kontext
wird weiter unten zu besprechen sein.)

[26] Aber nicht nur dort – wofür wenigstens ein Beispiel gegeben sei: «Ich be-
sah die Gruppe [= die Laokoon-Gruppe; J. S.] des Nachts beim Scheine der
Fakkeln, die Flammen zitterten in der Luft und in dem abentheuerlichen Spiele
von Schatten und Licht fingen die Körper an sich zu bewegen und lebten vor
meinen Augen; die Schlangen schlugen ihre gräßlichen Knoten um des Vaters
und der Kinder Glieder (...)» (Romano, 1. Bd., S. 10); zu vergleichen mit: (...)
*bei dem täuschenden Fackelglanze schien sich der ganze verstümmelte Olymp
umher plözlich zu beleben (...) mächtig bäumten sich die Drachen um den
kämpfenden Laokoon und die sinkenden Söhne* (13. Nw.; S. 112).

Liebenden kommen läßt. Die entscheidende Stelle liest sich in den ‹Nacht-wachen› folgendermaßen:

In seiner Seele war alles fest und entschieden, doch floh er seinen eige-nen Umgang, um dem dunklen Gefühle keine Worte zu geben, und sich nicht gegen sich selbst erklären zu müssen. So suchte er, gegen sich ge-heimnisvoll, Ponces Landgut auf, und trat in Donna Ines Zimmer; sie erkannte ihn rasch, und die weiße Rose blühete zum erstenmale roth und glühend auf, und die Liebe belebte Pygmalions kaltes Wunderbild. Die Abendsonne brannte durch Laub und Blüthen, und Ines schob kindlich schuldlos den Wangenpurpur dem Himmelsfeuer zu, das sie anstrahlte: dann ergriff sie bebend die Harfe, und wie Juan ihr Spiel mit der Flöte begleitete, hub das verbotene Gespräch ohne Worte an, und die Töne bekannten und erwiederten Liebe. (5. Nw.; S. 45)

Und im ‹Romano›, in der Novelle von Paolo und Francesca:

«Paolo hatte es sich selbst geschworen, ihr niemals seine Liebe durch Worte zu offenbaren und er hielt streng auf seinen Eid. Wenn Sie allein beisammen waren, ergriff er die Flöte und begleitete ihr Spiel auf der Guitarre – aber hier entstand ein Gespräch zwischen ihnen, zarter, als es die Worte auszudrükken vermochten. Sie griff leise in die Saiten und entlokte ihnen zärtliche Klagen, dann weheten wie aus der Ferne die sanften Töne der Flöte her und schienen die rührenden Klänge zu um-schlingen und vereint mit ihnen leise zu verhallen.»[27]

Einige weitere Beispiele: «Starr wie eine Bildsäule» steht Paolo, als er Francesca wiedersieht (als Frau seines Bruders); *starr wie eine Bildsäule* steht Juan am Schluß der Geschichte von den *Brüdern*. «In dem düstern Haine auf kaltem Boden» liegt Paolo «in einer starren Fühllosigkeit», nach der schrecklichen Entdeckung; Juan sinkt im entsprechenden Augen-blick *bewußtlos auf den Stein nieder*, dann stürzt er *hinaus ins Freie* (was auch Paolo tut). Vor allem aber weist das letzte Bild des *schreklichen Nachtstücks* am Ende der ‹Brüder› wieder zurück auf den ‹Romano›, allerdings nicht auf die Novelle von Paolo und Francesca, sondern auf einen Traum des Helden Romano selbst:

Da wurde das schrekliche Nachtstück[28] beleuchtet. Der schöne Knabe lag schon im festen Todesschlummer auf dem Boden, und aus Ines Brust floß der purpurrothe Strom und haftete auf dem schneeweißen Schleier wie vorgestekte Rosen (5. Nw.; S. 47) – heißt es in der fünften *Nacht-wache*, und in Romanos Traum:

«Sie deutete mit der Hand nach dem östlichen Himmel, an dem in dem Augenblicke die Morgenröthe glühend emporstieg, und wie eine ferne

---

[27] Romano, 2. Bd., S. 65 f.

[28] «Nachtstük» ist übrigens auch der Titel eines Sonetts im ‹Romano› (2. Bd., S. 117 f.).

himmlische Musik in seinem Herzen wiedertönte. Plözlich aber blikte sie erschrokken auf ihn nieder, und aller Glanz war verschwunden, er fühlte sich schmerzlich getroffen, und als er sich betrachtete, floß ein Strom Blut aus seiner Brust und färbte ihr weißes Gewand.»[29] Noch näher steht dieser melodramatischen Stelle allerdings ein anderes Todesbild aus den ‹Nachtwachen›: dasjenige, mit dem der Teufelskampf am Totenbett des Freigeistes endet:

(. . .) und ein purpurrother Blutstrom färbte das weiße Sterbegewand des schlafenden Freigeistes. (2. Nw.; S. 15)

2. ‹Kunst und Natur›

Im Folgenden handelt es sich wieder um ausgesprochen Faktisches, genauer: um wiederkehrende Bezugnahmen auf bestimmte, und zwar höchst spezielle, wenn man so will: banale Fakten. Es liegt ja in der Natur dieser Untersuchung, daß sie ihren Leser mit sehr speziellen und ‹faktischen›, hegelsch gesprochen: sehr partikularen Dingen befassen und das Allgemeine geradezu scheuen muß: je ‹allgemeiner› irgendein Charakteristikum ist, um so gleichgültiger ist es in unserem Zusammenhang – sehr im Gegensatz zu der in den Wissenschaften, heute mehr denn je, vorherrschenden, vielfach sicher auch ganz legitimen Auffassung. Es war ja gerade die Schwäche z. B. der Franz Schultzschen Argumentation, daß sie unbedenklich mit Merkmalen operierte, die in gewissen Grenzen, insbesondere gewissen Gattungsgrenzen, allgemein verbreitet, ja z. T. geradezu zeittypisch waren: Merkmalen wie «humoristisch-ironische Technik», «desillusionierende Seitensprünge», «Vorliebe für nächtliche Stimmungen und Szenerien» usw. So ist, um ein Beispiel aus dem Vorigen zu geben, die Polemik gegen Kotzebue – in den ‹Nachtwachen› einerseits, den vorgeführten Klingemannschen Veröffentlichungen andererseits – sicher ein Indiz von schwächerer Beweiskraft als etwa die Bezugnahme auf den Schluß des ersten wie des zweiten ‹Ödipus›; denn die Kenntnis Kotzebues war damals allgemein und der Spott über seine Stücke namentlich unter den selbst literarisch Tätigen weit verbreitet, während eine Kenntnis jener beiden Dramenschlüsse sicher nur bei einem – damit verglichen – kleineren Kreis von Autoren vorausgesetzt werden kann. Überlegungen dieser Art führen einen dazu, gerade auf die Spiegelungen von

---

[29] Romano, 2. Bd., S. 31. Der erste Satz des Zitats enthält überdies Anklänge an den Schluß der 1. Nw.: *(. . .) sie ist der erste süße Laut vom fernen Jenseits, und die Muse des Gesanges ist die mystische Schwester, die zum Himmel zeigt. So entschlummerte Jakob Böhme, indem er die ferne Musik vernahm, die Niemand, ausser dem Sterbenden hörte.* (1. Nw.; S. 9)

‹punktuellen› und möglichst ‹ausgefallenen›, ‹nebensächlichen› Fakten, d. h. solchen, deren Kenntnis lediglich innerhalb eines möglichst kleinen Kreises von Zeitgenossen vorausgesetzt werden kann, besonders achtzugeben. Freilich ist, wie früher schon angedeutet, der Text unseres Buches alles andere als reich an solchen punktuellen und hinreichend speziellen Faktenreflexen. Einer der wenigen, die es gibt, zugleich einer der auffälligsten, ist die ebenfalls schon erwähnte Stelle über die *Nachtuhren* des Samuel Day.

(1) *Nachtuhren*

Der Leser erfährt von dieser merkwürdigen Erfindung am Ende der sechsten *Nachtwache*, in der vorher erzählt wurde, wie der Nachtwächter *in der lezten Stunde des Säkulums* es sich hatte einfallen lassen, *mit dem jüngsten Tage vorzuspuken und statt der Zeit die Ewigkeit auszurufen, worüber viele geistliche und weltliche Herren erschrocken aus ihren Federn fuhren und ganz in Verlegenheit kamen, weil sie so unerwartet nicht darauf vorbereitet waren*, und wie er damit, bei nicht eintretendem Jüngsten Tag, den Zorn und die Rache der höchsten zuständigen Behörden auf sich gezogen habe:

Damit indeß ein ähnlicher Lerm nicht wieder für die Folge zu besorgen, so wurden durch eine Kabinettsordre die von Samuel Day erfundenen watchmanns noctuaries eingeführt, wodurch ich von einem singenden und blasenden Nachtwächter auf einen stummen reduzirt wurde, wobei man zum Grunde anführte, daß ich durch mein Blasen und Rufen mich den Nachtdieben verriethe, und es deshalb als unzweckmäßig abgeschafft werden müsse (6. Nw.; S. 55 f.). Dazu findet sich am Fuß der Seite, durch einen Stern hinter *reduzirt wurde* mit dem Text in Beziehung gesetzt, die recht detaillierte Sacherläuterung: *Diese Nachtuhren sind so eingerichtet, daß der Nachtwächter jedesmal in ein bis dahin verstektes Loch, das erst bei der bestimmten Stunde hervorrükt, einen Zettel stekt, zum Belege, daß er regelmäßig umhergegangen ist. Am Morgen schließt dann ein Polizeyoffizier die Uhr auf, um zu sehen, ob in jedem einzelnen Loche der Zettel sich vorfindet.*

Soweit die Originalfußnote in den ‹Nachtwachen›, deren Angaben übrigens, wie gleich zu zeigen sein wird, auf authentischen zeitgenössischen Nachrichten basieren. Es ist kaum anzunehmen, daß ein großer Teil der literarisch-belletristisch tätigen Zeitgenossen von dieser technischen Neuerung Kenntnis genommen hat (und überdies so beeindruckt von ihr war, daß er sie in seine literarische Produktion eingehen ließ). Um so wichtiger wird das nun zu besprechende Indiz, ein Detail von kaum zu überbietender Geringfügigkeit, wenn man es an und für sich betrachtet: eine Erwähnung offensichtlich derselben «Nachtuhren» in einer sehr viel späteren Schrift August Klingemanns, dem dritten Band von ‹Kunst und Natur› (1828). Thema des ganzen Abschnitts ist das Theater in Kassel und seine Einrichtung, die dem reisenden alten Theatermann imponiert. In diesem Zusammenhang kommt er auch auf die Art der nächtlichen Bewachung und, mit einer Ausführlichkeit und einem Interesse, die als solche bereits auffällig sind, auf die zur Kontrolle der Wächter installierten Uhren zu sprechen:

«Die Vorsichtsmaaßregeln gegen Feuersgefahr betreffend, hat man, zur Controllirung der angestellten, und das Haus durchvisitirenden Wächter, die in London erfundenen Nachtuhren, sehr zweckmäßig angewendet, welche einen Mechanismus enthalten, vermöge dessen sich unter einem oben angebrachten schmalen Einschnitte, von einer halben Stunde zur andern, in dem verschlossenen Innern fortrückend kleine Kästchen vorschieben, welche, die von den Wächtern, insofern dieselben ordnungsmäßig ihren Umgang zur Nacht gemacht haben, hineingesteckten, numerirten Marken emthalten müssen, wenn der Theaterinspector am darauf folgenden Morgen die Uhr eröffnet und Nachsicht anstellt. Wo eine Nummer in dem bestimmten Kästchen abgeht, da ist auch sofort der saumselige Wächter ausgemittelt und überwiesen, und wird durch Arrestation, oder bei nachfolgender Contravention durch Cassirung bestraft.»[30]

Ich lasse auch diese Parallelstelle ohne Kommentar, um zwei weitere Parallelen aus demselben Werk anzuschließen, die beide von ähnlicher Art sind; jede von ihnen auf ein bestimmtes, verhältnismäßig punktuelles und nicht sehr bekanntes Faktum bezogen, die eine auf ein literarisches, die andere auf ein naturhistorisches.

(2) Mandandane

Es scheint, daß auch damalige Leser mit diesem Namen nicht allzu viel anfangen konnten: an der Stelle in den ‹Nachtwachen›, wo er auftaucht, steht eine Fußnote und erläutert: *G ö t h e ' s Triumpf der Empfindsamkeit* (8. Nw.; S. 75). Dieselbe Fußnote aber erscheint, von unwesentlichen Abweichungen abgesehen, auch in ‹Kunst und Natur› beim Auftreten desselben Namens: «S. Göthe's: Triumph der Empfindsamkeit.»[31]

Der springende Punkt ist beidemale das Motiv der lebensgroßen weiblichen Puppe, die der Prinz in Goethes genanntem Stück als eine Art Andachtsbild mit sich herum führt und die der von ihm geliebten Königin, der wahren Mandandane, nachgebildet ist: das Ganze ein Spott auf die Empfindsamkeit, ebenso wie die Figur des «Directeur de la nature», die in Kisten mitgeführte «Reisenatur» und die Figur des Merkulo, der

---

[30] Kunst und Natur; Blätter aus meinem Reisetagebuche. 3. Bd. Braunschweig 1828, S. 399.

[31] 3. Bd., S. 240.

den Prinzen als Kavalier und Fachmann für die «Effekte» des Natürlichen
begleitet.[32] Beidemale wird die «ausgestopfte Mandandane» (Kunst und
Natur, III 240), der *zusammengeflickte Popanz* (8. Nw.) zu metaphorischen Zwecken herangezogen. Sprachliche Koinzidenzen, die über den
Namen «Mandandane» hinausgingen, gibt es nicht, weshalb die Kontexte
hier wegbleiben können.

(3) Erasmus Darwin

Um so überraschender sind die sprachlichen Übereinstimmungen im folgenden Fall, in dem es um eine naturhistorische Hypothese geht, die in
die Vorgeschichte der Deszendenztheorie gehört (der im Folgenden genannte Erasmus Darwin ist übrigens der Großvater ihres eigentlichen
Begründers). Der betreffende Passus in den ‹Nachtwachen› ist der Anfang
des schon öfter herangezogenen *Prologs des Hanswurstes zu der Tragödie: der Mensch:*

*Ich trete als Vorredner des Menschen auf. Ein respektives zahlreiches
Publikum wird es leichter übersehen, daß ich meiner Handthierung nach
ein Narr bin, wenn ich für mich anführe, daß nach Doktor Darwin eigentlich der Affe, der doch ohnstreitig noch läppischer ist als ein bloßer Narr,
der Vorredner und Prologist des ganzen Menschengeschlechts ist, und daß
meine und Ihre Gedanken und Gefühle sich nur blos mit der Zeit etwas
verfeinert und kultivirt haben, obgleich sie ihrem Ursprunge gemäß doch
immer nur Gedanken und Gefühle bleiben, wie sie in dem Kopfe und
Herzen eines Affen entstehen konnten. Doktor Darwin, den ich hier als
meinen Stellvertreter und Anwald aufführe, behauptet nämlich, daß der
Mensch als Mensch einer Affenart am mittelländischen Meere sein Dasein
verdanke, und daß diese blos dadurch daß sie sich ihres Daumenmuskels
so bedienen lernte, daß Daumen und Fingerspitzen sich berührten, sich
allmählig ein verfeinertes Gefühl verschaffte, von diesem in den folgen-*

---

[32] Als Antizipation Garlieb Merkels, «nur durch eine Italienische Endung ein
wenig idealisirt», wird dieser Merkulo in einer humoristisch-satirischen Zu-
schrift gedeutet, die am 2. 2. 1802 (anonym) in der ‹El. Welt› erschien und in
der auch die wahre ebenso wie die falsche Mandandane vorkommt. Sie gibt
sich als Brief des Königs Andrason aus Goethes Drama an den Herausgeber
der Zeitung und will ihm die Methode «an die Hand geben», wie Merkel-Mer-
kulo zur «Unterhaltung» des Publikums dienen könne: indem man ihn nicht
etwa «ernsthaft» nehme, sondern als «allegorische Figur, als bloße Maske», als
«das fratzenhafte Geschöpf einer scherzenden Fantasie». Ich bin überzeugt, daß
der Brief von Klingemann stammt – schon die Art, Merkel als Beitrag zur komischen Literatur zu würdigen, liegt völlig auf der Linie der Klingemannschen
Polemiken gegen Merkel (siehe oben S. 42 und S. 45, Anm. 51) – will ihn aber
hier nicht als Argument anführen, um die Beweisführung nicht durch selbst noch
Beweisbedürftiges zu belasten.

den Generationen zu Begriffen überging und sich zulezt zu verständigen Menschen einkleidete, wie wir sie jezt noch täglich in Hof- und anderen Uniformen einherschreiten sehen. (8. Nw.; S. 72 f.). Auch hierzu gibt es eine Originalfußnote; sie bezieht sich auf die erste Nennung des Doktor Darwin und lautet: S. dessen Gedicht über die Natur.

Auch der Verfasser von ‹Kunst und Natur› weiß von dem Naturgedicht des Doktor Darwin, ja, er weist sogar mit derselben Folge von Buchstaben darauf hin, und wieder handelt es sich um die Hypothese von der Affenart am Mittelländischen Meere und ihrem Daumenmuskel. Kontext ist ein Exkurs über den Tanz und insbesondere die Pantomime, der Klingemann vorwirft, «die Tanzkunst in ein Aftergebiet» hinüberzuführen, «in welchem sie sich nie, auf eine ihr würdige und höhere Weise geltend machen kann»:

«Wenn übrigens nach D o c t o r D a r w i n s poetischer Hypothese (s. dessen Gedicht über die Natur) das Menschengeschlecht von einer Affenraçe am mittelländischen Meere abstammt, welche durch eine fortgesetzte kleine Manipulation, vermöge welcher sie den Daumenmuskel mit den Fingerspitzen in eine immer geschicktere Berührung brachte, erst ein verfeinertes Gefühl erhielt, von diesem aber zu Begriffen u.s.w. überging; so dürfte bei jener Raçe sich die Pantomime in ihrer ganzen Selbstständigkeit, als die sublimste Kunst ausgebildet haben, und wer weiß, ob wir nicht einmal, in jene Lage zurückversetzt, wieder zu ihr zu greifen gezwungen werden dürften.»[33]

Hier sind nun ganze Wortfolgen identisch: angefangen von dem Hinweis «s. dessen Gedicht über die Natur» über die Affenraçe bzw. -art «am mittelländischen Meere» bis zu ihrem «verfeinerten Gefühl», von dem aus sie dann «zu Begriffen überging». Darüber hinaus aber ist beiden Stellen eine charakteristische Ungenauigkeit gemeinsam. Denn wie schon Michel in seinem Kommentar zur bewußten Stelle in den ‹Nachtwachen› hervorgehoben hat, wird die Hypothese von der Affenart am Mittelmeer von Erasmus Darwin nicht eigentlich vertreten, sondern nur mit einer gewissen Distanz referiert – als Ansicht von Buffon und Helvetius – und auch dies nicht innerhalb des Gedichtes selbst, sondern in den gelehrten Fußnoten, mit denen es angereichert ist.[34] Das führt auf die Frage, ob nicht schon zwischen Erasmus Darwin's Lehrgedicht und den

---

[33] Kunst und Natur, 3. Bd., S. 64.

[34] «(...) these philosophers, with Buffon and Helvetius, seem to imagine, that mankind arose from one family of monkeys on the banks of the Mediterranean; who accidentally had learned to use the adductor pollicis (...)», heißt es im Original (The Temple of Nature; or the Origin of Society. London 1803, S. 54). (Der Rest entspricht im wesentlichen den beiden obigen Referaten.) Vgl. auch Michel, a. a. O., S. 156.

‹Nachtwachen› eine Zwischenstation, eine Rezension etwa oder sonst irgendeine Form von Berichterstattung, anzunehmen ist, die dem ‹Nachtwachen›-Verfasser als Quelle vorgelegen hat; eine Frage, die sich auch deshalb nahelegt, weil man sich den Kreis der deutschen Leser, die das englische Original[35], ein kostbar ausgestattetes Buch mit Kupfern nach Zeichnungen von Füßli, in Händen hatten, ohnehin eher begrenzt denken muß.

(4) Quellenkritisches und Entstehungsgeschichtliches

Die fragliche Zwischenstation läßt sich nun in der Tat nachweisen, und zwar in einer Zeitung, die auch Klingemann damals zu lesen mancherlei Veranlassung hatte: im ‹Freimüthigen›. Hier erschien am 2. März 1804 unter der Überschrift ‹Englische Literatur› ein Bericht über «Doctor Darwins ‹Tempel der Natur›», in dem als ein Beispiel unter anderen für die «Bockssprünge» des englischen Autors auch die Hypothese von der Affenart am Mittelmeer vorgeführt wird – ganz so, als ob sie Darwins eigene Hypothese wäre, und mit Formulierungen, die keinen Zweifel daran lassen, daß der Verfasser der ‹Nachtwachen› seine Kenntnis über sie hierher bezog:

«Einer Affenart am Ufer, (welchem?)[36] des Mittelländischen Meeres dankt der Mensch, als Mensch seinen Ursprung. Gelegentlich lernte nehmlich diese Affenart, was man bei andern gewöhnlichen Affenarten indeß nicht findet, sich des starken Muskels des Daumens, welchen wir die Maus nennen, so zu bedienen, daß Daumen und Fingerspitzen sich berührten. In den nachfolgenden Affengenerationen wurde nun dieser Muskel immer größer, stärker und thätiger. Aus seiner Thätigkeit entsprang insonderheit verfeinertes Gefühl, durch dies verfeinerte Gefühl, klare Begriffe, – und so wurden stufenweise aus Affen, – Menschen.»

Dies ist nicht das einzige Anzeichen dafür, daß der ‹Freimüthige› bei der Entstehung unseres Buches eine gewisse Rolle spielte. Hinzu kommt eine andere naturhistorische Hypothese, die der Verfasser ebenfalls hier fand, und zwar ebenfalls in dem Bericht über E. Darwins Lehrgedicht, nämlich die sonderbare Ansicht, *daß die ersten Insekten nur Staubfäden an Pflanzen waren, die sich durch ein Ohngefähr von ihnen trennten*[37],

---

[35] Eine deutsche Übersetzung erschien erst 1808.

[36] Die Zwischenfrage ist typisch für den bissigen, spöttischen Ton, der den ganzen Artikel beherrscht und der überhaupt der in der Berichterstattung des ‹Freimüthigen› vorherrschende war.

[37] So die betreffende Fußnote in den ‹Nachtwachen› (9. Nw.; S. 81; einleitend heißt es dazu: *Irgend ein Naturforscher stellt die Hypothese auf, daß [...]*); und der Bericht im ‹Freimüthigen›: «Ein gewisser Naturforscher, welcher sich beson-

und vor allem: hier fand er die Nachricht von der Erfindung des Samuel Day: die Nachricht von den «watchman's noctuaries». Damit man vergleichen kann mit dem eingangs zitierten ‹Nachtwachen›-Text (und um die Fußnoten nicht allzu sehr anschwellen zu lassen), sei auch sie – oder wenigstens ihre wichtigsten Passagen – hierhergesetzt:

«Der Engländer Samuel Day Esqu. hat im vorigen Jahre von der Engl. Regierung ein Patent über gewisse Uhren erhalten, die er watchman's noctuaries oder labourer's regulators nennt. (...) Er ging von der Idee aus, daß die jährlichen Nachtdiebstäle in London mehr als zwei Millionen Pfund Sterling betrügen (...) Erstlich verrathen sich diese Aufseher der nächtlichen Sicherheit durch ihren Ausruf der Stunden (...) zweitens giebt ja niemand auf dieses Schreien genau Acht (...) Zu diesem Zweck erfand er vorerwähnte Uhren, um eine Controlle für die Nachtwächter abzugeben. Das Zifferblatt derselben liegt horizontal und ist versteckt, und nur durch ein kleines Loch an der Thür (...) sieht die jedesmalige Stundenzahl heraus. Unter der Ziffer sind noch 4 kleine Löcher in dem Zifferrad, für die vier Viertelstunden der Stunde. In diese Löcher wird nun von dem Nachtwärter, so oft er an der Uhr ankommt, ein Zeichen eingesteckt (...). An den beiden Enden der Runde eines Nachtwächters werden nun zwei solche Uhren aufgestellt (...) So muß er die Nacht über immer herumgehen, indem ihm am Morgen vom Polizeiofficier alle Zeichen nachgezählt werden, und sein Rufen unterbleibt ohne Nachtheil für die Schlafenden. Die Uhr selbst innen aufschließen kann er nicht, denn dazu führt allein der Polizeiofficier den Schlüssel.»[38]

Aus diesen Befunden ergeben sich zunächst einige Anhaltspunkte für die Entstehungsgeschichte unseres Buches: zumindest für Teile der sechsten, achten und neunten *Nachtwache* kann gesagt werden, daß sie jeden-

---

ders auf diesen Gegenstand geleget, findet es gar nicht unmöglich, daß die ersten Insekten, Staubfäden und Staubnarben waren, welche, wer weiß wodurch von ihrer Mutterpflanze getrennt wurden (...)». (Die von Michel in diesem Zusammenhang herangezogene Stelle aus Henrik Steffens' ‹Beyträgen zur innern Naturgeschichte der Erde› (siehe Michel, a. a. O., S. 157), steht demgegenüber so fern, daß sie als Vorlage – angesichts der eben vorgeführten Parallele – nicht mehr in Betracht kommt.)

[38] Literarischer und artistischer Anzeiger. Als Beilage zum Freymüthigen oder Scherz und Ernst 1804. No. X. (Erschienen ebenfalls um Anfang März, wie u. a. daraus hervorgeht, daß in derselben Nummer eine Einsendung vom 26. 2. 1804 steht und in der folgenden eine Notiz über die feierliche Beerdigung Immanuel Kants in Königsberg, die am 28. 2. 1804 stattfand.) – Die von Michel (S. XVI) nachgewiesene Beschreibung derselben Erfindung im ‹Magazin aller neuen Erfindungen, Entdeckungen und Verbesserungen›, hrsg. v. Seebaß und Baumgärtner, Leipzig [1804], ist zweifellos – ihrer ganzen Formulierung nach – nicht die Quelle des ‹Nachtwachen›-Verfassers gewesen, wird übrigens auch von Michel nicht dafür gehalten.

falls nach Anfang März 1804 entstanden sind. Das fügt sich zu einer Beobachtung, die man unmittelbar am Text selbst machen kann: in der sechsten *Nachtwache*, innerhalb der Gerichtstagsrede, ist vom *seeligen Kant* die Rede; Kant war am 12. 2. 1804 gestorben, die Totenfeier für ihn (28. 2. 1804) ein in den Zeitungen um Anfang März vielbesprochenes Ereignis. Andererseits ist, wie früher bemerkt, bereits am 21. 7. 1804 der Vorabdruck in der ‹Eleganten Welt› erschienen, zugleich mit der Ankündigung, daß das ganze Buch zur Michaelismesse herauskommen werde. All das deutet auf die Zeit von Frühjahr bis Sommer 1804 als den Zeitraum, in dem jedenfalls Teile des Buches – darunter so wichtige wie der *Prolog des Hanswurstes zu der Tragödie: der Mensch* – entstanden und das ganze Werk vollendet wurde.

Weiter aber ergeben sich von hier aus neue Argumente für den Beweisgang dieser Untersuchung. Der Verfasser der ‹Nachtwachen› hat sich als jemand erwiesen, der einerseits keineswegs zu den Anhängern der Kotzebue-Partei gehörte, vielmehr zu ihren Verächtern, andererseits aber keine Bedenken hatte, ihr Hauptorgan, den ‹Freimüthigen› – wie oft, muß natürlich offen bleiben – in die Hand zu nehmen und darin zu lesen. Beides zugleich wird man nicht von allzu vielen unter den überhaupt in Frage kommenden Autoren der Zeit annehmen können, wohl aber von Klingemann, dem alten Gegner Kotzebues und vor allem Garlieb Merkels, des Mannes, der seit dem Herbst 1803 die Redaktionsgeschäfte der Zeitung führte. Klingemann hatte gerade damals sogar besonderen Anlaß, sich mit dem ‹Freimüthigen› zu beschäftigen: gerade eben war eine kleine, anonyme, außerordentlich scharfe Spottschrift gegen Kotzebue und Merkel erschienen, deren Resonanz im ‹Freimüthigen› ihn interessieren mußte, denn sie stammte von ihm selbst. Die Schrift – die den Gegenstand des nächsten Abschnitts bilden wird – ist denn auch im ‹Freimüthigen› besprochen worden; die Rezension, von Merkel selbst herrührend, kurz und giftig, erschien in der Nummer vom 23. Februar 1804, genau acht Tage vor dem Artikel über Erasmus Darwin's ‹Temple of Nature›.

3. ‹Freimüthigkeiten›

Der volle Titel der Schrift, um die es sich handelt, lautet, ebenso lang wie beziehungsvoll: «Freimüthigkeiten. Ein Seitenstück zu den Expektorazionen und zugleich ein blöder Mitbewerber um den vom Herrn v. Kotzebue ausgesetzten Preis für das beste Lustspiel». Als Erscheinungsort ist «Abdera» angegeben, was nach Merkels Rezension bereits für «die alberne Schiefheit des Ganzen» zeugt, denn: der angebliche Druckort «sollte ohne Zweifel ein witziger Scherz seyn, aber kann man einem Buche etwas Schlimmeres nachsagen, als daß es ein ‹Abderitisches› Produkt ist?»[39] Was den Titel betrifft, so enthält er insgesamt drei Anspielungen, die alle in dieselbe Richtung zielen: eine auf die Zeitung, die Kotzebue begründet hatte und für die er immer noch als Mitherausgeber, neben Merkel, und als Beiträger eifrig tätig war, als diese Satire erschien; eine auf ein anonym erschienenes, antiromantisches und antigoethisches Pamphlet mit dem Titel ‹Expektorazionen›, als dessen Verfasser man mit großer Wahrscheinlichkeit Kotzebue vermuten konnte und auch sehr früh schon vermutet hat; und schließlich eine Anspielung auf den Preis, der von Kotzebue wirklich ausgeschrieben worden war, nämlich in der ersten Nummer des ‹Freimüthigen›.[40]

Die Frage der Verfasserschaft läßt sich in diesem Falle ohne umständliche Prozeduren, sozusagen mit einem Streich, lösen: am 14. April 1803 ist ein Vorabdruck aus dem Stück mit dem Namen des Verfassers – dem Namen August Klingemann – in der ‹Zeitung für die elegante Welt› erschienen: ein Ausschnitt aus der Mitte des Stücks, ungefähr sechs Seiten der späteren Buchausgabe umfassend[41]. Der Text dieses satirischen Lustspiels, dieser «musikalischen Travestie», wie es im Vorabdruck genannt wird, bietet so viele und vielfältige Beziehungen zu den ‹Nachtwachen›, daß ihre Darstellung als solche bereits Probleme neuer und eigener Art

[39] (Wirklicher) Erscheinungsort und Erscheinungsjahr (laut Kaysers Bücherlexikon): Lüneburg 1804.

[40] Erschienen am 3. 1. 1803. Zu Anfang des Ausschreibungstextes Variation und Zitation des Friedrich Schlegelschen Satzes «Der Mensch ist von Natur eine ernsthafte Bestie» (aus der ‹Lucinde›; von Kotzebue auf die Deutschen der letzten Jahre bezogen). Auf denselben Satz wird auch in den ‹Nw.› angespielt: *Was soll es auch überhaupt mit dem Ernste, der Mensch ist eine spashafte Bestie von Haus aus (...)* (8. Nw.; S. 74). – Der Preis blieb unvergeben; eine Beurteilung der (14) eingesandten Stücke, zweifellos ebenfalls von Klingemann mit Interesse gelesen, erschien im Februar 1804 in No. VI des ‹Anzeigers› zum ‹Freimüthigen›.

[41] Abgedruckt im Anhang der vorliegenden Monographie (S. 122 ff.); dort auch eine Zusammenstellung der geringfügigen Varianten der Buchausgabe gegenüber dem Vorabdruck. Zu ihnen gehört die Änderung der Szenennummer: statt «Fünfte Szene» heißt es in der Buchausgabe: «Dritte Handlung. (Auf der Bühne.) Erste Szene.» (Abgesehen von einer stummen Szene – dem Durchzug der Kinder aus den ‹Hussiten vor Naumburg› von Kotzebue, mit dem die «zweite Handlung» schließt – ist die Szene auch im Buchtext die fünfte «auf der Bühne» stattfindende geblieben; eingeschaltet ist nach jeder «Handlung» ein «Zwischenspiel» im «Parterre».) Geändert hat sich während der Zeit zwischen Vorabdruck und Buchedition auch der Titel des Ganzen: als solcher erscheint im Vorabdruck: «Der Dichter»; ebenso in einem erhaltenen Brief Klingemanns vom 26. 4. 1803, in dem er das Stück unter Hinweis auf die Probe in der ‹El. Welt› zum Verlag anbietet (Stadtarchiv Braunschweig; abgedr. in: Braunschweiger Magazin, Jg. 1923, Sp. 21).

aufwirft. Ich versuche sie zu lösen, indem ich von einer Charakteristik
des Lustspiels ausgehe, überhaupt der Darstellung dieses kaum bekannten und schwer zugänglichen Werkchens den Vorrang gebe und die not-
wendigen Bezugnahmen auf die ‹Nachtwachen› stärker als bisher in den
Hintergrund und in den Fußnotenapparat verweise.

«Wenn Sie Lust haben das Stück zu verlegen», schreibt Klingemann in
dem Brief, der sich hierzu erhalten hat, «so steht es zu Ihren Diensten;
es ist durchaus satirisch und besonders gegen die Herren Merkel u.
Kotzebue gerichtet (...)». Beide Herren kommen selbst innerhalb des
Stückes vor, jener unter dem Namen Theobald, dieser dagegen als Hilarius[42]. Die Identität Theobalds wird u. a. durch ein kalauerndes Wortspiel
in der Szene, die auch in der ‹Eleganten Welt› erschien, enthüllt: «Ach
ich habe die Prosa g a r l i e b, m e r k e auch, daß ich ganz für sie geschaffen bin!»[43] und diejenige des Hilarius durch zahlreiche Nennungen Kotzebuescher Stücke, durch Hinweise auf das oben erwähnte
Preisausschreiben – «Eben dieser», sagt Theobald einmal über Hilarius,
«zur Zeit unser berühmtester Dichter, hat einen Preis von 100 Friedrichs-
d'oren auf das beste Lustspiel gesetzt»[44] – aber auch durch Epitheta wie
das soeben zitierte, das auch im Personenverzeichnis bereits auftaucht:
das des «berühmtesten Dichters» oder auch des «beliebtesten Dichters»[45].

---

[42] Die Namengebung dürfte zurückgehen auf eine «Justus Hilarius» unter-
zeichnete satirische «Bittschrift» im ‹Freimüthigen› vom 4. 2. 1803, in der eine
«christliche Fürbitte» für «hülfsbedürftige Jünger des Apollo – das heißt: für in-
solvente Studenten, welche sich der Selbstanschauung, oder der rein poetischen
Poesie widmen», an die Buchhändler gerichtet wird. Als «rühmliches Beispiel»
wird dabei der Buchhändler Dienemann in Penig genannt, der im Verlauf von
wenigen Monaten einen Roman, ein musikalisches Taschenbuch und «den Anfang einer kritischen und poetischen Zeitschrift, A p o l l o n genannt, (bekla-
genswerther Gott!) sauber gedruckt geliefert» habe, ohne sich durch den «tra-
gikomischen» Inhalt dieser Produkte «in seinem edlen Eifer, das akademische
Elend auf seine und der Lesewelt Kosten zu mindern, stören zu lassen»; der
junge Mann, der sich «auf den Titelblättern der eben genannten drei Werke hinter dem Nahmen Julius Werden [Pseudonym für F. Th. Mann; J. S.] verstecken
zu wollen affektirt», sei «nehmlich ein Student, welcher...» (es folgen einige
stereotype Verbalinjurien). Polemik gegen den Verlag Dienemann ist übrigens
auch sonst im ‹Freimüthigen›, ebenso wie in Merkels Frauenzimmer-Briefen,
nicht selten, auch nicht verwunderlich, bei der pro-romantischen Ausrichtung,
die der Verlag namentlich durch die Mitarbeit der beiden «Brüder» Werden
(F. Th. Mann und F. G. Winzer), zweier wahrer Schlegel-Anbeter, erhielt.

[43] Siehe Anhang, S. 123. (Die Sperrungen bereits im Original, im Vorabdruck ebenso wie in der Buchausgabe.)

[44] S. 74.

[45] So S. 17 f., mit Bezug auf einen angeblichen «Hyperboreer»: «Einer von
denen, für die unser beliebtester Dichter dasjenige opferte, was ihm am liebsten

Diesem Paar gegenübergestellt sind Apollo und Amor, die fremd und verstört durch die prosaische Zeit, das «aufgeklärte Zeitalter», das Zeitalter, in dem die «Humanität» als «schöne Tugend»[46] gilt, irren. Apollo, von Theobald eingefangen und in moderne Kleidung gesteckt, ebenso wie Amor, muß lernen, in Prosa zu sprechen, was im Dialog des Stückes so realisiert wird, daß er erst in jambischen Trimetern, dann in fünffüßigen, dann in vierfüßigen Jamben spricht und zuletzt den Sprung auf die «flache Erde» der Prosa tut: «Nun, ist es Dir so recht?»[47] Zwischen diesen beiden Paaren stehen Max, Theobalds Famulus und Repräsentant der gesunden Mitte und menschlichen Normalität, sowie das «natürliche Clärchen», die Verkörperung des Kotzebueschen Mädchenideals, die auch durch Apollos wieder in Trimetern gesprochene Paränese nicht dazu zu bewegen ist, aus ihrer sträflichen Verirrung zurückzukehren zur Natur, auch von ihrer Liebe zu Hilarius nicht lassen will und dafür von Apollo in einen Lorbeerbaum verwandelt wird.

Hinzu aber kommt nun, ganz in der Art des Tieckschen ‹Gestiefelten Katers›, das Publikum im Parterre, das in den Zwischenspielen über die Bühnenvorgänge räsonniert, übrigens auch über das eigene Mitspielen in diesem Lustspiel reflektiert, ebenfalls ganz wie in Tiecks ‹Gestiefeltem Kater› – wobei auch dieser Bezug zum Gegenstand der Reflexion wird: «Selbst daß wir hier miteinander reden, ist schon im gestiefelten Kater vorgekommen» bemerkt einer der Bürger im «dritten Zwischenspiel». Unterstützt, beraten und mehr noch: in Ratlosigkeit versetzt wird das Publikum bei seinen kritischen Erörterungen durch Arlequin oder (wie er von den bürgerlichen Dialogpartnern selbst genannt wird) Hanswurst[48], der sich unter das Publikum gemischt hat, um Rache zu nehmen

---

war – den Beniamin seiner Laune, seinen Esel!» (Anspielung auf Kotzebues ‹Hyperboräischen Esel›) – oder S. 95 f.: «(...) und ich finde es überhaupt unverantwortlich, daß ein allgemein beliebter Schriftsteller so unanständig vor dem Publikum behandelt wird». Vgl. dazu 4. Nw.; S. 31 f.: «*O besäßen doch dieses dein Talent manche von unsern beliebten Schriftstellern!*» rief ich aus, «*Ihre Werke könnten dann immerhin Ephemeren bleiben, wären sie selbst doch unsterblich, und könnten ihre ephemerische Schriftstellerei ewig fortsetzen, und bis zum jüngsten Tage beliebt bleiben.*» (Siehe auch oben S. 46).

[46] S. 31, S. 92 und ähnlich öfter. Vgl. 13. Nw.; S. 110: *unser aufgeklärtes Jahrhundert,* 9. Nw.; S. 79: *Hier No. 1 ist ein Beleg zur Humanität, der mehr als alle Schriften darüber gilt (...),* 1. Nw.; S. 6: (...) *in dieser kalt prosaischen Zeit* (...) und ähnliche Stellen.

[47] S. 67 (ebenfalls in der im Vorabdruck erschienenen Szene enthalten; siehe Anhang, S. 124).

[48] Auch in den ‹Nw.› kommen beide Benennungen vor: die deutsche und die der commedia dell'arte, auch die letztere übrigens in derselben Form (die ja nur eine von sehr vielen möglichen ist): *Arlequin* (4. Nw.; S. 36).

dafür, daß dieses Publikum für seinen «derben Spaß und Scherz» ein «zu ästhetisch Herz» hat, wie er im «Prolog» erklärt. Drum sei er – heißt es in diesem Knittelvers-Prolog –

> «auch von hier vertrieben,
> Und es ist nichts als die Wehmuth geblieben.
> Aus Rache will ich nun aber keine Ordnung ehren,
> Und hier das Oberste zu unterst kehren!»[49]

Im noch leeren Theater umherleuchtend, stellt er dann die Folgen der letztvergangenen Theateraufführung fest, einer Aufführung von Kotzebues bekanntem Stück ‹Menschenhaß und Reue›:

> «Auch scheine ich bis an die Knie im Wasser zu stehn;
> Alles ist wie in ein Meer versunken
> Und dort liegt gar der Soufleur ertrunken!
> Zur Grabschrift ruht auf dem Kasten, bei meiner Treue,
> Der Anschlagezettel von Menschenhaß und Reue!
>
> So hat Dich, Du unschuldig Blut,
> Auch hingerafft die Thränenfluth!»[50]

Damit ist das Thema eingeführt, das im Folgenden dann auf vielen Ebenen variiert wird, namentlich auch auf der physiologischen: «Ich gebrauche diese Kotzebueschen Stücke», sagt einer der Zuschauer (S. 16), «ordentlicherweise als eine Brunnenkur, bei katharralischen und moralischen Verstopfungen, und habe sie in beiden Fällen probat gefunden», und ein anderer, in einer späteren Situation (S. 100), als Arlequin das Weinen lernen soll und erklärt, in seinem Leben nichts anderes gelernt zu haben als lachen: «O dafür haben wir Zugmittel! Leset ihm eine Szene aus einem Kotzebueschen Stücke vor; die muß Wirkung thun.»[51] Es ist dies ein Höhepunkt innerhalb der Handlung der «Zwischenspiele»: Arlequin soll hinausgeworfen werden, weil er «kein Mensch» sei und «noch nicht eine einzige Thräne vergossen» habe. Bedingungen werden gestellt, unter denen er bleiben möge: «So zwingt ihn zu weinen; und dann mag er seinen Platz behalten», schlägt Lukas vor, und Johannes

---

49 Vgl. im *Prolog des Hanswurstes zu der Tragödie: der Mensch: Ich hoffe indeß das alte Schicksal, unter dem bei den Griechen selbst die Götter standen, darin abzugeben, und die handelnden Personen recht toll in einander zu verwirren (...)* (8. Nw.; S. 75 f.).

50 Vgl. 9. Nw.; S. 80: *No. 8 unter den Wahnsinnigen habe dadurch, daß er bei vernünftigen Tagen es mit der Rührung in seinen Komödien so übermäßig betrieb, seine Vernunft gänzlich weggeschwemmt.*

51 Vgl. 15. Nw.; S. 126: *(...) obgleich sich eine Thräne leicht zu Tage fördern läßt, blos durch starkes Hinschauen auf einen Fleck, oder durch mechanisches Lesen Kotzebuescher Dramen (...)*

antwortet: «Ja, vor unseren Augen soll er weinen, das gehe ich ein; und einen gerührten Hanswurst[52] will ich allenfalls dulden.» Dann wird er dazu verurteilt, eine «Apologie der Thränen» zu halten, worauf er erwidert: «O wozu zwingt Ihr mich! Ein Hanswurst in Trauerkleidern[52] ist ein betrübter Anblick», um schließlich doch die von ihm verlangte Apologie zu halten, wobei Johannes zu Demonstrationszwecken, auf Bitten Arlequins, die «Stellung des Laokoon» einnimmt (S. 100 ff.). Aber schon im ersten Zwischenspiel hatte es einen Aufruhr gegeben, als Arlequin entdeckt wurde (S. 23):

«**Alle.**
Hinaus mit dem Hanswurst! Wir wollen nicht lachen, wir wollen weinen!

Markus.
Corrigere mores! Sittenverbesserung, Sittenverbesserung wollen wir; moralische Streiche und Stöße – keine Narrenpossen!

Tobias.
Wir wollen nicht über uns lachen, wir wollen über uns weinen, und über die Kotzebueschen Stücke! – Comedia quasi vitae imago! Wir sind rührende Gegenstände und keine lächerliche.»[52]

Arlequins Gegenmittel ist Nieswurz, die er schon vor Beginn des Stückes auf dem Theater ausstreut und während der Unterhaltung immer wieder aus seiner Schnupftabaksdose anbietet, gelegentlich auch mit Erfolg: einem der Zuschauer kommen «die gescheitesten Dinge» nach wiederholtem Niesen «auf einmal sehr albern und abgeschmackt» vor, ein anderer fühlt sich so «erstaunlich von Sinnen gekommen», daß er «Lust hätte, ein Kotzebuesches Stück auszupfeifen» (S. 22). Johannes dagegen, dem das Weinen «ganz zur anderen Natur geworden» ist, vermag seinen Widerstand auch gegen eine gewaltsam eingezwungene «Prise aus Arlequins Dose» aufrechtzuerhalten: «Er nieset nicht! Laßt ihn, der alte Verstand hat zu tiefe Wurzeln bei ihm geschlagen und läßt

---

[52] Vgl. zu allen diesen Stellen den Hanswurst im *Marionettenspiel* der 4. Nw.: *Ueber das Leben und den Zeitkarakter macht er die höchst albernen Bemerkungen, daß beide jezt mehr rührend als komisch seyen, und daß man jezt weniger über die Menschen lachen als weinen könne, weshalb er denn auch selbst ein moralischer und ernsthafter Narr geworden, und immer nur im edlen Genre sich zeige, wo er vielen Applaus bekäme.* (4. Nw.; S. 33 f.). (Zur Erklärung und – falls nötig – Entschuldigung aller dieser Selbstwiederholungen sei auf den kurzen Zeitabstand zwischen beiden Werken hingewiesen sowie auf die doppelte Anonymität, in deren Schutz der Autor sich der Sorge, um jeden Preis und an jeder Stelle ‹neu› zu erscheinen, enthoben fühlen konnte. Überdies treten die Repititionen natürlich in ihren originalen Kontexten bei weitem nicht so konzentriert auf wie in diesem Referat.)

sich nicht ausrotten.»[53] (S. 54) Auf etwas höherer Ebene wird dieselbe
Diskussion um Ernst und Scherz, Lachen und Weinen auf der Bühne
geführt, etwa zwischen Theobald und Apollo (S. 71 ff.): Theobald
wünscht von Apollo «begeistert» zu werden, aber «lieber ins Kleine», wie
er ihm erklärt, nach dem Scheitern eines ersten Versuchs, der ihm sein Ge-
hirn «zu enge» und die Kunst wie einen «Riesen» erscheinen ließ:

«Theobald.
(...) um die Sache ins Große zu treiben, scheint ein gigantischer Körperbau
nöthig zu seyn, – und ich bin von Natur klein[54], wie Ihr seht!

Apollo.
So erklärt Euch zuvor näher über die Gattung, die ihr erwählt habt!

Theobald.
O die Gattung ist ganz gutmüthig[54], und ich meine ein Ding, das halb lustig,
halb rührend ist, wodurch man weder zu heftig erschüttert, noch zu sehr auf-
geweckt wird, und sich dabei besinnen muß, ob man lieber lachen oder weinen
möchte; kurz, wobei man beständig auf einer glücklichen Mittelstraße bleibt.
Ihr habt mich begriffen, nicht wahr?

Apollo.
Eure Theorie ist wirklich etwas verwirrt, und ich weiß noch nicht was ihr wollt!

Theobald.
Nun denn, mit klaren Worten; ich meine ein solches Ding, das man bei uns
gewöhnlich ein Lustspiel zu nennen pflegt.

Apollo.
Jetzt komme ich Euch auf die Spur! – Eine Komödie also. – Etwa im Geiste des
Aristophanes?[54]

Theobald.
Der Himmel behüte uns vor dem Aristophanes[54], der ist noch unsittlicher, wie
Friedrich Schlegel! Auch hat man jetzt die Injurienklage[55] gegen solche Dichter,
die die Leute persönlich auf das Theater zu bringen wagen! (...)»

Dies etwa ist es, was man über das «Lustspiel» im Sinne der Merkel-
Kotzebueschen Ästhetik erfährt. Was Begriff und Funktion der «Rührung» nach den Ansichten dieser Ästhetik betrifft, so erhält man dazu
eine genauere Aufklärung im nächstfolgenden «Zwischenspiel» (S.100ff.):

---

[53] Vgl. dazu in den ‹Nw.› die schon früher berührte Gegenüberstellung: *wei-*
nen wie Kotzebue und niesen wie Tiek (12. Nw.; S. 100).

[54] Vgl. 4. Nw.; S. 29: *Die kleinen Wizbolde und gutmüthigen Komödien-*
verfasser dagegen, die sich nur blos in den Familien umhertreiben, und nicht,
wie Aristophanes, selbst über die Götter sich lustig zu machen wagen, sind
mir herzlich zuwider (...).

[55] Das Motiv der «Injurienklage» wird wenig später, im dritten «Zwischenspiel» (S. 92), noch einmal ausgespielt, mit Bezug auf das vorliegende Stück

sage nicht Kotzebue selbst, daß er «sehr wohl wisse, daß die Rührung nicht der Zweck der Kunst sei!» Arlequin ist es, der daran erinnert, und Johannes, der treuste Kotzebue-Anhänger unter den Zuschauern, fügt ergänzend hinzu: «Seine Stücke haben die Rührung n e b e n h e r , wie der Laokoon und die Niobe; das kann selbst kein Schlegelianer widerlegen: die Rührung n e b e n h e r schadet keinem Kunstwerke.» Die nähere Ausführung dieser Theorie der Rührung gibt dann wieder – ironischerweise – Arlequin, in seiner «Apologie der Thränen» und mit Hinweisen auf den als Laokoon posierenden Johannes:

> «Ein Kunstwerk in der Harmonie
> Spricht zu dem einzelnen Sinne nie;
> Doch hören wir auf uns ästhetisch zu freun,
> So treten sogleich die Thränen ein,
> Und dieses ist, mit Eurer Gunst,
> Die edle Humanität in der Kunst;
> Dem Kunstwerk schadet sie nicht mehr,
> Dieweil sie kommt nur nebenher!
> Dergleichen sieht selbst Schlegel ein,
> Er müßte sonst von Sinnen seyn.
> Schaut nur den Herrn Johannes an,
> Er leidet sehr, der arme Mann;
> Hier sind der thierischen Natur
> Wir nun ganz nahe auf der Spur,
> Die Freiheit ließen wir in der Kunst zurück,
> Bei der Rührung entflieht sie im Augenblick;
> Der Mensch ist ja nicht frei allein,
> Er will zu Zeiten auch gepeinigt seyn!
> Seht nur, wie Herr Johann sich quält,
> Es scheint daß ihm der Athem fehlt (. . .)»[56]

selbst («Etwas sehr boshaft bleibt indeß das Ganze immer. Sollte man den Verfasser nicht injuriarum belangen können?» Worauf ein anderer Zuschauer meint, «aus Schonung für seine Familie» könne man «schon etwas durch die Finger sehen; – er soll Familie haben!») – aber auch in den ‹Nw.›, dort mit noch größerer Ausführlichkeit: im Schlußteil der 7. Nw., der im Inhaltsverzeichnis den Untertitel *Injurienklage* erhält und in dem erzählt wird, wie die schriftstellerischen Versuche des Nachtwächters ihm *in kurzem mehr denn fünfzig Injurienprozesse* (7. Nw.; S. 62) eingebracht haben.

[56] Zu vergleichen ist hier die unmittelbare Fortsetzung des Gedankens über die *gutmüthigen Komödienverfasser* in den ‹Nw.› (siehe Anm. 54): *eben so wie jene schwachen gerührten Seelen, die statt ein ganzes Menschenleben zu zertrümmern, um den Menschen selbst darüber zu erheben, sich nur mit der kleinen Quälerei beschäftigen, und neben ihren Gefolterten den Arzt stehen haben, der ihnen genau die Grade der Tortur bestimmt, damit der arme Schelm, obgleich geradebrecht, doch mit dem Leben zuletzt noch davon gehen kann* (4. Nw.; S. 29).

Als Arlequin schließlich, mit einer Anspielung auf den Laokoon-Aufsatz von Alois Hirt, behauptet, er merke gerade, daß den Laokoon-Johannes «der Schlag gleich rühren wird», bricht das ganze Parterre in Tränen aus, und es «entsteht eine Pause», während welcher Johannes «seine natürliche Stellung» wieder einnimmt. Nach einigen kunstkritischen Zwischenbemerkungen der Zuhörer setzt Arlequin seine «Apologie» fort: mit noch stärkerer Ironie, die aber niemand merkt, schildert er, wie wohltätig z. B. nach dem «wilden Wallenstein», dem «Frevler», dem jeglicher «mit Lust» zuschaue, der Kotzebuesche Ritter Bayard wirke: «Im Augenblick weint jedermann; / Und weint man erst, so ist bekannt, / Schont man die Fliege an der Wand!» Am Schluß hat er die Herzen seiner Zuhörer gewonnen:

«Tobias.
Der Hanswurst soll bleiben; er ist ein Mensch, und unser Bruder!

Johannes.
Wir lassen ihn nicht! Er ist gerührt, und die Wehmuth erstickte zuletzt seine Stimme.

Arlequin.
(lacht boshaft ins Fäustchen[57].)

Alle.
Er weint heftig. Bravo Hanswurst!
(Ende des dritten Zwischenspiels.)»

Zu diesen Themen – Lustspiel, Rührung, Lachen, Weinen – die der ganzen Anlage des Stückes gemäß die Dominante darstellen, treten einige Seitenthemen, auch sie Stück für Stück zugleich in den ‹Nachtwachen› nachweisbar. So etwa der Kontrast zwischen antiker Kunst und modernem Banausentum, hier, im Lustspiel, wie es nahe liegt, vor allem als szenisches Gegenüber gestaltet: in den Dialogen zwischen Theobald und Apoll, Hilarius und Apoll. Auch von bildender Kunst ist dabei die Rede, auf eine Weise, die sehr an den Besuch im Antikenkabinett in den ‹Nachtwachen› erinnert: man sei «übel umgegangen» mit «Euren Bildsäulen», sagt Hilarius zu Apollo: die «Neueren» hätten «so viel daran geflickt und ausgebessert, daß man oft in Zweifel steht, ob irgend ein Arm oder Bein nicht untergeschoben ist und bloß für ächt ausgegeben wird» (S. 80) – und der Nachtwächter zu dem *kleinen Dilettanten* im Antikensaal: *O Freund, was die Kunstärzte der neuern Periode auch immer heilen und flicken mögen, sie bringen doch die von der tückischen*

---

[57] Vgl. in den ‹Nw.› den Abgang des Hanswursts nach dem dritten Akt des *Marionettenspiels: Nun lacht er in der Stille hämisch ins Fäustchen und geht ab.* (4. Nw.; S. 36, wo statt «lacht» der offensichtliche Druckfehler «lachte»).

*Zeit verstümmelten Götter, wie z. B. diesen daliegenden Torso, nicht
wieder auf die Beine* (13. Nw.; S. 110). Später will Hilarius den Kopf des
Apollo näher untersuchen, muß ihn dabei aber bitten, sich ein wenig
zu bücken, da er «so hoch nicht reichen kann» (S. 85), ähnlich wie der
kleine Dilettant im Antikensaal an einer *medicäischen Venus ohne Arme,
mühsam hinauf*klettert, *um wie es schien, ihr den Hintern, als den bekanntlich gelungensten Kunsttheil dieser Göttin zu küssen* (13. Nw.;
S. 109). Hilarius ist dann von dem Ergebnis seiner Untersuchung wenig
befriedigt, eher irritiert: es gebe «da nichts wie reine Formen», Apollo
sei «ja gar nicht nach den Regeln der Anatomie erschaffen». Er möchte
deshalb den Kopf seinem «Freunde Gall zur Untersuchung übersenden»
– ein Witz, der zwar nicht in der Antikensaal-Episode wiederkehrt, dafür aber in dem Bericht über die Streitigkeiten um das aufgefundene
Teufelshaupt zu Anfang der ‹Nachtwachen›: *In dieser allgemeinen Ver-
wirrung und bei der Ungewißheit, ob man ein ächtes Teufelshaupt vor
sich habe, wurde beschlossen, daß der Kopf dem Doktor Gall in Wien
zugesandt würde, damit er die untrüglichen satanischen Protuberanzen
an ihm aufsuchen möge.* (3. Nw.; S. 17)[58]
Dazu kommt, eng zusammenhängend mit dem eben besprochenen
Themenmaterial, die Klage über die Ungunst der Zeit den Dichtern gegenüber, eine Klage, die ja auch durch die ‹Nachtwachen› hindurchgeht,
angefangen vom ersten Kapitel – wo der Nachtwächter zu dem *ver-
unglückten Poeten* hinaufruft: «‹. . .› *schade nur daß dir deine Nachtwachen in dieser kalt prosaischen Zeit nichts einbringen, indeß die mei-
nigen doch immer ein Uebriges abwerfen. Als ich noch in der Nacht
poesirte*[59], *wie du, mußte ich hungern, wie du, und sang tauben Ohren;
das letzte thue ich zwar noch jetzt, aber man bezahlt mich dafür. O
Freund Poet, wer jezt leben will, der darf nicht dichten!*» (1. Nw.; S. 6) –
bis zum Höhepunkt in der achten *Nachtwache,* in der *Himmelfahrt des
Dichters* und seinem *Absagebrief an das Leben,* von dem der Erzähler

---

[58] Derselbe Witz kommt übrigens in den ‹Freimüthigkeiten› noch einmal
vor: in der 4. Szene des 1. Akts, wo Hilarius dem «natürlichen Clärchen» «in
den Haaren herumwühlt» und auf die Proteste, die sie ihrer Frisur wegen erhebt, antwortet: «Es sind Gallsche Experimente! Ich sammele Erfahrungen für
diesen meinen Freund, und war eben bemüht Euern Naivetätsknoten zu finden.» (S. 43). (Auch hier wird man, angesichts so ungenierter Ausnutzung desselben Einfalls in zwei so dicht aufeinander folgenden Veröffentlichungen, die
besondere Situation des anonym bzw. pseudonym publizierenden Schriftstellers
bedenken müssen.)

[59] Dieselbe ungewöhnliche Wortbildung begegnet auch in den ‹Freimüthigkeiten› (S. 11): «Und es wird überhaupt kinderleicht dadurch – das Poesiren
meine ich!» (sagt einer der Bürger über die rührende Wirkung von Kindern auf
der Bühne).

sagt: *Dies war die lezte zurükgebliebene Asche von einer Flamme, die in sich selbst ersticken mußte.* (8. Nw.; S. 71) In den ‹Freimüthigkeiten› ist es, naheliegenderweise, Apollo, dem diese Klage in den Mund gelegt wird: «Wahrlich, ich war nicht selten im Begriffe, meine Unsterblichkeit[60] für ein Linsengerichte zu verkaufen, wenn die Unsterblichkeit nur überhaupt hier unten im Preise wäre», sagt er zu Amor (S. 87), der erstaunt ist, den Gott der Dichter «in Pension gesetzt» zu sehen, ja sogar im Begriffe, «die Unsterblichkeit aufzugeben». «Die Umstände! – Die Zeit!» erklärt ihm Apollo: «O ich hätte nicht geglaubt, daß die Zeit so unverschämt in die Unsterblichkeit[60] sich mischen würde! – Doch sag mir, was bin ich jetzt? Ein unglückliches Mittelding zwischen Himmel und Erde, schwebe ich bald auf- bald abwärts, und finde nirgends eine Heimath. Wo ich jemals einen Geist mit göttlichem Feuer entzündete, da verzehrte er sich in der eigenen Flamme [!], und seine Mitwelt erkannte die hohe Beglaubigung nicht, die er aussprach: so machte meine Begeisterung nur Unglückliche, und der höchste Flug wurde für sie das tiefste Verderben!» Und auf Amors Ermahnung, er möge zu sich selbst zurückkehren und sich erheben: «Ach hätten die Griechen ihre Götter nicht an Essen und Trinken gewöhnt, so stände es jetzt besser um sie. Aber hungern kann ich nun einmal nicht mehr lernen.» (S. 89 f.)

Hinzu treten schließlich die Gemeinsamkeiten in der Art, wie das Theater selbst, mit allem was dazugehört: Bühne, Schauspieler, Rollen, zum Thema gemacht wird, besonders die Übereinstimmung in der Art, Theater und Realität vergleichsweise aufeinander zu beziehen, die Bühne als Bild des Lebens zu betrachten – «Comedia quasi vitae imago!» hieß es an der schon angeführten Stelle aus dem ersten «Zwischenspiel» – aber auch Leben und Tod als Metaphern für Bühnenvorgänge zu verwenden oder auch: die ganze Weltgeschichte als «Komödie» anzusehen. «Ich glaube es ist gar kein Dichter dabei im Spiele», sagt Tobias, als im dritten «Zwischenspiel» die Frage aufkommt, von wem das Stück wohl sein

---

[60] Abgesehen von den in den Zitaten selbst unmittelbar abzulesenden Korrespondenzen, wäre auch zum Thema «Unsterblichkeit» in beiden Werken vieles zu sagen. Daß es zu den Lieblingsthemen der ‹Nachtwachen› gehört, weiß jeder Leser dieses Buches; für die Berührungen mit dem Lustspieltext nur noch ein Beispiel aus dem Gespräch Apollos mit Hilarius: Hilarius: «Ihr habt doch die Idee mit der Unsterblichkeit aufgegeben?» Apollo: «Wenn ich mich mit Euch verbinden sollte, müßte ich mich wol zuletzt dazu bequemen.» Hilarius: «Ei freilich, schiebt das ja nicht auf, es ist ein entsetzlicher Gedanke um die Unsterblichkeit, an den ich mich gar nicht einmal erinnern darf, ohne ganz betäubt davon zu werden!» (S. 85 f.) (Zu vergleichen mit dem Dialog zwischen dem Nachtwächter und dem Mann, der nicht sterben kann, besonders der schon öfter (zuletzt Anm. 45) berührten Stelle, an der Kotzebue die entgegengesetzte Eigenschaft zugeschrieben wird (4. Nw.; S. 31 f.).)

möge (S. 93), «und es führt sich ganz von selbst auf; ohngefähr wie die Weltgeschichte!» Und in den ‹Nachtwachen› erklärt der Nachtwächter selbst dem Unbekannten, der nicht sterben kann, es sei *doch spaßhaft und der Mühe werth, dieser großen Tragikomödie der Weltgeschichte bis zum lezten Akte als Zuschauer beizuwohnen* (4. Nw.; S. 32), während er in seiner Rede zum Ende des Säkulums die *ganze Weltgeschichte* einen *albernen Roman* nennt, *in dem es einige wenige leidliche Karaktere, und eine Unzahl erbärmlicher giebt,* um dann fortzufahren: *Ach, euer Herr-gott hat es nur in dem einzigen versehen, daß er ihn nicht selbst bearbei-tete, sondern es euch überlies daran zu schreiben* (6. Nw.; S. 53). Im vier-ten Akt des Lustspiels eilt Max, von Amors Pfeil verwundet, mit den Worten herein: «Ich laufe wie verrückt durch das Stück, und bin verlo-ren, wenn ich nicht in Poesie gesetzt werde!» (S. 113)[61], und in der letzten Szene des fünften Akts wird er «immer schwächer», so daß Theobald ihn fragt: «Was Teufel, Ihr werdet doch nicht sterben wollen; wir haben ja ein Lustspiel angekündigt!» Worauf Max antwortet: «Ich kann mir nicht anders helfen, und fühle in der That einen solchen übeln Zustand, daß ich mit guter Manier aus dem Stücke zu kommen suchen muß» (S. 124 f.) – was dann in den ‹Nachtwachen› wieder anklingt in den Worten der todessehnsüchtigen Ophelia: *Gottlob, daß ich aus dem Stücke heraus-komme und meinen angenommenen Namen ablegen kann* (14. Nw.;

---

[61] Auf «Reflexionen» dieser Art hat bereits, mit eben diesem Zitat, W. Pfeif-fer-Belli im ersten, bibliographischen Teil seines Aufsatzes über «Antiroman-tische Streitschriften und Pasquille» (Euph. 26, Jg. 1925, S. 602–630) hingewie-sen, in dem er auch (unter 20 f) das oben besprochene Lustspiel, ohne die Ver-fasserschaft zu erkennen, aufführt und kurz charakterisiert. Bemerkenswerter-weise hat Pfeiffer-Belli auch bereits, wenn auch aus z. T. falschen Erwägungen, an die Möglichkeit einer Identität des Verfassers mit dem Dichter der ‹Nacht-wachen› gedacht, der für ihn – ebenso wie noch im Nachwort zu seiner ‹Nacht-wachen›-Ausgabe von 1947 – F. G. Wetzel hieß. (Falsch ist seine Deutung der Ortsanspielung im Dialog zwischen Hilarius und Apollo (S. 81 f.): das dort genannte, von den Musen bevorzugte «kleine sächsische Städtchen», von dem Hilarius sagt, er habe es «nie recht leiden mögen», ist nicht, wie Pf.-B. voraus-setzt, Penig, sondern Weimar, wie aus der Fortsetzung hervorgeht: «‹Seid ihr wol die Gegend passirt?› Apollo: ‹Ihr waret damals gerade abwesend!› Hi-larius: ‹Thut mir leid; habe viel dadurch verloren! – Jetzt ist mir der Ort ver-haßt, denn es wohnt da ein gewisser – ich habe seit langer Zeit gegen ihn ge-schrieben und geschrien, daß mir die Brust davon heiser geworden ist! Denkt nur, er hat gar nicht darauf geantwortet, und ich befürchte beinahe lächerlich geworden zu seyn!›» – alles eindeutig auf Weimar zielend, wo ja nicht nur «ein gewisser –» wohnte, gegen den Kotzebue sich heiser schrie, ohne je Antwort zu erhalten, sondern auch, zumindest zeitweise, Kotzebue selbst, so daß Apollo Grund hat zu der Feststellung, daß Hilarius «damals gerade abwesend» gewe-sen sei.)

S. 123), aber auch in denen des Unbekannten, der nicht sterben kann:
*O schon seit vielen Menschenaltern habe ich mich bestrebt aus dem
Stücke herauszuspringen, und dem Direktor zu entwischen* (4. Nw.;
S. 38).

Am Ende des letzten Lustspielaktes sinkt Max, der sich immer mehr
als Allegorie des Publikums enthüllt hat, zu Boden und gibt den Geist
auf, während im Parterre «gepocht und gepfiffen» wird, «so daß das
Stück nicht ausgespielt werden kann, und der Vorhang fallen muß». Nach
einer letzten Diskussion im Parterre, in der es darum geht, ob das Stück
noch hätte weitergehen sollen, weitergehen können, und nach dem Weg-
gang der Zuschauer sieht Arlequin sich in der Lage, vor einem im doppelten Sinne fehlenden Publikum[62] seinen «Epilog» zu halten:

> «Geneigtes Publikum, ich spreche zu Dir,
> Obgleich ich Dich nicht mehr finde allhier;
> Denn auf dem Theater bist Du vorhin verblichen,
> Und im Parterre hast Du dich fortgeschlichen;
> Existirst Du nun nicht noch zum drittenmal,
> So ist's mit dem Epiloge ein kritischer Fall!
>
> Allein, da Fichte es bündig darthut,
> Wie die ganze Welt nur im Ich beruht,
> So rede ich mein Ich an, und denke dabei
> daß es allhier das Publikum sei!»

Damit ist das philosophische Zeitphänomen angedeutet, das wie bei
Tieck, wie bei Jean Paul, den Hintergrund aller dieser poetischen Spiele
mit dem Motiv der ad infinitum fortgesetzten Selbstreflexion bildet: die
Philosophie des transzendentalen Idealismus. Auch die ‹Nachtwachen›
sind bekanntlich reich an Reflexen dieser Philosophie; auch hier ist es vor
allem – in einer sehr stark an Jean Pauls ‹Clavis› erinnernden Weise –
das Fichtesche System, auf das, direkt oder indirekt, Bezug genommen
wird: direkt an einer Stelle des Besuchs im Tollhaus, wo es von dem sich
für den *Weltschöpfer* haltenden Wahnsinnigen heißt, er habe *eben so gut
sein konsequentes System wie Fichte, und nimmt es im Grunde mit dem
Menschen noch geringer als dieser, der ihn nur von Himmel und Hölle ab-
trennt, dafür aber alles Klassische rings umher in das kleine Ich, das jeder*

---

[62] Vgl. dazu in den Hamlet-Variationen der 14. Nw. den Ausruf: *... laß
uns lieben und fortpflanzen und alle die Possen mittreiben – blos aus Rache,
damit nach uns noch Rollen auftreten müssen, die alle diese Langweiligkeiten
von neuem ausweiten, bis auf einen lezten Schauspieler, der grimmig das Pa-
pier zerreißt und aus der Rolle fällt, um nicht mehr vor einem unsichtbar dasizenden Parterre spielen zu müssen.* (14. Nw.; S. 121).

*winzige Knabe ausrufen kann, wie in ein Taschenformat zusammen-
gedrängt. Jeder vermag jezt aus der unbedeutenden Hülse, wie es ihm
beliebt, ganze Kosmogonien, Theosophien, Weltgeschichten und dergleichen samt den dazu gehörigen Bilderchen herauszuziehen.* (9. Nw.;
S. 83). Sogar das Wortspiel, das hier kurz vorher über den Idealisten und
den Realisten gemacht wird – jener laboriere *an einer gläsernen Brust,
und dieser an einem gläsernen Gesäße, weshalb er sein Ich niemals setzt,
was jenem eine Kleinigkeit ist* (9. Nw.; S. 79) – findet sich im Lustspiel,
im Epilog des Hanswurstes, vorgebildet, in erheblich breiterer Ausführung, von der wenigstens ein Stück hier wiedergegeben sei, als letzte
Probe aus diesem satirischen Possenspiel:

> «Zuerst, wie es aus der Wissenschaftslehre erhellt,
> **Setzt sich das Ich; darauf setzt es die Welt.**
> In der Poesie muß es umgekehrt seyn,
> Und das Ich geht hinter dem Publikum drein;
> Denn wo das Publikum nicht existirt,
> Ist die poetische Person übel angeführt.
> Aus diesem Grunde ersuche ich Dich inständig drum:
> Setze dich geneigtes Publikum!»

4. ‹Der Schweitzerbund›

Die letzten Indizien, die hier mitzuteilen sind, und wohl auch die über-
raschendsten, finden sich an einer Stelle, an der man zunächst wenig zu
finden erwartet (die denn auch während der Entstehung dieser Arbeit die
längste Zeit ununtersucht geblieben ist): in dem mißglückten und von
vornherein glücklosen Versuch einer eigenen dramatischen Bearbeitung
des Wilhelm Tell-Stoffes, den Klingemann unter dem Titel ‹Der Schweitzerbund› veröffentlichte, und zwar noch gegen Ende des Jahres 1804,
etwa um dieselbe Zeit, zu der auch Schillers ‹Wilhelm Tell› im Druck erschien, nachdem er zuvor in Weimar (März 1804), in Mannheim und,
mit ungeheurem Erfolg, in Berlin (Juli 1804) über die Bühne gegangen
war. Außerdem aber war im selben Jahr bereits der ‹Wilhelm Tell› des
Veit Weber erschienen, von Klingemann selbst in einer früher erwähnten
Rezension in der ‹Eleganten Welt› (7. 6. 1804) besprochen. Dies also war
die Situation, in der nun sein eigenes Schweizer-Drama – in einem ob-
skuren Leipziger «litterarischen Magazin» – herauskam. «Ein literarischer
Bajazzo-Streich», schrieb mit unverkennbarer Schadenfreude der Rezen-
sent des ‹Freimüthigen› in der Nummer vom 22. November 1804: «Nachdem Schillers Pegasus seinen Kunstflug vollendet hat, und Veit Weber
auf seinem bekannten romantisch-historischen Seile hingeschwanket ist,
siehe da kommt – Hr. Klingemann und zeigt, indem er auch die Befrei-

ungs-Geschichte der Schweiz in Dialogen zerarbeitet, daß er – weder fliegen noch tanzen kann.»

Wichtig für uns zunächst: wir geraten mit diesem dramatischen Werk unmittelbar in die Entstehungszeit auch der ‹Nachtwachen›. In der Staats- und Universitätsbibliothek Hamburg wird ein Brief Klingemanns aufbewahrt, in dem er das Drama dem Hamburger Verleger Benjamin Gottlob Hoffmann anbietet. Er bezeichnet es darin als einen «drama- tischen Roman» – offenbar mit Rücksicht auf die lockere, episch aus- ufernde Form des Ganzen – «der die Geschichte des S c h w e i t z e r - b u n d e s in zwei Theilen darstellt, wovon der erste A r n o l d a n d e r H a l d e n und der zweite den S t u r z d e r V ö g t e enthält», und teilt mit, daß er «der Vollendung» dieses Werkes «nahe» sei. Der Brief, auf den Hoffmann negativ geantwortet haben muß, trägt das Datum: 26. 6. 04. Am 21. 7. 1804 erscheint, wie erinnerlich, der Vorabdruck aus den ‹Nachtwachen› in der ‹Zeitung für die elegante Welt›, vorgestellt als «Fragment aus einem noch ungedruckten Roman», der «zur Michaelis- messe herauskommen» werde. Für Teile der sechsten, achten und neun- ten Nachtwache ergab sich uns als Terminus post quem die Zeit um Anfang März 1804 (aufgrund der direkten Benutzung von Informatio- nen, die um eben die Zeit im ‹Freimüthigen› erschienen waren). All das deutet darauf hin, daß beide Werke, der ‹Schweizerbund› und die ‹Nachtwachen›, eine Zeitlang nebeneinanderher gearbeitet wurden. So war es in der Tat, und daß es so war, hat seine Spuren hinterlassen, wie man bei genauerer Betrachtung der beiden Werke bemerkt; Spuren, von denen ich meinen würde, daß sie geeignet sind, die Kette der hier vorge- legten Beweisglieder endgültig zu schließen.

Es handelt sich vor allem um eine Reihe von Stellen, die jeweils am Anfang eines ‹Nachtwachen›-Kapitels stehen. Die Reihe beginnt mit dem Beginn der zehnten Nachtwache, wo man plötzlich, nachdem man sich bisher ausschließlich in einer rein städtischen Umgebung befunden hat, wie sie zum Lebens- und Pflichtenkreis eines, wenn auch sonderbaren Nachtwächters paßt, mit einem Bild winterlicher Natur konfrontiert wird:

Alles ist kalt und starr und rauh, und von dem Naturtorso sind die Glieder abgefallen, und er streckt nur noch seine versteinerten Stümpfe ohne die Kränze von Blüthen und Blättern gegen den Himmel. Die Nacht ist still und fast schrecklich und der kalte Tod steht in ihr, wie ein un- sichtbarer Geist, der das überwundene Leben festhält. (10. Nw.; S. 87). Auch von einem Bettler hört man, der *ohne Dach und Fach* mit dem Schlummer kämpft, der ihn *süß und lockend, in die Arme des Todes legen* will. Im Gegensatz zu den Reichen in ihren *Schlafkammern* ruhe *dieser Vogelfreie*, heißt es dann von demselben Bettler befremdlicher- weise, *der alten Mutter noch unmittelbar an der Brust, die eigensinnig*

und launisch, wie jede Alte, bald ihre Kinder erwärmt und bald sie er-
drückt. Es folgt die Schilderung seines Todes durch Erfrieren – *Da ist
das Gesicht schon starr und kalt, und der Schlaf hat die Bildsäule seinem
Bruder in die Arme gelegt* – und darauf in abrupter Wendung ein *Der
Traum der Liebe* überschriebenes Stück, in dem auf ziemlich chaotische
Weise von einer toten *Geliebten*, von *weißen* und *roten Rosen* und dem
Grabhügel der Geliebten die Rede ist, über dem *ihre Gestalt ewig jugend-
lich und bekränzt* einherschwebt.

Man könnte versuchen. in diesem wie Scherben durcheinanderliegen-
den Haufen von Motiven irgendein eigentümliches Kompositionsgeheim-
nis aufzufinden – und man hat das natürlich auch versucht – aber man
kann sich die Mühe sparen. Denn alle diese Motive sind Stück für Stück
und bis in einzelne Formulierungen hinein aus dem ‹Schweitzerbund›-
Drama übernommen. Hier ist dem wackeren Arnold an der Halden, der
Titelgestalt des ersten Teiles, die düstere Figur des Heinrich von Wolfenschieß gegenübergestellt, der Arnolds Braut liebt, sich ihrer mit Gewalt zu bemächtigen sucht und dadurch an ihrem Tode schuldig wird,
denn sie wird, kaum daß durch sie selbst das Verbrechen des Wolfenschieß bekannt wird, nach nur zu berühmten Mustern von ihrem eigenen
Vater, Walter von Beroldingen, erstochen. Wolfenschieß, der überdies
noch als Verräter an der schweizerischen Sache gezeichnet ist, lebt seither
in wilder Verzweiflung auf seinem Schloß, gepeinigt von Gewissens-
qualen und Ahnungen eines gerechten Gerichts (das ihn auch bald erei-
len wird, in Gestalt Arnolds an der Halden, der am Schluß des ersten
Teils als Rächer seiner Braut auftreten und den Frevler und einstigen
Freund im Zweikampf umbringen wird). In einer der letzten Szenen des
ersten Teils sieht man Wolfenschieß mit seinem Waffenträger Peter, «an
einem Tische mit Pokalen», immer wieder trinkend, schließlich das Fen-
ster aufreißend und in die nächtliche Gebirgslandschaft hinausblickend:

«Da draußen liegt die Welt erstarrt, mit ihren Gräbern und Leichen
im Schooße – die Berge stehn versteinert da im todten Eismeere – wie
rauh alles und wie kalt – eine Schneewolke liegt wie ein Baartuch in dem
Thale ausgebreitet (...) da bauen sich Gräber über Lebenden auf und
drunter heult die sterbende Verzweiflung! – – Was ist das Alles? –
Nichts! – Hier in dem Feuerstrome ersäuf' ich die Verzweiflung, den
Tod, die Ewigkeit und das Gericht!»[63]

Damit beginnt eine Partie von einigen Seiten Länge, in der man alles
wiederfindet, was soeben aus dem Anfang der zehnten *Nachtwache* vorgeführt wurde: die Bilder der *starren*, *kalten* und *rauhen* Natur, die *alte*

---

[63] Der Schweitzerbund. Erster Band. Arnold an der Halden. Leipzig 1804,
S. 182. Ähnliche Naturbilder im 2. Bd., S. 140 ff.: «Versteinert Berg' und Wälder
stehen; (...) Zwar prangt dort kein Frühling mit farbigen Kränzen (...)».

Mutter (in metaphorischem Sinne[64]), die *Rosen*, die tote *Geliebte*, die Vision ihrer vorübergleitenden *Gestalt*, schließlich sogar den *süßen*, aber gefährlichen *Schlummer*, der den in der Winternacht draußen Ausruhenden in die Arme des Todes bettet, nur daß alle diese Dinge hier in völlig vernünftiger Ordnung aufeinander folgen. «Hört auf zu freveln»- mahnt der Waffenträger den weinberauschten Ritter, «und gedenkt der schönen Kinderjahre, als ihr noch schuldlos an der grünen Alpe spieltet, euch unter muntre Heerden mischtet, und zu des Hornes vaterländischen Tönen sangt. – Da war die alte Mutter Euch noch lieb, Ihr küßtet ihre Blumen, die wie Kinder sie umspielten, und sahet der Zukunft hoffnungsvoll entgegen. Kann nichts dies Bild in Eurem Gemüthe wieder anfrischen?» Wolfenschieß darauf: «Es ist verraucht! – Das kehrt mir nimmer wieder. Auch keine Liebe mehr – alles todt! Sieh, da geht die Gestalt vorüber im Leichentuch, in der Brust eine blutende Wunde – sie sieht so ernst – und ist so schön – aber blaß! – (er nimmt den Pokal). Sieh, auch da schwimmt das Bild in dem Golde, mit den Rosen an der Brust; – aber die Rosen sind Blut! –» Es folgt eine Szene zwischen Geßler und Landenberg, dem anderen der beiden Reichsvögte, und darauf eine, in der Arnold an der Halden und der Minnesinger Hadloub zusammen auftreten und Herberge im Stall des Schlosses Wolfenschieß suchen, wobei sich ein Gespräch mit dem Knecht über Erfrorene anspinnt, von denen sie auf ihrem Wege hörten: «Marie Jesus!» sagt der Knecht: «Was mögen jetzt die Pilger leiden, die auf dem St. Gotthardus sich versteigen!» Hadloub: «Das liegt am Tage! – Und so heimlich weiß es einen zu beschleichen; erst naht die Müdigkeit, ein süßer Schlummer – die Augen sinken schon, man kann nicht widerstehen: der Arme setzt sich nieder – o weh, jetzt fesselt ihn der Schlaf, noch hört man Athemzüge, doch der Hauch erfriert vor Nase und Munde – jetzt ist's geschehen, da sitzt die Leiche vor mir, und Arme und Beine erstarret wie zu Eis!»[65]

Der nächste Fall solcher Anleihe bei der gleichzeitig entstehenden dramatischen Arbeit findet sich am Anfang der zwölften *Nachtwache*. (Die zehnte ist inzwischen mit dem Schauerromanmotiv der lebendig begrabenen Nonne schlecht und recht zu Ende gebracht, darauf das extrem kurze, auch sonst völlig aus dem Rahmen fallende elfte Stück eingelegt worden, das die Heilung eines Blindgeborenen schildert, notdürftig verklammert mit dem Vorausgehenden als *Bruchstück aus der Geschichte des Unbekannten im Mantel*, der in der vorigen *Nachtwache* mit einigen wenigen Worten eingeführt wurde: offenbar ein schon bereitliegendes

---

[64] Ein im ‹Schweizerbund› auch sonst mehrfach wiederkehrendes Bild, besonders S. 28 des 1. Teils, wo die Schweizer selbst «der alten Mutter Erde Kinder» genannt werden.
[65] Ebda., S. 189 f.

Stück, vielleicht wirklich, wie öfter vermutet worden ist, von einem anderen Verfasser stammend.[66]) Die zwölfte *Nachtwache* beginnt mit der ausdrücklichen Erklärung, den *Unbekannten im Mantel hier mitten in seiner Erzählung* unterbrechen zu wollen, woran sich eine Reflexion anschließt, deren Anfang wir bereits früher einmal berührt haben[67] und deren Fortsetzung zu den meistumrätselten Anspielungen unseres Textes gehört:

... und es wäre nicht übel zu wünschen daß mancher große Dichter und Schriftsteller sich selbst zur rechten Zeit unterbrechen möchte, so auch der Tod in der rechten Stunde das Leben großer Männer – Beispiele liegen nahe.

Oft erhebt sich der Mensch wie der Adler zur Sonne und scheinet der Erde entrückt, daß Alle dem Verklärten in seinem Glanze nachstaunen; – aber der Egoist kehrt plözlich zurük und statt den Sonnenstrahl wie Prometheus geraubt zu haben und zur Erde herabzuführen, verbindet er den Umstehenden die Augen, weil er glaubt es blende sie die Sonne.

Wer kennt den Sonnenadler nicht, der durch die neuere Geschichte schwebt! –

Über die Identität dieses *Sonnenadlers* sind mancherlei Vermutungen angestellt worden. Franz Schultz etwa dachte an Herder[68]: eine Vermu-

---

[66] Dafür spricht nicht nur der simple Stil, die kurzen Sätze und Absätze, der seraphische Ton, die Anklänge an Klopstock (nicht nur an Jean Paul), an Empfindsamkeit und ihr entsprechende Frömmigkeit (*Ich wagte den Ewigen zu denken!*), sondern auch die nicht gewöhnliche einführende Bemerkung des Erzählers, er *liebe* das Selbst, das jene Geschichte erlebte, darum möge *er selbst reden* (11. Nw.; S. 95). Genaueres zu sagen, scheint mir einstweilen, solange nicht noch weitere Materialien auftauchen, kaum möglich, weshalb ich auch auf Mitteilung eigener Vermutungen zur Verfasserschaft dieser vier Seiten (in Michels Ausgabe) lieber verzichte.

[67] Siehe oben S. 32 f.; inzwischen ist verständlicher geworden, warum gerade Schillers ‹Wilhelm Tell› Klingemann zu so unfreundlichen Worten veranlaßte wie der dort zitierten Erinnerung an Raffael, der nach Vollendung seines Meisterwerks den Pinsel habe ruhen lassen.

[68] Veranlaßt durch einen ähnlichen Gedanken und ein weniger ähnliches Bild in einer anonym erschienenen, Wetzel zugeschriebenen Schrift: Fischers Reise von Leipzig nach Heidelberg im Herbst 1805. Görlitz 1808. Dort heißt es über Goethe, Genien wie er (ich zitiere nach Schultz, op. cit., S. 294 f.:) «sollten nie alt werden, ein gütiger Gott sollte sie, wie Göthe selbst von Winkelmann sehr schön sagt, auf dem Gipfel des Lebens, in der höchsten Blüthe vollendeter Kraft hinwegnehmen», und weiter, in metaphorischer Ausführung desselben Gedankens: daß «der Geist der über Erdgewölke und Zeitsturm hoch erhaben, im Äther reiner Vollendung schwebt, ... nur zuletzt nach dem Boden zu sinken scheint, wie nach einer schönen Sage der Paradiesvogel», und schließlich von Herder, daß er «ein geborener König und Prophet, größer war, als das ganze Jahrhundert».

tung, die von vornherein wenig für sich hat, da es zwar zuerst, am Anfang der kleinen Digression, um *große Dichter und Schriftsteller* geht,
dann aber offensichtlich um eine andere Kategorie, die ihnen mit einem
so auch gegenübergestellt und mit dem Stichwort *große Männer* bezeichnet wird, was auf Größen der allgemeinen Völker- und Staatengeschichte
hindeutet, ebenso wie der Ausdruck *neuere Geschichte.* Wer gemeint ist,
geht aus dem Prolog zum zweiten Teil des ‹Schweizerbundes› hervor,
der in einer langen Folge von mühelos gereimten Stanzen und mit ver-
blüffend Schillerschem Pathos die Beziehung zur gegenwärtigen welt-
geschichtlichen Stunde herstellt, von der Entwicklung der Französischen
Revolution als einem «großen Possenspiele» spricht, dem der «Weltgeist lachend» zusehe – darauf wird zurückzukommen sein – um sich
dann dem «Einen Mann» zuzuwenden, auf den das Jahrhundert «verwiesen» worden sei (ich zitiere die letzten vier Strophen):

«Weh dem Jahrhundert; wie ward es betrogen!
Auf Einen Mann verwiesen vom Geschick,
Der, gleich dem Aar, zum Sonnenkreis entflogen,
Im Glanz sich zeigte dem erstaunten Blick;
Der, trotzend des Geschickes wilden Wogen,
Von Tapferkeit begleitet und vom Glück,
Im Kampf mit widerstrebenden Gewalten,
Den Erdkreis schien von neuem zu gestalten.

Ein heller Stern schien über ihm zu schweben,
Vom Schicksal auserkohren trat er auf,
Kein Feind vermocht’ ihm wild zu widerstreben,
Nichts hemmte ihn in seinem kühnen Lauf;
Wo Felsen in die Wolken sich erheben,
Da kämpft’ er unaufhaltsam sich hinauf –
Bis er, der nie den Sieger noch gefunden,
Im eignen Busen wurde überwunden.

Da sank, der kühn sich über sich entschwungen,
Im raschen Sturze tief zu sich herab,
Und was dem Bürger göttlich war gelungen,
Fand in des Herrschers Brust ein stilles Grab.
Es welkt der Lorbeer, den er sich errungen,
Zum dürren Zepter wird der Feldherrnstab;
So prangt er traurig groß dort auf dem Throne,
Mit des erschlagnen Königs blut’ger Krone.

O wenn von ihrer Höhe Götter fallen,
Dann mag ringsum der weite Erdkreis zittern,
Ihr Sturz wird durch die Nachwelt wiederhallen,
Das kommende Jahrtausend noch erschüttern;

> So wird's von ihm durch alle Zeiten schallen,
> Der Nam' am Sarkophag wird nie verwittern,
> Und einst wird ihn mit seiner Thaten Früchten
> Die Nemesis der Weltgeschichte richten!»[69]

Es ist offensichtlich derselbe Adler, der hier wie dort der Sonne ent-
gegenfliegt und dessen Bahn dann eine so unrühmliche Wendung nimmt,
Bonaparte also, der übrigens auch gegen Ende derselben zwölften *Nachtwache* direkt genannt wird – als zweites Beispiel für die Bedeutung des
Essens: er habe den *Julius Cäsar* in sich aufgenommen, nicht jedoch
den *Geist des Brutus* (12. Nw.; S. 105), was wieder auf denselben Mangel zurückverweist, den auch das Sonnenadler-Gleichnis ausspricht. Übernommen worden ist hier, am Anfang der zwölften *Nachtwache*, wie man
sieht, nicht nur das Motiv des sich zur Sonne erhebenden Adlers selbst,
sondern auch das Nachstaunen derer, die seinem «Glanz» von unten her
zusehen, ebenso wie der Hinweis auf die Gegenkraft im «eigenen Busen»,
die den, «der kühn sich über sich entschwungen, / Im raschen Sturze tief
zu sich herab» sinken ließ, also – in weniger poetischer Ausdrucksweise
– den «Egoismus»[70]. Das Thema ‹Französische Revolution› wird später,
in der fünfzehnten *Nachtwache*, noch einmal aufgenommen, aber dem
einmal gewählten modus procedendi gemäß ist zunächst der direkt folgende Fall von ‹Anleihe› bei dem dramatischen Nebenwerk zu erwähnen, nämlich der Anfang der dreizehnten *Nachtwache*, wo man sich
einem Naturbild gegenübersieht, das an seiner Stelle vielleicht noch
befremdlicher ist als das des winterlich *starren Naturtorsos* in der
zehnten *Nachtwache*: der Nachtwächter steigt *den Berg hinauf*, der *am
Ausgange der Stadt* liegen soll, sieht draußen *die alte Fee, die Erde*, liegen und sich vorbereiten auf ein neues Aufstehen als *eine junge Nymphe*,
unten im Tale aber bläst *ein Hirte das Alphorn, und die Töne* sprechen *so lockend von einem fernen Lande, und von Liebe und Jugend und*

---

[69] Op. cit., 2. Bd., S. 9 f.

[70] Ein Lieblingsthema Klingemanns, das fast nach Art einer fixen Idee in
seinen Schriften wiederkehrt, vom ‹Romano›, wo von der «fürchterlichen Herr-
schaft des Egoismus» (I, 85) die Rede ist, bis zu ‹Kunst und Natur›, wo es über
die aufwendige Einrichtung eines Theatersaals heißt, sie sei «auch nichts anders,
als ein E g o i s m u s , wie er in dem großen Bühnenwesen so oft zur Erscheinung kommt», woran sich ein längerer Exkurs schließt (II, 384 f.). Das Beispiel
Napoleon begegnet nochmals (1820) in einem Vortrag Klingemanns über
Raupachs ‹Die Fürsten Chawansky› (abgedr. in: Euph. 26, 1925, S. 260 ff.): «Vor
allen Dingen ist es der Egoismus, der die seltensten Erscheinungen in dieser
Rücksicht hervorzuführen im Stande ist; und wie der schrecklichste und größeste
Mensch unseres Zeitalters als ein natürlicher Sohn der vollendeten Selbstsucht
erscheint, so ist auch Sophie in der Hauptsache nichts anderes als eine kecke
Egoistin.» (a. a. O. S. 267).

Hoffnung – ebenso «lockend», wie sie in den szenischen Gemälden des ‹Schweitzerbundes› immer wieder sprechen[71]! Und ebenso wie Hadloub in einer Szene des ‹Schweitzerbundes› einen alphornblasenden Hirten mit einem Lied begleitet[72], so dichtet hier der Nachtwächter, als die Töne des Alphorns *so lockend* sprechen, *zu ihrer Begleitung* einen *Dithyrambus über den Frühling*, in dem vom Sinken des *letzten Glätschers*, von *Sennenhütten* und *gefleckten Herden* die Rede ist, die an den *Abhängen* der Berge *kleben* (13. Nw.; S. 107 f.).

Damit ist die Reihe der direkt vom Nachbarwerk her inspirierten Kapiteleingänge beendet; eine Reihe, wie sie in der Literaturgeschichte nicht allzu häufig begegnet, erklärbar zweifellos nur durch die besonderen Bedingungen, unter denen beide Werke entstanden. Es waren Bedingungen, die in fast allen Stücken von denen abweichen, mit denen der Literarhistoriker ‹normalerweise› zu rechnen hat: ‹normalerweise› hat er es mit Werken zu tun, in denen der Autor mit seinem eigenen Namen auftritt, überdies in den meisten Fällen mit der Erwartung, daß man ihn schon kennt und sich, sei es auch nur innerhalb eines gewissen Kreises von Lesern, für seine Werke interessiert, so daß er auch mit der Möglichkeit vergleichenden Lesens rechnen kann und muß. ‹Normalerweise› – so fragwürdig diese Norm auch sein mag – sind die Werke, mit denen der Literarhistoriker sich befaßt, auch auf etwas mußevollere und weniger gehetzte Weise entstanden als diese beiden, von denen das eine, wie wir sahen, noch im März 1804 in statu nascendi war und im Juli bereits dem Publikum der ‹Eleganten Welt› angekündigt wurde, das andere dagegen, noch Ende Juni 1804 erst der Vollendung «nahe», geradezu im Wettlauf mit einem überlegenen Konkurrenten entstand. *Die Unsterblichkeit ist widerspänstig, die Verleger zahlen bogenweis, und die Honorare sind heuer schmal*: dieser Satz des Poeten aus der letzten *Nachtwache* (16. Nw.; S. 135), mindestens dieser eine Satz dürfte aus der Erfahrung des Autors gesprochen sein: der Erfahrung eines Autors, der mittellos und ohne Aussicht auf eine Anstellung von seinen Universitätsstudien, ohne eigentlichen ‹Abschluß›, nach Hause gekommen war, übrigens auch bereits «Familie hatte»[73], wie es in den ‹Freimüthigkeiten›

---

[71] Zwei Proben nur: «Rudolf: ‹Horch das Alphorn tönt!› Werner: ‹Es ist ganz still ringsum – die Sonne geht unter!› Rudolf: ‹Ich hör's doch lieblich in der Ferne spielen!› (tiefe Stille.) Rudolf: ‹Der Ruf wird immer lockender, und will mich zu den blauen Bergen hinziehn!›» (2. Bd., S. 95) – «Arnold: ‹(...) Ich glaube, hätte ich einmal nur das Alphorn hören können, ich wäre gesundet, denn gar schmerzlich sehnte ich mich stets nach den Tönen, und in allen meinen Träumen schienen sie mich nach den Bergen einzuladen.›» (1. Bd., S. 25)

[72] 1. Bd., S. 117 f.

[73] Freilich nicht im Sinne ‹geordneter Familienverhältnisse›: die Geburt einer Tochter (Clara Mathilde Klingemann, unter diesem Namen später berühmte

von deren Autor heißt, und auf die Einkünfte aus seiner Feder schlechthin angewiesen war.

Gelegentliche, wenn auch weniger entscheidende Anklänge an das Nachbarwerk, kleinere Funkenüberschläge gleichsam, gibt es dann noch öfter:
nicht in der vierzehnten *Nachtwache,* die den schon in der neunten angekündigten *Wonnemonat im Tollhause* enthält – die Liebesgeschichte mit
der wirklich wahnsinnig gewordenen Ophelia-Darstellerin des *Hoftheaters* – wohl aber gleich zu Anfang der fünfzehnten, wo der aus dem
Tollhaus Vertriebene auf merkwürdig weite Reisen geht und bei der
alten Mutter selbst, der auch im ‹Schweitzerbund› so gern berufenen, zu
Gast ist, die *noch Wurzeln in ihrem Schooße* hat und *der durstigen Lippe
in der dargebotenen Felsenschaale den frischen brausenden Trank des
stürzenden Wasserfalls* reicht (15. Nw.; S. 126). Auch der Rheinfall wird
genannt, als letzte unter den *Herrlichkeiten,* die dem Armen dank seines
Freibillets für die ganze Natur offenstehen, und zwar mit einem Bild, das
auch im ‹Schweitzerbund› vorkommt: von einer *köstlichen krystallenen
Halle* ist hier die Rede, dort von einem «krystallenen Bogen» oder auch
einem «Haus von Krystall»[74]. Überhaupt sind es, wie sich denken läßt,
vor allem die Naturbilder, in denen die beiden Werke sich berühren, wobei sie gelegentlich auch, in gewissen Lieblingsbildern und -formeln, mit
früheren Publikationen zusammentreffen. Charakteristisch etwa die Vorliebe für fliegende oder gleitende Lichterscheinungen: da «fliegt das
Mondlicht über Wald und See und um die silberhellen Glätscher, die wie
Geister sich erheben» (Schweitzerbund, I 46), da *flog ein Wetterleuchten
luftig und rasch durch die öden Straßen* (2. Nw.; S. 10); *neugierig gleitete* – so heißt es in der 16. *Nachtwache* (S. 140) – *das Mondlicht an den
halbverwitterten Schildern und Verzierungen hinab,* und im ‹Schweitzerbund› (I, 81): «(...) flüchtig gleitet Mondlicht nur an den Felsen nieder
und fliegt über die fernen Glätscher!» Aber auch die uns von früher her
bekannte Vorstellung von der zweiten, höheren Welt, die in den ‹Nachtwachen› zweimal, in der ersten und in der letzten, und außerdem in dem
Aufsatz über die ‹Jungfrau von Orleans› von 1805 vorkam, kann man in
diesem Drama oder «dramatischen Roman» von 1804 noch einmal finden:

Schauspielerin, gest. 1837) ist für den 25. 2. 1803 bezeugt, für den 29. 9. 1805 die
Heirat mit ihrer Mutter, Sophie Caroline Rückling, geschiedener Ehefrau des
Buchhändlers Schröder, bei dem Klingemanns erste literarische Produktionen
erschienen waren. Klingemann hatte inzwischen (1805) die kümmerliche Stellung eines «Adjunkts» bei seinem Vater, der «Registrator» beim «Obersanitätskollegium» war, sowie die Anwartschaft auf dessen Stelle bekommen, die er
am 8. 4. 1806 erhielt.
[74] 2. Bd., S. 43 (ähnlich 1. Bd., S. 171: «wie ein krystallner Bogen») und
2. Bd., S. 141. Bezugsobjekt ist in allen diesen Fällen ein gefrorner Wasserfall,
was besonders die Bilder von «Halle» bzw. «Haus» verständlicher macht.

hier in einer Formulierung, die der in der letzten *Nachtwache* besonders nahesteht: Wolfenschieß ist es, der in der letzten Szene des ersten Teils, der Szene seines Todes, sagt: «Ein Schicksal umschwebt den Menschen, das er nie ergründet und oftmals scheint gar wunderbar die Geisterwelt in die irdische hinabzulauschen! –»[75]

Genug der Parallelstellen! Nur eine letzte tiefergehende Beziehung ist hier noch zu erwähnen, die zur Aufhellung der Hintergründe unseres Haupttextes und zu seiner ‹Ortsbestimmung› nicht unwichtig ist: die schon angekündigte Wiederaufnahme der zeitgeschichtlichen Thematik gegen Ende der ‹Nachtwachen› – im vorletzten Kapitel – die wieder in dem großen Prolog zum zweiten Teil des Schweizerbund-Dramas ihre vollere, sozusagen üppiger instrumentierte, vielfach auch deutlicher formulierte Parallele findet: die französische Revolution als *große Tragikomödie*, wie es in den ‹Nachtwachen› (15. Nw.; S. 129) heißt, *in der ein König unglücklich debütirte, und der Hanswurst, als Freiheit und Gleichheit, lustig Menschenköpfe, statt der Schellen schüttelte*, als «großes Possenspiel», wie im Prolog zum ‹Sturz der Vögte›, dem zweiten Teil des ‹Schweizerbundes›, gesagt wird[76]. Um den ganzen Kontext zu geben (es sind die drei Strophen, die den bereits zitierten unmittelbar vorausgehen), zugleich als weitere Probe für die Fähigkeiten unseres Autors auch in diesem Genre, dem Genre des feierlichen Theaterprologs à la Schiller oder auch, mit einem wenig glücklichen, aber gebräuchlichen Terminus gesprochen, der Schillerschen ‹Gedankenlyrik›:

> «Den späten Enkel wird die Zeitgeschichte
> Ein abenteuerliches Mährchen dünken,
> Er hält die wundervollen Kunden für Gedichte,
> Wie Völker rasch sich heben, rascher sinken;
> Wie Glück und Unglück Eines Stammes Früchte;
> Gleichlockend Tugend und Verbrechen winken;
> Wie alles was die Menschheit ehrt und schändet
> In einem großen Possenspiele endet.

[75] 1. Bd., S. 192 f. Die betreffende Stelle in der 16. Nw.: *Ein Poet meinte, die zweite Welt lausche in die untenliegende herunter* (S. 133). Und die analoge Stelle im Aufsatz in der ‹El. Welt› vom 7. 5. 1805: «(...) und das zweite Leben schaut hell und leuchtend in das Irdische hinein (...)».

[76] Ganz ähnlich hat sich Klingemann auch in einem gleichzeitigen Artikel über ein gerade erschienenes Charlotte Corday-Drama ([Christine Westphalen:] Charlotte Corday, Hamburg 1804) geäußert: «(...) ich meines Theils fürchte, daß der poetische Genius sich auf immer von diesem Momente der Geschichte abwenden werde (...). Sollte je die tragische Muse sich einst an ihn wagen, so muß sie einen noch kältern und blutdürstigern Karakter annehmen, als in den klassischen Tragödien der Franzosen herrschend ist, in denen selbst der Mord noch vom Zeremoniell begleitet wird, und es ließe sich dann allenfalls ein neues Genre von tragischen Possenspielen erwarten.» (‹El. Welt› v. 23. 10. 1804).

Umsonst stürzt hier ein Königsstamm vom Throne,
Es färbt umsonst den Boden Herrscherblut,
Umsonst sinkt in den Staub die heil'ge Krone,
Umsonst kämpft gegen sich der Bürger Wuth,
Es dient der Himmel selbst umsonst dem Hohne,
Umsonst ist Tugend, Tapferkeit und Muth;
Die Gottheit selbst, die schaudernd sich abwendet,
Wird von den Rasenden umsonst geschändet.

Der Weltgeist sieht dem großen Possenspiele
Wild lachend zu; – es tobet Gallia,
Verhöhnt der Menschheit heiligste Gefühle,
Es scheint das Ende aller Dinge nah;
Jetzt sinkt auch in dem stürmischen Gewühle
Der Freiheit höchster Stolz – Helvetia,
Und jene, die der Freiheit Glück besingen,
Sie sind's die ihm die Sklavenfesseln bringen.»[77]

Das «Umsonst», das in der Rhetorik dieser Verse wie ein dumpfer
Glockenschlag immer wieder ertönt, ist auch der Tenor des Passus in den
‹Nachtwachen›, der auf das obige Zitat folgt, eingeleitet durch den Zwi-
schenfall bei der Aufführung der Judith-und-Holofernes-Geschichte als
Marionettenspiel: den Aufruhr der *zuschauenden Bauern*, die mit dem
abgeschlagenen hölzernen Haupte des Holofernes vor das Haus ihres
Schulzen ziehen und *nichts weniger als seinen Kopf von ihm* fordern, dann
aber durch eine Rede des Nachtwächters (der zu dieser Zeit noch keiner
ist) beruhigt und sogar vollkommen umgestimmt werden. *Was hat euch
dieser arme Kopf gethan*, fragt er, das *hölzerne blutige Königshaupt*
hochhaltend, mit mehr als doppelsinnigem Bezug, *daß ihr so mit ihm
umspringt; er ist das mechanischste Ding auf der Welt und es wohnt nicht
einmal ein Gedanke in ihm. Fordert doch von diesem Kopfe keine Freiheit, da er selbst nichts Analoges davon in sich enthält.* (15. Nw.; S. 130).
Und es folgt ein Hinweis auf Marionettenspiele *von noch fehlerhafterer
Natur*, die der Redner und Marionettendirektor in seinem Kasten habe –
*wo der Dichter dem Stoffe nicht gewachsen war, und er nach Art poli-
tischer Poeten, die Republik an der er dichtete, zu einer Despotie ver-
pfuschte*, was natürlich wieder auf Napoleon zielt. Ähnliche Zeitanspie-
lungen stecken in dem anschließenden Absatz über die so rasch um-
gestimmten Bauern – sie geben nach Beendigung der Rede *das Revo-
luziniren gutmüthig wieder auf* und lassen *dagegen ihren Schulzen hoch-
leben* – und in den allgemeinen Betrachtungen über die *Menschheit*, die
sich so *leicht in das Entgegengesezteste* finde: *ja ich glaube sie kann sich,
wenn sie heute ein leichtes Band, das sie fesselte, zerrissen hat, morgen*

---

[77] 2. Bd., S. 7–9.

mit eben dem Enthusiasmus in Ketten werfen lassen. Einer der droben zuschaut, muß mit dem Volke Mitleid haben. Besonders letzteres ist bezeichnend für Tonart und Perspektive dieser Geschichtsbetrachtung (die beide wiederum typisch sind für die Gattung ‹Satire›, deren Name denn auch nicht zufällig einige Zeilen tiefer auftaucht, im Zusammenhang mit einem *strengen Zensuredikt,* wonach *alle Satire im Staate ohne Ausnahme verboten sei, und man sie schon zum voraus in den Köpfen konfiscire*): Geschichte nicht als Tragödie, aber auch nicht als reine Komödie, sondern als Mischung von beidem, betrachtet von einem *droben* gelegenen Standpunkt aus, als Gegenstand des Mitleids und zugleich des Gelächters oder, in der Sprache des Prologs zum zweiten Teil des ‹Schweitzerbunds›: als Gegenstand, von dem «die Gottheit selbst» sich «schaudernd» abwendet, und zugleich auch wieder als «Possenspiel», dem der Weltgeist «wild lachend» zusieht.

IV. Schluß

Fassen wir kurz zusammen, was sich, über die bloße Zuschreibung als
solche hinaus, an Einsichten über das Werk, über seine Situation und
seinen literarischen Rang ergeben hat! Um mit dem letzten Punkt zu beginnen: Dieses Buch ist – so hat sich gezeigt – alles andere als das Werk
eines ‹Originalgenies›. Das ist freilich auch früher schon gesehen worden,
z. B. von Eduard Berend, der 1912 in seiner Widerlegung der Frankschen
Brentano-These schrieb, Frank überschätze «den Wert der Nachtwachen
gewaltig». Gewiß sei «das Werk ein glücklicher Wurf; man mag es sogar
mit Haym zu den geistreichsten Produktionen der Romantik rechnen», von
«dichterischer Gestaltungskraft» aber sei doch nur «sehr wenig darin zu
spüren», schrieb Berend, und er fuhr fort: «Vor allem fehlt es dem
Werke – und das war wohl der Hauptgrund, warum es bei den Zeitgenossen so wenig Beachtung fand – an durchgreifender Originalität.»[1]
Eben dies ist die Eigenschaft, die Klingemanns literarische Produktionen
auch sonst, eigentlich durchweg zeigen und die ihm auch von seinen
Freunden bescheinigt wurde, ja in ihren Kreisen geradezu sprichwörtlich
gewesen zu sein scheint. Als Brentano im Dezember 1802 von seinem
Freund Winkelmann, dem Mediziner – demselben, dem der zweite Band
von Klingemanns ‹Romano› gewidmet ist – gewisse briefliche Ratschläge
erhält, die ihm unsinnig erscheinen, und gleichzeitig einen Brief seiner
Großmutter Sophie Laroche mit Vorschlägen zu einer Reise, die er nicht
zu tun gedenkt, da schreibt er an Savigny: «Winkelmanns Zettel erhielt
ich in einer witzigen Vergesellung mit beiliegendem Brief der Laroche.
Wenn Klingemann alle Dichter nachahmt, so ist es doch nicht schön von
Winkelmann, meine alte Großmutter nachzuahmen; ist in seinen Vorschlägen nicht die größte Aehnlichkeit mit den vom Himmel herabgefal-
lenen Vorschlägen der Großmutter für ihn und mich zu Reisen, die wir
gar nicht machen wollen?»[2]

---

[1] Eduard Berend, a. a. O. (Euph. 19. Bd., 1912), S. 798.

[2] Das unsterbliche Leben. Unbekannte Briefe von Clemens Brentano. Hrsg.
v. W. Schellberg und F. Fuchs. Jena 1939. S. 283. In einer vorausgehenden Passage desselben Briefes und in anderem Zusammenhang, innerhalb einer Serie
von burlesk-satirischen Steckbriefen, in der auch Winkelmann, Schelling und
die beiden Schlegel charakterisiert werden, kennzeichnet Brentano Klingemann
als einen «von den vielen Schülern des Philadelphia [Name eines berühmten
Taschenspielers; J. S.], die auf ihrem Zettel in jeder Stadt nur des Wirtshauses
Namen ausfüllen, ein Mietpferd borgen und sich für ein Freibillet bei dem
Apotheker Lausesalbe kaufen» (a. a. O., S. 280).

«Wenn Klingemann alle Dichter nachahmt»: er hat es getan, zumindest ansatzweise, indem er nicht eben weniges von den literarischen Haupterzeugnissen der Epoche aufgriff und – sagen wir es ruhig, trotz der Verdikte einer dieses Wort verpönenden, immer noch vom Geniebegriff faszinierten Ästhetik – nachahmte: den Tieckschen ‹Gestiefelten Kater› in den ‹Freimüthigkeiten›, den ‹Sternbald› im ‹Romano› – wo auch die im ‹Athenäum› erschienenen Sonette auf Kunstwerke ihren Nachhall in einer ähnlich langen Reihe von Sonetten auf Kunstwerke finden – den F. Schlegelschen ‹Brief an Dorothea› und zugleich die ‹Fragmente› des ‹Athenäums› in den ‹Fragmenten›, die unter dem Titel ‹Poesie› und mit der Adresse ‹An Louise› im ‹Memnon› erschienen, das ‹Athenäum› selbst in der Zeitschrift ‹Memnon›, Schillers ‹Luise Millerin› in dem «Karaktergemählde» ‹Selbstgefühl›, Schillers rhetorische Lyrik, insbesondere den ‹Wallenstein›-Prolog, im Prolog zum zweiten Teil des ‹Schweitzerbundes› und die Jean Paulsche romanhaft-erzählende Satire, besonders den ‹Luftschiffer Giannozzo› – wie schon der erkannte, der hierfür das beste Ohr gehabt haben dürfte, nämlich Jean Paul selbst – in den ‹Nachwachen›. Wieviel hier, auf allen Ebenen, reinste Jean Paul-Nachahmung ist, braucht an dieser Stelle nicht mehr ausgeführt zu werden, da es bereits auf meisterliche, ebenso knappe wie hinreichende Weise ausgeführt worden ist: in Michels Einleitung zu seiner Edition der ‹Nachtwachen›. Auch hier hat bereits Eduard Berend das Richtige gesehen, wenn er gegen Schultz (und gegen manche spätere Interpreten) schrieb, er müsse «Michel beistimmen, der kaum übertreibt, wenn er in den Nachtwachen eine so starke Beeinflussung durch einen bestimmten Autor, nämlich Jean Paul, konstatiert, wie sie in der gesamten deutschen Literaturgeschichte nicht häufig aufzuzeigen sei»[3]. Um nur an einiges zu erinnern, anknüpfend an Dinge, die im Vorhergehenden berührt wurden: jeanpaulisch ist etwa die Form der eingelegten ‹Rede›[4], wie sie uns zuletzt in der Passage über die *revoluzionirenden* Bauern begegnete, eine Form, die ja nicht nur hier, sondern ebenso in der Rede des Nachtwächters über das *Jüngste Gericht* am Ende des Säkulums, in der Verteidigungsrede wegen der *Injurienklage*, in der *Rede des steinernen Crispinus über das Kapitel de adulteriis* (was für ein jeanpaulischer Titel!), in der *Leichenrede am Geburtstage eines Kindes*, in der *Apologie des Lebens* usw. begegnet; jeanpaulisch sind die zuletzt zitierten Überschriften selbst, ebenso wie die Anlage des Inhaltsverzeichnisses, in dem man sie als Untertitel für Teile einzelner *Nachtwachen* findet; jeanpaulisch ist auch die Verwendung eben dieses Wortes – *Nachtwache* – anstelle von «Kapitel» (in den Überschriften: *Erste Nachtwache, Zweite Nachtwache* usw.[5]); jeanpaulisch ist die Fichte-Kritik durch satirisch-

---

[3] A. a. O., S. 798.

[4] Vgl. hierzu besonders die Reden Schoppes im ‹Titan›.

[5] Vergleichbar ist hier nicht nur das aus den großen Romanen Jean Pauls

spaßige reductio ad absurdum, wie wir sie auch in den ‹Freimüthigkeiten› wiederfanden, vor allem aber die reductio ad absurdum im Wortsinne: die Weiterführung bis zur Konsequenz des Wahnsinns, wie sie etwa im *Monolog des wahnsinnigen Weltschöpfers* begegnet, der auf die ‹Clavis Fichtiana› ebenso zurückweist wie auf das Schicksal Schoppes; jeanpaulisch sind viele der Wortspiele, z. B. das eingangs zitierte: der Erzähler habe statt des einen Trauerspiels, das er *nicht erwartet hatte, ihrer zwei* gefunden, das *rükgehende vom Verleger* und den erhängten *Tragiker* selbst; jeanpaulisch sind aber auch ganz konkrete Einzelmotive, wie etwa der *schwarze Vogel* des Pförtners in der zehnten *Nachtwache*, der auf die entsprechend formulierten Fragen seines menschenhassenden Herrn immer nur krächzt: «*Mensch!*» und der seinen Vorfahren hat in der sprechenden Dohle im ‹Titan›, der Roquairol einige poetische Zeilen beibringt, damit sie in seinem Trauerspiel ‹Der Trauerspieler› (nicht etwa: ‹Der Mensch›!) den Chor abgebe. Ich nenne dieses eine, schon von Michel nachgewiesene Jean Paul-Motiv deshalb, weil es von Klingemann selbst einmal ausdrücklich erwähnt wird – in seiner Rezension des ‹Titan›, die am 7. Juli 1803 in der ‹Eleganten Welt› erschien. Der Zusammenhang läßt zugleich erkennen, welche von den Figuren des ‹Titan› den stärksten Eindruck auf den Verfasser gemacht hat:

«Unter den männlichen Karakteren ist R o q u a i r o l der vorzüglichste; und zwar nicht, wie es oft wol der Fall zu seyn pflegt, ein Phantom in Jean Pauls Humor gehüllt, sondern aus der Tiefe des Lebens selbst hervorgerufen und ein kolossales Denkmal für ein großes Kapitel aus der Zeitgeschichte. Dieses spielen und verspielen seiner Selbst ist bis zum leisesten Hauche in sich getreu, und schon bei seinem ersten Auftreten ist es klar, daß dieser furchtbare Verschwender des Höchsten und Heiligsten in den Marionettenspielen, die er überall mit sich selbst aufführt, zuletzt seine eigene Figur, und wo möglich auch die seines Mitspielers, zerschlagen muß. – Der Onkel, der ihm bei seinem Trauerspiele zu dem untheilnehmenden mechanischen Chorsänger verhilft, gehört schon mehr zu den Phantomen, ob er gleich etwas von einer grellen Wahrheit an sich hat. Er ist fast eben so mechanisch wie seine Dohle, besonders in seinem Hasse.»[6]

---

bekannte Verfahren, sondern auch – wieder – der ‹Giannozzo› mit seinen Kapitelüberschriften: «Erste Fahrt», «Zweite Fahrt» usw.

[6] ‹Brief an eine Dame bei Übersendung des Titan von Jean Paul›. – Klingemann hat während der Zeit seiner regelmäßigen Mitarbeit an der ‹El. Welt› jede der größeren Jean Paulschen Publikationen in verständnisvollen und eindringlichen Besprechungen gewürdigt: den ‹Titan› in dem eben zitierten Artikel vom 7. 7. 1803, die ‹Flegeljahre› in dem eingangs herangezogenen ersten der ‹Briefe über die neuesten Werke der deutschen schönen Literatur› (7. 6. 1804), die ‹Vorschule der Ästhetik› in der Nummer vom 21. 3. 1805, das ‹Freiheitsbüchlein› in der vom 6. 8. 1805.

Roquairol – mit diesem Namen ist die tiefere, allgemeiner-historische Dimension unseres Themas angedeutet, die Dimension, in der das Einzelphänomen der ‹Nachtwachen› und ihres Autors zusammenhängt mit einem «großen Kapitel aus der Zeitgeschichte»: das Problem des Histrionentums, der «Universalität» ohne festen Kern und der ständigen, gleichsam Natur gewordenen Schauspielerei, des «unheiligen Schlemmens und Prassens in Gefühlen», wie es im ‹Titan› von Roquairol heißt[7]; ein Problem, das ja namentlich auch, nach Roquairols eigenen Worten in seinem Absagebrief an Albano, dasjenige gewisser «Romanen- und Tragödienschreiber» ist, «die alles, Gottheit und Menschheit, tausendmal durch- und nachgeäfft haben»[8]. Auch in den ‹Nachtwachen› wird es hinlänglich deutlich thematisiert, nicht nur in dem so oft ausgespielten Motiv des *Marionettenspiels*, das auch in dem eben zitierten Absatz aus dem ‹Titan›-Artikel auftaucht, sondern auch in weniger metaphorischen Formulierungen, etwa wenn dem Nachtwächter am Ende der neunten *Nachtwache*, des *Tollhaus*-Kapitels, vom Doktor Oehlmann versichert wird, sein Wahnsinn sei, *gerade wie bei andern eine Indigestion durch zu häufigen physischen Genuß, durch übertriebene intellektuelle Schwelgerei entstanden*, oder wenn er selbst später, in der Erzählung von seinem *Wonnemonat im Tollhause*, über sich und seine in der Hamletrolle geschriebenen Briefe an Ophelia sagt: *In solchen und dergleichen Fragmenten habe ich mich abgearbeitet, und mich ordentlich methodisch auszuschreiben gesucht, wie mancher Dichter, der seine Gefühle so lange auf dem Papiere von sich giebt, bis sie zuletzt alle abgegangen sind, und der Kerl selbst ganz ausgebrannt und nüchtern dasteht* (14. Nw.; S. 117): eine Stelle, die dem Roquairolschen Vorbild, wie überhaupt die ganze Hamlet-Ophelia-Episode[9], besonders nahekommt.

Das Problem als solches und zugleich als spezifisch künstlerisches ist uns aber bereits früher begegnet: im ersten Band des ‹Romano› (1800), in der Klage des Helden über seine «fürchterliche Empfänglichkeit», die so weit gehe, daß er sich oft aus sich selbst «verliere» und «in einem anderen Wesen wiederfinde», daß es ihm sei, als schwebte er «oben über dem Ganzen und stelle chemische Prozesse in der Geisterwelt an», trennend und vereinigend, «bald burlesk, bald groß und kühn wie es mir die Laune eingiebt» – als ein «Meister in der Kunst des Amalgamirens»[10].

---

[7] 55. Zykel.

[8] 88. Zykel.

[9] Auch sie beginnt, wie Roquairols Trauerspiel im ‹Titan›, mit dem Spiel von Dramenrollen und endet, wie dieses, mit einem wirklichen Tod: dem Tod der zur Ophelia gewordenen Ophelia-Darstellerin.

[10] Auch hierzu gibt es eine merkwürdige Parallele, zumindest ein gewisses Analogon, in Brentanos Briefen: «Klingemann ist ein geistiger Mechanikus, der unendlich, aber nicht unbeschreiblich ist. Seine Kunst ist mehr Astronomie als

Aber «mein eigenes Selbst geht dabei zu Grunde und verliert sich in die Allgemeinheit meiner Geschicklichkeit», hieß es am Schluß des zitierten Absatzes mit einer Formulierung, die inzwischen an Relief gewonnen hat, und am Ende des ganzen Briefes, aus dem er stammt, wird für dasselbe Dilemma der Begriff des «Virtuosen»[11] eingeführt. Gleichgültig, ob man solche Sätze, denen noch manche ähnliche zur Seite zu stellen wären, als ‹Bekenntnisse› nimmt oder nicht: sie zeigen, daß Dinge wie Virtuosentum, *intellektuelle Schwelgerei*, universelle «Empfänglichkeit» Gegenstände der Reflexion für diesen Autor waren.

Gerade in der Frage: ‹Bekenntnis oder nicht?› wird man sich ja, nach allem eben Gesagten, kaum vorsichtig genug verhalten können. Man wird z. B., um auf die ‹Nachtwachen› zurückzukommen, angesichts des grimmigen Hohngelächters über die Menschheit im Ganzen, das der Nachtwächter so oft anstimmt, nicht ignorieren können, daß auch der Luftschiffer Giannozzo immer wieder in dasselbe Hohngelächter ausbricht. Wenn der Nachtwächter das Gefühl hat, als ob er sich *in der Nacht unter dem zugedeckten Monde, weit ausdehnte, und auf großen schwarzen Schwingen, wie der Teufel über dem Erdball schwebte,* und die Lust ihn ankommt, alle Schläfer unter ihm *mit eins* aufzurütteln und das *ganze Geschlecht im Negligée anzuschauen* (12. Nw.; S. 105.), wird man nicht außer acht lassen dürfen, daß Giannozzo sich mit ganz ähnlichen Gefühlen immer wieder, und zwar wirklich, über den Erdball erhebt. Auch die große, zornige, ‹nihilistische› Rede am Schluß wird man nicht so ‹existentiell› nehmen dürfen, wie das mehrfach, besonders natürlich in nachexistenzialistischer Zeit, geschehen ist – nicht als Zeugnis eines «Einzelnen», als Bezeugung seiner «Verzweiflung» und seiner «illusionslosen Existenznähe» – wird vielmehr auch hier bedenken müssen, wie viel von diesem Pathos schon vorgegeben, schon formuliert war; und man wird sich in diesem Fall nicht nur an Jean Paul, sondern etwa auch an die letzten Worte des Talbot in Schillers ‹Jungfrau› erinnern, darüber hinaus aber auch an die ganze, große und für einen eingefleischten Theatermann wie unseren Autor immer noch durchaus lebendige Tradition der Rhetorik.

Sowohl die theatralischen als auch die rhetorischen Elemente in den ‹Nachtwachen› wird man – auch dies gehört zum Fazit unserer Unter-

---

Poesie der Sternbilder. Er wird die Seelen und ihre Sphären und ihre Glut nach angenommenen Systemen berechnen und sich wundern, wie man die Höhe aus der Ferne weiß.» (Jena, Dezember 1801, an einen unbekannten Empfänger. In: Clemens Brentano: Briefe. Hrsg. v. F. Seebaß, 1. Bd., Nürnberg 1951, S. 95).

[11] «Da hast du wieder einen langen Brief voll Reflexionen – Nicht wahr? Ich bin noch eben so modern – wirst du sagen. Aber darum komme ich auch nie zu reiner Poesie und werde beständig ein Virtuose in der Kunst und im Leben bleiben.» (Romano, 1. Bd., S. 145).

suchung – möglichst realistisch sehen müssen: nicht bloß als Gleichnis für Weltanschauliches, sondern als Einsatz schon bereitliegender und, zumal für einen Theaterkenner wie Klingemann, verfügbarer Mittel. Ein neues Licht fällt von den Ergebnissen unserer Untersuchung her insbesondere auf die schon öfter gesehenen[12] formalen (sprachlichen, kompositorischen, den Aufbau wie die Bauteile betreffenden) Berührungen mit der Welt des Theaters und ihrer Konventionen. Ich erinnere nur an die eingelegten ‹Solonummern› wie den *Prolog des Hanswurstes zu der Tragödie: der Mensch*, der sich ja überhaupt im Laufe der Untersuchung als ein Kernstück des Buches herausgestellt hat und nicht zufällig als Probe für das Ganze in der ‹Eleganten Welt› erschienen sein dürfte, den *Monolog des wahnsinnigen Weltschöpfers* oder jenes auf den Zwischentitel *Der Traum der Liebe* folgende Prosastück, dessen sonderbare Beziehung zur Szene von Wolfenschießens Ende im ‹Schweitzerbund› wir kennenlernten, womit sich auch die Elemente einer ganz bestimmten Art von dramatischer Rollenpartie in ihrer Identität enthüllten: die Elemente des typischen Wahnsinns- und Verzweiflungsmonologs à la King Lear oder besser noch: à la Franz Moor (V. Akt), also jener Art von dramatischer Rede, wo sich dem Helden die Sinne und die Worte verwirren und er, die Augen wild und «graß» ins Nichts oder in die Nacht gerichtet, anfängt zu «phantasieren». Man höre nur, um sich die Art, wie dergleichen auf damaligen Bühnen gegeben wurde, zu vergegenwärtigen, und zugleich als Beispiel für Klingemanns Verhältnis zu diesen Dingen, die folgende Schilderung von Ludwig Devrients Spiel in der Rolle des Franz Moor aus einer später, anläßlich eines Devrientschen Gastspiels in Braunschweig im Herbst 1822 entstandenen Tagebuchaufzeichnung:

«Dritter Act – Trauerkleidung; Hermelinmantel; den gebietenden Grafenstern blitzend auf der Brust. Das Genie macht sich Luft mit der wachsenden Leidenschaft – der Geist fängt an den Körper zu vergessen; die höhere organische Kraft entbindet sich und der Künstler hat festen Boden gewonnen. Von nun an steigt es durch alle Scenen bis zum Schlusse in genialem Aufschwunge – Phantasie spiegelt sich in Phantasie, und Dichter und Künstler beginnen mit einander stürmend um den Preis zu ringen. Die Dämonen seiner Frevel dringen auf den Verbrecher ein – entsetzlicher Moment, wo er sich ihrer Gewalt allein überlassen wähnt – der Mord schleicht hinter ihm drein, und er schreckt vor seinem fallenden Dolche zusammen. Darauf die Scene mit Daniel; die ganz aus jener Welt herübergeholte Erzählung des Traums – das Gebet, wo den Worten die G e d a n k e n ausgehen, und er mechanisch in steigender Todesangst fortredet, daß die Töne zuletzt unzusammenhängend von den Lippen w e g f l a t t e r n – – hier war mehr als Wahrheit – mehr, mehr als Vollendung, und der Beifall der ergrif-

---

[12] Vor allem von Dorothee Sölle-Nipperdey: Untersuchungen zur Struktur der Nachtwachen von Bonaventura (Palaestra, 230). Göttingen 1959.

fenen Menge wurde zum Aufruhr, ja zum Geschrei! – Das Mimische an sich war dabei schauerlich groß; das Auge leuchtete in der Raserei in Flammen auf, und erlosch zum Hipokratischen Verkohlen mit der Abspannung, Alles aufgebender Verzweiflung; – dazu das Gorgonenartig, wilde Haupthaar, dessen gelösete Lokken, wie Schlangen der Furien, Antlitz und Brust umwanden – – alles dieses im entsetzlichen Zusammenhange, lieferte ein Bild, entworfen und vollendet mit F l a x m a n n s c h e r Künheit, und dem, was man Theaterspiel benennt, ganz und gar entrückt; so daß alles Andere dagegen nur gemacht schien, und selbst Ifflands Darstellung wie ein Schatten in der Erinnerung verdunstete. –»[13]

Das «Mimische» ist auch in den ‹Nachtwachen› immer wieder «schauerlich groß»: nicht nur in der eben erwähnten Partie, wo auf den Zwischentitel *Der Traum der Liebe* zunächst die Vision der toten Geliebten über dem Grabhügel folgt, sodann mit einem *Horch!* wieder flüchtig zur Situation des Nachtwächters zurückgelenkt, aber gleich wieder im visionären Stil fortgefahren wird: *Tanzmusik und Todtengesang – das schüttelt lustig seine Schellen! Rüstig immer zu* (10. Nw.; S. 91), sondern auch in der Szene am Bett des *sterbenden Freigeists*, wenn dort die Rede des Pfaffen *mächtig* anschwillt *wie ein Strom* und er dem Sterbenden das Jenseits malt *in kühnen Bildern, nicht das schöne Morgenroth des neuen Tages*, sondern, *wie ein wilder Höllenbreugel, die Flammen und die ganze schaudervolle Unterwelt des Dante* (1. Nw.; S. 7), oder auch in der Schlußrede des Nachtwächters auf dem Friedhof, die mit der Anrede an den vom Boden aufgenommenen *Wurm* beginnt und sich dann, nachdem der Redner *stark und wild genug* geworden ist, um den Deckel von der Grabkammer des Vaters zu heben, mit einem neuen Anlauf und in einer neuen – der *zornigen* – Tonlage bis zu den Sternen erhebt, um schließlich mit dem dreimal pointiert ans Absatzende gesetzten *Nichts!* auszuhallen.

Das alles ist – in einem unverächtlichen Sinne des Wortes – Theater, und zwar in einem Maße, das weit hinausgeht über bloße Struktur-

---

[13] August Klingemann: Kunst und Natur. Blätter aus meinem Reisetagebuche. 3. Bd., Braunschweig 1828, S. 344 f. – Der hier erwähnte englische Bildhauer und Illustrator Flaxman war in Deutschland vor allem durch A. W. Schlegels Aufsatz ‹Über Zeichnungen zu Gedichten und Joh. Flaxman's Umrisse› (Athenäum, II, 2, 1799) bekannt geworden, in dem besonders die Dante-Illustrationen Flaxman's, aber auch die zu Homer und Aischylos, gewürdigt werden. Eine Anspielung auf den polemischen Anfang dieses Aufsatzes («Nichts ist gewöhnlicher unter uns als Kupferblätter und Blättchen zu Gedichten, besonders zu Schauspielen und Romanen, theils zu den Ausgaben derselben, theils zu Taschenbüchern in den kleinsten Formaten») in der 9. Nw.; S. 83: *Schon Schlegel hat es sehr auf die kleinen Bilderchen abgesehen, und ich muß gestehen, daß mir eine große Iliade in Sedez herausgegeben, nimmer behagen will (. . .).*

analogien. Es ist Theater im Sinne eines Grundzuges, den man nicht tref-
fender kennzeichnen kann als mit dem Terminus «mimisch», eines Grundzuges, auf den man in den großen Reden unseres Textes ebenso stößt wie
in den knappen, präzisen Andeutungen von Gesten, Haltungen, Stellun-
gen, die immer wieder gegeben werden: da knien *unbeweglich die drei*
Knaben und die blasse Mutter vor einem Altare – die Gruppe der Niobe
mit ihren Kindern – in stummes angstvolles Gebet versunken (2. Nw.;
S. 12), da redet ein Liebhaber *rhetorischen Bombast* und spricht *in einem*
Athem von Liebe und Treue; das Frauenbild dagegen zweifelte gläubig,
und machte viel künstlichen Händeringens (3. Nw.; S. 18), da ist der
Stadtpoet gerade *in einer tragischen Stellung begriffen, die eine Hand in*
den Haaren, die andere hielt das Blatt, von dem er wahrscheinlich seine
Unsterblichkeit sich vorrezitirte (1. Nw.; S. 6), da ist ein *auf dem Gottes-*
acker sich herumtreibender *junger Mensch* damit beschäftigt, *durch hefti-*
ges Gestikuliren und Deklamiren sich in eine mäßige Verzweiflung zu
bringen, setzt sich eine Pistole an die Stirn und drückt ab, aber die Pistole
ist ungeladen, und der junge Mann selbst steht, wie er am Ende des
Kapitels – mit einer *Danksagungsverbeugung* für den *wieder angehefteten*
falschen Zopf – dem Nachtwächter erklärt, *am Hoftheater* und *suchte*
sich nur hier am Grabe durch mäßiges Rasen in den Karakter eines Selbst-
mörders zu versetzen, den er *morgen darzustellen habe* (12. Nw.; S. 105).
Dieser mimische Grundzug, der durch das ganze Buch hindurchgeht, auch
durch die Reden des Nachtwächters, der ja ebenfalls ‹Figur› ist, ebenfalls
seine typischen Gesten, Posituren und ‹Tonfälle› hat – dieser mimische
Grundzug des Werkes ist offenbar auch schuld daran, daß die Versuche,
den Autor selbst bei einer bestimmten ‹Aussage›, einer bestimmten welt-
anschaulichen, sei es ‹nihilistischen› oder ‹pessimistischen› oder ‹pro-
testantischen› oder sonstwie gearteten ‹Position› zu behaften, um von da
aus etwa zu Schlüssen über seine Identität zu gelangen, zu so wider-
sprüchlichen, unsicheren und wenig befriedigenden Resultaten geführt
haben: man ‹faßt› einen Autor nicht leicht, bei dem das (sicher in jedem
Stück Literatur vorhandene) mimische Element so sehr dominiert.

    Klingemann selbst scheint sich über diese Eigenart seiner Begabung
ziemlich bald im klaren gewesen zu sein. Schon unter den literarischen
Publikationen der Frühzeit überwiegen, wie wir sahen, die dramatischen
Produktionen die erzählerischen, von denen übrigens die erste, die
‹Ruinen im Schwarzwalde› (1798–1799), auf weite Strecken ein ‹dialogier-
ter Roman›, oft sogar in regelrechte Dramenszenen eingeteilt ist, im
Untertitel denn auch nicht als Roman bezeichnet wird, sondern mit einem
romantisierenden Terminus als «Arabeske». Dies Werk selbst, das alles
andere als eine Arabeske im Schlegelschen Sinne ist, konnte hier ebenso
wie ‹Albano der Lautenspieler› (1802) beiseitebleiben, da beide sich, wie
angedeutet, in völlig anderen literarischen Gattungen bewegen als die

‹Nachtwachen›, beide in Gattungen, die zu dem gehören, was man heute etwa als Konsumliteratur bezeichnen würde, im Gegensatz zum ‹Romano› (1800–01), der ja schon durch seine Vorbilder eine gewisse Höhenlage erreicht und durch Nennungen von Namen wie Goethe, Hans Sachs, Dante und durch seine Kunst- und Künstlerthematik Anlaß zu Vergleichen bot. *Die Unsterblichkeit ist widerspänstig, die Verleger zahlen bogenweis und die Honorare sind heuer sehr schmal:* wir zitierten diesen Satz aus der letzten der *Nachtwachen* schon einmal, aber noch nicht seine Fortsetzung: *da wirft dergleichen Schreiberei nichts ab, und ich will mich wieder in die Dramen werfen* (16. Nw.; S. 135). Lassen wir es dahingestellt, wie weit bei der Niederschrift dieser Worte Gedanken an die eigene schriftstellerische Laufbahn des Schreibers im Spiel waren und was für Gedanken (ausschließen läßt sich dergleichen ebensowenig wie beweisen), und stellen wir nur fest: Klingemann warf sich seit 1804 tatsächlich in die Dramen, verfaßte mühelos ein Stück nach dem andern – darunter vier über Figuren, die auch in den ‹Nachtwachen› genannt werden: ein Ödipus-, ein Moses-, ein Hamlet- und ein Ahasver-Drama[14] – und wurde mit ihnen für eine gewisse Zeit einer der meistgespielten Bühnenautoren Deutschlands. Nur ein Teil seiner Stücke wurde, einzeln oder in Sammeleditionen, gedruckt – unter ihnen auch die eben genannten[15] – viele dagegen in Abschriften an die Direktoren z. T. bedeutender Theater gesandt, die nicht *bogenweis* zahlten wie die Verleger, sondern nach Maßgabe ihres Interesses, ihrer Finanzkraft und der zu erwartenden eingespielten Eintrittsgelder. Über den eigentlich literarischen Wert seiner Dramen hat er selbst recht nüchtern geurteilt: «(...) übrigens streichen Sie in dem Ding was Sie wollen», schreibt er einmal, am 10. September

---

[14] Über die Ödipus- und die Hamlet-Stellen in den ‹Nw.› wurde oben gehandelt. Moses wird erwähnt in der 9. Nw.; S. 85: *(...) und erkannte in aller dieser gepriesenen Weisheit zulezt nichts anders als die Decke die über das Mosesantlitz des Lebens gehängt ist, damit es Gott nicht schaue* (ähnlich auch schon im ‹Romano›, 1. Bd., S. 264: «(...) so ertrug Moses das Anschauen Gottes nicht und er musste sich abwenden als der Herr an ihm vorüber ging»); *der ewige Jude* in der 4. Nw.; S. 32: *(...) halte ich dich für den ewigen Juden, der, weil er das Unsterbliche lästerte, zur Strafe schon hier unten unsterblich geworden ist, wo alles um ihn her vergeht.*

[15] Moses. Ein dramatisches Gedicht in 5 Akten. Helmstädt 1812. – Hamlet. Leipzig und Altenburg 1815. – Oedipus und Jokaste. In: Theater, 3. Bd., Stuttgart 1820. – Ahasver. Braunschweig 1827. – In gewisser Hinsicht gehört auch, als fünftes Stück mit einer in den ‹Nw.› genannten Figur, Klingemanns ‹Faust›, eines seiner erfolgreichsten Stücke (gedr. Leipzig und Altenburg 1815), in diese Reihe, nämlich im Hinblick auf die Rolle des Teufels, die übrigens in der Uraufführung am 29. 11. 1811 in Breslau von Ludwig Devrient verkörpert wurde, auch auf Gastspielreisen Devrients eine seiner Erfolgsrollen wurde.

1822, bei Übersendung eines Columbus-Dramas aus früherer Zeit, «das ist aufgedunsener Jugendquark, worauf ich nichts mehr gebe. Überhaupt bezweifle ich, daß ich jemals ein eigentlich dramatisches Talent gehabt; höchstens bin ich nur Theaterschriftsteller eine Zeit gewesen.»[16]

Doch nicht diese spätere Zeit mit ihren starken und letztes Endes doch *ephemerischen* Erfolgen – *ephemerisch* wie diejenigen Kotzebues, mit dem Klingemann sich schließlich, kurz vor dessen Tode, noch aussöhnte[17] – interessiert uns hier, sondern das Jahr 1804 mit seinem Paradoxon eines Buches, das zu Lebzeiten seines Autors so gut wie unbekannt blieb, auf das er selbst vielleicht später «nichts mehr gab» und das dann doch das einzige nicht ephemere seiner Werke werden sollte, sich selbst, aber nicht den Namen seines Autors der Nachwelt überliefernd. Eine Paradoxie, die sich noch weiter zuspitzt, wenn man sich fragt, ob das Buch wohl jemals so berühmt geworden wäre, wie es dann hundert Jahre später geworden ist, wenn es n i c h t unter dem Pseudonym Bonaventura, sondern unter dem Namen seines Autors erschienen wäre. Das aber führt zugleich auf eine weitere, für die Erkenntnis seines Charakters wichtige Frage: konnte denn dieses Buch unter dem Namen seines Autors erscheinen? Hätte es auf dem Titelblatt heißen können: ‹Nachtwachen. Von August Klingemann› und dann genauso anfangen können, wie es anfängt – nämlich mit der Überschrift «Erste Nachtwache» und dem ersten Satz des Textes: *Die Nachtstunde schlug; ich hüllte mich in meine abenteuerliche Vermummung, nahm die Pike und das Horn zur Hand* usw. – und so fortfahren können bis zum Schluß, bis zur Rede des Nachtwächters auf dem Kirchhof? Ganz undenkbar ist es nicht, aber doch schwer vorstellbar. Es wäre etwa so, wie wenn Jean Pauls ‹Giannozzo› erschienen wäre mit dem Titelblatt «Luftfahrten. Von Jean Paul» und unmittelbar darauf die erste Kapitelüberschrift – «Erste Fahrt» – und das erste Kapitel selbst gefolgt wären, darauf wieder das zweite Kapitel und so fort bis zum letzten Kapitel, der «Vierzehnten Fahrt». Was auf diese Weise deutlich wird, ist eine an sich sehr einfache, aber doch beachtenswerte Eigenschaft unseres Buches, ein eigentümlicher Mangel und zugleich eine eigentümliche Konsequenz seiner ganzen Anlage: es fehlt in diesem Buch jeder, auch der geringste Ansatz zu einer ‹Vorstellung› der Hauptfigur, wie sie im Fall des Jean Paulschen ‹Giannozzo› ja schon im Titel gegeben ist: ‹Des Luftschiffers Giannozzo Seebuch›, des weiteren in der ‹Vorrede›, die von Jean Paul selbst unterzeichnet ist, sogar mit seinem vollen Namen, über-

---

[16] Staats- und Universitätsbibliothek Hamburg, Handschriftenabteilung.

[17] Kunst und Natur, Bd. 1, S. 466: «Eine frühere literarische Differenz zwischen uns, wurde Gesprächsweise ausgeglichen (...)». Unmittelbar darauf eine «Nachschrift» über die soeben eingetroffene Nachricht von Kotzebues Ermordung am 23. 3. 1819.

dies noch datiert ist: «Berlin, den 1sten Ostertag 1801» und deren erster Satz lautet: «Der ganze komische Anhang wird von der Geschichte eines Reisenden nicht zu Wasser, sondern zu Luft gefüllt.» Es ist – so ließe sich diese Eigenart der ‹Nachtwachen›, sowohl ihrer Anlage als ihrer Publikationsweise, vielleicht am anschaulichsten beschreiben – wie wenn Jean Paul nur den Giannozzo-Text selbst, nur das «Seebuch», publiziert hätte, überdies aber statt des erläuternden, ja sogar ‹vorstellenden› Titels, den ich eben zitierte, einen so wortkargen wie den Titel unseres Buchs gewählt hätte – einen Titel, der noch dazu auf die Benennung der einzelnen Kapitel zurückgreift – also wenn er etwa den Titel ‹Luftfahrten› gewählt hätte, und überdies seinen eigenen Namen verschwiegen und statt dessen ein Pseudonym auf das Titelblatt hätte setzen lassen. Kürzer gesagt, zugleich anknüpfend an das, was oben über die Welt gesagt wurde, in der Klingemann sich bewegte: er gibt nur die ‹Rolle› selbst, nicht einmal ein Personenverzeichnis, geschweige denn eine Einführung, auch keine Szenen- oder Regieanweisungen, denn jedes Wort, auch das über Ort und Stunde, auch das über die *abenteuerliche Vermummung* der Hauptperson Gesagte, ist ja ein Wort dieser Hauptperson selbst, ist Bestandteil dieser einen ‹Rolle›. Eben damit legte er den Grund für ein Mißverständnis oder genauer: die Möglichkeit eines Mißverständnisses, das wir hier nicht mehr ausführlich zu erörtern und zu belegen brauchen: für die Möglichkeit, das Buch als unmittelbare Äußerung des Autors selbst, als Äußerung «Bonaventuras», zu verstehen und hinter diesem Namen die Gestalt eines Mannes zu sehen oder zu suchen, der den Inhalt dieses Buches oder doch einen Teil davon, vielleicht nicht gerade die nächtlichen Gänge mit Pike und Horn, aber doch manches andere von dem hier Mitgeteilten selbst erlebt und erlitten habe. Bezeichnend für dieses Mißverständnis, mindestens aber ihm förderlich gewesen, ist bereits die nicht selten, auch auf manchen Neuausgaben zu findende Formulierung des Titels: «Die Nachtwachen des Bonaventura»[18]; eine Formulierung, die jedenfalls doppeldeutig ist, einerseits auf den Verfasser hinweist, andererseits die Vorstellung, Bonaventura sei selbst jener Nachtwächter, zumindest nicht ausschließt.

Es ist nun nicht zu bestreiten – und damit komme ich zu den positiven Qualitäten des Buchs – daß ihm die Durchführung dieser ‹Rolle› vortrefflich gelungen ist, wie ja nicht zuletzt die Wirkungsgeschichte beweist, eben durch die starken, wenn auch späten Wirkungen, die von ihm ausgingen. Ebenso wie der Pfaffe am Bett des *sterbenden Freigeists* bis zuletzt *seiner Teufelsrolle getreu* bleibt, ebenso bleibt der Nachtwächter selbst von der ersten bis zur letzten *Nachtwache* seiner Rolle getreu: der Rolle

---

[18] Dies der Titel der Ausgaben von Franz Schultz (Leipzig 1909) und von Renate Riemeck (Wedel 1946, später: Frechen/Köln 1955).

des bärbeißigen, in allen Bereichen der Gesellschaft ‹unmöglichen› Sonder-
lings und Querkopfs, der über alle Zünfte und Stände – Pfaffen, Dokto-
ren, Juristen, Philosophen, Bauern, Minister und Fürsten – seinen Spott
ausgießt und in allen Metiers, mit denen er es versucht hat, als Poet,
Bänkelsänger, Schauspieler und Marionettendirekteur, gescheitert ist,
sogar im Tollhaus nicht lange geduldet wird und schließlich als Nachtwächter eine einigermaßen zu ihm passende Stelle gefunden hat. Er selbst
bezeichnet seine Rolle einmal als die eines *satirischen Stentors* (1. Nw.;
S. 6), womit zugleich die Gattung genannt ist, in deren Rahmen und mit
deren Maßen das Werk am ehesten zu beurteilen ist, wenn man ihm ge-
recht werden will: als Satire erreicht es unstreitig einen gewissen Rang,
den man sogar in Anbetracht der nicht gerade großen Zahl von guten
deutschen Satiren beachtlich nennen kann, während es in den eigentlich
erzählerischen, insbesondere den novellistischen Partien schwach, z. T.
ausgesprochen dilettantisch ist. Es reflektiert ja gelegentlich auch selbst
auf diese seine charakteristische Schwäche, mit einer Selbstironie, die wieder für das Buch im ganzen und zugleich für die Intelligenz seines Autors
spricht, z. B. am Anfang der sechsten *Nachtwache*, nachdem die Geschichte von den zwei Brüdern zu Ende gebracht ist: *Mir ists nun einmal
nicht gegeben, und die kurze simple Mordgeschichte hat mich Schweiß
und Mühe genug gekostet, und sieht doch immer noch kraus und bunt
genug aus* (6. Nw.; S. 48).

Ironien dieser Art, mit der in ihnen sich manifestierenden Reflexion des
Werks auf sich selbst, sind es zugleich, wodurch das Buch formal mit der
Romantik zusammenhängt – der Jenaer Romantik, der Romantik der
Tieckschen Lustspiele und des Schlegelschen Ironiebegriffs, die in Fichtes
‹Wissenschaftslehre› ihr philosophisches Zentrum hatte. Dazu kommen
die entsprechenden Beziehungen auf der thematischen Ebene: die direkten
Anspielungen auf Fichtes Philosophie, die Hinweise auf das Ich als das
Behältnis, in das die Welt zusammengedrängt sei wie *eine große Iliade* in
ein *Taschenformat* (9. Nw.; S. 83), so daß *alles in uns selbst* liegt und
außer uns nichts Reelles ist, wie Hamlet an Ophelia schreibt (14. Nw.;
S. 118), aber auch die Reflexionen über das eigene Dasein als Rolle innerhalb eines Schauspiels, wie wir sie in so viel breiterer, variationen-
reicherer Ausführung in den ‹Freimüthigkeiten› wiederfanden, schließlich
auch und nicht zuletzt die Anknüpfungen an Shakespeare und das Lieb-
lingsdrama der Frühromantik, den ‹Hamlet›. Dies also wäre, neben Jean
Paul und nach ihm, der zweite Fixpunkt für eine historische Ortsbestimmung: Fichte und nicht Schelling, von dem in der Tat, wie Dilthey erkannte, «keine Spur» zu finden ist, die frühere Romantik und nicht die
spätere, von Mythologie, Naturphilosophie, Magnetismus, Somnambu-
lismus und Ähnlichem bestimmte, mit einem Wort: die Romantik der
‹Athenäums›-Periode, freilich schon verblaßt und im Begriff, zur Reminis-

zenz zu werden, wie sie es ja für den Autor selbst unter der Wirkung der
räumlichen wie der zeitlichen Distanz allmählich wurde. Alle diese Beziehungen sind denn auch im Werk selbst nur mit entsprechend blassen,
verwischten Zügen ausgedrückt, treten aber doch deutlich hervor auf dem
Hintergrund der gesamten literarischen Entwicklung des Autors: der
übrigen Werke, von denen im vorigen die Rede war, des gescheiterten
Versuchs, selber eine Zeitschrift in der Nachfolge des ‹Athenäums› zu
begründen, der biographischen Fakten, die wir andeuteten: des Aufent-
halts in Jena während der ‹Athenäums›-Periode, der Beziehungen zu
Brentano und zu August Winkelmann, dem Freunde Brentanos, der in
dessen Briefen aus der Jenaer und der Göttinger Zeit eine merkwürdig
dominierende Rolle spielt[19].

Als weiteres für die Bestimmung des historischen Orts wichtiges Datum
ergab sich eine negative, polemische Beziehung: die zu Kotzebue und zum
Kotzebueschen Familiendrama, auch sie freilich hineingehörend in den
oben angedeuteten Zusammenhang mit Jena, sich herschreibend aus der

---

[19] Winkelmann ist übrigens nicht nur im ‹Memnon›, sondern auch in Musen-
almanachen und dgl., meist anonym oder pseudonym, mit literarischen Beiträgen aufgetreten, überdies als Verfasser von medizinischen Fachschriften; er starb
1806, erst sechsundzwanzigjährig, als Professor der Medizin in Braunschweig.
– Brentano betreffend, sei hier nur erinnert an die seit E. Frank (1912) vieldis-
kutierte ‹Godwi›-Parallele: *Ein paarmale jagte man mich aus Kirchen, weil ich
dort lachte, und eben so oft aus Freudenhäusern, weil ich drin beten wollte*
(7. Nw.; S. 58), wozu erstmals von E. Frank herangezogen wurde: ‹Godwi›,
2. Teil, 27. Kap.: «(...) nirgends möchte ich so gerne laut sprechen oder pfei-
fen, als in der Kirche, nicht um gehört zu werden, sondern um es zu hören, –
ich möchte auch wohl gerne in einem lüderlichen Hause beten (...)»; eine
Parallele, die zweifellos als Reminiszenz zu beurteilen ist (woran Berend, a. a.
O., S. 800, noch zweifelte), denn natürlich kannte Klingemann den ‹Godwi›.
Auch sonst erinnert ja manches an Brentano, so etwa in der Geschichte von den
zwei Brüdern der Name *Ponce*, die spanische Szenerie und besonders ein Detail aus der Schilderung der schlafenden Ines: *(...) und in das Saitenspiel (...)
schlangen sich braune Lockenkränze* (5. Nw.; S. 46, vgl. das ‹Godwi›-Gedicht:
«Um die Harfe sind Kränze geschlungen»). Manches deutet übrigens darauf
hin, daß Klingemann in dieser Geschichte, ebenso wie in ihrer Puppenspiel-
Variante in der 4. Nw., dem Jenaer Studienfreund noch dichter auf den Leib
rückt und Einzelheiten aus Brentanos und Sophie Mereaus Liebesleben ausplau-
dert; so schon die etwas sonderbare Einführung des Don Ponce: *Sein Bruder
Don Ponce dagegen war jungfräulich mild*, die auf die beiden Brentanoschen
Vornamen Clemens und Maria anspielen könnte, u.a.m. (Die Frage nach der
Identität der übrigen Personen bleibt ein Feld für reizvolle, aber einstweilen
unbeweisbare Vermutungen). – Auch daß er mit der Karolina der 4. Nw. auf
die berühmteste Trägerin dieses Namens hinzielt – mit naheliegenden Konse-
quenzen für die Identität von Ehemann und Liebhaber – ist ihm zuzutrauen.

Zeit des Verkehrs im Kreise der Romantiker (die ja alle in wenigen Dingen so einig miteinander waren wie in der Verachtung Kotzebues und der Ansicht, daß er zu «annihilieren» sei), aber doch mit erheblich kräftigeren Zügen ausgeprägt in der Handschrift der ‹Nachtwachen›, entsprechend der unverminderten, ja eher noch gesteigerten Aktualität des Themas. Denn wie oben, im biographischen Abriß, kurz gezeigt: der Kampf zwischen der «neuen» und der «alten» Schule, zwischen der pro- und der antiromantischen Partei war in vollem Gange um das Jahr 1804, zumal seit sich im ‹Freimüthigen› Kotzebues und Merkels und in der ‹Eleganten Welt› Karl Spaziers zwei Zentren gebildet hatten, die nun wie Bastionen einander gegenüberstanden: hier das Zentrum der ‹Alten›, der Antiromantiker, derer, die Autoritäten wie Wieland gegen die Schlegelianer, gelegentlich auch gegen Goethe ausspielten; dort das Zentrum der ‹Neuen›, wo man für Tieck und gegen Kotzebue plädierte, wo auch Jean Paul mit Wohlwollen und Verständnis rezensiert wurde – während er im ‹Freimüthigen› ausgesprochen mißgünstig besprochen zu werden pflegte – wo gelegentlich auch Autoren wie A. W. Schlegel, Jean Paul selbst, Brentano auftraten, und nicht nur gelegentlich, sondern als regelmäßiger Mitarbeiter[20] August Klingemann. Damit dürfte aber auch die unmittelbare Vorgeschichte unseres Buchs einigermaßen, wenn auch nicht ohne einen Rest von Unsicherheit, aufgehellt sein. Denn es liegt zumindest nahe, anzunehmen, daß F. Dienemann, der junge Verleger, als er mit seinem Roman-Unternehmen ins Stocken geraten war und sich entschloß – wie Varnhagen schreibt – «an einige ihm dem Namen nach bekannte Anhänger der neuen Schule zu schreiben und sie dringend um Beiträge zu bitten, die er stracks und gut bezahlen wollte», nicht nur an die von Varnhagen genannten Autoren, sondern auch an den von ihm nicht genannten Klingemann schrieb; wobei auch daran zu denken ist, daß Dienemann in der ‹Eleganten Welt› häufig für seine Verlagsartikel durch Annoncen werben ließ. Und es liegt weiterhin nahe genug, anzunehmen, daß Klingemann auf dieses Anerbieten einging. Auch an den früher erwähnten Antagonismus zwischen dem Verlag Dienemann und dem ‹Freimüthigen› wird man dabei denken müssen, insbesondere an die Polemik gegen Dienemann, die am 4. Februar 1803 im ‹Freimüthigen‹ erschienen und mit dem Pseudonym «Justus Hilarius» unterzeichnet war. Ganz zweifellos wußte Dienemann, daß er hier etwas mit Klingemann gemein-

---

[20] Die Bedeutung seiner Mitarbeit für diese Zeitung geht u.a. aus einem Brief hervor, den nach dem Tode Karl Spaziers (19. 1. 1805) dessen Witwe, die die Zeitung zusammen mit ihrem Schwager Mahlmann fortführte, an Klingemann schrieb (am 25. 1. 1805) und in dem es heißt: «Ich weiß, wie Spazier Ihre Theilnahme anschlug, wie Ihr Name ihm wohlthat, wenn er ihn fand unter den Sachen, die einliefen.» (Abgedruckt in: P. Zimmermann, a. a. O., Braunschw. Magazin, Jg. 1923, Sp. 23 f.)

sam hatte, nämlich dieselben Feinde: die «Herren Merkel und Kotzebue»; die Fehde zwischen ihnen und Klingemann hatte in den Spalten der ‹Eleganten Welt› und des ‹Freimüthigen›, ebenso wie in Merkels Frauenzimmer-Briefen, einen zu sichtbaren und zu ausführlichen Niederschlag gefunden, als daß sie einem Verleger, der so wie Dienemann an diesen Dingen beteiligt war, hätte entgehen können. Denkbar sogar, daß er schon vorher, etwa um den Anfang des Jahres 1803, mit Klingemann – oder auch dieser mit ihm – Beziehungen angeknüpft hatte. Nicht nur eine Anspielung auf die Zeitschrift ‹Apollon› in den 1803 entstandenen ‹Freimüthigkeiten›[21] kann einen solchen Gedanken nahelegen, sondern auch der Name, unter dem Kotzebue in den ‹Freimüthigkeiten› erscheint: der Name «Hilarius», der ja vielleicht, sogar wahrscheinlich auf eben diese speziell gegen Dienemann gerichtete Polemik im ‹Freimüthigen› vom 4. Februar 1803 zurückgeht. Zumindest zeigt beides zusammen, daß Klingemann schon 1803 von Dienemanns Verlag Notiz genommen und ein gewisses Interesse für ihn gewonnen hatte. Dafür freilich und zugleich dafür, daß er insbesondere auch von dem ‹Romanen-Journal› desselben Verlages Kenntnis genommen hatte, spricht noch ein weiterer Umstand: wie früher schon erwähnt, war in diesem ‹Journal von neuen deutschen Original Romanen›, als erste Lieferung des ersten Jahrgangs übrigens, ein Werk seines Braunschweiger Jugendfreundes Franz Horn[22] erschienen, übrigens keineswegs die einzige Publikation Franz Horns im Verlag Dienemann. All das zeigt jedenfalls, daß der Peniger Verlag für Klingemann im Jahr 1804 keine unbekannte Größe war und daß, sollte Dienemann n i c h t in jener Notlage auch an Klingemann geschrieben haben, er doch seinerseits sehr wohl auf den Gedanken kommen konnte, sich wegen des Drucks der ‹Nachtwachen› an den jungen Dienemann zu wenden. Freilich deuten doch die Spuren einer gewissen Eile, namentlich vom Anfang der zehnten *Nachtwache* an (s. o.), darauf hin, daß der Autor unter dem Druck einer Terminverpflichtung dem Verleger gegenüber arbeitete, womit es wahrscheinlicher wird, daß die Anknüpfung – auch in diesem Falle – von Dienemann ausging.

Die Polemik gegen Kotzebue, die Fehde mit Merkel, mit ihrem langen, zähen Hin und Her von Angriffen und Gegenangriffen, Erklärungen und Gegenerklärungen, das gegen beide gerichtete satirische Lustspiel, das

---

[21] «Theobald: ‹(...) Kennst du den Apollo?› Max: ‹Das wunderliche Journal, von dem Ihr meintet, daß nichts daraus werden würde?›» (S. 27). Ein Hinweis auf diese Anspielung bereits bei Michel (a. a. O., S. VII); ferner bei Pfeiffer-Belli, a. a. O. (Euph. 26. Bd., 1925), S. 615.

[22] Viktors Wallfahrten. Penig 1802. Im selben Verlag waren von F. Horn außerdem zwei Seneca-Übersetzungen, ‹Thyestes› (1802) und ‹Die Trojanerinnen› (1803), sowie eine Schrift ‹Über Carlo Gozzi's dramatische Poesie› (1803) erschienen.

Klingemann als «blöden Mitbewerber um den vom Herrn v. Kotzebue ausgesetzten Preis» in die Welt hinausschickte – all das zeigt aber noch eines: es zeigt, daß die ‹Rolle›, von der oben die Rede war, die Rolle des streitbaren, überall Händel anfangenden *Kerls*, wie sie in den ‹Nachtwachen› durchgeführt ist, sicher nicht zufällig von ihrem Autor gewählt wurde, er selbst nicht ohne Beziehung zu ihr war, kurz: daß diese Rolle des *satirischen Stentors* ihm ‹lag›. Ich erinnere auch an den – früher schon einmal herangezogenen – Anfang des ersten der Klingemannschen ‹Literaturbriefe› (desselben Briefs, in dem er die ‹Flegeljahre› den Lesern und namentlich den Leserinnen der ‹Eleganten Welt› vorstellt): «Ich soll den Harnisch ablegen, fordern Sie, und nur gleichsam im Tanzkleide mit Ihnen durch das Gebiet der schönen Literatur umherstreifen! Wahrlich das ist in unserer Zeit schwer zu versprechen; indeß mag es seyn, weil eine Frau es fordert. Ich hoffe aber doch auf Ihre Nachsicht, wenn mich meine Unart, Händel zu suchen, dann und wann unerwartet überraschen sollte.»[23] Ähnlich hatte er schon 1802, in der Schrift über Schillers ‹Jungfrau von Orleans›, geschrieben, als er im Begriff war, sich dem eigentlichen Thema dieser Schrift zuzuwenden, übrigens ebenfalls in Briefform: «Erlauben Sie mir dabei aber einen eigenen Weg, weil ich von je her das Kriegführen sehr geliebt habe. – Wir wollen nämlich hören, was Merkel, wenn er sich nur selbst getreu bleiben will, über diese Tragödie sagen muß.»[24] Auf einem satirischen Kupferstich mit der Unterschrift ‹Versuch auf den Parnaß zu gelangen›, der 1803 in einer Publikation aus dem Kreis um Merkel und Kotzebue erschienen ist und der die ganze Gesellschaft der Romantiker und Romantikanhänger in Karikaturen zeigt, findet man Klingemann denn auch entsprechend dargestellt: als Figurine in kindlicher Kleidung, zum Zeichen seiner jugendlichen Unreife, mit einem «Fallhütchen» auf dem Kopf und einem gezogenen Degen in der Hand, den er gegen den gewaltig vor ihm aufragenden Merkel zückt. Im Text des Pasquills, der als Erläuterung des Kupferstichs angelegt ist, heißt es dazu: «Der größre M a n n mit der bloßen K l i n g e / Glaubt von sich selber Wunderdinge, / Spricht sehr laut und gewaltig viel, / Schreibt über Kunst und Komödienspiel, / Und stellt mit ritterlichem Sinn / Sich zum ungleichen Kampfe hin, / um – –», und darauf folgt in Prosa eine Anspielung auf den Klingemannschen «Brief an den Herrn Garlieb Merkel», der im Intelligenzblatt der ‹Eleganten Welt› vom 22. 1. 1803 erschienen war: «einem naseweisen, ihn verfolgenden Kritiker seine l i t e r ä r i s c h e E x i s t e n z z u b e w e i s e n »[25].

---

[23] ‹El. Welt› v. 7. 6. 1804.
[24] Über Schillers Tragödie: Die Jungfrau von Orleans, Leipzig 1802, S. 47 f. (Vgl. auch oben S. 41).
[25] Ansichten der Literatur und Kunst unsres Zeitalters. 1. Heft. Mit einem

«Wahrlich das ist in unserer Zeit schwer zu versprechen» – die Art, wie hier das endgültige Ablegen des «Harnischs» verweigert wird oder wie am Ende desselben Aufsatzes der Erfolg Kotzebues auf den «Dilettantismus» zurückgeführt wird, der «in jeder Rücksicht den Karakter der Zeit» ausmache[26], läßt nun doch, zusammen mit vielen ähnlichen, mit vollem Namen gezeichneten Äußerungen Klingemanns, Züge einer gewissen – wenn nicht Originalität, so doch – Individualität erkennen. Unverkennbar ist vor allem ein entschiedener Hang zur Polemik, der sich immer wieder in Ausfällen gegen die Zeit und ihren «Karakter» Luft macht: so wenn er etwa, um nur an einige weitere Beispiele aus den Artikeln in der ‹Eleganten Welt› zu erinnern, in einem ‹Postskriptum› den spätaufkläre-

Kupfer. Deutschland 1803. (Seiten- und zeilengetreuer Neudruck: Weimar (Gesellschaft der Bibliophilen) 1903, hrsg. v. G. Witkowski. Danach – S. 38 – das Zitat). In der dichtgedrängten Gruppe von sechs kleinen Figuren, in der Klingemann steht, befinden sich übrigens außer ihm die drei Herausgeber des ‹Apollon›, Sophie Bernhardi und eine in der Erläuterung als «geistlicher Herr» bezeichnete und entsprechend gekleidete Figur, der zwei Verse aus den ‹Letzten Worten des Pfarrers zu Drottning› als Spruchband in den Mund gelegt sind. Bild und Text lassen darauf schließen, daß die Urheber des Pasquills nicht wußten, daß Schelling der Verfasser dieses Gedichts war, vielmehr vermutlich der Meinung waren, es sei, ebenso wie die anderen unter demselben Pseudonym am selben Ort erschienenen Gedichte, von einem wirklichen Pfarrer verfaßt; das Ganze jedenfalls ein Anzeichen dafür, daß im Jahr 1803 die Identität jenes im Schlegel-Tieckschen Musenalmanach aufgetretenen Bonaventura weithin unbekannt war. Ob Klingemann durch Betrachtung dieses Kupfers oder Lektüre der Erläuterung, wo direkt auf ihn jener «geistliche Herr» folgt, zur Wahl des Pseudonyms für die ‹Nachtwachen› angeregt wurde? Möglich ist es, aber nicht sehr wahrscheinlich, schon in Anbetracht der offenbar sehr geringen Verbreitung dieses Pasquills (vgl. G. Witkowski im Nachwort des Neudrucks, S. 59, über die «ungemeine Seltenheit» der Schrift).

[26] Anlaß ist das Erscheinen von Kotzebues ‹Erinnerungen aus Paris im Jahre 1804›. Nachtragsweise sei hier vermerkt, daß auch der Kotzebuesche Parisaufenthalt, über den dieser schon in einer Artikelserie im ‹Freimüthigen› (16. 1. – 14. 4. 1804) berichtet hatte, seinen Niederschlag in den ‹Nachtwachen› gefunden hat, nämlich in der Antikensaal-Episode, besonders an der Stelle, wo der *kleine Dilettant* an einer *medicäischen Venus ohne Arme, mühsam hinaufklettert, um, wie es schien, mit gespiztem Munde und fast thränend, ihr den Hintern, als den bekanntlich gelungensten Kunsttheil dieser Göttin zu küssen* (13. Nw.; S. 109). Im ‹Freimüthigen› vom 26./27. 3. 1804 war Kotzebues Bericht über seinen Besuch in der «Gallerie der Antiken, Statüen, Büsten, Basreliefs» des «Museum Napoleon» erschienen, wo es zur Venus von Medici heißt: «Was kann ich denn dafür, daß diese V e n u s mir wie ein ganz artiges Kammermädchen vorkommt, die von dem jungen Herrn von Hause im höchsten Negligé überrascht wird, und sich seinem lüsternen Blicke nicht ganz ernstlich zu entziehen sucht? (...)»

rischen Berliner Kreis um den ‹Freimüthigen› als «unwillkührliche Beiträge zur grotesk komischen Literatur unsers Zeitalters» bezeichnet und
gleichzeitig beklagt, daß «das Komische sich so sehr unter uns verlohren
hat, daß selbst Herr von Kotzebue es nicht durch einen Preis von 100
Friedrich-d'oren wiederzufinden vermogte», so daß man die «etwanigen
Reste aus allen Winkeln zusammensuchen» müsse[27]; wenn er den Weg
schildert, auf dem Ludwig Tieck es mit dem Zeitalter «verdarb», diesem
Zeitalter, «in dem man nur verständig und mit Mäßigung fortgeführt,
nicht aber wild fortgerissen werden will»; oder wenn er in demselben
Artikel über Tieck das Ideal einer Komödie entwirft, die es darauf anlegte,
«sich dem herrschenden Zeitgeschmacke auf eine boshafte Weise anzuschmiegen, und diesen so gleichsam durch sich selbst zu vernichten», wobei es nichts ausmachen würde, «wenn die s o g e n a n n t e n G e b i l-
d e t e n auch die Nase dabei rümpften»[28]. Womit zugleich ein weiterer
Zug angedeutet ist, der offenbar ebenfalls zur Individualität dieses Autors
gehört: die Lust am Possenspiel im doppelten Sinne des Wortes: einmal
in dem des volkstümlichen komischen Theaterstücks[29], wie er selbst eines
in den ‹Freimüthigkeiten› vorgelegt hatte, freilich ohne jedes Echo – also
jener Art von Stück, für die die Figur des Harlekin oder Hanswurst
charakteristisch ist und von der auch in den ‹Nachtwachen› so oft die
Rede ist – zum anderen aber auch im Sinne der Redewendung vom ‹Possen›, den man jemandem spielt, im Sinne von ‹Schabernack› und ‹hinters
Licht führen›, wobei eine Beimischung von Bosheit nicht ausgeschlossen
ist. All dies wird ja von dem Hanswurst in Klingemanns Lustspiel ad
oculos demonstriert, namentlich in der «Apologie der Thränen», wo er
nichts anderes tut, als sich «dem herrschenden Zeitgeschmacke auf eine
boshafte Weise anzuschmiegen», und zwar mit bestem Erfolg: alles
klatscht und ist gerührt, er aber «lacht boshaft ins Fäustchen» und geht
ab (wozu sich im Puppenspiel in der vierten *Nachtwache* die fast wörtliche Entsprechung vom *hämisch ins Fäustchen* lachenden Hanswurst
fand). Aber auch Klingemanns schon so früh bezeugte Vorliebe für Theaterspiel überhaupt, für Maske und Kothurn, für Verkleidung, *abenteuerliche Vermummung* und Verstellung wird man im selben Zusammenhang
sehen dürfen. Höchst bezeichnend eine der wenigen Kindheitserinnerun-
gen in seinen Schriften, die Schilderung einer der ersten Begegnungen

---

[27] ‹El. Welt› v. 23. 10. 1804.
[28] Einige Worte über Ludwig Tieck. Auf Veranlassung seines Lustspiels:
Oktavianus. (‹El. Welt› v. 6./8. 9. 1804).
[29] Noch 1809 schreibt er an den Hamburger Theaterdirektor F. L. Schmidt:
«Ich hätte Lust, mich der Ausarbeitung einer derben Posse zu unterziehen, die
in Deutschland ganz untergegangen ist (...)» (Hermann Uhde [Hrsg.]: Denk-
würdigkeiten des Schauspielers, Schauspieldichters und Schauspieldirektors
Friedrich Ludwig Schmidt, Stuttgart ²1878, S. 277.)

des Knaben mit dem Theater: «Herrn Pauly erinnere ich mich übrigens noch in meiner Knabenzeit als Heldenspieler in Braunschweig gesehen zu haben, und der Moment in seinem F i e s k o, wo er mit verstellter Stimme und tief in den Mantel verhüllt, den alten Doria, unter dem Balkon seines Pallastes stehend, warnt, verfolgte mich die ganze Nacht darauf, bei einer heftig gereizten Phantasie, mit Fieberträumen.»[30] ‹Die Maske› lautet der Titel eines seiner Jugenddramen, eben des Dramas, das als erstes seiner Stücke aufgeführt wurde – auf Goethes Veranlassung, wie erwähnt – und mit dem er zum erstenmal einen gewissen Erfolg hatte. Auch an die Faszination durch den ‹Schwarzen Ritter› in Schillers ‹Jungfrau von Orleans› wird man in diesem Zusammenhang erinnert, an den Versuch, «dem schwarzen Ritter durchs Visir zu schauen», dem er 1805 einen ganzen Aufsatz widmete, nachdem er dasselbe Thema schon in seiner ‹Jungfrau von Orleans›-Schrift von 1802 behandelt hatte. Aber auch an die Art seines literarischen Auftretens wird man hier denken dürfen: an das anonyme Erscheinen schon jenes Trauerspiels ‹Die Maske›, an den fingierten Brief des Königs Andrason aus Goethes ‹Triumph der Empfindsamkeit›, in dem Merkulo, alias Merkel, als «der Polichinell unserer Literatur» der Aufmerksamkeit des Herausgebers der ‹Eleganten Welt› empfohlen wird, an die Art, wie er sein satirisches Lustspiel gegen Merkel und Kotzebue hinausgehen ließ – anonym und mit sichtlicher Freude an der Rolle des «blöden Mitbewerbers um den vom Herrn v. Kotzebue ausgesetzten Preis» – und schließlich auch an die Wahl des Pseudonyms «Bonaventura», das er zweifellos aus dem Schlegel-Tieckschen Musenalmanach kannte, sei es direkt, durch eigene Lektüre, oder indirekt, durch eine Rezension des Almanachs, und das er dann für die Publikation der ‹Nachtwachen› benutzte, vielleicht im Gedanken an das «schauderhafte, mitternächtliche Gemählde», als das die ‹Letzten Worte des Pfarrers zu Drottning› in einer Rezension in der ‹Eleganten Welt› bezeichnet werden[31], aber wahrscheinlich, ohne zu wissen, wer jener erste Bonaventura war; denn nach allem, was die reiche Überlieferung zur Jenaer Romantik erkennen läßt, gehörte Klingemann sicherlich nicht, auch während seiner Jenaer Zeit nicht, zum engeren Kreis um die beiden Herausgeber des Almanachs. Auch von den ersten Einreihungen der ‹Nachtwachen› (zusammen mit den Almanach-Gedichten) unter die Werke Schellings in gelehrten Nachschlagewerken, bei Meusel und Raßmann,

---

[30] Kunst und Natur, 3. Bd., Braunschweig 1828, S. 79.
[31] ‹El. Welt› v. 16. 3. 1802, wo es heißt: «D i e l e t z t e n W o r t e d e s P f a r r e r s z u D r o t t n i n g auf See l and von Bonaventura sind ein schauderhaftes, mitternächtliches Gemählde», der Name «Bonaventura» also genannt wird. Die Verfasserschaft der (anonym erschienenen) Rezension ist mir unklar.

wird er, längst in Amt und Würden eines Theaterdirektors und entsprechend beschäftigt, kaum Kenntnis bekommen haben: das Werk war vergessen, hatte schon zur Zeit seines Erscheinens nicht das geringste Aufsehen erregt, und eine Veranlassung, sich als sein Verfasser zu erkennen zu geben, bestand für ihn in jenen frühen Jahren ebensowenig wie zu seinen späteren Lebzeiten.

Wahrscheinlich, ohne zu wissen, wer jener erste Bonaventura war: so wird man sagen müssen, denn ganz läßt es sich natürlich nicht ausschließen, d a ß er es wußte – womit sich die Wahl des Pseudonyms «Bonaventura» für die ‹Nachtwachen› als ein Schelling (und zugleich einer großen späteren Leserschaft) gespielter ‹Possen› darstellte; ein Possen, für den allerdings einstweilen keinerlei Grund ersichtlich oder auch nur zu vermuten wäre. Denn nichts in den erhaltenen Dokumenten läßt irgendetwas erkennen von einer persönlichen Beziehung zwischen den beiden Männern, die da eine Zeitlang in derselben Universitätsstadt lebten, der eine als berühmter Philosoph und Professor, der andere als schriftstellernder, mit den Schwierigkeiten eines debütierenden Autors (7. Nw.; S. 59) kämpfender Jurastudent, der gelegentlich die Vorlesungen des berühmten Professors besucht haben mag. Es ist auch – die unwahrscheinliche Möglichkeit einmal vorausgesetzt, daß er «es wußte» – schwer einzusehen, worin der Witz eines solchen ‹Possens› bestanden haben könnte, in was für einer Schädigung des ersten Bonaventura oder was für einem Vorteil für den zweiten, es sei denn, man nimmt (um das Spiel der abenteuerlichen Kombinationen noch ein Stück weit fortzusetzen) einmal an, daß dieser durch die Berühmtheit des ersten gleichsam incognito in die Unsterblichkeit einzugehen gedachte, von der in den ‹Nachtwachen› so oft die Rede ist, von der der Poet in der letzten Nachtwache sagt, sie sei widerspänstig, während ein anderer, an früherer Stelle auftretender, der schon berühmt geworden ist, freilich auf fragwürdige Weise, dem Nachtwächter erklärt: Mein Freund! – sagte er – ich seze der Unsterblichkeit nach, und werde von ihr nachgesezt! Er selbst wird es wissen, wie schwer es ist berühmt zu werden, wie noch unendlich schwerer aber zu leben. Worauf er erzählt, auf welche Weise ihm schließlich das eine wie das andere gelungen sei: er habe gefunden, daß er Kants Nase, Göthens Augen, Lessings Stirn, Schillers Mund, und den Hintern mehrerer berühmter Männer habe, habe darauf aufmerksam gemacht – mit Erfolg: er fand Eingang – habe sodann an große Geister um alten abgelegten Trödel geschrieben, und das Glück habe ihm so wohl gewollt, daß er jetzt in Schuhen einherschreite in denen einst Kant eigenfüßig ging, am Tage Göthens Hut auf Lessings Perücke setze, und zu Abends Schillers Schlafmütze trage. Ja, er sei noch weiter gegangen und habe weinen wie Kotzebue und niesen wie Tiek gelernt; es sei auch keine Spiegelfechterei, wenn er erzähle, daß jemand, vor dem er einst wie Göthe mit verkehrt gesetztem Hute und in den Rockfalten ver-

borgenen Händen einherwandelte, ihm *die Versicherung gab, das amüsire*
ihn mehr, als Göthens neueste Schriften (12. Nw.; S. 100 f.): das Ganze
eine bemerkenswerte Variation des Themas von der Nachahmung «aller
Dichter», die wie eine Selbstpersiflage des Autors klingt (zugleich beinahe
wie eine Vorahnung des Weges, auf dem er selbst *Eingang* finden sollte
bei einem späteren Publikum: mit Schellings Decknamen und einer Fülle
von Anleihen aus den Arsenalen Jean Pauls, aus dessen *poetischer Schatz-*
kammer, um die Dankesworte des Teufels (S. 148) nochmals zu zitieren),
und die zumindest eines sehr deutlich zeigt: daß es auch für den Autor der
‹Nachtwachen› ein ‹Thema› war.

Doch wie gesagt: wahrscheinlicher ist es, nach allem, was die Quellen
besagen, daß er «es» nicht wußte, daß er nur das Pseudonym als solches
kennengelernt hatte, es aufgriff, vielleicht fasziniert durch den geheimnis-
vollen, dem ursprünglichen Wortsinne nach ja auch verheißungsvollen
Klang dieses Namens, und es benutzte, um hinter dieser *vorgehaltenen*
Göttermaske (14. Nw.; S. 116) seine eigenen Spiele zu treiben. Er mochte
besondere Gründe zu einer solchen, besonders schwer zu durchschauen-
den Tarnung haben, Gründe, die vielleicht mit mancherlei persönlichen
Indiskretionen zusammenhängen, wie wir sie andeuteten, sicher aber
auch mit der alten Freude am Versteckspiel als solchem, die sich in so
vielen Äußerungen dieses Autors bekundet, aber auch durch eine Äußerung ü b e r ihn, und zwar eine aus allernächster Nähe stammende, bezeugt
wird: durch das Denkmal, das ihm sein Freund Winkelmann im Anhang
zu Brentanos ‹Godwi›, in den ‹Nachrichten von den Lebensumständen des
verstorbenen Maria›[32] (1801), gesetzt hat, wo der Reihe nach die Freunde
des «verstorbenen Maria» gewürdigt werden, mit einer Feierlichkeit, die
Winkelmann auch sonst eigen war, die aber hier durch den epitapharti-
gen Charakter dieses Anhanges eine Art Rechtfertigung erhält: erst Ludwig Tieck, dann Friedrich Schlegel und Johann Wilhelm Ritter und zuletzt auch Klingemann, jeder von ihnen durch die Anfangsbuchstaben
seines Namens gekennzeichnet. «Von einer andern Seite berührte ihn die
seltene Erhabenheit in Kl. Gemüthe», so beginnt Winkelmann (der sich
als Verfasser des Ganzen nicht nennt, aber in den Briefen Brentanos als
solcher genannt wird) die Würdigung seines Jugendfreundes, um dann
diesen selbst anzureden: «Trefflicher Spiegel Deines Zeitalters! Dich
weckte schon in früher Jugend der Genius, mit versteckten Erfindungen
dem Irrthume zu begegnen – was Du geschrieben, ist eine stille Persiflage
der herrschenden Schwäche –» und darauf folgt eine Reihe von Sätzen,
die den Vorwurf mangelnder «Originalität», indem sie ihn zurückweist,
nochmals bezeugt, als einen bereits damals, im Jahre 1801, erhobenen

---

[32] Godwi oder das steinerne Bild der Mutter. Ein verwilderter Roman von
Maria. Zweiter Band. Bremen 1802. S. 437.

Vorwurf: «mit kluger Mäßigung verhüllst Du Dein Vorhaben und Deine Originalität – viele sind Dir begegnet, ohne Dich zu erkennen – unbesonnene Kritiker tadeln Deine Werke, die sie dem Aeußern nach beurtheilen» – eine Reihe von Sätzen, die man, ebenso wie das feierlich-prophetische «die Nachwelt wird Dir danken» am Schluß dieser Gedenktafel, als Äußerung der Freundschaft eher denn als Äußerung der Kritik wird beurteilen müssen.

In einem seiner kürzeren Artikel in der ‹Eleganten Welt›, einer Rezension eines Werkes über die römische Geschichte, das sich der Form der «Totengespräche» bedient, die «Geister des Cicero, Cäsar, Brutus, der Gracchen usw.» hervorruft und sie «über das für und wider ihrer Handlungsweise in größern, zum Theil gehaltvollen Reden streiten» läßt, erklärt Klingemann, es sei zu bedauern, daß diese noch vor einigen Jahrzehnten in Deutschland so beliebte Art von «Dialogen» in letzter Zeit nicht weiter kultiviert worden sei – zu bedauern deshalb, weil «sie bei einigen, die sonst sehr empfindlich sind, das s c h e i n b a r e der poetischen Form für sich haben, und die Nemesis der Geschichte hinter dieser vorgehaltenen Larve kühner und schneller richten darf, so wie die Aegypter ihre Könige, wenn sie verstorben waren, der strengen Waage des Todtengerichts überantworteten»[33]. Damit, in gewisser Weise aber auch schon in den Worten Winkelmanns, ist ein weiteres Motiv für ein Auftreten mit «vorgehaltener Larve» angedeutet, das auch bei der Veröffentlichung der ‹Nachtwachen› mitgespielt haben dürfte, ebenso wie beim späteren Schweigen des Autors: die Rücksicht auf gewisse «sehr empfindliche» Leser, die Rücksicht auch auf Zensoren und einflußreiche Beamte an Fürstenhöfen wie demjenigen, an dessen «Obersanitätskollegium» Klingemann 1806, nach langer Wartezeit, eine Anstellung als «Registrator» erhielt und dem er auch später, auch als Theaterleiter, Rechenschaft schuldig blieb. Es gab in den ‹Nachtwachen› bedenkliche, ‹starke› Stellen genug, an denen solche «empfindlichen» Leser Anstoß nehmen konnten (unter ihnen diejenigen, die sich in der späteren Wirkungsgeschichte des Buches in einem anderen Sinne als seine ‹stärksten› Stellen erweisen sollten): angefangen von der Szene zwischen dem *sterbenden Freigeist*, der sich bis zuletzt *stark* hält, *wie Voltaire*, und dem in seiner *Teufelsrolle* auf ihn einredenden *Pfaffen*, über die *Weltgerichts*-Rede in der sechsten *Nacht*wache, die viele *geistliche und weltliche Herren erschrocken aus ihren Federn* fahren läßt, und ähnliche Reden, wie die in der vorletzten *Nacht*wache über das *hölzerne blutige Königshaupt*, das nur ein Marionettenhaupt ist, und den Draht, der als *Minister* fungiert, bis hin zu der *zornigen* Rede auf dem Kirchhof und ihrer Frage, ob etwa *über diesem zertrümmerten Pantheon ein neues herrlicheres* aufsteige, *in dem sich die*

---

[33] ‹El. Welt› v. 30. 7. 1805.

kolossalen ringsumher dasizenden Götter wirklich aufrichten können,
ohne sich an der niederen Decke die Köpfe zu zerstoßen. Es sind namentlich die satirischen Stellen des Buches, die ein Auftreten hinter «vorgehaltener Larve» aus derartigen Gründen nahelegten, darunter auch und nicht
zuletzt die Stellen, an denen die Satire versucht, der «Nemesis der Geschichte» zu Hilfe zu kommen und in ihrem Namen «kühner und schneller» zu «richten».

Anhang

Der folgende Ausschnitt aus dem später unter dem Titel ‹Freimüthigkeiten› gedruckten Lustspiel – über dieses siehe oben: Kapitel III, Abschnitt 3 – erschien in der ‹Zeitung für die elegante Welt› vom 14. April 1803 (45. Stück, Spalte 353–355). Die Szene wird im Buchabdruck als die erste der dritten «Handlung» bezeichnet, ist aber auch dort im wesentlichen die fünfte des ganzen Stücks geblieben (vgl. das oben dazu Ausgeführte); die weiteren Abweichungen der Buchfassung (= B) von diesem Vorabdruck verzeichnet der angefügte Kritische Apparat, unter Absehung von Änderungen der Interpunktion, vollständig.

«Ausstellung aus einer noch ungedruckten musikalischen Travestie:
der Dichter,
von August Klingemann.

Fünfte Szene.
Apollo, modern gekleidet, mit der Lyra in der Hand. Theobald.

Theobald.
Vortreflich! Kotzebues Wildfang, wie er leibt und lebt. Ihr müßt nur
5 etwas mehr Behendigkeit annehmen und nicht wie auf Kothurnen einherschreiten; man befindet sich bei uns ganz auf der flachen Erde, und damit gut. Gebt acht, wir bilden uns! Jedes Zeitalter hat seine Sitten.

Apollo.
O warum ward uns doch Unsterblichkeit zu Theil,
10   Und warum deckten seines Tempels Trümmer nicht
Zugleich den Gott, daß dies Geschlecht er schauen muß!

Theobald.
Das sind kritische Fragen! Ich bedaure Euch; denn es muß einem Gotte sehr üble Laune machen, wenn er keinen Tempel mehr hat. Indeß ist doch
15 noch vieles zu gewinnen. – Fürs erste legt diese steife Sprache ab – ich glaube es sind Trimeter! Alles muß jetzt behende und natürlich seyn; es versuchten es seit kurzer Zeit zwar einige Dichter, ihre Schauspiele in Jamben zu schreiben, aber man liebt das doch im Ganzen nicht. Leichter

Dialog, Prosa, das ist die Hauptsache, alles Prosa! Ich glaube, Ihr könnt
gar nicht in Prosa reden? 20

Apollo.
Nur Harmonie beseelt der Dichtkunst hohes Werk;
Vom Himmel wurde sie zu Euch herabgesandt!

Theobald.
Das ist Mystik, womit wir nichts zu schaffen haben. Glaubt mir, mit sol- 25
chen Ideen kommt man jetzt nicht durch; Ihr müßt plan und verständlich
seyn, daß Euch die Kinder in der Wiege begreifen. Wir machen jetzt
solche erstaunliche Fortschritte in der Popularität, daß uns in kurzer Zeit
vielleicht sogar die unvernüftigen Thiere verstehen lernen. Davon wußte
man zu Eurer Zeit nichts. Folgt mir, ich meine es gut mit Euch; seht wie 30
anständig Ihr nicht schon geworden seid, seitdem Ihr Euch zu einer sittlichen Kleidung bequemtet. Versucht es nun auch mit der Prosa, es wird
Euch nicht gereuen.

Apollo.
Laß sehn, wie weit es eure Thorheit treibt! 35

Theobald.
Es wird Euch schwer, ich merke es; das war noch ein fünffüßiger Jambus
– indeß gebt den Muth nicht auf; Prosa ist die Seele der Poesie. Ich beur-
theile z. B. nie einen Vers, ehe ich ihn nicht zuvor in Prosa übersetzt habe,
da kommen aber auch die Schönheiten recht zur Sprache. – Laßt uns 40
gleich zur Probe einen Versuch anstellen! Ihr sagtet vorhin: «Nur Harmonie belebt der Dichtkunst hohes Werk!» H a r m o n i e ? Das ist My-
stizismus! – M u s i k ? ist auch noch zu poetisch! – Habt Geduld, wir
wollen das Wort schon herunter bringen! – S y l b e n m a a ß ! Das ist
der rechte Ausdruck. – In Prosa aufgelöst hat also der Vers folgenden 45
Sinn: «Nur durch das Sylbenmaaß entsteht ein Gedicht!» – Der Gedanke
ist klar und verständlich. – Jetzt laßt uns den Nachsatz beurtheilen:
«Vom Himmel wurde sie zu euch herabgesandt!» – Das giebt einen schie-
fen Sinn; denn das Sylbenmaaß mit dem Himmel zusammenzustellen, ist
wol sehr lächerlich! Ein gut prosaischer Sinn findet gleich den Fehler. 50
Seht, so bin z. B. mit Göthens «Braut von Korinth» umgegangen, und
habe sie ganz heruntergebracht. – Ach ich habe die Prosa g a r l i e b,
m e r k e auch, daß ich ganz für sie geschaffen bin! –

Apollo.
Beinahe überzeugst Du mich! 55

Theobald.
Herrlich! Das sind nur noch vier Füße. Wir gehen immer weiter zurück,
und kommen gewiß zuletzt ganz aus der Poesie heraus. Faßt Euch ein
Herz! Ein kühner Sprung, und es ist vorbei!

60
Apollo.
Nun, ist es Dir so recht?

Theobald.
Vortreflich! Jetzt sind wir auf der Erde! Das ist die rechte Manier, die
Jederman versteht. Ach was es für ein Vergnügen ist, natürlich zu seyn!

65
Apollo.
Ich fühle mich recht edelmüthig gestimmt, und bin gleichsam zu Hause,
wie unter einer guten Familie!

Theobald.
Jetzt legt nur noch das Instrument ab, das Ihr tragt! Es ist geschmacklos,
70 und Niemand spielt es. – Die Guitarre ist jetzt das allgemein beliebte
Instrument; die Damen haben sogar ihre Schoßhündchen darum abge-
schaft! (er reicht ihm statt der Lyra eine Guitarre.)

Apollo.
Dies leichte luftige Saitenspiel kam noch nie in meine Hand!

75
Theobald.
Das wird sich finden! Ich will Euch die Guitarrenschulen von D o a s s y
und B o r n h a r d t zum eigenen Unterrichte mittheilen! – So seid Ihr
denn nun mit Gottes Hülfe modern geworden, und ich würde Euch überhaupt rathen, ganz aus der alten Mythologie herauszutreten; denn da
80 sie doch nun einmal nicht wieder in Aufnahme kommen wird, so müßt
Ihr immer in elenden Umständen bleiben! – Mit dem alten Wesen ist es
ganz vorbei, und sollten wir ja ein Mal an eine neue Mythologie denken
wollen, so ist bereits dazu die Physik als Grundlage vorgeschlagen.

Apollo.
85 Du hast eine so verständliche überzeugende Manier, daß es einem kinderleicht wird, sich darin zu finden!

Theobald.
Das ist eben das Höchste in unserer Methode, daß man den Kopf gar
nicht dabei anzustrengen braucht. Eine kritische Untersuchung z. B. wie
90 ich sie anzustellen pflege, könnte man selbst im Schlafe vollenden, so natürlich folgt darin ein Satz aus dem andern. – Wie gesagt, schüttelt Eure
Unsterblichkeit ab; es ist recht angenehm unter uns zu leben, und im
Gegentheile scheint es doch traurig mit einem Gotte zu stehen, der in
einem abstrakten Begrif zusammengeschrumpft ist!»

Z. 2 in der Hand] *fehlt in B*   Z. 7 acht] Acht B   Z. 17 seit kurzer Zeit]
seit kurzem B   Z. 18 man liebt das doch im Ganzen nicht] das waren Fehl-
schüsse über das dramatische Ziel hinaus B   Z. 29 sogar] *fehlt in B*
Z. 35 Laß sehn wie weit es eure Thorheit treibt!] Wo flohst du hin der Künste
goldne Zeit! B   Z. 42 belebt] beseelt B   Z. 43 Habt] O B   Z. 44
S y l b e n m a a ß] Sylbenmaß B, *wo auch sonst die Sperrungen fortgefallen*
sind, außer der in Z. 52 f.   Z. 46, 49 Sylbenmaaß] Sylbenmaß B   Z. 47
klar] gut B   Z. 48 euch] Euch B   Z. 50 gut prosaischer] gutprosaischer
B   Z. 51 bin] bin ich B   Z. 52 g a r l i e b] g a r l i e b B   Z. 58 Euch]
fehlt in B   Z. 64 Jederman] Jedermann B   Z. 69 f. Es ist geschmacklos,
und Niemand spielt es] Es ist eine alte Lyra, die Niemand mehr spielt, und
Jedermann muß das geschmacklos finden B   Z. 76 D o a s s y] Doissy B
Z. 83 dazu die Physik] die Physik dazu B   Z. 94 einem] einen B   Z. 94
abstrakten Begrif] abstrackten Begriff B

In der Reihe Edition Beck liegen außerdem vor:

Paul Rilla, Lessing und sein Zeitalter

1973. 464 Seiten. Paperback DM 19.80

Das Lessing-Buch Paul Rillas, des großen Kritikers und Polemikers, erscheint mit dieser Ausgabe zum ersten Mal in der Bundesrepublik. Es ist die «große Lessing-Deutung» (Hans Mayer) eines marxistischen Literaturwissenschaftlers und gewiß eines der bedeutenden literaturhistorischen Werke, die im Deutschland der Nachkriegszeit erschienen sind.

Albrecht Schöne, Emblematik und Drama im Zeitalter des Barock

2., überarbeitete und ergänzte Auflage. 1967. VIII, 240 Seiten. Mit 63 Textabbildungen und 2 Tafeln. Paperback DM 19.80

«... der bedeutendste Beitrag zur Erforschung des deutschen Barockdramas seit ... Benjamins Arbeit über den ‹Ursprung des deutschen Trauerspiels› ... Das Buch vermittelt Erkenntnisse, die eine Revision etlicher Interpretationen barocker Dichtung erzwingen werden.»
Mitteilungen des Deutschen Germanistenverbandes

Christian Wagenknecht, Weckherlin und Opitz

Zur Metrik der deutschen Renaissancepoesie. Mit einem Anhang: Quellenschriften zur Versgeschichte des 16. und 17. Jahrhunderts. 1971. VI, 126 Seiten. Paperback DM 19.80

Die Arbeit erneuert die verschollene Gattung der gelehrten Polemik. Sie beweist, mit methodisch neu fundierten Argumenten, daß die bis heute fortwirkende Versreform von Opitz sich *nicht* gegen eine tonbeugende Mißhandlung der deutschen Sprache in der Versdichtung der deutschen Renaissancepoeten, zumal Weckherlins, gerichtet hat.

J. M. van Winter, Rittertum

Ideal und Wirklichkeit. 1969. 108 Seiten mit 29 Abbildungen im Text und 31 Abbildungen auf Tafeln. Paperback DM 14.80

Verlag C. H. Beck München